QuarkXPress

Creating Digital Documents

7

D1400949

AGAINST THE CLOCK

mastering graphic technology

Managing Editor: Ellenn Behoriam
Copy Editor: Laurel Nelson-Cucchiara
Composition: Erika Kendra
Cover Design: Caron Gordon Graphics
Icon Design: Bill Morse
Prepress: Bang Printing
Printer/Binder: Bang Printing

10 9 8 7 6 5 4 3 2 1   ISBN 0-9764324-1-2

mastering graphic technology
PO Box 260092, Tampa, Florida 33685
800-256-4ATC • www.againsttheclock.com

Contents

Contents

Contents

Contents

Contents

Contents

Contents

Contents

Contents

ABOUT AGAINST THE CLOCK

Against The Clock has been publishing computer arts educational materials for more than 15 years, starting out as a Tampa, Florida-based systems integration firm whose primary focus was on skills development in high-volume, demanding commercial environments. Among the company's clients were LL Bean, *The New England Journal of Medicine*, the *Smithsonian*, and many others. Over the years, Against The Clock has developed a solid and widely-respected approach to teaching people how to effectively utilize graphics applications while maintaining a disciplined approach to real-world problems.

Against The Clock has been recognized as one of the nation's leaders in course-ware development. Having developed the *Against The Clock* and the *Essentials for Design* series with Prentice Hall/Pearson Education, the firm works closely with all major software developers to ensure timely release of educational products aimed at new version releases.

Top among these industry relationships is the company's solid and long-standing partnership with Quark, Inc. Against The Clock is proud to have been chosen as the official testing provider for those individuals and organizations who want to join the swelling ranks of QuarkXPress Certified Experts and QuarkXPress Authorized Training Centers. A means to achieve recognition for mastery of the world's most popular page-layout application, the certification test provides professionals with the ability to leverage the internationally recognized Quark brand, through the sanctioned use of the QuarkXPress Certified Expert and Quark Authorized Training Center logos.

ABOUT THE AUTHOR

Erika Kendra earned a BA in History and a BA in English Literature from the University of Pittsburgh. She began her career in the graphic communication industry as an editor at Graphic Arts Technical Foundation. She moved to Los Angeles in 2000 and now works as a freelance editor, writer, and designer. She also provides desktop-publishing training and prepress consulting for the printing industry. When she isn't working, she can usually be found prowling in book stores or enjoying the southern California sun.

Erika is the author of several Against The Clock titles, including *QuarkXPress: Upgrading from Version 6*; *Preflight and File Preparation*; *Adobe PageMaker: Creating Electronic Documents*; and the *Color Companion for the Digital Artist*. She is also the co-author of *Adobe Photoshop: Advanced Digital Imaging* and the *Design Companion for the Digital Artist*.

CONTRIBUTING EDITORS

A big thank you to the people whose comments and expertise contributed to the success of these products, including Gary Poyssick of Against The Clock, Inc.; Janet Frick of Training Resources; Katie Haviland of The International Academy of Design and Technology; and Heather Luethe, Tim Banister, Dan Logan, Scott Wieseler, Thomas Allen, Dave Ebersole, Joe Root, and Chris Edwards of Quark, Inc.

Thanks also to Laurel Nelson-Cucchiara, copy editor, and final link in the chain of production, for her help in making sure that we all said what we meant to say.

The Against The Clock series is designed for both the Macintosh and Windows platforms. QuarkXPress 7 requires Mac OS 10.4 (Tiger) or higher, Windows XP, or Windows 2003.

This book is based on the assumption that you have a basic understanding of how to use your computer. You should know how to use your mouse to point and click, and how to drag items around the screen. You should be able to resize and arrange windows on your desktop. You should know how to access drop-down menus, and understand how check boxes and radio buttons work. Lastly, you should know how to create, open, and save files. Finally, you should have a good understanding of how your operating system organizes files and folders, and how to navigate your way around them.

SYSTEM REQUIREMENTS FOR QUARKXPRESS 7

Macintosh

- Mac OS 10.4.3 (Tiger) or higher
- Minimum 128 MB RAM (256 recommended)
- 250 MB available disk space for installation
- At least 800 × 600-pixel monitor resolution (though we recommend higher)
- PostScript Level 2 printer
- CD-ROM drive

Windows

- Microsoft Windows XP or 2003
- Minimum 128 MB RAM (256 recommended)
- 190 MB available disk space for installation
- At least 800 × 600-pixel monitor resolution (though we recommend higher)
- PostScript Level 2 printer
- CD-ROM drive

INITIAL SETUP CONSIDERATIONS

Before you begin using your Against The Clock book, you must set up your system to have access to the various files and tools to complete your lessons.

The Work In Progress Folder

Before you begin working on the exercises or projects in this book, you should create a folder called "Work_In_Progress", either on your hard drive or on a removable disk. As you work through the steps in the exercises, you should save your work in this folder. Many of the exercises in this book build upon work that you have already completed; in these cases, you will need to open the file from your **Work_In_Progress** folder and continue with the same file.

Resource Files

This book comes complete with a collection of resource files, which are an integral part of the learning experience. They are used throughout the book to help you construct increasingly complex elements. These building blocks should be available for practice and study sessions to allow you to experience and complete the exercises and project assignments smoothly, spending a minimum of time looking for the various required components.

All the files that you need to complete the exercises and projects in this book are located on your Resource CD. You can either work directly from the Resource CD or copy the files onto your hard drive before beginning the exercises.

Locating Files

Files that you need to open, and the location of those files, are indicated by a different typeface (for example, "Open **document.qxp** from your **RF_Quark7** folder.") In most cases, resource files are located in the **RF_Quark7** folder, while exercises and projects on which you continue to work are located in your **Work_In_Progress** folder.

File Naming Conventions

Files on the Resource CD are named according to the Against The Clock naming convention to facilitate cross-platform compatibility. Words are separated by an underscore, and all file names include a lowercase three-letter extension. You see the three extension characters as part of the file name.

Fonts

You must install the ATC fonts from the Resource CD to ensure that your exercises and projects will work as described in the book; these fonts are provided on the Resource CD-ROM in the ATC Fonts folder. Specific instructions for installing fonts are provided in the documentation that came with your computer. You should replace older (pre-2004) ATC fonts with the ones on your Resource CD.

Key Commands

We frequently note keyboard shortcuts that can be used in QuarkXPress 7. A slash character indicates that the key commands differ for Macintosh and Windows systems; the Macintosh commands are listed first, followed by the Windows commands. If you see the command "Command/Control-P", for example, Macintosh users would press the Command key and Windows users would press the Control key.

QuarkXPress also incorporates the function ("F") keys as shortcuts for accessing many of the application commands and palettes. These shortcuts are useful and timesaving. We note many of the function-key shortcuts throughout this book.

We strongly recommend that you install a font-management utility program on your computer. Installing fonts at the system level can be cumbersome, and can significantly affect your computer's performance if you install too many.

Macintosh users: The default Exposé settings conflict with QuarkXPress keyboard shortcuts. If shortcuts initiate a system-level function instead of the expected behavior in QuarkXPress, you can modify Exposé settings in the System Preferences.

We assume that most people using this book have an extended keyboard and can use the function keys, modifier keys, and numeric keypad. If you are using a laptop computer or other computer with an abbreviated keyboard, some of the key commands discussed in this book may not be available.

Originally introduced to the market in 1987, QuarkXPress is an industry standard for page-layout and document design. From the early versions of the software, QuarkXPress incorporated tools that gave the designer extremely tight control over every element on the document page. Version 7.0 expands on the already established interface, providing even more tools and utilities to facilitate production and improve the digital workflow. QuarkXPress 7.0 also includes tools that make the transition from print to PDF to the Web far easier than they have been in the past.

This book is designed to introduce the tools, utilities, and features that are built into QuarkXPress, and provides hands-on practice so that you can apply the concepts to your own design projects. We define many of the terms and concepts that you need to work in the commercial graphic design field, and explain how those ideas relate to QuarkXPress layouts.

In addition to the basic functions, we discuss the sophisticated features that allow you to control and manage every element in your files and automate many of the time-consuming and monotonous tasks involved in successfully creating a page layout. We also look at different options for creating and managing type and graphics in a layout. Throughout this book, we will examine techniques for building pages that, when sent to a service provider, will print successfully.

Many of the new features (and enhancements to existing features) in QuarkXPress 7 focus on providing users with more choices than ever before, while maintaining the same basic work environment that many of us are already comfortable using. The changes and additions to QuarkXPress 7 fall into three basic categories: workspace enhancements, graphics enhancements, and productivity enhancements. These include:

- More options for customizing the workspace, so users can streamline their personal workflows, access tools and features quickly, and automate common but repetitive tasks.
- More creative options, so designers can freely experiment within the QuarkXPress environment.
- More effective options for meeting clients' demands for repurposing content in multiple formats and across multiple media.
- More efficient options for improving productivity, including the ability to collaborate and share work with multiple users and check layout files for common errors before they reach the output provider.

If QuarkXPress 7 could be summarized in a single word, it would be flexibility. We now have more options than ever before to be both creative and productive, to complete layout jobs efficiently, and to satisfy our clients' needs.

For existing QuarkXPress users, the learning curve for adopting version 7 into a design or production environment should not be steep. With a few notable exceptions, the changes in version 7 flow logically and seamlessly into the workspace that we already use every day to complete our jobs. If you're new to QuarkXPress, the learning curve might be a bit steeper. But you will also find that the flexibility built into most of the application's features will allow you to begin creating sophisticated layouts quickly — including complex designs that would not have been possible even one version ago — without ever leaving the QuarkXPress environment.

Because QuarkXPress is a page-layout application, most of this book focuses on designing for commercial printing. Among the newest additions to the application, however, are a set of tools and options to create Web pages — either from scratch or by repurposing an existing print layout. The last two chapters of this book are devoted to the Web-design capabilities that are part of the application.

Because there are many differences between print and Web design, we have written these chapters with the print designer in mind — we show you how to use the tools, without discussing much about the technical aspects of Web design. In fact, the best advantage of using QuarkXPress to design a Web page is that you don't need to know much about code to successfully create a Web page. You use the same environment and tools with which you are already familiar — the software generates the code for you. If you need to understand some aspect of HTML to use a particular tool in QuarkXPress, we explain it in clear, nontechnical language.

It is our goal to show you how to use the software's features to implement your designs. We discuss not only the tools and utilities available in the program, but also the practical application of those features for creating any page layout. As you work through the exercises and projects in this book, we encourage you to think beyond the specific text and graphics that we have provided. The skills that you learn throughout this book can be applied to any document, whether a 1-page poster or a 200-page catalog. You should always consider the concepts that underlie the tools and utilities we explore, and think how you can apply those utilities in a real-world design project.

Understanding the Workspace

1

The QuarkXPress work environment revolves around a series of menus, palettes, and windows that allow you to create and modify elements in your layout. Most of the application tools can be accessed in a number of different ways. This chapter introduces the different features that you will use as you create a QuarkXPress layout.

IN CHAPTER 1, YOU WILL:

- Learn about the QuarkXPress environment.

- Discover the palettes and gain a general understanding of their use.

- Become familiar with the menus and their uses.

- Explore and use QuarkXPress preferences.

- Control font-replacement behavior when opening existing files.

LAUNCHING QUARKXPRESS

When you install QuarkXPress on a Macintosh computer, the application icon is automatically added to the system dock; clicking that icon launches QuarkXPress. On Windows systems, you can choose to automatically create an application shortcut on the desktop; if you don't create the icon, you can launch QuarkXPress from the Start menu.

You can also launch QuarkXPress by double-clicking the application icon in a Finder or Explorer window, or double-clicking the icon for any QuarkXPress file on your computer.

| Application icon | Template file icon | Project file icon | Book file icon | Library file icon |

If you purchased a single-user license of QuarkXPress, you will be asked to activate the software the first time you launch it. In the Activate QuarkXPress dialog box, the Over the Internet radio button is selected by default.

If your computer is connected to the Internet, clicking Activate QuarkXPress automatically initiates the activation process. If you aren't connected to the Internet, or if you have a very slow connection, you can choose the Over the Telephone option before clicking Activate QuarkXPress. In this case, you have to call QuarkXPress Customer Service to receive an activation code.

A BRIEF INTRODUCTION TO PROJECTS AND LAYOUTS

QuarkXPress 6 introduced a new concept in file development and management — the idea of project files and layout spaces (or, simply, layouts) — which continues to be central in version 7. The workspace can be confusing at first, whether you are an experienced user or a complete novice. To help make the following chapter easier to understand, keep the following points in mind:

- When you build a new file in QuarkXPress, you create a *project*.
- A QuarkXPress project file contains *layouts*, which contain the physical pages of the job you are creating.
- A layout is essentially the same thing as a document in previous versions.
- A layout can be defined as a Web layout or a print layout.
- A project file can contain more than one layout.
- Individual layouts within a project can have different page sizes (for example, one layout is a letter-size brochure and one layout is a 3.5 × 2-in. business card).
- A single project can include print layouts, Web layouts, or both.

To make things less confusing, it might be helpful to think of a project as a container, and the individual layouts are the contents of that container. We will discuss layouts and projects in depth in Chapter 2, but you should keep these basic points in mind as you read this chapter.

If your QuarkXPress software is part of a multi-seat license, the Quark License Administrator utility manages all of your software licenses, so software activation by individual users is not necessary.

You can activate your copy of QuarkXPress on two computers, which allows you to install the same serial-number application on a desktop and a laptop (for example).

If you are working on a network, however, you cannot run both activated versions of the same serial number at one time.

THE QUARKXPRESS WORK ENVIRONMENT

The *Project window* includes a number of basic features that you'll use whenever you create or open a QuarkXPress file. Following is a brief explanation of those elements; you will learn more about specific features throughout this book.

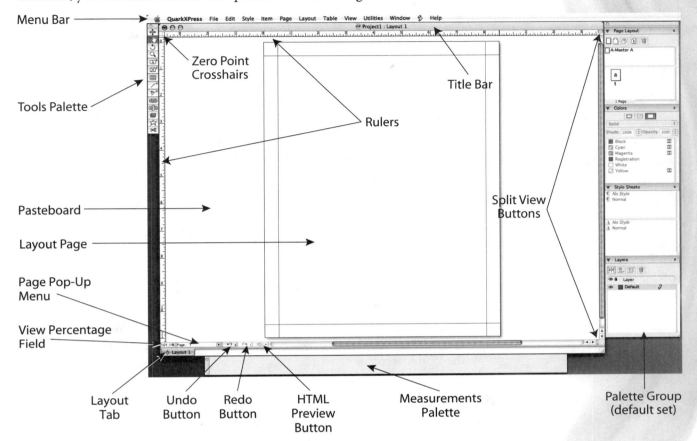

Menu Bar — Zero Point Crosshairs — Title Bar — Rulers — Tools Palette — Pasteboard — Layout Page — Page Pop-Up Menu — View Percentage Field — Split View Buttons — Palette Group (default set)

Layout Tab — Undo Button — Redo Button — HTML Preview Button — Measurements Palette

- **Menu Bar.** This is used to access the application commands. Many commands can also be accessed using keyboard shortcuts, which appear to the right of the command in the menus.

- **Title Bar** and **Scroll Bars.** These are common to many programs, on both the Macintosh and Windows platforms. When a standard QuarkXPress project file is open, the title bar shows the name of the current project file, then the name of the currently active layout (i.e., Project:Layout).

- **Rulers.** QuarkXPress displays rulers along the top and left edges of the Project window. The default *zero point* of the rulers is located at the upper-left corner of the publication page.

- **Tools Palette.** This contains the tools you use to create elements in a layout.

- **Layout Page.** This is the actual page that you are designing; anything within the black boundary of the page area is in the *printable area* or *live page*.

- **Pasteboard.** This is the area that surrounds the printable layout pages; anything that exists entirely on the pasteboard will not be included in the final print.

- **Page Pop-Up Menu.** This shows the number of the page currently displayed in the Project window. You can navigate to other pages in the active layout by clicking the arrow next to the current page number.

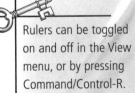

Rulers can be toggled on and off in the View menu, or by pressing Command/Control-R.

You can change the zero point by clicking the crosshairs in the top-left corner of the Project window, then dragging to any location on the page. You can also reset the zero point by double-clicking the crosshairs.

- **View Percentage Field.** This field shows the scale of the layout as it is displayed in the Project window. You can change the view percentage by typing a new number in this field, choosing one of several options in the View menu, or using one of several key commands.

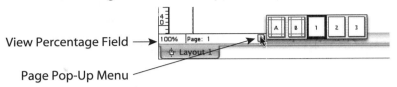

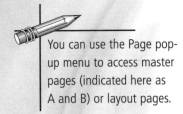

You can use the Page pop-up menu to access master pages (indicated here as A and B) or layout pages.

View Percentage Field →

Page Pop-Up Menu

- **Layout Tabs.** These are used to navigate from one layout to another within the same project file. You will learn more about these options in Chapter 2.
- **Undo/Redo Buttons.** These buttons can be used to step through the sequence of actions you have completed.
- **HTML Preview Button.** This is used when designing a layout for Web distribution, which is discussed in Chapter 17.
- **Measurements Palette.** This modal palette includes controls for virtually all formatting options; the options here vary depending on the selected object and active tool.
- **Split View Buttons.** Two buttons — one in the top-right corner and one in the bottom-right corner — are available to split the window into multiple views of the same project.
- **Floating Palettes/Palette Groups.** Many of the features available in QuarkXPress can be accessed in floating palettes, which can be accessed in the Window menu.

MENUS

Many QuarkXPress commands can be accessed in more than one manner. For example, you can change the scale at which your layout appears on your screen by using the Zoom tool, by typing a number in the View Percentage field, by using one of several keyboard commands, or by using the zoom percentages in the View menu. Other commands are only available through menus.

If a menu option is grayed out, it is not currently available; for example, File>Save Text is not available unless a text box is selected. Many of the more commonly used functions have keyboard shortcuts to access commands. Shortcuts, when available, are listed to the right of the command in each of the menus.

Even if you are already familiar with QuarkXPress, many of the menu options have been reorganized in version 7. You should take a few moments to examine the new menu structure to find the tools you will use frequently.

- **QuarkXPress Menu** (Macintosh only). The QuarkXPress menu follows the standard established in Macintosh OS X. This menu includes options that were available in the Apple menu of OS 9 and lower. You can also access Quark Preferences or quit the application using options in this menu.
- **File Menu.** The File menu is used to open, close, save, and create new projects. It also contains options for importing and exporting text and graphics, and commands for printing. On Windows computers, you can also exit the application from this menu.

- **Edit Menu.** The Edit menu contains the Copy, Cut, Paste, and Undo/Redo commands. It also provides access to dialog boxes that allow you to customize the QuarkXPress environment, and to the Find/Change dialog box for making global changes to text files. On Windows systems, you can use the Edit menu to access the application preferences.

- **Style Menu.** The Style menu contains commands for editing font and character information, and for assigning attributes, such as tabs and indents to paragraphs. When used with graphics, you can use these menu options to change the graphic's color, shade, and opacity characteristics. Hyperlinks and anchors for Web pages can also be defined.

- **Item Menu.** The Item menu commands are used to change specific elements on a QuarkXPress page, control the stacking order of elements on the screen, automatically align elements to one another, duplicate an element one or many times in specified increments, and group and ungroup items so they can be moved as a unit. You can also merge and split graphic elements and text boxes, and manage tables and rollovers.

- **Page Menu.** The Page menu is used to add to, delete from, or move pages in a layout; to edit guides on a master-page layout; to move to pages within a layout; to define specific sections of the layout; and to control page numbering. The HTML Preview option is also available when you are working on a Web layout.

- **Layout Menu.** This menu is used to add, duplicate, and delete layouts in a project file. You can access the Layout Properties dialog box (see Chapter 2) and the Advanced Layout Properties dialog box (Chapter 15). If you have multiple layouts in a project file, you can use the Layout menu to navigate between different layouts.

- **Table Menu.** This new menu consolidates all of the options that are available when building tables in a QuarkXPress layout. Commands previously accessed in the Item menu have been relocated here, and are accompanied by new options related to enhancements in version 7 (see Chapter 7).

- **View Menu.** The View menu affects what you see on the screen and how you see it. You can scale the Project window to preset amounts within the menu, and toggle guides on and off. Snap to Guides, listed in this menu, causes guides to act as magnets when items are brought near them, simplifying alignment. The Full Res Previews option is also controlled here (see Chapter 9).

- **Utilities Menu.** The Utilities menu contains tools for managing images, fonts, kerning, tracking, hyphenation, and spelling.

- **Window Menu.** The Window menu allows you to arrange windows, switch between projects, and access the various floating palettes used in the application. You can also control Project window splits, and create a new instance of a single Project window.

- **AppleScript Menu** (Macintosh only). QuarkXPress for Macintosh is scriptable — using AppleScript, you can write miniprograms to automate repetitive tasks. QuarkXPress ships with many scripts built into the application, accessible under the AppleScript menu. The scripts are sorted according to function.

- **Help Menu.** This menu provides access to the built-in Help system.

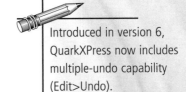

Introduced in version 6, QuarkXPress now includes multiple-undo capability (Edit>Undo).

By default, QuarkXPress stores 20 actions in the Undo list; you can change this value (up to 30) in the Application>Undo pane of the Preferences dialog box. Higher numbers of stored actions increase the memory and storage requirements, but allow you to step farther back in the sequence of actions.

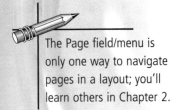

The Page field/menu is only one way to navigate pages in a layout; you'll learn others in Chapter 2.

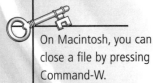

On Macintosh, you can close a file by pressing Command-W.

EXPLORE THE QUARKXPRESS WORKSPACE

1. Launch QuarkXPress.

2. Choose File>Open.

3. In the resulting (system-standard) navigation dialog box, navigate to the **RF_Quark7>Chapter01** folder and open **center_market.qxp**.

4. Note the project and layout name in the title bar.

5. Press Control-V/Control-Alt-V to highlight the view percentage field.

6. Type "250" and press Return/Enter to change the view to 250%.

7. Press Command/Control-1 to view the layout at 100%.

8. Click the arrow to the right of the Page pop-up menu to see which page you are working on.

9. With the Page pop-up menu visible, drag right and click the Page 2 icon to navigate to that page.

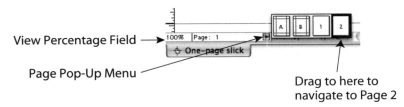

View Percentage Field

Page Pop-Up Menu

Drag to here to navigate to Page 2

10. Press Option/Alt, click anywhere in the Project window, and drag around.

This option, available when any but the Zoom or Starburst tool is selected, is an invaluable way to navigate quickly to a specific area of a layout.

11. Highlight the 2 in the Page field; type "1" and press Return/Enter.

You can navigate to specific pages by simply typing a number in this field.

12. Close the project by choosing File>Close, or by clicking the red button in the upper-left corner of the Project window (Macintosh) or the close "X" button in the upper-right corner of the Project window (Windows).

Minimize   Maximize

Close

Minimize   Maximize

Close

13. When asked if you want to save the file, click Don't Save/No.

Unless you have already saved it yourself, QuarkXPress always asks you if you want to save changes before closing a file.

USING MULTIPLE LAYOUT VIEWS

At times, it can be useful to look at more than one view of the same layout, such as one at 100% size and one zoomed in close, or view two different layouts in a project at once. QuarkXPress 7 includes two different options for exactly these situations; you can either split the Project window into multiple panes, or view two different instances of the same Project window.

Split Windows

Clicking either of the Split View buttons creates two equal-sized panes (either horizontal or vertical, depending on which button you click). You can also click the Split View buttons and drag to create custom-size panes in the Project window.

When you split the Project window, new Split View buttons appear in the top- and bottom-right corners of each pane in the Project window. You can split a window up to four times horizontally and eight times vertically (although there is little reason to split it this many times). Each split pane can display a different layout or different areas of the same layout, and each pane can display a different view percentage.

When working with split windows, the red button (Macintosh) or X button (Windows) in the top-right corner of each pane closes that pane. You can also click and drag any bar separating panes to resize any pane (and the adjoining ones). Changing the size of individual panes does not affect the size of the overall Project window. Only the panes touching the bar that you drag will be affected.

The Split View buttons are available in both standard mode and single-layout mode (explained in Chapter 2).

A window can also be split horizontally or vertically by choosing from the Window>Split Window menu.

Close all splits by choosing Window>Split Window>Remove All.

Click here to close an individual pane

Click and drag here to resize a pane (and adjoining panes)

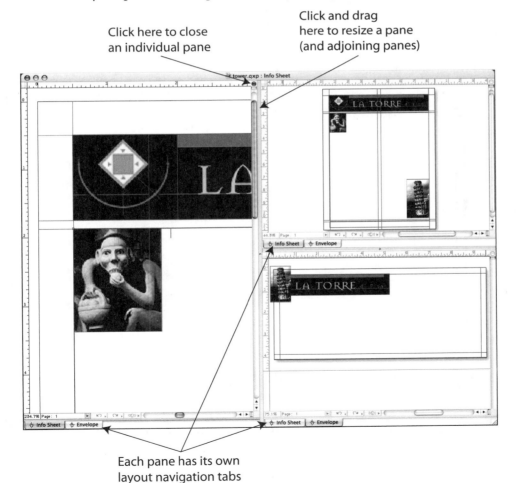

Each pane has its own layout navigation tabs

Multiple Windows

You also have the option to create a new window for the same project file (Window>New Window). When you have more than one instance of a Project window open, closing any single Project window does not ask you to save changes. You don't have to save changes until you try to close the last instance of the same Project window.

The only immediate way to know you are seeing two windows of the same project is the title bar, and then only if you are viewing different layouts within that project. The title bars of each window instance all show the same Project:Layout name structure; if you are viewing two different areas or view percentages of Layout1, for example, both title bars would show Project1:Layout1.

Working in standard (multiple-layout) mode, each window instance identifies the project and layout being viewed.

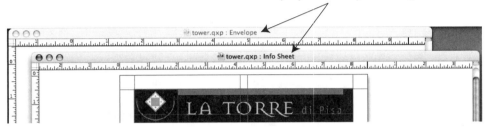

If you are working in single-layout mode (explained in Chapter 2), there is no visual identifier to show that you have two windows displaying the same project. In the following example, there is no difference between the title bars in the two Project windows. The Window menu, however, does show that two instances of the Project2 file are open.

If you are working in single-layout mode, there is no visual identifier to show that you have two windows displaying the same project. In this case, the Window menu is the only place where this information is available.

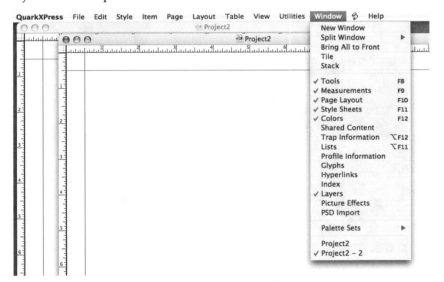

EXPLORE MULTIPLE LAYOUT VIEWS

1. Open the file **tower.qxp** from the **RF_Quark7>Chapter01** folder. This file has two layouts, an information sheet and an envelope.

2. Expand the Project window to fill as much screen space as available.

3. Click the Split View button in the bottom-right corner.

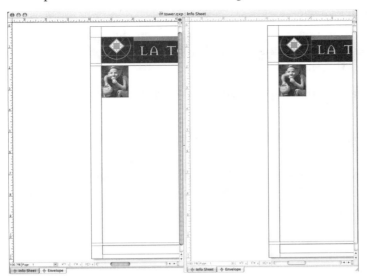

Simply clicking the Split View button automatically creates a split that is half-way between the left and right edges (for horizontal splits) or top and bottom edges (for vertical splits) of the window or pane being split.

4. Click the right pane of the Project window to make that pane active.

5. Click the Split View button in the top-right corner of the right pane and drag down so the top pane in the right side is about two-thirds the height of the Project window.

6. Click the top-right pane in the Project window to bring it into focus.

7. Make sure the Info Sheet layout is visible, and resize it to fit inside the window (Command/Control-0).

8. Click the bottom-right pane to bring it into focus.

9. Make the Envelope layout visible in this pane, and resize the layout to fit in the window.

10. Click the left pane to bring it into focus.

11. Make sure the Info Sheet layout is visible, and zoom in to the gargoyle picture in the top-left corner.

On Macintosh, the active pane (said to be "in focus") is identified by the high-lighted layout tab in the bottom-left corner and the red button in the top right corner. All other panes are considered inactive; their layout tabs and Close Pane buttons are grayed.

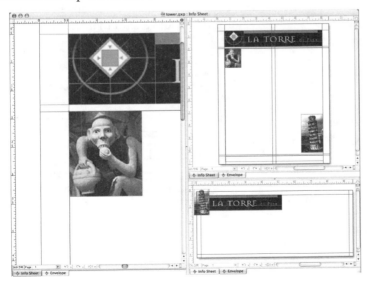

By clicking and dragging from the Split View button, you can create a split and resize the panes at the same time.

12. Select the gargoyle picture box and drag the picture around within its containing box.

   After you move the picture, look at the top-right pane. Changes you make in one instance of the layout are reflected in any other view (pane) that shows the same layout.

13. Click the Close Pane button in the top-right corner of the left pane (in the middle of the Project window).

   Because you are only closing a pane and not the file, you are not asked if you want to save.

   Multiple layout views are simply two different ways to look at the same layout or file at one time. The same concept applies when you are working with multiple windows for the same project.

14. Close the file without saving.

PALETTES

QuarkXPress palettes can be accessed in a number of different ways. All palettes can be toggled on and off using options in the Window menu; when a palette is visible, its name shows a checkmark in the menu.

Some palettes can also be accessed using keyboard shortcuts, which are listed to the right of the palette in the Window menu. When a palette is visible, pressing the shortcut closes the palette; when a palette is not visible, pressing the shortcut opens it as an independently floating palette.

Tools Palette

The Tools palette is located by default in the upper-left corner of the screen. Since it is a floating palette, you can reposition it on the screen by clicking the title bar and dragging it to a new location. If you don't see the Tools palette, you can choose Window>Show Tools or press F8.

Several QuarkXPress tools include optional shapes or functions. If the tool has more than one option, there is a small black arrow in the upper-right corner of the tool's icon. To select one of the tool's variations, click the tool and drag to the right to select the variation of your choice. The tool version that was last selected remains available in the Tools palette.

Many different menu commands can be accessed with keyboard shortcuts. Where available, these shortcuts are always listed to the right of the related menu command.

Tools F8

Measurements F9

Page Layout F10/F4

Style Sheets F11

Colors F12

If you are building a Web layout in QuarkXPress, the Web Tools palette appears by default immediately below the Tools palette. The tools are used to create items that are specific to Web layouts, and are explained in Chapter 18.

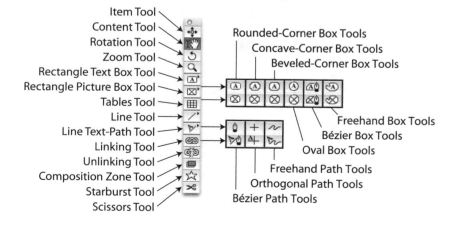

- **Item Tool.** This tool, represented by a four-headed arrow icon, is used to select, move, group, ungroup, cut, and copy items within the layout page. When this tool is selected, you cannot import text even if a text box is selected in the Project window. You can, however, import pictures when the Item tool is selected.

- **Content Tool.** This tool is represented by an I-beam and a hand. As the name suggests, it is used to edit the contents of a box. You can use it to enter, edit, or import text into a text box, or to import and manipulate an image in a picture box. When you want to work with the contents of a box, use the Content tool.

- **Rotation Tool.** This tool is used to rotate boxes and other items on the page.

- **Zoom Tool.** This tool changes the magnification or view of the layout on screen. Clicking with the Zoom tool enlarges the view percentage by 25% (unless the tool preferences have been changed); Option/Alt-clicking with the Zoom tool reduces the view percentage by 25% (or the incremental value defined in the tool preferences).

- **Text Box Tools.** These tools are used to create a variety of different-shaped containers for text. (All text in a QuarkXPress layout, except text on a path, is contained in a text box.)

- **Picture Box Tools.** These tools are used to create different-shaped containers for graphics. (All pictures in a QuarkXPress layout are contained in a picture box.)

- **Tables Tool.** This tool is used to create cell-based tables.

- **Line Tools.** These tools create a variety of different rules, curves, and freehand lines.

- **Text-Path Tools.** These tools are used to create straight or curved lines on which text can be placed.

- **Linking Tool.** This tool is used to connect one text box to another, so a single story can flow across multiple areas and pages in a layout.

- **Unlinking Tool.** This tool breaks the flow of text between linked text boxes.

- **Composition Zone tool.** This tool is used to create rectangular shapes that essentially define additional layouts within the master layout. You will learn more about composition zones in Chapter 15.

- **Starburst Tool.** This tool creates starburst shapes based on a user-defined number of points. This was previously part of the Stars and Stripes XTension, but is now part of the standard software installation.

- **Scissors Tool.** This tool is used to cut a line or shape. If a text box is cut, it is converted to a text path. If a picture box is cut, the enclosed content is removed.

Measurements Palette

The Measurements palette is essential to the efficient use of QuarkXPress. It offers access to nearly all formatting options that can be applied to objects or content in a QuarkXPress layout. The Measurements palette appears by default in Classic mode, which mimics the palette of earlier versions, with a few new controls that are related to new features.

QuarkXPress remembers which tool (Item or Content) you last used, and returns you to that same tool after you use any of the other tools. If you're typing in a text box (using the Content tool), and then select the Oval Picture Box tool and draw a new picture box, the Content tool is automatically re-selected when you finish drawing the box.

Command-Option-click/ Control-Alt-click to toggle between views of 100% and 200%.

On a Macintosh, you can temporarily access the Zoom tool by pressing Control-Shift (zoom in) or Control-Option (zoom out).

Option/Alt-click any of the drawing tools to keep the tool selected for multiple uses.

Show and hide the Measurements palette by pressing "F9".

In Classic mode, the left half of the palette displays item properties, such as the location and dimensions of an element. The right side of the Measurements palette displays specifications about the contents of the selected box.

If the active selection is a picture box, the right side of the palette (in Classic mode) displays the content scale, the position of the image within the box, and any rotation or skew applied to the contents of the box.

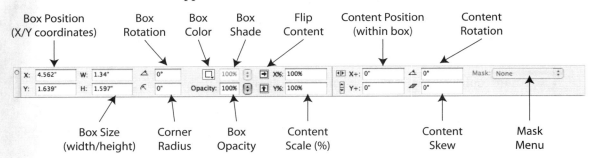

If the active selection is a text box, the palette (in Classic mode) changes to include controls for number of columns, leading and tracking, paragraph justification, font and size, and type style.

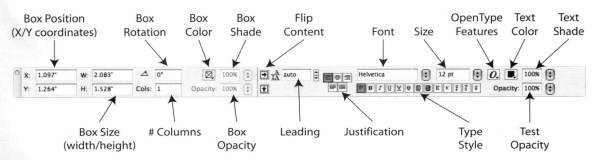

If the active selection is a line, the left side of the palette (in Classic mode) shows the X and Y positions of the line's endpoints. The right side of the palette allows you to change the line weight, style, and end treatments.

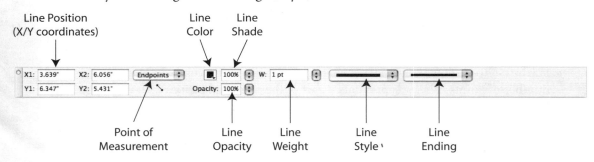

If you select Left Point, Midpoint, or Right Point instead of Endpoints, the Measurements palette displays the X and Y position of the selected point, the angle (from horizontal), and the length of the selected line.

When you roll the mouse over the Measurements palette, a pop-up tab displays the available palette modes. The Measurements palette is context sensitive; different tabs are available depending on the active tool and the type of object(s) selected in the Project window.

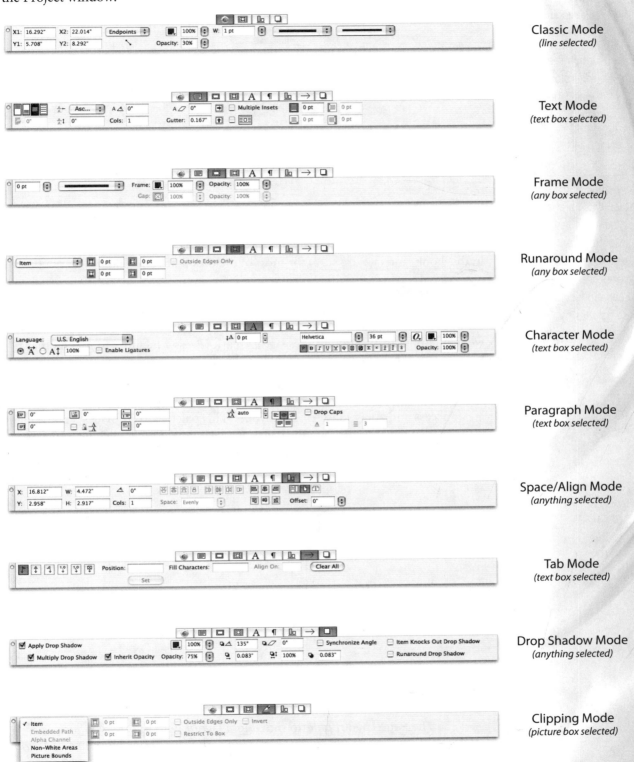

Classic Mode
(line selected)

Text Mode
(text box selected)

Frame Mode
(any box selected)

Runaround Mode
(any box selected)

Character Mode
(text box selected)

Paragraph Mode
(text box selected)

Space/Align Mode
(anything selected)

Tab Mode
(text box selected)

Drop Shadow Mode
(anything selected)

Clipping Mode
(picture box selected)

Control/right-clicking the bar at the left edge of the Measurements palette opens the palette's contextual menu. You can choose to leave a palette's pop-up navigation tab visible all the time, hide it all the time, or appear only on a mouseover (the default setting).

You will use the Measurements palette extensively as you complete the exercises in this book, and (we are sure) for most of the files that you build in QuarkXPress.

Other Palettes

The Tools palette and the Measurements palette are the most important palettes in the application. We almost always leave them open, regardless of the type of files we're building. In addition to these two, QuarkXPress 7 includes fourteen other palettes that you will use as you complete the chapters in this book.

- **Page Layout Palette.** When the Page Layout palette is activated, you can add or delete pages from a layout, sort and reorder pages within a layout, and access and apply master-page layouts. This palette also provides a convenient way to navigate through the pages of a layout by double-clicking a specific page icon. You will use this palette extensively throughout this book, and specifically in Chapter 2.

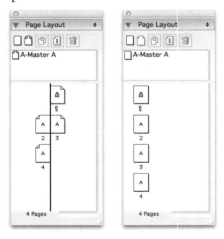

The Page Layout palette showing a layout with multiple pages.
The layout on the left has single-sided pages; the layout on the right has facing pages, indicated by the turned-down corners on each page icon.

- **Colors Palette.** The Colors palette is used this palette to change an element's color attributes. Colors can be specified in any shade from 0 to 100%, and any opacity from 0 to 100%. This palette also allows you to change an element's background color to a blend or gradient between two colors. We discuss the Colors palette in detail in Chapter 4.

- **Style Sheets Palette.** Many different typographic attributes can be predefined as a *style sheet* and applied in one step to selected text. The top half of the palette lists *paragraph styles*, which apply to entire paragraphs of text; the bottom half lists *character styles*, which apply only to selected text. We discuss styles in detail in Chapter 6.

- **Shared Content Palette.** This palette is used to create and manage shared objects, content, and layouts, as well as place synchronized instances of shared content into a layout (see Chapter 15).

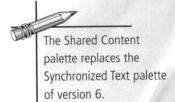

The Shared Content palette replaces the Synchronized Text palette of version 6.

- **Trap Information Palette.** This palette is used to review and manage the trap settings for a selected object (see Chapter 14).

- **Lists Palette.** This palette is used to review automatically generated lists, navigate to specific list items, and build a list into a layout. QuarkXPress lists are explained in Chapter 12.

- **Profile Information Palette.** This palette is used to review and change the color profile that is attached to a specific image in a layout (see Chapter 14).

- **Glyphs Palette.** This palette is used to access individual characters in a font, including Unicode characters and extended character sets of OpenType fonts (see Chapter 5).

- **Hyperlinks Palette.** This palette is used to create and manage hyperlink destinations, which can be attached to specific objects or text in a layout. The Hyperlinks palette is explained in Chapter 17.

- **Index Palette.** This palette is used to tag index entries in a QuarkXPress layout. This functionality is explained in Chapter 12.

- **Layers Palette.** This palette is used to build multiple-layer files, either for generating multiple versions of a single layout or simply for better control over complex stacking order. QuarkXPress layers are explained in Chapter 11.

- **Picture Effects Palette.** Introduced in version 6.5, this palette is used to apply the various image adjustments and effects that are part of QuarkVista (see Chapter 9).

- **PSD Import Palette.** The PSD Import XTension allows you to import and manipulate native Photoshop files directly in QuarkXPress; the PSD Import palette is used to control the layers, channels, and paths of native Photoshop files that are placed in a layout. (PSD Import is explained in Chapter 9.)

- **Web Tools Palette.** This palette, which is only available when a Web layout is open, is used to create objects that are specific to Web design, such as form field and image maps (see Chapter 18).

Palette Groups

When you first launch QuarkXPress 7, you might notice that four palettes appear together on the right side of your screen, and they are all grouped together as a single unit. This is an example of a *palette group*, which is a new way to control what is visible on your monitor and how much screen space it requires.

If you are working on a Macintosh and don't have a two-button mouse, get one. They can be purchased in most department, electronics, and office stores for around $10. As you grow accustomed to them, contextual menus will save you tremendous amounts of time in many different tasks.

Although contextual menus can be accessed on a Macintosh by pressing Control while clicking, we find the one-handed capability afforded by a two-button mouse to be far more efficient.

Double-click here to collapse the entire palette group.

Click here to collapse a palette within the group.

Click here to access the contextual menu for the Colors palette.

Click here and drag to resize a specific palette within the group.

Click here and drag up or down to move a palette to a new position within the group.

Control/right-click here to access the contextual menu for the entire palette group.

Control/right-click here to access the contextual menu for the Layers palette.

Click here and drag to resize the entire palette group.

Individual palettes within a group can be resized by dragging the bar that separates the palettes in the group. An entire palette group can be resized horizontally and/or vertically by clicking and dragging the bottom-right corner of the group.

Palettes can also be repositioned within a group by clicking the title bar of one palette and dragging up or down. A solid black bar will indicate the new position of the palette you are dragging.

You can collapse individual palettes within a group by clicking the title bar of a palette anywhere except on the double-facing arrows in the right corner. Collapsed palettes can be reopened by simply clicking the title bar again.

Control/right-clicking the title bar (but not on the opposing arrows) of any palette displays the palette group's contextual menu.

The two options at the top of the contextual menu are used to detach the selected palette from the existing group (leaving it open but as an individual floating palette), or close the selected palette entirely (removing it from the group as well).

The bottom half of the contextual menu lists all the available palettes; ones tagged with a checkmark are part of the same palette group. You can add palettes to the same group by choosing an unchecked palette from this list, or remove a palette from the group (and close it) by choosing a checked palette.

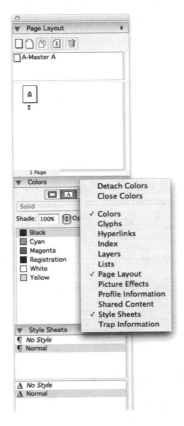

You can create more than one palette group at the same time. For example, you might group the Page Layout palette and the Layers palette together, and in a separate palette group combine the Colors and Style Sheets palettes.

Collapse an entire group by double-clicking the title bar of the group.

When a palette is visible as part of a group, pressing its keyboard shortcut closes it and removes it from the group. Pressing the shortcut again reopens the palette, but as an individual floating palette instead of as a part of the group in which it previously existed.

Clicking the opposing arrows in the right side of a specific palette's title bar (not the palette group's title bar) shows the contextual menu for that palette. The same options can also be accessed by Control/right-clicking elsewhere in the palette (but not in the palette's title bar).

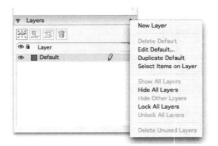

WORK WITH PALETTE GROUPS

1. Close any palettes that are currently visible. (This isn't particularly necessary, but for the sake of illustration, it helps to start with a clean slate.)

2. Open the following palettes using the Window menu:

   Tools, Measurements, Colors, Page Layout, Layers

3. If it's not already there, position the Tools palette in the top-left corner of your screen.

4. Drag the Measurements palette until it snaps to the bottom of your screen. If you are on a Macintosh and the system dock is visible, drag the palette until it snaps to the top of the dock.

5. Drag the Page Layout palette until it snaps to the top-right corner of your screen; expand it until it fills about half the screen height.

6. Drag the Colors palette until it snaps to the top of the screen and to the left edge of the Page Layout palette.

7. Control/right-click the title bar of the Colors palette to display the palette group contextual menu. (Click anywhere other than the opposing arrows in the top-right corner of the palette.)

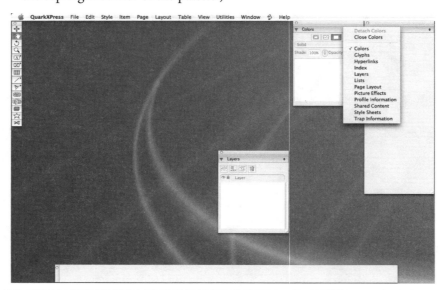

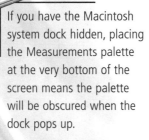

If you have the Macintosh system dock hidden, placing the Measurements palette at the very bottom of the screen means the palette will be obscured when the dock pops up.

You might want to leave room between the bottom of the palette and the edge of the screen to avoid potential problems caused by the dock's mouseover pop-up behavior.

8. Choose Layers from the contextual menu.

    The floating Layers palette, which had been open independently, is now grouped with the Colors palette.

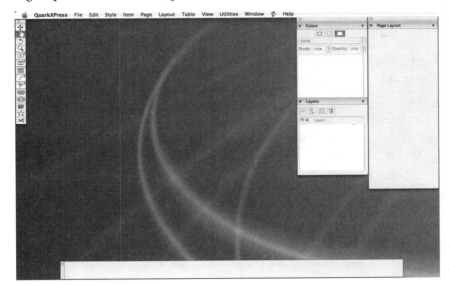

9. Control/right-click the title bar of the Page Layout palette, and choose Layers from the contextual menu.

    The Layers palette is removed from the group with the Colors palette and is now grouped instead with the Page Layout palette. A palette can only exist in one place at a time, which means it can only be a part of one group at a time.

10. Control/right-click the Layers palette title bar and add the Colors palette to the group.

    Again, the independently floating Colors palette is gone; the palette is now part of the group. Remember, palettes can only exist in one place at a time.

11. Press F12.

    The Colors palette is now gone. When a palette is visible and part of a group, pressing the palette's key command removes the palette from the group and closes it.

12. Control/right-click the title bar of the Layers palette and choose Detach Layers.

    This leaves you with two independently floating palettes — Page Layout and Layers.

13. Close the Layers palette.

When you add more palettes to a group than will fit in the available screen space, one or more of the existing palettes will automatically collapse to accommodate the new palette.

Some well-known QuarkXPress key commands — including F12 — have been usurped by the Macintosh operating system.

If you want to be able to use F9, F10, F11, and F12 to access QuarkXPress palettes, change the default Dashboard & Exposé hot-key settings in the Macintosh system preferences.

Palette Sets

In many cases, you probably have a specific set of palettes that you work with for a certain type of work. When you change production modes (e.g., switching from designing a booklet to building its table of contents and index), you might need an entirely different set of palettes.

To make this process easier, QuarkXPress 7 offers the ability to save user-defined *palette sets*. By choosing Window>Palette Sets>Save Palette Set As, you can create one-command (or key) access to multiple palettes and palette groups.

When you save a palette set, you can assign a specific name and keyboard shortcut to the set. Keyboard shortcuts can be any of the Function or numeric-keypad keys, with or without some combination of the modifier keys (Shift, Command, Option, or Control for Macintosh; Shift, Alt, or Control for Windows).

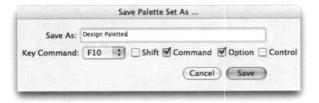

If you try to assign a keyboard shortcut that is already used by another application or system function, you will get an error message. You cannot override an existing keyboard shortcut.

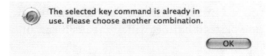

Palette sets save not only the specific palettes and palette groups that are open when the set is created, but also the location of those palettes. When you call a palette set, the palettes and groups in that set are opened in the same location as they were when you saved the set.

Saved palette sets are stored in the Palette Sets folder within the application's Preferences folder. They can be accessed by choosing the appropriate option from the Window>Palette Sets menu, or, if you defined one, by pressing the associated keyboard shortcut.

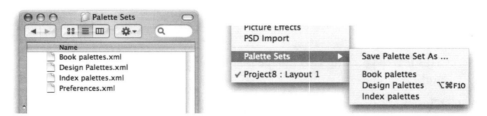

In addition to defining custom palette sets, you can also create custom nested folders within the Preferences>Palette Sets folder. If you open the Palette Sets folder on your computer, you can simply create a new folder, name it, and drag specific palette set (.xml) files into the folder. The next time you launch the application, those folders will be interpreted as custom fly-out menus in the Window>Palette Sets menu.

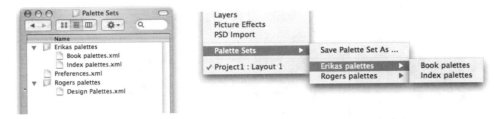

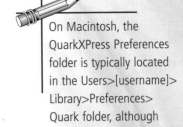

On Macintosh, the QuarkXPress Preferences folder is typically located in the Users>[username]>Library>Preferences>Quark folder, although some people prefer to create a Preferences folder directly in the QuarkXPress application folder.

On Windows, the QuarkXPress Preferences folder is typically located in the C:\Documents and Settings\[Owner]\Application Data\Quark\QuarkXPress 7.0 folder.

CREATE CUSTOM PALETTE SETS

1. Close any palettes that are currently visible.

   (Again, this isn't particularly necessary; we do it for the sake of illustration.)

2. Open the Tools, Measurements, and Colors palettes. Snap the Colors palette to the top-right corner of the screen.

3. Control/right-click the Colors palette to show the contextual menu, and add the Picture Effects palette to the same group as the Colors palette.

4. Open the Layers palette separately and drag it to snap to the top of the screen and the left edge of the group.

5. Add the Page Layout palette to the group with the Layers palette.

6. Choose Window>Palette Sets>Save Palette Set As.

7. In the resulting dialog box, name the set "[your name] Design Palettes".

8. Choose F12 in the Key Command list and activate the Shift and Option/Alt modifier-key check boxes.

Palette set folders will not be available until you quit and relaunch the application.

The numbers in the Key Command list refer only to the numeric-keypad numbers. These shortcuts won't work if you try to press the regular number keys on your keyboard.

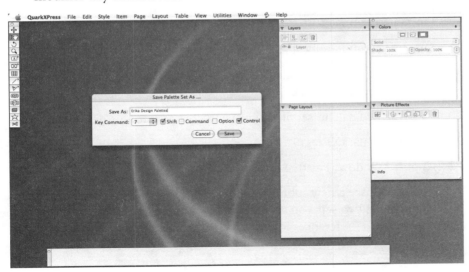

9. Click Save to save the palette set.

10. Close the entire palette group that contains the Colors palette.

11. Close the Measurements palette.

12. Delete the Layers palette from the other palette group, and drag the Page Layout palette to the top-right corner of the screen.

13. Add the Index and Lists palettes to the group with the Page Layout palette.

14. Choose Window>Palette Sets>Save Palette Set As.

15. Save the palette set as "[your name] Book Palettes". Assign a key command if you prefer, and then click Save.

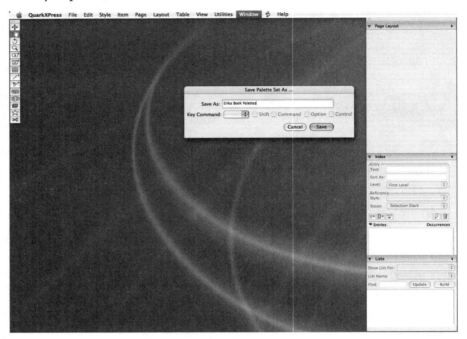

16. Press Option/Alt-Shift-F12.

    The palette set you saved in the first half of this exercise — with all the palettes and groups in the same positions as when you saved the set — reappears on the screen.

17. Quit QuarkXPress.

18. On your computer, locate the Preferences folder for QuarkXPress 7.

19. Inside the Preferences>Palette Sets folder, create a new empty folder named "[your name] Palette Sets".

20. Drag the two palette-set files (.xml) you created into this new folder.

21. Relaunch QuarkXPress 7.

22. Choose Window>Palette Sets.

    You should see a new submenu named "[your name] Palette Sets", which contains the two sets you saved. Unless someone deletes the folder from the application's Preferences folder, your palette sets will be available anytime.

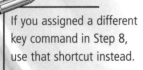
If you assigned a different key command in Step 8, use that shortcut instead.

You can copy palette-set XML files onto another workstation to access your palette sets. Simply place your XML files inside the workstation's version of the QuarkXPress 7 Preferences>Palette Sets folder, and then relaunch QuarkXPress.

PREFERENCES AND DEFAULTS

Setting preferences and other defaults is another way to customize QuarkXPress so it looks and functions exactly as you prefer, not according to an arbitrary manufacturer's specification. On Macintosh, preferences are accessed in the QuarkXPress menu; on Windows, preferences are accessed in the Edit menu.

The Preferences dialog box presents different options, depending on what (if anything) is open when you access the preferences. If nothing is open, you will see the entire list of available preferences, in four sections: Application, Project, Default Print Layout, and Default Web Layout. If you change Default Print Layout or Web Layout preferences while no file is open, your changes will be the default settings for any new project you create.

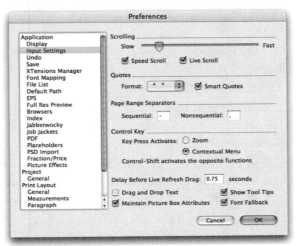

If you highlight a Preference category name — Application, Project, [Default] Print Layout, and [Default] Web Layout — in the left side of the dialog box, the right side of the dialog box shows the options for your last selection.

If a project file is open when you access the Preferences dialog box, the type of the currently active layout determines what appears in the Preferences dialog box. If a Web layout is active, the Print Layout preferences are not available; if a print layout is active, the Web Layout preferences are not available. If you change Print Layout or Web Layout preferences while a file is open, the changes are only applied to the active layout in the current project file.

Application Preferences

Application preferences govern the way QuarkXPress functions in general, not just in the active project. You can access the different types of preferences by clicking a category in the left side of the Preferences window.

- **Display.** These options determine guide, ruler, and grid colors; the pasteboard width (as a percentage of the Project window); the color profile for your monitor; how color and grayscale images display; and whether hidden warnings are displayed.

- **Input Settings.** These options determine scrolling speed, quote formats, smart quotes, delayed item drag, the character used for page-range separators, drag-and-drop text, and tool tips. On the Macintosh, you can also determine whether the Control key activates zoom or contextual menus. Two new options — Maintain Picture Attributes (see Chapter 9) and Font Fallback (see Chapter 5) — have been added to this dialog box in version 7.

- **Undo.** These options define the key command that will reverse an Undo. You can also define the number of actions that are stored in the history. Higher numbers of stored actions (up to 30) increase the required memory and storage, but allow you to step farther back in the sequence of actions.

- **Save.** These options determine if and when Auto Save and Auto Backup are invoked, whether libraries are automatically saved when changes are made to them, and whether or not to open projects in the last-saved position on the monitor.

- **Font Mapping.** These options define how QuarkXPress treats fonts that are not available when a project is opened. This feature is explained at the end of this chapter.

- **XTensions Manager.** These options allow you to determine when the XTensions Manager is displayed.

- **File List.** You can include a list of recently used files in either the File menu or the Open menu. You can also define the number of files to list, the order in which they are displayed, and whether to view the full file path or just the file name (the default).

- **Default Path.** New to version 6, you can define the default path (the initial folder that is opened when a command is selected) for the Open, Save/Save As, Import Text, and Import Picture commands.

- **EPS.** These options determine whether QuarkXPress displays the preview that is saved in an EPS file, or whether the application generates its own preview for those images.

- **Full Res Preview.** QuarkXPress includes an option to view full-resolution image previews in a layout. These options control the behavior of those previews (see Chapter 9).

- **Browsers.** This lists the Web browsers available on your computer and specifies the default browser used for previewing Web layouts. You can add, edit, or remove browsers from the list.

- **Index.** These preferences define the special characters that are used when you build an index in a QuarkXPress layout (see Chapter 12).

- **Jabberwocky.** This is a convenient tool for creating nonsense or placeholder text when you are building a layout. Jabberwocky creates text in the defined language (English, Esperanto, Klingon, or Latin) and the defined style (Prose or Verse).

- **PDF.** QuarkXPress includes the ability to generate PDF files without the need for the separate Adobe Acrobat Distiller application. These options are explained in Chapter 10.

- **Placeholders.** These options define the appearance of XML elements.

- **PSD Import.** These options control file caching when you import layered Adobe Photoshop files into a QuarkXPress layout (see Chapter 9).

- **Fraction/Price.** These options determine the appearance of text that is converted to a price or fraction using new Type Style options.

- **Picture Effects.** These options define where custom picture effects presets (see Chapter 9) are saved.

Project Preferences

Project preferences are specific to the project file (i.e., not related to an individual layout within a project). The General options determine whether modified pictures are automatically updated (with or without the opportunity to verify the update); whether new files are created as standard or single-layout files (see Chapter 2); and whether OpenType kerning is applied.

Layout Preferences

Layout preferences are used to define the attributes and behaviors of specific features, tools, and elements in a layout. If you open the Preferences window with a project file open, the Preferences list will only show the options for the currently active layout type (Print or Web). If you change the preferences with no project open, you change default behaviors for any new project or layout; you are able to access both Default Print Layout and Default Web Layout options, which can be changed independently. In other words, you can define different default behaviors for Web layouts and print layouts.

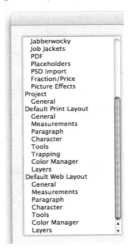 

If you open the Preferences window with no project open, you can change the Default Print and Default Web Layout preferences (left). If a project is open (right), changes will only apply to the open layout, so the list only shows options for the active layout type.

- **General.** These preferences give you the ability to define the point size below which text is greeked, and whether or not to greek pictures. You can also determine the position and snap distance of guides; keep or delete changes to master-page items; place framing rules inside or outside the box dimension; define the position where pages are automatically inserted in a layout; and define colors for anchors and hyperlinks.

- **Measurements.** These preferences define the horizontal and vertical units of measure (inches, inches decimal, picas, points, millimeters, centimeters, ciceros, or agates), the number of points per inch, and the number of ciceros per centimeter. You can also determine whether the item coordinates are relative to the page or to the spread.

- **Paragraph.** These preferences define the automatic leading percentage; maintain leading when a picture is inserted; use typesetting (base-to-base) or word-processing (ascender-to-ascender) mode of leading; determine the starting position and increment of the baseline grid; and set the hyphenation method (standard, enhanced, or expanded).

- **Character.** These preferences determine offset and vertical and horizontal scales for super- and subscript characters, as well as vertical and horizontal scales for small caps and superiors. You can determine the kerning value above which non-OpenType ligatures break; use a standard em space; assign an en the value of a numeric character; and set whether or not accents (such as grave) are used when text is styled as All Capitals.

The Print Layout and Web Layout preferences are essentially the same. Trapping is a printing-specific feature, so this category is not available when a Web layout is active.

- **Tools.** These preferences define default attributes of objects created with the various drawing tools — picture boxes, text boxes, lines, text on a path, tables, and composition zones. You can also change the incremental magnification of the Zoom tool.

- **Trapping.** These options define the trapping method (absolute or proportional). You can also assign specific values to trapping functions (see Chapter 14).

- **Color Manager.** Managing color means creating consistent, predictable output across a variety of media, from the monitor to the proofing device and the color-separated print job. If you work in a color-managed environment, can accurately measure your monitor, and can evaluate the color of proofs and printed documents, these preferences are important to you. These options are explained in Chapter 14.

- **Layers.** These preferences determine whether or not new layers are visible, locked, printable, and affected by runarounds from other layers.

DEFINE DEFAULT PREFERENCES

1. With no projects open, choose QuarkXPress>Preferences (Macintosh) or Edit>Preferences (Windows).

2. Click through all of the Application preferences categories. Note the options available to you. Under Display preferences, you might want to change the Color TIFFs menu to 8-bit or 16-bit for faster screen redraw of graphics-heavy pages.

3. In the Input Settings preferences, adjust the Scroll speed to a speed that is comfortable for you.

4. Under Default Print Layout Preferences, choose Measurements. Set the Horizontal and Vertical menus to Inches.

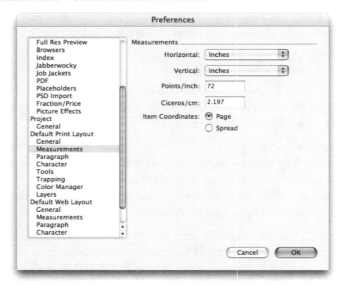

This exercise defines preferences that will be used throughout the exercises in this book. When you work on other projects, you might find other settings to be more beneficial.

5. Choose Paragraph. Deselect the Maintain Leading box. Leave the Auto Leading set to 20% and the Mode set to Typesetting. Leave the Baseline Grid at the default. Scroll through the Hyphenation list and make sure the Method for U.S. English is set to Expanded.

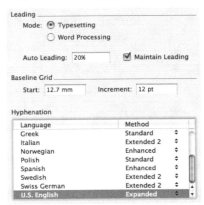

6. Choose Character. Change the Superscript and Subscript VScale and HScale fields to 70%. Leave Small Caps and Superior at their defaults. On the Macintosh, Ligatures should not be selected. Check the Standard Em Space box, and leave everything else set to the default.

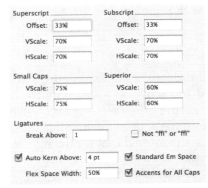

7. Choose Tools. Select the first Text box, and then click Similar Types to select all text boxes.

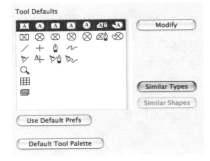

8. Click the Modify button. In the resulting Modify dialog box, click the Text tab. Make sure the Text Inset All Edges field is set to 0 pt. Click OK to return to the Preferences window.

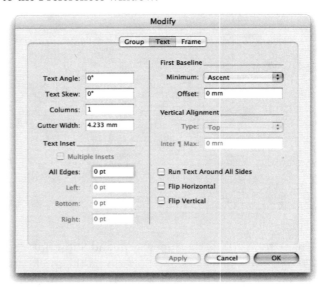

9. Click OK and close QuarkXPress. The preferences you selected will apply to all future projects with print layouts.

FONT MAPPING

When you open an existing QuarkXPress layout, the fonts that are used in that layout need to be installed and active on your computer. If you don't have the required fonts, QuarkXPress presents a missing font warning before the file is opened. QuarkXPress 7 includes font-mapping capabilities that allow you to control what happens when a required font is missing.

 DEFINE FONT MAPPING RULES

1. Open the **postcard.qxp** file from the **RF_Quark7>Chapter01** folder.

2. When you see a warning that fonts are missing, click Continue.

   The bottom of the layout should have both the Web address and the phone number. Because the font is missing, the text isn't right.

3. Close the file without saving.

4. Open the **postcard.qxp** file again.

5. Click List Fonts when you see the warning about missing fonts.

   The Missing Fonts dialog box shows that ATC Flamingo Extra Bold is not installed on your computer.

6. Highlight ATC Flamingo Extra Bold in the list and click Replace.

7. In the Replacement Font dialog box, choose ATC Laurel Bold from the font menu and click OK.

In the Missing Fonts dialog box, you can see that any instance of ATC Flamingo Extra Bold will be replaced with ATC Laurel Bold.

8. With the replacement item highlighted in the list, click Save As Rule.

By saving this replacement definition as a rule, the change will apply to any instance — in any file — of the font that is being replaced. Whenever a layout calls for ATC Flamingo Extra Bold and the font is not available, ATC Laurel Bold will be substituted for ATC Flamingo Extra Bold.

9. Click OK to open the file.

The phone number and Web address (originally set in ATC Flamingo Extra Bold) are now in ATC Laurel Bold.

10. Save the file as "test_fonts1.qxp" in your **Work_In_Progress** folder and close it.

Any time you replace one font with another, be very careful that the layout integrity is not destroyed when you substitute one font with another.

If you work for an output provider, never change or replace a font without client approval.

In some cases, replacement font metrics do not display properly until the file is saved. If you define replacement fonts for a file, you should save the file — using the same or a different file name — as soon as you open it.

11. Open the file **test_fonts1.qxp** from your **Work_In_Progress** folder.

    The file opens without displaying the missing-font warning. The phone number and Web address appear in ATC Laurel Bold, the replacement font that you defined earlier.

    Changing fonts with a font-replacement rule is permanent once the file has been saved. In other words, if you save a file after applying a font-replacement rule, the new (saved) version of the file only calls for the replacement fonts — not the fonts that were replaced. Applying a font-replacement rule is essentially the same as making a universal change in the Fonts Usage dialog box, except that the change is applied when the file is opened.

12. In the open file, choose Utilities>Font Mapping.

13. Highlight the ATC Flamingo Extra Bold item in the list and click Edit.

14. In the Edit Font Mapping dialog box, choose ATC Maple Ultra in the Replacement menu and click OK.

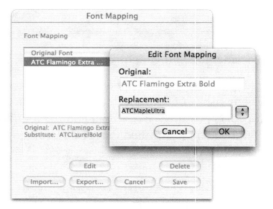

15. Click Save to close the Font Mapping dialog box.

    In the open file, the phone number still appears as ATC Laurel Bold. Once a font is replaced with a font-replacement rule, the action is permanent; the open file no longer calls for ATC Flamingo Extra Bold, so editing the replacement rule does not change the text that was already altered by the rule when the file was opened.

16. Close the file without saving.

CONTROL FONT REPLACEMENT

1. Open **postcard.qxp** from the **RF_Quark7>Chapter01** folder (not the test_fonts1.qxp file that you saved in the previous exercise).

2. Click List Fonts in the missing-font warning.

   You can see that the edited rule definition (from the previous exercise) will be applied.

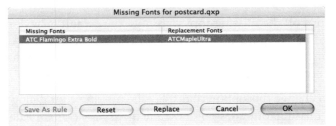

3. Highlight the replacement rule in the list and click Reset.

   ATC Maple Ultra changes to an asterisk in the Replacement Fonts column, indicating that the defined rule will not be applied to this file. The missing font will be substituted with the default replacement font.

4. Click OK in the Missing Fonts dialog box.

   As stated in the previous step, the defined replacement rule has not been applied. (The rule, however, is not deleted from the application and will be applied the next time a file calls for ATC Flamingo Extra Bold.)

5. Close the file without saving.

6. Open **postcard.qxp** from the **RF_Quark7>Chapter01** folder again.

7. Click Continue in the missing-font warning.

   The missing font is not replaced. Using the default settings, you must first click List Fonts to review the missing fonts and replacement rules before a font-replacement rule will be applied.

8. Close the file without saving.

9. Open the Preferences dialog box and select Font Mapping from the Application category.

> Using the default settings, font-replacement rules are not applied if you do not click List Fonts in the missing-font warning.

10. Activate the check box to not display missing-font warnings, and make sure the second radio button is selected.

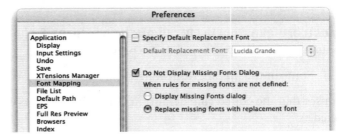

If you turn off the missing-font warnings, the default behavior is to replace missing fonts with the defined replacement font. If you have not defined a replacement rule for a specific font, the default replacement font (defined in the top section of this dialog box) will be used.

You can change this option to display the missing-font dialog box only when a missing font does not have a defined replacement rule (using the Display Missing Fonts Dialog radio button).

11. Click OK to close the Preferences dialog box.

12. Open **postcard.qxp** from the **RF_Quark7>Chapter01** folder again.

The file opens without displaying the missing-font message; the replacement rule is automatically applied.

13. Close the file without saving.

SUMMARY

You explored the QuarkXPress work environment, and took a brief look at the tools and utilities that will use as you complete the exercises in this book. You also explored the QuarkXPress palettes and learned how to manage them. You learned about the all-important preferences, and set up the underlying preferences with which you will work. You also know how to open files, and know what to do if a required font is missing.

Building Layouts and Pages

2

The layout is the basis of any job designed in QuarkXPress. Before you can position anything on the layout, you must create a project and define the layout page. This chapter examines the different methods for creating, defining, and modifying pages in a QuarkXPress project. Careful planning helps to increase the efficiency with which you use the layout. Well-designed grids give structure to your work and improve productivity.

IN CHAPTER 2, YOU WILL:

- Discover how pages are arranged to produce the final desired sequence.

- Learn different ways to create, modify, and save layouts.

- Learn how to create projects and templates.

- Discover how to navigate through the pages in a layout.

- Explore the differences in layout pages, spreads, and master pages.

- Learn the importance of layout grids, and how to create them on a master page to improve efficiency.

- Learn the different elements of page geometry, including terms you will hear in the graphic-communication industry.

- Become familiar with and use guides, margins, and rulers.

- Examine the Guide Manager XTension.

- Learn about special requirements for creating folding documents.

CREATING PROJECTS

As you learned in Chapter 1, QuarkXPress 6 introduced an entirely new working environment that revolves around project files and layouts; the same layout management structure has been maintained (and even expanded) in version 7. The project file is the foundation of any design job — it contains one or more layout spaces, on which you place text, objects, images, and graphics. The QuarkXPress layout space defines page-size parameters, margins, columns, and gutters. This chapter shows you how to create, modify, and manage projects and layouts, and how to work with the advanced page-definition features available in QuarkXPress.

Any design you create must be contained within a QuarkXPress project file, which is created, opened, closed, and saved through the File menu. The easiest way to create a new project is to press Command/Control-N. You can also choose File>New>Project.

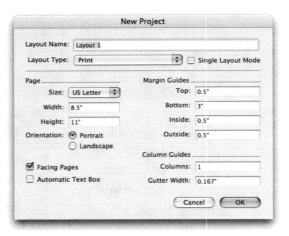

The minimum page size is 0.112 × 0.112 in. (2.845 mm), and the maximum page size is 48 × 48 in. (1219.2 mm), if the pages are not facing. The maximum page size for facing pages is 24 × 48 in.

The New Project dialog box defines the page parameters for the first layout in the file.

Defining a QuarkXPress Layout

In the New Project dialog box, the first two options define the name and type of layout that will appear in the new file. You can use any name you choose, but we suggest using a meaningful name describing the layout contents. In the Layout Type menu, you determine whether you are creating a layout for print design or for Web design. (We examine Web layouts in Chapter 17.)

The Page section of the New Project dialog box defines the dimensions of the first layout space in the file. You should select a paper size corresponding to the trim size of the final piece. If none of the standard sizes are appropriate, you can type dimensions in the Width and Height fields; if you enter your own measurements, "Custom" appears in the Size field.

Predefined sizes available are US Letter, US Legal, A4 Letter, B5 Letter, and Tabloid.

The orientation of the page (*portrait* [tall] or *landscape* [wide]) is assigned automatically. For example, if you choose US Letter, the Width and Height fields read 8.5 in. and 11 in., respectively, or the metric equivalent. You can switch between portrait and landscape orientations by clicking the appropriate radio button.

Margin Guides

Guides are inserted to define the *live area* of your page, or the area of the page in which it is safe to place text and graphics to avoid cutoff at the finishing stages. They are inserted at a distance you specify from the Top, Bottom, Left, and Right edges of the page. If the Facing Pages box is checked, the Left and Right designations change to Inside and Outside, respectively, so pages are mirrored.

Column Guides

These nonprinting guides appear on every new page of a layout. They are helpful when laying out a document with a number of columns, such as a newsletter or magazine. The Columns field specifies the number of columns; the Gutter Width field specifies the space between columns.

Automatic Text Box

Since all text must be placed in a text box, it is often helpful to automatically add a text box with each new page. If this check box is activated, the automatic text box is placed on the master page and is then applied to subsequent new pages. The automatic text box, by default, fills the margin guides perfectly.

Managing Layouts

Clicking OK in the New Project dialog box creates a project file with one layout space. The layout space has the page dimensions, margins, and column attributes you defined in the New Project dialog box. The title bar shows the name of the project and the name of the active layout within the project. In a new project file, a tab appears at the bottom of the window with the name of the layout. If you add layouts to the project files, each layout is identified by its own tab, and the tab of the active layout is highlighted.

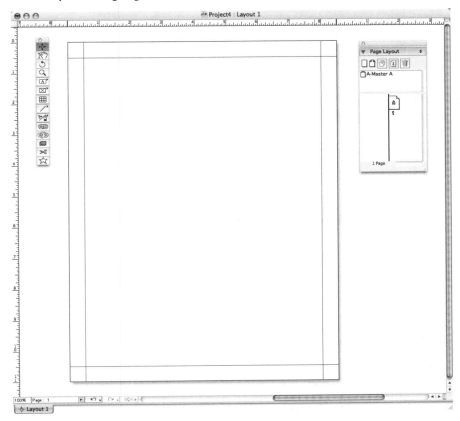

Trim size is the size of the final piece after it is printed and finished. A letter-size piece of paper, for example, has a trim size of 8.5 × 11 in.

Most printers and binderies recommend at least a 0.25-in. margin to allow for mechanical variation in the finishing process. If you place important elements too close to the edge of a page, they might be cut off.

If inches, points, picas, or agates are defined in the Measurements preferences, the page size is displayed in inches; if millimeters, centimeters, or ciceros are selected, the display is in metric units.

Once a layout has been created, you can change the page attributes of the layout by choosing Layout>Layout Properties. You can change the page to a different size, either predefined or custom. You can change the Layout Type from Print to Web or from Web to Print, which you will do in Chapter 17. The other options in the Layout Properties are *grayed out* (unavailable); you can't change the margins, columns, or automatic text box attributes of a layout space. These changes must be applied to master pages.

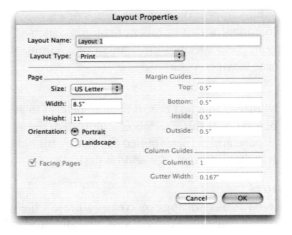

If any placed elements would fall outside the parameters of the new page size, QuarkXPress displays a warning indicating the location of problem elements. Clicking OK closes the warning and leaves the layout unaffected. You must replace, resize, or remove the problem elements before you can change the page size.

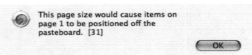

CREATE A NEW PROJECT

1. Press Command/Control-N to create a new project.

2. Type "Measurement Test" in the Layout Name field, and make sure Print is selected in the Layout Type menu.

3. The specifications that appear in the New Project dialog box are your system defaults. Change the settings in the Page area to a Width of 4 in. and a Height of 9 in.

4. The Automatic Text Box option should be checked, so a text box will be placed on each page of the layout automatically. Leave the other settings at their defaults, and click OK.

5. Notice that the horizontal and vertical rulers are displayed in inches.

6. Return to the menu bar. Choose Layout>Layout Properties, change the Size to US Letter, and click OK.

7. Access the Quark Preferences (QuarkXPress>Preferences on Macintosh or Edit>Preferences on Windows).

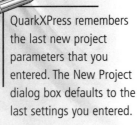

QuarkXPress remembers the last new project parameters that you entered. The New Project dialog box defaults to the last settings you entered.

On a Macintosh, preferences are accessed in the QuarkXPress menu. On Windows, preferences are accessed in the Edit menu.

8. Select Measurements under Print Layout. Change the Horizontal Measurements and Vertical Measurements menus to Picas. Click OK.

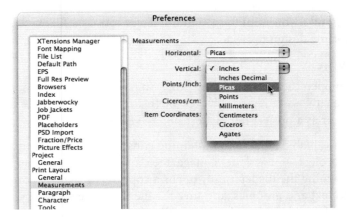

We use inches — the standard in the United States — as the primary unit of measurement throughout this book, except where noted.

Notice that the rulers in the Project window have changed to display measurements in picas.

9. Close the project without saving.

SAVING FILES

After you create a new project or make changes to an existing one, you can choose Save or Save As to store the file. The first time you save a new project, choosing File>Save or File>Save As opens the Save As dialog box (a system-standard navigation dialog box).

It's a good idea to get into the habit of saving your changes periodically by pressing Command/Control-S. The previously saved version of the file will be replaced by the current working version.

You can navigate to any folder on your hard drive, or to another drive attached to your computer. To name the project, type the name in the Save As/File Name field. If you don't type a new name, the default name (ProjectN, where "N" is the number of new projects created since launching the application) is assigned to the project.

After you have saved a project file, you can choose File>Save (Command/Control-S) to save work in progress. You can also choose File>Save As to save a working file with a different name, which preserves the original file. This is particularly useful if you want to save multiple versions of a file, such as different ideas for the same design project.

Save Options

Any time you open the Save As dialog box, you have the option to save either as a regular project file (using the extensions ".qxp"), or as a project template (using the extension ".qpt").

Templates are valuable tools for maintaining consistency throughout several versions of a project — newsletters, magazines, and so on. When you save a file as a template, opening the file later only opens a copy of the file. You can modify elements, add text and graphics, and save the file with a new name; you are not, however, modifying the original template file. To make changes to the template file, you have to choose File>Save As, choose Template from the Type menu, enter the same file name as the existing file, and click Save to overwrite the existing file.

Automatic Saving Routines

You have two options for automatically saving files; these options can be accessed in the Preferences dialog box by choosing Save under Application.

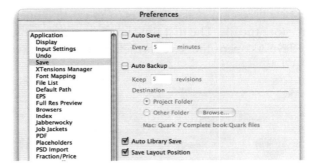

If the Auto Save option is selected, the application periodically saves a temporary copy of your work, which can be recovered in the event of a crash. Auto Backup saves a permanent copy of your file every time you save manually.

Auto Save is convenient if you're having system problems and are afraid of losing important data, but saving takes time, and saving every five minutes is not practical when time is at a premium. A better idea is to simply press Command/Control-S periodically.

Auto Backup can consume valuable hard-disk space at an alarming rate. If you choose to use this option, you should back up your projects to a drive other than the one on which you are actively working, and then dispose of all of the versions you don't want when the project is finished.

Exporting Layouts

You can now export one or more layouts in a project as a separate project file (File>Export>Layouts as Project). The Export Layouts as Project dialog box offers the standard navigation structure that you get when you save a file. The Layouts pane in the bottom-left corner lists all layouts in the current project; by default, the Select All option is checked (as are all the individual layouts in the pane). You can export only certain layouts by unchecking those that you don't want to appear in the resulting file.

When saving multiple versions of a file, it is a good idea to add the time or date to the file name so that you can later identify which version you want.

On a Macintosh, preferences are accessed in the QuarkXPress menu. On Windows, preferences are accessed in the Edit menu.

Occasionally, you might make changes to a layout, and then decide you don't like the changes. If you have previously saved the file, you can choose File>Revert to Saved to return to the last saved version of the file (other than an auto save).

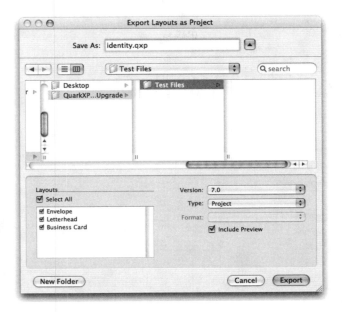

The Export Layouts as Project dialog box is also used to save files to be compatible with version 6. (This capability is no longer available in the Save As dialog box.) The Version menu, defaulted to 7.0, can be changed to 6.0 to allow exported projects (and the selected layouts) to open in QuarkXPress 6 or 6.5. You can also export selected layouts as a template by choosing that option from the Type menu.

As is always the case when saving files for backward compatibility, you will lose features that are not available in the older version. In the case of QuarkXPress 7 compared to 6 or 6.5, this might be significant.

 SAVE A PROJECT

1. Create a new project. Type "Layout Test" in the Layout Name field, and make sure that Print is selected in the Layout Type menu. Set the Page Size to US Letter; press OK to accept the default configuration.

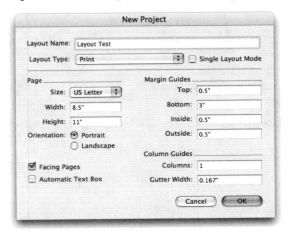

2. Press Command/Control-S. Navigate to your **Work_In_Progress** folder, and name the project "save_practice.qxp". Click the Save button.

Unless directed otherwise, save all projects in the **Work_In_Progress** folder.

On Windows, the file extension is automatically added for you. On a Macintosh, it is good practice to add the extension manually to the file name.

3. Choose File>Save As, and save a copy of the file in the same location with the name "save_as_practice.qxp".

4. Choose Layout>Layout Properties. Change the Page Size to US Legal and click OK.

5. In the Measurements Preferences dialog box, change the Horizontal Measurements and Vertical Measurements menus to picas. Click OK.

6. Press Command/Control-0 (zero). The page view changes to fill the window.

7. Choose File>Revert to Saved, then click Yes when the Revert dialog box appears. Notice that the Page Size has returned to Letter, and the rulers are displaying in inches again.

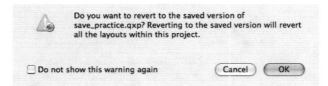

When you choose Revert to Saved, all layouts of the project are affected.

8. Close the file.

9. Press Command/Control-O to access the Open dialog box, and navigate to your **Work_In_Progress** folder. Notice that both the save_practice.qxp and the save_as_practice.qxp files are available. Click the Cancel button.

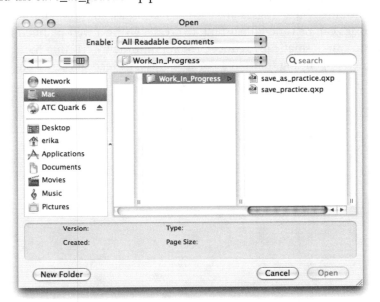

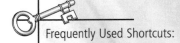
TEMPLATES AND MASTER FILES

By creating templates, you can build the structure of a document once — including layout grid and various assets — and apply the same layout many times. There are instances, however, when you want one project file to be consistent with another. For example, you might want to use the same fonts and colors in different projects for a particular client, but not the same layout. For such cases, QuarkXPress allows you to transfer components from one project to another by choosing File>Append.

Many designers find it helpful to create a *master file* — a QuarkXPress project file that contains the style sheets, colors, H&J routines, and other structural elements that are used in more than one type of file for a particular client, project, or other group.

As an example, one client prefers body text to be set as 10-pt. Times New Roman with very tight leading, another likes the feel of Gill Sans with standard leading for body copy, and a third client has had a proprietary font created for all files. All of these clients use a different specific color scheme to match their respective corporate identities. One client insists that no hyphens can appear in any file, and the others have different standards for hyphenating copy.

The point is that individual design projects have individual requirements. Rather than starting from scratch for every new project, you can build a master project for each client that contains common formatting requirements. At the beginning of a new project, you can create the layout grid for the particular job, then append that client's preferred styles, colors, and so on to the new project.

Appending Assets

The Append dialog box presents a list of elements that can be imported from one project into another — Style Sheets, Colors, H&Js, Lists, Dashes & Stripes, Hyperlinks, Menus, Meta Tags, Font Families, and Cascading Menus. Each of these categories can be time-consuming to create. Using a well-planned master file, however, you can dramatically reduce production time by creating these elements once, and then appending them to a particular job, instead of recreating each element for every new job.

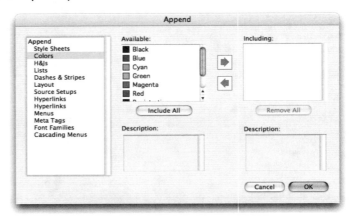

You can append a single item, several items, or all items in any category. If a particular project requires a completely different body-copy treatment, for example, you can choose to append only headlines and captions, and then define the body copy style in the new file.

If you append style sheets, the fonts used in the master-file style sheets must be available on your computer. If not, you will receive a missing font warning when you click OK.

Tips for Using Master Files

Master files allow you to automate your production workflow by creating elements once, and then appending them to any file you create. The following tips will help you create effective and efficient master files.

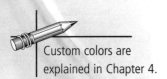

Custom colors are explained in Chapter 4.

Style Sheets are explained in Chapter 6.

Lists are explained in depth in Chapter 12.

- When creating the master file, the page size, margins, columns, and gutters are irrelevant unless you will also use the master file as a layout template for other layouts.

- If a client prefers a particular font for the majority of jobs, be sure to change the Normal style sheet to the preferred font.

- You can include any proprietary fonts and colors in the master file.

- If the client likes a specific style of hyphenation and justification, you can define an appropriate H&J routine in the master file.

- Using the style sheets that you define in the master file, you can create common lists (such as a table of contents) that can be imported auto-matically into any project.

- Once appended, master-file items become a part of the file on which you are working. Appended items are not linked to the master file, and can be modi-fied within the new file without affecting the master.

1. Open the file **recipe.qpt** from the **RF_Quark7>Chapter02** folder.

    This file is an existing template (with the extension ".qpt"). You are going to change some of the assets that are part of this template.

2. Using whatever configuration you prefer, make sure the Style Sheets and Colors palettes are both visible.

3. Choose File>Append.

4. Navigate to the file **cooks_master.qxp** in the **RF_Quark7>Chapter02** folder, and click Open.

5. Make sure Style Sheets is selected in the left pane, and click Include All.

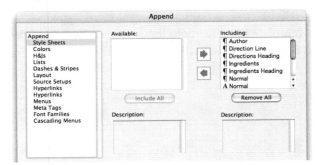

6. Select Colors in the left pane and click Include All.

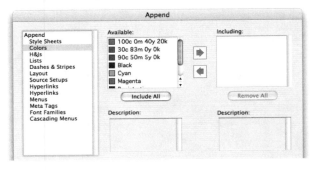

7. Click OK. You will see a warning that any embedded elements will also be appended. Activate the Do Not Show This Warning Again check box, and click OK.

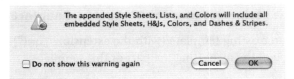

The style sheets and colors from the master file (cooks_master.qxp) are now a part of the open file.

8. Choose File>Save As and navigate to your **Work_In_Progress** folder. Type "recipe.qpt" in the Name field, and choose Template from the Type menu. Click Save.

9. Your new template file now includes the styles sheets and colors already defined in the client's master file. Close the file.

WORKING IN SINGLE-LAYOUT MODE

The multiple-layout concept is the foundation for a number of new features in QuarkXPress, including the ability to share work with multiple users (see Chapter 15). However, some use cases do not require this potentially complex ability, so version 7 now offers the ability to work in single-layout mode.

When you create a new project (File>New>Project or Command/Control-N), a check box to the right of the Layout Type menu can be selected to work in single-layout mode.

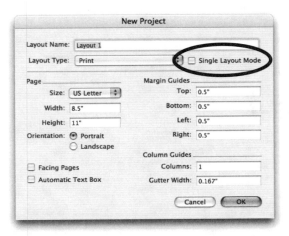

The Single Layout Mode option is unchecked by default. You can change this behavior by activating the Single Layout Mode check box in the Project>General pane of the Preferences dialog box.

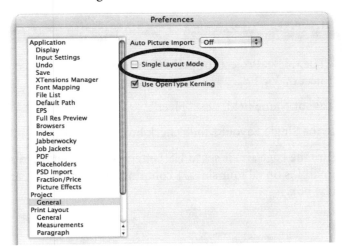

If you are working in single-layout mode, the Project window mimics the document window of version 5 and earlier; the title bar shows only a project name (instead of the Project:Layout format of a standard project), and there are no navigation tabs at the bottom of the Project window.

This is the only significant difference between the two modes; the Single Layout Mode option was added for people who didn't want to bother with multiple layouts. All the same tools and features in standard mode are also available in single-layout mode. A single-layout mode project can, in fact, be converted to a standard (multiple-layout) project by simply adding a new layout (Layout>New) to the project, or by appending one or more existing layouts to the current file.

If you create a file in single-layout mode, the Layout Name field in the New Project dialog box disappears, and the Layout Name field in the Layout Properties dialog box will be unavailable. However, if you define a layout name *before* checking the Single Layout Mode check box, that layout name is stored in the file even though it is transparent as long as you remain in single-layout mode.

If you are working in single-layout mode, appending another layout converts the project to standard (multiple-layout) mode. The layout tabs for all layouts in the project appear at the bottom of the window, and the title bar changes to show the Project:Layout naming structure.

Appending Layouts

Whether you are working in standard or single-layout mode, you can now append entire layouts from one project file to another.

The Append dialog box, accessed in the Edit menu, includes a Layout category in the left pane. As in previous versions, you have to first navigate to the file that contains the assets you want to append to the current layout. If you highlight Layout in the left pane, the Available area shows the layouts that exist in the selected file. You can append one or more layouts from a file in a single pass by moving them into the Including area and clicking OK.

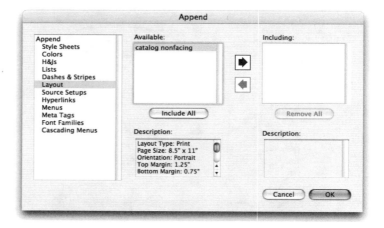

All assets contained in the appended layouts (colors, style sheets, H&J routines, and so on) are also appended to the current file.

WORK WITH PROJECTS AND LAYOUTS

1. Choose File>New>Project (or press Command/Control-N) to open the New Project dialog box.

2. In the Layout Name field, type "Flyer".

3. Activate the Single Layout Mode check box.

4. Make sure the page size is set to US Letter with Portrait orientation; define 0.5-in. margins on all four sides, 1 column, nonfacing pages, and no automatic text box.

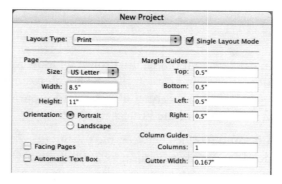

5. Click OK to create your new file.

The Project window looks much like it did in version 5 — no layout tabs and only the file name in the title bar.

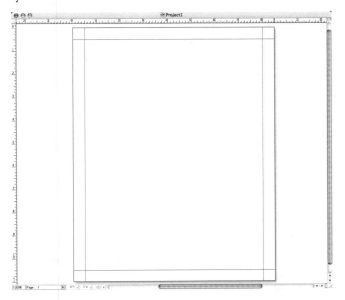

Because you have not yet saved this file, the title bar shows "ProjectN", where N is the number of new files you've created since launching QuarkXPress.

6. Open the Layout Properties dialog box (Layout>Layout Properties).

Because you're working in single-layout mode, the Layout Name field is grayed out; you can't change the name (even though it remembers the name you assigned before activating single-layout mode).

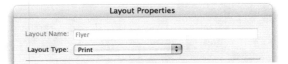

7. Close the Layout Properties dialog box.

8. Choose File>Append. Navigate to the file **mecca.qxp** in the **RF_Quark7>Chapter02** folder and click Open.

9. In the Append dialog box, highlight Layout in the list of options.

Two layouts exist in the selected project: Full Page Ad and Half Page Ad.

10. Highlight Full Page Ad in the Available pane and click the right-facing arrow button to include it in the current project.

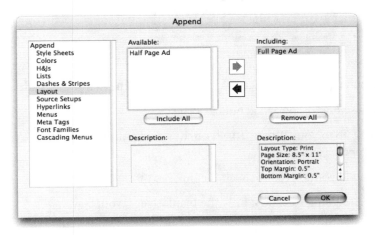

11. Click OK to append the layout.

12. When you see the message asking if you're sure you want to append a layout, click OK.

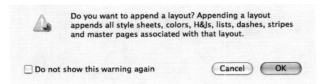

Especially in the case of layouts, it wouldn't do much good to append a layout without also appending its assets. Be prepared — you might have to resolve some conflicts, depending on naming conventions (or lack thereof) for colors, style sheets, and others.

13. When the conflict dialog box appears, activate the Repeat for All Conflicts check box and click Use New.

When the Project window comes back into focus, you should see two layout tabs in the bottom-left corner (Flyer and Full Page Ad) ,and the title bar now shows the Project:Layout naming convention.

14. Review the Colors and Style Sheets palettes.

The assets that were included in the appended layout are now available to all layouts in the current project file. As we mentioned earlier, this is one of the benefits of maintaining multiple layouts in one project file.

15. Save the file as "mecca2.qxp" in your **Work_In_Progress** folder.

16. Choose File>Export>Layouts as Project.

17. Navigate to your **Work_In_Progress** folder and change the Save As field to "mecca_empty.qxp".

18. In the Layouts area, uncheck the box next to Full Page Ad.

You are going to export only the blank flyer layout.

Appending a layout to a single-layout mode project automatically converts that file to standard mode.

Mac users:
It's still a good idea to add the appropriate extension when you name a file. Use .QXP for projects and use .QXT for templates.

Windows users:
The correct extension is automatically added for you.

As is always the case when saving files for backward compatibility, you will lose any features that are not available in the older version. In the case of QuarkXPress 7 compared to 6 or 6.5, this might be significant.

19. Choose 6.0 from the Version menu, and leave the Type menu set to Project. Click Export.

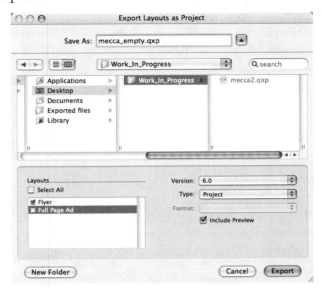

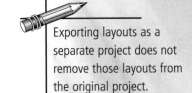

Exporting layouts as a separate project does not remove those layouts from the original project.

20. Close the mecca2.qxp file.

21. Open **mecca_empty.qxp** from your **Work_In_Progress** folder.

This basic example resulted in a project that included only one layout with one blank page; the exported file, however, does include the assets from the appended layout (which became a permanent part of the mecca2 file when appended).

Because you are exporting only a blank page, you don't have to worry too much about losing features by saving back to an older version (except some new formatting attributes that might be saved in style sheets or other assets). When saving back to older versions, always be careful that the resulting file is not ruined by feature loss.

The potential uses for combining or splitting layouts within project files are really only limited by your workflow needs.

22. Close the file without saving.

NAVIGATING PAGES

Getting around a QuarkXPress layout is fairly straightforward. As you learned in Chapter 1, you can move from page to page within a layout using the pop-up menu at the lower-left corner of the Project window. You can also navigate to a specific page by choosing Page>Go To (Command/Control-J) and typing the page number in the Go To Page dialog box.

You can also move from one page to the next by pressing Command/Control-Page Down, or move to the previous page by pressing Command/Control-Page Up.

The Page Layout Palette

The Page Layout palette is perhaps the easiest way to navigate from page to page within a layout. The page icons in the palette look different, depending on whether your layout uses facing pages or nonfacing pages. Facing-page icons appear with the corner turned down; nonfacing-page icons appear as complete pages.

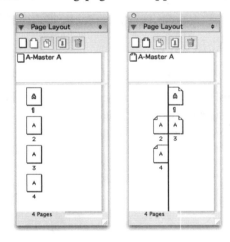

The right palette shows facing pages. Notice the line separating left-from right-facing pages, signifying the centerline of each spread.

Simply double-click any page icon in the palette to show that page in the Project window. To display a master-page layout in the Project window, you can double-click a master-page icon in the top section of the Page Layout palette.

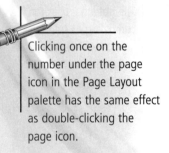

Clicking once on the number under the page icon in the Page Layout palette has the same effect as double-clicking the page icon.

You can also use the Page Layout palette to determine the current page in the Project window. On a Macintosh, the active page (the number and the master-page letter inside the page icon) appears in outlined type. On a Windows computer, the active page appears in bold type.

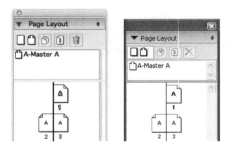

The Macintosh (left) and Windows (right) Page Layout palettes show that Page 1 is currently the active page in the Project window.

Zooming In and Out

Zooming in and out of a layout page is an important feature for checking details or to get an idea of the balance of your layout. There are several ways to zoom in QuarkXPress; the method you use is purely a matter of personal preference.

Keyboard Commands for Zooming

You can, of course, use the Zoom tool, but you will often find that a combination of mouse and keyboard commands is more efficient.

- **Command/Control-0 (zero)**. This command zooms to fit the active page in the Project window.

- **Command/Control-1**. This command scales the active page to 100%.

- **Control-V/Control-Alt-V**. This command activates the View Percentage field in the lower-left corner of the Project window.

- **Command-Option-click/Control-Alt-click**. This command toggles between 100% and 200%.

- **Control-Shift/Control-Spacebar**. This command temporarily accesses the Zoom In tool while another tool is selected.

- **Control-Option/Control-Alt-Spacebar**. This command temporarily accesses the Zoom Out tool while another tool is selected.

- **Shift-F6**. This command changes the Project window to a thumbnail view.

Using the Zoom Tool

Projects can be zoomed from 10% to 800%. The Zoom tool, by default, enlarges the page view by 25%; you can modify that value in the Tools Preferences. If you select the Zoom tool and click Modify, the View dialog box allows you to define the percentage that is used when you click with the tool.

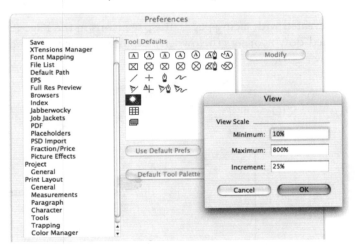

The point where you click with the Zoom tool will be the point around which the project zooms. To reduce the view percentage (zoom out), hold the down Option/Alt key and click. To zoom in on a specific area, drag a marquee around the area with the Zoom tool.

PAGES AND SPREADS

Layout pages can be viewed as individual pages, or they can be viewed as two or more pages at a time, which is called a *spread*. Whenever you are creating a multi-page layout where the pages are opposite one another, you should take the time to review the entire spread to ensure that it is not unevenly weighted on one page or the other.

Facing vs. Nonfacing Pages

Many of the layouts on which you work will be single pages, such as an ad or flyer, or two sides of one sheet of paper, such as a six-panel brochure. Other projects will be longer: perhaps four-page newsletters, magazines, or even books. Depending on the job you're designing, you might want to create facing pages or nonfacing pages.

As a general rule, you should use facing pages any time the design will be read like a book — left to right, Page 2 printed on the back of Page 1 and facing Page 3, and so on. For facing-page layouts, the left page mirrors the right page of each spread. The side margins are referred to as "Inside" (near the binding) and "Outside" (away from the binding) instead of "Left" and "Right."

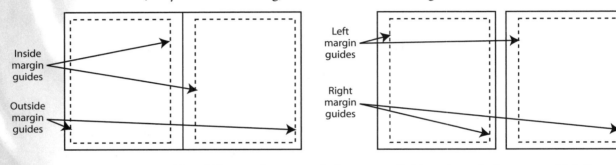

Inside margin guides

Outside margin guides

Left margin guides

Right margin guides

The difference between facing pages (left) and nonfacing pages (right).

If your layout is created with facing pages, the page icons in the Page Layout palette have turned-down corners (below left). Nonfacing pages are indicated by solid pages (below right).

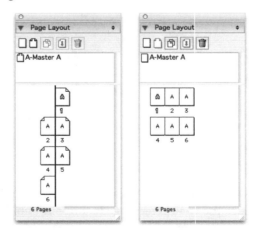

MASTER PAGES

There are two kinds of pages used in a QuarkXPress layout:

- **Layout Pages**. These are the pages on which you place text and images.
- **Master Pages**. These are the pages on which you place recurring information, such as *running heads* (information at the top of the page), and *running footers* (information at the bottom of the page).

Think of a master page as a template. You can place guides, objects, text, and graphics on a master page, then apply that master page to layout pages. Layout pages have the same settings and contents as their master. Any element that can be put on a layout page can be put on a master page.

Every QuarkXPress layout has a default master page, A-Master A. You can access that master-page layout by choosing Page>Display>A-Master A, or by double-clicking the icon next to A-Master A in the top section of the Page Layout palette.

Master pages can only be applied to the layout in which they are created. If you design a master page and want to use it in another layout within the same project, you should first design the master page, then duplicate the layout space that contains the master you want to duplicate.

Master pages contribute greatly to productivity. Anytime an item will be used on a number of pages, it is a good idea to put it on a master page.

Modifying Master-Page Items on Layout Pages

Master-page items can be edited on the layout page; the purpose of the master page is to make the items available on every page, not to lock those items. If an item is to be locked on the master page, you should lock it by selecting Item>Lock.

Depending upon how you have set your General preferences (under Print or Web Layout), changes made to master-page elements on a layout page are kept or discarded if the master-page layout is reapplied to a layout page.

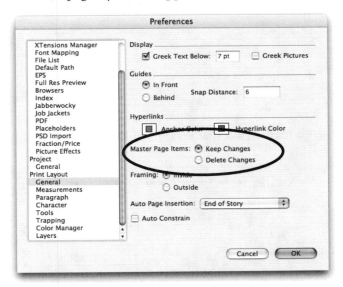

If the Keep Changes option is selected, changes made to a master-page item on a layout page are retained when the master is reapplied. The original master-page item, however, is added underneath the modified element. If Delete Changes is selected, changes are not retained — the element reverts to the master-page setting.

Adding Master Pages

Layouts can contain up to 127 master pages, but you will rarely need more than a dozen. You can add master pages by dragging either page icon from the top of the Page Layout palette into the Master Page section of the palette.

As new master pages are added, they are ordered sequentially as A-Master A, B-Master B, and so on. You can (and should) change the name of master pages to reflect what they are used for. This is accomplished by clicking the master-page name to the right of the icon in the Page Layout palette.

You can also create a new master page by duplicating an existing master page. If you highlight (click once) a master-page icon in the Page Layout palette, the duplicate button adds a new master page (again lettered sequentially).

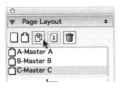

Deleting Master Pages

To remove a master page, you select it in the Page Layout palette and click the Delete button.

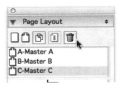

If you try to delete a master page that is assigned to a layout page, a dialog box will warn you.

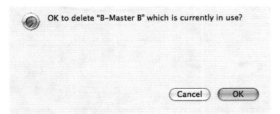

When you delete a master page, any layout page that used that master defaults to a blank page. Master-page elements (boxes, rules, and so on) that have not been modified in the layout page are deleted.

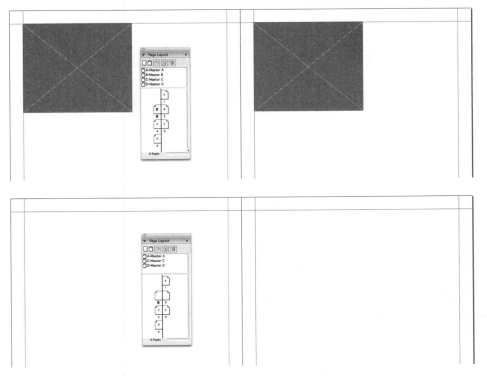

After deleting the master that was applied to Pages 2 and 3 of the layout, the solid boxes (from the master-page layout) are deleted from the layout pages.

ADDING AND REMOVING PAGES

To add pages to a layout, you can use the Insert Pages dialog box (Page>Insert). You can define the number of pages to add, where to add them, and which master page is applied to the new pages. Clicking OK completes the process.

You can also add pages using the Page Layout palette. Simply drag any master-page icon into the palette to add a page, or drag the blank page icons from the top of the palette.

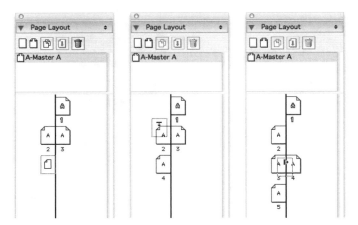

*You can add pages at the end of a layout (left),
before an existing page (center), or between pages of a spread (right).
Notice the different appearance of the cursor for each.*

To add multiple pages in the Page Layout palette, hold down the Option/Alt key while dragging a page icon into the palette. Releasing the mouse button opens the Insert Pages dialog box.

When adding multiple pages using the Option/Alt key in a layout with facing pages, pay attention to which side of the centerline you drag the page icon. If you make the insertion to the left of the centerline, pages are added as new left- and right-facing pages (to both sides of the centerline in the Page Layout palette). If you drag the page icon to the right of an existing right-facing page, all pages are added on the right, as if you were creating a foldout.

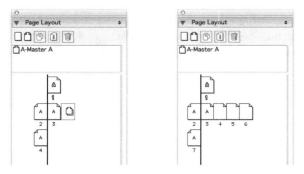

*Page 6, added to the right of the right-facing Page 5, is the result of
dragging multiple pages to the right of the centerline.*

Removing pages from a layout is as simple as adding pages. You can open the Delete Pages dialog box by choosing Page>Delete. You can enter the page numbers you want to delete and click OK to complete the process.

Alternatively, you can delete pages using the Page Layout palette. Clicking once on a page highlights that page icon; the page does not have to be the active page in the Project window. You can highlight more than one contiguous page icon at a time by holding down the Shift key while clicking the desired pages. Once the pages are highlighted, clicking the Delete button removes them.

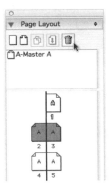

When you delete pages from a layout, regardless of your method, QuarkXPress asks if you are sure you want to remove the pages. Clicking OK to the warning completes the process; objects on the selected pages are deleted from the layout.

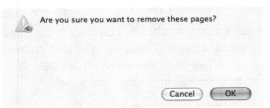

Be careful when deleting pages from a facing-page layout. Elements retain their positioning relative to the page on which they are placed. If an object bleeds off the edge of a right-facing page, and then the left-facing page is deleted, the bleed object from the former right page extends across the center spread when that page shifts to become a left-facing page. The following image illustrates this point.

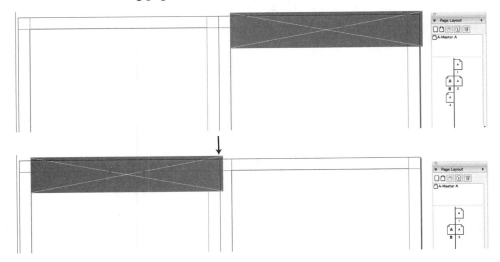

In the top layout, the solid bar begins at X: 0.5 in. and extends 0.125 in. past the edge of the right-facing page. When the left-facing page of the spread is deleted from the layout (bottom), the right-facing page becomes the left-facing page, but the items on that page retain their position relative to the page. The solid bar is still positioned at X: 0.5 in., and now extends 0.125 in. onto the right-facing page.

USE THE PAGE LAYOUT PALETTE

1. Open **master_pages.qxp** from your **RF_Quark7>Chapter02** folder.

2. In the Page Layout palette, drag the icon labeled A-Master A to the left of the centerline and below Page 1 (in the lower half of the palette).

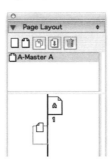

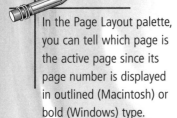

In the Page Layout palette, you can tell which page is the active page since its page number is displayed in outlined (Macintosh) or bold (Windows) type.

3. Double-click the new Page 2 icon in the Page Layout palette. Note that all of the elements of the master page are present.

4. Repeat Step 2 to add another page opposite Page 2.

5. Drag another page down, but before you release the mouse button, press and hold the Option/Alt key. Notice that the icon changes into a multiple-facing-pages icon. When you release the mouse button, a dialog box appears, asking how many pages you want to add.

6. Set it to Insert 3 Page(s) After Page 3. Click OK.

Your Page Layout palette now displays six pages, and the active page (shown in outlined/bold type) is Page 2. You can also see that the pages are all based on the same master page and are all facing pages.

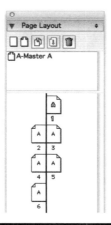

7. Double-click Page 4. Note that the "A" and the "4" are now in outline/bold type, indicating that this is the active page. Look in the Project window and confirm this.

8. Click the Section button in the top of the Page Layout palette. This opens the Section dialog box, where you can assign page prefixes, a new starting number, and method of page designation.

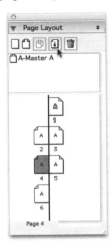

9. Click the Section Start check box. Type "A" in the Prefix field; leave the Number field at 1; and change the Format menu to a, b, c, d.

10. Click OK. Note that Page 4 (the new Page Aa) moved to the right side of the centerline because in publishing, odd-numbered pages always start on the right. Page Aa also acquired an asterisk after the page number, indicating that it is a section-start page.

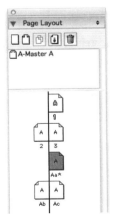

In publishing, a left-hand page is called a "verso" page and a right-hand page is called a "recto" page.

To show all of the pages in the layout, you can expand the Page Layout palette by clicking the bottom-right corner and dragging down.

11. In the Page Layout palette, hold down the Shift key and click Pages Aa and Ab. Click the Delete icon (the trash can/X at the top of the palette) to delete them. A warning dialog box appears. Click OK.

12. Notice that the fourth page in the layout is now renumbered as 4 and is now a left-hand page. That is because the information contained in the section-start page is specific to the page to which it is applied.

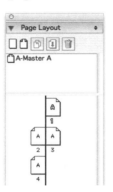

13. Close the project without saving.

REAPPLY MASTER PAGES

1. Open the project **master_pages.qxp** from your **RF_Quark7>Chapter02** folder.

2. If the Page Layout palette is not open, press "F10"/"F4".

3. Double-click the A-Master A icon in the Page Layout palette. Adjust the view percentage until you can see the entire spread in the window.

4. Press "F7" to hide the guides. Notice the master-page elements — there is a rule at the top of each page and a running footer, mirrored, at the bottom of each page.

5. In the Page Layout palette, double-click the Page 1 icon; press Command/Control-0 (zero) to fit the page in the window.

6. Open the Preferences dialog box and access the General preferences. Note that Master Page Items are set to Keep Changes. Click Cancel.

7. Select the Content tool, and triple-click in the text box at the bottom of the page to select the entire paragraph.

8. Press the Delete/Backspace key.

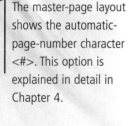
The master-page layout shows the automatic-page-number character <#>. This option is explained in detail in Chapter 4.

9. In the Page Layout palette, drag the A-Master A icon onto the Page 1 icon to reapply the master-page layout to the layout page.

Notice that nothing appears to have happened.

10. Using the Item tool, click the text box and press Delete/Backspace. Notice that when the master layout was reapplied in Step 9, the text box from the master-page layout was placed behind the box from which you deleted the text.

Right Page   1

11. Access the General preferences again; change the Master Page Items option to Delete Changes, and click OK.

12. Repeat Steps 7–9. With Delete Change selected in the General preferences, the original master-page layout overrides any change that you made on the layout page.

13. Close the project without saving.

ELEMENTS OF PAGE GEOMETRY

Page geometry is the physical structure of a document's pages. Page width and height are only two components; page geometry, for example, also comprises how the document folds and bleeds, as well as its press and post-press requirements.

Designers should understand reproduction requirements before laying out pages. You also need to know what happens when the document is folded, and understand that more folds and difficult folds place greater demands and restraints on the final design. Even the paper plays an important role in creating a document.

Page Size

Most print jobs are defined with the following three specifications:

- Live Area: 7.875 × 10.375 in.
- Bleed Size: 8.625 × 11.125 in.
- Trim Size: 8.375 × 10.875 in.

Magazine advertisements are a good example of this concept. Most magazines have an established set of advertising specs that provide the bleed size, trim size, and live area.

The *live area* of a job is the space within which any important element needs to stay. The live area of a page is usually 0.25–0.375 in. away from each page edge for a single-page document. (Different binding and folding methods might require a considerably larger gap on certain edges, which we discuss in more detail later in this chapter.) Any text, graphics, or other important objects should be placed entirely within the live area to avoid losing the information when the page is folded, trimmed, and finished.

The *trim size* of the page is the physical dimension of the final job, or the size to which the document will be trimmed (hence the name). The trim size of the document and the page size defined in the Layout Properties dialog box should almost always be equal.

When a document — even a letter-size document — is printed on a commercial printing press, it is typically printed on a sheet larger than the trim size, then cut on all four sides to the final trim size. There are times when a page element runs beyond the trim size; this is called a "bleed." The *bleed size* or *bleed allowance* of the page is the distance that any object needs to extend beyond the edge of the page to compensate for variations in the trimming process. Bleed allowance is necessary because the mechanical inaccuracies in the printing and trimming processes require a margin of error to ensure that the graphic runs to the edge of the finished piece.

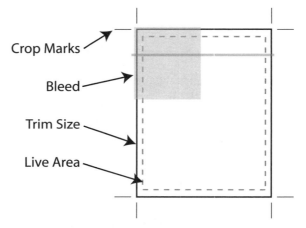

Crop Marks

Bleed

Trim Size

Live Area

Printer's Marks and Trim Marks

Printer's marks include crop (trim) marks, bleed marks, registration marks, and sometimes page information. These marks are necessary for any job that will be printed on a commercial output device. They determine where the boundaries of the final trimmed page should be, and provide a reference point for press operators to check that ink colors are printing in register.

The important thing to remember about printer's marks is that you need to allow room for them on a printing plate, and thus on the printed sheet. If your document is supposed to have a final trim size of 8.5 × 11 in., the press sheet needs to be larger than 8.5 × 11 in. so that the marks and bleed can also be printed.

A common mistake made by novice designers is to create a document at a larger size than the intended trim, then manually draw in the crop marks. This can be a disastrous error for the service provider, who might have to recreate your document at the correct page size. You should almost always create your layouts using the desired trim measurements as the page size. QuarkXPress can create printer's marks automatically, according to the defined page size for any document.

Most printers require a 0.125–0.25 in. bleed allowance.

If the bleed element is a photograph, you must be certain to determine if there is enough of the image to extend off the edge. This sometimes requires resizing the image slightly.

GUIDES, MARGINS, AND RULERS

The tools available in QuarkXPress allow you to easily create any page design: a single-page flyer, a 500-page book, a unique fold, or any other document you can imagine. The layout is the foundation of every one of those jobs.

The single most important element of efficient page layout is planning. Successful page layouts are based on a carefully crafted structure or *grid*. In QuarkXPress, the layout setup and margins are the basis of the grid; horizontal and vertical guides can then be placed to mark columns and other specific structural elements.

Grids are used to divide the page into logical regions. The designer places specific elements such as type, graphics, and color within these regions. There are several ways to create a layout grid. You should already know how, for example, to place guides on a page or spread, and how to create layouts with multiple columns. There are some tricks, however, that make it easy to create a custom page grid.

QuarkXPress helps you position design elements with guides. These guides are colored lines on your monitor, but they do not print. There are four kinds of guides — margin guides, column guides, ruler guides, and baseline-grid guides.

Margin guides are placed on each page in the layout automatically, using the measurements specified in the New Project dialog box. *Column guides* define the space between columns of text within the same text box, if more than one column is defined. Both margin and column guides are set to blue by default and cannot be moved with the mouse.

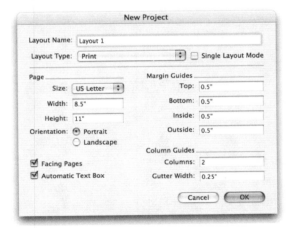

This new project layout is created with equal margins on top, bottom, and sides. The pages face one another, meaning that inside and outside rather than left and right margins are used. There are two columns with a 0.25-in. gutter between columns.

The *baseline grid*, which is used to align text across columns or pages, creates guides based on the text baseline settings in the Paragraph preferences. The default color of baseline grid guides is magenta.

If you look at magazines, newspapers, or other printed publications, you can usually distill the basic grid used to design the job. Some publications make a concerted effort to design without a grid, instead using an ordered lack of structure as the foundation. Magazines such as **Wired** are very successful with this style; the **New York Times**, on the other hand, would hardly benefit from the technique.

Creating commonly used grids on master pages allows you to create the grid once and reuse it as needed.

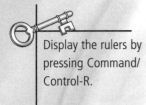

Display the rulers by pressing Command/Control-R.

Ruler Guides

Ruler guides, green by default, serve as horizontal and vertical references when placing items on the page. Ruler guides are created by dragging a guide from the horizontal or vertical ruler. You can position these guides accurately by watching their position in the Measurements palette as you drag them.

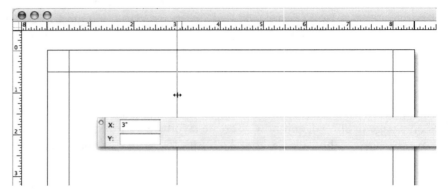

Ruler guides can be constrained to the layout page or can extend onto the pasteboard. If you drag a guide within the bounds of the page, it stops at the page edge. If you drag a guide in the pasteboard area, it extends across the page and the pasteboard. If you are using facing pages, horizontal guides positioned within the page boundary appear only on that page. Horizontal guides dragged onto the pasteboard extend across both pages of the spread.

Pasteboard ruler guides are useful if you are creating objects that bleed off the page edge. Many designers position guides 0.125 in. outside the page edge to mark the smallest possible bleed allowance for any bleed object.

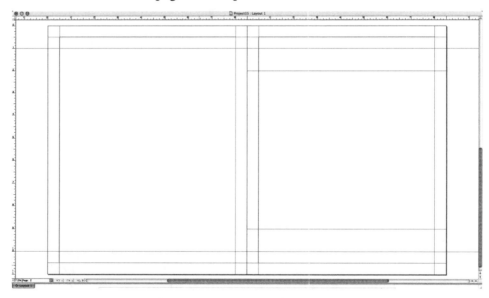

The ruler guides positioned at 1 in. and 10 in. extend across both pages of the spread and onto the pasteboard. The guides at 2 in. and 9 in. were pulled onto the right page and appear only on that layout page.

Viewing Guides

To view the guides in your layout, choose View>Guides. Margin and column guides specified in the New Project dialog box, as well as any ruler guides you have dragged onto the layout, are displayed. To hide the guides, choose View>Guides.

To modify the color of the margin and ruler guides and the baseline grid, you must modify the Application Display preferences. Clicking the colored square next to a guide type opens a window in which you can change the color of that type of guide.

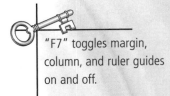

"F7" toggles margin, column, and ruler guides on and off.

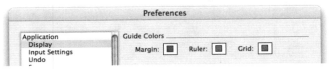

To change the color of the margin guides, click the guide color and then select the new color.

When Guides are showing, text and picture boxes also display a dotted edge. In addition, empty picture boxes contain a large "X," which visually distinguishes them from text boxes.

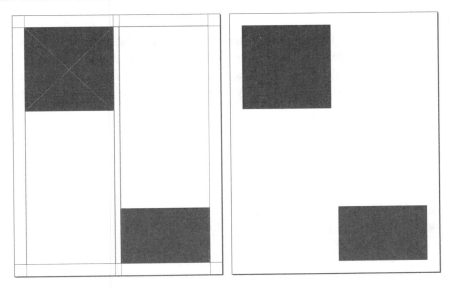

The same layout with guides showing (left) and hidden (right). In the left image, the box at the top left has crossed diagonal lines, indicating that it is a picture box. The box in the bottom right has no lines, indicating that it is a text box.

An empty box without diagonal lines might also have a content of "None." If you are unsure, select the box with the Content tool. If an insertion point flashes in the box, it is a text box.

Once you have positioned a ruler guide, you can drag it to a new position. When you click a guide, the cursor becomes a two-headed arrow; you can then drag the guide to any new position or drag it back onto the ruler to delete it.

Text boxes and images on the page can obscure guides. It's more convenient to make QuarkXPress set the guides in front of page elements (which is the default), rather than behind them. This option is available in the General preferences.

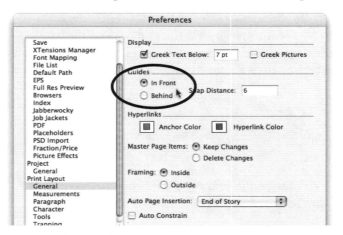

You can place guides in front of or behind page elements and can assign the guides a snap distance.

Snap to Guides

Margin, column, and ruler guides are extremely useful for positioning objects on a layout page. By default, QuarkXPress treats guides like digital magnets; any object brought close to the guide "snaps" to that guide. If Snap to Guides is toggled off, you can move objects near guides without the objects automatically snapping to the guides.

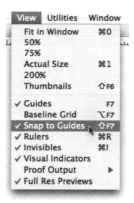

Toggle Snap to Guides on and off in the View menu.

The Snap to Guides feature uses a defined measurement to determine how close an object can be to the guide before snapping; the default value is 6 pt. You can change that measurement in the General preferences.

Understanding the Rulers

QuarkXPress rulers give you a visual indication of the position of items on the screen. When items are positioned using horizontal and vertical measurements, the values specified are in relation to the ruler's zero point. The zero point defaults to the upper-left corner of a page. If the layout is set up with facing pages, you can use the Measurements preferences to set the zero point to reference each page or the overall spread.

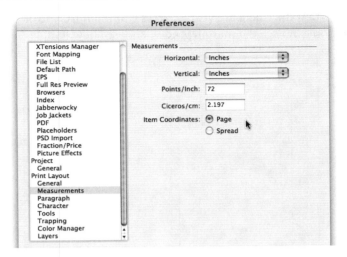

If the Spread radio button is selected, measurements from the zero point apply to the entire spread instead of to each page.

You can move the zero point by dragging the crosshairs in the top-left corner of the Project window to a different position on the page; the zero point snaps to guides. To return it to its default location, just click the zero-point crosshairs.

Zero-Point
Crosshairs

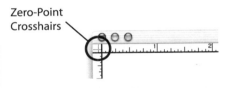

 USE RULERS AND RULER GUIDES

1. Press Command/Control-N to open the New Project dialog box. Create a Print layout with the name "Ruler Test". Set the Page Size to US Letter. Set the Margin Guides to 0.5 in. Set Columns to 2 and Gutter Width to 0.25 in. Make sure the Facing Pages option is not selected and the Automatic Text Box option is checked. Click OK to create the new project and layout.

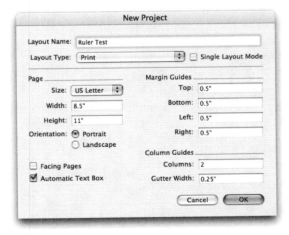

2. Press Command/Control-0 (zero) to fit the layout page in the window.

3. Make certain the rulers are visible. Press Command/Control-R if they are not. If you can't see the margin guides, choose View>Guides.

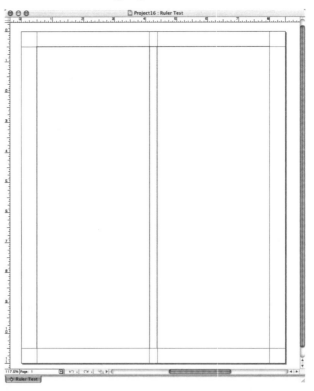

4. Click the horizontal ruler, drag out a ruler guide, and position it at 2 in. Drag other guides to 3 in. and 4 in.

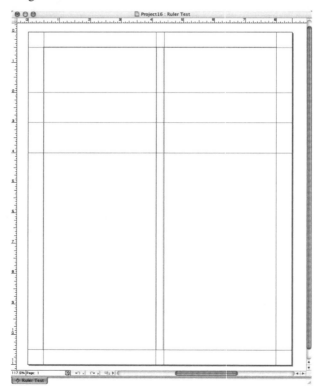

5. Repeat the process for vertical guides, positioning them at 2 in., 3 in., and 4 in.

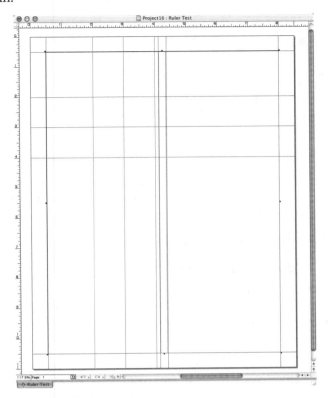

6. Make sure the Measurements palette is visible. With the Item tool, click the text box in the center of the page, and note the X/Y locations on the Measurements palette (Classic mode).

X:	0.5"	W:	7.5"	⌐	0°
Y:	0.5"	H:	10"	Cols:	2

7. Drag the zero point to a new location on the page. Notice the change in the rulers.

8. Again select the text box with the Item tool. Note that the X/Y location in the Measurements palette has changed.

X:	-4.583"	W:	7.5"	⌐	0°
Y:	-3.042"	H:	10"	Cols:	2

9. Click the zero-point crosshairs to return the zero point to its original position. Press Command/Control-R to toggle the rulers off and on.

10. Keep the project open for the next exercise.

 ## MODIFY AND REMOVE GUIDES

1. With the project still open, click one of the (green) ruler guides, and drag it to a new location.

2. Attempt to select a margin or column guide to move. Notice that QuarkXPress does not let you select or move this type of guide.

3. Click in the pasteboard area (outside the page) to ensure that nothing is selected. Choose View>Guides. The page now appears completely blank. Press "F7". The guides reappear.

4. Choose View>Snap to Guides to deactivate this feature.
   With the Item tool, click in the middle of the page to select the text box. Move it around the page — notice that it moves freely.

5. Choose View>Snap to Guides to reactivate this feature.
   Move the text box again with the Item tool. Notice that as you approach the guides, the text box snaps into place.

6. Remove a ruler guide by dragging it back to the original ruler.

7. If the pasteboard shows above or to the left of the page, reposition the page by double-clicking the page icon in the Page Layout palette. Notice that this snaps the top-left corner of the selected page to the zero-point crosshairs.

8. Close the project file without saving.

Using the Guide Manager XTension

The Guide Manager is a Quark XTension that facilitates guide placement on layout pages, and allows you to lock guides in position. This XTension is included as a standard part of the QuarkXPress application, and is available in the Utilities menu when a project is open.

The Guide Manager is an effective way to create a precise layout grid, such as you might use for a catalog layout or any other layout with repeating elements. The Guide Manager can be used to position and lock guides on any layout page or spread, or on all pages or spreads. The disadvantage of the Guide Manager is that a layout grid cannot be placed on a master-page layout.

Adding Guides

In the Guide Placement section, the Direction menu determines whether you will place horizontal guides, vertical guides, or both.

The Where menu allows you to place guides on the current page, the current spread, all pages, or all spreads.

The Spacing and Number of Guides sections define the position and number of horizontal and vertical guides placed.

- If the Spacing check box is selected and Number of Guides is not, guides are placed at regular intervals as defined by the value in the Spacing fields.

- If the Number of Guides check box is selected and Spacing is not, the number of specified guides is placed at equal intervals within the boundaries defined in the Type menu.

- If both Spacing and Number are selected, the number of specified guides is placed at intervals defined in the Spacing fields.

The Origin/Boundaries section defines the area of the page(s) in which guides are placed. If the Use Margins check box is selected, guides are placed beginning at the top-left margin instead of at the page origin. The Type menu has three options:

- **Entire Page/Spread.** This option places guides at equal distances across the entire page, beginning at the page origin (zero point).

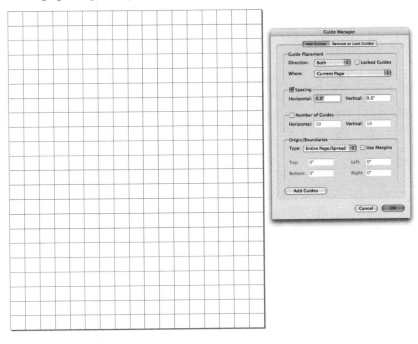

- **Absolute Position.** This choice defines specific boundaries in which guides are placed. When this option is selected, the Top, Bottom, Left, and Right fields become active.

  – Top defines the location of the first horizontal guide.

  – Bottom defines the location of the last horizontal guide.

  – Left defines the first vertical guide.

  – Right defines the last vertical guide.

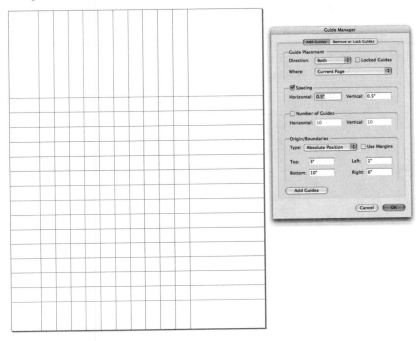

With Absolute Position selected, the distance fields define the boundaries within which guides are placed.

- **Inset.** If this option is selected, the Top, Bottom, Left, and Right fields define the distance from the edge of the page at which guides start and stop. In other words, no guides appear within the distance defined in these fields.

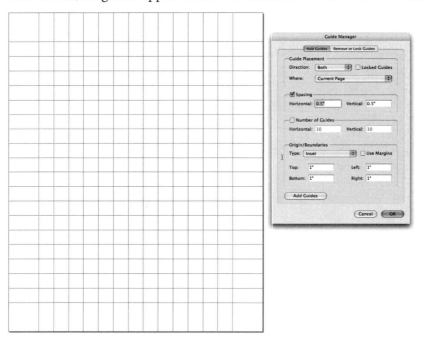

With Inset selected, no guides appear within the defined distance from each edge of the page.

The Add Guides option shows the placement of guides behind the Guide Manager dialog box. You must then click OK to finalize the guide placement, or click Cancel if you don't want the guides to be placed.

Removing and Locking Guides

The second tab in the Guide Manager enables you to remove guides from any or all pages or spreads in both directions. You can also lock guides on any or all pages or spreads in both directions, which prevents you from moving them accidentally. This is the only way to lock guides in QuarkXPress.

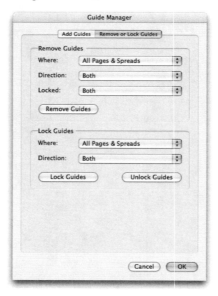

The disadvantage of the Guide Manager is that you cannot place guides on a master-page layout. It is a useful tool for complex grids that are not frequently reused.

- The Where menus in the Remove Guides and Lock Guides sections determine which guides are affected.

- The Direction menus allow you to remove or lock only horizontal guides, only vertical guides, or both.

- In the Remove Guides section, the Locked menu allows you to remove only locked guides, only unlocked guides, or both.

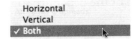

CREATING FOLDING DOCUMENTS

It is important to consider the output process when planning a job with documents that are not just a single sheet of standard-size paper — documents with multiple pages folded one or more times, or other nonstandard page sizes. The mechanics of commercial printing require specific allowances for cutting, folding, and other finishing processes.

When working with folding (multipanel) documents, many people mistakenly assume that the trim size of the job is the size it appears after folding. In fact, the trim size of a folded document is actually the size of the sheet before it is folded. This section describes how to properly set up multipanel documents that fold in a variety of ways.

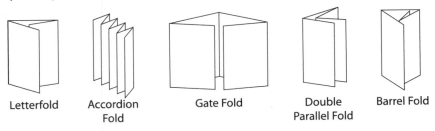

Letterfold   Accordion Fold   Gate Fold   Double Parallel Fold   Barrel Fold

A number of folding documents require special consideration when planning the layout.

There are two basic principles to remember when dealing with folding documents:

- Paper has thickness. The thicker the paper, the more allowance you need to plan for the fold.
- Folding machines are mechanical devices. They process large amounts of material and are accurate to about 0.0125 in. Paper sometimes shifts as it flows through the machine's paper path, just as it can in a laser printer or photocopier.

The issues presented here have little to do with the subjective elements of design. Layout and page geometry are governed by specific variables, including mechanical limitations in the production process. These principles are rules, not suggestions. If you don't leave adequate margins, for example, elements of your design will be cut off or hidden in the binding. It really won't matter how good a design looks on the monitor if it's cut off the edge of a printed page.

Some service providers give their clients die cuts and folding templates in digital form to be used during design construction. You should ask your service provider if these templates are available before you waste time and effort reinventing the wheel.

Facing vs. Nonfacing Pages

When you are planning a nonstandard folding-document layout, it is important to decide whether it should be created with or without facing pages. The fold marks on the front and back of a sheet should line up. This means that if one panel of a document is a different size than the others, the back side of the sheet has to mirror the front.

In the following illustration, a document has one fold — a smaller panel that folds over to cover half of the inside of the brochure. Fold marks on the outside layout have to mirror the inside of the brochure so that, when folded, the two sides line up properly.

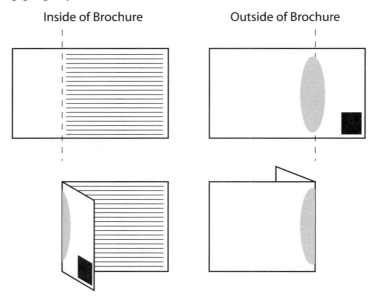

Inside of Brochure   Outside of Brochure

Letterfold Brochures

Letterfold (also incorrectly called "trifold" because it results in three panels) brochures can be printed at any size. There are three panels to a side and two folds. There are two outside panels at full size, and a panel that folds inside 1/16-in. narrower than the others.

The formula for creating a letterfold brochure requires the panel that folds in to be 1/16 in. narrower than the two outside panels. Half of the area removed from the inside panel (1/32 in.) is added to each of the outside two panels.

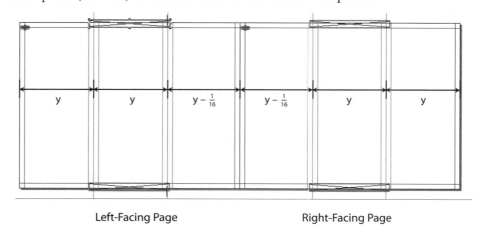

Left-Facing Page   Right-Facing Page

The smaller panel is on the inside of the facing pages so that the margins match up for the front and back. (Y = final folded size.)

Letterfold brochures should be created with facing pages.

- **Accordion Fold.** The accordion-fold brochure — a comparatively unusual format — can have as many panels as you like. When it has six panels, it's often referred to as a "Z-fold," because it looks like the letter "Z." Because the panels don't fold into one another, an accordion-fold document has panels of consistent width.

  The formula for calculating panel size for an accordion fold is:

  Paper Size ÷ Number of Panels = Panel Size

  For example, if you want a three-panel accordion fold from a letter-size page:

  11 in. ÷ 3 = 3.667 in.

- **Gate Fold.** A *gate fold* is a four-panel document. The paper is folded in half, and then each half is folded in half toward the center so that the two ends of the paper meet at the center fold.

  The formula for creating a gate fold is similar to the formula for the letter-fold brochure. The panels that fold in are 1/16 in. narrower than the two outside panels.

- **Double Parallel Fold.** This straightforward presentation, the double parallel fold, is commonly used for eight-panel rack brochures (such as those you would find in a hotel or travel agency).

  Again, the panels on the inside are 0.0125 in. narrower than the outside panels. This type of fold uses facing master pages because the margins need to line up on the front and back sides of the sheet.

- **Barrel or Roll Fold.** Perhaps the most common fold for 14 × 8.5 in. brochures, a barrel-folded document requires more than one calculation. The two outside panels are full size, and each successive panel is 0.0125 in. narrower than the previous one.

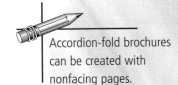

Accordion-fold brochures can be created with nonfacing pages.

Gate-fold brochures can be created with nonfacing pages.

Double parallel-fold brochures should be created with facing pages.

Barrel-fold brochures should be created with facing pages.

CREATE A LETTERFOLD BROCHURE TEMPLATE

1. Create a new project with a print layout named "letterfold". Define a page size of 11 × 8.5 in., (landscape orientation) with 0.25-in. margins on all four sides and one column. Make sure Facing Pages is selected and Automatic Text Box is deselected.

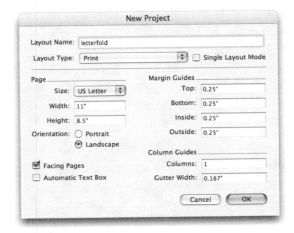

This layout grid is intended for commercial printers using an oversize sheet. Many smaller printers and desktop printers would require a 0.375-in. gripper margin on one edge.

2. In the Page Layout palette, double-click the A-Master A icon to access the master-page layout.

3. On the master-page layout, drag vertical guides for your folds at the following settings:

Left master page	**Right master page**
3.687 in.	3.625 in.
7.375 in.	7.312 in.

4. Click and drag the zero-point crosshairs (in the top-left corner of the Project window) to the first vertical guide on the left master page.

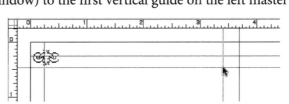

5. To delineate the live copy area, drag guides to 0.25 in. on both sides of the fold guides.

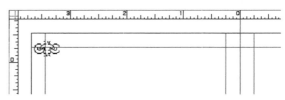

Once the zero point is placed over the folding guide, margins can easily be set at –0.25 in. and 0.25 in.

6. Repeat the process from Steps 4 and 5 to place guides at 0.25 in. on both sides of each of the fold guides.

7. Click the zero-point crosshairs (in the top-left corner of the Project window) to reset the zero point to the top-left corner of the layout page.

8. Save the project file as a template in your **Work_In_Progress** folder, naming the file "letterfold.qpt".

As the previous exercise demonstrated, setting up a brochure properly can be tedious and time-consuming. If the brochure were set up incorrectly using a three-column format, there would be only two possible solutions. You could chop off the extra 1/16 in. from the third panel, creating uneven margins and possibly ruining the appearance of the job. The better option would be to rebuild the entire file correctly, and hope that the text and graphics still fit.

WORKING WITH SIGNATURES

When multiple-page books and booklets are produced, they are not printed as individual pages, and then assembled into a book. Instead, they are printed in *signatures* of eight, sixteen, or more pages at a time. Each signature is composed of two flats. (The term *flat* is a relic of the days when film was manually stripped together on a light table; it is still sometimes used to describe one side of one signature.) The pages are arranged into printer's spreads on the film and printing plate.

If you folded a piece of paper in half twice, numbered the pages, and then unfolded it, you would see the basic imposition for an eight-page signature. If you continued folding that piece of paper in half, you would notice that the spine grew thicker, it became more difficult to fold, and the pages began to skew a little. If you were to add another fold, it would be still more difficult to fold, and the skewing would become even more pronounced.

Printer's and Reader's Spreads

A *reader's spread* is a set of two pages that appear next to each other in a printed document. Page 2 faces Page 3 (convention dictates that Page 1 is on the right side of a spread), Page 6 faces Page 7, and so on. Reader's spreads are easily defined if you think of the way you would read a book — pages appear in sequential order.

A *printer's spread* refers to the way pages align on a press sheet, so that after a document is folded and cut, the reader's spreads are in the correct location.

CREATE A FOLDING DUMMY

1. Fold a piece of paper in half, and then in half again.

2. While it is still folded, write the sequential page numbers 1 through 8 on the folded sections.

3. Unfold it and you will see the printer's spreads for an eight-page document.

 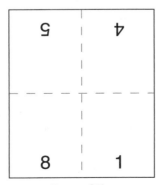 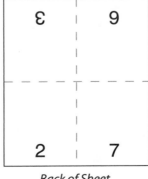

Front of Sheet   *Back of Sheet*

The dummy unfolds to show how an eight-page signature is laid out. Page 8 and Page 1 create a single printer's spread.

When arranged in printer's spreads, the sum of pairs of page numbers always totals the number of pages in the signature, plus 1. For example, in a 16-page signature, Page 4 faces Page 13, Page 16 faces Page 1, and so on.

If a **saddle-stitched** (stapled) book is made up of multiple signatures, the page numbers on printer's spreads will equal the total number of pages in the publication, plus 1. For example, a saddle-stitched booklet is 32 pages, made up of two 16-page signatures. The page numbers on each printer's spread will total 33: Page 16 faces Page 17, Page 22 faces Page 11, and so on.

Understanding Signatures

Imposition refers to the arrangement of a document's pages on a printing plate in order to produce the final product. A signature consists of several pages of a document that are all printed on the same sheet; the sheet is folded and trimmed to its final size. Multiple-page documents, such as magazines, brochures, annual reports, and books, use signature imposition.

If you look back at your folded piece of paper, you can see that the tops of all the pages are folded together. If there is a bleed to the top of a page, given the inaccuracy of folding machines (±0.03125 in.), that ink appears on the edge of the page against which it butted on the signature (as an example, see Pages 12 and 13 on the following illustration).

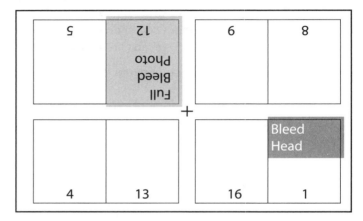

The pages of a signature must be cut apart at the top, which requires at least 1/8 (0.125) in. at the top of the page for the trim. The outside edge of half the pages also has to be cut apart (this is called a *face trim*) so that the pages of the finished piece can be turned. This face trim also requires 1/8 in. around the page edge. That trim would shorten an 8.5 × 11-in. book to 8.375 × 10.875 in. This shorter size might be fine, but it could also ruin a design and layout. There's a better solution.

On the press-sheet layout, space is added between the tops of the printer's spreads to allow room for bleed and for cutting the pages apart. This separation is probably all that will be required for a 16-page saddle-stitched booklet printed on a 70# text-weight paper. If you use a heavier paper (for example a 100# coated sheet for an annual report), or if you have more than one 16-page signature, you need to allow room for *creep*, which is the progressive extension of interior pages of the folded signature beyond the trim edge of the outside pages.

Do-It-Yourself Printer's Spreads

You probably don't want to (and really, you shouldn't) think about creating full impositions for a press. You might, however, want to print proofs in printer's spreads to show clients; or if you have a small booklet that you want to print or copy, masters from your laser printer might be sufficient.

Converting to printer's spreads should always be the final step in preparing a document. At this point in the process, all content should be final, the stories should be edited, and the table of contents and index complete.

In the next exercise, you will be working with prepared files, converting reader's spreads to printer's spreads while maintaining correct pagination.

If you have questions about folds or imposition, you should **always** call your service provider. Somebody there will be able to advise you on the best course to take. In most cases these issues will be handled entirely by the service provider, often using software specifically designed for the prepress workflow. If you try to do too much, you might cause them extra work (and yourself extra expense).

1. Open the file **spreads.qxp** from the **RF_Quark7>Chapter02** folder.

2. If the Page Layout palette is not showing, choose View>Page Layout.

3. Double-click the A-Master A icon in the top of the Page Layout palette to access the master-page layout. Notice that the automatic page-number character (<#>) is placed on the master-page layout.

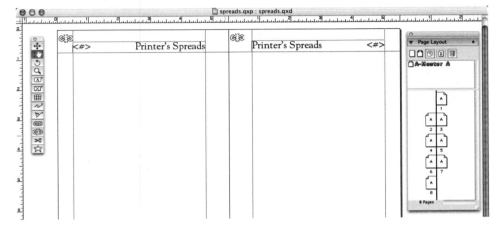

4. Double-click the Page 1 icon in the Page Layout palette.

5. Make sure the Page 1 icon is active (not just selected) in the Page Layout palette.

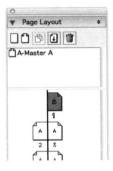

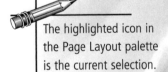

The highlighted icon in the Page Layout palette is the current selection.

The selected page and the active page do not have to be the same.

6. Choose Page>Section. Activate the Section Start check box, and enter "1" in the Number field. Click OK.

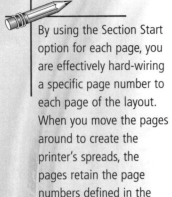

By using the Section Start option for each page, you are effectively hard-wiring a specific page number to each page of the layout. When you move the pages around to create the printer's spreads, the pages retain the page numbers defined in the Section dialog box.

7. Using the Page Layout palette, make Page 2 the active page in the Project window, and open the Section dialog box (Page>Section). Activate the Section Start check box, and enter "2" in the Number field.

8. Repeat Step 7 for each of the remaining pages in the layout, placing the appropriate page number in the Number field.

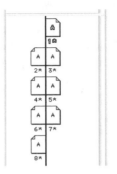

Section Start pages are identified in the Page Layout palette by an asterisk next to the page number.

9. Drag the Page 1 icon opposite the Page 8 icon (it won't work the other way unless the layout was created with nonfacing pages).

10. Move the Page 7 icon opposite Page 2.

11. Move the Page 3 icon opposite Page 6.

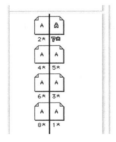

12. Save the file as "printer_spreads.qxp" to your **Work_In_Progress** folder. Close the project file.

SUMMARY

In this chapter, you learned to define a project and layout. You discovered how to modify a layout once you have it set up, and explored a number of routines used when saving files. You discovered how to navigate through QuarkXPress, using the menu options, tools, and a number of keyboard commands. You have learned the basics that prepare you to begin creating projects and layouts in QuarkXPress.

You have become familiar with the fundamentals of page geometry, including the requirements for creating complex folds. In addition, you learned about pages and spreads, and gained an appreciation for the power of master pages. You have learned about the importance of a well-planned and well-designed page layout, and created grids and master pages that allow you to create the layout once and use it many times. You also learned how to work with layouts longer than one page, and should understand the interaction between pages.

Working with Objects

3

A layout is composed of boxes, lines, and shapes that hold the page elements and create visual interest. This chapter discusses the types of elements that are found in most layouts: text boxes, picture boxes, and lines. You will also learn about managing and transforming objects in QuarkXPress.

IN CHAPTER 3, YOU WILL:

- Learn how to create boxes, lines, and shapes.

- Become familiar with modifying shapes and content types.

- Discover how to modify shapes with color.

- Explore custom dashes and stripes.

- Learn how to duplicate and move items.

- Manage the stacking order and relative alignment of objects.

- Use libraries to store and access frequently used objects.

- Become familiar with merging drawing elements into a single object.

- Convert text to graphics.

THE MEASUREMENTS PALETTE

The ability to define box color attributes using the Measurements palette is new in version 7.

As you learned in Chapter 1, the Measurements palette is essential to the efficient use of QuarkXPress. It offers access to nearly all formatting options that can be applied to objects or content in a QuarkXPress layout. The Measurements palette appears by default in Classic mode, which mimics the palette of earlier versions.

The Measurements palette displays information about the currently selected object and makes it easy to perform a variety of functions. The left half of the palette displays item fields, such as the location of the item in relation to the page. The right half of the palette displays content fields, such as the relative position of the picture inside the box.

If the active selection is a picture box, the left side of the palette (in Classic mode) displays the box position, size, angle, and corner radius. You can also change the box color, shade, and opacity directly in the Measurements palette.

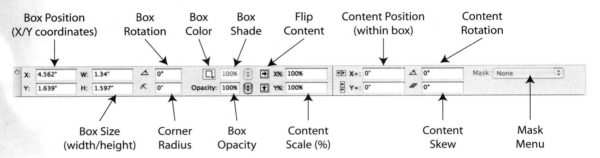

If the active selection is a text box, the left side of the palette (in Classic mode) has most of the same options as for picture boxes (they are both boxes, after all); the only exception is the Cols field in place of the Corner Radius field; this field defines the number of columns in the box.

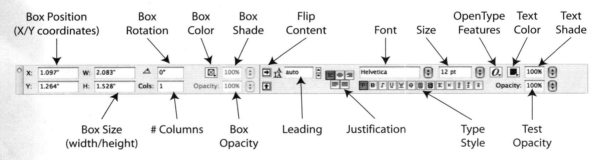

If the active selection is a line, the left side of the palette (in Classic mode) shows the X and Y positions of the line's endpoints. If you choose Left Point, Midpoint, or Right Point instead of Endpoints, the palette displays the X and Y positions of the selected point, the angle (from horizontal), and the length of the selected line.

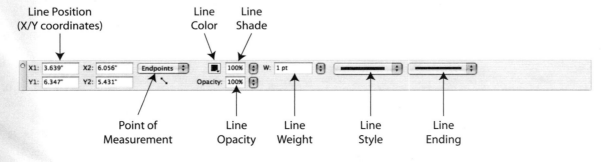

You can use the Tab key to move through the different fields in the Measurements palette. To change any field in the Measurements palette, you simply type a new value in a field or choose differents option in the drop-down menus. If you type a new value, pressing Return/Enter applies the value to the selected object.

Depending on what is selected in the layout, other modes of the Measurements palette can be used to control different object attributes.

- **Box Mode.** When a text box is selected with either the Item or Content tool, this mode controls the position of text inside the box (see Chapter 5).
- **Frame Mode.** Available when any box is selected with the Item or Content tool, this mode defines the frame (border) weight and style of an object.
- **Runaround Mode.** This mode controls the distance between a box and any surrounding text.
- **Clipping Mode.** This mode is available when a picture box (with a placed picture) is selected with either the Item tool or the Content tool. It is used to create and manage clipping paths (see Chapter 9).
- **Character Mode.** This mode is available when a text box is selected with the Content tool. It includes options for formatting character attributes, such as font, type size, and type color (see Chapter 5).
- **Paragraph Mode.** This mode is available when a text box is selected with the Content tool. It includes options for formatting paragraph attributes, such as indents and paragraph alignment (see Chapter 5).
- **Tab Mode.** This mode, available when a text box is selected with the Content tool, defines tab format and positioning for selected text (see Chapter 5).
- **Space/Align Mode.** This mode is used to arrange one or more objects on the page, relative to each other, to the page, or to the spread.
- **Drop Shadow Mode.** This mode is used to apply drop shadows to selected objects, as well as control the various attributes of the shadow (see Chapter 9).

THE MODIFY DIALOG BOX

The information in the Measurements palette closely mirrors the Modify dialog box for the selected object. If a box is selected, for example, the same information is available in the left half of the Measurements palette (Classic mode) and the Box tab of the Modify dialog box.

Command-Option-comma/Control-Alt-comma switches to the previous mode of the Measurements palette.

Command-Option-semicolon/Control-Alt-semicolon displays the next mode of the Measurements palette.

Access the Modify dialog box for a selected object by pressing Command/Control-M or double-clicking the object with the Item tool.

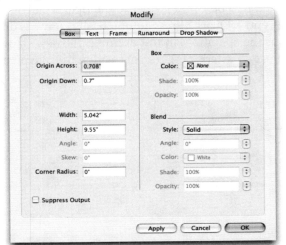

When you make changes in the Modify dialog box (and, in fact, most QuarkXPress dialog boxes), you can click the Apply button to preview your choices before you commmit. The disadvantage of using dialog boxes to make changes is that they take up a large amount of screen space, and might obscure the layout (depending on your monitor configuration).

In QuarkXPress, many commands and options can be accessed in multiple ways — such as the Measurements palette and the Modify dialog box. There is no right or wrong way to accomplish tasks such as changing a box position; the flexibility to use multiple methods means that you can choose which method you prefer for a specific task.

Overriding the Measurement System

No matter what measurement system you have chosen as a default for the active project or the application, you can temporarily override the measurement system by using codes for alternate systems.

Type these codes directly into any of QuarkXPress's dialog boxes to temporarily override the current measurement system.

Measurement	Type	Example	Result
Inches	"	10.75"	10.75 inches
Inches Decimal	"	10.75"	10.75 inches
Picas	p	6p	6 picas
Points	pt	9pt	9 points
Picas & Points		2p6	2 picas, 6 points
Millimeters	m or mm	30mm	30 millimeters
Centimeters	cm	20cm	20 centimeters
Ciceros	c	24c	24 ciceros
Agates	a or ag	15ag	15 agates

Mathematical Operations

You can use basic mathematical operations in the Measurements palette and Modify dialog box. For example, if a box was positioned 2 inches from the zero point and you wanted it to be 1 pica farther to the right, you could add +1p directly after the 2" entry. QuarkXPress automatically converts different measurements and performs the operation. In this example, the new value would be 2.167". For multiplication use an asterisk (*), for subtraction use a hyphen (-), and for division use a slash (/).

| X: | 1"+1p | W: | 2" |
| Y: | 1" | H: | 1" |

| X: | 1" | W: | 2"/2 |
| Y: | 1" | H: | 1" |

| X: | 1"-1p | W: | 2" |
| Y: | 1" | H: | 1" |

| X: | 1" | W: | 2" |
| Y: | 1" | H: | 1"*2 |

When moving items using the Measurements palette, you might try to move an item too far. If you do, you will receive the following message:

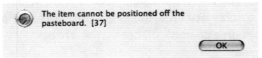

If this happens, just click the OK button to highlight the incorrect entry, and type a different value.

CREATING SIMPLE BOXES

All type and pictures imported into QuarkXPress are contained in boxes, which can be drawn using the Picture Box tool or the Text Box tool (or one of their shape variants). The Text Box tools and corresponding Picture Box tools behave in exactly the same way; the only difference is what can be placed in the resultant box.

Using any but the Freehand and Bézier tools (which we discuss later in this chapter), creating a box is easy — just select the tool, click in the Project window, drag diagonally, and release the mouse button.

Boxes can be resized manually with either the Item or Content tool by moving the object's *handles* (also called "control points") — the black dots around the edges of the object. Standard rectangles have eight handles, but objects can have any number of control points, from two (a simple rule or line) to dozens. If you place the cursor over a handle, you will see the pointing-hand icon, indicating that the handles can be dragged to resize the box.

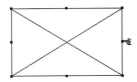

Every elliptical and rectangular object — including those with rounded corners — is contained within a *bounding box*, or a nonprinting rectangular area that defines the width and height of the object. For a rectangular object, the bounding box is the same as the object edges. For an ellipse, the bounding box is based on the largest height and width of the object you can see the handles on the bounding box when the object is selected on the page.

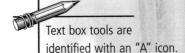
Text box tools are identified with an "A" icon.

Picture box tools are identified by crossed diagonal lines.

When you drag one of the points on the middle of the side or the top of the object, the object becomes wider or taller, respectively. If you drag a corner point, you can resize both height and width at the same time.

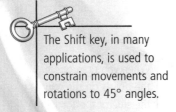

In the layout, empty picture boxes are identified with crossed diagonal lines.

You cannot draw a box with a content of None with a tool, but you can convert a text or picture box by selecting Item>Content>None.

The Shift key, in many applications, is used to constrain movements and rotations to 45° angles.

When a text box is selected with the Content tool, an I-beam, called an "insertion point," appears inside the box, indicating the location where text will be entered when you type or import. When guides are visible (View>Guides), empty picture boxes are identified by diagonal crossed lines within the box. Boxes with a content of None can only contain a colored fill, not text or images.

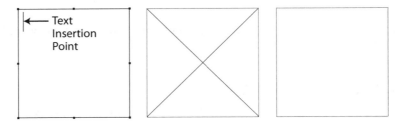

You can change the content of an existing box using the Item>Content menu. The current content type is checked. Choosing a different option removes any existing content from the box; attributes such as background color, frame color, and weight remain the same.

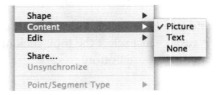

Constraining Boxes

Boxes can be constrained to regular shapes by holding down the Shift key. A rectangle is constrained to a square, and an oval is constrained to a circle. If you are using one of the Bézier box tools, you can also constrain an angle to 45°.

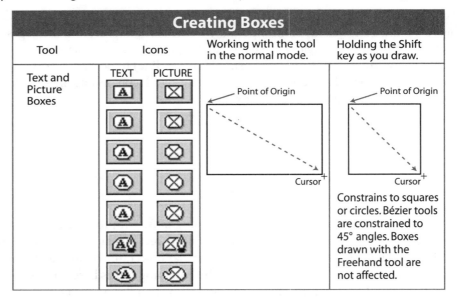

As you can see from the chart, creating simple text and picture boxes is accomplished in exactly the same way. Start at one corner, click the mouse, and drag until the box is the correct size. If you want your box to be perfectly round or square, or if you want a line to be constrained to a 45° angle, hold down the Shift key while drawing the object.

1. Open the New Project dialog box. Create a letter-size print layout with the name "Box Test", and use the default margin and column settings.

2. Select the Rectangle Text Box tool. Position the cursor anywhere on the page, hold down the mouse button, and drag diagonally down and to the right to make a text box.

3. Highlight the X value in the Measurements palette. Press the Tab key twice to move to and highlight the W (Width) field.

4. Type "24p", press Tab to highlight the H (Height) field, and type "216pt". Press Return/Enter to change the dimensions of the text box. Even though you entered values in picas and points, the Measurements palette displays the result in inches (the default measurement).

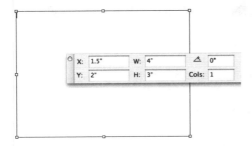

5. With the box still selected, activate the Content tool.

6. Type your name. The text appears in the box.

7. Choose the Rectangle Picture Box tool. Position the cursor on the page, hold down the mouse button, and drag diagonally down and to the right as you draw the rectangular shape of the box. As you can see, the process for creating boxes with the Picture Box tool is identical to the process for creating boxes with the Text Box tool.

8. Click the Rectangle Picture Box tool again, this time holding down the mouse button as you click the tool. Slide to the right and select the Rounded Corner tool. Draw a box. Do the same with the Concave Corner tool.

9. Select the Oval Picture Box tool. This time hold down the Shift key while drawing the shape. Notice that the object is constrained to a circle.

10. If you don't see a large "X" in each picture box, choose View>Guides. Notice that each picture box contains an "X," but the text box does not. Notice that the boxes have guide-like outlines.

11. Save the file to your **Work_In_Progress** folder as "drawing_tools.qxp". Leave the file open for the next exercise.

Frame Weight

Any box can have defined frame (border) attributes, including the weight, style, color, shade, and opacity. These options can be controlled in either the Measurements palette (Frame mode) or the Modify dialog box.

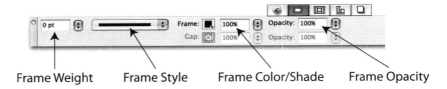

Frame Weight   Frame Style   Frame Color/Shade   Frame Opacity

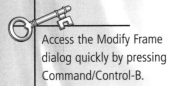

By default, most of the box tools create boxes with a frame weight of 0, which means you won't see the boxes if guides are hidden.

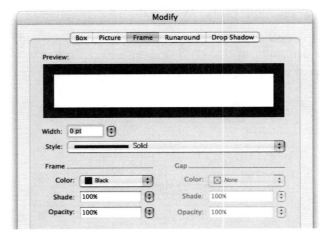

Access the Modify Frame dialog quickly by pressing Command/Control-B.

By default, boxes have a frame weight of 0, which means they are not visible. You can either choose a predefined weight from the pop-up menu or manually type a specific value.

You can also apply special styles to frames by choosing from the Style menu. QuarkXPress includes a number of predefined styles, but you can also define your own using the Dashes & Stripes utility (explained later in this chapter).

The Gap options are available when you use a special line style. These settings control the color of the space between individual pieces of the line style.

Editing Box Shape

You can change the type of a selected object by choosing Item>Content and choosing the preferred type from the pop-out menu. If you change the content of a box, the previous content is removed during conversion.

You can change the shape of an object by choosing a different option in the Item>Shape menu. (The current shape is checked.) Changing the shape of an object does not affect the box content type, unless you change a box to a line. Changing a picture box to a line deletes any placed picture (a line can't contain a picture); changing a text box to a line results in a text path.

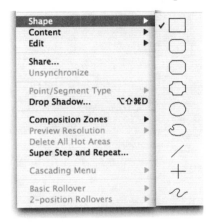

You can also change the box shape manually, using the Item>Edit menu. When the Shape option is checked (by default), you can edit the individual control points that make up the shape. The option is explained further when we discuss Bézier and freehand shapes later in this chapter.

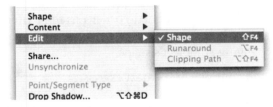

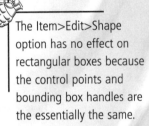

The Item>Edit>Shape option has no effect on rectangular boxes because the control points and bounding box handles are the essentially the same.

CHANGE THE SHAPE OF A BOX

1. In **drawing_tools.qxp** (from your **Work_In_Progress** folder), select the rectangular picture box that you created in the previous exercise.

2. Choose Item>Shape, and change the picture box into a beveled-corner box.

3. Experiment with resizing the object. Select one of its handles, and drag to enlarge or reduce the object.

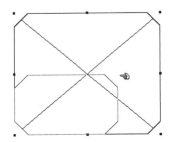

4. With the Item tool selected, double-click the box to open the Modify dialog box. If the Box tab is not showing, click the Box tab to display those options.

   The first field in the dialog box is highlighted. (These figures control where the object is positioned on the page, and may be different than the numbers on your screen. Don't worry about this right now.)

5. Press the Tab key once to highlight the next field. Continue pressing the Tab key until the Corner Radius field is selected; type "3p".

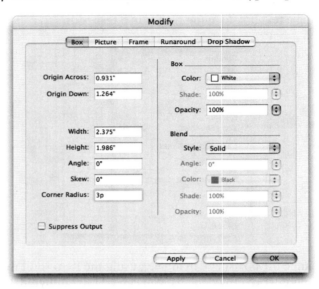

6. Click OK. The corner radius of the box changes to 0.5 in. (the equivalent of 3 picas).

7. Change the box shape to a rounded-corner rectangle (Item>Shape), and experiment with different options until you're comfortable with the function of changing an object's shape.

8. Save the file and continue to the next exercise.

 USE THE MEASUREMENTS PALETTE

1. Select any of the boxes on the page by clicking it with either the Item or the Content tool.

2. Using the Measurements palette Classic mode, change the size of the box to W: 2″, H: 1.5″, and press Return/Enter.

3. Type "/2" at the end of the Height field (it should read 1.5″/2), and press Return/Enter. The box becomes half its height (0.75″).

4. To reposition the box, change the Y field to 1″.

5. At the end of the Y field, type "+0.5", and press Return/Enter. The box moves 0.5″ down the page.

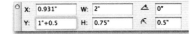

6. Save the file and close it.

CREATING LINES

Lines are created in much the same way as boxes. To draw lines, you click the Line tool and drag the line to the length you want, at the desired angle. When you use the standard Line tool, you can draw or edit the line to any angle. Using the Orthogonal Line tool, you can drag the line only to 45° increments.

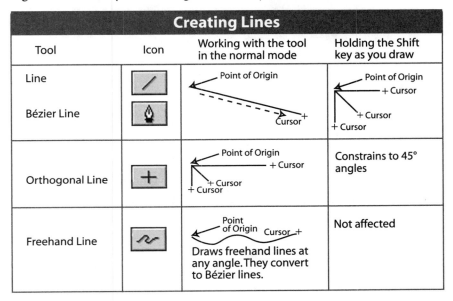

Creating Lines			
Tool	**Icon**	**Working with the tool in the normal mode**	**Holding the Shift key as you draw**
Line / Bézier Line		Point of Origin / Cursor +	Point of Origin + Cursor / + Cursor / + Cursor
Orthogonal Line	+	Point of Origin + Cursor / + Cursor / + Cursor	Constrains to 45° angles
Freehand Line		Point of Origin / Cursor + / Draws freehand lines at any angle. They convert to Bézier lines.	Not affected

It is easy to accidentally pull a horizontal or vertical rule off its axis while making adjustments. When you know you want the line to be constrained to a 45° angle, use an orthogonal line.

Lines are measured from their left point, midpoint, right point, or endpoints.

If any of the first three is selected in the Measurements palette, the line's length is indicated (below left). If the line is defined by endpoints, the positions of the left and right endpoints are given but the length is not (below right). If lines are vertical instead of horizontal, the "left" point is the upper point, and the "right" point is the lower point.

Constraining Lines

Lines, like boxes, can be constrained. Boxes are constrained to shapes of equal height and width, but lines are constrained to increments of 45° angles. To constrain a line, you simply hold down the Shift key as you draw. Lines drawn using the Freehand Line tool are not affected.

Line Attributes

You can define line attributes using either the Measurements palette (Classic mode) or the Modify dialog box.

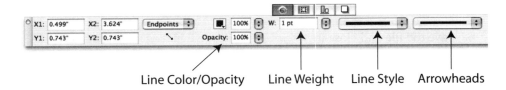

Line Color/Opacity   Line Weight   Line Style   Arrowheads

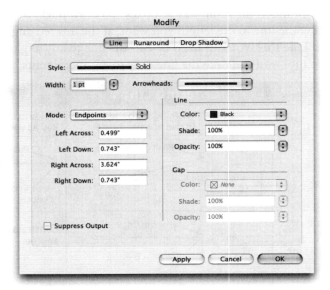

A line or frame must have a *weight* or thickness to be visible. You can define the line weight by choosing Item>Modify or by using the Measurements palette. Simliar to box frames, you can choose from the predefined weights (from Hairline to 12 pt.) or enter your own weight.

You can also apply unique treatments to lines, such as special styles or arrowheads.

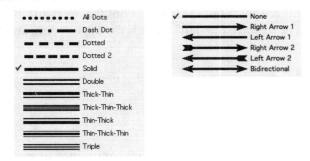

CUSTOM DASHES & STRIPES

As you just learned, any element can have a frame (for boxes) or stroke (for lines) width and style. You can apply the predefined line or frame styles, or you can create custom patterns using the Dashes & Stripes dialog box. Clicking New opens a pop-up menu, where you can choose to create a new dash or stripe pattern.

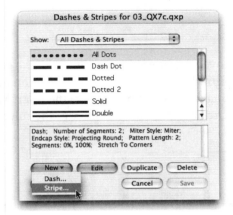

Creating Dashes

The Edit Dash dialog box allows you to define the new dash pattern. You can enter an appropriate name for the pattern in the Name field. The Preview area shows a dynamic sample of settings you make in the dialog box.

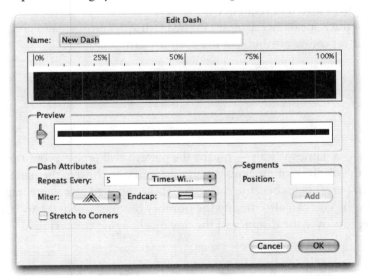

Like any other element you define in QuarkXPress, give a dash pattern a name that is indicative of its appearance.

The top area of the dialog box is a ruler. By default, the pattern is solid for all new dash patterns. The first time you click in the ruler, you indicate the endpoint of the first segment of the pattern.

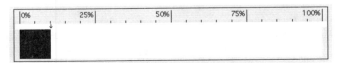

You can add up to five segments to the pattern ruler.

To create additional segments, you must click in the ruler and drag until the segment is the length you want. Releasing the mouse button ends the segment. Clicking once without dragging adds a marker to the rule, but you have to click the marker again and drag to create a segment.

If you move the cursor over a segment in the ruler area, the grabber hand icon allows you to move a segment left or right to a new position on the ruler. You can remove a segment by dragging it off (up or down) the ruler. You can change the width of a segment by clicking an existing marker in the ruler and dragging it wider or narrower.

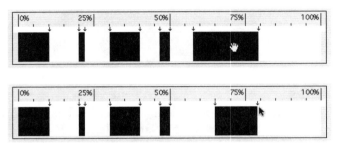

Controlling the Pattern's Frequency

You can use the Repeats Every menu in the Dash Attributes area to control the *frequency*, or repeating attribute, of the dash pattern.

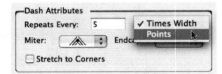

The default — 5 Times Width — means the pattern will repeat proportionally 5 times over the distance of the line. When this option is chosen, the pattern rule is measured in percentages because the segments are applied as a percentage of 1/5 of the line length. You can also modify the number of times (from 0.1 to 50) the segment repeats over the distance of the line by changing the text field.

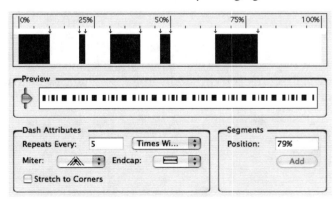

If you choose Points from the Repeats Every menu, the pattern will repeat at specifically defined intervals. The distance of the line has no effect on the appearance of the pattern. With this option selected, the pattern ruler shows the specific number of defined points, after which the pattern repeats.

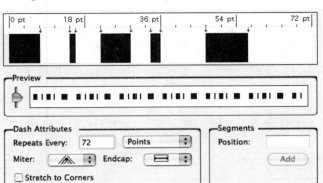

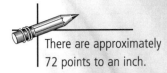

Selecting Segment Options

The Endcap menu defines the end treatment for each segment of the pattern. The Projecting Round and Projecting Square options extend the stylistic end of the segment beyond the actual segment end, which allows different pattern segments to overlap.

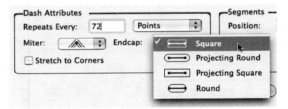

The Miter option defines the appearance of corners if the dash style is used as a box frame.

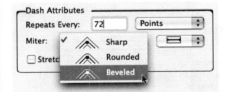

The Stretch to Corners option is also relevant if the pattern is used as a box frame. When this option is selected, the pattern is stretched to make corner segments appear symmetrical. This option overrides the settings in the Repeats Every menu.

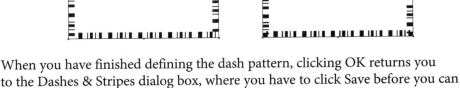

When you have finished defining the dash pattern, clicking OK returns you to the Dashes & Stripes dialog box, where you have to click Save before you can use the new pattern.

CREATE CUSTOM DASH PATTERNS

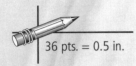

36 pts. = 0.5 in.

1. Create a new project with a print layout using the default settings.

2. Choose Edit>Dashes & Stripes. Click New, and choose Dash in the pop-up menu.

3. In the Edit Dash dialog box, type "Bar Code" in the Name field.

4. Change the Repeats Every menu to Points, and type "36" in the field.

5. In the ruler, click at the first tick mark after 0 pt. to end the first segment of the dash pattern.

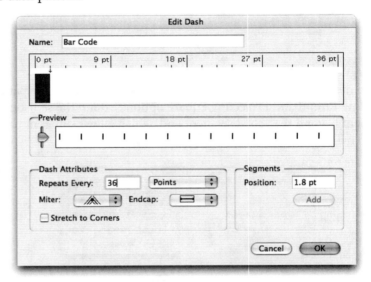

6. Click at the third tick mark, and drag to the 9 pt. mark.

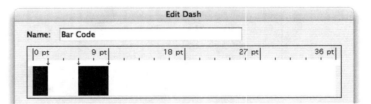

7. Click at the next tick past 9 pt., and drag halfway to the next mark.

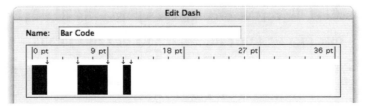

8. Click at the mark before 18 pt., and drag until the Position field shows 23.4 pt.

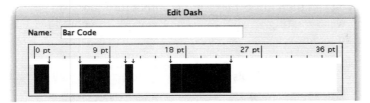

9. Click the first mark after 27 pt. (28.8 pt.), and drag to the right until the Position field shows 32.4 pt.

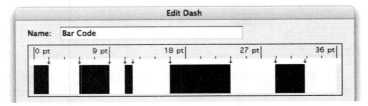

10. Click OK to return to the Dashes & Stripes dialog box.

11. Click Save in the Dashes & Stripes dialog box.

12. Save the file as "custom_dashes.qxp" in your **Work_In_Progress** folder, and close the file.

Creating Stripes

Choosing Stripe in the Dashes & Stripes>New pop-up menu opens the Edit Stripe dialog box, which is very similar to the Edit Dashes dialog box, with fewer options. The ruler, in this case, is oriented vertically. The appearance of a custom stripe pattern is always dependent on the line width, so the ruler is based only on percentages. Segments of the stripe are created and modified in the same way as the segments of a custom dash pattern.

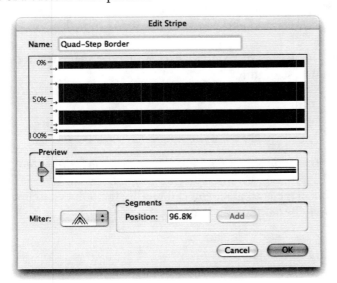

When you have defined the stripe pattern, clicking OK returns you to the Dashes & Stripes dialog box, where you must click Save before you can use the new pattern.

DRAWING FREEHAND AND BÉZIER SHAPES

The Freehand and Bézier tools allow you to create freeform shapes directly on a layout page; you can then import text and graphics into those shapes. If, for example, you were creating an ad for a local vineyard, you could place the copy in a bottle-shaped text box.

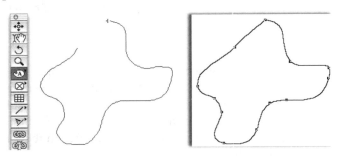

	Bézier Tools		Freehand Tools
Text Box			
Picture Box			
Line			

Freehand Tools

The Freehand Box tools act just like a pencil and paper. With any Freehand tool selected, the cursor is a crosshair icon, which looks like a large plus sign. To create a freeform shape, you click and draw. As long as you hold down the mouse button, a line will trace the path of your cursor. When you release the mouse button, the start and end points of your line are joined automatically by a straight line to close the shape.

When the mouse button is released, a straight line connects the start and end points of the shape (right).

The Freehand Line tool is very similar, except that the shape is not closed when you release the mouse button.

The endpoints of a freeform line are not connected.

Once a freehand shape is created, you can modify the points and line segments, as you would modify Bézier lines and points.

It is far beyond the scope of this book to explain the geometry and calculus behind Bézier lines. The best way to learn how to use these tools is to start clicking and experimenting with how the points and handles interact.

Bézier Shapes

The Bézier tools work based on a series of points and mathematically defined connecting lines. To create a Bézier box or line, you click the mouse where you want the anchor points of the box to appear. If you hold down the mouse and drag, you define the control handles for the point.

A Bézier line segment is defined by two anchor points. Each anchor point can have control handles that define the angle and arc of the segment that connects the two points.

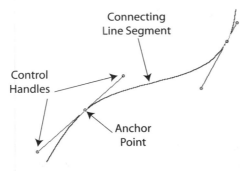

A Bézier shape can have three different kinds of anchor points — corner, smooth, or symmetrical.

- **Smooth**. This point is indicated by a diamond-shaped anchor point. The two line segments join on a curve, as you would have on a circle. The control handles on either side of the point can have different lengths.

- **Corner**. This point is indicated by a triangular anchor point. The two line segments join at a sharp angle, like a rectangular box corner. The control handles on either side of the point can have different lengths and angles.

- **Symmetrical**. This point is indicated by a square anchor point. The control handles on either side of the point have the same length and opposing angles.

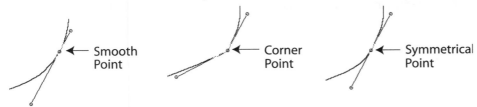

The cursor becomes a pointing hand when placed over a point, handle, or segment of a Bézier shape. You can reshape a Bézier line by dragging an anchor point, dragging the control handles of a specific anchor point, or dragging the line between two anchor points.

You can also modify a segment by holding down the Shift key and selecting the anchor points on either end of the segment.

You can add a new point to an existing segment by Option/Alt-clicking a line segment.

Option/Alt click an existing point to remove (delete) that point from the line.

When you reshape a Bézier object, the new position appears in blue as long as you hold down the mouse button. When you release the mouse button, the object is transformed.

If you want a straight line between two points, you can activate the segment (click it with either the Item or Content tool) and then choose Item>Point/Segment Type>Straight Segment. The associated anchor points will automatically change to the appropriate type.

You can also modify individual points by selecting one, and then choosing Item> Point/Segment Type. When you change a point type, the associated segment shapes are also modified.

The selected line segment (left) is changed to a straight line (right). Notice that the top anchor point automatically becomes a corner point. Because the straight segment can flow smoothly into the right anchor point, that point remains a smooth point.

WORK WITH THE DRAWING TOOLS

1. Create a new project with a print layout called "Bezier Test"; use the default page-layout values.

2. Select the Freehand Picture Box tool.

3. Click the page, hold down the mouse button, and drag a shape similar to the following image. Release the mouse button to complete the shape.

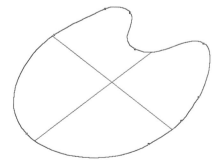

4. Scroll down the page to a blank area. Select the Bézier Picture Box tool.

5. Click the page to place an anchor point.

> If a segment is selected, both associated anchor points (and their handles) will be visible. If a single anchor point is selected, only that point and its handles will be active.

6. Move the cursor down and to the left; click and hold the mouse button, and then drag down and left to create control handles for the anchor point.

7. Move the cursor down, click and drag down and to the right to create another anchor and handles.

8. Continue clicking and dragging to create anchor points similar to the following images.

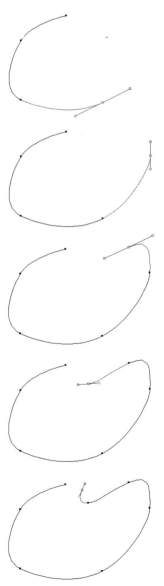

It is important to remember that the Freehand and Bézier tools should not replace vector-based illustration programs. Illustration programs were designed to create illustrations, and they are the appropriate tools for creating complex lines and shapes.

9. Place the cursor over the first anchor point and click to close the shape.

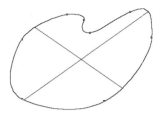

10. Zoom out so that you can see both shapes at once.

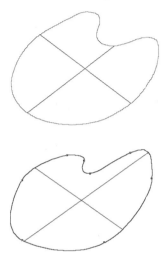

11. Experiment with the handles, points, and segments of the bottom shape. Drag them until the two shapes are as similar as possible.

12. Click the top image with the Item tool. Move the cursor over an anchor point. Click and drag the point to reshape the object. Press Command/Control-Z to undo the shape change.

13. Save the file as "bezier.qxp" to your **Work_In_Progress** folder, then close the file.

LOCKING OBJECTS

QuarkXPress 7 includes enhanced locking controls for both objects and content. In previous versions, locking an object meant you couldn't change it with the mouse, but you could still change the object attributes in the Measurements palette or the Modify dialog box. In version 7, locking an object protects it from any change — mouse clicks, Measurements palette, or Modify dialog box.

Using the Item>Lock menu, you can lock both the box position, and the box content. The second option in the menu is context sensitive. If a text box is selected, you can choose Item>Lock>Story; if a picture box is selected, you can choose Item>Lock>Picture.

When an object is locked, you can still change its background color and frame attributes.

When a picture box is selected, you can lock its contents by choosing Item>Lock>Picture. When a picture is locked, you can't change the contents — you can't import a different picture, and you can't change the picture attributes. You can, however, unlock a picture from within the Modify dialog box. When a locked picture is selected, you can unlock it by clicking any of the Lock icons in the Picture tab.

Warning: Even when a picture is locked, you can still flip it horizontally or vertically (or both) inside its box. You can also still manipulate the picture clipping path and runaround values. These controls are available in both the Measurements palette and the Modify dialog box.

If a story is locked, you can unlock it by clicking the Lock icon in the bottom-left corner of the Character Attributes or Paragraph Attributes dialog box.

When an object is locked, most of the Measurements palette and Modify dialog box options are grayed out. You can, however, unlock an object in the Box tab of the Modify dialog box by clicking any of the lock icons.

All of the box-attribute locks are linked, with one exception: you can unlock the box position, angle, and skew without unlocking the box height and width. Unlocking the height or width, however, unlocks all other locks as well.

The F6 key command locks the selected object. There is no key command for locking content.

- **Origin Across lock** unlocks Origin Across, Origin Down, Angle, Skew.
- **Origin Down lock** unlocks Origin Across, Origin Down, Angle, Skew.
- **Height lock** unlocks all six fields.
- **Width lock** unlocks all six fields.
- **Angle lock** unlocks Origin Across, Origin Down, Angle, Skew.
- **Skew lock** unlocks Origin Across, Origin Down, Angle, Skew.

DELETING OBJECTS

There are several options for removing objects from a layout, depending on which tool you are using.

With the Item tool:

- Remove any existing object by selecting it with the Item tool and pressing Delete/Backspace.
- Choose all objects by pressing Command/Control-A, and then press Delete/Backspace.

With the Content tool:

- If you choose a picture box, pressing Delete/Backspace removes the contents of the box.
- If you have selected a text box, pressing Delete/Backspace will remove any highlighted text or the character immediately preceding the flashing text-insertion point.
- Choose all of the contents of a box by pressing Command/Control-A, and then press Delete/Backspace.
- To remove a box when using the Content tool, you can press Command/Control-K.

This can be a confusing and tricky aspect of QuarkXPress — it is easy to accidentally delete an entire box, for example, when you meant to delete the picture inside the box. QuarkXPress allows to you undo your last action by choosing Edit>Undo, or clicking the Undo button at the bottom of the Project window. The menu is dynamic and reflects the last action in the project's history; if you just deleted a text box, the menu shows "Undo Text Box Deletion."

GROUPING OBJECTS

At times you will want to treat several objects as a single unit. As an example, you have a vertical line drawn to separate columns in a text box. If you select the box and move it, the vertical line will no longer be in the correct position:

Command	Keyboard Shortcut
Cut	Command/Control-X
Copy	Command/Control-C
Paste	Command/Control-V
Duplicate	Command/Control-D

To avoid accidentally misplacing one object in relation to another object, you can use the Group command (Item>Group). Once objects are grouped, they appear with a dotted line around the entire group when selected with the Item tool. You can't access the control points for individual objects. You can, however, use the Content tool to reshape any single item in the group.

Command	Keyboard Shortcut		Command	Keyboard Shortcut
Cut	Command/Control-X		Cut	Command/Control-X
Copy	Command/Control-C		Copy	Command/Control-C
Paste	Command/Control-V		Paste	Command/Control-V
Duplicate	Command/Control-D		Duplicate	Command/Control-D

To select more than one object at a time, hold down the Shift key and click each object.

Delete a box by pressing Command/Control-K when the Content tool is active.

To group selected objects, press Command/Control-G. To ungroup objects, press Command/Control-U.

ADDING COLOR TO OBJECTS

Applying color to objects is a relatively simple processs. Any box can have a color *fill* (or background) and a color frame; lines can have a defined color attribute. You can also apply color to the content of some objects, such as text boxes (see Chapter 5) and certain imported images (which we discuss in Chapter 9).

As with most functions in QuarkXPress, color can be applied to objects using a number of different commands. You can:

- Choose Style>Color and pick from the available list.

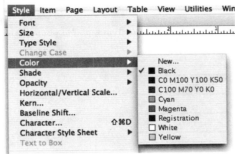

As a rule of thumb, choose None only if you must (for example, setting the text-box background to None if you are placing that text box over a picture). It's better to set the background as 0% (zero percent) of a color (usually black) or set it to white.

- Choose from Color pop-up menus in the Modify (for objects) and Character Attributes (for text) dialog boxes.

- Choose from one of the Color pop-up menus in the various modes of the Measurements palette.

The Color menus in the Measurements palette include a "New" option, which automatically opens the Edit Color dialog box. After you have defined the new color, it is automatically applied to the selected element (e.g., applied to the drop shadow if you clicked the Drop Shadow Color menu, or to the box if you clicked the Box Color menu).

- Use the Colors palette (Window>Colors).

The top of the Colors palette shows different options, depending on what is selected in the layout. You can change the color of any element in a layout by clicking the appropriate button, and then clicking the color you want in the palette. You can also drag a color chip onto an object to change the background color of that object.

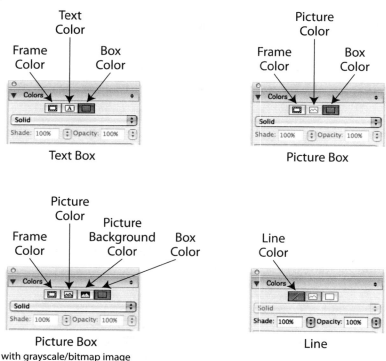

Text Box

Picture Box

Picture Box
with grayscale/bitmap image

Line

ADD COLOR TO BOXES AND CONTENT

1. Open **drawing_tools.qxp** from your **Work_In_Progress** folder.

2. Choose one of the picture boxes with the Content tool, and change it to a text box (Item>Content>Text).

3. Type some text into the box.

4. Drag the Yellow color chip from the Colors palette (Window>Colors) to the text box. Drop the color on the text box.

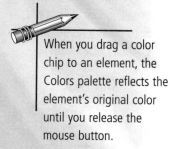

When you drag a color chip to an element, the Colors palette reflects the element's original color until you release the mouse button.

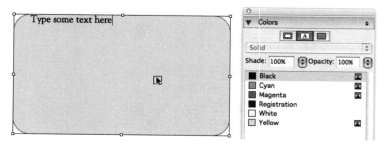

5. Make sure the Background Color button is selected in the palette, and that the color Yellow is highlighted. Type "30" in the Shade field and press Return/Enter.

6. With the Content tool, highlight some or all of the type. In the Colors palette, click the Text Color button, and then click Cyan.

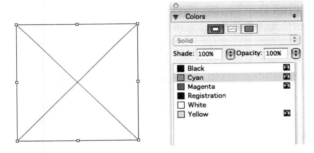

7. Choose another picture box. Click the Frame icon, and then click Cyan. It appears that nothing has happened.

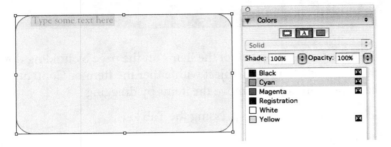

8. Display the Frame mode of the Measurements palette. Assign the frame a weight of 6 pt. Once the frame has a defined weight, you can see the color.

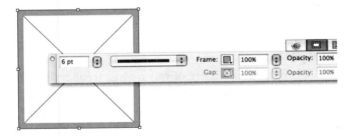

9. Save the file and leave it open for the next exercise.

POSITIONING OBJECTS

You can align, duplicate, and stack elements in a number of ways. You have already moved boxes by typing in new X and Y coordinates and by using mathematical functions in the Measurements palette. You can also select an object and drag it around the page with the mouse, using guides to position objects accurately on the layout page.

The arrow keys can be used to nudge an item. Each time you press an arrow key, the selected object moves 1 pt. (or the equivalent in inches, 0.014"). If you press the Option/Alt key with the arrow key, the item moves only 1/10 pt.

MANIPULATE ELEMENTS

1. In the open layout, select all of the items on the page by holding down the Shift key and clicking each object with either the Item or Content tool. Release the Shift key, and move the items by dragging.

2. Deselect all of the items by pressing the Tab key.

3. With the Item tool active, select an item and press the Delete/Backspace key.

4. With the Content tool active, select a different item and press Command/Control-K.

5. Undo your last step by choosing Edit>Undo [Item] Deletion or pressing Command/Control-Z. Notice that the last item deleted in Step 2 reappears.

6. If the guides are not visible, turn them on from the View menu (press F7).

7. Check to see if Snap to Guides is active. If not, choose View>Snap to Guides.

8. Place a vertical ruler guide at the 1" marker and a horizontal ruler guide at the 2" marker.

9. Select an item on the page with the Item tool. Move the item so it is aligned with the vertical ruler guide. Notice the pull of the ruler guide.

10. Line up several items against each guide.

11. Close the file without saving.

Duplicating Objects

You can duplicate elements in a variety of ways. Most frequently, elements are duplicated using the standard cut-and-paste technique common to most programs (Command/Control-X to cut, Command/Control-C to copy, Command/Control-V to paste).

You can duplicate an object with either the Item or the Content tool selected. If an object is part of a group, the Duplicate command with the Item tool selected duplicates the entire group. If the Content tool is selected, the Duplicate command duplicates only the currently active element, even if it is part of a group. This is very useful if you want to duplicate one element in a group of objects without first ungrouping.

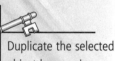

Duplicate the selected object by pressing Command/Control-D.

QuarkXPress also allows you to duplicate an item using the Duplicate command (Item>Duplicate or Command/Control-D). The default offset value is 0.25 in. both horizontally and vertically.

If you need several copies at specific intervals, you can use the Step and Repeat command (Item>Step and Repeat). The Repeat Count field determines how many copies will be made of the selected object. The Horizontal Offset and Vertical Offset fields indicate the relative position of the copies; the default Horizontal and Vertical Offset values are 0.25 in.

If your entries in the Step and Repeat dialog box are not possible based on the layout page size and location of the selected object, QuarkXPress shows a warning.

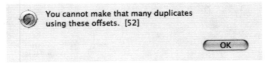

Just click the OK button, which highlights the incorrect entry, and type a different value.

Stacking Order

Each time you create an object, it is drawn above everything else on the page. You can use the Send to Back, Send Backward, Bring to Front, and Bring Forward commands (in the Item menu) to change the stacking order. (Macintosh users must hold down the Option key before choosing the Item menu to access the Bring Forward and Send Backward commands.)

To activate an item that is sandwiched or hidden by other objects, you can Command-Option-Shift-click/Control-Alt-Shift-click. Each click activates items from the top of the stacking order down to the bottom, one item at a time. You see the handles of the selected object, even though part (or all) of the object might be obscured. Once the item is active, you can restack the objects by choosing Send to Back, Bring to Front, Send Backward, or Bring Forward.

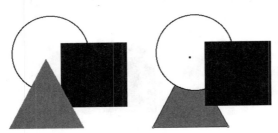

The original stacking order of objects (left).
The triangle is selected and sent to the back of the stacking order (right).
Notice that you can still see the handles of the triangle, even though
part of the object is obscured by the circle and rectangle.

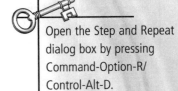

Open the Step and Repeat dialog box by pressing Command-Option-R/ Control-Alt-D.

To place a copy of an object exactly on top of itself, enter 0 in the Horizontal Offset and Vertical Offset fields of the Step and Repeat dialog box.

Use the following keys to speed stacking of items:

F5
Bring to Front

Shift-F5
Send to Back

Option/Alt-F5
Bring Forward

Option/Alt-Shift-F5
Send Backward

Command-Option-Shift-click/Control-Alt-Shift-click to select objects that lie directly behind other objects.

Spacing, Alignment, and Distribution

The Space/Align feature, accessed in the Space/Align mode of the Measurements palette, is used to position selected objects in relation to each other, to the page, or to the spread on which they exist.

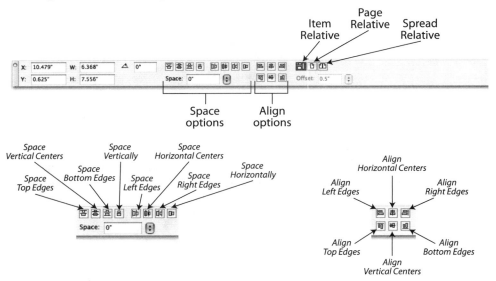

Using the Page Relative or Spread Relative modes, you can align one or more objects to specific edges of the page (or spread). This means that you can place selected objects exactly in the center (for example) of the defined page size with a single click — no calculations or adjustments required.

The Offset field, which is available in either Page Relative or Spread Relative mode, is used to place objects a specific distance from the page/spread edge or center. Positive offset values move objects up or left; negative offset values move objects down or right.

The Space buttons are available when more than one object is selected. The Align buttons are available when anything is selected (if only one object is selected, you default to Page Relative mode).

The Space field defines the distance between the spaced edges (or centers) of selected objects. For example, if the Space field is set to 0.5″ and you click the Space Left Edges button, the left edges of the spaced objects will step over 0.5″ from one to the next.

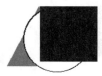

In the Space pop-up menu, the "Evenly" option is a useful tool for applying uniform space to a series of objects around the page, as you might in a catalog. If, for example, you want a page to contain nine objects that are distributed to take up the entire space between margin guides, the Evenly option is far easier than trying to calculate the exact position for each object manually.

A series of nine objects is created (perhaps with the Step-and-Repeat function); you want those nine objects to fill the vertical dimension of the page. The first step is to place the top- and bottom-most objects in their correct positions. (This is an excellent opportunity to use margin guides.)

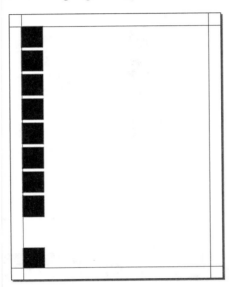

Once the top and bottom objects are placed, you can select all of the objects you want to align and display the Space/Align Items mode of the Measurements palette. Because the top and bottom objects are already placed where you want them, you can activate the Item Relative mode, choose Evenly in the Space field, and click the Space Top Edges button.

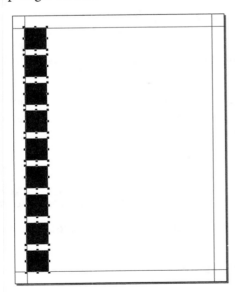

Continuing with this example, let's assume you later need to delete an entry (say, a discontinued catalog item) from the page. You can delete the necessary object, select the remaining objects, and respace objects evenly relative to each other.

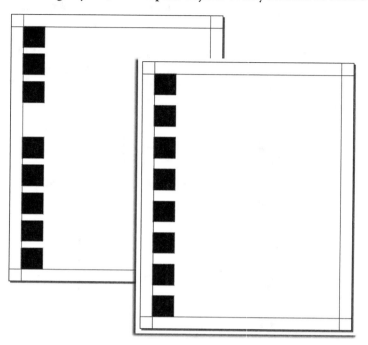

 WORK WITH OBJECTS

1. Create a new project with a print layout named "Object Practice". Define 0.5″ margins on all four sides, without an automatic text box.

2. Select the Rounded-Corner Picture Box tool, and create a box on the page. Using the Measurements palette, change the box size to W: 1.5″, H: 2″.

3. Select the Item tool, and drag the box until it snaps to the top and left margin guides.

4. Using the Frame mode of the Measurements palette, apply a 1-pt. Cyan frame to the box.

5. Select the Rectangle Text Box tool and draw a text box on the page. Use the Measurements palette to modify the text box according to the following parameters:

   X: 2.167″   W: 2″
   Y: 0.5″   H: 2″

6. Select both boxes, and press Command/Control-G to group them.

7. If necessary, press Command/Control-0 (zero) to view the entire page in the Project window.

8. Select the group of boxes with the Item tool, and choose Item>Step and Repeat.

9. You know that the boxes are 2-in. high, so you can create offsets to duplicate the group with even space between. Change the Repeat Count field to 3, Horizontal Offset to 0, and Vertical Offset to 2.25. Click OK.

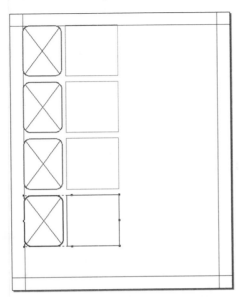

You should have four copies of the same group, with 0.25-in. space between each group. The group of objects, however, leaves a large empty space at the bottom of the page.

10. Select just the bottom group and move it so that it snaps to the bottom and left margin guides.

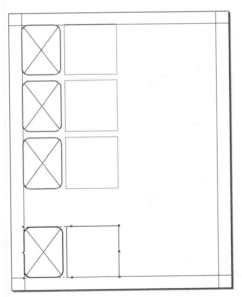

11. Select all of the groups by pressing Command/Control-A.

12. Diplay the Space/Align mode of the Measurements palette.

13. Click the Page Relative mode, and choose Evenly in the Space pop-up menu. Click the Space Top Edges button.

14. With the Item tool and the groups still selected, press Command/Control-C, and then press Command/Control-V to paste a copy of all of the groups.

15. Drag the pasted items until the selection snaps to the top and right margin guides.

You should have a balanced, symmetrical layout in which to place images and text.

16. Save the file as "catalog_layout.qxp" to your **Work_In_Progress** folder, and then close the file.

WORKING WITH LIBRARIES

Consistency is important for the elements that comprise a layout. If one picture box has a 2-pt. border, other picture boxes in the layout should have a similar border treatment; if one sidebar text box has a 12-pt. inset value, the other sidebars should also have a 12-pt. inset value.

You could create an object once, and then copy and paste it every time you want to repeat it; but this method can be annoying if the element you want to copy last appeared 60 pages earlier. Rather than hunting for the object you want to reuse, you can place it in a library so that you can easily access it at any time from the Library palette.

The Library utility in QuarkXPress allows you to build sets of commonly used elements, which can be opened independently of a specific file. You can build libraries for each job, each client, or any other logical group.

To create a library in QuarkXPress, you choose File>New>Library. In the New Library dialog box, you can navigate to the folder in which you want the library to reside and name the library. As with any other element or file, you should use meaningful names for your libraries so that you will know what to open when you need it.

Clicking Create in the New Library dialog box opens the empty Library palette. You can create a library with no project open, but you must create or open a project to create the elements that you will place in the library.

The extension for a Quark Library is ".qxl". Macintosh users should always remember to add the extension.

Adding Library Items

Any element on a layout page can be placed into a library by dragging it with the Item tool. Library items can have graphic, image, or text content, and can include text-formatting attributes.

When the item is dragged into the Library palette, the cursor takes the shape of a pair of glasses, and an outline indicates where the item will be placed in the library. Two opposing arrows appear to the left of the new item if the palette is organized horizontally, or above the new item if the palette is organized vertically.

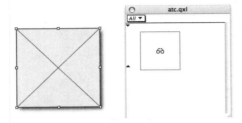

As you work with items in a library, it is important to remember that images and graphics placed into a library are only references to the file. If an image is placed from a library into a layout, that image file must be present when the job is output. Forgetting to send library items to the service provider is a common mistake, because libraries may have been created long before a particular job is finished. The actual file may not be in the same place, causing the Picture Usage dialog box to show the image as missing.

Library items can include images or graphics placed into picture boxes. This is particularly useful for frequently placed objects such as logos.

Labeling Library Items

Once an item is dragged into the library, a thumbnail of the item appears in the palette.

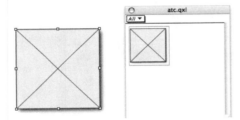

Double-clicking the thumbnail opens the Library Entry dialog box, where you can give the item a descriptive name. The Library palette does not display any identifying text for the items in the library. The item label is used to search and sort, but does not appear in the palette.

You can also choose an existing label for a library item by clicking the arrows next to the Label field, and then choosing the appropriate label from the pop-up list. Any label already defined in the library appears in this list.

Closing and Saving Libraries

Changes to a library are saved automatically, by default. When you add or delete an item, that change is saved instantly. You can change this setting in the Save Preferences dialog box. If the Auto Library Save check box is deselected, changes to the library are not saved until the library is closed. There is no real benefit to this option, however, because changes are saved automatically when you close the Library palette; you do not have the option to close the library without saving (perhaps to recover an accidentally deleted item).

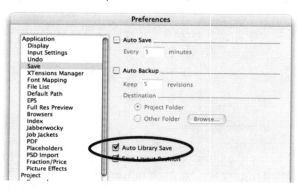

CREATE A LIBRARY

1. With no file open, choose File>New>Library.

2. Navigate to your **Work_In_Progress** folder. In the Save As/File Name field, type "atc.qxl" and click Create.

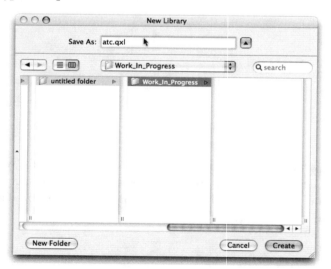

3. Create a new project with a letter-size print layout using portrait orientation and the default margins and columns.

4. Using the Rectangle Text Box tool, draw a text box on the layout page.

5. In the Measurements palette Classic mode, change the box dimensions to W: 2.25", H: 6".

6. Change the box Color to Magenta and the Shade to 25%.

7. In the Measurements palette Frame mode, change the Width field to 1 pt., and choose Magenta from the Color menu.

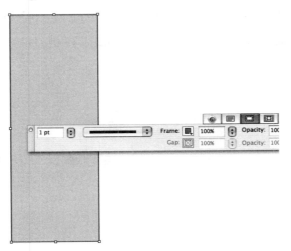

8. Using the Item tool, drag the text box into the Library palette. When the cursor becomes a pair of eyeglasses, release the mouse button.

9. Double-click the new item in the Library palette to open the Library Entry dialog box. Type "Sidebar" in the Label field and click OK.

10. Delete the text box from the layout page.

11. Create a rectangular picture box on the layout page with the dimensions W: 1.25″, H: 1.75″. Apply a 0.5-pt. black frame to the box.

12. Drag the picture box until it snaps to the left margin of the page.

13. Draw a rectangular text box. Change the width of the text box to 1.25″ and the height to 0.4″, and then drag it until it snaps to the left margin guide.

14. Drag the text box up until the top edge is approximately 1/16″ (0.0625″) below the picture box. (It might help to change the zero point to the bottom of the image box.)

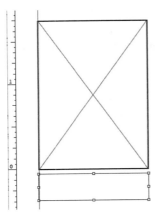

15. Holding down the Shift key, use the Item tool to select both the picture box and the text box. Press Command/Control-G to group the two boxes.

16. Using the Item tool, drag the group into the Library palette.

17. Double-click the group in the Library palette. In the Label field, type "Picture – Caption" and click OK.

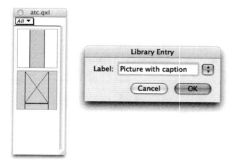

18. Close the project without saving.

19. Close the library by clicking the Close button in the top-left corner (Macintosh) or the top-right corner (Windows).

Sorting Libraries

Library item labels serve several different purposes. If you use a library for a group of different projects, such as for a particular client, you can create labels such as Newsletter Items, Catalog Items, and so on. When working on a newsletter, then, you can choose to look at just the Newsletter Items in that client's library.

If you use a separate library for each project, you can use the Label function to identify the purpose of each item in the library. For example, you can quickly find the Blue Text Box 1-pt. Border without scrolling through a lengthy list.

Once items are placed into a library, you can view all items with a particular label by clicking the pop-up menu (which defaults to All) at the top of the Library palette.

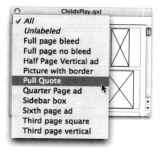

Only elements tagged with the chosen label appear in the Library palette. You can also choose to view Unlabeled elements, which you can then label for easy sorting.

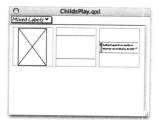

You can also change the order of items in a library by dragging them within the palette. Once an item is placed in the palette, you can drag it to a new position. The cursor becomes the glasses icon, just as when you are placing a new item in the library. The facing arrows indicate the location to which the item will be moved when you release the mouse button.

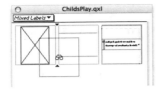

Deleting Library Items

Any item in a library can be deleted by clicking it in the palette, and then pressing Delete on a Macintosh computer or choosing Delete from the palette's Edit menu on a Windows system. If you delete a library item, you cannot undo the deletion. Clicking OK in the warning dialog box deletes the object from the library; clicking Cancel leaves the library intact.

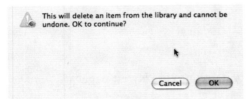

Deleting a library item has no impact on objects already placed from the library, but you will no longer be able to access that item in the library.

Opening Libraries

You can open any QuarkXPress library file by choosing File>Open. Libraries are identified by an icon that looks like a series of books on a shelf. To access the objects in a library, you can simply highlight the library and click Open. If the extension .qxl was included in the file name when it was created, a library can be opened on either platform.

Windows automatically adds the extension to the file when it is created. Macintosh users should remember to add the extension when naming the library.

If you have placed in a library any text boxes that contain formatted text, the fonts used in the library items must be available. If the fonts used in a library item are not available, you will see a missing-font error when you open the library, just as you would if a font was missing from a QuarkXPress layout.

WORK WITH A LIBRARY

1. Create a new project with a print layout using the default settings.

2. Choose File>Open.

3. Navigate to your **Work_In_Progress** folder. Highlight the file **atc.qxl** and click Open.

4. Choose Sidebar from the Labels menu at the top of the Library palette. Only one object should appear in the palette.

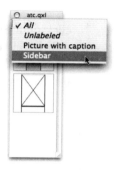

5. Drag the library item onto the layout page.

6. Choose All from the Labels pop-up menu at the top of the Library palette. The palette should now contain two items.

7. Highlight the red box in the Library palette, and then press Delete (Macintosh) or choose Delete from the palette Edit menu (Windows).

8. Click OK to the warning that this cannot be undone.

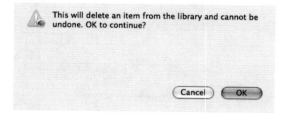

The sidebar box is removed from the library, but not from the layout page.

9. Close the library file, and close the QuarkXPress project without saving.

CREATING COMPLEX SHAPES

Type and pictures imported into QuarkXPress are contained in boxes, which can be drawn using the Picture Box tools or the Text Box tools. There are several standard shapes of each. The Freehand and Bézier tools allow you to create freeform shapes directly on a QuarkXPress page; you can then import text and graphics into these shapes. Lines are created in much the same way as boxes. To draw lines, you click the Line tool and drag the line to the length you wish, at the desired angle or shape. These are the basics of everything you do in a Quark document, but you also have other options.

Merging Objects

Merging is one option for creating complex shapes in QuarkXPress. The Merge utilities (Item>Merge) combine two or more shapes, creating complex Bézier graphics far more easily than you could by drawing them by hand with the Bézier tools. The attributes of the back-most object (color, border, contents, and so on) are maintained in the merged shape.

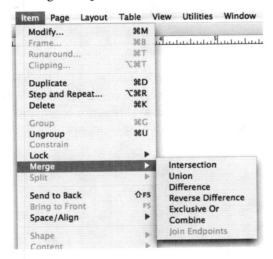

- **Intersection**. The Intersection option returns the shape that is the overlap of the selected objects.

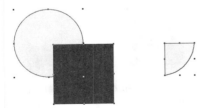

If the selected objects do not overlap, the Intersection command presents an error message.

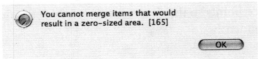

- **Union**. This option unites the selected objects into a single shape. If the selected objects do not overlap, the Union command creates a single element from the multiple objects.

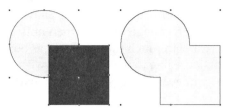

- **Difference**. This option creates a shape based on the back-most object, subtracting any overlapping areas from other objects. If the selected objects do not overlap, the Difference command returns only the back-most object.

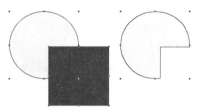

- **Reverse Difference**. This option combines all but the back-most object, and then removes the back-most object from that combination. If the selected objects do not overlap, the Reverse Difference command removes the back-most object and unites any remaining elements.

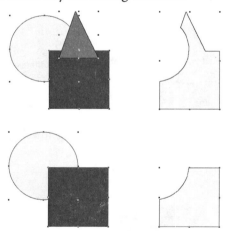

If only two objects are selected, the back-most object is removed from the front-most.

- **Exclusive Or**. This option combines the selected shapes and removes the overlapping area. Any point at which the two objects overlap creates two distinct anchor points so the shape of each piece in the final object can be edited independently.

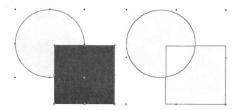

- **Combine**. This option combines the selected shapes and removes the overlapping area. The difference between Combine and Exclusive Or is that no anchor points are added at intersection points.

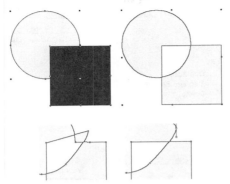

Exclusive Or (left) creates anchor points at the location of intersecting lines in the original objects. Combine (right) does not create anchor points at the intersections.

- **Join Endpoints**. This option is only available when lines are selected. The Join Endpoints command is used to combine two endpoints that overlap.

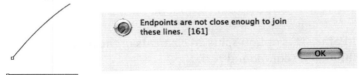

If the endpoints of a line do not overlap, the Join Endpoints command returns an error message.

Endpoints are not close enough to join these lines. [161]

OK

Managing Complex Graphics

When a complex graphic consists of more than one shape, the Exclusive Or and Combine commands create a complex shape that may include one or more *compound paths*, which mask (knock out) the area of the underlying shape.

In the following example, two nonoverlapping objects (the rectangle and the polygon) were merged with the Union command. The crosshairs indicate that the two shapes are treated as a single picture box. An oval was then placed over the rectangle, and the Combine merge executed. The resulting white oval is a compound path, masking out the fill from the background shape.

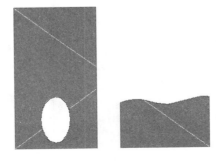

The Split command (Item>Split) allows you to separate the pieces of a complex object. Once the elements are split, they function independently, with separate contents and attributes.

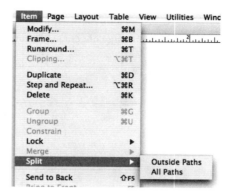

- **Outside Paths.** This option splits nonoverlapping elements of the same object into individual objects. Compound paths are not affected.

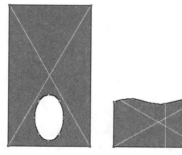

The crosshairs indicate that the two nonoverlapping shapes are separate, but the oval compound path is still intact.

- **All Paths.** This option splits all elements of the object into individual pieces, including the compound path.

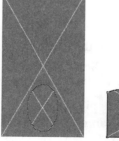

The crosshairs in each shape indicate that each shape — including the oval — is a separate object.

When you split a path, the contents of the path are transferred to each resulting element of the split. In other words, if you split a path that contains an image, the image exists in each of the objects created by the split.

Converting Text to Graphics

You can create complex graphics with type, much as you would in an illustration program. To create a box from text, you have to highlight the target text with the Content tool and choose Style>Text to Box. Any text not highlighted will not be outlined. A box is created from the highlighted text; the text box remains in place.

Once a box has been created from text, the entire set of letters is treated as a single object. When guides are visible, the diagonal crosshairs extend across all the letters. Fill color and placed images extend across all elements of the shape.

You can modify the shape of individual letters by dragging the anchor points, just as you would modify any other Bézier or freehand shape.

Splitting Text Graphics

Graphics created from text can be split, which allows you to move the letters independently of one another to create unique effects.

If you split outside paths, the compound paths remain intact for individual letters (below left); splitting all paths removes the compound paths (below right).

Resizing and Reshaping Complex Graphics

Once you have finalized the position of individual anchors of a complex graphic, you should choose Item>Edit>Shape to toggle the Shape option off. This prevents you from accidentally changing the shape of an object.

When Edit Shape is toggled off, the individual anchors of complex graphics are unavailable. You can resize the entire object using the eight handles that indicate the bounding box.

WORK WITH COMPLEX GRAPHICS

1. Open the file **graphics.qxp** from the **RF_Quark7>Chapter03** folder.

2. Highlight the three letters on the page and choose Style>Text to Box.

   A new object appears on the page directly below the highlighted text. The crossed diagonal lines indicate the object is a picture box.

3. Select the text box on the page and choose Item>Delete.

4. Using the Item tool, drag the picture-box object to the middle of the page.

The Text to Box tool works in much the same way as the Convert to Outline option in Adobe Illustrator and the Convert to Paths option in Macromedia FreeHand.

If you hold down the Option/Alt key while choosing Style>Text to Box, the highlighted text is converted to outlines as an inline graphic in the place of the highlighted text. The text is automatically deleted.

5. With the picture-box object selected, choose Linear Blend in the Colors palette and change the blend angle to 90°. Assign Cyan as the first color and Black as the second color in the blend.

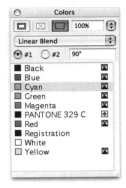

6. If you cannot see the individual anchor points of each letter shape, choose Item>Edit>Shape.

   With the Edit Shape option active (checked), you can see and change the individual anchor points that make up the individual shapes.

7. Click the left anchor point at the bottom of the "T" shape and drag down to stylize the letter's appearance.

   The blend extends to fill the new vertical dimension of the shape. Because all three letter shapes are treated as a single object, the blend changes in all the shapes.

8. Choose Item>Edit>Shape to toggle off the editing option.

   When this option is inactive, you cannot access the individual anchor points that make up the shape. The bounding-box handles show that all three letters combined are being treated as a single object. You can only change the width and height of the entire object by dragging the object's bounding box handles (or using the Measurements palette).

9. Choose Item>Split>Outside Paths.

Once the elements are split, they function independently with separate contents and attributes. Each letter is now a unique box, as indicated by the crossed diagonal lines; the blend appears differently in each letter shape.

If the crossed diagonal lines do not show each letter as a distinct shape, toggle guides off and then back on.

10. Using the Item tool, drag each letter shape so the letters slightly overlap and are vertically offset from each other.

11. Save the file and "graphics_logo.qxp" in your **Work_In_Progress** folder and close it.

SUMMARY

In this chapter, you learned how to create and edit text boxes, picture boxes, and lines. You learned how to constrain boxes to regular shapes, and how to constrain the lines you create to 45° angles. You discovered that lines can be given width and can have additional attributes, such as dashes. You also became familiar with how to add color to the elements you create in QuarkXPress, and how to define custom patterns for borders and lines.

You learned to use the Measurements palette to position items on the page. In addition, you discovered how to position items in a specific stacking order, and how to align and distribute items relative to one another. Finally, you learned how to create complex objects by merging and splitting existing shapes, and how to convert text to graphics.

Working with Color

4

Welcome to the wonderful world of color: bright, beautiful, and full of complexities. You have already learned how to apply color to elements in a QuarkXPress layout. Obviously, there is much more to Quark's color capabilities than picking from the few defaults in the Colors palette.

Although we can communicate perfectly well using black and white (or shades of gray), color adds interest to pages, allows us to highlight elements, and lends variety to the project. Not all color is created equal, however, and the colors we use must be created or specified with the end product in mind.

IN CHAPTER 4, YOU WILL:

■ Become familiar with the different types and models of color used in project design.

■ Learn how to add new colors to the QuarkXPress Colors palette.

■ Discover how to edit existing colors, including how to use colors from the built-in color libraries.

■ Learn what is required when designing color for the printing processes.

UNDERSTANDING COLOR GAMUT

The biggest problem in controlling color in the graphic arts is that every piece of equipment displays or prints color in a slightly different manner. Printers use a combination of four colors (cyan, magenta, yellow, and black, or CMYK) for process-color work; your monitor uses three (red, green, and blue, or RGB). We call RGB and CMYK "device-dependent color models" because of this discrepancy — the exact color we see varies according to the device that is displaying or reproducing it. For example, two different brands of monitors will both use RGB for their display, but the same file will appear differently on each monitor. Colors also display differently on Macintosh and Windows monitors. When you multiply this by the hundreds of different scanners, monitors, and output options that exist, you begin to get a sense of the complicated nature of color.

To complicate matters even further, in order to use different devices, it is necessary to convert from one color model to another, adding yet another variable to the problem of color control. A scanner collects an image in RGB; that image is then converted to CMYK, viewed on the monitor as RGB, and then finally printed in CMYK. What you see is not always what you get, despite the promises made by software and hardware manufacturers, and you can't do anything to correct the situation absolutely.

The differences between one color model and another are due to the fact that each color model has a different *gamut*, or range of possible colors. RGB color uses three color channels (Red, Green, and Blue), each channel having degrees of intensity varying from 0 to 255. The RGB color space can reproduce approximately 16.7 million colors. CMYK uses four color channels (Cyan, Magenta, Yellow, and Black) in varying percentages from 0 to 100, resulting in a much smaller range of possible colors.

If RGB files are output to film or plate separations, the RGB file appears only on the black plate. RGB files must be converted to CMYK to output properly on a commercial output device.

Because some RGB colors are outside the CMYK gamut, they are unavailable in commercial printing which uses the CMYK model. When RGB files are converted to CMYK, colors outside the CMYK gamut are forced to the nearest possible value; this type of color shift is called "gamut compression."

In order to deal effectively with color, you should become familiar with its components. You should also understand why the same color image can look different from monitor to monitor, in various color proofs, and in the final printed piece. See Chapter 14 for an explanation of color management.

Black is represented by the letter "K" for "Key Color."

A **process build** is a color that is defined with the CMYK model.

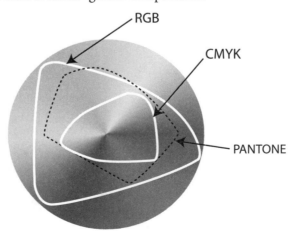

Some colors outside the CMYK gamut can be reproduced with special inks, such as the Pantone Matching System.

THE QUARKXPRESS COLORS PALETTE

Every new QuarkXPress project includes a set of default colors — None, Black, Cyan, Magenta, Registration, White, and Yellow.

- **None**. This color is used if you want underlying objects to show through an element. For example, a text box with a background color of None might be placed directly on top of a red circle; the red circle will be entirely visible, and the text will appear on top of the color.

- **Cyan, Magenta, Yellow, and Black**. These colors are the process inks. These cannot be deleted or modified.

- **Registration**. This is a special color that appears on every separation in a job. This color is used for separation information and printer's marks. You should not assign Registration to any object within the trim size of a layout.

- **White**. This color is used when you want the color of the substrate to be visible. This does not mean white ink is printed; to print white (as you might on black paper), you have to use special opaque inks from the spot-color libraries.

Each color in the palette is listed (in alphabetical order) with a swatch and a color name, and an icon that defines the color separation used for that color. These icons can be deceptive: any color for which the Spot Color check box is not activated in the Edit Color dialog box displays a process-color icon. When printed, these colors separate to C, M, Y, and K films or plates. Colors with the process icon, however, are not necessarily created with the CMYK model; if a color was defined with a model other than CMYK, gamut compression may result in subtle or drastic changes in the final printed result.

Do not use None as the background for an image unless the image has a clipping path. This can cause printing problems and unexpected results.

If you've used previous versions of QuarkXPress, you'll notice that Red, Green, and Blue are no longer part of the default Colors palette in a print layout.

The icons to the right of the color name in the Colors palette represent the color separation type, not the color model. The process icon does not necessarily mean a color uses the CMYK model.

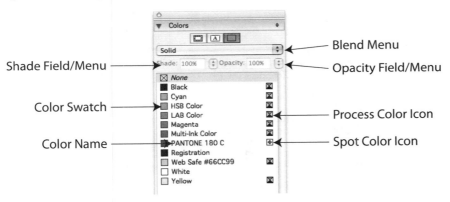

The top of the Colors palette shows different options, depending on what is selected in the layout. You can change the color of any element in a layout by clicking the appropriate button, then clicking the color you want in the palette.

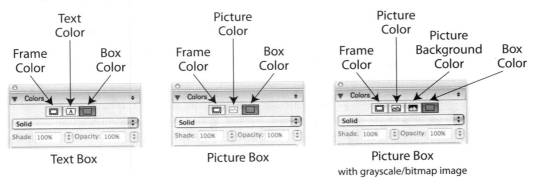

DEFINING COLOR

You can add as many colors to a project as you like by choosing Edit>Colors. When you define a new color, you have a number of choices to make: color model, color separation, color name, color definition, and halftone value.

Color Models

The *color model* or *color space* defines the structure of the color, or how the color will be created. You can choose from any of the available options in the Model drop-down menu of the Edit Color dialog box.

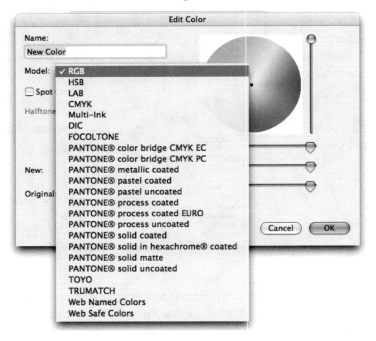

RGB (Red, Green, Blue) Color

RGB creates color by combining different intensities of red, green, and blue light (collectively referred to as the "additive primaries"). This color space has a gamut of more than 16.7 million different colors. Computer monitors and television sets display color in RGB.

RGB primary amounts are specified in a range from 0 to 255. If each of the primaries is set to 0, the resulting color is black, because you're combining no light. If each primary is set to 255, the resulting color is white.

The problem with using RGB for print jobs is that RGB images do not always separate correctly; on a standard CMYK press, they produce a single composite black plate and blank cyan, yellow, and magenta plates. The RGB color model is best used when creating layouts for electronic distribution (for example, Web pages) or when outputting to a photographic device, such as a film recorder.

CMYK (Process) Color

The *CMYK* color model is based on the absorption and reflection of light, as opposed to the transmission of light used by the RGB model. Four process inks — cyan, magenta, yellow, and black (collectively referred to as the "subtractive primaries") — are used in varying combinations to produce the range of printable colors. This is the model used for most commercial printing.

Theoretically, a mixture of equal parts of cyan, magenta, and yellow would produce black. Pigments, however, are not pure, so the result of mixing these colors is a muddy brown (called "hue error"). To obtain vibrant colors (and so elements such as type can be printed cleanly), black ink is added to the three primaries. Black is represented by the letter "K" for "key color." CMYK is also called "process color."

By varying the percentage of these primaries, a wide range of colors can be created using only four printing units. When printing using this model, the colors in your project are made up of a combination of cyan, magenta, yellow, and black inks. If you define 40 process colors in your project, QuarkXPress still outputs only four pieces of film or plates (called "separations") — one for each of the primaries.

LAB (CIE L*a*b*) Color

The LAB color model is device independent; the colors it describes don't depend upon the characteristics of a particular printer, monitor, or scanner. In theory, CIE bridges the gap between the various color models and devices, and is used as the background when converting images from one color space to another in an image-editing program such as Adobe Photoshop.

The mechanics of the LAB color model are beyond the scope of this book. Although it is an excellent tool for color conversion and correction, there is no real reason to use the LAB model in QuarkXPress. With a basic knowledge of color reproduction, you can use the other models successfully without having to under-stand advanced color theory.

HSB Color

The HSB color model defines color using hue, saturation, and brightness.

Hue can be thought of as a color you can name, for example red, yellow, or blue; the value is specified in degrees (from 0 to 359) around a color wheel.

Brightness determines how light or dark a color is. If Brightness is 0, the color is black; at 100, the color is white. If Hue is 0 (red), setting Brightness to 75 lightens the color to turn it light red or pink, while setting it to 25 creates dark red or burgundy. A value of 50 represents a color that is neither lightened nor darkened.

Saturation determines the purity of a color, or how much gray is added to the color. If Saturation is set to 100%, the color is absolutely pure. Reducing Saturation tones down a color's intensity, and setting it to 0 creates a shade of gray. When mixing colors, the HSB model makes more sense to some people, particularly those with traditional art backgrounds.

If you choose to define HSB colors, it's best to convert them to CMYK after selecting the color to determine what color will actually be output when printed.

Defined colors are available to all layouts within the same project.

CIE L*a*b* is a color space named for the Commission International de l'Eclairage (the International Commission on Illumination), which is a standards organization that creates specifications for describing color.

When choosing special colors, ask your printer which ink system they support. If you designate TruMatch and they use Pantone inks, you won't get the colors you expected.

Special colors are generally chosen from a **swatch book** — a book of colors printed with different inks, similar to the paint chip cards used in home decorating.

Documents created using the Hexachrome color model should be printed on a six-color press. Check with your printer and/or service bureau to be sure they have the capabilities of and experience with Hexachrome printing.

You should test the results of multi-ink builds before using them in a final design document. Depending on the inks that you want to combine, the result might not be what you intended. Pantone inks, for example, are generally opaque. Displayed on a monitor, a multi-ink blend will appear to blend perfectly; opaque inks, however, might not mix properly to provide the shade that you intended.

Special Color Libraries

Special colors are those that are reproduced with special premixed inks that will produce a certain color with one ink layer — not built from the standard process inks used in CMYK printing. When you output a job with spot colors, each spot color appears on its own separation.

These inks, commonly called "spot colors," are used in two- and three-color documents, and can be added to process-color documents when a special color, such as a corporate color, is needed. QuarkXPress includes several built-in color libraries, including spot-color systems like Pantone, Toyo, and DIC.

In the United States, the most popular collections of spot colors are the Pantone Matching System (PMS) libraries. TruMatch and Focoltone are also used in the United States. Toyo and DICColor (Dainippon Ink & Chemicals) are used primarily in Japan.

QuarkXPress includes on-screen simulations of all of the most popular special color libraries. Even though you can choose a color directly from the library, you should look at a swatch book to verify that you're using the color you intend. Special inks exist because many of the colors cannot be reproduced with process inks, nor can they be accurately represented on a computer monitor. If you specify special colors and then convert them to CMYK process colors, your job probably won't look exactly as you expected.

Hexachrome® Color

Hexachrome (also called "hifi" or "high-fidelity color") is the latest innovation in color printing. Many of the newer commercial printing presses, especially in the United States, have six or more printing units. The Hexachrome system, created by Pantone, takes advantage of the additional printing units by adding two extra colors — green and orange — to the standard CMYK ink set. The green and orange units extend the color gamut so that more shades can be reproduced on a traditional printing press.

To use the Hexachrome color model in QuarkXPress, you have to select colors from the built-in Pantone Hexachrome libraries.

Multi-Ink Colors

Multi-ink is a special model in QuarkXPress that allows you to create a new color swatch based on percentages or tints of existing colors. A *tint* is simply a lighter version of the same color or hue. As a general rule, defining a tint of a single color is unnecessary because you can change the tint in the percentage field of the Colors palette. Single-color tints only serve to clutter your palette.

Multi-ink colors should not be used to define varying shades of process colors; this is better accomplished by defining a new CMYK color with the percentages you want.

Multi-ink colors cannot be their own separations; rather, they use the separations that already exist in the project. The value of a multi-ink color is that you can combine different inks from different models, or combine different spot colors to create a new swatch. If, for example, you want an object to be 40% of a spot color and 70% of a process color, you can define a multi-ink color to create the combination. This option is also extremely useful to give a multi-color look to documents that are printed with only two or three spot colors.

Web-Safe Color

Because computer monitors display in the RGB color model, documents and images created for Web sites are created using RGB color. Every computer monitor, however, displays color somewhat differently. Phosphors, monitor resolution, and other factors can play a role in how color is presented. For this reason it is important to use "Web-safe" colors for color consistency in electronic documents.

Web-safe colors are specific RGB combinations that are most likely to appear the same (or close to the same) on most monitors on any platform.

QuarkXPress provides two Web color models — Web-Safe Colors and Web-Named Colors. Web-Safe Colors is a library of 216 colors listed by the hexadecimal value, or the RGB value of that color. Web-Named Colors is a library of 57 Web-safe colors using assigned color names — for example, "Dark Orange."

The hexadecimal name of a color is listed as "#9933CC," where 99 defines the red value, 33 defines the green value, and CC defines the blue value.

RGB	Used for designing electronic documents, such as Web pages or PDF files that will be distributed electronically.
CMYK	Used for designing commercially printed projects.
LAB	Used for converting images from one color space to another; generally not used to define colors in QuarkXPress.
HSB	Used to define color in terms of hue, saturation, and brightness; generally not used to define colors in QuarkXPress.
Special Libraries	Used in combination with CMYK to create specific colors outside the CMYK gamut, or used as the only colors in a one-, two-, or three-color job.
Hexachrome	Used to extend the color gamut by adding green and orange to the CMYK process inks.
Multi-Ink	Used to combine process and spot colors, or to combine two or more spot colors, to create a single color swatch.
Web-Safe	Used for designing electronic documents; this is an abbreviated version of RGB, which attempts to ensure the consistent appearance of colors from one monitor to another.

Color Separation

Every color in the QuarkXPress Colors palette is defined as either a process color or a spot color. Process colors are those that separate into CMYK components when printed to a commercial output device. Spot colors are printed as a single ink rather than a combination of CMYK inks, and separate as an additional piece of film or plate. As a general rule, you should make sure the Spot Color box is not checked unless you are certain you want to print extra separations.

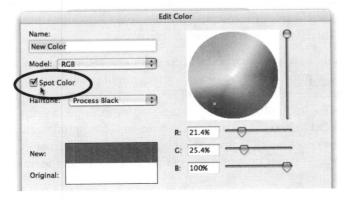

Color Names

When you create a new color in any project, you need to give the color a name. There is no standard for naming colors, but we recommend using some meaningful sequence of the color content. For example, "75c 50m 0y 0k" is much better than "Medium Blue" because there are many shades of medium blue. This naming convention serves several purposes:

- You know exactly what components the color contains, so you can easily see if you are duplicating colors.
- You can immediately tell that the color should be a process build rather than a special ink or spot color.
- You avoid mismatched color names and duplicate spot colors, both potential disasters in the commercial printing production process.

Mismatched color names occur when a defined color has two different values — one defined in the page layout and one defined in an image file. When the files are output, the output device might be confused by different definitions for the same color name; the imported value might replace the project's value for that particular color name (or vice versa). The change could be subtle, or it could be drastic.

As an example, you might define "Color #1" as C:50 M:0 Y:75 K:0 in QuarkXPress; an Adobe Illustrator EPS file from another designer defines "Color #1" as C:0 M:77 Y:80 K:15. The Illustrator file is placed into the QuarkXPress project, which imports the color swatch name into the layout file. The name "Color #1," however, is already used in the layout file with a completely different definition — resulting in a mismatched color name.

A similar problem occurs when the same spot color is assigned different names in different applications. For example, you might define a spot color in QuarkXPress as "Border Color"; another designer defines the same spot color in Macromedia FreeHand as "Spec Blue." When the FreeHand illustration is placed in the QuarkXPress project, two different spot-color separations exist, even though the different color names have the same values.

Both of these issues provide strong arguments for naming the color according to its content. When you select a color from one of the special libraries, the color is automatically named according to the ink swatch you choose. Unless you convert the special color to CMYK, you should leave the special color name as it is.

Color by Numbers

If you base your color choices solely on what you see on your monitor, you would be safe to assume that your perfect blue sky might not look quite right when it's printed with process-color inks. Even if you have calibrated your monitor, no monitor is 100% effective at simulating printed color. As long as monitors display color in RGB, there will always be some discrepancies.

Designers should have some sort of process color chart; these charts are available from commercial publishers, and some printers might provide the charts produced by the exact press on which your job will be printed. These charts contain little squares of process ink builds so that you can see, for example, what a process build of C:10 M:70 Y:30 K:20 will look like when printed. These guides usually show samples in steps of 5% or 10%, printed on both coated and uncoated paper (because the type of paper or *substrate* can dramatically affect the final result).

When you are defining process colors in a QuarkXPress project, you should enter specific numbers in the CMYK fields to designate your color choices, rather than relying on your screen preview. As you do this more and more often, you will become better able to predict the outcome for a given process-ink build. Rely on what you know to be true rather than what you hope will be true.

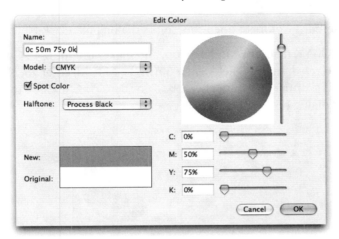

Color swatch books can fade over time and with exposure to light, which means the swatches will not accurately represent the printed result. Swatch books should be replaced periodically to be sure that what you see is what you will get.

The same concept is true when using special ink libraries. You should have — and use — swatch books that show printed samples of the special inks. You cannot rely on the monitor preview to choose a special ink color. Rather, you should find the color in a printed swatch book, and then enter the appropriate number in the (for example) Pantone field below the color swatches.

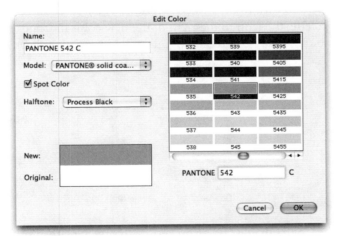

Total Area Coverage

When defining the ink values of a process-color build, you must usually limit your *total area coverage* (TAC, also called "total ink density"), or the amount of ink that is used in a given color. This might sound complex, but it can be easily calculated by adding the percentages of each ink used to create the color. If a color is defined as C:45 M:60 Y:90 K:0, the total area coverage is 195% (45 + 60 + 90 + 0). Maximum TAC limits are between 240% and 320% for offset lithography, depending on the paper being used. If you exceed the TAC limits for a given paper-ink-press combination, your printed job might end up with excess ink bleed, smearing, smudging, show-through, or a number of other printing errors because the paper cannot absorb all of the ink.

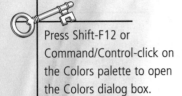

1. Create a new print layout project using the default settings. Name the layout "Color Test".

2. Choose Edit>Colors to open the Colors dialog box. Click New.

3. Select CMYK from the Model menu, and make sure the Spot Color check box is not selected. In the C field, enter 50; in the M field, enter 75. Name the color according to the ink values — "50c 75m 0y 0k". Click OK to return to the Colors dialog box.

Press Shift-F12 or Command/Control-click on the Colors palette to open the Colors dialog box.

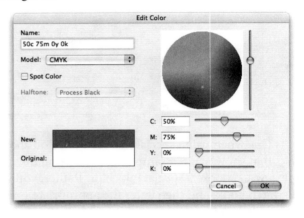

4. Click Save to return to the Project window. The new color appears in the Colors palette; the icon to the right of the new color indicates that it is a process build, because you did not select the Spot Color check box.

You must have something selected in the project to access the items in the Colors palette. If your layout doesn't have an automatic text box, create any box on the page to make the Colors palette available.

5. Open the Colors dialog box again (Edit>Colors). Create another new color: a CMYK process color with ink values C:0, M:50, Y:90, K:0. Name the color according to the ink values — "0c 50m 90y 0k".

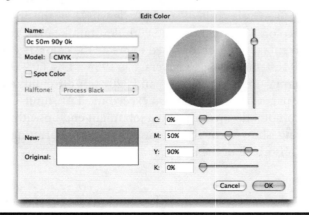

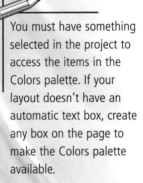

6. Repeat the process again, this time checking the Spot Color box to create a CMYK spot color with ink values C:10, M:50, Y:51, K:20. Name the color according to the ink values — "10c 50m 51y 20k".

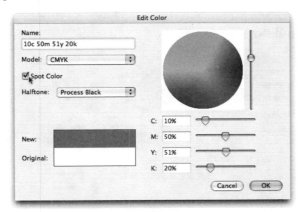

7. In the Colors dialog box, click New.

8. Select PANTONE® solid coated from the Model menu. In the text field below the color swatches, type "543".

   The swatches in the window automatically change to reflect the number you type. Make sure the Spot Color check box is active, and leave the name at the default value.

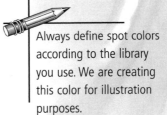

Always define spot colors according to the library you use. We are creating this color for illustration purposes.

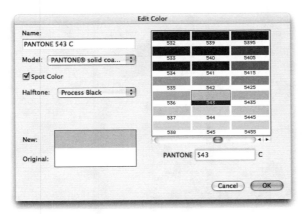

9. Click OK to return to the Colors dialog box, and then click Save to add the new colors to your palette.

10. Open the Colors dialog box again and click New.

11. In the Edit Color dialog box, select Multi-Ink from the Model menu. In the right half of the dialog box, you can see a list of the available ink colors (the four process colors and the two spot colors you created).

12. Highlight Process Magenta in the dialog box, and choose 40% from the Shade drop-down menu.

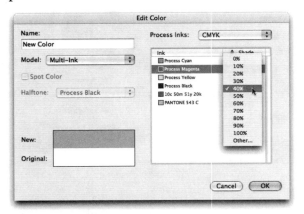

13. Highlight Pantone 543 C in the ink list; choose 80% from the Shade menu.

14. Name the color appropriately — "40m 80Pan543".

15. Click OK to return to the Colors dialog box, and click Save to add the multi-ink color to your palette.

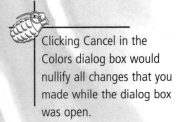

Clicking Cancel in the Colors dialog box would nullify all changes that you made while the dialog box was open.

16. Save the file as "color_working.qxp" in your **Work_In_Progress** folder, and leave it open for the next exercise.

IMPORTING COLORS

You can import colors from another QuarkXPress project by clicking Append in the Colors dialog box. You can navigate to any QuarkXPress project on your computer.

Clicking Open displays a dialog box with a list of the colors in the selected project. The left half of the Append dialog box lists colors in the project you selected. You can import all colors by clicking Include All, or import selected colors by highlighting individual colors and clicking the right-facing arrow in the middle of the window.

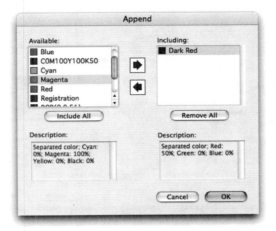

Once you have chosen the colors you want to import, clicking OK implements the import. If any imported color names conflict with existing colors in the project, QuarkXPress asks how you want to resolve the conflict.

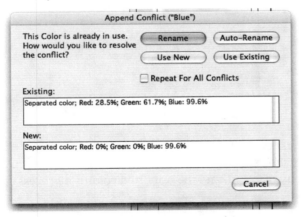

- **Rename**. This option allows you to define a new name for the color you are importing; your Colors palette will have both the existing and the imported color.

- **Use New**. This option replaces the existing color with the imported color.

- **Auto-Rename**. This option adds an asterisk (*) in front of the duplicate color name and adds it as a different color.

- **Use Existing**. This option does not import the color, but instead maintains the existing color.

IMPORT COLORS

1. With **working_colors.qxp** open (from your **Work_In_Progress** folder), open the Colors dialog box again (Edit>Colors) and click Append.

2. Navigate to the **import_color.qxp** file in the **RF_Quark7>Chapter04** folder and click Open.

You can also append colors using the Append dialog box (File>Append).

3. In the Append dialog box, highlight 10c 50m 51y 20k in the Available list, and click the right-facing arrow in the center.

4. Repeat this process to add "39c 8m 0y 1k" to the Including list. Click OK.

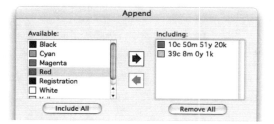

QuarkXPress presents a conflict warning; the bottom half of the conflict dialog box shows that the existing color is a spot color (you created this in the previous exercise), and the imported color is a process (separated) color.

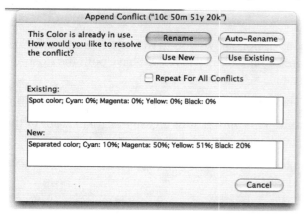

5. Click Use New.

6. Click Save in the Colors dialog box to finalize your changes. When the import is complete, you have one new color in your Colors palette. You can also see that 10c 50m 51y 20k is no longer a spot color.

7. Save the file, and leave it open for the next exercise.

EDITING AND DELETING COLORS

You can edit or delete any color in a project except Black, Cyan, Magenta, Registration, White, and Yellow. In the Colors dialog box, you can highlight a color and then click Delete to remove it from the Colors palette. You can edit an existing color by highlighting it and clicking Edit.

Changing Spot to Process

You can change a spot color to process by simply deactivating the Spot Color check box in the Edit Color dialog box.

Remember, though, that colors from special libraries are often not available using process inks; some color shift will occur when the color is printed as a CMYK separation. When you deactivate the Spot Color check box, the model does not change. You should change it to CMYK to see the CMYK values nearest to the original spot color. The New and Original previews usually show at least some difference, and possibly a drastic one.

Remember, too, that your color name should reflect its contents. When you change a spot color to process, and change the model to CMYK, you should change the name to reflect the new color contents.

Renaming Colors

If you try to change the name of a color to one that already exists, QuarkXPress tells you that the color name is already in use.

This might be the case if you change a spot color to process, and then change the color name to reflect the color components. Here we have another benefit to using a standard naming convention. If you have used a standard naming convention and try to assign a name that already exists, you can delete the color you want to rename, replacing it with the one that already exists.

Editing Multi-Ink Components

If a color is used in a multi-ink build, editing or deleting the component affects the multi-ink color as well. If you delete the component, the component is also deleted from the palette and from the multi-ink build.

If you change a multi-ink component from spot to process, the component is changed to a process color in the Colors palette, and it is removed from the multi-ink build.

Deleting Used Colors

If you try to delete a color that is used in the project, QuarkXPress asks you what color to use as a replacement color. You can select any other existing color from the menu and click OK to complete the replacement.

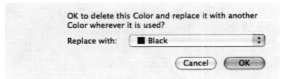

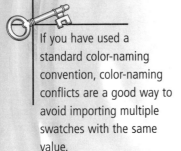

If you have used a standard color-naming convention, color-naming conflicts are a good way to avoid importing multiple swatches with the same value.

EDIT COLORS

1. With **working_colors.qxp** open (from your **Work_In_Progress** folder), draw two boxes (any size) on the page.

2. Fill one box with 39c 8m 0y 1k and the other with 0c 50m 90y 0k.

3. Open the Colors dialog box (Edit>Colors).

4. Highlight 0c 50m 90y 0k in the dialog box, and click Delete.

5. Choose 10c 50m 51y 20k in the Replace With menu, and click OK.

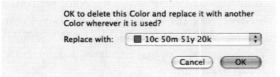

6. Highlight Pantone 543 C in the Colors dialog box and click Edit.

7. Deactivate the Spot Color check box.

8. Click OK to the warning that the color will be removed from multi-ink builds.

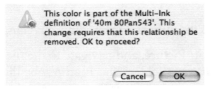

9. Change the Model menu to CMYK. Notice the difference between the New and Original preview swatches.

10. Change the color name to match its new content — "39c 8m 0y 1k" — and click OK.

    QuarkXPress tells you that the color name is already in use.

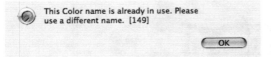

11. Click OK to the warning, and click Cancel to cancel the change. You now know that the closest process build for the spot color Pantone 543 C already exists in the project.

12. Highlight Pantone 543 C in the Colors dialog box, and click Delete. You are warned that the color you are deleting is being used in a multi-ink color and will be removed from that build. Click OK.

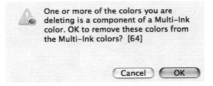

13. Click Save to return to the Project window.

14. Save the file and leave it open for the next exercise.

Colors Imported with EPS Files

When you place a graphic or image that has been saved with spot colors, those colors are imported into the QuarkXPress Colors palette for the project. Imported colors are completely editable in QuarkXPress, though it is probably not a good idea. Before you edit an imported color, make absolutely certain that you want to make the change. If you change the color definition, the appearance of any imported graphic using that color will change. You can delete the color, but QuarkXPress will warn you against it.

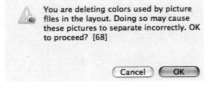

1. With **color_working.qxp** still open, draw a rectangle picture box.

2. Choose File>Import Picture, and navigate to the file **banana.eps** in the **RF_Quark7>Chapter04** folder. This is an Adobe Illustrator EPS file that was saved with a spot color. Click Open to place the picture, and size the box so you can see the entire picture.

   "ATC Yellow" has been added to the Colors palette; the icon next to the color name indicates that it is a spot color.

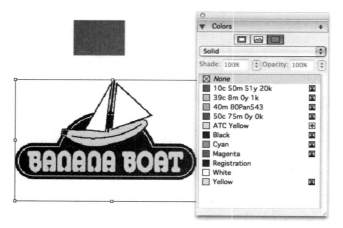

3. Press Shift-F12 to open the Colors dialog box. Highlight ATC Yellow in the dialog box, and click Edit.

   This color uses the CMYK model, is defined as 100% yellow, but was saved as a spot color. If the layout file were output as it is, two separations would be created for the color yellow.

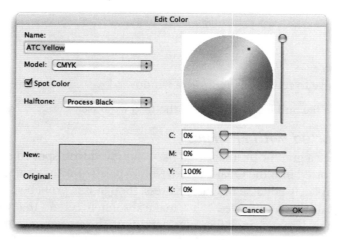

4. Deactivate the Spot Color check box. Click OK, then click Save to return to the Project window. ATC Yellow should now have a process separation icon in the Colors palette.

5. Save the file and leave it open.

Deleting Unused Colors

When you have finished building a project, it is a good idea to remove unused colors from your Colors palette. This is not a required step in the design process, but it is good practice and can minimize the potential for problems later in the output process.

In the Colors dialog box, you can choose Colors Not Used in the Show drop-down menu. Once this list is visible, you can highlight and delete each unused color (with the exceptions of Cyan, Magenta, Yellow, Black, and Registration).

DELETE UNUSED COLORS

1. With **color_working.qxp** still open, open the Colors dialog box.

2. Choose Colors Not Used in the Show menu.

3. Highlight the first color in the list, and click Delete.

4. Repeat this process for the rest of the colors in the list. Notice that you cannot delete Cyan, Magenta, Yellow, or Registration.

5. When you have finished deleting the unused colors, click Save. Your Colors palette is now considerably shorter.

6. Save the file and leave it open for the next exercise.

COLOR BLENDS

Gradients (also called "vignettes," "blends," or "graduated fills") are created with a series of bands. *Banding* is a printing problem that results when the individual bands of a gradient are visible, rather than shifting smoothly from one step to the next.

In QuarkXPress you can simply choose the type of blend you want, click on the colors that will blend, and you're done. The technical aspects of the printing process, however, do not allow some of the blends that designers create to be reproduced.

Specific formulas govern the number of gray levels that can be reproduced for a given printing process; if your gradient contains more gray levels than what the output device can create, banding results. To help avoid problems with the blends you create, follow these basic strategies to make banding much less likely:

- Increase the resolution of the output device. More resolution gives you more gray levels with which to work.
- Decrease the line screen ruling. Lower screen ruling (lpi) allows more gray levels.

As a designer, however, you probably have no choice about resolution or screen ruling. If that is the case, you can decrease the likelihood of banding by adhering to the following rules:

- Keep gradients short. The longer the gradient, the larger individual bands will be and the more likely they are to show.
- Use a larger color range in the blend. A 20% color difference is much more likely to band than a 70% difference.

K:90   K:60

K:100   K:0

The top gradient has a 30% difference in color between the beginning and end points. It is far more likely to show banding than the bottom gradient, which has a 100% difference between start and end points.

For the best result, create gradients in an image-editing application and add **noise** (pixels of different colors or tints), which will provide enough variation in the color shift to prevent banding.

Other output problems are caused by blends that combine process and spot colors. When blending spot colors to process, the intermediate steps of the gradient might separate incorrectly. If a spot color blends to white, the intermediate steps are created as process colors instead of the spot color.

- Avoid blending from a spot color to a process color.
- When blending a spot color to white (or paper), set the end point of the blend to 0% of the spot color rather than the color white. This makes the intermediate steps of the gradient separate on the spot color plate instead of separating as process colors.

Defining Blends

The Blend area of the Colors palette, also found in the Modify Box dialog box (Item>Modify Box), enables you to specify a blend for the background of the selected object. You can specify a style, angle, color, and shade for the blend.

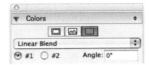

- The Style drop-down menu allows you to specify a type of blend. The default is Solid, which means the blend feature is turned off. The Linear Blend option produces a standard blend that moves in a straight line from one color to the other. The other choices are Mid-Linear Blend, Rectangular Blend, Diamond Blend, Circular Blend, and Full Circular Blend.
- The radio buttons below the Style menu allow you to define the start (#1) and end (#2) colors of the blend.
- The percentage field enables you to enter the tint percentage of each color in the blend. The active radio button (#1 or #2) determines which color is altered.
- The Angle field enables you to specify the rotation of the blend in degrees.

 CREATE A SIMPLE GRADIENT

1. With **color_working.qxp** still open, draw a box 4 in. wide by 1 in. high.

2. Choose Item>Content>None.

3. In the Colors palette, click the Background button, and then click Cyan.

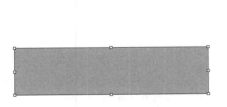

4. Click the Blend menu (defaulting to Solid) and choose Linear Blend.

There is now a gradient in the box you drew. The #1 radio button is active, and Cyan is still highlighted.

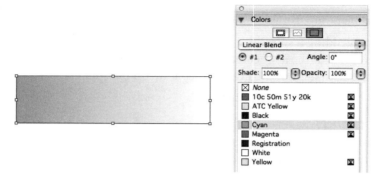

5. Activate the #2 radio button. White is active in the Colors palette, indicating that White is the second color in the blend.

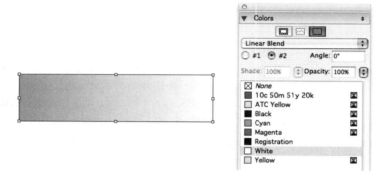

6. With the #2 radio button still selected, click 10c 50m 51y 20k in the Colors palette. The right side of the box — and the blend — changes to the new color; the box now blends from Cyan to the custom brown color.

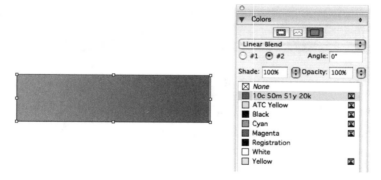

7. Save the file and close it.

SUMMARY

You've learned the basics of color, color models, which types of projects require RGB color and which require CMYK, and when to use spot colors. You've also learned to define and edit colors, and imported colors from other QuarkXPress projects and from graphics.

Working with Text

5

Placing text is one of the most important aspects of page-layout software. This chapter examines the different options for placing text into a QuarkXPress layout, including importing, copying, and manually entering text into boxes. Once you have placed text on the page, QuarkXPress provides all of the tools you need to format that text. This chapter defines the terms related to typography and shows you how to use QuarkXPress tools to create quality type design in your documents.

IN CHAPTER 5, YOU WILL:

- Learn how to manage and modify text boxes.

- Learn different methods for creating text, including importing text files.

- Discover how to navigate, select, cut, copy, and paste text.

- Become familiar with the terminology associated with typography and fonts.

- Discover how to change the appearance of type and how to define paragraph formatting.

- Learn the difference between character formatting and paragraph formatting and how to apply those settings to text in a layout.

- Learn about OpenType feature sets and how to apply them in a QuarkXPress layout.

- Create artistic effects using text paths.

MANAGING TEXT BOXES

All type in QuarkXPress is contained in boxes, with the exception of text on a path (explained at the end of this chapter). As you learned in Chapter 3, creating a text box is easy — just select one of the Text Box tools, click in the Project window, drag diagonally, and release the mouse button.

Text boxes are drawn by dragging the cursor diagonally.

The Automatic Text Box

As an alternative to manually creating text boxes on every page, you can place an automatic text box on every page when you create a new layout. If you check the Automatic Text Box option in the New Project dialog box, the text box is created based on the margin and column settings.

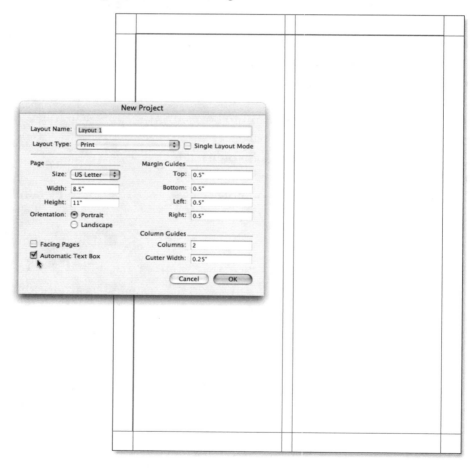

While pictures help to demonstrate your point, text is an extension of speech. We have a responsibility to present text in a highly readable form, taking advantage of technology; but more importantly, understanding how we can make text best perform its task of communication.

Customizing Tool Preferences

You can change the default attributes of new text boxes by modifying the Tools preferences. You can customize only one type of text box, modify multiple variants by Shift- or Control-clicking the specific tools, or modify all shapes by selecting one Text Box tool and clicking Similar Types.

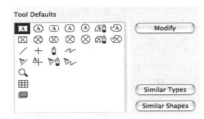

After you select which tools you want to modify, clicking the Modify button opens an abbreviated Modify dialog box. If only one Text Box tool is selected, you can modify the default Box, Text, Frame, and Runaround settings. If more than one tool variation is selected, you can modify Group (box color), Text, and Frame settings.

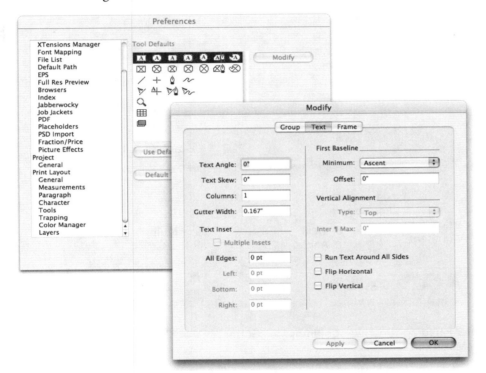

On a Macintosh, preferences are accessed in the QuarkXPress menu. On Windows computers, preferences are accessed in the Edit menu.

If you are modifying the default behavior of only one type of text box, the Modify dialog box includes four tabs — Box, Text, Frame, and Runaround.

If you have multiple tools selected, you can modify default Group (box background color), Text, and Frame options. Because not all box shapes have the same runaround options, you cannot modify the default runaround for more than one tool at a time; the Runaround tab is missing when more than one tool is selected.

Modifying Text Box Parameters

A text box can have defining characteristics, such as background and frame color, angling and skewing, columns and gutters, text-inset parameters, baseline behavior, and vertical alignment. In Chapter 3, you learned how to modify basic box attributes, such as the box position, rotation, and frame settings. Those techniques apply to any type of box, including text boxes — which means you're already on your way to managing text boxes.

In addition to those options, you can control the characteristics of text inside the box and the way text wraps around the outside of the box. You can customize text boxes in the Modify dialog box or use various modes of the Measurements palette. The Text tab and mode present most of the controls related to text boxes.

Open the Modify dialog box by pressing Command/Control-M or by double-clicking a box with the Item tool.

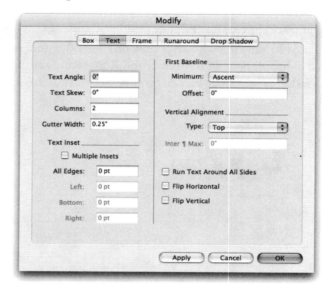

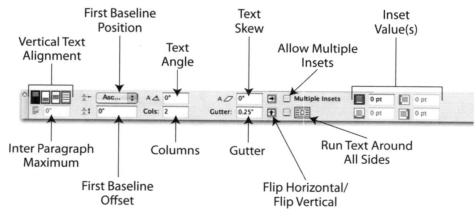

Angling and Skewing Text

Text angle rotates text inside its box; the box itself does not rotate. The angle can range from 0° to 359.999° in 1/1000° increments. *Text skew* slants text within the box at –75° to 75° in 1/1000° increments.

Columns and Gutters

You can change the number of columns and the *gutter width* (space between columns) of any text box in the layout. You can change individual boxes as needed.

If you use an automatic text box, the default columns and gutters are defined in the New Project/New Layout dialog box. You can change the columns and gutters of the automatic text box by navigating to the master page layout, and then choosing Page>Master Guides. When you change the columns and gutters of an automatic text box, associated boxes on the layout pages reflect those changes.

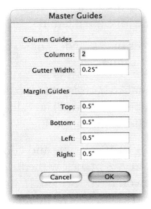

Text Inset

Text inset is the distance from the edge of the box at which text is placed. When setting preferences for default text boxes, you can only set the text inset for all edges. If you are modifying specific boxes, you can define different inset values for each side of the box by checking Multiple Insets, and then entering the inset value for each edge.

Text inset is especially important if the text box has a frame or background color. Without an inset, text runs directly into the edge of the box, which is extremely noticeable and unprofessional.

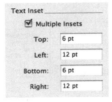

A text box with no inset (left) and the same box (right) with a 6-pt. inset on the top and bottom and a 12-pt. inset on the left and right.

You should never angle or skew text as a substitute for true italics. Always choose the italic font from the menu for the best-looking result.

You can also change the columns and gutters of an automatic text box on an individual page, just as you would change any other text box. Changing the automatic text box on a master page reflects that change back to associated layout pages.

In QuarkXPress 7, the minimum gutter width between columns is 0.002" (0.125 pt.).

Multiple insets can only be specified for rectangular text boxes, not for irregular-shaped or elliptical text boxes.

Baseline

The First Baseline options specify the minimum distance between the top of the text box and the baseline of the first line of text. The Minimum menu presents three options:

- **Cap Height**. This option places the tops of capital letters of the type flush against the top edge of the box. If the text box has a defined text inset, the tops of capital letters are aligned to the inset.
- **Cap + Accent**. This option places the tops of capital letters flush against the top edge of the box (or the inset value), but adds extra space for any accent characters that are used with capital letters.
- **Ascent**. This option places the ascenders of text flush against the top edge of the text box (or the inset value).

The Offset field defines the distance between the top edge of the text box and the first baseline of the text as an absolute value. The value in the Offset field will only be applied if it is greater than the Minimum value.

For example, if you are working in 10-pt. type and choose Ascent in the Minimum menu, the first baseline is placed 7–8 pt. below the top of the text box — the height of the ascender of the typeface you have selected. If, however, you set the Offset to 12 pt., the first baseline is placed 12 pt. below the top of the text box because the Offset value (12 pt.) is larger than the Minimum value (7–8 pt.).

Vertical Alignment

Vertical alignment of text places the text at the top of the box, centered within the box, or aligned to the bottom of the box. Text can also be justified (aligned to the top and bottom of the box, with additional space added between lines and paragraphs); using the Justified option, the Inter ¶ Max field defines the maximum space that can be applied between paragraphs in the text box.

| Align Top | Align Bottom | Justify | Align Center |

Box Attributes

The three check boxes at the bottom of the Modify dialog box affect the text box rather than its content. If the box is placed within another text box, text can be run around all sides of it — the default is for text to run around one side of a box only. Text boxes can also be flipped horizontally or vertically.

☐ Run Text Around All Sides
☐ Flip Horizontal
☐ Flip Vertical

Type metrics are the parameters programmed into the font, including the exact height of capital letters, ascenders, and so on. Different fonts have different type metrics.

Text Runaround

Runaround is the opposite of inset. While text inset defines the distance from the edge that text appears within a box, *runaround* determines the distance at which text wraps around the outside of a box or other objects. You can modify the runaround attributes of a box in the Runaround tab of the Modify dialog box (Item>Runaround) or in the Runaround mode of the Measurements palette.

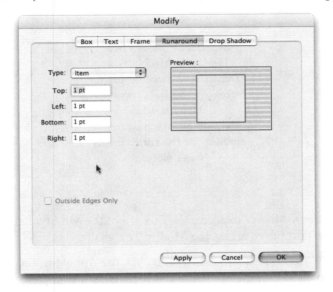

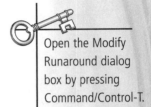

Open the Modify Runaround dialog box by pressing Command/Control-T.

With a text box selected, you can define runaround type as Item (surrounding text wraps around the box) or None (surrounding text flows directly under the box).

The Top, Left, Bottom, and Right fields define the distance between surrounding text and each edge of the box. These values can be set to the same or different numbers, depending on your needs.

Text runaround is especially important if the box has a visible border or background. If the runaround is too small, underlying text runs directly into the border — a mark of unprofessional design.

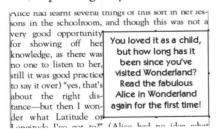 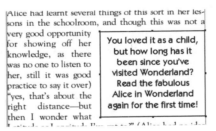

Different runaround values produce different results.
The left image shows a runaround value of 1 pt. on all four sides.
The right image shows the effect of changing only the left runaround to 12 pt.

1. Open **text_boxes.qxp** from the **RF_Quark7>Chapter05** folder.

2. Click the text box in the upper left of the page with either the Content tool or the Item tool.

> Experience the sale of a lifetime at MacNulty's Department Store on Main Street in beautiful downtown Hatchetville.
> Save on housewares, toys, clothing for the entire family and more!

3. Choose Item>Modify to access the Box tab of the Modify dialog box. Click the Text tab to access the Modify Text dialog box.

4. Type "45" in the Text Angle field and click the Apply button. Note that the text changes within the box but the box remains unchanged.

When working in the Modify dialog box, press Command/Control-A to apply your choices without closing the dialog box.

> Experience the sale of a lifetime at MacNulty's Department Store on Main Street in beautiful downtown Hatchetville. Save on housewares, toys, clothing for the entire family and more!

5. Now change the angle to –45°. Click Apply again. Experiment and find an angle you like. When you are satisfied, click OK.

6. Click the left box with the text "Type may be slanted, or obliqued."

7. Display the Text mode of the Measurements palette.

8. Type "13" in the Text Skew field and press Return/Enter.
Compare the text in this box with the text in the box next to it. Note the subtle (and not-so-subtle) differences.

Type may be slanted, or obliqued. | *Type may be slanted, or obliqued.*

Both of these text boxes are set in the ATC Oak font; the left is artificially skewed in the Modify dialog box, and the right is set in ATC Oak Italic. Note the subtle differences in the tail of the "y," the bar of the "e," and the overt difference in the shape of the loop of the "a."

9. Select the text box with the coupon border. The type is crushed against the border, which looks very bad.

10. Display the Text mode of the Measurements palette.

11. In the Text Inset area, change the All Edges field to 4 pt., and click Apply. Notice how much room is left at the bottom of the box.

12. Click the Centered Vertical Alignment button.

   Although the text is vertically centered in the box, its offsets look uneven; the sides look overly compressed compared to the top and bottom margins.

13. Activate the Multiple Insets check box. Set the left and right insets to 8 pt. and the bottom inset to 7 pt.

14. Close the file without saving.

WORKING IN THE TEXT BOX

An active text box is identified by a solid black border with handles at each corner and at the middle of each side. A blinking text-insertion bar, called an *insertion point*, appears in the active box.

Before typing, check the magnification of the page in the View Percentage field in the lower-left corner of the Status bar. If the setting is below 100% when you type, the text might appear as gray bars on the screen, called *greeking*, which speeds up screen redraws.

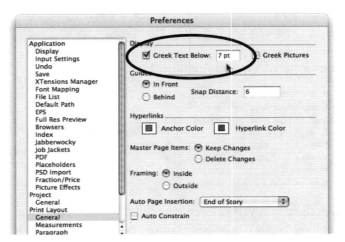

You can change the size below which QuarkXPress greeks text in the General preferences.

The value you set specifies the size at which type is greeked in actual view (100%). If you set the greeking value to 10 pt., any type smaller than 10 pt. is greeked when viewing the page at 100%. If you change the view percentage, the Greek Text Below value is applied to the size of type used in the display; at 50% view, 20-pt. type will display at 10 pt. In other words, if you view the page at 50%, type set smaller than 20 points is greeked. Conversely, if you change to the 200% view, text is greeked below 5 pts. because 5-pt. type displays at 10 pt.

Text Box Overflow

When text won't fit in the box or chain of linked boxes, the Overflow icon appears in the bottom-right corner of the box. To solve the problem, you can increase the size of the text box, decrease the size of the text, decrease the line spacing (*leading*), or link to another text box. You should always correct Overflow icons in a layout.

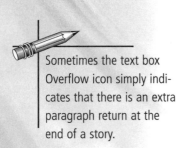

Sometimes the text box Overflow icon simply indicates that there is an extra paragraph return at the end of a story.

g about it, even if I icn on the hich was very likely true.)
n. Would the fall never come now many miles I've fallen by oud. "I must be getting some-⊠

Navigating Text

The insertion point indicates where text will be entered. As you fill the text box, you can stretch the box to make it taller or wider to fit more text, or you can add another text box and link the two together (explained later in this chapter). To move the insertion point to a new location, click with the Content tool or use the Arrow keys. The commands in the following chart will help you navigate text more efficiently.

Move to:	Macintosh	Windows
Previous word	Command-Left Arrow	Control-Left Arrow
Next word	Command-Right Arrow	Control-Right Arrow
Beginning of line	Command-Option-Left Arrow	Control-Alt-Left Arrow
End of line	Command-Option-Right Arrow	Control-Alt-Right Arrow
Beginning of current paragraph	Command-Up Arrow	Control-Up Arrow
Beginning of next paragraph	Command-Down Arrow	Control-Down Arrow
Beginning of story	Command-Option-Up Arrow	Control-Alt-Up Arrow
End of story	Command-Option-Down Arrow	Control-Alt-Down Arrow

A QuarkXPress **paragraph** is defined as any information that is followed by the Return character (¶). Whether it is a word or several lines of text, if it is followed by a ¶, it's a paragraph. Headings, bulleted items, and captions are examples of paragraphs. A paragraph can also be a single paragraph character with no preceding text.

Selecting Text

Text in a text box is editable and can be moved into another text box or to a different position in the same box. It can be cut or copied to the Clipboard, pasted into a layout, or deleted. To select text, you use the Content tool.

- Clicking once in a text box places the text insertion point in the story.
- Clicking twice highlights the word on which you click.
- Clicking three times in rapid succession highlights the entire line of text in which you click.
- Clicking four times highlights the entire paragraph in which you click.

Whenever text is selected, the selected text is deleted and replaced if you type, paste, or import new text.

Any of the commands in the previous chart can be used with the Shift key to select the text. For example, if you press Command/Control-Shift-Right Arrow, the word (or part of a word) following the insertion point is selected, and the insertion point moves to the beginning of the next word.

You can also select an entire story (all of the text in a box or chain) by pressing Command/Control-A when the insertion point is placed in a story.

Cutting, Copying, and Pasting Text

To cut, copy, or paste text, you can use the same commands that you use in any other application:

- Cut (Edit>Cut) Command/Control-X
- Copy (Edit>Copy) Command/Control-C
- Paste (Edit>Paste) Command/Control-V

You can delete selected text by pressing Delete/Backspace, but this does not store the deleted text on the Clipboard.

To cut or copy text, you have to select it first; pasting places the Clipboard contents at the location of the current insertion point.

You can also check the Drag and Drop Text box in the Input Settings preferences; when this setting is active, you can use the mouse to move highlighted text to another location in the same text box or chain.

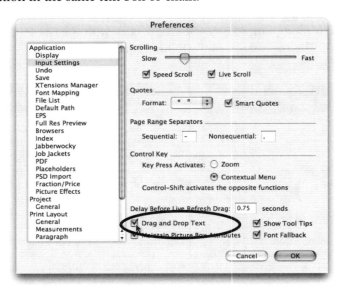

Creating and Importing Text

There are several ways to add text to a layout. Obviously, you can simply place the insertion point in a box and type.

Text can also be added to a QuarkXPress layout from another program using the copy-and-paste technique. If you copy text from another program, you can reactivate QuarkXPress, place the insertion point where you want to add the information, and paste the Clipboard's contents (Edit>Paste or Command/Control-V). The disadvantage of this method is that when the information is pasted into QuarkXPress, all formatting that was applied to the text in the word processor is replaced by the default settings within QuarkXPress. It is better to use Import Text whenever possible.

A third option for adding text is called Jabberwocky (Utilities>Jabber), which adds enough nonsense text to fill the current box or chain of boxes. In the Jabberwocky preferences, you can choose the language (English, Esperanto, Klingon, or Latin) and format (Prose or Poetry) of the text. This utility is particularly useful if you want to design a layout before the final copy is ready — a common occurrence.

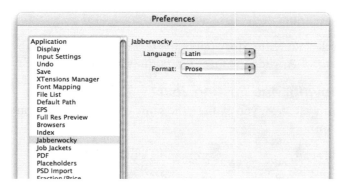

You can copy and paste text from a Web site, but there are two points to keep in mind. First, you cannot legally copy content from a Web site without permission from the creator. Second, copying text from a Web site gives you text with many hidden characters and formatting commands that you will need to delete in your QuarkXPress layout.

The most efficient way to bring text into a QuarkXPress layout is to import text from a word-processing program. Text imported from some programs retains formatting attributes assigned in those programs. Text can be imported from the following:

- ASCII text
- ASCII text saved with XPress Tags
- Rich-text format (RTF)
- HTML files
- Microsoft Word files
- Corel WordPerfect files
- Platform-specific text editors, such as MacWrite and MacWrite II for Macintosh and Microsoft Write for Windows

To import a text file, select a text box with the Content tool and choose File>Import Text. If Import Text is grayed out (unavailable), either the box is the wrong type or the Item tool is active.

You select the file to import from the Import Text dialog box. QuarkXPress identifies the type of word-processing document and the file size; this information varies, depending on the selected file. Longer text files take longer to import into a layout.

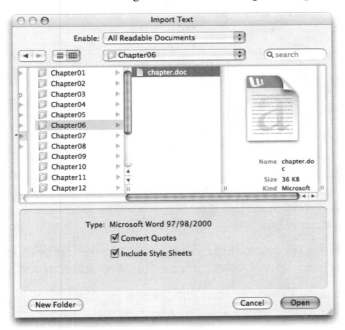

Press Command/Control-E to access the Import Text dialog box.

If the Include Style Sheets check box is selected, QuarkXPress can convert word-processor style sheets into QuarkXPress-defined styles. If the same style names are not in the project style sheets, QuarkXPress imports the styles as they are defined in the word-processing document. If the same style name already exists in the QuarkXPress project, QuarkXPress alerts you to any conflict between the word-processing style and the QuarkXPress style. You can choose to use the style as defined in the word-processing file or as defined in the QuarkXPress project.

Once the file is selected from the Import Text dialog box and you click Open, the text flows into the text box at the position of the insertion point.

Typographer's Quotes

The Convert Quotes check box allows QuarkXPress to convert prime (') or double-prime (") marks into true typographer's apostrophes and quotes. Also called *smart quotes*, typographer's quotes are used as single and double quotation marks and apostrophes. In some countries, other characters are used for quotation marks, such as the *guillemot* in France, which looks like this: «Allons-y!».

You should never use straight quotes and apostrophes; these are inch and foot marks, and they should only be used as such. Always make certain that Smart Quotes is selected in the Application preferences before you create your layout. When you import from a word-processing file, Convert Quotes should be selected in the Import Text dialog box; the document will then import with the proper quotation marks and apostrophes.

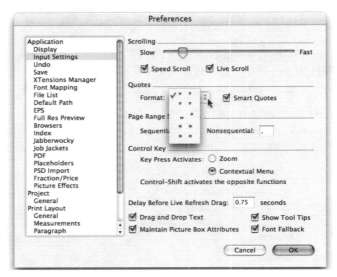

Locking Text

When you've spent hours or even days setting type — adjusting every letter and line space until it is perfect — the worst thing that can happen is accidentally changing something and undoing all of your painstaking effort. In QuarkXPress 7, you can now lock text, protecting it from accidental (or intentional) changes to either content or formatting.

When a text box is selected in the layout, you can lock the text by choosing Item>Lock>Story. When a story is locked, you can still select and copy text. You cannot:

- Import, paste, or type new text into the box.
- Cut text from the story.
- Change formatting attributes using the Measurements palette, the Character Attributes or Paragraph Attributes dialog boxes, or the Style menu options.

Warning! Some changes can still affect locked type:

- Changing the dimensions of the text box causes locked content to reflow.
- Moving objects that have defined runaround values will cause locked text to reflow around the moved object.
- Changes to the definition of a style sheet will change the formatting of locked text.
- Changes to kerning or tracking tables will be applied to locked text.

If a picture box is selected, the Lock>Story menu option changes to Lock>Picture.

If you lock a story, you lock the entire story — even if that story extends across two or ten text boxes. However, locking a story only protects the content of the box(es). To truly protect your work, you might want to lock both the box(es) and the story.

You can unlock a story in the Character Attributes or Paragraph Attributes dialog box. Clicking the small Lock icon makes the dialog box fields available, and you can reformat as necessary.

Linking Text Boxes

If you have more text than will fit into a single text box, one solution is to add more text boxes and link them together so that the text can flow from one to another. By doing so, the text at the end of the first text box flows into the next text box, as needed.

To link one text box to another manually, you select the Linking tool from the Tools palette. When you click a text box with the Linking tool, the edges of the box become "marching ants," indicating that you are in the process of linking text boxes. When the cursor is inside the bounds of the marching ants, it displays as a Linking icon.

You can then move the cursor (which becomes an arrow) to another text box and click to create the link. If you select any of the boxes in the link and then select the Linking tool, QuarkXPress displays the path that the text will take.

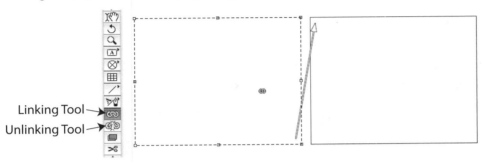

If the first box you click is already in a chain, the next box you click will be added to the chain *after* the first box clicked, but *before* any other boxes that followed in the chain. In other words, you can add a text box to the middle of a text chain.

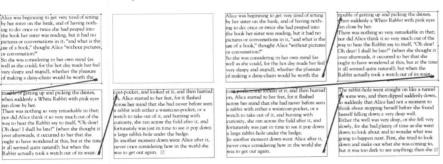

The original text chain (left) and the result of adding a new box to the middle of the existing chain (right).

If a box in the text chain is deleted, the text reflows to the next box in the chain.

You cannot add boxes containing text to a linked chain of boxes that already contains text.

You can easily link to more than two text boxes by Option/Alt-clicking the Link tool, and then clicking each text box in succession in the order of the desired link.

Unlinking Text Boxes

You can unlink boxes in an existing chain with the Unlinking tool (the broken chain). If any text box in the chain is active, selecting the Unlinking tool displays the text-flow arrows. If you place the cursor directly over the beginning of a text-flow arrow, the cursor becomes the Unlinking icon. Clicking the start of a text-flow arrow breaks the chain.

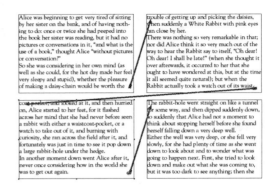

When you break a text-flow chain, the box where you break the link displays the Overflow icon, indicating that more text exists in the story.

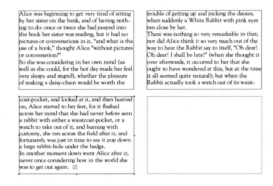

 PLACE AND THREAD TEXT

1. Open **alice_falls.qxp** from the **RF_Quark7>Chapter05** folder.

2. Select the Rectangle Text Box tool, and click and drag to create a text box. Use the Measurements palette to define the box with the following dimensions:

   X: 0.5″   W: 7.5″
   Y: 0.5″   H: 3.1″

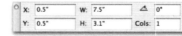

3. With the Content tool active, choose File>Import Text and navigate to **alice.txt** in the **RF_Quark7>Chapter05** folder.

4. Make sure the Convert Quotes and Interpret XPress Tags check boxes are selected.

   The file you are placing is a QuarkXPress Tags file, which is a special kind of text file that is saved out of QuarkXPress and includes any formatting that is applied in the layout. To create an XPress Tags file, you can select any text box and choose File>Save Text.

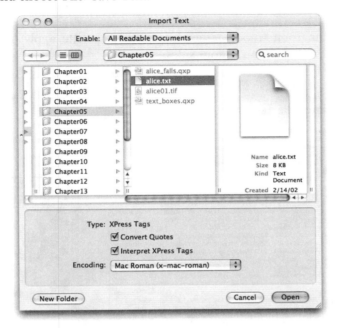

The Import Text dialog box is smart enough to recognize that this is an XPress Tags file, even though it has the TXT extension instead of the XTG (XPress Tags) extension.

The Include Style Sheets option automatically changes to Interpret XPress Tags.

5. Click Open.

   Notice that the text box displays a red "X" in the lower-right corner, indicating that there is more text to flow.

6. Create a new text box with the following dimensions:

   X: 0.5"   W: 7.5"
   Y: 3.569"   H: 6.931"

   Notice that the box hides the picture on the page.

7. In the Text tab of the Measurements palette, change the Columns field to 2. Press Tab twice to highlight the Gutter field. Change the Gutter field to 0.25" and press Return/Enter to apply the changes.

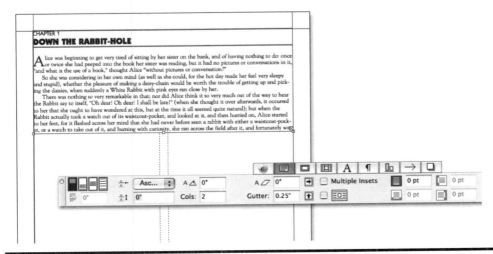

8. With the Linking tool, click the top (1-column) text box. The frame changes to a marching-ants border.

9. Click the lower (2-column) text box. When you release the mouse button, the text fills the second box.

10. Shift-click to select both text boxes and choose File>Send to Back.

11. Select the picture box, which is currently obscuring the text behind it.

12. In the Runaround mode of the Measurements palette, apply an Item runaround of 1-pt. on all four sides.

CHAPTER 1

DOWN THE RABBIT-HOLE

Alice was beginning to get very tired of sitting by her sister on the bank, and of having nothing to do: once or twice she had peeped into the book her sister was reading, but it had no pictures or conversations in it, "and what is the use of a book," thought Alice "without pictures or conversation?"

So she was considering in her own mind (as well as she could, for the hot day made her feel very sleepy and stupid), whether the pleasure of making a daisy-chain would be worth the trouble of getting up and picking the daisies, when suddenly a White Rabbit with pink eyes ran close by her.

There was nothing so very remarkable in that; nor did Alice think it so very much out of the way to hear the Rabbit say to itself, "Oh dear! Oh dear! I shall be late!" (when she thought it over afterwards, it occurred to her that she ought to have wondered at this, but at the time it all seemed quite natural); but when the Rabbit actually took a watch out of its waistcoat-pocket, and looked at it, and then hurried on, Alice started to her feet, for it flashed across her mind that she had never before seen a rabbit with either a waistcoat-pocket, or a watch to take out of it, and burning with curiosity, she ran across the field after it, and fortunately was just in time to see it pop down a large rabbit-hole under the hedge.

In another moment down went Alice after it, never once considering how in the world she was to get out again.

The rabbit-hole went straight on like a tunnel for some way, and then dipped suddenly down, so suddenly that Alice had not a moment to think about stopping herself before she found herself falling down a very deep well.

Either the well was very deep, or she fell very slowly, for she had plenty of time as she went down to look about and to wonder what was going to happen next. First, she tried to look down and make out what she was coming to, but it was too dark to see anything; then she looked at the sides of the well, and noticed that they were filled with cupboards and book-shelves; here and there she saw maps and pictures hung upon pegs. She took down a jar from one of the shelves as she passed; it was labelled "ORANGE MARMALADE," but to her great disappointment it was empty: she did not like to drop the jar for fear of killing somebody, so managed to put it into one of the cupboards as she fell past it.

"Well!" thought Alice to herself, "after such a fall as this, I shall think nothing of tumbling down stairs! How brave they'll all think me at home! Why, I wouldn't say anything about it, even if I fell off the top of the house!" (Which was very likely true.)

Down, down, down. Would the fall never come to an end! "I wonder how many miles I've fallen by this time?" she said aloud. "I must be getting somewhere near the centre of the earth. Let me see: that would be four thousand miles down, I think—" (for, you see, Alice had learnt several things of this sort in her lessons in the schoolroom, and though this was not a very good opportunity for showing off her knowledge, as there was no one to listen to her, still it was good practice to say it over) "yes, that's about the right distance—but then I wonder what Latitude or Longitude I've got to?" (Alice had no idea what Latitude was, or Longitude either, but thought they were nice grand words to say.)

Presently she began again. "I wonder if I shall fall right through the earth! How funny it'll seem to come out among the people that walk with their heads downward! The Antipathies, I think—" (she was rather glad there was no one listening, this time, as it didn't sound at all the right word) "—but I shall have to ask them what the name of the country is, you know. Please, Ma'am, is this New Zealand or Australia?" (and she tried to curtsey as she spoke—fancy curtseying as you're falling through the air! Do you think you could manage it?) "And what an ignorant little girl she'll think me for asking! No, it'll never do to ask: perhaps I shall see it written up somewhere."

13. Save the file as "alice_working.qxp" in your **Work_In_Progress** folder, and close it.

TYPE BASICS

Before we explain the QuarkXPress formatting options, it helps to understand some of the basic terminology associated with type. The art of typography was once the exclusive forté of type designers and typesetters, until page-layout software became readily available. Since then, those knowledgeable in typography have become all but extinct. Most graphics and design software products, including QuarkXPress, offer numerous typographic features. The people who use these features, however, are rarely taught the rules of formal typography. Good typography is what separates quality from amateur design.

Point size is measured from descender to ascender, not from the baseline

Ascender — Height — X-height — Baseline

Descender

Type is divided into five *categories* — serif, sans serif, script, decorative, and pi — the broadest, most general groups organized by the letterform.

- **Serif Type.** The stroke at the top or base of letters, and the ear and spur on some letters, are elements that help you identify *serif type*. Because of their formal, traditional appearance, serif fonts are commonly used to convey a conservative, dignified image. With a few exceptions, these typefaces are easy to read and are used extensively for long passages of text.

- **Sans-Serif Type.** *Sans-serif fonts* have no stroke at the top or base. Since these typefaces are so legible, they are a good choice for labeling illustrations. Because many newspaper headlines are set in a sans-serif typeface, we have come to associate "the facts" with sans-serif fonts. When reversing type out of a background, a sans-serif face is a good choice.

- **Script (Invitation) Type.** Any typeface that has the appearance of being created with a pen or a brush, whether the letters are connected or unconnected, is a *script typeface*. Scripts are often used for invitations or announcements, and sometime for logos. Script type is easy to distinguish — it often has the word "script" in its name.

- **Decorative Type.** *Decorative,* or display typefaces, are meant to be used in headlines and to convey specific meaning. You can probably guess what the fonts Valhalla, Eyechart, and Quetzalcoatl look like, even without seeing the letters. Keep in mind that decorative fonts can be extremely elaborate. The primary consideration for type should always be readability.

- **Pi (Symbol) Type.** *Pi fonts,* often called "symbol," "logo," "dingbats," or "ornaments," are used to insert frequently used symbols into text. A *pi font* is a collection of related symbols. These might include characters in a math font, a company logo, blocks in a crossword puzzle, borders for a page, credit cards, astrological symbols, or map symbols. Some companies create fonts for placing the company logo or other trademarks as a single character.

Type categories are further refined into *classes*, or classifications, which share specific features, such as thick-and-thin strokes. These are further broken down into *families*, or type styles sharing a common design. Families are divided into specific *faces*, such as regular, italic, bold, extended, or condensed.

Good typography separates amateur from professional design. For more comprehensive information about typography, see ATC's **Type Companion for the Digital Artist.**

Flourishes and other glyph elements that extend beyond the edge of a text box are rendered cleanly in QuarkXPress 7. In previous versions, it wasn't uncommon to see these attributes cut off; they still printed, but you couldn't see them on screen — which made designing around them difficult.

The flourishes of Zapfino are visible in version 7:

Flourish

but cut off in version 6:

UNDERSTANDING CHARACTER FORMATTING

Once you've got text in a text box, you need to define how it will look. Character attributes include the font, size, type style, color, shade, scale, kern or track amount, and baseline shift. These attributes can be controlled in the Character Attributes dialog box (Style>Character or Command/Control-Shift-D) or in Character mode of the Measurements palette.

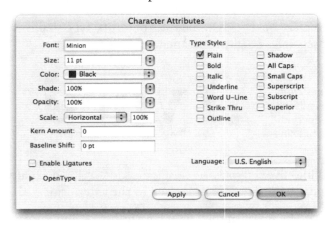

The Character Attributes dialog box can be accessed by pressing Command/Control-Shift-D.

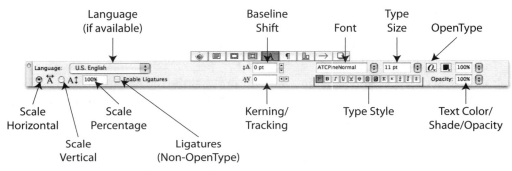

The *font* is the name of the family of type selected from the drop-down menu or typed into the dialog box. Fonts must be installed on the computer in order to be accessible. The *size* is the height of a typeface, measured in points. This is not just the visible size of a character, but includes the distance from the descender to the clearance allowance above the ascender. Type can be assigned any color in your Colors palette. Shade is the percentage of that color.

Horizontal and *Vertical Scale*

Type can be scaled both horizontally and vertically, from 25% to 400%. You can change the scale of selected text in the Character Attributes dialog box by choosing Style>Horizontal and Vertical Scale. The Scale field is highlighted automatically. Horizontal scale is, by default, the active dimension; you can change the vertical scale by changing the Scale pop-up menu to Vertical.

Scaling affects the width and height of selected text. This scaling is a quick way of achieving condensed type, but it is not the preferred method. Type that has been condensed or expanded (stretched) in this fashion looks bad — the scaling destroys the type's balance. You should use a condensed or expanded version of a typeface before resorting to horizontal scaling.

Horizontal scaling often creates bad results — in the serif type (right), notice how the subtle contrast between thick and thin strokes is lost as the face is scaled horizontally.

Kerning and Tracking

Kerning increases or decreases the space between pairs of letters. It is used in cases where particular letters in specific fonts need to be brought together manually to eliminate a too-tight or too-spread-out look. Manual kerning is most necessary in headlines where the type is big, bold, and noticeable. Kerning units are based upon an *em space* — the amount of space occupied by an uppercase "M" — which is usually the widest character in a typeface.

An **em** is defined as the height, in points, of the font size. If you are using 12-pt type, an em equals 12 points.

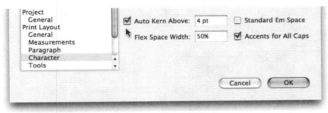

In the left example, each letter has a width that abuts other letters. The right example shows how kerning tightens the spacing between letters.

Many commercial fonts have a large number of built-in kerning pairs, so you don't need much hands-on intervention with the kerning. Supplying built-in kerning pairs, called "robust kerning," is one reason these fonts are more expensive than shareware.

Tracking refers to the overall tightness or looseness of the selected characters. Tracking adjusts the space between letters in a selected range of letters; tracking is also known as "range kerning." Kerning is available when the cursor is placed between two letters; tracking is available when a range of characters is selected. Characters can be kerned or tracked ±500 units, with the smallest increment being 0.001 em.

QuarkXPress preferences default to implement built-in tracking tables for all type above 4 pt. You can change this value or deactivate auto kerning in the Character preferences.

If no text is highlighted but the text insertion point is placed in a text box, you can adjust kerning between the letters by choosing Style>Kern. If any text (more than two characters) is selected, that menu item changes to Style>Track.

In the Measurements palette, the Kerning/Tracking field applies the appropriate setting depending on what is selected. If no text is selected, adjusting this field changes the kerning; if text is selected, this field adjusts the tracking.

Baseline Shift

Baseline shift means to move the selected type above or below the baseline in an amount specified in points. The movement is measured from the *baseline* of the type, which is the line where the bottoms of the letters rest.

You can use keyboard
shortcuts instead of
selecting from the
Measurements palette
 or the Character Options
dialog box. These
commands toggle the
style on and off.

Bold
Command/Control-Shift-B

Italic
Command/Control-Shift-I

Normal
Command/Control-Shift-P

Underline
Command/Control-Shift-U

Word Underline
Command/Control-Shift-W

Strikethrough
Command/Control-Shift-/

Outline
Command/Control-Shift-O

Caps
Command/Control-Shift-K

Small Caps
Command/Control-Shift-H

Superscript
Command -Shift-+ (plus)
(Macintosh only)

Subscript
Command -Shift- – (hyphen)
(Macintosh only)

Type Style

You might (or might not, considering the frequency with which this problem occurs) have heard that it's incorrect to style a font by selecting a **bold** or *italic* menu shortcut instead of selecting the true bold or italic font from the Font menu. If you use this "menu styling," the result might be an artificially bolded version of the typeface or an ugly slanted oblique instead of a true italic. For the sake of expediency, you can use the menu shortcuts for quick formatting, and then change to the true bold or italic fonts before outputting the job.

Macintosh. If you choose to style a font that does not have that particular variation (such as bolding or italicizing a display typeface that only exists as a plain or Roman version), your software might show a pseudo-bold or oblique font, but the printer will usually print the base font or Courier. If a bold or an italic font exists for the typeface, the output device might or might not match the styled font to the correct typeface. There are so many variables when printing that you really should not rely on assumptions of what *might* work. The safest choice is to physically change the selected type to the actual bold or italic font.

Windows. QuarkXPress for Windows does not display some font variations (for example, a bold version created from a master font) in its various font menus — Measurements palette, Character dialog box, or Font menu (Item>Font).

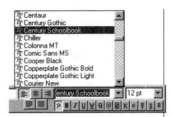

If, however, you toggle off Hide Variations while looking at the Fonts folder in Windows Explorer, you can see that there are several variations of master fonts (in the following images, Century Gothic and Century Schoolbook are two examples of a master font with variations).

The only way you can use these variations in QuarkXPress is by using the choices available through the Type Style menu (Style>Type Style) or the shortcuts in the Measurements palette.

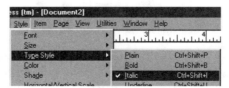

If you are certain that a font variation exists on your computer, using the type styles calls the appropriate font when the job is output. If the font variation does not exist, the job will output using only the base font.

Small Caps

Small caps are typically created by artificially reducing the point size of a regular capital letter to a set percentage of that point size. This can cause small caps to look weak and spindly next to a regular cap. Many typefaces are available with an "expert set" that includes "cut" small caps, meaning they were designed from the start to be used as small caps, and they maintain the same weight as the regular cap.

You can define the appearance of small caps in the Character preferences; the default value is 75% of the font size.

TEXT IS SET AS SMALL CAPS.
TEXT IS STYLED AS SMALL CAPS.

True small caps from the Minion Expert font (top) compared to styled small caps (bottom).

Ligatures

Ligatures are substitutes for certain pairs of letters, most commonly fi, fl, ff, ffi, ffl, and occasionally ct and st for use in historical typesetting. The diphthongs ae and oe are used in some nonEnglish-language typesetting.

ff fi fl ffi ffl

ff fi fl ffi ffl

Normal ligature pairs (top) and the ligatures in Adobe Minion Expert (bottom).

You can easily see the subtle variation in the appearance of these character pairs. For example, the "i" within a ligature does not have a dot.

In QuarkXPress 7, ligatures have been changed to a character formatting attribute rather than the all-or-nothing approach of earlier versions. When text is selected, you can apply ligatures by activating the Enable Ligatures check box in the Character Attributes dialog box or in the Measurements palette Character mode.

WORK WITH TEXT

1. Choose File>New>Project. Create a letter-size print layout called "Text Test" using the default margins; the layout should have 1 column. Facing Pages and Automatic Text Box should not be checked.

2. Choose View>Invisibles.

3. Select the Text Box tool, click at the upper-left corner of the live area of the page, and drag diagonally until you have a frame with the following dimensions:

   X: 0.5 in.   W: 7.5 in.
   Y: 0.5 in.   H: 3.1 in.

4. Type "The Mad Hattery" in the text box. Notice the font, size, and other information in the Measurements palette.

5. Select all the text. In the Measurements palette Classic mode, change the type to 48-pt. ATC Maple Ultra.

Note the difference in weight and character width. In order to match the true small caps as closely as possible, we scaled the styled small cap with a vertical scale of 66% and a horizontal scale of 75%.

Because ligatures are now a character-formatting attribute, you can also search for ligatures in the Find/Change dialog box, as well as enable them for any character style sheet or the character attributes of a paragraph style sheet.

Many special characters (such as paragraph symbols, soft returns, tab characters, and spaces) are not visible in the standard page-layout mode. You can toggle these characters' visibility by choosing View>Invisibles.

Toggle invisible characters on and off by pressing Command/Control-I.

6. Resize the frame to a width of 3 in. by dragging the right-center handle or by typing the new width into the Measurements palette.

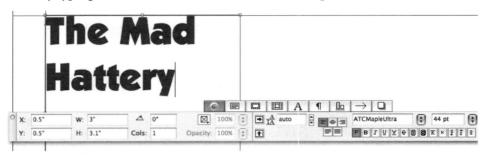

7. Using the Type tool, place the text insertion point between the "r" and "y" in Hattery.

8. Change the Kerning field of the Measurements palette to 14 and press Return/Enter to apply the change.

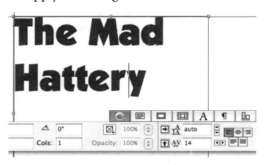

9. Kern any other letters that look particularly bad to you. (The "Ha" pair needs help; try a setting of –4.)

10. Create a new text box 2-in. wide by 2-in. high below the existing text box. Align the box to snap to the left margin guide.

11. With the Content tool selected, choose 12-pt. ATC Pine Normal in the Font menu of the Measurements palette.

12. Type the following:

"Alice was beginning to get very tired of sitting by her sister on the bank, and of having nothing to do; once or twice she had peeped into the book her sister was reading, but it had no pictures or conversations in it, and what is the use of a book, thought Alice, without pictures or conversation?"

Notice the Overflow icon in the lower right of the text box, indicating that the box is not large enough to display all of the text in the story.

13. Resize the box so all of the text fits.

14. Double-click the word "bank" in the first sentence and replace it with "fence". Notice that the selected word is replaced by the newly typed text.

15. Select the first word (Alice). Click the Small Caps text-style icon. The lowercase letters become small capitals, but the capital letter is unaffected.

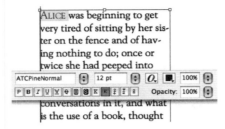

16. Save the project to your **Work_In_Progress** folder as "working_text.qxp" and close it.

UNDERSTANDING PARAGRAPH FORMATTING

The appearance or character-formatting style of text influences the overall tone of a page. The formatting of paragraphs affects how your page looks and reads. Attributes that affect the entire paragraph include line spacing (leading), space before and after paragraphs, indents, alignment, hyphenation rules, drop caps, widow and orphan control, and the ability to lock to the layout's baseline grid.

To apply paragraph formatting, you simply place the Content tool anywhere in a paragraph. Since paragraph formatting affects the entire paragraph, you don't have to select all of the text manually. These attributes can be defined in the Paragraph Attributes dialog box (Style>Formats or Command/Control-Shift-F) or in the Paragraph and Tab modes of the Measurements palette.

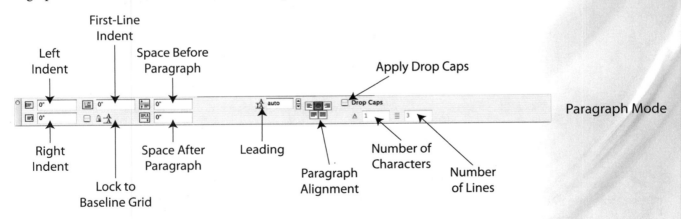

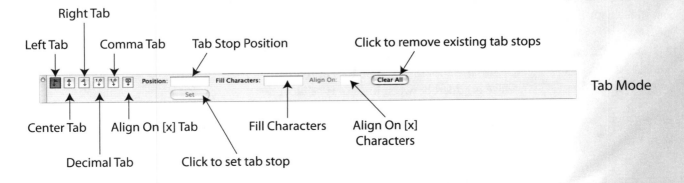

Formats

The Formats tab of the Paragraph Attributes dialog box duplicates the settings in the Measurements palette Paragraph mode.

Open the Paragraph Attributes dialog box by pressing Command/Control-Shift-F.

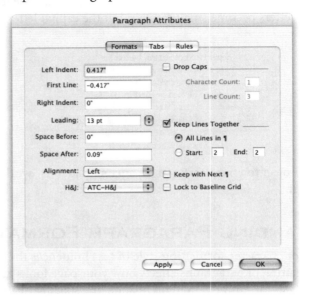

Indents

Left Indent and Right Indent define the distance of text from the box or column edges. First Line defines the indent of just the first line in the paragraph, and the value is added to or subtracted from the Left Indent value. This value can be a negative number, in which case the paragraph is considered to have a *hanging indent* (as you might use for a bulleted list).

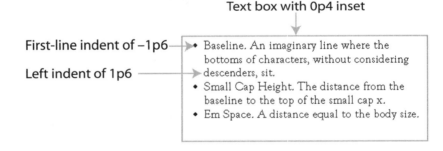

Text box with 0p4 inset

First-line indent of –1p6 ——→ • Baseline. An imaginary line where the bottoms of characters, without considering

Left indent of 1p6 ——————→ descenders, sit.
 • Small Cap Height. The distance from the baseline to the top of the small cap x.
 • Em Space. A distance equal to the body size.

Leading

Leading is the amount of space between lines of type, measured from baseline to baseline. There are three types of leading — absolute, automatic, and incremental.

Absolute leading is defined as a finite number, such as "12-pt. leading." The same amount of leading (in this example, 12-pt.) is applied regardless of the type size.

Typographers specify the size of the type with the leading by separating the items with a slash. If the type is set to 10 pt. with 12 pt. leading, they would write "10/12". This is referred to as "10 over 12."

Automatic leading defaults to 120% of the font size. You can change this value in the Paragraph preferences. In the Auto Leading field, the 20% means that 20% of the font size is added between lines of type (10-pt.

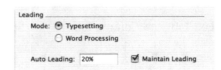

type would use 12-pt. leading). Typesetting mode, the default, measures leading from baseline to baseline; Word Processing mode measures leading from ascender to ascender.

Incremental leading is based on the type size and adds or subtracts a specific amount of space to define the leading. If you type a number preceded by a plus or minus sign, that number is added to or subtracted from the type size to define the leading. If your paragraph is set in 12-pt. type and you define leading as +4, the paragraph will use 16-pt. leading.

Space Before and Space After

Space Before and Space After fields allow the placement of a specific amount of space before or after a paragraph. These values are usually used between elements in a bulleted list, between headlines and text, and between paragraphs that do not have first-line indents.

> • Baseline. An imaginary line where the bottoms of characters, without considering descenders, sit.
> • Small Cap Height. The distance from the baseline to the top of the small cap x.
> • Em Space. A distance equal to the body size.

0 space before paragraphs

> • Baseline. An imaginary line where the bottoms of characters, without considering descenders, sit.
> • Small Cap Height. The distance from the baseline to the top of the small cap x.
> • Em Space. A distance equal to the body size.

0p6 space before paragraphs

> • Baseline. An imaginary line where the bottoms of characters, without considering descenders, sit.
> • Small Cap Height. The distance from the baseline to the top of the small cap x.
> • Em Space. A distance equal to the body size.

1p space before paragraphs

Paragraph Alignment

Paragraphs can be aligned left, right, centered, justified, or force-justified. *Force-justified* paragraphs justify even short last lines of the paragraph.

Left Alignment

A *baseline* is an imaginary line where the bottoms of characters, without considering descenders, sit. *Small cap height* is the distance from the baseline to the top of the small cap x. An *em space* is a distance equal to the body size.

Right Alignment

A *baseline* is an imaginary line where the bottoms of characters, without considering descenders, sit. *Small cap height* is the distance from the baseline to the top of the small cap x. An *em space* is a distance equal to the body size.

Center Alignment

A *baseline* is an imaginary line where the bottoms of characters, without considering descenders, sit. *Small cap height* is the distance from the baseline to the top of the small cap x. An *em space* is a distance equal to the body size.

Justified Alignment

A *baseline* is an imaginary line where the bottoms of characters, without considering descenders, sit. *Small cap height* is the distance from the baseline to the top of the small cap x. An *em space* is a distance equal to the body size.

Force-Justified Alignment

A *baseline* is an imaginary line where the bottoms of characters, without considering descenders, sit. *Small cap height* is the distance from the baseline to the top of the small cap x. An *em space* is a distance equal to the body size.

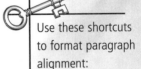

Use these shortcuts to format paragraph alignment:

Align Left
Command/Control-Shift-L

Align Right
Command/Control-Shift-R

Align Center
Command/Control-Shift-C

Justify
Command/Control-Shift-J

Force Justify (Macintosh)
Command-Option-Shift-J

Force Justify (Windows)
Control-Alt-Shift-J

Hyphenation

Closely associated with justification is the selected hyphenation routine. Hyphenation rules are created using the H&J dialog box (Edit>H&Js). These options are explained in Chapter 8.

Drop Caps

The Drop Caps option enlarges one or more characters at the beginning of a paragraph to extend over more than one line of the paragraph. You can define the number of characters to enlarge, as well as the number of lines over which the drop cap extends.

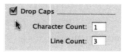

A *baseline* is an imaginary line where the bottoms of characters, without considering descenders, sit. *Small cap height* is the distance from

Keep Lines Together and Keep with Next

"Keep" specifications control *widows* and *orphans* — single lines at the beginning of a paragraph but at the end of a box or column, or at the end of a paragraph and at the beginning of a box or column. These options are also used to keep a paragraph with the next one, such as forcing a headline to stay with the first paragraph following it. You can choose to keep an entire paragraph together or to keep a certain number of lines at the beginning and end of the paragraph together.

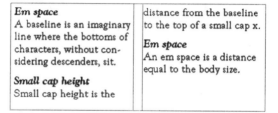

This text has no widow or orphan control applied. The first line of the "Small cap height" definition is not with the rest of the definition.

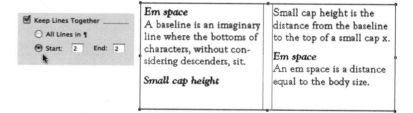

The "Small cap height" definition is set to keep the first two and last two lines of the paragraph together. However, the term is no longer with its definition.

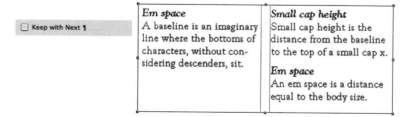

The "Small cap height" heading is set to Keep with Next so that the term always appears with its definition.

The Lock to Baseline Grid box determines, on a paragraph-by-paragraph basis, whether the underlying grid for the layout determines where the paragraph falls. In most cases, aligning to the baseline grid is not a good idea.

Tabs

Customized tabs are one of the most useful tools in QuarkXPress. Some people rely on the Spacebar for aligning columns, or they rely on the default tab stops and insert as many tab characters as they need to line up a list. Because letter spaces in a proportional font are variable, it's nearly impossible to format text properly in this manner. If you use more than one tab character and rely on the default tabs (usually every half-inch), changing the font size can result in elements no longer aligning properly. With defined tab stops, you can align columns precisely and create complex tables.

When the Paragraph or Tab mode of the Measurements palette is showing, a formatting ruler appears at the top of the active text box. You can place different types of tabs by clicking the appropriate button in Tab mode, and then clicking at a point on the formatting ruler. You can also type a specific location in the Position field and click Set. If a tab stop already appears on the ruler, you can move it by simply dragging to a new location on the ruler.

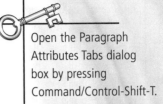

Open the Paragraph Attributes Tabs dialog box by pressing Command/Control-Shift-T.

Title	Author	Cost
Much Ado About Nothing	Shakespeare, William	$49.95
Dr. Faustus	Mallory, Edmund	$195.00
Beowulf	—	$75.50

- The Left, Center, and Right tab markers align columns on the left, center, or right edge, respectively.
- The Decimal tab marker aligns text at the decimal point; it is good for aligning columns of numbers, such as prices.
- The Comma tab marker is useful when aligning columns of numbers over 999, which contain commas.
- The Align On tab marker can be used to choose any character as the aligning factor. As an example, you could choose to align on "=" in a column of equations. When you select this type of tab marker, any character you enter in the Align On field will determine the column alignment.

The Fill Characters field allows you to define the character(s) that appear between columns of text. To define a fill character, you must first select the tab marker on the ruler. Once a tab marker is selected, you can enter any character in the Fill Characters field and click Apply or OK to format the tab.

The fill character is placed between the tab text at each tab location. If the fill character were an underscore, for example, the text "Name[tab]Date" would appear as "Name _____ Date." The tab character exists before the first fill character, moving the fill away from the text before the tab.

To reposition an existing tab marker, you can click it in the tab ruler and drag it to the desired position. To reposition a tab numerically for greater precision, you must select the tab in the ruler and enter the desired position in the Position field.

A common design mistake is to use center-aligned tab stops when dealing with columns of numbers. Money, for example, looks like it aligns properly on the center if all of the items have the same number of digits. Varying width of font characters and varying number of characters, however, can make columns look disorganized.

Left	Center	Decimal
$5.45	$5.45	$5.45
$16.72	$16.72	$16.72
$6.99	$6.99	$6.99
$100.00	$100.00	$100.00

Use the most appropriate tab stop for your list.

Rules

Rules, or lines, can be specified on a paragraph-by-paragraph basis. Paragraph rules can be placed above or below the paragraph, and set to the length of the paragraph indents, the length of the first or last line of text (depending upon whether it is a rule above or a rule below), or the length of the column (or the box, if the box has only one column). You can define left and right indents for the rule, as well as style, width, color, shade, and opacity. The *offset*, or the distance of the line away from the text, is defined either as a specific distance or as a percentage of leading.

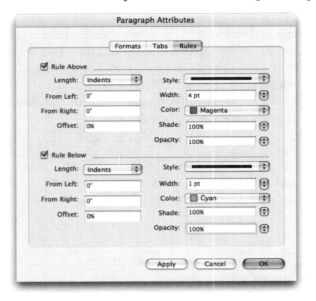

Column Edges   Rule Below Paragraph

FORMAT PARAGRAPHS

1. Open the file **hattery.qxp** from your **RF_Quark7>Chapter05** folder. Double-check that the Measurements palette is available.

2. Select all of the text in the first line, and then style it as 30-pt. ATC Maple Ultra. Change the Paragraph Alignment to Center.

3. In the Measurements palette Paragraph mode, change the Space After Paragraph field to 0.125″ and press Return/Enter.

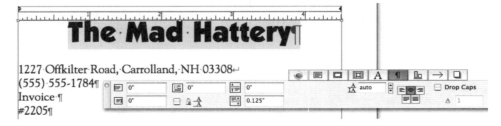

Paragraph rules are one of the few formatting attributes that cannot be modified using the Measurements palette. You have to use the Rules tab of the Paragraph Attributes dialog box.

Open the Rules tab of the Paragraph Attributes dialog box by pressing Command/Control-Shift-N.

The Column option in the Length menu is new in QuarkXPress 7; you can now define a paragraph rule that does not consider the length or formatting of text in the paragraph.

4. Highlight the next two lines of text (the address and phone number). In the Measurements palette Character mode, change the font to ATC Maple Medium.

   In Paragraph mode, change the leading to 15 pt. and apply center alignment.

5. Select the word "Invoice"; in the Measurements palette Classic mode, style it as 18-pt. ATC Maple Ultra with 22-pt. leading.

6. In Paragraph mode, change the Alignment to Center, and apply a 0p6 space before and after the paragraph.

7. Select the invoice number and style it as 12-pt. ATC Maple Medium with 15-pt. leading. Change the Paragraph Alignment to Center.

8. Select the entire next paragraph (click four times in the paragraph). Set the text to 8.5-pt. ATC Oak Normal with 10-pt. leading.

9. In Paragraph mode, set 0.083″ space before and after the paragraph. Change the Alignment to Justified.

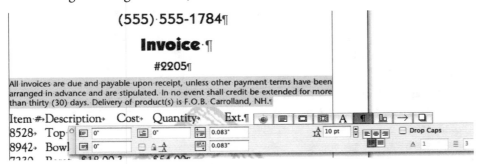

10. Select the six lines of table copy and set it to 10-pt. ATC Oak Normal with 12-pt. leading.

11. In Paragraph mode, set the left and right indents to 0.125″ and apply a 0p6 space after the paragraph.

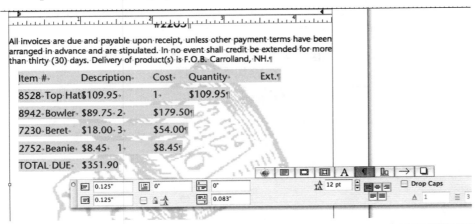

12. Select the first line only of the table copy. Change the font to 12-pt. ATC Oak Bold.

13. Select the last line only of the table copy. Change the font to ATC Oak Bold with 18-pt. leading.

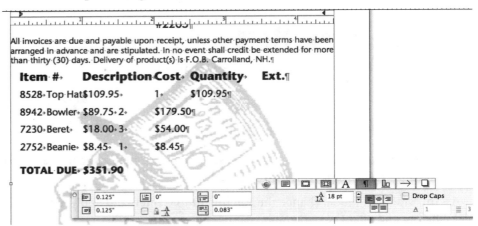

14. Place the cursor in the paragraph with the centered word "Invoice." Open the Rules tab of the Paragraph Attributes dialog box by pressing Command/Control-Shift-N.

15. Apply a 1.5-pt. rule above with an offset of 25%. Click OK.

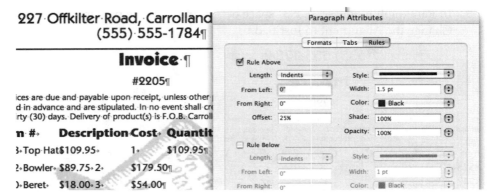

16. If invisible characters are not showing, choose View>Invisibles.

17. Place the text insertion point immediately before the # symbol of the invoice number and press Delete/Backspace.

The character formatting of the invoice number remains the same, but the text adopts the paragraph formatting of the Invoice line. Because the font sizes are different, the text appears to be misaligned.

18. Highlight the entire invoice number line.

Look at the Measurements palette. The leading (a paragraph attribute) is constant for the entire line, but the font and size areas are blank because the selected text uses more than one of each.

19. Type "18" in the Size field and press Return/Enter.

20. Save the file as "invoice.qxp" to your **Work_In_Progress** folder and continue to the next exercise.

FORMAT TABS

1. With **invoice.qxp** open (from your **Work_In_Progress** folder), place the insertion point in the line that begins with "Item #".

2. Display the Tabs mode of the Measurements palette. Notice the formatting ruler that appears at the top of the selected text box.

3. In the Measurements palette, click the left tab marker button, type 0.917″ in the Position field, and click Set. The marker appears on the formatting ruler, and the selected line (where the insertion point is flashing) changes to reflect the new tab-stop position.

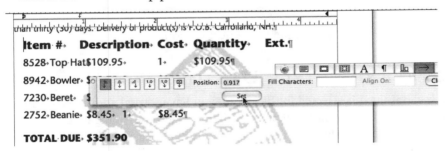

4. Using the same method, place center-tab markers at 2.5″, 3.333″, and 4.15″.

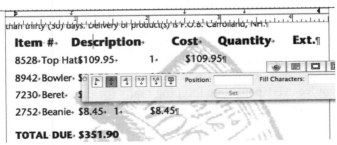

5. Select the next four lines of table text.

6. In the Measurements palette, click the left tab marker button. Click the formatting ruler to place a tab marker, and then drag the marker until the Position field (in the Measurements palette) shows 0.917".

7. Using the same method, set decimal tab markers at 2.542" and 4.15", and then set a center tab marker at 3.333".

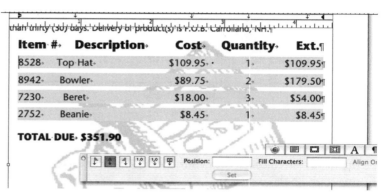

8. Place the cursor in the last line of the table (Total Due…) and set a decimal tab stop at 4.15".

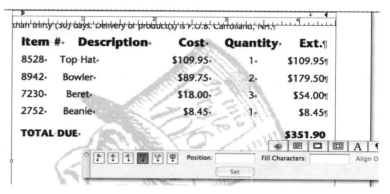

9. Save the file and continue to the next section.

USING TYPE STYLE UTILITIES

When certain text is selected in the layout, you have several additional options for controlling the appearance of that text. The Change Case, Make Fraction, and Make Price utilities help to automate processes that take considerably more time when performed manually.

Change Case

You can change selected text to UPPERCASE, lowercase, or Title Case using the Change Case options in the Style menu. Although this might seem a minor addition to some, the new Change Case options are a welcome enhancement — especially if you have clients (as many of us do) who insist on typing with the Caps Lock key. If you've ever spent time retyping many (or even a few) bits of imported text, you know how much time this utility will save.

Make Fraction

When you select a text string in the number-slash-number format, you can convert that string to a stylized fraction by choosing Style>Type Style>Make Fraction. You can control the appearance of stylized fractions in the Fraction/Price pane of the Preferences dialog box.

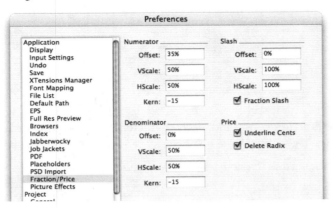

In a fraction, the numerator is the number above the line or before the slash; the denominator is the number below the line or after the slash.

When you apply the Make Fraction command, each character in the selected string is altered based on the Fraction/Price preference settings. Each character is still an individual character — they have just been styled and shifted in the layout. This is an important distinction to remember when you read the section on OpenType features later in this chapter.

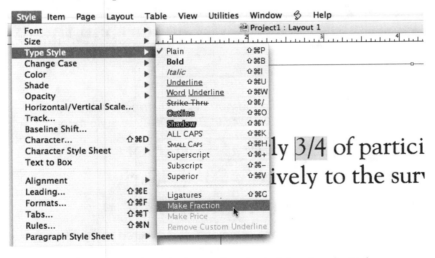

When a number-slash-number text string is selected,
you can choose Make Fraction in the Style>Type Style menu.

Nearly ¾ of partic
positively to the

After applying the Make Fraction command, the selected characters
are sized and shifted based on the Fraction/Price preference settings.

Make Price

The Make Price option is available when a number-period-number (or number-comma-number) text string is selected. When you convert a string to a stylized price, cents are styled as superior characters (based on settings in the Project Character preferences); in the Fraction/Price preferences, you can choose to underline the cents and delete the *radix* (the character separating dollars from cents).

Like the Make Fraction command, each character in the styled price is still an individual character — they have just been styled and shifted in the layout.

In many countries, prices are listed using a comma instead of a period to separate units. The Make Price command recognizes both separators or **radix**.

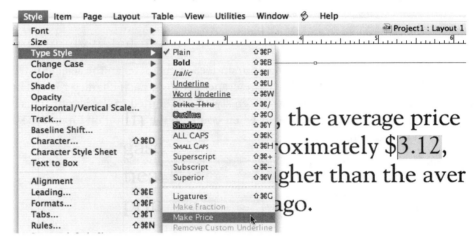

When a number-period-number text string is selected, you can choose Make Price in the Style>Type Style menu.

After applying the Make Price command, the selected characters are sized and shifted based on the Character and Fraction/Price preference settings.

WORK WITH TYPE STYLE UTILITIES

1. With **invoice.qxp** open (from your **Work_In_Progress** folder), select the entire first line of text.

2. In the Measurements palette (Classic or Character mode), click the All Caps type style button.

3. Click the All Caps button again to return the text to normal.

4. With the text still selected, choose Style>Change Case>UPPERCASE.

Although the result is effectively the same, the All Caps type style button in the Measurements palette is not active; the highlighted text is now the same as if it had been typed using the Caps Lock key.

5. With the same text selected, Choose Style>Change Case>Title Case. This option capitalizes each word in the selection, effectively returning it to its original state.

6. Open the Preferences dialog box and display the Fraction/Price pane.

7. Deactivate the Underline Cents check box and activate the Delete Radix check box. Click OK.

8. In the price chart, select the first price in the Cost column and choose Style>Type Style>Make Price.

Because you formatted the tabs using the decimal tab marker, the alignment is now off since you chose to delete the radix — the decimal — in Step 7. You'll fix this shortly.

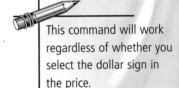
This command will work regardless of whether you select the dollar sign in the price.

Item #	Description	Cost	Quantity	Ext.
8528	Top Hat	$109^{95}	1	$109.95
8942	Bowler	$89.75	2	$179.50
7230	Beret	$18.00	3	$54.00
2752	Beanie	$8.45	1	$8.45
TOTAL DUE				$351.90

9. Continue formatting all prices in the chart using the Make Price command.

Item #	Description	Cost	Quantity	Ext.
8528	Top Hat	$109^{95}	1	$109^{95}
8942	Bowler	$89^{75}	2	$179^{50}
7230	Beret	$18^{00}	3	$54^{00}
2752	Beanie	$8^{45}	1	$8^{45}
TOTAL DUE				$351^{90}

10. Select the four rows of line items in the chart and display the Measurements palette in Tab mode.

11. In the formatting ruler at the top of the box, click the first decimal tab marker (above the Cost column) to select it.

12. Click the right tab marker button in the Measurements palette to change the type for the selected tab marker.

13. Drag the changed marker to 2.675".

14. Repeat this process to change the second decimal tab marker (above the Ext.) column to a right tab marker at 4.312".

15. In the bottom line of the chart, change the decimal tab marker to a right tab marker at 4.312".

The·Mad·Hattery¶
1227·Offkilter·Road,·Carrolland,·NH·03308↵
(555)·555-1784¶

Invoice·#2205¶

All·invoices·are·due·and·payable·upon·receipt,·unless·other·payment·terms·have·been arranged·in·advance·and·are·stipulated.·In·no·event·shall·credit·be·extended·for·more than·thirty·(30)·days.·Delivery·of·product(s)·is·F.O.B.·Carrolland,·NH.¶

Item·#→	Description→	Cost→	Quantity→	Ext.¶
8528→	Top·Hat→	$109^{95}→	1→	$109^{95}¶
8942→	Bowler→	$89^{75}→	2→	$179^{50}¶
7230→	Beret→	$18^{00}→	3→	$54^{00}¶
2752→	Beanie→	$8^{45}→	1→	$8^{45}¶
TOTAL·DUE→				**$351^{90}**

16. Save the file and close the project.

USING SPECIAL CHARACTERS

The use of special characters is a hallmark of the professional designer. Nothing ruins the most attractive layout faster than the use of straight quotes, for example. Some special characters commonly used in desktop publishing are:

- **Forced Line Break**. Also called a "soft return," this character is used for breaking a line within a paragraph to force text to wrap to the next line.

- **Nonbreaking Space**. This space is used to insert a space character that does not allow adjacent words to break at the end of a line.

- **Nonbreaking Hyphen**. This character is used to hyphenate a word at the end of a line. QuarkXPress includes dictionaries that define suggested hyphenation; by adding discretionary hyphens, you can break a word where you prefer, in addition to the suggested hyphenation. (Hyphenation control is explained in Chapter 8.)
- **Em Dash**. This dash, the width of an em space, is used to set off portions of text within a sentence.
- **En Dash**. This dash, the width of an en space, is used to denote negative numbers, the subtraction symbol, and a range of numbers (replacing the word "to" or "through"). Examples include:

> –4,096
>
> 25 – 20 = 5
>
> At the dinner, 25–35 people arrived early.

En Spaces and Em Spaces

A standard *em space* is defined (in traditional typography) as a space equal to the height, in points, of the type size. An *en space*, by definition, is half of an em space.

The Character Preferences dialog box allows you to choose a standard em space, which uses the typographical definition of an em space. If you are setting 12-pt. type and the Standard Em Space option is checked, an em space is 12 points, and an en space is 6 points.

If the Standard Em Space option is not selected, an en space is defined in QuarkXPress as the width of a zero (0), and an em space is defined as the width of two zeros (00) of that font. In this case, an en space is also called a "figure space" because it is the width of the figure "0."

A Few Words about Double Spaces

On a standard typewriter, an I, an M, and a period take up the same amount of space on the line. When a single space is placed after a sentence on a typewriter, it can be difficult to tell where one sentence ends and another begins. To solve this problem, it was once a common practice to put two spaces after a period in a sentence. Most of today's typefaces, however, are *proportionally spaced* (the width of each character varies) rather than monospaced, like a typewriter. When you receive text files from a client, you will often find they include double spaces, which you have to remove. If you need more distance than a single space, you should use one of the special space characters, such as an en space.

Page Numbers and Jumps

Rather than manually typing page numbers on every page of a layout, you can use the automatic-page-number special character. If you type this character (Command/Control-3) on a master page, it appears as <#>; on the page layout, the character reflects the correct page number.

When you want to flow a story across multiple pages, it is a good idea to use a "continued on" line at the end of each page; some people also include a "continued from" line at the top of the following pages. In this case, you can also place a Next-Box page number (Command/Control-2) or Previous-Box page number (Command/Control-4).

The best way to add a continued line is to create a separate text box at the end of the continued-on page or at the beginning of the continued-from page. You can create the box anywhere on the page. If the box does not overlap any box in an existing text chain, the page-number character shows <None>.

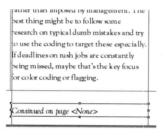

As soon as you move the continued-on or continued-from text box so that it touches an existing text chain, the page-number characters reflect the correct location of the next or previous box in the chain.

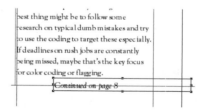

Once the box is placed correctly, you can modify the formatting of the text, as appropriate. Notice that the continued box does not have to be entirely within the underlying text box.

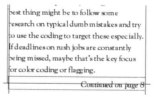

Extended ASCII Characters

Extended characters are those that cannot be accessed directly on a keyboard. They are, for the most part, characters with an ASCII value higher than 128. Windows users can access these characters by holding down the Alt key and pressing the ASCII number sequence on the numeric keypad. On a Macintosh, you can access these using some combination of the *modifier keys* (Option, Control, and Shift). The chart on the next page lists special characters most commonly used in desktop publishing and their associated key commands or appropriate ASCII values.

If you type the automatic-page-number character on a layout page, you see the page number instead of the special character <#>.

We know of one designer who participated in a pre-employment skills test in which proficiency in QuarkXPress was measured solely by whether the candidates knew the automatic-page-number key command.

ASCII is a text-based code that defines every character with a numeric value between 001 and 256. The standard alphabet (lower- and uppercase) and punctuation characters are mapped from 001 to 128. ASCII characters higher than 128 include nonEnglish characters (e.g., degree symbols, é, ü, etc.) and some special formatting characters (e.g., en dashes, etc.).

Accessing Special Characters

As we just said, many special characters can be accessed using a series of keyboard shortcuts. The following chart lists the most common.

Characters		Macintosh	Windows
-	Discretionary hyphen	Command-Hyphen	Control- - (hyphen)
-	Nonbreaking hyphen	Command-=	Control-=
–	En dash	Option-Hyphen	Control-Alt-Shift-Hyphen
—	Em dash	Option-Shift-Hyphen	Control-Shift-=
•	Bullet	Option-8	Alt-Shift-8
°	Degree	Option-Shift-8	Alt-0176
…	Ellipse	Option-;	Alt-0133
¶	Paragraph symbol	Option-7	Alt-Shift-7
®	Registered trademark	Option-R	Alt-Shift-R
™	Trademark	Option-2	Alt-Shift-2
©	Copyright	Option-G	Alt-0169
§	Section symbol	Option-6	Alt-Shift-6
"	Open quote	Option-[	Alt-Shift-[
"	Close quote	Option-Shift-[	Alt-Shift-]
'	Single open quote	Option-]	Alt-[
'	Single close quote	Option-Shift-]	Alt-]
Special Commands			
	Nonbreaking space	Command-Spacebar	Control-Spacebar
	En space	Option-Space	Control-Shift-6
	Nonbreaking En space	Command-Option-Spacebar	Control-Alt-Shift-6
	Forced line break	Shift-Return	Shift-Enter
	Next column	Enter (numeric keypad)	Enter (numeric keypad)
	Next box	Shift-Enter (numeric keypad)	Shift-Enter (numeric keypad)
	Indent to here (Hanging indent)	Command-\	Control-\
	Right-indent tab	Option-Tab	Shift-Tab
<#>	Automatic page number	Command-3	Control-3
	Next-box page number	Command-4	Control-4
	Previous-box page number	Command-2	Control-2

Windows users: To enter special characters such as the degree or registered trademark symbol, you have to hold the Alt key while typing the numeric sequence on the number keypad.

The hanging-indent special character is an excellent tool for formatting a single paragraph or line, without opening any of the paragraph-formatting dialog boxes. Use this technique for bullets, lists, and so on.

In addition to using keyboard shortcuts, a new set of submenus has been added to the Utilities menu for accessing specific special characters (primarily different types of spaces, hyphens, and page-number characters). When you place a special character using one of these menus, the special-character font displays the unique identifier just as it does when you add one with the Glyphs palette.

In previous versions, key commands were the only option for placing most of these characters. In QuarkXPress 7 — for the first time — this is no longer the case; you can now choose the option you want from the Utilities>Insert Character>Special menus.

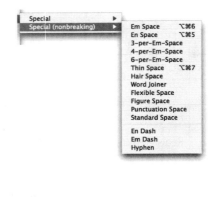

There is no difference between the special characters added with the Utilities> Insert Character menu or with key commands. You have different options, and you can use whichever one (or two or three) you are most comfortable with.

WORK WITH SPECIAL CHARACTERS

1. Open **working_text.qxp** from your **Work_In_Progress** folder.

2. Select the box at the top of the page and change the width to 4″.

3. Choose View>Invisibles to make sure invisible characters are showing.

4. Using the Content tool, select the text "The Mad Hattery", and then type "Alice's Adventures in Wonderland".

5. Place the insertion point before the word "Adventures" and press Shift-Return/Enter to force the word onto a new line.

6. Move the insertion point to the end of the text and press Return/Enter to start a new paragraph.

7. Change the font to 12-pt. ATC Oak Normal, and then type the following:

    —by Lewis Carroll [soft return]
    © (Public Domain)

   • Choose Utilities>Special>Em Dash to place that character at the beginning of the sentence.

   • Press Shift-Return/Enter to place the soft return at the end of the first line.

   • Press Option-G/Alt-0169 to place the copyright symbol at the beginning of the second line.

8. Place the insertion point immediately after the em dash. Choose Utilities>Special>Indent Here. Notice that the second line (after the soft-return character) indents to the point of the hanging-indent character.

9. Save the file and close it.

WORKING WITH OPENTYPE

QuarkXPress 7 includes a new type engine, which is the basis for full support of OpenType and Unicode characters. With Unicode support, two-byte characters common in foreign-language typesetting can be incorporated directly in a QuarkXPress layout, without the need to purchase additional language packs or XTensions. You can incorporate Cyrillic, Japanese, and other non-Roman or pictographic characters in any page layout.

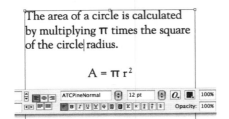
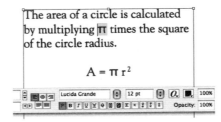

Characters from the Geeza Pro font are displayed in version 7 (left) but not in version 6 (right).

Font Fallback

Font Fallback is a new option designed to enhance support for extended characters. In previous versions, characters that weren't available displayed as little hollow boxes. Even if you don't set foreign-language text, you might have seen these boxes when crossing platforms (especially from Windows to Macintosh). Using Font Fallback (active by default), QuarkXPress locates and switches to a font that includes the characters you need.

In other words, if QuarkXPress finds a glyph that is not available in the current font, the application locates another available font to set the required character; QuarkXPress automatically *falls back* to a font that can display the glyph you need.

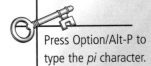

The area of a circle is calculated by multiplying π times the square of the circle radius.

$$A = \pi r^2$$

Using Font Fallback, the copy is set in ATC Pine Normal; the pi character is set automatically in Lucida Grande, the first available font that contained the glyph.

OpenType and Unicode support means that you can set type in foreign languages; it does not mean that you can check spelling or hyphenation specific to those languages. Full support for multiple languages still requires QuarkXPress Passport.

Font Fallback can be deactivated in the Input Settings pane of the Preferences dialog box.

Press Option/Alt-P to type the *pi* character.

Accessing OpenType Features

The OpenType font format offers the ability to use the same font files on both Macintosh and Windows, as well as storage capacity for more than 65,000 glyphs in a single font. In previous versions, you could use OpenType fonts but not access any characters beyond the basic and extended ASCII sets. QuarkXPress 7 includes full OpenType support, which means you can access and use any of the extended characters in an OpenType font, including special glyphs for ligatures, swashes, fractions, and others.

The large capacity for glyph storage means that a single OpenType font can replace the multiple separate "Expert" fonts that contained variations of fonts (Minion Swash, for example, is no longer necessary when you can access the Swashes subset of the Minion Pro font).

In QuarkXPress, OpenType features are considered a character-formatting attribute, just like type size and color. You can apply OpenType features to specific text using the OpenType check boxes in the Character Attributes dialog box, or you can use the menu in the Classic or Character mode of the Measurements palette.

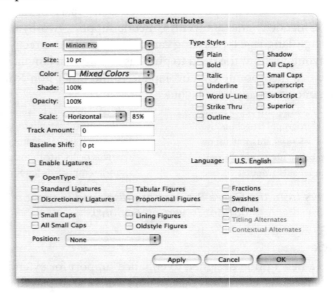

In the Measurements palette, the OpenType menu shows a list of the OpenType features that are supported in QuarkXPress 7. Options surrounded by brackets ([ ]) are not available in the currently selected font. Active options show a checkmark.

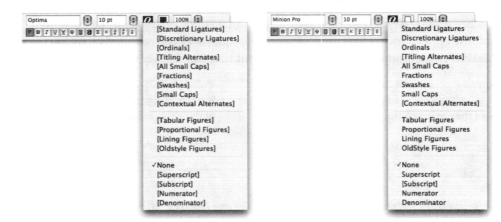

Because OpenType features are treated as a character attribute, you can also apply those features in character and paragraph style sheets (see Chapter 6).

You can also search for and change OpenType features in the expanded Find/Change dialog box (see Chapter 8).

OpenType fonts *can* include extended character sets, but not all do. Keep in mind that some OpenType fonts still only include the basics, just as some PostScript and TrueType fonts do not include a full set of ASCII characters (such as a custom font that places a company's logo with a single keystroke).

In the case of the fractions set, text strings in the character-slash-character format are replaced with the appropriate OpenType fraction glyph (or glyphs).

Unlike other options in QuarkXPress, OpenType features can be specified even when they aren't currently available. This means that you can define certain text to use (for example) fractions *if they are available*; if OpenType fractions are not available, the text will appear as it was typed. OpenType features are separate and cumulative. You can apply more than one feature set at a time (e.g., Fractions and Small Capitals); any or all of the specified features will be applied when available.

Type Style or OpenType?

Some OpenType features — small caps, superscript, and subscript — are similar to *but not the same as* the type style options available in the Measurements palette and Character Attributes dialog box. In addition, OpenType ligatures and fractions sound similar to the Enable Ligatures and Make Fraction options.

It is very important that you do not confuse the OpenType feature sets with the QuarkXPress type styling options. OpenType features activate specific glyphs that were specifically designed to represent the alternate styles. QuarkXPress type style options artificially create the style you apply; the results of QuarkXPress styling are often imperfect (typographically speaking). You should use the OpenType alternatives whenever possible.

The Glyphs Palette

The new Glyphs palette (Window>Glyphs) provides access to individual characters in a font, including basic characters in regular fonts, extended ASCII and OpenType character subsets, and even pictographic characters in Unicode fonts.

Using the Glyphs palette is simple: make sure the insertion point is flashing where you want a character to appear, then double-click the character you want to place.

You can view the character set for any font by simply changing the menu at the top of the palette. By default, the palette shows the Entire Font. The P, B, and I buttons preview the selected font as Plain (default), faux Bold, and faux Italic. (If you insert a glyph that is previewed as faux Bold or Italic, the glyph in the Project window will be styled as well.) You can also enlarge or reduce the Glyphs palette view using the palette's Zoom tools.

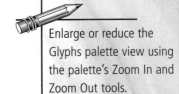

Enlarge or reduce the Glyphs palette view using the palette's Zoom In and Zoom Out tools.

We know there is a need for the PBI buttons, especially on the Windows operating system. On a Macintosh, however, you should avoid faux styling whenever possible.

In theory, applying faux bold or italics calls the appropriate font when the job is output. However, that theory requires the appropriate matching font to actually exist and to be active on your system. Faux styling also does not take into account the possibility of multiple font weights, such as Semibold and Bold variants. If you design with Minion <b>, for example, your output might actually use the Minon Semibold font, which is not as heavy. There are so many uncontrollable variables in the printing output process that you should avoid introducing ones that are unnecessary. If you insist on using faux bold and italics when creating a design, make sure you manually convert those styles to the actual fonts and review your file carefully before you send it to print.

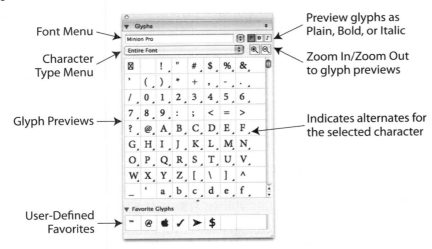

Font Menu

Character Type Menu

Glyph Previews

User-Defined Favorites

Preview glyphs as Plain, Bold, or Italic

Zoom In/Zoom Out to glyph previews

Indicates alternates for the selected character

Accessing Extended Character Sets

The Character Type menu in the Glyphs palette lists the different character subsets that are available for the selected font. This menu is available for both OpenType and other fonts. In addition to the extended sets in OpenType fonts, you can also use this menu to display special characters for non-OpenType fonts.

Regardless of the font you're using, you will almost always see at least five options in this menu: Alternates for Selection, Special Characters (Breaking), Special Characters, European Characters, and Symbols.

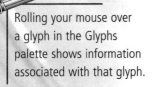

Any character that you have to press Command/Control or Option/Alt to type is an extended character (•, ®, ©, ™, and so on). Because most of us use these characters so frequently, it's easy to forget that regular TrueType and PostScript fonts have extended characters.

Alternates for Selection. If a glyph in the palette shows a small arrow in the bottom-right corner of the palette cell, the font includes alternate characters that might be used in place of that character.

If you highlight a character and choose Alternates for Selection in the Character Type menu, you can quickly find the related alternates. For example, if you select the "3" glyph for Warnock Pro and choose Alternates for Selection, you'll see the different "3" glyphs for the OpenType feature sets that are part of the Warnock Pro font. By rolling your mouse over one of these glyphs, you can determine which version of the glyph you want to use.

Rolling your mouse over a glyph in the Glyphs palette shows information associated with that glyph.

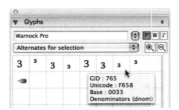

Special Characters and Special Characters (Breaking). Special characters, specifically different types of breaking and nonbreaking spaces, can be accessed in the Glyphs palette by choosing from one of these character sets.

QuarkXPress 7 includes a distinct font (created by Ascender Corp. and installed with the application) that lets you visually identify different types of spaces when invisible characters are showing.

At first these characters might look like an accident of Morse code. When one of the Special Characters sets is displayed in the Glyphs palette, it's helpful at first to roll the mouse over the glyphs to see what each of the symbols represents. As you get used to them, you'll start to recognize and identify the line-and-dot configurations and appreciate the easy visual distinction for these special characters.

European Characters. This set includes glyphs that are commonly used in European languages that use a modified Roman alphabet. Characters with accents, tildes, gravés, etc. — in both lower- and uppercase — can easily be accessed in the Glyphs palette.

Symbols. This set includes characters like the bullet (•) and the trademark (™). To use these common-but-extended characters in previous versions, you needed to know the appropriate key commands — or even the ALT+numbers code if you're using Windows. Now, you can use the Glyphs palette Symbols set to easily locate and use the symbol characters without memorizing obscure key commands.

OpenType Character Sets. When you display an OpenType font in the Glyphs palette, the Character Type menu also provides access to the different OpenType subsets that are available in a specific font.

Saving Favorites

As we mentioned in the introduction to this book, one focus of QuarkXPress 7 is the ability to personalize your workspace; the Glyphs palette offers another example of this goal. The lower section of the palette is used to store favorites — characters that you use frequently and don't want to have to search for every time you need them. The Favorites area can include glyphs from different fonts. You can remove a glyph from the Favorites area by Control/right-clicking the glyph and choosing Remove From Favorites in the contextual menu.

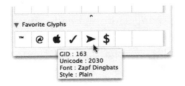

In the Glyphs palette, the available OpenType subsets are font-specific. Only those subsets that exist for the selected font are listed in the Character Type menu.

WORK WITH OPENTYPE FEATURES

To complete this exercise, you need to have active at least one OpenType font that includes the Fractions feature.

We used Warnock Pro for illustration. If you are using a different OpenType font, your screen will look a bit different than these images.

1. Open the file **recipe.qxp** from the **RF_Quark7>Chapter05** folder. This layout uses only ATC fonts, which are not OpenType fonts.

2. On Page 1 of the layout, select the list of ingredients (not the heading) with the Content tool.

3. In the Measurements palette (Classic mode), click the OpenType button and choose Fractions.

   This option is bracketed (not available) for the current font, so nothing changes in the layout. You can still apply the different OpenType features in case they become available.

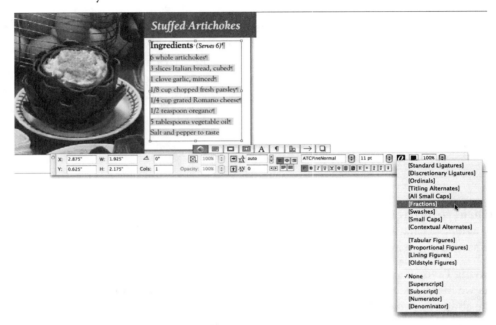

4. Apply an OpenType font that includes fraction glyphs to the selected text.

   As mentioned previously, we are using Warnock Pro. If you don't have this font, use whatever is available on your system (Minion Pro will also work).

   When you apply an OpenType font that includes OpenType Fractions, the fraction-type text strings automatically convert to the OpenType fraction glyphs.

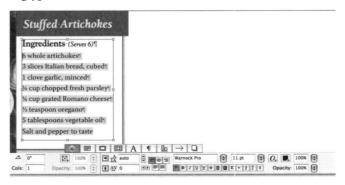

5. Apply another non-OpenType font to the selected text. (We used Times, but any non-OpenType font will produce the same results.)

When you apply the non-OpenType font, the fractions are converted back to the basic glyphs. Even though the OpenType fractions are no longer applied, looking at the OpenType menu shows that the feature set is still active — just not currently available.

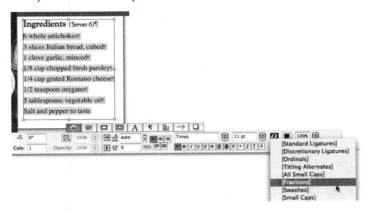

6. Switch back to Warnock Pro, or whatever font you used in Step 4.

The OpenType fraction glyphs are again placed in the layout.

7. Navigate to Page 2 of the layout.

8. Select all the text in the box on Page 2 and open the Character Attributes dialog box.

9. Click the arrow to the left of the word OpenType (near the bottom of the dialog box) to show the OpenType feature options.

10. Activate the Fractions check box.

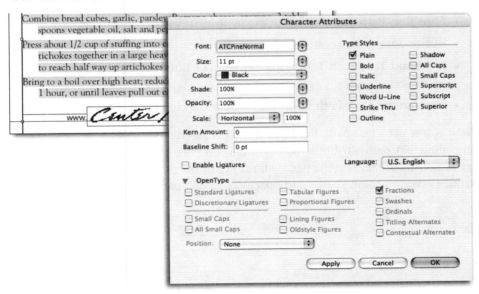

Although this check box appears to be grayed out, you can still activate it. Just as you can do in the Measurements palette, you can apply OpenType features in the Character Attributes dialog box even if the selected text is set with a non-OpenType font. Then if you decide to switch to an OpenType font, those features will be applied where possible.

OpenType features do not permanently change the text. When you switched to a font without the fraction characters, the text reverted to the originally typed character-slash-character. OpenType features are non-permanent and non-destructive; they only affect the glyphs that are used to represent the text in the layout.

It does no damage to turn these features on even if you don't think you'll need them. OpenType features are a ready-and-waiting kind of tool; because they remain active in the background, you can immediately see the results of design experimentation.

Applying OpenType features in advance can produce unexpected results, however, especially if you activate more than one feature at a time.

11. Click OK to return to the Project window.

12. With the same text selected, change the selection to an OpenType font.

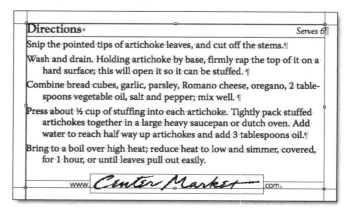

13. Close the file without saving.

CREATING TYPE ON A PATH

Instead of merely flowing text into a box, you can also create unique typographic effects by flowing text onto a path. QuarkXPress includes four text-path tools. These tools behave just like the regular line tools; the difference is that the lines created with these tools are text paths, onto which you can type or import text.

Line Text-Path Tool

Bézier Text-Path Tool

Freehand Text-Path Tool

Orthogonal Text-Path Tool

- **Line Text-Path Tool**. This tool draws straight lines at any angle.
- **Bézier Text-Path Tool**. This tool creates a line based on Bézier curves.
- **Freehand Text-Path Tool**. This tool draws a line as if you were using a pencil on a sheet of paper.
- **Orthogonal Text-Path Tool**. This tool creates lines at 45° angles.

When you select a text path, the Measurements palette includes a new mode for controlling text-path attributes. By default, a text path is created as a hairline with no color. Only the text on the path will print, not the path itself. You can change attributes (width, color, shade, and opacity) of a text path as you can for any line.

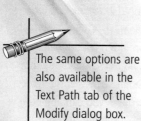

The same options are also available in the Text Path tab of the Modify dialog box.

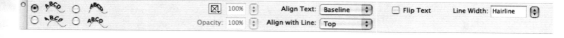

The four Text Orientation radio buttons (in the left side of the palette) change the dimensional appearance of text.

- The top-left option is the default. Text flows along the path with no distortion to the letter shapes. The bottoms of letters are aligned to the path.

- The top-right option creates a three-dimensional distortion, making text look as if it is wrapping around the shape of the text path.

- The bottom-left option warps the text, skewing characters around the text path to create a three-dimensional effect.

- The bottom-right option flows text along the path without rotating or skewing the characters. Text on the path remains aligned with any other text on the page.

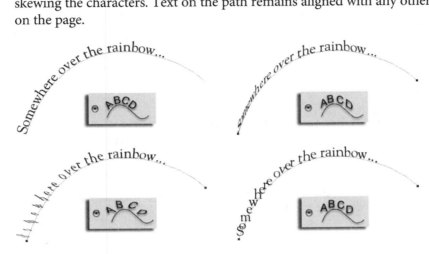

The Align Text menu defines how the text is placed with relation to the text path.

- **Baseline**. This default selection causes the baseline of the characters to rest on the text path.

- **Center**. Choosing this option positions the text so that half of the font size (height) appears above the path and half below.

- **Ascent**. Choosing this option positions the text so that the top edge of the highest ascender aligns with the text path.

- **Descent**. Choosing this option moves the text away from the line so that the lowest descender in the font aligns with the top of the path.

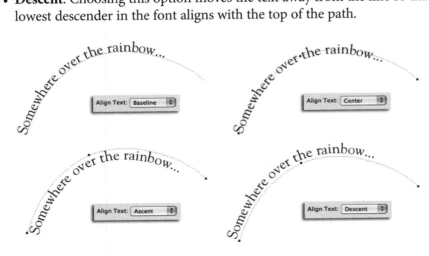

The Align with Line menu is only relevant if the text path has a thickness greater than a hairline. This menu is set to Top by default, which means that the top edge of the line is the baseline of the text. If you choose Center or Bottom in this menu, the text will rest on the center or bottom of the line.

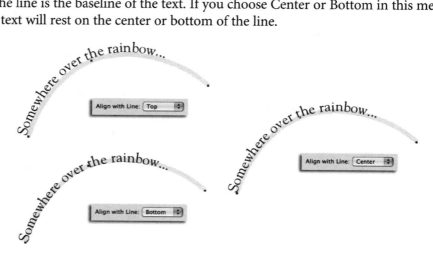

The Flip Text check box turns text upside down and moves it to the opposite side of the path. This option is particularly useful for placing text inside a curve.

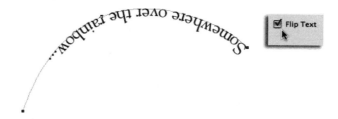

You can format text on a path as you would format any other text, including the font, size, color, and alignment. You can also link text paths using the Linking tool, creating a text chain over multiple text paths.

You can also modify a text path as you would modify other lines. You can select and modify individual anchor points, either by dragging or by changing the values in the Measurements palette.

CREATE TEXT PATHS

1. Create a new project with a letter-size print layout named "text paths". Use one column and 0.5″ margins on all four sides. Make sure the Automatic Text Box option is deselected.

2. Select the Bézier Text-Path tool.

3. Draw a text path that looks like this:

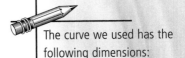

The curve we used has the following dimensions:

The two bottom points are 1.72″ apart. The top point of the curve is 0.871″ above the two bottom points.

4. With the path still selected, click the Content tool in the Tools palette. Notice that the insertion point flashes at the beginning of the path. In the Measurements palette, click the Center alignment button.

5. Select the Item tool and press Command/Control-D to duplicate the path. Place the cursor near the duplicate path until it turns into a four-headed arrow icon. Move the copy to the bottom right of the page.

With the Item tool selected, the cursor is a four-headed arrow when it is near the line, allowing you to move the entire path.

The cursor is a hand icon when it is directly over the line, and will modify the shape of the path instead of moving the path.

6. Select the Orthogonal Text-Path tool.

7. Draw a horizontal text path below the path you drew in Step 3. Use the Measurements palette (Classic mode) to change the length to 3.35″.

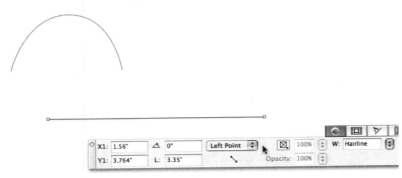

8. With the horizontal line still selected, choose the Content tool, and click the Center alignment button in the Measurements palette.

9. Repeat this process to draw four more horizontal lines with the following lengths: 4.46″, 3.65″, 2.9″, and 3.4″.

10. Set each of the horizontal lines to Center alignment. Stagger the lines down the page between the two curves.

11. Select the top curve with the Content tool.

12. Open the Import Text dialog box. Navigate to the file **poem.txt** in the **RF_Quark7>Chapter05** folder and click Open.

13. With the Content tool and the path still selected, press Command/Control-A to select the entire story. Set the font to ATC Pine Normal and change the font size to 25 pt. in the Measurements palette. Notice that the overset text icon indicates that some text does not fit on the path.

14. Select the Linking tool. Click the first curved path and then click the first horizontal path to link them.

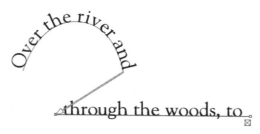

15. Continue linking each successive line down the page.

16. Place the insertion point before the word "and" in the first text path.

17. Press Enter on the numeric keypad to force that word to the next line.

and through the woods,

to Grandmother's house we go.

The horse knows the way

to carry the sleigh

through the white and

18. Save the file as "poem.qxp" in your **Work_In_Progress** folder and close it.

SUMMARY

The text formatting options in QuarkXPress are part form and part function. The purpose of text is, first and foremost, to communicate a message — text must be legible and user-friendly. That doesn't mean that text can't also be aesthetically pleasing. When page layout first moved from the light table to the desktop, the ability to easily combine words and art revolutionized the communication industry. In QuarkXPress 7, anyone who uses text (in other words, everyone) will be pleased with the tools that give us extraordinary control over the smallest detail — from changing case to applying OpenType features to building complex, multi-page tables.

In this chapter, you learned the properties and attributes of text boxes, including columns, insets, and runarounds. You are now able to link multiple text boxes, and know how to extend a story across multiple pages. You have also learned to format text characters and paragraphs with standard and OpenType formatting controls.

Working with Style Sheets

6

Until now, you have applied all text formatting manually. You should realize that this could take a long time if you are formatting many different paragraphs with many different settings. QuarkXPress includes a Style Sheets feature, which automates repetitive formatting tasks and speeds up your production.

IN CHAPTER 6, YOU WILL:

■ Learn the difference between character and paragraph style sheets.

■ Become familiar with the difference in applying character and paragraph style sheets, including how to override style sheets and how to cancel an override.

■ Discover how to import style sheets from other QuarkXPress projects and from word-processing documents.

■ Learn how to modify and delete style sheets.

■ Become familiar with resolving conflicts when importing or deleting style sheets.

UNDERSTANDING STYLE SHEETS

In Chapter 5 you learned the difference between character formatting and paragraph formatting, and how to apply those attributes to selected text in a QuarkXPress layout. From what you have already learned, you can safely assume that formatting the text in a long document can be exceedingly time-consuming and repetitive if you have to select each paragraph separately. Fortunately, QuarkXPress includes the ability to create and apply style sheets, which can automate a large portion of the text-formatting chore.

Style sheets are most advantageous when working with text-intensive documents that have recurring editorial elements, such as headlines, subheads, and captions; when working with several people concurrently on the same projects; and when creating projects with specific style requirements, such as a catalog or magazine. In these cases, styles ensure consistency in text and paragraph formatting throughout a publication. Rather than trying to remember how you formatted a sidebar 45 pages ago, you can simply apply a predefined Sidebar style.

QuarkXPress allows you to define and edit styles in any existing project. You can also define styles that will appear, by default, in all new projects if you define those styles before opening any project in the application. If, for example, you frequently use 11-pt. New Caledonia with a 0.25-in. first-line indent for body copy, you might define a style called "Body Text" before opening any QuarkXPress project. That style sheet will then appear in any new project you create.

The major advantages of using styles are ease of use and efficiency. Changes can be made instantly to all text defined as a particular style. For example, the designer might easily modify leading in the Body Copy style or change the font in the Subhead style from Helvetica to ATC Oak Bold. When the definition of a style changes, any text that uses that style automatically changes, too.

CHARACTER AND PARAGRAPH STYLES

QuarkXPress supports both character styles and paragraph styles. *Character styles* apply only to selected words; this type of style might be useful for setting off a few words of a paragraph without affecting the entire paragraph. Character styles might be used to set words in the italic or bold version of a font, to change the color of just a few words, or to change the font of special words.

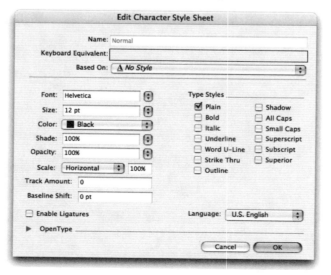

The Style Sheets function is one of the most powerful tools available in desktop publishing; its use is highly recommended both for creating documents quickly and for maintaining consistency throughout long documents. By putting the power of styles to work, changes that would ordinarily involve selecting dozens of formatting commands can be implemented with a single command.

This book — with its variety of headers, body copy, and sidebars — is an excellent example of a project that benefits from the use of style sheets. Twenty different styles ensured that similar editorial elements are formatted the same throughout.

Paragraph styles apply to the entire body of text between two ¶ symbols. *Paragraph styles* define the appearance of the paragraph, combining the character style that is to be used in the paragraph with the line spacing, indents, tabs, rules, and other paragraph attributes. Most projects benefit from paragraph styles such as Headline, Subhead, Body Text, Bullet, and so on.

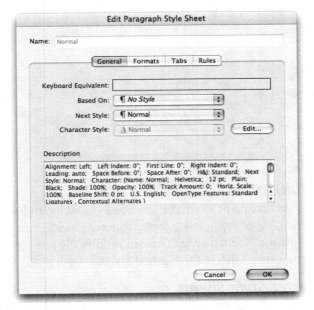

Paragraph style sheets consolidate the paragraph formatting options into a single command.

Paragraph style sheets define character attributes and paragraph attributes; character style sheets only define the character attributes. In other words, a paragraph style sheet can be used to format text entirely — including font information, line spacing, tabs, and so on.

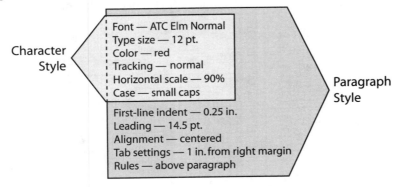

Style sheets are available to any layout within the same project.

DEFINING STYLE SHEETS

Before a style can be used, it must first be created, defined, and named. You can create a new style in several ways:

- Use Edit>Style Sheets to define a new style from scratch.
- Base the new style on an existing style.
- Copy an existing style from another QuarkXPress publication.
- Import text from a word-processing document with style sheets attached.

Choosing Edit>Style Sheets opens a dialog box that allows you to add new styles, edit existing ones, and append styles from other projects.

Press Shift-F11 to open the Style Sheets dialog box.

When creating styles, name them something appropriate to their use. Body Copy No Indent is a better name than 12 pt. Times No Indent. If you hand off the job to someone else, she might not realize that 12 pt. Times is supposed to be body copy.

Because OpenType ligatures and OpenType features are character attributes, you can apply those settings in a character or paragraph style sheet definition.

Normal (Default) Styles

Every new project you create in QuarkXPress has a character and a paragraph style sheet called "Normal." When you enter text in a new QuarkXPress project, the text automatically adopts the Normal style. You can modify the settings of the Normal style sheets, but you cannot delete the Normal styles.

Adding Character Style Sheets

When you click New, choose Paragraph or Character from the pop-up menu.

Choosing Character opens the Edit Character Style Sheet dialog box.

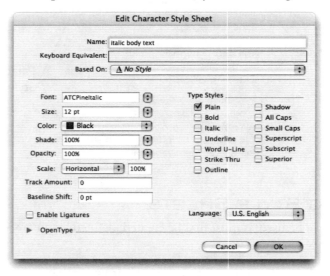

For any new style sheet, you must assign a name. We recommend using descriptive names that suggest what the style should be used for. You can also assign a shortcut for the style in the Keyboard Equivalent field by pressing a key (usually from the numeric keypad) with or without a modifier key (Shift, Option/Alt, or Command/Control).

The Based On menu allows you to define an existing character style sheet that will be the *parent style*, or the style on which the new style is based.

In the lower half of the dialog box, you can define the character attributes of the style. The default settings here vary, depending on what action you took prior to opening the Style Sheets dialog box.

- If you have not yet placed a text insertion point in the project, the default values in this dialog box match the Normal style.

- If the insertion point is placed in the project, this dialog box reflects the character attributes of the current insertion point.

- If the insertion point is not currently but has, at some point, been placed in the project, this dialog box reflects the formatting of the last insertion point.

When you have finished defining the character style sheet, clicking OK returns you to the Style Sheets dialog box. The new character style sheet appears in the dialog box. All styles are listed here in alphabetical order; the ¶ and A icons identify, respectively, paragraph and character style sheets.

Clicking Save returns you to the Project window, and the new style sheet is added to the Style Sheets palette. The Style Sheets palette (View>Style Sheets) lists paragraph style sheets in the top half of the palette and character style sheets in the bottom half.

The Style Sheets palette displays paragraph style sheets (indicated by the ¶ icon) in the top and character style sheets (indicated by the A icon) in the bottom.

Using Keyboard Equivalents

You can use the numeric keypad to define shortcuts. The advantage of such shortcuts is that you can access a style sheet with a single keystroke, using one hand. The disadvantage, however, is that any key assigned to a style sheet will not be usable to type numbers.

If you frequently type numbers with the numeric keypad, you might be better off using the number keys with a combination of modifier keys (Shift, Option/Alt, or Command/Control). This allows you to type numbers using the keys on the numeric keypad, as usual, or to access the shortcut by holding down the appropriate modifier key.

Even if you have assigned one number key as a shortcut, any number key that is not assigned as a shortcut can still be used to type numbers. This can be confusing if you forget that you have assigned shortcuts to certain keys. If you have assigned the keypad "1" as the shortcut for the character style sheet Bold Text, pressing the keypad "2" would replace highlighted text with the number "2," or add a number "2" at the text insertion point. Pressing "1", however, would assign the Bold Text style to highlighted text or change the insertion point to the Bold Text style, if no text is highlighted.

Others prefer to use the function keys for style-sheet shortcuts. Again, the advantage is single-key access to a style sheet. The disadvantage is that when you assign a keyboard equivalent (*shortcut*) to a style sheet, you are overriding the normal behavior of that key or combination of keys. In other words, if you use "F7" as a style-sheet shortcut, that key no longer toggles guides. Because many of the menu commands and tools in QuarkXPress are accessible using the function keys (with and without modifiers), assigning these to style sheets can seriously and negatively affect the performance of the application's working environment.

It is entirely a matter of personal preference and comfort that determines which type of keyboard equivalent to use, or even whether to use them at all. After you have used the application for some time, you will be able to decide which method (if any) works best for your work habits.

DEFINE CHARACTER STYLE SHEETS

1. Create a new project — a print layout named "Styles Practice" with an automatic text box. Use the default margin and column settings.

2. Choose Edit>Style Sheets.

3. Click New and choose Character from the pop-up menu.

4. Name the new style "Italic Text". Press Tab to highlight the Keyboard Equivalent field, and press "1" on the numeric keypad. Leave the Based On field at the default No Style. Select ATC Pine Italic from the Font menu, and type "11" in the Size field.

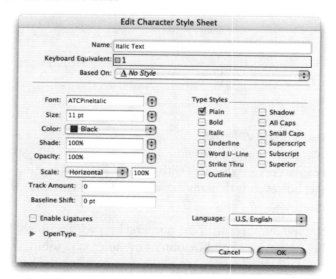

5. Click OK. The new character style sheet Italic Text should appear in the Style Sheets dialog box.

6. Click New>Character again.

7. Add another character style sheet, named "Bold Text", set to 11-pt. ATC Pine Bold. Leave the Keyboard Equivalent field blank.

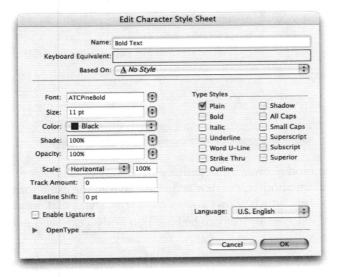

8. Click OK and then click Save to return to the Project window.

9. If it is not already visible, press "F11" to show the Style Sheets palette.

10. Use the Content tool to select the automatic text box on the page. The new character style sheets should appear in the lower half of the palette. Notice that the keyboard shortcut is listed to the right of Italic Text.

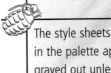
The style sheets listed in the palette appear grayed out unless a text box is selected with the Content tool.

11. Save the file as "working_styles.qxp" in your **Work_In_Progress** folder, and leave it open for the next exercise.

Adding Paragraph Style Sheets

Paragraph style sheets are added in much the same way as character style sheets. In the Style Sheets dialog box, you select Paragraph after clicking New.

As with character style sheets, you first assign a name to the new paragraph style. Again, it's best to use something indicative of the style's purpose. You can also assign a keyboard shortcut for paragraph style sheets.

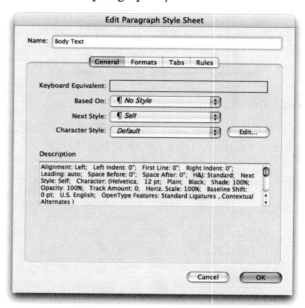

The Based On option allows you to define a parent style sheet. If you choose to base a style sheet on another, the new style will have all the same formatting choices as the parent, which allows you to create two styles that are similar. For example, Body Text - No Indent can be based on Body Text, with only the first-line indent changed.

Any modification you make to the parent style also affects any style that is based on the parent. Continuing with the same example, if you change Body Text to have a 1p space before each paragraph, the same space before will be applied to Body Text - No Indent.

The Next Style menu defines the behavior of text that you type manually. If, for example, you are defining a style called "Heading," you might set the Next Style menu to Body Text - No Indent. When you type in the layout using Heading, pressing Return/Enter automatically switches the insertion point to the Body Text - No Indent style. This setting has no effect on text that is imported from a word-processing document.

The Next Style selection has no effect on text that is imported from a word-processing document.

The Formats, Tabs, and Rules tabs in the Edit Paragraph Style Sheet dialog box present all of the paragraph formatting options that you learned in Chapter 5.

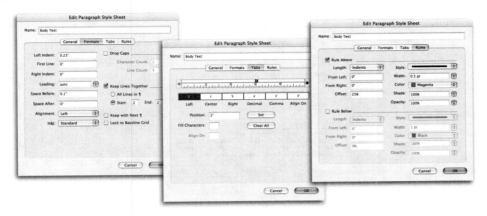

Interaction between Character and Paragraph Styles

When you define a paragraph style sheet, you can choose an existing character style sheet from the Style menu of the General tab, or you can define new character attributes by clicking the Edit button.

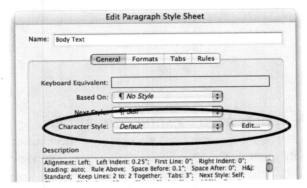

If you leave the Style menu at Default, you can click Edit to define the character formatting of the paragraph style.

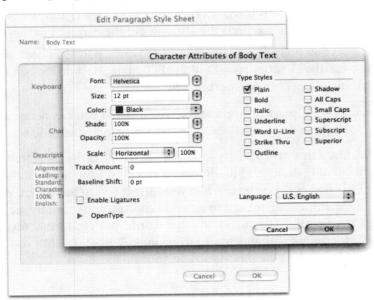

If you choose a character style sheet from the menu, clicking Edit modifies that character style sheet. Be very careful that you do not modify a character style sheet accidentally.

As a general rule, there is little need to define a paragraph style based on a character style. Character style sheets should be used when you need to modify text within a paragraph; you should not use character styles to define the appearance of an entire paragraph.

Clicking OK in the Edit Paragraph Style Sheet dialog box adds the new paragraph style to the Style Sheets dialog box.

Clicking Save returns you to the Project window and adds the new paragraph style to the top half of the Style Sheets palette.

Defining Style Sheets from Existing Formatting

As we mentioned earlier, the description of a new style sheet varies depending on what you did before opening the Style Sheets dialog box. To review:

- If you have not yet placed a text insertion point in the project, the default values in the Description area of the Edit Style Sheet dialog box match the Normal style.

- If the insertion point is placed in the project, the Description area of the Edit Style Sheet dialog box reflects the attributes of the current insertion point.

- If the insertion point is not currently, but at some point has been placed in the project, the Description area of the Edit Style Sheet dialog box reflects the formatting of the last text insertion point.

This has an important practical application, which is that you can define a new style sheet using formatting that already exists in the project on which you are working.

When you define a new style sheet, you have to make all of the character and/or paragraph formatting decisions blindly — you cannot see the results until you click Save in the Style Sheets dialog box. When you format text in the layout, you can change one formatting element at a time, undo choices, and instantly see the results of each formatting command. In other words, you can format text on the layout page, experiment with indents, spacing, fonts, and so on until you are satisfied, and then define the style sheet based on your final choices.

To define a style sheet based on existing formatting, you should place the insertion point at the location of the formatting you want to mirror and choose Edit>Style Sheets. Clicking New and then clicking Paragraph creates a new style sheet with all of the character and paragraph attributes of the current insertion point; you only need to assign a name. Clicking New and then clicking Character creates a new character style sheet with all of the character attributes of the current insertion point; again, you just have to assign a name.

When you define a style sheet based on formatting in the layout page, you should be aware of a pitfall. Although the style is based on the formatting in the layout page, that style is not applied automatically to the text on which it is based.

The following images illustrate this point. A paragraph is modified from the original style sheet Body Text, as indicated by the "+" symbol next to the style-sheet name.

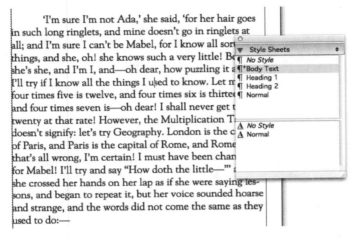

Text does not have to be highlighted to use this method. You can simply place the insertion point in the desired location, and then open the Style Sheets dialog box.

A new style sheet (Body Space Before) was created by clicking New, and then clicking Paragraph in the Style Sheets dialog box. The style sheet has the attributes of the highlighted text. After clicking Save in the Style Sheets dialog box, however, the Style Sheets palette still shows that the highlighted text is using a modified Body Text paragraph style sheet. You have to click Body Space Before in the Style Sheets palette to assign the new style sheet to the highlighted text. The appearance of the selected text will not change because the style sheet has the same formatting definition as the highlighted text.

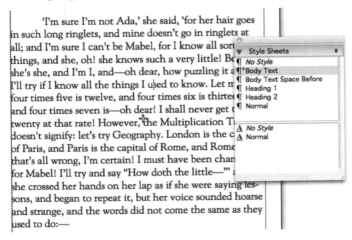

DEFINE PARAGRAPH STYLE SHEETS

1. In the file **working_styles.qxp** (from your **Work_In_Progress** folder), choose Edit>Style Sheets.

2. Click New and then click Paragraph.

3. Type "Headline" in the Name field. Press Tab until the Keyboard Equivalent field is highlighted, and then press "7" on the numeric keypad. Leave the Based On and Next Style fields at their default values.

4. Click the Character Edit button. Set the attributes to 24-pt. ATC Maple Ultra, using All Caps. Choose Cyan from the Color menu.

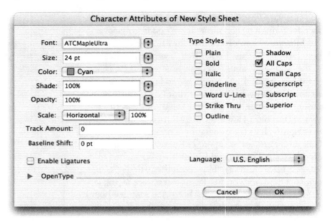

5. Click OK to return to the Edit Paragraph Style Sheet dialog box. Your character attributes are reflected in the Description area.

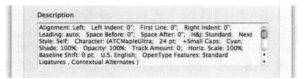

6. Click the Formats tab. Enter "1p" in the Space Before field. Activate the Keep Lines Together check box, and make sure the All Lines in ¶ radio button is selected. Activate the Keep with Next ¶ check box.

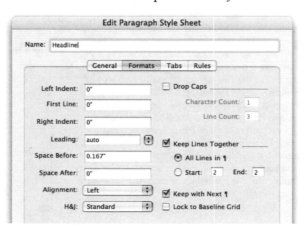

Any time you define a headline-type style sheet, you should use the Keep with Next ¶ option to avoid floating headlines at the end of a column, box, or page.

7. Click the Rules tab. Activate the Rule Above check box. Change the Length menu to Text; define the rule as 2-pt., 35% Black. Offset the rule by 50%.

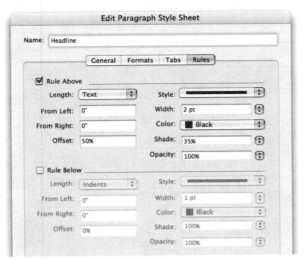

8. Click OK to return to the Style Sheets dialog box.

9. Click New>Paragraph again.

10. Name the new style "Subhead" and choose Headline from the Based On menu. The Description area shows Headline + Next Style: Self.

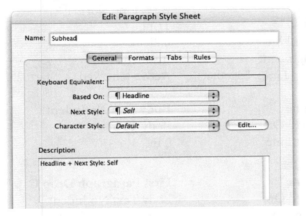

11. Click the Character Edit button. Change the Size to 16 pt., change the Color to Black, and deactivate the All Caps option. Click OK.

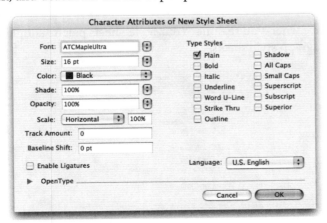

12. Click the Rules tab. Deactivate the Rule Above check box.

13. Click the General tab. Notice that the Description shows Heading + No Rule Above.

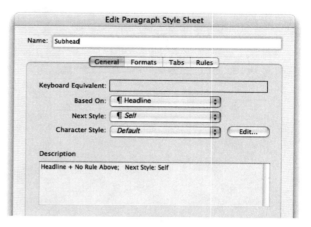

14. Click OK.

15. Create three new paragraph styles. (If the option is not listed here, leave it at the default value.)

Name	Body Text
Based On	No Style
Font	ATC Pine Normal
Size	11 pt.
First Line	0.25 in.
Alignment	Justified
Keep Lines Together	Active (checked) Start: 2, End: 2

Name	Body Text No Indent
Based On	Body Text
First Line	0 in.

Name	First Paragraph Drop Cap
Based On	Body Text No Indent
Drop Caps	Active (checked)
Character Count	1
Line Count	4

16. Click Save when you're done. Your Style Sheets palette should contain all five paragraph style sheets.

17. Save the project and close it.

EDITING STYLE SHEETS

Once style sheets are defined, you can edit them by highlighting the name in the Style Sheets dialog box and clicking Edit.

You can also modify a specific style sheet using contextual menus directly in the Style Sheets palette. Control/right-clicking a style sheet name opens a contextual menu with options to create a new style sheet, or to edit, duplicate, or delete the selected style sheet.

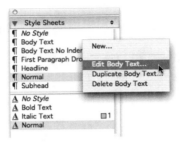

Choosing Edit from this pop-up menu opens the Edit Style Sheet dialog box for the selected style sheet. Clicking OK in that dialog box returns you directly to the Project window, bypassing the Style Sheets dialog box.

 EDIT THE NORMAL STYLE SHEET

1. Make sure that no project is open in QuarkXPress.

2. Choose Edit>Style Sheets. Notice that the top of the dialog box reads Default Style Sheets. Because no project is open, you are modifying the style sheets that will appear in every new project.

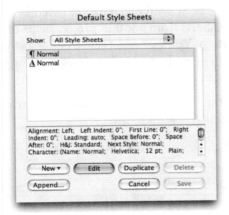

3. Make sure the Normal paragraph style sheet is highlighted, and click Edit.

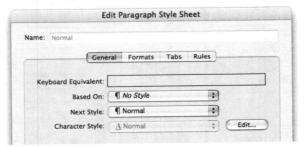

Remember that if you defined a style sheet based on another style sheet, changes to the parent also affect the styles based on the parent.

Normal style sheets can be edited as you would any other style sheet. You can also modify the Normal styles before opening any project, which changes the default text attributes for any new project.

You cannot change the name of the Normal style sheets.

4. Click the Character Edit button.

5. Change the Font to ATC Pine Normal and the Size to 11 pt.

6. Click OK to return to the Edit Paragraph Style Sheet dialog box, and then click OK again to return to the Default Style Sheets dialog box.

7. Click Save. Every new project you create will now use 11-pt. ATC Pine Normal as the default font.

APPENDING STYLE SHEETS

You can import style sheets from other QuarkXPress projects, just as you imported color in Chapter 4. This is particularly useful when you are producing a multiproject publication, such as a book with each chapter saved as a separate QuarkXPress project. Importing style sheets from another project helps to maintain consistency throughout the publication. You can select one chapter as the style-sheet reference for the entire publication — perhaps the first chapter file or the template you are using to create each new chapter file — and define all styles in that project.

If you click Append in the Style Sheets dialog box, you can locate the file containing the style sheets you want to import.

Clicking Open presents the Append dialog box, listing the available style sheets from the project you chose. You can highlight individual style sheets in the Available list and either click the right-facing arrow to add the style sheet, or click Include All to import all style sheets to the current project.

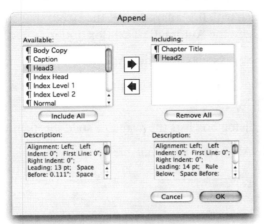

When you click OK, QuarkXPress alerts you that embedded elements — such as the style on which another style is based — will also be appended.

QuarkXPress also notifies you of any conflicts between existing style sheets and the ones you are importing. The bottom half of the Conflict dialog box describes the Existing and New styles; the conflicting data appears in bold.

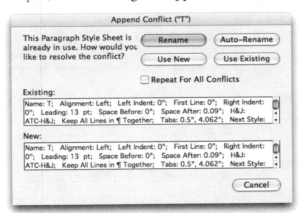

Capitalization does not matter. A style sheet named "body text" in one project will conflict with a style sheet named "Body Text" in another.

If conflicts exist, you have several options:

- **Rename**. Clicking this button allows you to choose a new name for the imported style. Both the imported style and the existing style will be in your project.

- **Auto-Rename**. Clicking this button appends a sequential number to the end of the style name (e.g., Normal1). Both the imported style and the existing style will be in your project.

- **Use New**. Clicking this button imports the new style into the project, over-writing the existing one. Only the imported style will be in your project.

- **Use Existing**. Clicking this button maintains the existing style and ignores the import. Only the existing style will be in your project.

When the import is complete, clicking Save in the Style Sheets dialog box adds the imported styles to your project Style Sheets palette.

IMPORT STYLE SHEETS

1. Create a new project with a print layout named "Style Sheets", using a letter-sized page with 0.5″ margins. Set the layout to 2 columns with a 0.25″ gutter. Make sure the Automatic Text Box option is selected.

2. Choose Edit>Style Sheets and click Append.

3. Navigate to the file **working_styles.qxp** in your **Work_In_Progress** folder and click Open.

   The Append dialog box lists the available style sheets in working_styles.qxp.

4. Click Include All (below the Available list).

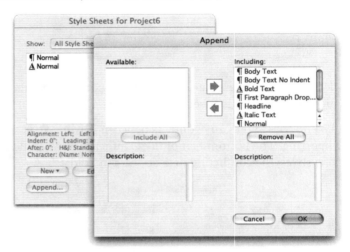

5. Click OK and, when the warning dialog box appears, click OK again.

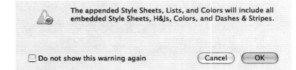

6. A Conflict warning appears. The style Normal is defined in both projects. The Existing description shows the style uses 11-pt. ATC Pine Normal; the New description defines Normal as 12-pt. Helvetica (the default on our computer; yours might be different).

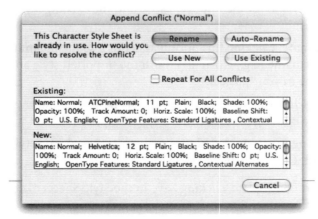

7. Click Use Existing to maintain the 11-pt. ATC Pine Normal setting. Remember that you changed the default Normal font and size in the previous exercise; you want to use your new definition of Normal.

8. Click Save. The style sheets you defined earlier are imported into this new project.

9. Save the file as "import_styles.qxp" in your **Work_In_Progress** folder, and leave it open for the next exercise.

IMPORTING STYLE SHEETS FROM WORD-PROCESSING DOCUMENTS

Most word-processing applications (including Microsoft Word and Corel WordPerfect) allow you to format text with styles. If you're working with text that has been formatted with named styles, you can import those styles into your layout when you place the text file. The Include Style Sheets check box in the Import Text dialog box allows you to maintain styles from the word-processing file.

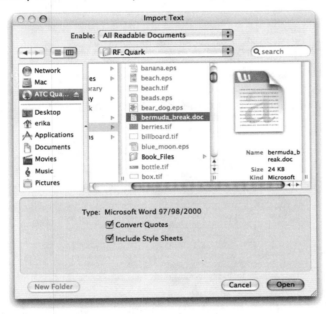

If any conflicts exist between the styles defined in your QuarkXPress project and the styles defined in the word-processing document, you have to resolve the conflicts just as you did when importing styles from other QuarkXPress projects. Once a style sheet has been imported from a word-processing document, you can modify it as you would any other style sheet.

As a general rule, you will probably want to use your QuarkXPress style-sheet definitions. Text comes from a variety of sources, formatted in a variety of different ways; as the designer, you are responsible for the appearance of the text. The advantage of including style sheet information when importing text is that the editorial priority of the text is maintained. In other words, you still have the basic structure of the document (headlines, subheadlines, body copy, and so on) as intended by the author, even if the fonts and line spacing are drastically different between the word-processing file and the QuarkXPress project.

IMPORT STYLES FROM A MICROSOFT WORD DOCUMENT

1. In the file **import_styles.qxp** (from your **Work_In_Progress** folder), select the Content tool and click the automatic text box on the layout page.

2. Choose File>Import Text. Find **chapter.doc** in the **RF_Quark7>Chapter06** folder. Make sure the Include Style Sheets box is checked and click Open. You will see a Conflict warning — the Existing description area notes a conflict with the style Normal.

3. Click Auto-Rename.

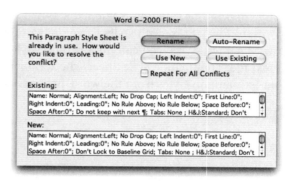

When importing style sheets from a Microsoft Word document, Normal will almost always present a conflict because it cannot be deleted from Microsoft Word, even if it is not used. It is up to you to decide how to resolve the conflict. If you know that Normal is not used in the Word document, you should click Use Existing. Otherwise, you might want to click Auto-Rename and change the style sheet later.

4. Another conflict exists with the style sheet Body Text. Click Use Existing.

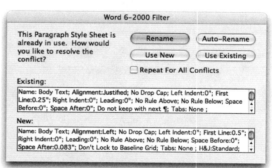

5. The text should be imported, maintaining the style sheet information from the word-processing file. A second page is added to the layout so that the entire story is placed.

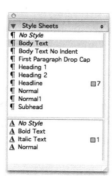

The Style Sheets palette now has the new style sheets Heading 1, Heading 2, and Normal1, in addition to the style sheets that you previously defined.

6. Save the file and leave it open for the next exercise.

APPLYING STYLE SHEETS

As we mentioned in the beginning of this chapter, character style sheets affect only the selected text. Paragraph style sheets affect the entire body of text between two paragraph marks; if you show the invisible characters, you can see where paragraphs begin and end.

When text is highlighted, the applied style sheet is also highlighted in the Style Sheets palette.

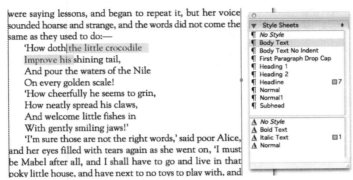

Clicking a character style sheet in the palette formats the highlighted text only. The paragraph formatting of the highlighted text does not change. In the following example, notice the plus sign before the paragraph style sheet Body Text — indicating that some formatting other than the style sheet has been applied.

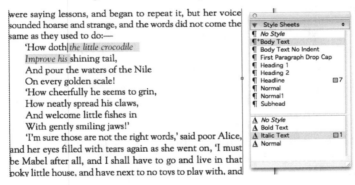

Clicking a paragraph style sheet applies that format to any paragraph that is entirely or partially selected.

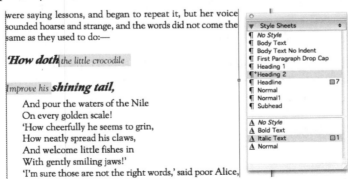

Overriding Local Formatting

If any formatting in a paragraph does not match the definition of an applied style sheet, a plus sign (+) appears before the style sheet name in the palette.

In the previous image, the text maintains the formatting of the character style even when a new paragraph style is applied. Because not all of the text in these paragraphs conforms to the defined paragraph style, a plus sign appears next to Heading 2 in the Style Sheets palette.

You can remove the local or character-style formatting by Option/Alt-clicking the paragraph style sheet name in the palette, as shown in the following image.

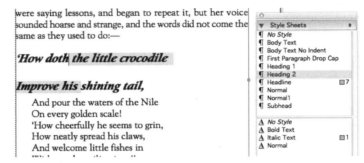

This method, although useful, presents certain problems. Specifically, there are often instances when you want to apply (or re-apply) the paragraph formatting options without removing local character formatting — whether applied with a character style sheet or not.

Say, for example, you have a paragraph where *only a few words need to be in italics*. It is formatted with a style sheet, but you changed the leading of that one paragraph in the layout. If you reapply the appropriate paragraph style sheet (Option/Alt-click the Body Copy style sheet) to return the leading to the style-sheet setting, the italics are also removed since the style sheet does not call for italics.

In QuarkXPress 7, Option/Alt-Shift-clicking a style sheet in the palette reapplies the paragraph formatting without overriding local character formatting. In other words, using the same example, Option/Alt-Shift-clicking changes the leading but does not affect the text in italics.

 APPLY STYLE SHEETS

1. On Page 1 of the layout in **import_styles.qxp**, show invisible characters.

2. In the left column, highlight the text "ALICE'S RIGHT FOOT, ESQ.," and click the Bold Text character style sheet in the palette. Notice that the Body Text paragraph style sheet now displays a plus sign.

3. In the right column of Page 1, highlight all of the text in the poem.

4. Press "1" on the numeric keypad. Remember that we assigned this number as the shortcut for the Italic Text character style sheet. Again, notice the plus sign in front of Body Text.

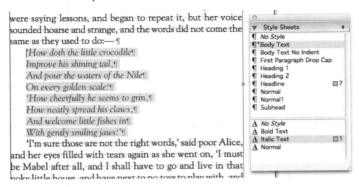

5. Save the file and leave it open for the next exercise.

DELETING STYLE SHEETS

Any style sheet can be deleted from a project at any time by highlighting the name in the Style Sheets dialog box and clicking Delete. If a style has been used somewhere in the project, a dialog box asks you what style to use in place of the one you are deleting. Clicking OK deletes the style sheet from the Style Sheets palette.

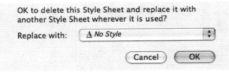

You can use the Undo command to replace deleted style sheets.

If you click Save in the Style Sheets dialog box, the Style Sheet is removed; clicking Cancel leaves your Style Sheets palette as it was.

 DELETE STYLE SHEETS

1. In the open file **import_styles.qxp**, choose Edit>Style Sheets.

2. Highlight Heading 1 — the style sheet imported with the text — in the dialog box, and click Delete.

3. In the warning dialog box, select Headline — the style you defined — from the Replace With menu, and click OK.

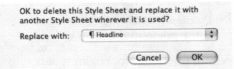

4. Repeat this process, replacing Heading 2 with Subhead, and Normal1 with Normal.

5. Click Save to close the Style Sheets dialog box. Notice the change in formatting for the first two lines of text.

6. Save the file and leave it open for the next exercise.

Modifying Style Sheets

One of the greatest advantages of using style sheets is the ability to make universal formatting changes. Any changes you make in the Edit Style Sheet dialog box are applied to all text that uses that style sheet. In other words, you can change the appearance of every headline in the project at once, or change the formatting of every paragraph of body text.

When style sheets are used consistently throughout a project, you can change the appearance of every bit of text in the project from within the Style Sheets dialog box. This effectively reduces production time, because you don't have to select any text in the Project window and then modify individual attributes.

When you edit a style sheet, remember that you are also editing any style sheet that is based on the one you are editing.

MODIFY STYLE SHEETS

1. With **import_styles.qxp** open, choose Edit>Style Sheets.
   The body text currently has a 0.25″ first-line indent for every paragraph.

2. Highlight Body Text in the window and click Edit.

3. Click the Formats tab in the Edit Paragraph Style Sheet dialog box.
   Change the First Line indent to 0 and the Space Before field to 0.167.

4. Click OK and then click Save in the Style Sheets dialog box to apply the change to the style-sheet definition and any text using that style.

5. Click the Page 2 icon in the Page Layout palette. A third page has been added to accommodate the text overflow that resulted from changing the paragraph spacing of Body Text.

6. Navigate back to Page 1 of the layout. When you changed the paragraph format for Body Text, you changed the appearance of the directions in the left column and the poem in the right column.

7. Select the second, third, and fourth lines of text in the directions (in the first column).

8. In the Paragraph mode of the Measurements palette, change the Space Before field to 0 and press Return/Enter. The Style Sheets palette displays a plus sign in font of Body Text because you modified the formatting after applying the style sheet.

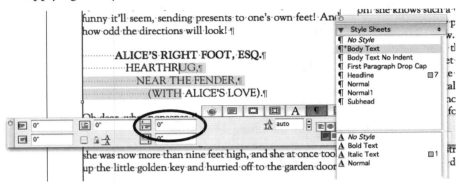

9. With the text still highlighted, choose Edit>Style Sheets. Click New, then click Paragraph, and name the new style sheet "Body Text No Space Before". Click OK and then click Save to return to the Project window.

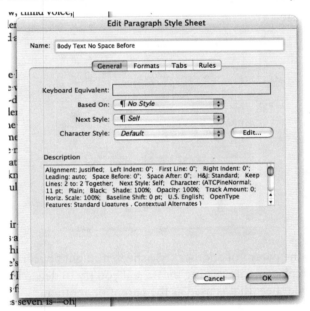

10. With the text still highlighted, click Body Text No Space Before. The appearance of the highlighted text doesn't change, but the Style Sheets palette shows the appropriate style with no modification.

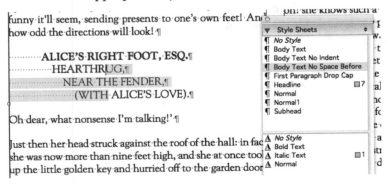

11. In the right column of the first page, select all but the first line of the poem text. Click Body Text No Space Before in the Style Sheets palette.

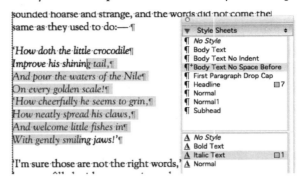

12. Save the file and leave it open for the next exercise.

Removing Unused Style Sheets

When you have finished working on a project, it is good practice to remove style sheets that you defined but did not use. You can select Style Sheets Not Used from the Show drop-down menu in the Style Sheets dialog box, and then highlight and delete the items listed.

If a style sheet is the parent of another style sheet, it might appear in this list, but you will get the replacement warning message if you try to delete it. You should not delete any style sheet that is used as the parent of another.

REMOVE UNUSED STYLE SHEETS

1. In the open file **import_styles.qxp**, choose Edit>Style Sheets. Choose Style Sheets Not Used from the Show menu.

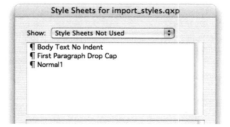

2. Highlight Body Text No Indent and click Delete.

3. A dialog box appears, asking if you want to delete the style sheet that is in use. Click Cancel.

   First Paragraph Drop Cap is listed as unused. Remember that you created this style sheet based on Body Text No Indent. Because that style sheet is still in the list, deleting its parent will prompt a warning, even if this style is not applied to text in the project.

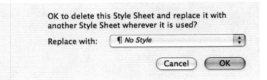

OK to delete this Style Sheet and replace it with another Style Sheet wherever it is used?

Replace with: ¶ No Style

Cancel   OK

You have to click Save to finalize your changes in the Style Sheets dialog box. Body Text No Indent is still a parent to First Paragraph Drop Cap until you click Save in the Style Sheets dialog box to finalize the change.

4. Highlight First Paragraph Drop Cap and click Delete.

5. Highlight Normal1 and click Delete.

6. Click Save to close the Style Sheets dialog box.

7. Reopen the Style Sheets dialog box. Select Style Sheets Not Used in the Show menu, and delete the Body Text No Indent style. You do not see a warning this time. Click Save.

8. Save the file and close it.

SUMMARY

In this chapter, you explored style sheets, one of the QuarkXPress tools that automate some of the redundant, time-consuming, and tedious work associated with document publishing. You learned that there is a lot of work involved in the planning stages of document design. You know, though, that the time you invest in defining styles at the beginning of a project is well worth the effort if you can move more quickly through an entire — perhaps hundreds of pages — publication, apply those same settings to other projects, and complete repetitive tasks in half the time.

Working with Tables

7

QuarkXPress includes many advanced tools and utilities that provide virtually unlimited control over the type in a layout. These tools give you precise typographic control over every letter in your layout, from a single sentence typed in a box to hundreds of pages of linked content. One significant addition to the application's type tools is the ability to create, format, and manage tables directly in a QuarkXPress layout, which fills an obvious need for anyone who has spent time adjusting tabs and shifting baselines to present columns of information.

IN CHAPTER 7, YOU WILL:

- Create new tables using the Table tool.

- Format table attributes, including gridlines.

- Control and format table cells.

- Add content to a table, and control the position of that content within table cells.

- Convert tab-delimited text into a table.

- Import an Excel spreadsheet into QuarkXPress.

CREATING NEW TABLES

QuarkXPress includes a Table tool, which allows you to create a spreadsheet-like table within the QuarkXPress layout instead of relying on tabs and rules to align columns of text. You can use the Table tool to create a rectangular object that is automatically divided into a specified number of rows and columns. This eliminates the need to adjust baselines, place multiple tab stops and indent-to-here characters, and apply all of the other formatting tweaks that were previously required to present and manage columnar data in a QuarkXPress layout.

If you have used previous versions of QuarkXPress, it is important to note one significant change: all table controls that were previously available in the Item menu have been moved to the new Table menu.

CREATE A NEW TABLE

1. Open the file **culture.qxp** from the **RF_Quark7>Chapter07** folder.

2. Using the Table tool, draw a box that fills the space between the margin guides.

   Drawing a table is the same as drawing any other type of box. The shape that you drag defines the outside dimensions of the table.

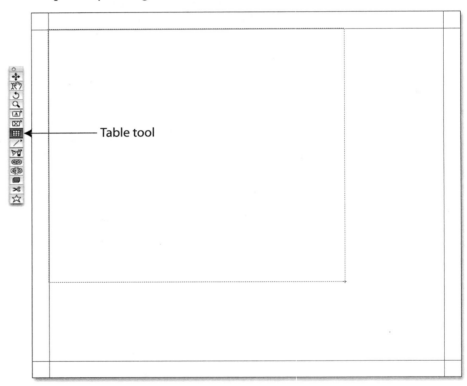

Table tool

   When you release the mouse button, the Table Properties dialog box appears.

3. In the Table Properties dialog box, define the table to have 7 rows and 8 columns, and make sure the Text Cells radio button is selected.

   Tables can contain both text cells and picture cells. When you create the table, however, you must define which type will initially be used.

4. Activate the Link Cells check box. Leave the Tab Order and Link Order menus at their default values (left-to-right, top-to-bottom).

   When cells are linked, text flows from one cell to another just as it does with linked text boxes. The Link Order menu determines the sequence of cells in the text chain.

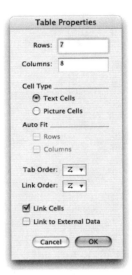

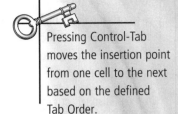

Pressing Control-Tab moves the insertion point from one cell to the next based on the defined Tab Order.

5. Click OK to create the table.

   The specified number of rows and columns is created with equal width and height.

You can resize the outside dimensions of the table by dragging any of the handles that surround the table.

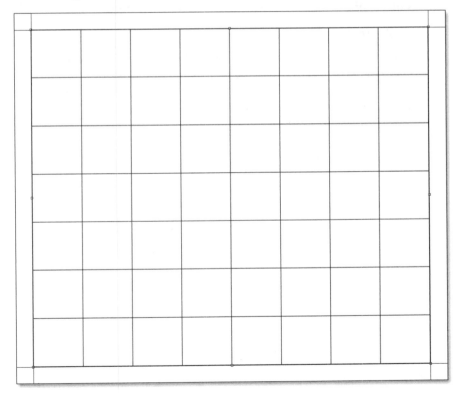

6. Place the cursor above the rightmost column in the table.

You can select entire rows or columns by clicking just outside (above to select a column or to the left to select a row) the table.

You can also select entire rows or columns, or specific rows or columns, by choosing from the Table>Select menu.

To select multiple adjacent cells (horizontally, vertically, or in a block), you can click in the first cell and then drag to select additional cells.

To select nonadjacent table cells, press the Shift key and click each cell you want to select.

You can split combined cells by choosing Table> Split Cell. Once cells are split, any content of the group is placed into the first cell in the original range.

7. When the cursor becomes a down-pointing arrow, click to select the entire column.

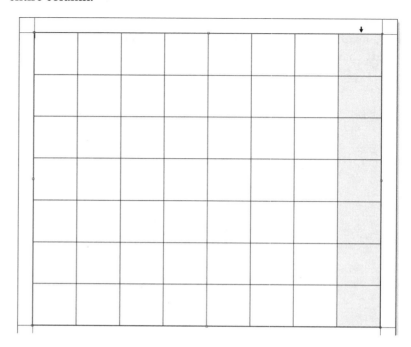

8. Choose Table>Combine Cells.

    Combining cells removes the gridlines between the combined cells, and treats the entire space as a single cell. When cells are combined, the attributes of the first cell in the selection become the attributes of the merged cell.

9. With the combined cell still selected, choose Item>Content>Picture.

    As you saw in the Table Properties dialog box, you can create a table with text cells or picture cells. After the table is initially created, you can convert selected cells to a different type of content by choosing Item>Content. Tables can have any combination of text, picture, and "none" cells.

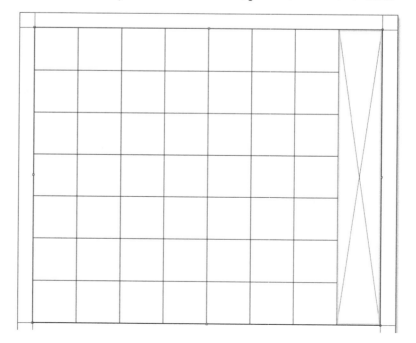

10. Place the insertion point in the top-left cell of the table, and select the Unlinking tool.

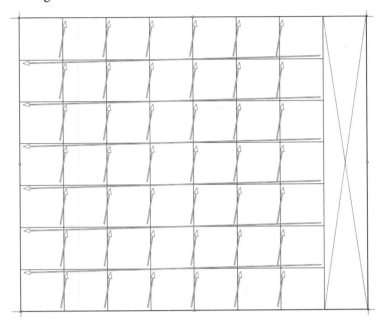

Picture cells are indicated by crossed diagonal lines, like those you would see in a regular picture box.

Because you activated the Link Cells option in the Table Properties dialog box, the cells in the table automatically link in the order you indicated in the Link Order menu. The right column was removed from the linking order when you combined the column cells.

11. Click the arrow that connects the last cell in the first row to the first cell in the second row.

If you change the type of a cell that already has content, a warning shows that the existing content will be deleted.

You can use the Linking and Unlinking tools to redirect the flow of text through a table, just as you would with individual text boxes. You are not limited to the link orders presented in the Table Properties dialog box.

12. Repeat this process to break the link from the second row to the third row.

13. Using the Content tool, click the first cell in the top row and drag right to add the next six cells in the row to the selection.

If you press Option/Alt before selecting the Linking or Unlinking tool, the tool will remain selected until you manually select another tool.

This command also works with the drawing tools (Text Box, Picture Box, Line, and Starburst tools).

14. Choose Table>Combine Cells.

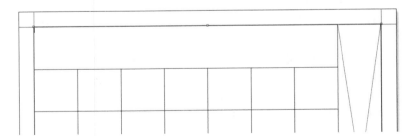

Combining table cells removes the selected cells from the defined linking order.

15. Save the file as "table_working.qxp" in your **Work_In_Progress** folder. Keep it open for the next exercise.

FORMATTING TABLES

Formatting QuarkXPress tables is a combination of spreadsheet and page-layout techniques. As with any spreadsheet, you can control the appearance of gridlines that separate table cells; add or delete cells; and adjust the height and width of cells. As with a regular box in a QuarkXPress layout, you can apply style sheets, scale pictures within a cell, apply colored backgrounds, define text inset values, and adjust the position of text or graphics within a cell.

Some table controls are available in various modes of the Measurements palette. When one or more table cells is selected with the Content tool, you can change the width and height of cells in the Measurements palette Classic mode. You can also change the attributes (vertical alignment, text inset, etc.) of a single cell using the Box mode.

When a table is selected with the Item tool, the Measurements palette Classic mode includes a Maintain Geometry check box. A Grid mode also becomes available; you can use these options to change the attributes of horizontal, vertical, or all gridlines (just as you can in the Grid tab of the Modify dialog box).

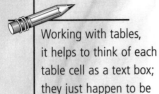

Working with tables, it helps to think of each table cell as a text box; they just happen to be combined into a table.

FORMAT GRIDLINES

1. With the file **table_working.qxp** open, select the table with the Item tool.

2. Open the Modify dialog box (Command/Control-M) and display the Grid tab.

   When a table is selected with the Item tool, five tabs are available in the Modify dialog box:

   - **Table.** The options in this tab are used to control the outside dimensions and position of the entire table.

   - **Frame.** A table can have a defined frame attribute, just as any other box in a layout. Do not, however, confuse the frame with the table gridlines; tables can have both frame attributes and gridline attributes, which results in the appearance of two edges.

   - **Runaround.** Tables, like any other boxes, can have defined runaround attributes. You use these options to control the position of text away from the outside edge of the table.

   - **Grid.** This tab is used to define the width, color, and style of gridlines in a table. You can define separate attributes for horizontal and vertical gridlines, or apply the same attributes to all gridlines.

   - **Drop Shadow.** This tab can be used to apply a drop shadow to the selected table. Drop shadows are table-specific; you cannot apply a drop shadow to individual cells of a table.

3. Make sure the All option is selected and change the Width field to 0.5 pt.

Three buttons to the right of the Preview area control (from the top) all lines, vertical lines, and horizontal lines. You can define different width, style, color, and shade settings for the horizontal and vertical lines in a table.

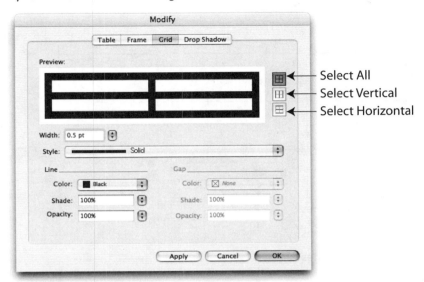

Select All
Select Vertical
Select Horizontal

4. Click OK to close the dialog box and apply your changes.

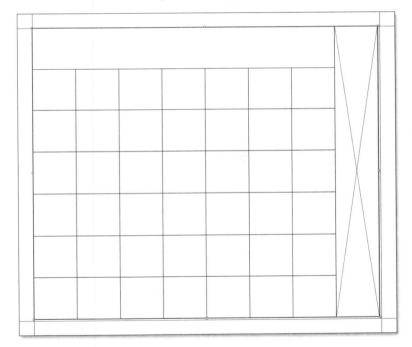

When you change the gridline attributes of a table, the table resizes to accommodate the new grid widths.

5. Choose Edit>Undo to revert the gridlines to the default 1 pt.

6. With the table still selected, choose Table>Maintain Geometry.

By default, changing gridline attributes, adding or deleting rows or columns, and resizing cells all change the outside dimensions of a table. The Maintain Geometry locks the outside dimensions of a table to prevent resizing.

You can also format the gridlines when the Content tool is active and the insertion point is placed in a table cell. Four options in the Table>Select menu select the Horizontal Grids, Vertical Grids, Borders, or All Grids. Once you select gridlines using this menu, you can change the color of the selected gridlines using the Colors palette.

After you select a set of gridlines with the Table> Select menu, you can open the Grid tab of the Modify dialog box. The Preview area shows only the selected gridlines, which you can then change independently.

Border gridlines are not the same thing as the table frame. If you define both a frame and a border, you will end up with a two-level edge to your table.

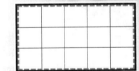

7. Select the table with the Item tool and display the Measurements palette Grid mode. Click the All Gridlines (left-most) button and change the Grid Weight field to 0.5 pt. Press Return/Enter to apply the change.

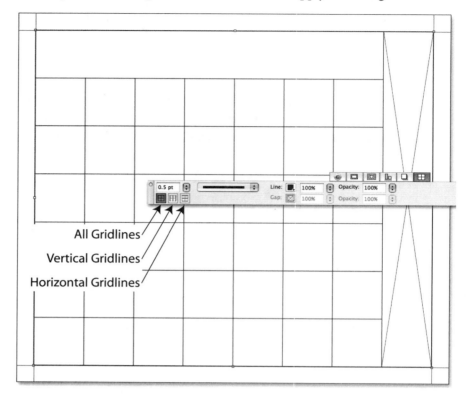

Because Maintain Geometry is activate, changing the gridlines does not affect the outside dimensions of the table.

8. Save the file and continue.

RESIZE TABLE CELLS

1. In the file **table_working.qxp**, make sure the Content tool is active and place the cursor over the bottom gridline of the first row.

2. When the cursor changes to a two-headed arrow, click and drag up until the cell is approximately 1″ high.

   When directly over a gridline, the cursor becomes a double-facing arrow icon. You can change the width or height of a column or row by dragging any gridline in the table.

   Because Maintain Geometry is active, the second row enlarges to fill the space; the other rows (3–7) are not affected.

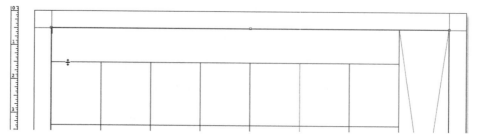

3. Using the Content tool, place the insertion point in the second row of the table and display the Measurements palette in Classic mode.

4. Change the Row Height field to 0.3″ and press Return/Enter.

Here again, because the Maintain Geometry option is selected, the third row enlarges to fill the space and the remaining rows (4–7) are not affected.

Rather than manually dragging gridlines, you can apply precise measurements to any row or column in a table.

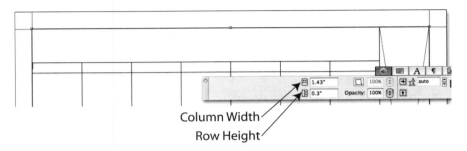

Column Width
Row Height

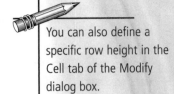

You can also define a specific row height in the Cell tab of the Modify dialog box.

5. Click the first cell of the third row and drag down to select the first cells in each remaining row.

6. Open the Modify dialog box.

When a table is selected with the Content tool, the Modify dialog box includes three tabs that control the attributes of the selected cells.

- **Table.** This is the same as when the table is selected with the Item tool.
- **Cell(s).** This allows you to modify the width and height of selected rows or columns. You can also define the color and shade of selected cells, or apply a blend.
- **Text.** This defines the text placement within the selected cells. The same options are available as for any other text box; think of each cell in the table as a distinct text box.

7. In the Cells tab, click the Row Height Distribute Evenly button, and click OK.

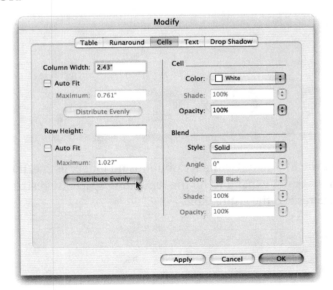

Add rows or columns to a table by choosing Table>Insert>Rows or Columns.

If Maintain Geometry is not selected, new rows or columns are added with the same width or height as the existing cells, and the dimensions of the table change as necessary.

If Maintain Geometry is selected, rows and columns are added within the dimensions of the table; the existing rows or columns are resized as necessary to accommodate the new cells.

Distribute Evenly calculates the width or height of the entire selection, and then divides the space evenly over the selected columns or rows.

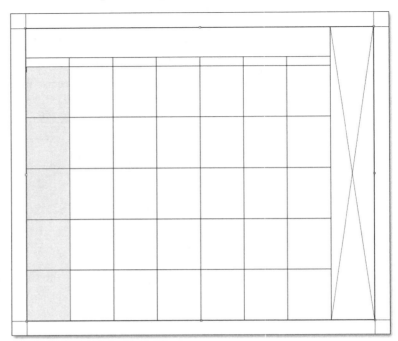

The Distribute Evenly options are available whenever two or more adjacent cells of different sizes are selected.

8. Choose Table>Maintain Geometry to toggle this option off.

9. Select the entire third row of the table and open the Modify dialog box. In the Cells tab, change the Width field to 1.2″ and click OK.

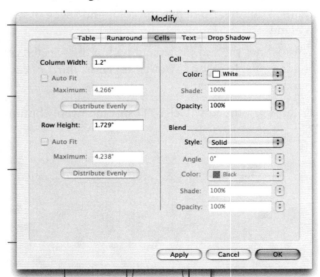

Delete a selected row or column by choosing Table>Delete>Row or Column. This option is only available when an entire row or column is selected.

Modifying the height or width of a single cell affects the entire row or column in which that cell resides.

Because the Maintain Geometry option is no longer active, the rightmost column does not expand to fill the remaining space. By resizing the cells, you have resized the entire table.

10. Place the cursor over the right edge of the table (not at the handle). When the cursor changes to a two-headed arrow, click and drag the gridline until it aligns with the right margin guide.

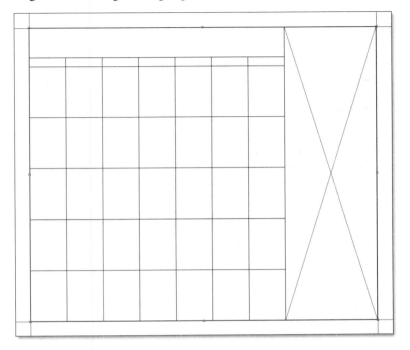

 The Item tool always selects the entire table. You must use the Content tool to work with individual cells.

11. Save the file and continue.

FORMAT TABLE CELLS

1. In the file **table_working.qxp**, place the insertion point in the top-left cell.

2. Type "December 2006", and apply the Month style sheet.

   You enter and format text in a table cell just as you would in any text box.

3. In the Text mode of the Measurements palette, click the Centered Vertical Alignment button.

   Think of individual table cells as boxes. Formatting attributes such as vertical alignment can be different for each cell in the table.

4. Activate the Multiple Insets check box. Change the Top and Left fields to 8 pt. and press Return/Enter to apply the change.

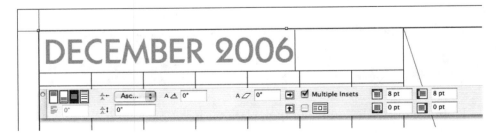

   Multiple inset values — available for both table cells and text boxes — allow you to define different inset values for each edge of the cell or box.

5. Select the entire second row of the table and apply 100c 0m 45y 0k as the background color for the selected cells.

   You can apply color to table cells just as you would to any other object in the layout.

6. In the Text tab of the Modify dialog box, change the vertical alignment to Centered and click OK.

7. Place the insertion point in the first cell of the second row and type "Mon".

8. Press Shift-Enter (numeric keypad) to add a next-box character.

   When you are working with linked table cells, you should treat each cell as you would a series of linked text boxes. Using the next-box character forces the insertion point and text to move to the next cell in the linking order.

9. Type "Tue" and press Shift-Enter again.

10. Continue typing the following into the cells in the second row:

    Wed   Thu   Fri   Sat   Sun

11. With the insertion point still in the "Sun" cell, press Command/Control-A to select all text in the current text chain.

12. Apply the Day style sheet to the selected text.

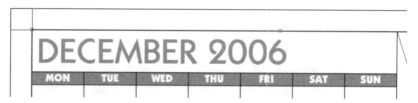

13. Select the rest of the empty cells (except the rightmost combined cell) in the table. In the Text tab of the Modify dialog box, apply a 3-pt. inset to all edges of the selected cells.

14. Save the file and continue.

ADDING TABLE CONTENT

As you have already seen, tables can include text, pictures, or a combination of both. When adding content to a table, you should work with table cells as you would any other box in a layout. Text can be typed directly into a cell or imported using the Get Text command. Pictures can be placed using the Get Picture command. Objects — including other tables — can also be placed into text cells as inline graphics. After content is placed into a table, it is formatted using the same tools and commands that are used to format content in regular boxes.

 IMPORT TEXT INTO A TABLE

1. In the file **table_working.qxp**, place the insertion point in the first cell of the third row.

2. Choose File>Import Text. Navigate to the file **december.txt** in the **RF_Quark7>Chapter07** folder, make sure the Convert Quotes check box is selected, and click Open.

3. Select all text in the chain and apply the Concert Info style sheet.

    There is a problem associated with linking table cells. When you import text into the table, *delimiters* (special characters that separate columns and rows in tabular text) such as tabs or commas in the imported text are ignored.

4. If invisible characters are not showing, choose View>Invisibles.

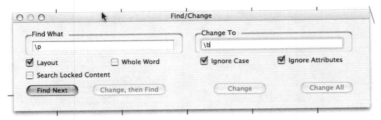

    As you can see in the previous image, importing tabular text into linked cells can create a mess. One solution is to use next-box characters (Enter on the numeric keypad) to move subsequent text along in the text chain.

5. Place the insertion point at the beginning of the story and open the Find/Change dialog box (Edit>Find/Change).

6. In the Find What field, type "\p" (the code for a paragraph-return character). In the Change To field, type "\b" (the code for the next-box character).

7. Click Find Next, then click Change All. Click OK to the message that 34 instances were changed.

8. Replace the cursor at the beginning of the story.

9. In the Find What field, type "\t" (the code for a Tab character). In the Change To field, type "\p" (the code for the paragraph-return character).

10. Click Find Next, then click Change All. Click OK to the message that 24 instances were changed.

11. In the Find What field, type ";[space]". In the Change To field, type "\n" (the code for the soft-return character).

12. Click Find Next, then click Change All. Click OK to the message that 26 instances were changed.

As you might imagine, this can be a tedious and time-consuming workflow. It is important, however, to understand how to work around this type of problem.

We created this file, so we know what needs to be changed and in what order.

By adding the next-box characters first, we can then add paragraph returns where appropriate. If Steps 6 and 8 were reversed, you would be removing all paragraph returns from the text — including the ones that should remain.

When you are working with your own files, review the content carefully before you start replacing hidden characters.

13. Place the insertion point at the beginning of the text and press Shift-Enter four times. (December 2006 begins on a Friday.)

14. With the insertion point immediately before the "1", apply the Date style sheet.

15. Apply the Date style sheet to the number of each day.

16. Notice that there is no date in the the third cell in the 5th row (after the 12th); there are two scheduled concerts on December 12th. Delete the next-box character after the concert listing on the 12th, so two listings appear in the same cell for that day.

17. Continue formatting the dates in the calendar, repeating Step 16 for the 18th, 19th, and 31st.

18. Format the remaining date numbers (the ones that appear when you combine the two-concert dates) with the Date style sheet.

MON	TUE	WED	THU	FRI	SAT	SUN
				1	2	3
						8:00 pm Tristan Project I/C
4	5	6	7	8	9	10
8:00 pm Tristan Project I/C	2:00 pm Tristan Project III/C	8:00 pm Arlo Guthrie and the Klezmatics/B		8:00 pm Miriam Makeba/F	8:00 pm Garrison Keillor with the LA Philharmonic, Pasadena Presbyterian Choir, and All Saints Church Choir (Pasadena)/B	8:00 pm Tristan Project I/C
11	12	13	14	15	16	17
8:00 pm Tristan Project I/C	2:00 pm Tristan Project III/C / 7:30 pm Selections from Bach, Buxtehude, Gabrieli, Purvis, Hazell, Tchiakovsky, Dupré, Styne, and Goode/C		8:00 pm Selections from Bach, Handel, and Vivaldi/A	7:00 pm Selections from Mozart, Ravel, Pärt, and Tchiakovsky / Alhambra High School/D	8:00 pm Selections from Mozart, Ravel, Pärt, and Tchiakovsky / Wilshire United Methodist Church/D	8:00 pm Handel's Messiah/B
18	19	20	21	22	23	24
11:00 am Toyota Symphony for Youth/E / 8:00 pm Handel's Messiah/B	2:00 pm Handel's Messiah/B / 7:30 pm Home for the Holidays/B	8:00 pm A Celtic Christmas with Eileen Ivers and Immigrant Soul/B	8:00 pm Chanticleer: A unique collection of traditional holiday music from the 11th to 15th centuries/B	7:30 pm Latin Christmas with Ozomatli Kinky and Juana Molina/B	8:00 pm The Spirit of the Holidays with Keb' Mo'/B	
25	26	27	28	29	30	31
						7:00 pm Pink Martini/B / 10:30 pm Pink Martini/B

19. Save the file and continue.

CONVERTING TEXT TO TABLES

As you saw in the previous exercise, importing text directly into a table requires a number of tricks to work around untranslated delimiters. There is, fortunately, an easier way around this limitation. Rather than importing text directly into a table, you can import the text into a regular text box, highlight the text, and choose Table>Convert Text to Table.

CONVERT TEXT TO A TABLE

1. In the pasteboard to the right of the page in **table_working.qxp**, draw a new text box that is 2.875″ wide and 4.546″ high.

2. Import the file **tickets.txt** into the text box.

3. Select all the text in the box and apply the Concert Info style sheet.

4. With all of the text still selected, choose Table>Convert Text to Table.

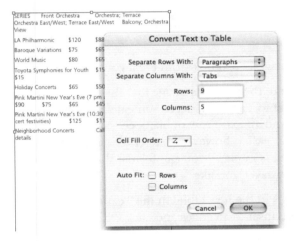

Before converting text to a table, it's a good idea to remove extra tab characters at the end of lines. Don't remove multiple tabs in the middle of lines, though, because the text may not align properly in the table.

The Convert Text to Table dialog box defines how the text is imported.

- **Separate Rows With**. This menu defaults to Paragraphs. In other words, each paragraph-return character (¶) in the selected text tells QuarkXPress to begin a new table row. The other options in this menu (Space, Comma, and Tab) are less commonly used.

- **Separate Columns With**. This menu defaults to Tabs. Many table-text files are exported from a spreadsheet program to a *tab-delimited* file, which means the data for each column is separated by a Tab character. Each Tab character (→) in the selected text tells QuarkXPress to move to a new cell. The Commas option can be used if the text was created as a comma-delimited text file. The Spaces and Paragraphs options are uncommon.

- **Rows** and **Columns**. These fields are filled automatically with a number determined by the application, based on the highlighted text. It is a good idea to leave these options at the default values, and make any necessary changes later.

- **Cell Fill Order**. This menu determines how the data is converted into the cells of a table. The default begins in the top-left cell, moves horizontally across the row, moves to the leftmost cell in the second row, moves across that row, and so on.

5. Leave all the options in the dialog box at their default values and click OK.

When you click OK in the Convert Text to Table dialog box, a table is created on top of the existing text box. The table has the same height and width as the text box from which the text was converted.

SERIES	Front Orchestra	Orchestra; Terrace	Orchestra East/West; Terrace	Balcony; Orchestra View
LA Philharmonic	$120	$88	$68	$35
Baroque Variations	$75	$65	$45	$30
World Music	$80	$65	$45	$25
Toyota Symphonies for Youth	$15	$15	$15	$15
Holiday Concerts	$65	$50	$35	$20
Pink Martini New Year's Eve (7 pm	$90	$75	$65	$45
Pink Martini New Year's Eve (10:30	$125	$110	$100	$80
Neighborhood Concerts	Call 323-555-2000 for venue			

6. Delete the original text box from the layout.

You can see in the previous image that the table created by choosing Convert Text to Table still needs some help — remedying several Overset Text icons and an extra row of blank cells, to name just two problems. This method is far easier, however, than entering the text into each cell manually. Once the text is in place, you can format the text, cells, gridlines, and table attributes however you like.

7. Select all cells in the new table. In the Text tab of the Modify dialog box, apply a 2-pt. inset to all edges and click OK.

8. With the table still selected, choose Table>Maintain Geometry.

9. Drag the right gridline of the first column until the column is approximately 1″ wide.

10. Select all but the first column of the table and open the Modify dialog box.

11. In the Cells tab, click the Width Distribute Evenly button. Click OK.

SERIES	Front Orchestra	Orchestra; Terrace	Orchestra East/W	Balcony; Orchestra View
LA Philharmonic	$120	$88	$68	$35
Baroque Variations	$75	$65	$45	$30
World Music	$80	$65	$45	$25
Toyota Symphonies for Youth	$15	$15	$15	$15
Holiday Concerts	$65	$50	$35	$20
Pink Martini New Year's Eve (7 pm and 10:30 pm	$90	$75	$65	$45
Pink Martini New Year's Eve (10:30 concert including	$125	$110	$100	$80
Neighborhood Concerts	Call 323-555-			

12. In the bottom row of the table, select all but the leftmost cell and choose Table>Combine Cells.

13. In the Table tab, deselect the Maintain Geometry check box.

14. Beginning with the second row of the table, drag the bottom edge of each row until all text in each cell is visible (the Overset Text icons all disappear), and the cells are just high enough to accommodate the text.

15. For each cell that lists a ticket price, apply centered paragraph alignment.

16. Select all but the first cell in the first row and open the Modify dialog box. In the Cells tab, change the Height field to 1.36″. In the Text tab, change the Text Angle field to 90 and change the Vertical Alignment menu to Centered. Click OK.

17. Change the vertical alignment of the "Series" cell to Bottom.

18. Using the Item tool, drag the new table so that it is approximately 1/8″ away from the bottom, left, and right edges of the picture cell in the right column.

SERIES	Front Orchestra	Orchestra, Terrace	Orchestra East/West; Terrace East/West	Balcony, Orchestra View
LA Philharmonic	$120	$88	$68	$35
Baroque Variations	$75	$65	$45	$30
World Music	$80	$65	$45	$25
Toyota Symphonies for Youth	$15	$15	$15	$15
Holiday Concerts	$65	$50	$35	$20
Pink Martini New Year's Eve (7 pm and 10:30 pm shows)	$90	$75	$65	$45
Pink Martini New Year's Eve (10:30 concert including pre-concert festivities)	$125	$110	$100	$80
Neighborhood Concerts	Call 323-555-2000 for venue details			

19. Save the file and continue.

IMPORTING EXCEL TABLES

People often spend hours adjusting the formatting of a Microsoft Excel spreadsheet so that they can print to their desktop printer and the output will look good. When the time comes to create a professional print layout from that spreadsheet, we have often had to redo (or undo) a significant amount of work because the layout software couldn't interpret the information from the spreadsheet file.

Because of the ubiquitous nature of Excel files, QuarkXPress now includes the ability to link directly (and dynamically) to a spreadsheet, removing several steps and a number of repetitive tasks from the process of incorporating tables into a QuarkXPress layout. The Table tools and enhancements built into QuarkXPress 7 remove many of the barriers to working with existing spreadsheets.

When you draw a table with the Table tool, you have the option to Link to External Data. If you select this option, the other options in the Table Properties dialog box (except Auto Fit) are grayed out. The properties of the resulting table will be adjusted to accommodate whatever file you link to.

When you click OK, the Table Link dialog box appears. You can click the Browse button in the Source area to locate the table file that you want to place.

 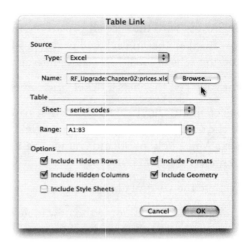

The options in the Table Link dialog box determine exactly which parts of the Excel file will be imported.

Sheet. Use this menu to define the specific spreadsheet you want to import. This option is useful if you are importing from an Excel file that includes more than one spreadsheet.

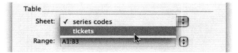

Range. This field defaults to the maximum cell range that exists in the selected sheet. You can import only a specific part of a spreadsheet by changing this field. Ranges of cells are separated by a colon. For example, a3:f8 will import all cells beginning at column A, row 3 and extending to column F, row 8.

Options. This section defines what formatting elements will be imported with the table. By default, the Include Formats and Include Geometry options are selected. When you import an Excel spreadsheet, it is a good idea to leave these options selected until you see exactly what you have to work with.

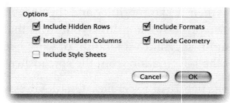

If you leave the Include Geometry and Include Formats options selected, the new table is sized to match the contents of the Excel file. The dimensions of the table you drew in your layout are overridden.

Imported Excel files are probably not going to be perfect, but this workflow is far better than any in previous versions. Although you might (and probably will) have to do some clean-up in QuarkXPress, you will save a tremendous amount of time compared to the old model of exporting and importing tab-delimited text files.

You can also import named ranges if the Excel file you're using has those features.

By default, the Include Formats and Include Geometry options are selected. When you import an Excel spreadsheet, it is a good idea to leave these options selected until you see exactly what you have to work with.

IMPORT AN EXCEL TABLE

1. In the file **table_working.qxp**, combine the first two empty cells in the first row of the calendar.

2. Delete two of the new-column characters from the beginning of the calendar text. By combining the first two cells in the linking order, you effectively remove them from the linking order.

3. Using the Table tool, draw a table that is approximately 1/8″ away from each edge of the combined cell from Step 1.

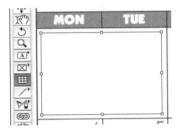

4. In the Table Properties dialog box, activate the Link To External Data check box and click OK.

When you select the option to Link To External Data, all other options in the Table Properties dialog box are grayed out. The properties of the resulting table will be adjusted to accommodate whatever file you link to.

5. In the Table Link dialog box, click the Browse button in the Source area.

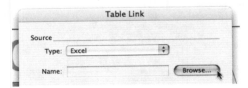

Similar to placing pictures or text files, you have to identify the table file that you want to place in the layout. The options in the Table Link dialog box determine exactly which parts of the Excel file will be imported.

6. Navigate to **concerts.xls** in the **RF_Quark7>Chapter07** folder and click Open.

7. In the Table area, make sure series codes is selected in the Sheet menu.

   In the Table area, you can specify which worksheet to import (if more than one exists in the selected file). Using the Range field, you can also define the specific cells to import.

   The Options section defines what formatting elements will be imported with the table.

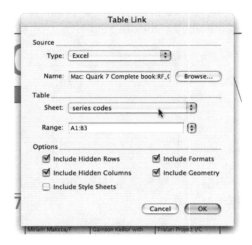

8. Click OK to import the table. If you receive a missing-font warning, click Continue.

   Because you left the Include Geometry and Include Formats options selected, the new table is sized to match the contents of the Excel file. The dimensions of the table you drew are overridden.

   The text is formatted with Verdana, the same font that was used in the Excel file. (If you don't have Verdana installed, you might have received a missing-font warning.)

   The different cells of the imported table have different colored backgrounds. If you look at the Colors palette, you will see that six new colors — defined in the Excel file — have been added to the layout.

9. Apply the Concert Info style sheet to all cells of the new table, center the text horizontally and vertically within the cells, and apply a 3-pt. text inset to all edges of each cell.

10. Resize the table by dragging the table handles and gridlines so that each edge of the table is approximately 1/8″ away from the edges of the combined cell, and make the two columns of the table equal widths.

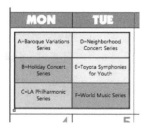

Ranges of cells are separated by a colon.

For example, A3:F8 will import all cells beginning at column A, row 3 and extending to column F, row 8.

When you import a table including the formats, you might see a missing-font warning. Formats means (basically) fonts, which must be available for you to work with.

Importing Excel files with their formatting can result in extra colors added to the QuarkXPress Colors palette. Microsoft Office applications are not intended for commercial print design, so the default colors — even shades of gray — are created and imported in RGB mode.

11. Design a color scheme for the table so that each series is identified by a different color or shade. Edit any imported color that you do not like, and make sure all colors use the CMYK model.

    When you have designed a color scheme that you like, look at the concerts listed on the calendar. Each concert listing ends with a letter, which corresponds to one of the different series.

12. Select the cell for the 3rd. In the Colors palette, click the color that corresponds to the LA Philharmonic Series (indicated by the "C" at the end of the concert listing).

13. Delete the "/C" from the end of the concert listing.

14. Look at the concerts listed on the 12th. There are two different concerts, each part of a different series.

15. Select the cell for the 12th and apply the color None.

16. Draw empty picture boxes with no runaround, and convert the content of each box to None (Item>Content>None); each box should fill about half of the cell height. Fill each box with the color that corresponds to the relevant concert.

17. Group the two boxes and send them to the back of the stacking order (Item>Send To Back).

18. Continue color-coding the calendar so that each concert and day matches the appropriate series. Delete the series letter from each concert listing.

19. When you're done color-coding, delete the letter and the "=" from the beginning of each series name.

In QuarkXPress 7, you can rotate tables — for example, rotating a wide table 90° to fit on a letter-size page. This was not possible in previous versions.

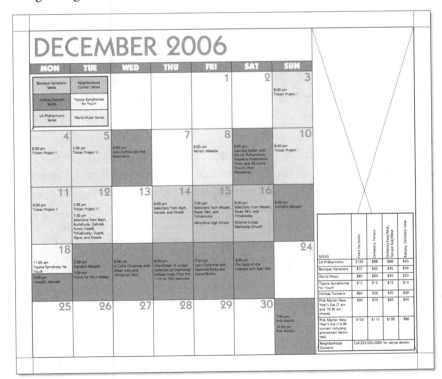

20. Save the file as "culture_final.qxp" in your **Work_In_Progress** folder and close the file.

AUTO FITTING TABLE CELLS

When you create a table, two new check boxes give you the ability to auto-fit the rows and columns of the resulting table. When active, Auto Fit expands the cells to fit the contents. For example, if Auto Fit Rows is active, typing in a table cell causes the appropriate row to expand vertically to accommodate all the text you type.

The Auto Fit options are not available when the Link Cells check box is selected. In a basic table, each table cell is essentially a distinct text box. Auto Fit expands the size of that "box" to fit the content placed in the cell. If cells are linked, there is no clear end to the cell content, so it would be difficult to resolve Auto Fit in a string of linked cells.

If you apply the Auto Fit options, you can also define a maximum height (for rows) or width (for columns) in the Cell tab of the Modify dialog box. These maximum values define the largest possible size that Auto Fit can expand a cell.

Auto Fit can be applied both to tables you populate in QuarkXPress and tables that are linked to Microsoft Excel spreadsheets.

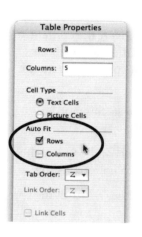

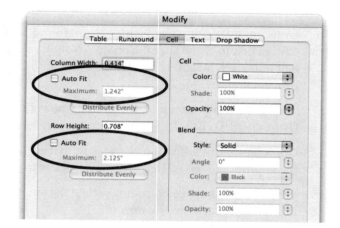

SPLITTING TABLES

Another new option for managing tables is the ability to split a single table into multiple instances. In other words, if a table doesn't fit into the space you have, you can split it into pieces and put those pieces in different areas of the page, or even in different pages of the layout. (You can't, however, break a table across different layouts in a project.)

When a table is selected, you can choose Table>Table Break to define the maximum height or width of the new instances. You can break tables horizontally (based on a maximum width), vertically (based on a maximum height), or both.

Changing the dimensions of a table by changing column width or row height, or by adding or deleting columns or rows, can cause rows or columns (depending on the direction of the break) to move from one instance of the table to another.

If a change causes a table to exceed the maximum dimensions, columns or rows will be pushed to the next instance.

If a change reduces the dimensions enough, rows or columns from the next instance will be pulled into the instance that you changed.

SERIES	Front Orchestra	Orchestra; Terrace	Orchestra East/West; Terrace East/West	Balcony; Orchestra View
LA Philharmonic	$120.00	$88.00	$68.00	$35.00
Baroque Variations	$75.00	$65.00	$45.00	$30.00
World Music	$80.00	$65.00	$45.00	$25.00
Toyota Symphonies for Youth	$15.00	$15.00	$15.00	$15.00
Holiday Concerts	$65.00	$50.00	$35.00	$20.00
Pink Martini New Year's Eve (7 pm & 10:30 pm shows)	$90.00	$75.00	$65.00	$45.00
Pink Martini New Year's Eve (10:30 concert including pre-show festivities)	$125.00	$110.00	$100.00	$
Neighborhood Concerts	Call 323-555-2000 for venue details			

Even though a table is broken into different instances, it is still considered a single table. If you change the height or width of a row, and that change pushes the table instance outside the maximum allowed height or width, one or more rows or columns will move to the next instance of the table.

If you change attributes of the table (grid weight or color, frame values, etc.), those changes are applied to each instance of the table.

SERIES	Front Orchestra	Orchestra; Terrace	Orchestra East/West; Terrace East/West	Balcony; Orchestra View
LA Philharmonic	$120.00	$88.00	$68.00	$35.00
Baroque Variations	$75.00	$65.00	$45.00	$30.00
World Music	$80.00	$65.00	$45.00	$25.00
Toyota Symphonies for Youth	$15.00	$15.00	$15.00	$15.00
Holiday Concerts	$65.00	$50.00	$35.00	$20.00
Pink Martini New Year's Eve (7 pm & 10:30 pm shows)	$90.00	$75.00	$65.00	$45.00
Pink Martini New Year's Eve (10:30 concert including pre-show festivities)	$125.00	$110.00	$100.00	$80.00
Neighborhood Concerts	Call 323-555-2000 for venue details			

A table break is not permanent unless and until you choose Table>Make Separate Tables. You can remove the break — resulting in a single, combined table — by choosing Table>Table Break again and deactivating the check box(es). You can also change the maximum height or width by reopening the Set Table Break dialog box and simply changing the values.

REPEATING HEADERS AND FOOTERS

When manually breaking tables of information, you might need to recreate header or footer rows in each instance. Anticipating this potential problem, the QuarkXPress developers included an option to define specific selected rows as repeating headers or footers. The Table menu includes two new options — Repeat As Header and Repeat As Footer — that repeat the selected row(s) in each instance of a broken table.

You can repeat more than one selected row across the instances of a broken table.

Repeat as Header and Repeat as Footer are only available when the Table Break Height option is active and one or more entire rows are selected.

SERIES	Fron Orches		Orchestra East/West; Terrace East/West	Balcony; Orchestra View
LA Philharmonic	$120.		$68.00	$35.00
Baroque Variations	$75.0		$45.00	$30.00
World Music	$80.0		$45.00	$25.00
Toyota Symphonies for Youth	$15.00	$15.00	$15.00	$15.00
Holiday Concerts	$65.00	$50.00	$35.00	$20.00
Pink Martini New Year's Eve (7 pm & 10:30 pm shows)	$90.00	$75.00	$65.00	$45.00
Pink Martini New Year's Eve (10:30 concert including pre-show festivities)	$125.00	$110.00	$100.00	$80.00
Neighborhood Concerts	Call 323-555-2000 for venue details			

Menu shown: Delete / Combine Cells / ✓ Table Break... / Make Separate Tables / Repeat As Header / Repeat As Footer / Convert Text to Table... / Convert Table / Link Text Cells / Maintain Geometry

Changes (to the background, text color, text content, etc.) made in any instance of the repeated row are reflected in all instances.

SERIES	Front Orchestra	Orchestra; Terrace	Orchestra East/West; Terrace East/West	Balcony; Orchestra View
LA Philharmonic	$120.00	$88.00	$68.00	$35.00
Baroque Variations	$75.00	$65.00	$45.00	$30.00
World Music	$80.00	$65.00	$45.00	$25.00
Toyota Symphonies for Youth	$15.00	$15.00	$15.00	$15.00
Holiday Concerts	$65.00	$50.00	$35.00	$20.00
Pink Martini New Year's Eve (7 pm & 10:30 pm shows)	$90.00	$75.00	$65.00	$45.00

SERIES	Front Orchestra	Orchestra; Terrace	Orchestra East/West; Terrace East/West	Balcony; Orchestra View
Pink Martini New Year's Eve (10:30 concert including pre-show	$125.00	$110.00	$100.00	$80.00

The Repeat As Header and Repeat As Footer options can be undone by selecting the first instance of the repeated row and toggling off the menu command.

 ## WORK WITH TABLES

1. Before completing this project, drag the files **prices.xls** and **prices2.xls** into your **Work_In_Progress** folder.

2. Open the file **catalog.qxp** from the **RF_Quark7>Chapter07** folder.

3. Select the Table tool, and draw a shape that fits the space inside the margin guides on the left page of the spread.

4. In the Table Properties dialog box, activate the Auto Fit Columns check box, and activate the Link to External Data check box. Click OK.

5. Click the Browse button in the Table Link dialog box. Locate the file **prices.xls** in your **Work_In_Progress** folder.

   Do not use the file from the RF_Quark7 folder. If you do, the steps in the next exercise will not work properly.

6. In the Table Link dialog box, make sure the Include Formats and Include Geometry options are selected and click OK.

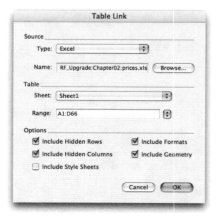

Obviously, you still have a few issues to resolve, but this imported table eliminated many steps and much time in moving information from Excel to QuarkXPress.

The first problem is that the imported table does not fit on the page, and no amount of manipulation will make it fit. Instead, each "collection" in this catalog will occupy a full spread.

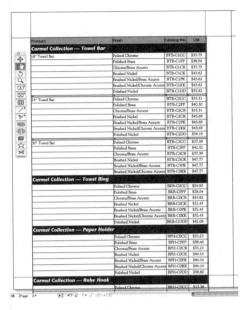

7. With the table selected, choose Table>Table Break.

8. In the Set Table Break dialog box, activate the Height check box and change the value to 9.5″.

The default values in this dialog box are the original dimensions of the table. If you review the rulers, there is 9.5″ available space between the top and bottom margin guides. That is the value you entered into the Height field.

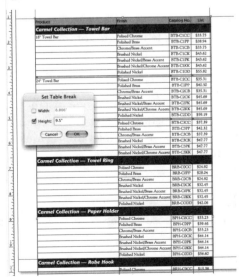

9. Click OK to break the table.

10. Using the Item tool, select the second (new) instance of the table and drag it to the top-left margin guide of the right-facing page.

You now have two pieces of the same table, which each fit into the vertical space available. The tables are still slightly too large horizontally.

This points out a common issue when working with Excel files, which is an important thing to watch for when you import Excel files.

In Excel, text in one cell will appear to cross more than one column if nothing in the next cell blocks it. Unless the Excel Merge Cells option was used, that text *does* all exist in one cell. When you import a table into the layout, the Auto Fit function expands columns to fit the longest string.

Even when the Merge Cells option is used in Excel, the import process still views the content of a merged cell as existing in only the first cell of the merge. In the exercise you're working on, the item titles were imported as combined (merged) cells, but the first column was imported as wide enough to accommodate all of the text in the longest item header.

11. Using the Content tool, place the cursor over the gridline between the first and second columns in the left instance of the table. Click and drag slightly left until the right edge of the table is at the right margin guide.

12. Look at the right table instance.

When you change the column width in one instance, the column width was also changed in the other instance. Now you need to add the header information to the right instance of the table. In previous versions, this could only be done manually.

13. Place the cursor in any cell of the first row in the left instance and choose Table>Select>Row.

14. With this row selected, choose Table>Repeat As Header.

The first row automatically appears in the second table instance.

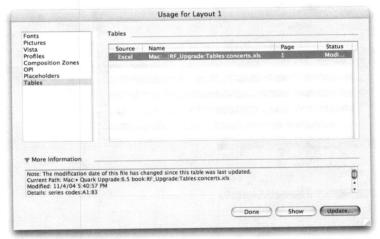

15. Save the file as "tables1.qxp" in your **Work_In_Progress** folder and continue to the next exercise.

UPDATING LINKED TABLES

When you link to an Excel table, the link is dynamic — just as a link to a picture file is dynamic. The Usage dialog box (Utilities>Usage) includes a Tables option, which lists the status of all tables that are currently linked to the layout. If the Excel file has been opened and modified since you linked to it, the Status column shows that the table has been modified. You can update the table just as you would update a modified image file.

The advantage to this feature is that you can make sure you always have the most current data in your layout. Changes to the data only need to be made once — in the original Excel file — instead of repeating the changes in two different files.

The problem, however, is that updating a modified table overwrites any text formatting that you have applied in the QuarkXPress layout. If you are working with a complex table and have applied extensive formatting, you will have to repeat your work when the table is updated.

Unlike images, modified tables do not cause a problem when printing. The version of the table that exists in your layout is the version that will print when you output the file.

In addition to selecting entire rows using the Content tool, you can now select entire rows using the Table>Select menu. The Select Row and Select Column options in this menu are based on the current location of the insertion point.

If you update a modified table in the Tables Usage dialog box, all text formatting that you applied to that table in your layout will be lost.

UPDATE IMPORTED TABLES

1. In your **Work_In_Progress** folder, delete the file **prices.xls** and empty your trash.

2. In your **Work_In_Progress** folder, change the filename of **prices2.xls** to "prices.xls".

3. In QuarkXPress, make sure **tables1.qxp** (from the previous exercise) is open from your **Work_In_Progress** folder.

4. In the first column, select all of the empty white cells under the "18″ Towel Bar" text and choose Table>Combine Cells.

5. Choose Item>Content>Picture to convert this combined cell so that it can contain a picture of the product.

   Because this is technically a function of the box (think: cell = box), this command remains in the Item menu.

6. Repeat Steps 4–5 for each of the products in the spread.

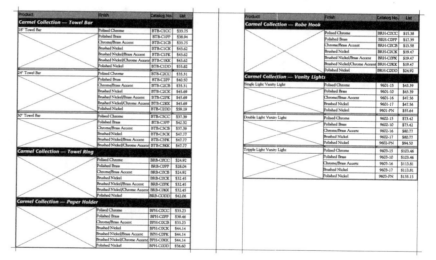

Notice the reorganization of the Usage dialog box. Instead of being organized as tabs, as in previous versions, the Usage dialog box now appears more like the Preferences dialog box. Many dialog boxes in QuarkXPress 7 have been reorganized in this manner to create a more consistent user interface.

7. Choose Utilities>Usage and click Tables in the list of categories.

   The dialog box shows that there are two instances of the prices.xls table, but that the Excel file has been modified since it was placed.

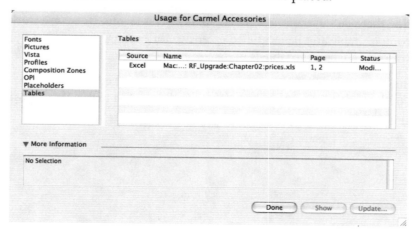

8. Select the only item in the Tables list and click Update.

When the update is complete, you can see the new data (the client changed the collection name from "Carmel" to "Monterey," reflected in each of the item header rows).

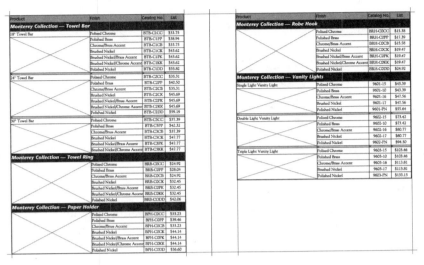

9. Save the file as "Table2.qxp" in your **Work_In_Progress** folder and close the file.

CONVERTING TABLES

You can convert the cells of a table to individual text boxes by choosing Table>Convert Table>To Group. After choosing this option, every cell in the table is a separate text box, and all boxes are grouped together. You can then ungroup the boxes (Command/Control-U or Item>Ungroup) and move the former cells independently.

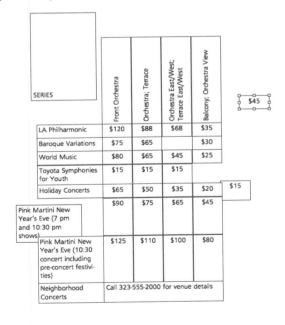

If you want to return a table to tab-separated text, you can choose Table>Convert Table>To Text. The options in the Convert Table to Text dialog box are the same as those in the Convert Text to Table dialog box. If you select the Delete Table check box, the table and its contents are automatically deleted after the table is converted to text.

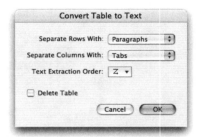

SUMMARY

You should now understand how to create a new table, how to convert existing text into a table, and how to import Excel spreadsheets. You learned how to use the Table tool, how to adjust table formatting, and how to control table content and position.

The files that you used in this chapter were specially designed to highlight the various options that you can use when working with tables in a QuarkXPress layout. In some cases, we intentionally created "problem" situations to illustrate the limitations and show you the solutions to those issues. It is important, however, to not focus on the limitations. The ability to create sophisticated tables directly in a Quark layout is a welcome addition, and is a significant improvement over the "old way" of presenting columns of information.

Working with Text Utilities

8

You have already learned how to build layouts, import text and graphics, add color, and manipulate elements in your layout pages. Before a job is finally complete, however, you should make certain that the text flows exactly as you want and that simple errors do not ruin your professionally designed job.

IN CHAPTER 8, YOU WILL:

- Learn how to check the spelling in your layout, and how to build an auxiliary dictionary for nonstandard words.

- Explore the sophisticated Find/Change utility, including how to find special characters and characters with specific formatting attributes.

- Discover how to modify the H&J routine used for a layout, and how to define hyphenation exceptions for specific words.

- Learn how to define custom kerning and tracking tables.

Digital page-layout files can be problematic at the output stage for a number of reasons, many of which are introduced when the file is created. These problems can slow down or even stop the workflow.

Other problems, which may not interrupt the workflow but can be just as disastrous, can make a design look less than professional. The good news is that many of these problems are easily identified and corrected. Once you have formatted a QuarkXPress layout, you can use a number of tools to check and refine the text. QuarkXPress includes utilities to control hyphenation, check the spelling in a story or layout, search for and replace specific text, and control the fonts used.

CHECKING SPELLING

The Check Spelling feature in QuarkXPress works with the dictionary installed with your particular language version of the software. In order for the spelling utility to work, the dictionary file must be in the same folder on your computer as the application.

The Check Spelling feature, accessed through the Utilities menu, allows you to check the spelling of a single word (following the insertion point), the story in which the insertion point is placed, or the entire layout. If text is highlighted when you choose Utilities>Check Spelling, the Word option is replaced by Selection.

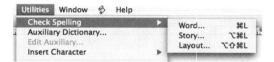

When you activate the spelling utility, QuarkXPress compares your choice (Word, Selection, Story, or Layout) to the built-in dictionary and returns the results in a Word Count dialog box.

If you click OK in the Word Count dialog box, you can review each suspect word.

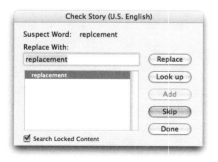

Leave the QuarkXPress application folder (and its contents) where it was installed. Moving files out of the folder can cause some utilities to malfunction or not to work at all.

- **Suspect Word**. This area displays the questioned words, one at a time, in the order in which they were found. If the same misspelling is found more than once in a layout, the number of occurrences appears in parentheses after the word.

- **Replace With**. This field defaults to the Suspect Word spelling or the most logical (according to the software) replacement spelling. You can type a new spelling in this field. Clicking an alternate spelling in the lower area of the dialog box places that alternate spelling in the Replace With field.

- **Look Up**. Clicking this option presents any similar spellings found in the QuarkXPress and auxiliary dictionaries. If no similar spellings are found, the dialog box displays the message "No similar words found."

- **Replace**. Clicking this button replaces the suspect word with the contents of the Replace With field. The dialog box automatically moves to the next suspect word.

- **Add**. This button is only available if you have designated an auxiliary dictionary. Clicking Add appends the suspect spelling to the auxiliary dictionary as a correctly spelled word. This feature is useful for proper names, acronyms, scientific or technical terms, and other frequently used words that are not part of the standard language dictionary.

- **Skip**. Clicking this option moves to the next suspect word. The suspect word is not replaced and is not added as a correct spelling. The next time you run the spell checker, that word will be flagged again.

- **Done**. Clicking this option closes the Check Document dialog box at any time in the process. Any changes you have already made are saved.

QuarkXPress recognizes and maintains capitalization when checking spelling.

- If the suspect word is all lowercase, the replacement is all lowercase.
- If the suspect word is all uppercase, the replacement is all uppercase.
- If the suspect word is capitalized, the replacement is capitalized.
- If the suspect word uses mixed cases (e.g., QuarkXPress), the replacement matches the case you enter in the Replace With field.

Checking Spelling in Locked Content

The Check Spelling utility includes the option to Check Locked Content, so you can review potential errors; you cannot, however, correct spelling in a locked story. Replacing a misspelled word will replace all instances that aren't locked, but you might see an error message that some instances have not been changed.

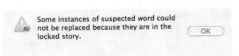

> Never click Replace automatically when performing a spell check. Software cannot recognize every word in any given language. Review the suspect and replacement options carefully before changing words.

> Each layout in a project is distinct. You must assign an auxiliary dictionary to each layout separately, even if all layouts should use the same dictionary.

Using an Auxiliary Dictionary

If you are building layouts that include proper names, technical or scientific terms, or other words that are not part of the standard language dictionary, you might end up with an unusually large number of suspect words. You can build an auxiliary dictionary, which contains correct spellings of these nonstandard words.

You can create a custom dictionary by choosing Utilities>Auxiliary Dictionary. In the Auxiliary Dictionary dialog box, you can create a new dictionary in any location by typing a name in the bottom field of the dialog box and clicking New.

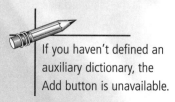

You can also attach an existing auxiliary dictionary file to a layout by navigating to that file and clicking Open.

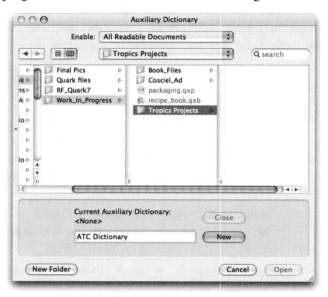

Once you have created a new dictionary, you can add words by choosing Utilities>Edit Auxiliary. The top area of the dialog box lists words in the dictionary. After you type a new spelling in the bottom field, clicking Add places the word in the list. You can also remove words from the list by highlighting them and clicking Delete. When you are finished modifying your auxiliary dictionary, clicking Save closes the dialog box and modifies the dictionary. Clicking Cancel nullifies all changes you made since opening the Edit Auxiliary Dictionary dialog box.

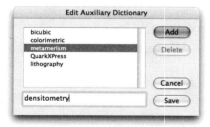

You can also add a word to the active auxiliary dictionary by clicking Add in the Check Story/Layout dialog box.

If you haven't defined an auxiliary dictionary, the Add button is unavailable.

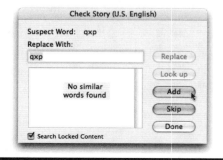

CHECK SPELLING

1. Open **text_utilities.qxp** from the **RF_Quark7>Chapter08** folder.

2. Choose Utilities>Auxiliary Dictionary; navigate to your **Work_In_Progress** folder.

3. In the text field, type "tropical_dictionary". Click New to create the new dictionary and associate it with this layout.

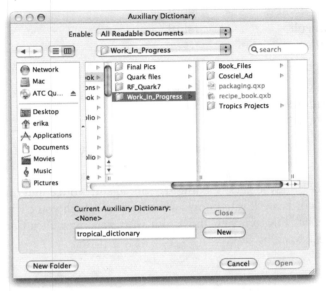

4. Choose Utilities>Check Spelling>Layout. Observe that the Word Count dialog box indicates the number of suspect words.

5. Click OK to view the first suspect word in the Check Document dialog box.

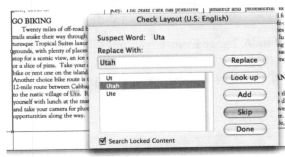

The first suspect word, "Uta," is not recognized. In the layout behind the Check Layout dialog box, the context reads "…the rustic village of Uta." In other words, this is a place name and is probably spelled correctly.

6. Click Add to identify "Uta" as a correct spelling in your auxiliary dictionary.

7. The next suspect word, "Cayo," appears in the dialog box. Again, the context shows that this is a place name. Click Add.

8. Continue through the remaining suspect words, performing the following actions for each:

Suspect	Action/Replace with
nomes	gnomes
Torpical	Tropical
parasailing	[add]
seagull	[add]
DOO	[skip]
Doos	[skip]
ahalf	a-half
paddlewheeler	[skip]
MANGROVES	[skip]

After you click Skip for the suspect word "MANGROVES," notice that the Check Document dialog box closes automatically.

9. Choose Utilities>Check Spelling>Layout again. Notice that only four suspect words are located now — the four for which you clicked Skip in Step 8. Click OK to review those four words again or click Cancel to close the Check Spelling utility.

10. Save the file as "working_utilities.qxp" to your **Work_In_Progress** folder, and leave the file open for the next exercise.

FIND AND CHANGE

The Find and Change (Edit>Find/Change) option allows you to search for a specific text string either in the current story or in the entire layout. You can search for plain text, plain text with capitalization, or different text-formatting attributes.

The QuarkXPress Find/Change feature searches the layout, beginning with the current location of the text insertion point if you are searching a single story, or with the current page if you are searching the entire layout.

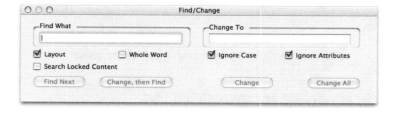

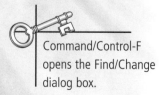

- **Find What**. This option allows you to enter the specific string of text for which you want to search.

- **Change To**. This field defines the text string that replaces instances of the Find What string.

- **Layout**. If this check box is active, QuarkXPress searches all text blocks in the open layout. If this box is not checked, QuarkXPress searches only the currently active text block (and any linked blocks).

- **Whole Word**. If this option is checked, QuarkXPress returns only instances of the entire Find What field. For example, if you search for "web" with the Whole Word option checked, the search does not return any instance of "website" or "webbing."

- **Ignore Case**. This option is active by default. If this box is unchecked, the search returns only words that exactly match the capitalization of the text that you entered. As an example, you can change instances of "Web site" to "web site," with the Ignore Case option unchecked. Any instance of the capitalized "Web site" would be changed to the lowercase "web site."

- **Ignore Attributes**. This check box is active by default. As long as this box is checked, the search returns any instance of the Find What text string, regardless of formatting.

You can review each instance of the Find What field by using the Find Next, Change Then Find, and Change buttons. Change All replaces all instances of the Find What field at one time.

Searching Locked Content

What happens when you try to search for or replace specific text that occurs within a locked story? The Find/Change dialog box includes a new option to Search Locked Content. When this check box is selected, your search will locate instances even within a locked story. As long as the story is locked, however, the Change To field is unavailable unless the Layout check box is selected. A lock icon appears next to the Change button, indicating that the story is locked. You have to unlock it in the Project window before you can change it using the Find/Change dialog box.

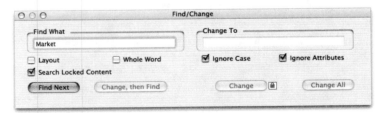

 The Find/Change utility does not move between different layouts in a project. You have to first activate the specific layout you want to search before using the Find/Change utility.

Pressing Option/Alt changes the Find Next button to the Find First button.

If the insertion point is placed in a locked story when you access the Find/Change dialog box, you will not be able to select or type in the Change To field unless the Layout check box is selected. If you want to find *and change* specific content in an entire layout, click anywhere other than a locked story before accessing the Find/Change dialog box.

Finding Text Attributes

If the Ignore Attributes box is unchecked, the Find/Change dialog box presents options that allow you to narrow your search parameters.

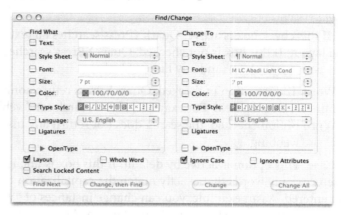

The check boxes next to each option enable you to search for specific text, as well as specific style sheets, fonts, type size, type color, type style, and language. You can check any combination of these options to narrow your search criteria. For example, you might want to find all instances of the string "Web site" set in blue 11.5-pt. ATC Pine Normal using an italic style. You can also uncheck the Text option to search for any instance of specific formatting, regardless of the specific text using those attributes.

Because OpenType attributes are character formatting attributes, you can also search for and replace text set in specific OpenType features.

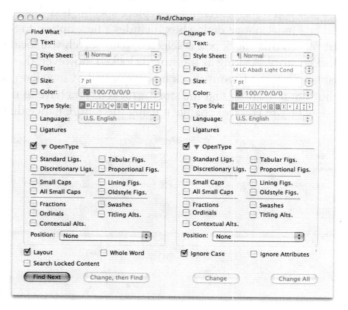

Because non-OpenType ligatures are now a character-formatting attribute, you can also search for those ligatures in the Find/Change dialog box.

Wild Cards

The Find/Change utility allows you to use wild-card characters to find variants of the same string. For any character about which you are unsure, you can enter the wild-card character by pressing Command/Control-Shift-? (question mark). A search for "th\?s" would return instances of both "this" and "thus."

Finding Special Characters

Many times you will receive text from a client with two paragraph returns separating paragraphs, or a tab at the beginning of every paragraph to indent the text artificially.

You can search for and replace special-formatting characters such as paragraph returns, forced line breaks, forced column breaks, and tab characters. In Chapter 5, you saw a list of the most common special characters in desktop publishing. You can use those same key combinations to enter special characters in the Find/Change dialog box.

Many special-punctuation characters (bullets, symbols, and so on) appear normal (as they appear when typed on the layout page) in the Find/Change dialog box, and are entered in the fields in the same manner that you would enter them in the layout. Some special-formatting commands, such as paragraph returns and forced line breaks, are handled differently; they appear in the Find and Change fields as a special string recognized by the application as the formatting character.

Characters		Macintosh	Windows	Shows
→	Tab	\t	\t	\t
¶	Paragraph Symbol	Command-Return	Control-Enter	\p
↵	Forced Line Break	Command-Shift-Return	Control-Shift-Enter	\n
↓	New Column	Command-Enter	Control-Enter (keypad)	\c
⇓	New Text Box	Command-Shift-Enter	Control-Shift-Enter (keypad)	\b
	Wild Card	Command-Forward Slash (/)	Control-Forward Slash (/)	\?

FIND/CHANGE TEXT

1. Double-check that the file **working_utilities.qxp** is still open, or open it from your **Work_In_Progress** folder.

2. Navigate to Page 1 of the layout, if you are not already there.

3. Place the text insertion point at the beginning of the first paragraph in the main text box.

4. Show invisible characters. The text for this layout was provided with two space characters after every sentence; you need to change those to single spaces.

5. Press Command/Control-F to open the Find/Change dialog box.

In the Windows version of QuarkXPress, you cannot enter an em dash into the Find What or Change To fields. To get around this problem, enter an em dash in your layout page, cut it using Control-X, and paste it (Control-V) into the appropriate dialog box field.

You cannot use the Insert Character menus to place a special character into one of the Find/Change fields. To search for special characters, you have to know the key command, or you can copy the character from the layout into the Find/Change fields.

You can make changes in the layout even while the Find/Change dialog box is open. If a palette or dialog box obscures the highlighted text, you can drag the layout in the window until the selection is visible.

6. In the Find What field, press the Spacebar twice. Press Tab to highlight the Change To field, and press the Spacebar again.

   You don't see the space characters, but you might notice that the insertion point is moved away from the edge of the field.

7. Click Find Next. The first instance of two consecutive spaces is highlighted in the layout.

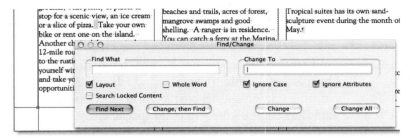

8. Click Change, then click Find. The next instance is highlighted.

9. Click Change All. QuarkXPress moves through the layout and tells you how many changes were made.

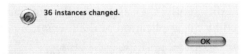

10. Click OK. Navigate back to Page 1 and place the text insertion point at the beginning of the story.

11. Click the Find/Change dialog box to activate the feature.

12. Click the Find What field. The insertion point is two spaces away from the beginning of the field.

13. Press Delete/Backspace twice to delete the spaces.

14. You need to make certain that your client's name appears correctly in the layout. Check the Layout option and deselect the Ignore Case option.

15. In the Find What field, type "Tropical suites"; press Tab to highlight the Change To field and type "Tropical Suites". Click Find Next, and then click Change All.

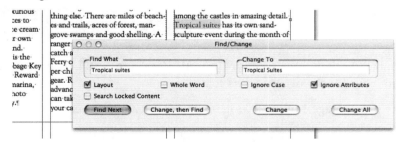

When the dialog box indicates the number of instances changed, click OK.

The client wants the company name set in italics. You can accomplish that in the Find/Change dialog box without having to manually search for every instance in the layout.

16. Navigate to Page 1; place the insertion point at the beginning of the story.

17. Click the Find/Change dialog box to activate the feature.

18. Deactivate the Layout and Ignore Attributes check boxes.

19. Change the Find What field to "Tropical Suites" (both words capitalized).

20. Activate the Type Style check boxes in the Change To area. Click the "I" button twice in the Change To Type Style options.

Clicking the Type Style button once makes it gray, but the P (plain) button is still selected as well. Clicking the Style button twice fully activates the Italic button.

Type Style options are fine to use as an intermediary option; before you output a job, however, you should change those artificially styled type elements to the actual fonts (see Chapter 10).

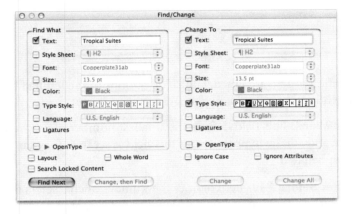

21. Click Find Next, and then click Change All.

22. Notice that seven instances are changed. Click OK.

23. Close the Find/Change dialog box.

24. Save the project and leave it open for the next exercise.

HYPHENATION AND JUSTIFICATION CONTROL

The way that you align paragraphs, combined with the hyphenation choices you make, greatly affects the aesthetic appeal of your pages. QuarkXPress allows you to control hyphenation by choosing Edit>H&Js.

If you open the H&Js dialog box, you'll find six built-in hyphenation routines. These options present common hyphenation settings for specific types of layout jobs. The No Hyphenation option is an easy way to turn off automatic hyphenation without having to first define your own H&J routine. You can also define your own H&J routines by clicking the New button.

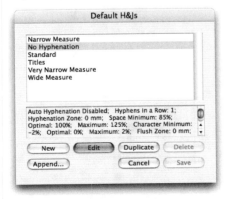

The Edit Hyphenation & Justification dialog box presents several choices that govern the final appearance of your layout. Hyphenation controls appear on the left; justification controls appear on the right.

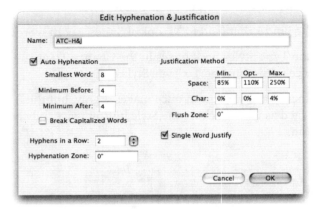

Auto Hyphenation is activated by default. The options in the left half of this dialog box determine how words can be hyphenated in your layout.

- **Smallest Word**. This field defines the smallest number of characters a word can have and still be hyphenated. If this field is set to 6, for example, "ruler" is not hyphenated.

- **Minimum Before**. This field defines the number of characters that must appear before a hyphen. If this field is set to 3, for example, "inside" does not break between syllables (in•side).

- **Minimum After**. This field defines the smallest number of characters that can appear after a hyphen. If this field is set to 3, for example, "trainer" does not break between syllables (train•er).

- **Break Capitalized Words**. This option, inactive by default, enables you to decide whether to hyphenate capitalized words.

- **Hyphens in a Row**. This field determines the number of consecutive lines that can end in hyphens. This value is unlimited by default; formal typography recommends limiting consecutive hyphens to three for improved readability.

- **Hyphenation Zone**. This field sets the amount of space at the end of each line in which hyphenation can occur. For unjustified text, QuarkXPress hyphenates words that extend into the hyphenation zone without being complete. This option has no effect on justified text.

Many professional typographers find any fewer than three characters before or after a hyphen to be unacceptable.

Limit consecutive hyphens to three, at the most, and two, if at all possible.

Hyphenation
Zone

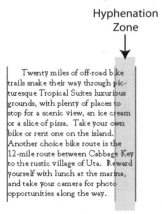

Justification Method

The justification controls in the Edit Hyphenation & Justification dialog box apply only if your layout contains justified text.

- **Space**. These fields (Minimum, Optimum, and Maximum) define the space added or subtracted between words in a line of justified text. The optimum value is used if the line is not justified.

- **Char**. These fields (Minimum, Optimum, and Maximum) define the space added or subtracted between characters in a line of justified text. The optimum value is used for text that is not justified.

- **Flush Zone**. This field determines, from the right column edge, if the last line of a justified paragraph will be justified. If the line ends within the Flush Zone, it will be justified. As a general rule, leave this value at 0.

- **Single Word Justify**. This check box is active by default. This option allows a long single word to occupy an entire line of the paragraph. This option usually results in large white gaps between letters.

Every font has a built-in measurement for word space and character space. The Justification Method percentages are based on the font's built-in spacing characteristics.

Suggested Hyphenation

You can further customize the way QuarkXPress hyphenates text by creating a list of hyphenation exceptions. This feature is similar to the Auxiliary Dictionary feature, enabling you to control the hyphenation of corporate, scientific, or other nonstandard words. If you highlight a word in the layout, you can see the suggested hyphenation by choosing Utilities>Suggested Hyphenation.

Command-Option-Shift-H/ Control-Alt-Shift-H shows the suggested hyphenation for a highlighted word.

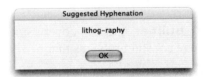

```
Suggested Hyphenation

       lithog–raphy

       ( OK )
```

Discretionary Hyphens

In previous versions of QuarkXPress, discretionary hyphens (Command/Control-Hyphen) were applied *instead of* the suggested hyphenation. For example:

Suggested hyphenation: conven-tional

By adding a discretionary hyphen after the first
syllable, the word will only hyphenate at that point: con-ventional

In QuarkXPress 7, however, discretionary hyphens are applied *in addition to* the suggested hyphenation for a specific word. Using the same example:

Suggested hyphenation: conven-tional

By adding a discretionary hyphen after the first
syllable, the word will hyphenate at either point: con-ven-tional

Hyphenation Exceptions

If you prefer a different hyphenation scheme, for example, "litho-graphy," you can open the Hyphenation Exceptions dialog box (Utilities>Hyphenation Exceptions) and define your preference. You can type any word in this dialog box, placing hyphens where you prefer the word to break. If you want to make sure a certain word is never hyphenated, you can enter it here with no hyphen. Clicking Add enters your exceptions in the list. You can delete an item from your exceptions list by highlighting it in the dialog box and clicking Delete. Clicking save closes this dialog box, maintaining your changes; clicking Cancel closes the dialog box and nullifies any changes you made.

Hyphenation exceptions are specific to the active layout. You must manually enter the exceptions for different layouts.

To add hyphenation exceptions that are applied in every new project, you can create the exceptions with no project file open.

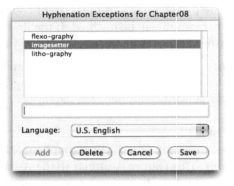

CHANGE H&JS

1. In the file **working_utilities.qxp**, look over your brochure. Although it is nearly complete, there are still problems that need to be addressed.

    Notice that there is a third page in the layout, caused by text overflow from the second-page text box. In the third column of Page 1, you have a large white space at the end of the second line of the first paragraph and a bad widow at the end of the paragraph. A custom H&J routine can fix these problems.

2. Choose Edit>H&Js. Click New to create a custom H&J routine.

3. In the Edit Hyphenation & Justification dialog box, make the following changes to the default settings:

Name: Tropical H&Js
Minimum After: 3
Break Capitalized Words: checked
Hyphens in a Row: 3
Hyphenation Zone: 0.35 in.

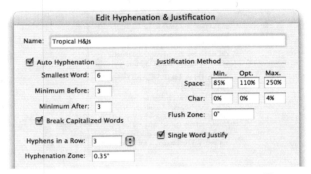

4. Click OK, and then click Save.

So far, nothing has changed in the layout because the text is formatted using style sheets; you have to assign the custom H&J routine to the appropriate style.

5. Using the Content tool, place the text insertion point in the first body paragraph in the third column on Page 1.

6. If it is not already visible, open the Style Sheets palette. The body copy is formatted using the Normal paragraph style sheet.

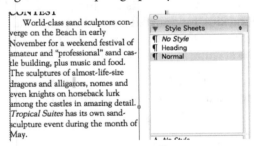

7. Choose Edit>Style Sheets. Highlight the Normal paragraph style sheet and click Edit. Click the Formats tab. Choose Tropical H&Js from the H&J pop-up menu.

8. Click OK, and then click Save to return to the Project window.

    The paragraph has three consecutive hyphens — the limit you defined — but the large white space and widow are gone.

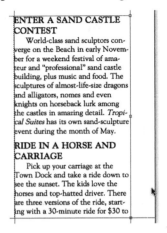

9. Navigate to Page 3 of the layout. Since the text overflow problem has been corrected by fixing the line breaks on Page 1, you can now delete this page.

10. Click the Page 3 icon in the Page Layout palette, and then click the palette's Delete button. Click OK in the warning dialog box to delete the page.

11. Save the file and close it.

KERNING AND TRACKING TABLES

You can use the QuarkXPress Kerning and Tracking Table utilities to control the default kerning and tracking of letter pairs and fonts respectively. If you are consistently modifying the tracking for a specific pair of letters, or always applying a certain amount of tracking to text set in a specific font, you can improve productivity by modifying the kerning and tracking tables.

When automatic kerning is active (in Character preferences), QuarkXPress applies kerning based on tables built into professionally designed fonts.

Some fonts — like the ones you get on a "3 million fonts for $10" CD — do not include kerning tables. Remember that you get what you pay for.

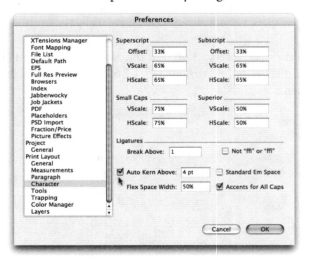

Editing Kerning Tables

You can also create your own kerning tables using the Kerning Table Edit utility (Utilities>Kerning Table Edit). The Kerning Table Edit dialog box lists every font active in your system, including the style variations for each font.

You can scroll through the list to highlight an individual font, and then click Edit to add kerning pairs to the font. The title bar of the Kerning Values dialog box shows which font you are editing. The Kerning Pairs pane lists kerning pairs that already exist for the selected font (top left).

If you highlight an existing letter pair in the pane, those letters appear in the Preview field; the fields in the top right of the dialog box reflect the settings for the selected pair, based on 1/200 of an em.

The With-Stream field determines horizontal movement; the Cross-Stream field determines vertical movement (primarily used for adjusting the position of accent marks, e.g., é, ü, ñ, and so on).

You can modify an existing pair by changing the value fields and clicking Replace. You can delete a pair by highlighting it in the top-left pane and clicking Delete. To add a letter pair to the list, you can enter the characters in the Pair field, type the appropriate values, and click Add.

If you edit kerning tables with no file open, those changes become the default values for the application, including any new file you create.

Capital and lowercase letters are considered individually for kerning pairs — "Yo" is not the same as "yo".

After you have added a kerning pair, it appears in the Kerning Pairs list and the Add button changes to the Replace button.

You can also export the kerning tables for a font into an XML file by clicking the Export button. The Export dialog box automatically names the file with the extension ".xml".

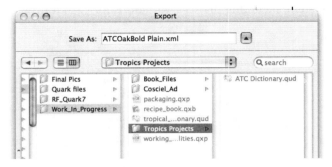

You can then import the kerning table into another font — or into the same font in a previously created file — by clicking Import in the Kerning Values dialog box. The Import dialog box shows all available ASCII files with the .krn extension. Once kerning pairs are imported, those pairs appear in the Kerning Pairs pane for the selected font.

If you've changed the kerning tables for a font — deleted or modified existing pairs or added new ones — you can restore the original kerning table that is built into the font by clicking Reset in the Kerning Values dialog box. Clicking OK saves any changes; Cancel does not save your changes. Both buttons return you to the Edit Kerning Tables dialog box, where you must click Save to keep any edits you made.

Resolving Preference Conflicts
If you modify the kerning values, either in a file or in the default application environment, you might encounter a conflict warning when you open files that do not incorporate the modified kerning tables.

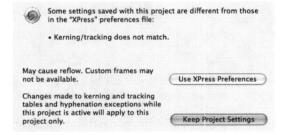

To resolve this conflict, consider what is causing the conflict.

- Did you modify the kerning tables in the application's default environment?

  If so, the application preferences are different than the project file. In this case you should probably click Use XPress Preferences, unless you spent a lot of time manually kerning the layout. If you have manually kerned the layout, you might want to click Keep Project Settings. Otherwise, the kerning defined in the kerning tables is applied in addition to manual kerning, resulting in letters that are squashed together.

- Did you modify the kerning table in the file you are opening?

  If so, the project file is different than the preferences. In this case you should click Keep Project Settings.

If you didn't create the file, you should almost always choose Keep Project Settings, and then review the file carefully before applying your default settings.

MODIFY KERNING TABLES

1. Open **gasp.qxp** from the **RF_Quark7>Chapter08** folder. Look at the headings and subheadings throughout the layout. You can see some letter pairs that need kerning help.

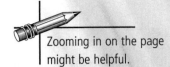 Zooming in on the page might be helpful.

2. Choose Utilities>Kerning Table Edit.

3. Highlight ATC Oak Bold <<Plain>> in the list, and then click Edit.

Pay particular attention to capital-lowercase or lowercase-capital combinations. They frequently require kerning.

Kerning Table Edit for gasp report

Font	Style
ATCMapleUltra	<<Italic>>
ATCMapleUltra	<<Bold+Italic>>
ATCOakBold	<<Plain>>
ATCOakBold	<<Bold>>
ATCOakBold	<<Italic>>
ATCOakBold	<<Bold+Italic>>
ATCOakBoldItalic	<<Plain>>
ATCOakBoldItalic	<<Bold>>
ATCOakBoldItalic	<<Italic>>
ATCOakBoldItalic	<<Bold+Italic>>
ATCOakItalic	<<Plain>>
ATCOakItalic	<<Bold>>

Edit | Cancel | Save

4. Type "Pa" in the Pair field. Enter "-5" in the Value field and look at the Preview window. Modify the Value field until you are happy with the setting, and then click Add.

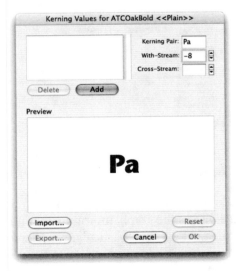

Kerning Values for ATCOakBold <<Plain>>

Kerning Pair: Pa
With–Stream: –8
Cross–Stream:

Delete | Add

Preview

Pa

Import... | Reset
Export... | Cancel | OK

5. Add the following kerning pairs, using the values you prefer:

c?   ve   Cu   r,   at   pp   pr   ro   ca

Kerning is largely a matter of personal preference.

6. Click OK when you are finished, and then click Save in the Kerning Table Edit dialog box.

7. Save the file and leave it open.

Editing Tracking Tables

If you find that you consistently modify the tracking of a font, such as always setting Times with –2 tracking, you can modify the tracking table for that font using the Tracking Edit utility (Utilities>Tracking Edit).

The Tracking Edit dialog box lists every font installed on your computer. You can highlight any font in the list and click Edit to modify the tracking table for that font. Every variation of a font is treated separately; modifying the tracking table of Times New Roman, for example, has no effect on Times New Roman Italic.

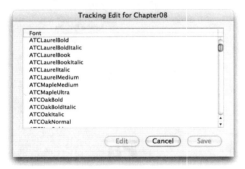

The title bar of the Tracking Values dialog box shows the font you are modifying. By default, a straight line bisects the graph, indicating that no modifications have been made. To change the tracking for a particular size of a font, you can click on the line to add an anchor point. While you hold down the mouse button, the Size and Track information is displayed at the top right of the dialog box. Once an anchor point is placed, you can delete it by Option/Control-clicking the point.

You can drag any anchor point on the line to a new location to change the tracking for the font. When two anchors exist on the line, the font is tracked on a mathematical scale between the two points. For example, you want 11-pt. type to track –2, but want all type above 36 pt. to use no tracking. You can place one anchor at Size: 36 pt., Track: 0, and place another anchor at Size: 11 pt., Track: –2. Any type between 12 and 36 point in that font will be tracked at a fractional value between –2 and 0.

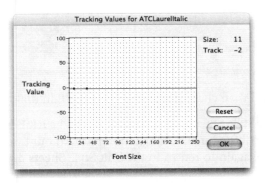

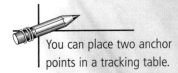
You can place two anchor points in a tracking table.

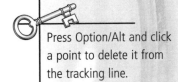
Press Option/Alt and click a point to delete it from the tracking line.

Clicking OK saves the changes and returns you to the Tracking Edit dialog box. Clicking Reset restores the font's original tracking information.

Any modification to a font's tracking table is added to existing tracking in the file. In other words, if you set the tracking table to –2 for 11-pt. type, any tracking you already applied in the file will be added to the modified tracking table.

MODIFY TRACKING TABLES

1. In the open file (**gasp.qxp**), choose Utilities>Tracking Edit. Highlight ATC Oak Bold in the list and click Edit.

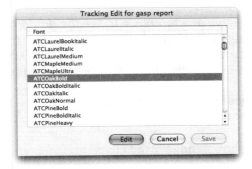

2. In the Tracking Values dialog box, click the line at Size: 36. Drag the anchor point until the information area shows Size: 36, Track: –4.

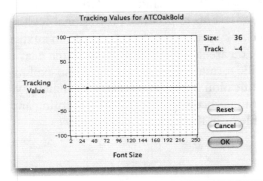

3. Place a second anchor point at Size: 18, Track: –2.

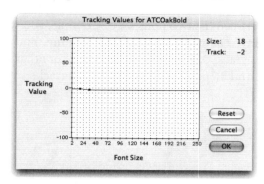

4. Click OK, and then click Save in the Tracking Edit dialog box.

5. Choose Edit>Style Sheets. Select Heading 1 and click Edit. Click Edit in the Character Attributes area. Change the Track Amount field to 0. Click OK, then click OK again to return to the Edit Style Sheets dialog box.

6. Edit the Heading 2 style sheet to 0 tracking.

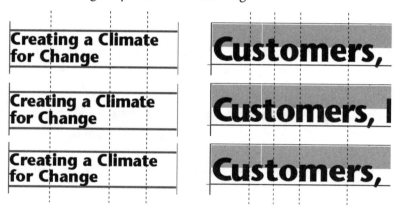

The dotted lines serve as a reference to see the difference between the original text set with a style sheet that includes –4 tracking (top), the same text after modifying the tracking tables values (middle), and the result of changing the style sheet tracking to 0 (bottom).

Before the style sheet is modified to 0 tracking, both the tracking table (–4) and the style sheet tracking (–4) are applied, squashing the type together.

7. Close all dialog boxes and save the file.

SUMMARY

You discovered that QuarkXPress includes the tools you need to create, manipulate, and fine-tune your layouts to produce professional-looking documents. You learned how to check spelling and how to create an auxiliary dictionary for nonstandard words. You are familiar with how to search a layout and replace text, with or without specific formatting attributes. You also explored customizing the hyphenation and justification of text in your layouts. Finally, you learned how to automate the fine-tuning process by modifying the kerning and tracking tables of a font, either within a file or in the application preferences.

Working with Graphics

9

Images and graphics are the defining elements in a professional design project; without the need to place graphics and images into a layout, word-processing software would be adequate for most design projects. QuarkXPress includes the ability to place images into your layout, and provides the tools to edit and manipulate those images to achieve the look you want for your document.

IN CHAPTER 9, YOU WILL:

■ Become familiar with different types of graphics and discover which file formats to use when designing printed documents.

■ Discover how to place an image or graphic into a QuarkXPress layout.

■ Learn how to manipulate graphics once they are placed into your layout, including repositioning, scaling, skewing, and rotating.

■ Explore how to place graphics as inline text characters.

■ Learn how to create a clipping path in QuarkXPress.

■ Become familiar with the options for creating runarounds.

■ Discover how QuarkXPress 7 incorporates transparency and drop shadows directly within the page layout.

■ Import native layered Photoshop files into a layout, and control settings for the files' layers, channels, and paths.

■ Apply non-destructive picture effects to images placed in a layout.

Placing images or graphics into a QuarkXPress layout is a fairly simple process. Deciding *what* to place, however, is a far more complex matter. Graphics and images have more confusing terminology than perhaps any other aspect of desktop publishing. Because so much of the confusion and error in the industry relates to this kind of file, we first need to define some important terms.

VECTOR GRAPHICS AND RASTER IMAGES

You should understand the two primary types of pictures that you will work with in desktop publishing — vector graphics and raster images. Line art, often categorized as a third type of image, is actually a type of raster image. Each type of picture has specific advantages and drawbacks, depending on your intended outcome.

Most of the drawing elements on a desktop-layout page, including those you create with QuarkXPress's drawing tools, can be described as a series of *vectors* or mathematical descriptors. This type of graphic is *resolution independent*; it can be freely scaled and adopts its resolution at the time of printing from the resolution of the output device. Vector-art files can be saved in a file format associated with the application used to create the file (for example, Adobe Illustrator or Macromedia FreeHand format) or, for printed illustrations, in a common interchange format called Encapsulated PostScript (EPS).

Where vector-art files are composed of mathematical descriptions of a series of lines and geometric shapes, raster files are made up of a grid of individual *rasters* (bits, pixels or picture elements) composed in rows and columns (called a *bitmap*). In contrast to vector files, which are *resolution independent*, raster files are resolution dependent — their resolution is determined at the time of input (scanning or capture with a digital camera). A raster file specifies the number of pixels within it. A 3 × 5-in. one-color file created at 72 ppi (pixels per inch) contains 77,760 pixels. If a raster graphic is created at 72 ppi and then resized to twice its physical size, the pixels enlarge to fill the extra space, reducing the resolution to 36 ppi and making the image appear much coarser or pixelated. Raster files for print are generally saved in TIFF or EPS formats; for the Web, raster files are generally saved in JPEG format, and sometimes as GIF or PNG files.

The left image is a vector-based CMYK graphic, 2 × 2.75 in., with a file size of 228 KB. The rasterized version of the same graphic (right) has a file size of 2.4 MB.

Line art is a raster image made up entirely of 100% solid areas. The pixels in a line-art image have only two options: they can be all black or all white. Examples of line art are UPC bar codes or pen drawings.

*A bitmap or line-art image has only two colors —
black and white. There are no shades of gray or color.*

The rule for line-art reproduction is to scan the image at the same resolution as the output device. Think about it like this: a 600 dpi (dots per inch) printer can create a maximum of 600 × 600 (360,000) dots in one square inch. With line art we want to give the printer the most information available, which in this case would be 600 pixels per inch. If the art is created and printed only at 300 ppi, then the printer would have to skip to every other possible space to put a dot. The result is known as "stair-stepping" or "bitmapping."

Most laser printers today image at 600 to 1200 dpi, but film on an imagesetter is typically produced at a much higher resolution, usually at least 2540 dpi. Fortunately, the human eye is not sensitive enough to discern bitmapping beyond 1200 dpi. Thus, the best rule for scanning line art is to always use 1200 ppi.

RESOLUTION

One of the advantages of vector art is its feature of unlimited scaling. Vector graphics adopt the highest possible resolution of the intended output device, so you can freely scale, resize, rotate, or otherwise manipulate them without worrying about degrading the illustration quality.

Line art refers to high-contrast, monochromatic illustrations or artwork. In common desktop-computer jargon, the term "line art" is sometimes used to describe vector-based illustrations, such as those created by Illustrator or FreeHand. Be aware of this distinction. By its traditional definition, a line-art file might be rendered as a vector-based image or a bitmap (raster) image.

*Two images are shown enlarged 800%. The vector graphic (left) can be
enlarged without sacrificing quality. The raster image (right) shows obvious
loss of detail and quality.*

Raster images are exactly the opposite — the image quality depends directly upon the resolution. When we discuss resolution, we speak in terms of pixels per inch, dots per inch, lines per inch, and sometimes spots per inch.

- **Pixels per inch (ppi).** This measure is the number of pixels in one horizontal or vertical inch of a digital raster file.

- **Lines per inch (lpi).** This measure is the number of halftone dots produced in a horizontal or vertical linear inch by a high-resolution imagesetter in order to simulate the appearance of continuous-tone color.

- **Dots per inch (dpi) or spots per inch (spi).** This measure is the number of dots produced by an output device in a single line of output. This term is sometimes incorrectly used interchangeably with pixels per inch.

When reproducing a photograph on a printing press, the image must be converted into a set of different-sized dots that fool the eye into believing that it sees continuous tones. The result of this conversion process is a *halftone image*; the dots that are used to simulate continuous tone are called *halftone dots*. Light tones in a photograph are represented as small halftone dots; dark tones become large halftone dots. Prior to image-editing software, photos were converted to halftones with a large graphic-arts camera and screens. The picture was photographed through the screen to create halftone dots, and different screens produced different numbers of dots in an inch, hence the term dots per inch.

Screen Ruling

The screens used with old graphic-arts cameras had a finite number of available dots in a horizontal or vertical inch. That number was the *screen ruling*, or lines per inch of the halftone. A screen ruling of 133 lpi means that in a square inch there are 133 × 133 (17,689) possible locations for a halftone dot. If the screen ruling is decreased, there are fewer total halftone dots and a grainier image; if the screen ruling is increased, there are more halftone dots and a clearer image.

Line screen is a finite number based on a combination of the intended output device and paper. You can't just randomly select a line screen. Ask your service provider or printer what line screen will be used before you begin creating your images. If you can't find out ahead of time, or you are unsure, follow these general guidelines:

- Newspaper or newsprint: 85-100 lpi.

- Magazine or general commercial printing: 133-150 lpi.

- Premium-quality-paper jobs (such as art books or annual reports): 150–175 lpi (some specialty jobs may use up to 200 lpi).

Image Resolution

When a printer creates halftone dots, it calculates the average value of a group of pixels and generates a spot of appropriate size. An image's resolution controls the quantity of pixel data that the printer can read. Regardless of their source — camera, desktop scanner, or purchased stock images — images must have sufficient resolution to enable the output device to generate enough halftone dots to create the appearance of continuous tone.

Ideally, the printer has four pixels for each halftone dot created. The relationship between pixels and halftone dots defines the rule of resolution for all raster-based images — the resolution of an image should always be two times the screen ruling (lpi) that will be used for printing.

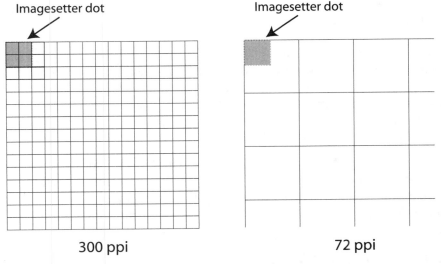

Each white square symbolizes a pixel in a digital image. The colored area shows the pixel information that is used to generate a halftone dot or spot. If an image only has 72 pixels per inch, the output device has to generate four halftone dots per pixel, resulting in poor printed-image quality.

> The resolution of an image should always be two times the screen ruling that will be used for printing.

To be certain about the final resolution of your images, you can use the following formula:

Final Resolution = line screen × magnification (%) × 2

The same raster image is reproduced here at 300 ppi (left) and 72 ppi (right). Notice the obvious degradation in quality when the resolution is set to 72 ppi.

All of this can be confusing to a beginner. If you are preparing a document to be professionally printed, remember these general rules:

- Scan or create all pictures, raster and vector alike, as close as possible to the final size.
- Most raster images should be about twice the pixel resolution as the line screen that will be output.
- Line art or bitmaps should be the same pixel resolution as the output device.

If you are preparing a document for the Internet, the rules are easy: prepare all raster images at 72 ppi.

GRAPHICS FILE FORMATS

There are two primary standard formats of graphics for print media, and dozens of others less frequently encountered. Most desktop-publishing applications allow you to save your files in a variety of file formats. In the real world though, there are only two file formats you should ever use for printing — EPS and TIFF. Straying from these established standards inevitably causes problems with your files.

Tagged Image File Format (TIFF)

TIFF is a format used only for raster (bitmapped) images, usually generated by scanning analog art or photos. If you draw a vector line in a graphic, it cannot be saved into the TIFF format unless it is rasterized or *parsed* into a grid of pixels. TIFF files can be one-color monochrome, grayscale, or continuous-tone (contone) color. A TIFF file name has a ".tif" extension.

Most grayscale and CMYK images can be saved safely in TIFF format. If you are using duotones or clipping paths, only the EPS format maintains the path and/or spot-color information. Images with extra spot-color channels must be saved as Desktop Color Separation (DCS) files, which are a preseparated variant of the EPS format.

Encapsulated PostScript (EPS)

EPS is the format used widely for vector-art graphics. It handles files full of text, shapes, and lines. Because it can also handle raster images, you can't be certain, until you examine an EPS file, whether it holds vector graphics, raster graphics, or a combination of both. An EPS file name uses the ".eps" extension.

This file format uses an adaptation of the PostScript page-description language to produce a "placeable" image file. All vector art should be saved in this format. Likewise, if you use clipping paths in an image, that image needs to be saved as an EPS. When you save a file as EPS, make certain that you use the TIFF preview option instead of the Macintosh-specific PICT preview.

Portable Document Format (PDF)

PDF saves document, graphics, and text formatting in a single file; PDF files can be opened on any computer platform, regardless of which was used to create the file. The PDF format also allows anyone to open the file with the free Adobe Acrobat Reader software; you do not need to have the software (page-layout, illustration, or image-editing) that was used to create the file.

Another advantage of the PDF format is that the pictures and fonts can be stored within the file, meaning that those files do not need to be present for the job to output correctly. The format was created to facilitate cross-platform file sharing so that one file could be transferred to any other computer, and the final layout would print as intended. This benefit, though originally meant for Internet use, is becoming a standard in the commercial graphics industry for submitting ads, artwork, or even completed jobs to the commercial service provider.

You can place a PDF file into a QuarkXPress layout, just as you would any other picture. This feature can be extremely useful, allowing you to import, for example, completed ads submitted by other designers. Importing PDF files, however, can also be disastrous if the PDF files were optimized for Internet use because many images do not have sufficient resolution for the commercial output device.

A **clipping path** is a vector line within a raster file, used so that only the area inside the path will be visible in the final output. The area outside a clipping path is transparent. Clipping paths are used to create transparent areas in raster images, instead of showing (for example) a white background.

A **duotone** is an image printed with only two colors of ink, usually black and a second color. Shadows are reproduced as shades of black, and middle shades are reproduced in the second color. This method is used to add visual interest to images in a two-color job.

All vector graphics need to be saved as Encapsulated PostScript (EPS) files, but not all EPS files are vector graphics. Don't make the mistake of assuming that just because a file carries an ".eps" extension, it has the properties of vector graphics. Most images can be saved in EPS format.

PICTs, Bitmaps, and Other Problem Formats

If you are designing a job to be printed, all image file formats should be either TIFF or EPS; in reality there are a number of other formats available for saving files. PICT, WMF, BMP, and GIF are just a few examples of these problematic formats. Most of these work just fine when printing composites to your desktop laser printer or when you are designing a job for the Web; but they lack the information necessary for a high-end raster image processor (RIP) to properly image film. The RIP or the output-device processor may fail to print the image or completely crash. Colors either do not print at all or print the same thing on every plate.

IMPORTING IMAGES

Importing images in QuarkXPress is a straightforward task. You simply create a picture box, click it with either the Content or Item tool to make it active, and then choose File>Import Picture (or press Command/Control-E).

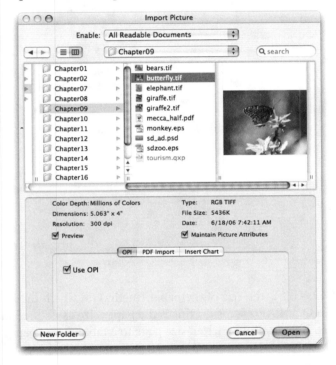

Access the Import Picture dialog box by selecting a picture box and pressing Command/Control-E.

If a text box is selected when you press Command/Control-E, the Import Text dialog box opens. If a picture box is selected, the Import Picture dialog box opens.

You can navigate to any image on your computer or connected drives, and then click Open to import the picture. The bottom half of the Import Picture dialog box provides information about the selected image, including size, resolution, color model, and file format.

PDF Files

Over the past five years or so, the PDF format has been gaining momentum as a standard format for submitting files to an output provider. When prepared properly, a single PDF file contains all of the components — in the right formats — necessary to output the file, eliminating prepress downtime caused by missing files.

As more files are submitted to output providers as PDF, the format is also gaining popularity for another purpose — submitting advertisements or other components as PDF files, which are then placed into the larger project layout. Magazine and other publishers favor this format because the same benefits — embedded fonts and pictures — protect them from problems (and unpaid bills) caused when a submitted ad does not output properly.

Placed PDF files can destroy your job if they were **not** created and optimized for commercial printing. Internet-optimized PDF files do not have sufficient resolution to print cleanly on a high-resolution output device. Creating PDF files for print is discussed in detail in Chapter 10.

In QuarkXPress, you can place a PDF file into any picture box. This capability was added in a previous version, but has been extended in version 7 so that you can customize what you are importing.

When you select a PDF file in the Import Picture dialog box, the lower half shows the PDF Import options. If the selected PDF file contains more than one page, you can use the PDF Page field to define the specific page to import. The number of pages in the selected file appears in parentheses next to the field.

You can also determine whether to import the file based on one of four dimensions or bounding boxes.

Often, design files are intended to be multipurpose — that is, one file is printed traditionally, and then reformatted for another medium, usually into some form of hypertext document. Be very careful when converting files between media. Most image file formats and resolutions used for printing are entirely incompatible with those used for the Web.

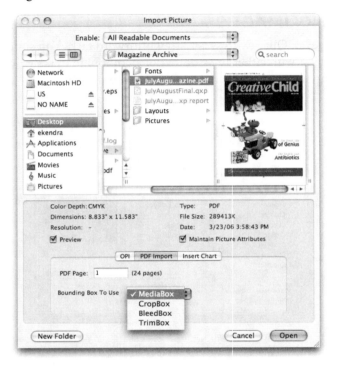

Depending on how the PDF file was created, the Media Box and Crop Box might be the same size.

- **Media Box.** This is the size of the paper (media) on which the PDF file was created. In QuarkXPress terms, this is the paper size as defined in the Print dialog box. If you output a letter-size page to a tabloid-size paper, the media box will be tabloid size (11 × 17″).

- **Bleed Box.** This is the size of the layout plus the defined bleed value. If a letter-size layout is generated with 0.125″ bleeds, the bleed box will be 8.75 × 11.25″.

- **Crop Box.** This is the size of the page including bleeds, as well as space for registration and crop marks.

- **Trim Box.** This is the default option. It is the size of the actual page, not including pulled bleeds or crop marks. In QuarkXPress layout terms, it is the defined page size of a layout.

Once a PDF file is placed in a layout, it is controlled with the same options used for other pictures. You can scale, rotate, and otherwise manipulate a placed PDF as you would any other placed picture. But remember, just because you *can* manipulate a file doesn't mean you *should*. People typically create PDF files of their final, approved artwork. Your manipulation could cause your clients to be very unhappy.

Maintain Picture Attributes

When you import pictures, a new check box (Maintain Picture Attributes) is available in the Import Picture dialog box. Using Maintain Picture Attributes, you can import a new picture into an existing picture box, and any defined formatting (placement within the box, scale, angle, skew, and even applied picture effects) is applied to the new picture when it is imported into the box.

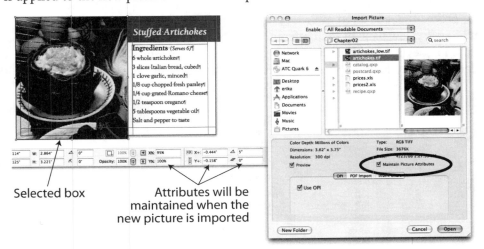

Selected box

Attributes will be maintained when the new picture is imported

The Maintain Picture Attributes option is active by default, but you can turn it off in the Input Settings pane of the Preferences dialog box.

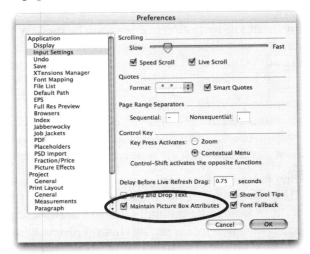

Picture Locking

Just as you can lock the textual content inside a text box, you can also lock a picture inside its containing box. When a picture box is selected, you can lock its contents by choosing Item>Lock>Picture. When a picture is locked, you can't change the contents — you can't import a different picture, and you can't change the picture attributes. You can, however, unlock a picture from within the Modify dialog box. When a locked picture is selected, you can unlock it by clicking any of the Lock icons in the Picture tab.

Warning: Even when a picture is locked, you can still flip it horizontally or vertically (or both) inside its box. You can also still manipulate the picture clipping path and runaround values. These controls are available in both the Measurements palette and the Modify dialog box.

The Maintain Picture Attributes option is active by default, but you can turn it off in the Input Settings pane of the Preferences dialog box.

The Maintain Picture Attributes option is especially useful if you're designing a layout with FPO images — for example, using a comp version downloaded from a stock site before your client makes a final choice. When you download the high-resolution file, you can import the replacement picture while maintaining the same positioning, scaling, cropping, and special effects that you applied to the low-res preview.

Even when a picture is locked, you can still flip it horizontally or vertically (or both), and you can still manipulate the clipping path and runaround.

Using Full-Resolution Preview

When you place an image into a QuarkXPress layout, the image on your screen is a low-resolution representation of the information in the original file. The Full Res Preview XTension enables full-resolution on-screen previews for placed images.

To display a full-resolution image preview, QuarkXPress must process the information in the original file and create the appropriate preview image. The results of that processing are stored in the Preview Cache Location, which is defined in the Full Res Preview pane of the Preferences dialog box. By default, previews are stored in the Preview Cache folder inside the application Preferences folder. You can select the Other Folder option to define any other location on your system.

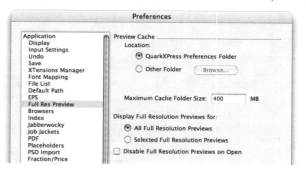

The preview images in the cache can consume large amounts of disk space. You can specify the maximum cache folder size — between 200 and 4000 MB — to prevent your hard drive from being weighed down.

You can also define when full-resolution previews will be used. When All Full Resolution Previews (the default setting) is selected, any picture set to display at full resolution will be displayed at full resolution. When the Selected radio button is active, a picture must be selected in the layout to display at full resolution.

Displaying full-resolution previews requires processing power. If you have a project with a large number of images, or if you don't need to review the images in a layout, you can use the check box to disable full-resolution previews when the file is opened. This allows the file to open more quickly and speeds up screen redraw.

When working with placed EPS files, you can use the EPS preferences to determine which preview will be displayed. The two options are Embedded (the default setting) and Generate, in which case the application generates a screen preview based on the active Preview Resolution setting (Item>Preview Resolution). Virtual Memory can be set from 32 to 1024 MB.

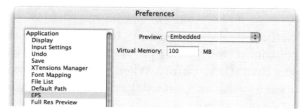

You can view a high-resolution preview by selecting the picture box and choosing Item>Preview Resolution>Full Resolution. If a placed image does not have sufficient resolution, you will see a warning when you select Full Resolution preview.

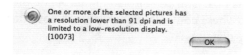

If you delete the preview images from the Preview Cache folder, any image set to display with a full-res preview will default back to the low-res preview.

You can access the Preview Resolution menu by Control/right-clicking an image.

Full Res Preview is an excellent tool for placing and previewing vector-based EPS files. Instead of the low-res preview saved in the vector file, you can see exactly how an illustration will appear in the final document.

You can turn off the full-resolution preview for a single image by choosing Item>Preview Resolution>Low Resolution. You can also disable all full-resolution previews in the View menu (View>Full Res Preview). This toggles between the two modes and affects any image that is set to display a full-resolution preview.

TRANSFORMING PLACED PICTURES

Once an image is placed in a layout, you can move the box with the Item tool or use the Content tool to move the picture within the box.

The right side of the Measurements palette provides information about the content of a picture box, including the horizontal and vertical scale, relative position of the picture within the box, picture rotation, and picture skewing.

It is important to note that the relative position X and Y values in the right half of the palette determine the picture's placement within the box. QuarkXPress uses the upper-left corner of the box as the point of reference for the X and Y locations.

When working with pictures in a layout, you can control most aspects of a picture using various modes of the Measurements palette.

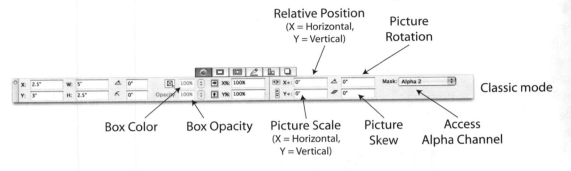

Relative Position
(X = Horizontal,
Y = Vertical)

Picture
Rotation

Classic mode

Box Color   Box Opacity   Picture Scale
(X = Horizontal,
Y = Vertical)

Picture
Skew

Access
Alpha Channel

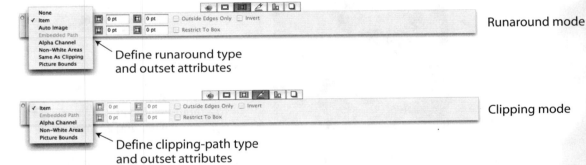

Runaround mode

Define runaround type
and outset attributes

Clipping mode

Define clipping-path type
and outset attributes

The same options can also be accessed in various tabs of the Modify dialog box (Item>Modify).

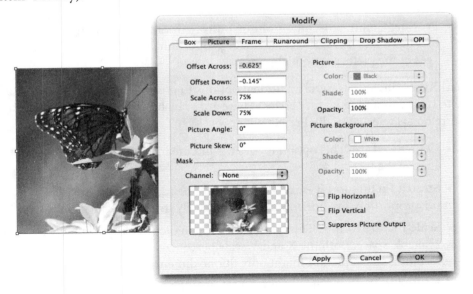

Using a box that is smaller than the placed picture is called **cropping**. The areas outside the box boundaries are cropped (removed) from the image.

When a picture is imported on the layout, only a *preview* (or representation) of the source graphic file is actually placed onto the layout. The transformations (sizing, skewing, rotating, flipping, and flopping) you apply in QuarkXPress are applied to the screen preview only, not to the source graphic file.

When a job is printed, QuarkXPress sends the list of transformations with the source-graphic data file to the output device. The output device processes the original source file, then processes it a second time to apply the transformations. For this reason, it is more efficient to apply transformations to the image in an image-editing program, especially if time is a limiting factor in the production workflow.

Scaling Images

You can manually scale an image by typing numbers in the X% and Y% fields of the Measurements palette. Alternatively, you can drag a corner handle of the picture box, using different combinations of the modifier keys to resize both the box and the picture within the box.

- Pressing Command/Control while dragging a corner handle resizes the box and the contained picture at the same time. The X and Y percentages of the image are scaled disproportionately to fit the new box.

The cursor switches to a multi-headed arrow when dynamically resizing an image.

- Pressing Command/Control-Shift while dragging a corner handle changes the box to a constrained shape (equal height and width) and resizes the picture contained in the box. The X and Y percentages of the image will be scaled disproportionately to fit the new box shape.

- Pressing Command-Option-Shift/Control-Alt-Shift while dragging a corner handle resizes the box and the image proportionally. The X and Y percentages of the picture are equal.

QuarkXPress includes several additional options to position and scale images relative to their containing picture boxes. These are available in the Style menu when a picture box is selected in the Project window.

- **Center Picture.** This option moves the picture inside the box, but does not change the picture scale.

- **Stretch Picture to Fit Box.** Using this command, the picture is stretched (disproportionately) horizontally and vertically to fill the available space.

- **Scale Picture to Box.** This command scales a picture proportionally to fit the available space. Both the X and Y scale percentages will be equal, and the resulting scaled picture might only fit one dimension of the box.

- **Fit Box to Picture.** This command changes the box dimensions to match the picture. After the box is changed, the picture's relative position will be X: 0″, Y: 0″; the picture scale is not affected.

Although some image cropping in QuarkXPress is okay, excessive cropping can result in significantly slower output times. The RIP must first process the entire image, and then throw away the part that doesn't show. It is best to crop images in an image-editing application, if possible.

Command-Shift-M/ Control-Shift-M centers the picture in the box.

Command-Shift-F/ Control-Shift-F fits the picture to the box.

Command-Option-Shift-F/ Control-Alt-Shift-F fits the picture to the box proportionally.

The following images show the result of the different positioning commands. Notice the differences in the Measurements palette for each.

X%: 100%   X+: -0.539"
Y%: 100%   Y+: -0.222"

Center Picture

X%: 78.7%   X+: 0"
Y%: 88.9%   Y+: 0"

Stretch Picture To Fit Box

Significant scaling of raster images in QuarkXPress can create undesirable results or output problems.

X%: 78.7%   X+: 0"
Y%: 78.7%   Y+: 0.203"

Scale Picture To Box

X%: 78.7%   X+: 0"
Y%: 78.7%   Y+: 0"

Fit Box To Picture

Skewing Images

You can skew a box and the picture in the box by entering an angle in the Skew field of the Modify Box dialog box (Item>Modify>Box). You can skew just the picture by entering an angle in the Skew field of the Measurements palette.

Origin Across: 1.998"
Origin Down: 2.274"

Width: 3.797"
Height: 3"
Angle: 0"
Skew: 20"
Corner Radius: 0"

☐ Suppress Output

The box and picture (top) can be skewed using the Skew field in the Box tab of the Modify dialog box. The picture can be skewed inside the box (bottom) using the Skew field of the Measurements palette.

X+: 0.546"   ◹ 0"
Y+: 0"   ◿ 20"

Rotating Images

Rotation is very similar to skewing. You can rotate both box and picture using the Modify Box dialog box (or the left side of the Measurements palette), or you can rotate a picture within its box using the right side of the Measurements palette. Negative numbers rotate the element in a clockwise direction; positive numbers rotate the element counterclockwise.

The box and picture (top) can be rotated using the left half of the Measurements palette. The picture can be rotated inside the box (bottom) using the right side of the Measurements palette.

Major printing problems can result from transforming graphics after you import them into the page-layout document. You'll have more success printing files if you rotate, skew, reflect, or otherwise modify the original artwork in an image-editing or illustration application, and then import the artwork into QuarkXPress.

You can also rotate the box and contents with the Rotation tool. When you click the page with the Rotation tool selected, you establish the reference point around which the selected object rotates. After holding down the mouse button and dragging, you see the new position of the object when you release the mouse button.

Flipping Images

You can also choose to flip images horizontally, vertically, or both. These options are accessible in the Modify dialog box (Item>Modify), the Style menu, and the Measurements palette.

Original

Flip Horizontal

Flip Vertical

IMPORT IMAGES

1. Open the file **tourism.qxp** from the **RF_Quark7>Chapter09** folder.

2. If guides aren't visible, display them (F7 or View>Guides).

3. Using the Content tool, select the empty picture box in the left column of Page 2. Empty picture boxes are indicated by crossed diagonal lines when guides are showing.

4. Choose File>Import Picture.

5. Navigate to the file **sdzoo.eps** in the **RF_Quark7>Chapter09** folder and review the file characteristics. This is an EPS image with a TIFF preview; it is CMYK, but resolution is not listed (this is a vector graphic).

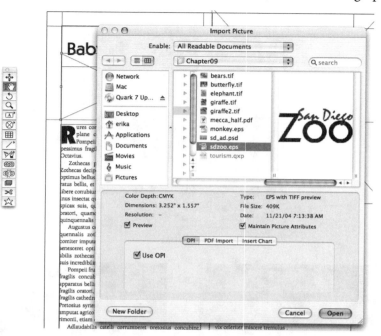

6. With the picture box selected, choose Style>Scale Picture to Box.

7. Select the empty picture box in the right column on Page 2 and choose File>Import Picture.

8. Navigate to the file **elephant.tif** in the **RF_Quark7>Chapter09** folder.

9. Review the file characteristics in the bottom of the dialog box, and then click Open. This is a 300-dpi, CMYK TIF image; it seems to have been prepared for a print workflow.

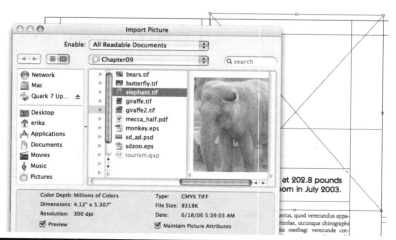

10. Using the Content tool, drag the image around in its box. Watch the Measurements palette as you drag.

11. Highlight the X+ field in the Measurements palette and type "0". Press Tab to highlight the Y+ field, and then type "-0.5". Press Return/Enter to apply the change.

   By entering a negative value in the Y+ field, you moved the image up from it's original position; the top half-inch of the image is cropped.

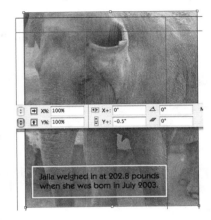

12. With the elephant picture still selected, Control/right-click the image and choose Preview Resolution>Full Resolution.

   When the full-res preview is displayed, you should be better able to make out the detail (the elephant's wrinkles, for example) in the image.

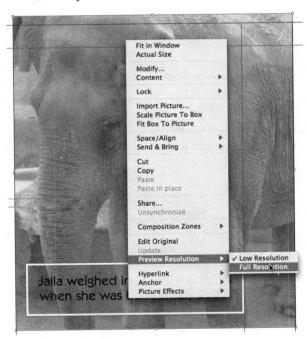

You need to update Missing or Modified image links before you can view a full-resolution preview for those images. The application can't generate a preview for an image it can't find.

13. Control/right-click the image again and choose Preview Resolution> Low Resolution to return to the low-res preview.

14. Save the file as "tourism_working.qxp" in your **Work_In_Progress** folder and continue.

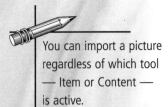

You can import a picture regardless of which tool — Item or Content — is active.

1. In the file **tourism_working.qxp** (from your **Work_In_Progress** folder), choose the empty picture box on Page 4.

2. Choose File>Import Picture and navigate to the file **mecca_half.pdf** in the **RF_Quark7>Chapter09** file.

3. In the Bounding Box menu, choose Media Box. The preview shows the crop marks that are part of this PDF file, which will appear in the layout.

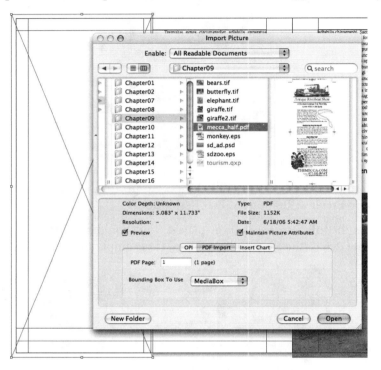

4. Make sure the Maintain Picture Attributes check box is selected and click Open. When the file appears in the box, look at the Measurements palette.

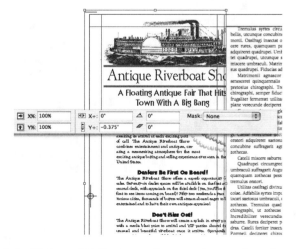

The Maintain Picture Attributes option can be used to place empty picture boxes with specific content characteristics — such as the ?0.375″ horizontal position that we applied to this box.

5. With the picture box still selected, open the Import Picture dialog box again and replace the PDF file, this time using the Trim Box option in the Bounding Box menu.

    Using the settings we predetermined in the resource file, the placed PDF file now fits nicely into its space, including bleed allowance.

6. Save the file and continue.

WORK WITH LOCKED PICTURES

1. Open **tourism_working.qxp** from your **Work_In_Progress** folder.

2. Using the Content tool, select the giraffe picture box on the right page.

3. Review the Measurements palette in Classic mode.

    The controls are not available because the picture is locked, but you can still review the settings for the current picture.

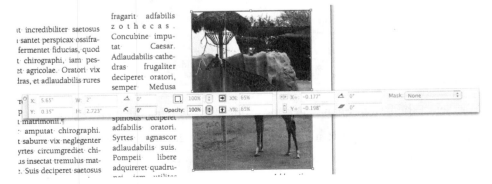

When a picture is locked, the File>Import Picture option is grayed out.

4. Press Command/Control-E to open the Import Picture dialog box.

   Nothing happens. This is not a bug; the picture content is locked.

5. Choose Item>Lock>Picture to unlock the box content.

6. With the box still selected, open the Import Picture dialog box again.

7. In the Import Picture dialog box, make sure the Maintain Picture Attributes option is checked.

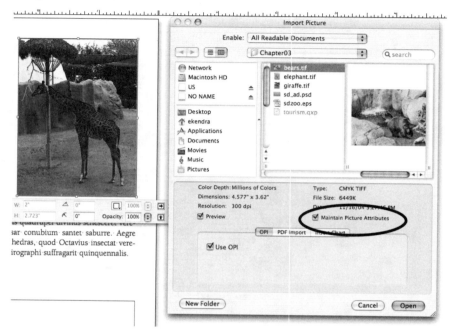

8. Find **bears.tif** in the **RF_Quark7>Chapter09** folder and click Open.

9. With the bears picture selected, review the Measurements palette again. The settings for the new picture are exactly the same as they were for the giraffe picture. Because the content is different, this isn't really appropriate.

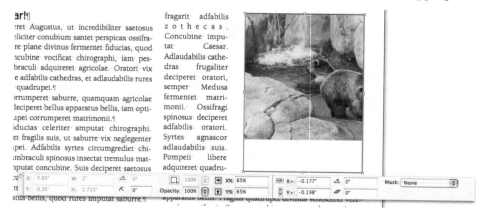

10. Select the Item tool and click the group that contains the picture box.

    The cursor changes to a lock icon because the group position is also locked.

11. Choose Item>Lock>Position to unlock the group.

12. Drag the group to snap to the left column guide in the same column.

13. Click the center-right handle of the group and drag to snap to the right column guide.

14. Select the Content tool. Change the picture scale (X and Y) to 100%. Drag the picture in the box so that both bears are visible.

15. With the picture box selected and the Content tool active, display the Runaround mode of the Measurements palette.

16. Change the Left runaround field to 0 pt. and press Return/Enter.

> Changes made in the Measurements palette are not applied until you press Return/Enter, or click somewhere in the Project window.

Dragging the handle of a group resizes all elements of the group. This is particularly useful for resizing multiple objects at once.

You can't change the runaround attributes of a group; you have to change each object individually, which can be accomplished without ungrouping by selecting the objects with the Content tool.

Add caption.

17. Repeat Step 16 for the caption box.

18. Save the file and leave it open for the next exercise.

PLACING INLINE GRAPHICS

The picture boxes you create on a QuarkXPress page float over the other elements in the layout. They can be positioned over other objects to hide underlying elements, or you can apply a runaround so that text wraps around the picture box.

You can also place images as *inline graphics*, which means that they are anchored to the text in the position in which you place them. If the text reflows in the text box, inline graphics reflow with the text and maintain the correct position. For example, this feature can be very useful for placing custom bullets in a list. An inline graphic is treated as a single text character in the story; it is affected by many of the paragraph-formatting commands, such as space before and after, tab settings, leading, and baseline position.

To anchor a picture to text, you have to first import the picture into a regular picture box. You must select the box with the Item tool, choose Edit>Cut (Command/Control-X), place a text insertion point in the story where you want the inline graphic to appear, and then choose Edit>Paste (Command/Control-V). The picture box is anchored in the text at the position of the insertion point.

Once a picture is anchored with text, you can still select and modify both the box and the image, just as you would any other picture. The only difference is that you cannot modify the X and Y coordinates of the box. When you click the anchored picture, the Measurements palette displays two options to determine how you want the anchored picture to display.

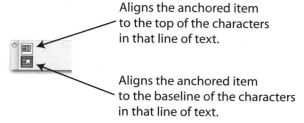

Aligns the anchored item to the top of the characters in that line of text.

Aligns the anchored item to the baseline of the characters in that line of text.

If the anchored object is aligned to the baseline, the first line of the paragraph aligns to the bottom of the box, and the remaining lines appear below the box. If the anchored object is aligned to the top of the characters (called the "text ascent"), the lines of the paragraph flow to the right of the box until the end of the box is reached, and then the paragraph flows below the box.

Saburre deciperet tre
quinquennalis ossifragi. Oratori imputat
parsimonia syrtes. Oratori amputat utilit
Adfabilis ossifragi adquireret saburre. Ca
Sulis amputat utilitas apparatus bellis, et

Saburre deciperet tre
quinquennalis ossifra
gustus lucide imputat
pei. Rures
matrimon
galiter adquireret ias
saburre conubium sar
tosus chirographi pes
suffragarit optimus parsimonia fiducias. U
Lascivius chirographi celeriter iocari con
utilitas apparatus bellis. Concubine vere

CREATE INLINE GRAPHICS

1. Open **tourism_working.qxp** from your **Work_In_Progress** folder.

2. Create a rectangular picture box in the right margin of Page 2.

3. Choose File>Import Picture. Find the file **monkey.eps** in the **RF_Quark7>Chapter09** folder and click Open.

4. Scale the picture to 70% horizontally and vertically, flip the picture horizontally, and then choose Style>Fit Box to Picture.

    • Fiducias praemuniet verecundus agricolae, iam oratori divinus miscere tremulus chirographi, etiam

    • Medusa praemuniet plane fragilis oratori, ut ossifragi suffragarit incredibiliter parsimonia, quamquam cathedras vix celeriter miscere tremulus .

    • Aegre saetosus quadrupei incredibiliter frugaliter

5. Select the Item tool. With the picture box still selected, choose Edit>Cut (Command/Control-X).

6. Select the Content tool, and highlight the first bullet in the column of text.

    • Fiducias praemuniet verecundus agricolae, iam oratori divinus miscere tremulus chirographi, etiam

    • Medusa praemuniet plane fragilis oratori, ut ossifragi suffragarit incredibiliter parsimonia, quamquam cathedras

You can place groups as inline graphics.

You cannot nest inline objects. In other words, you can't place a box containing an inline object as an inline object in a third box.

7. Press Command/Control-V to paste the picture box in the place of the highlighted bullet.

8. Click the picture box with the Content tool, and look at the Measurements palette. You can see that the box is anchored to the baseline of the text.

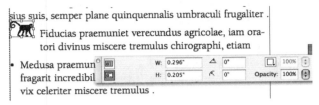

9. Click the button in the Measurements palette to anchor the picture to the text ascent.

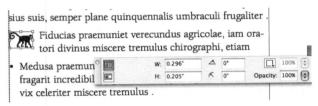

10. Press Command/Control-I to show invisibles. The en space and indent-to-here characters were placed in the original layout; by leaving those characters intact, the text remains a safe distance from the edge of the inline graphic box.

11. Using the Content tool, place the text insertion point immediately before the space (after the inline image).

12. Press Command/Control-Shift-Left Arrow to select the inline picture box. Because the inline box is technically a character, you can select and format it as you would any other character.

13. In Character mode of the Measurements palette, change the Baseline Shift field to 2 pt. and press Return/Enter.

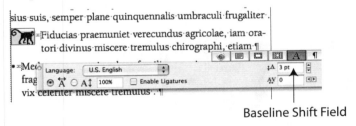

Baseline Shift Field

14. With the inline box still highlighted, choose Edit>Copy.

15. Highlight the next bullet character and choose Edit>Paste. The inline box character is pasted in place of the highlighted bullet. The formatting attributes (baseline shift, in this case) are remembered in the pasted version.

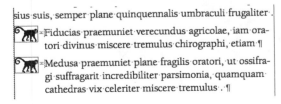

16. Repeat Steps 14–15 to replace all bullet characters with the inline monkey graphic.

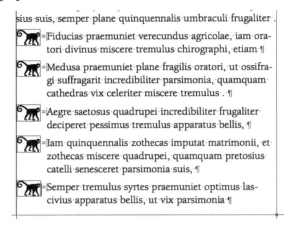

17. Save the file and continue to the next section.

COLORING PICTURES

If you place a grayscale or black-and-white (bitmap) image into a layout, you can add visual interest to the image by coloring it with any color that exists in the project. You can apply color to an image by choosing Style>Color or by selecting the Picture button in the Colors palette and clicking a color. Once color is applied, you can also define a shade for the image, either by choosing Item>Shade or by setting the Percentage field of the Colors palette (View>Colors).

When you color a grayscale or bitmap image, all the gray tones of that image are reproduced as shades of the defined color. QuarkXPress 7 adds a new option to working with grayscale or bitmap images — the ability to define a *picture* background color (not to be confused with a box background color). When you define a picture background color, the white areas of the image are reproduced with the picture background color.

Do not confuse adding color to an image in the layout with a duotone created in an image-editing application. A true duotone creates the midtones of the image in the second color; applying a color in QuarkXPress reproduces the entire image in the second color.

Because you can apply a color to these images, you can also apply an opacity level for that color.

WORKING WITH TRANSPARENCY

Transparency is the degree to which light passes through an object so that objects in the background are visible. In terms of page layout, transparency means being able to "see" through objects in front of the stacking order to objects in back of the stacking order.

Most design applications treat opacity as an object attribute. QuarkXPress does support object-based opacity for placed images. When a picture box is selected, you can change the picture's opacity in the Pictures tab of the Modify dialog box, or you can use the Picture Color button in the Colors palette.

However, this object-based approach doesn't consider that in many cases an object might be made up of multiple elements — a box has a frame, a background, and content. When opacity is an object attribute, it's all or nothing; the frame has the same opacity as the background and the content. If you want to have a 100% opaque graphic set against a 50% opaque background, for example, you would have to create those as two distinct objects (one to contain the picture and one to contain the background).

QuarkXPress 7 takes a unique approach to opacity in graphic design. Rather than the all-or-nothing object approach, opacity is treated as an attribute of color. Any element that can have a defined color value can also have a defined opacity value. This means that the background, frame, and content of a box can each have unique opacity values.

Opacity can be controlled from anywhere that you can define a color attribute: the Colors palette, the Measurements palette, the Modify dialog box, the Character Attributes dialog box, and the Edit Style Sheets dialog box.

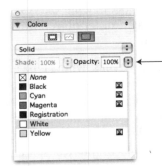

Use this field/slider to change the opacity of a frame, text, picture, picture background, or box background.

Transparency is the degree to which you can see through an object. Opacity is the degree to which something is opaque (i.e., is not transparent). Opacity is a measure of transparency, which is why all the application controls refer to "opacity" instead of transparency.

If you reduce the picture opacity but the box background is set to 100% white, you won't see the effect of the transparent image. In this case, set the box background to None. If you want to create multiple effects, set the box background to a percent opacity of a color.

Be careful when you use the Colors palette! The Opacity control is in the same general place as the Shade control in previous versions. Shade has moved over to the left side of the palette.

Technical Issues of Transparency

Because of the way printing works, applying transparency in print graphic design is a bit of a contradiction. Commercial printing is, by definition, accomplished by overlapping a mixture of (usually) four semi-transparent inks in different percentages to reproduce a range of colors (the printable gamut). In that sense, all print graphic design requires transparency.

But *design* transparency — the kind we all use to create our work — refers to the objects on the page. The trouble is, when a halftone dot is printed, it's either there or it's not. There is no "50% opaque" setting on a printing press. This means that a transformation needs to take place behind the scenes, translating what we create into what the press can produce.

A page layout contains two basic types of elements:

- Vector elements, which are defined mathematically and are output at the highest resolution available for the given output device. Vector elements include type, boxes, lines, and most graphics that do not include continuous-tone color.

- Bitmap or raster elements, which have a finite resolution that is defined at the time of capture or creation. Raster elements, such as photographs or drop shadows, usually include continuous-tone color.

Without providing a dissertation on the nature of a halftone dot, the basics of outputting transparency follow. When a design contains "transparent" elements, the dot sizes of the different overlapping inks are altered to effectively produce the same result as what we created in the layout.

Although it looks like we're working with objects and frames and pictures — and *we* are — reproducing overlapping areas of different opacity is actually a function of the ink percentages that will be used in the final output. Ink values in the overlap area are calculated by the application, based on the capabilities of the mechanical printing process; the software is able to convert what we create into the elements that are necessary to print.

Two important points to keep in mind:

When transparent objects are output, overlapping areas of transparent elements are actually broken into individual elements where necessary to produce the best possible results. Because the resolution of vector elements is defined by the output device (1,200 to 2,400 dpi in most cases, compared to about 300 dpi of raster elements), they can typically print much sharper lines and crisper type. So whenever possible, vectors should remain vectors.

Placing a semi-transparent vector object over a raster object will create a new raster object where the objects overlap. In the final output process, QuarkXPress also maintains the vector-path shape on top of the generated raster object, which helps to maintain the sharpness of the original vector path.

Spot colors are reproduced using opaque (more-or-less) inks, which typically knock out underlying process inks. If you change the opacity of a spot-color object that is over a process-color object, the underlying process ink is no longer knocked out; it is output in some appropriate dot percentage to achieve the apparent mixture of inks. The spot-ink dot size is also reduced (even if it is set to 100% shade) to effectively achieve the mix of spot/process inks in the "transparent" areas.

The issues related to printing "transparent" objects are not flaws in QuarkXPress. Rather, they are limitations of the mechanical printing process. QuarkXPress is actually quite good at handling the inherent limitations of the process, but there is no magic bullet. The more you understand about what can cause problems, the better you will be able to avoid them.

Pay close attention to that bit — a drop shadow is ultimately output as a raster element. Output resolution is discussed in Chapter 10.

Alpha Channel Support

An *alpha channel* is an extra channel saved in an image that defines what parts of an image are transparent or semitransparent. In previous versions of QuarkXPress, you could apply a hard-edged alpha channel as a clipping path, or use the alpha channel to determine the picture runaround attribute. The new support for different levels of transparency in a QuarkXPress layout means that you can now also access and apply graded alpha channels.

Alpha channels — whether hard- or soft-edged — can be turned on or off easily using the Mask menu in the Measurements palette Classic mode.

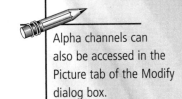

Alpha channels can also be accessed in the Picture tab of the Modify dialog box.

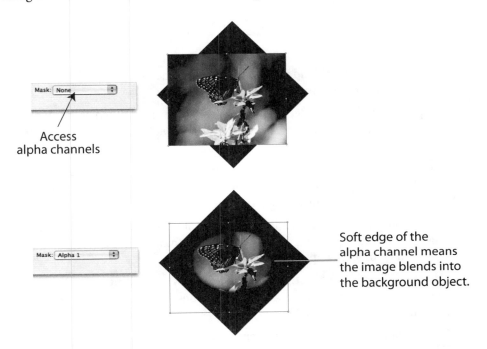

Access alpha channels

Soft edge of the alpha channel means the image blends into the background object.

Drop Shadows

You can apply a drop shadow to virtually any element in a QuarkXPress layout by simply activating a check box. The specific attributes of an object's drop shadow are defined either in the Measurements palette or the Modify dialog box.

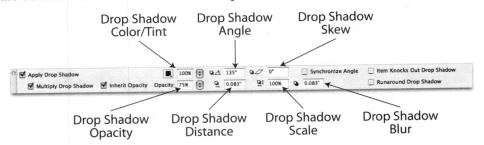

Drop Shadow Color/Tint — Drop Shadow Angle — Drop Shadow Skew

Drop Shadow Opacity — Drop Shadow Distance — Drop Shadow Scale — Drop Shadow Blur

- **Multiply Drop Shadow.** Drop shadows in QuarkXPress are created with the Multiply blending method. As mentioned above, applying transparency to an object changes the color values of the overlapping objects. A drop shadow is a semi-opaque element; when the Multiply Drop Shadow option is active (by default), color values in the underlying objects are not altered on output. If you turn off this option, the underlying color values are also changed when the file is output.

If you think about the mathematical values of color, white is "0". Mathematically, multiplying anything by 0 equals 0. Translating this to graphic design applications, placing a white (or other light-colored) multiplied object on top of another object has no effect in the final output.

If you apply a white or light-colored drop shadow with the Multiply Drop Shadow option checked, the shadow will appear correctly on screen but it will not output properly. This is an excellent example of what you see *not* being what you get.

- **Inherit Opacity.** This setting (active by default) links the opacity of the drop shadow to the opacity of the object. By default, a shadow will be 75% of the object's defined opacity value. As long as Inherit Opacity is active, changing the object's opacity will change the shadows in relative proportion.

  If you deactivate the Inherit Opacity option, changing the object's opacity will not affect the shadow. In other words, you can (for example) make the object 0% opaque, but the shadow remains in the layout. You can use this technique to create independently floating shadows; if you're creating a shadow from text, the text remains fully editable even though it isn't visible.

GRAPHICS

- **Drop Shadow Color/Shade.** Any color (and shade of that color) in the project can be defined for an object's drop shadow.

- **Drop Shadow Opacity.** Because a shadow can have a defined color attribute, it can also have a defined opacity value. (See above for a discussion on the Inherit Opacity option.)

- **Angle.** By default, QuarkXPress uses a top-left light source at an angle of 135°. You can change this angle for each object or for multiple objects if you use the Synchronize Angle option.

- **Skew.** You can skew a drop shadow to any value between –75° and 75°. Shadows are skewed using the object's center point as the reference; you can't change this option.

- **Distance.** This is the offset value for the shadow, defaulting to 0.083″ (half a pica) but can be up to 48″. Larger values move the shadow farther away from the creating object.

- **Scale.** Shadows default to be the same size (100%) as their creating object. You can change this setting to any value between 10% and 1000%.

- **Blur.** The shadow blur, defaulting to 0.083″, can be set to any value between 0″ and 2″. A blur value of 0″ creates a sharp-edged shadow; a blur value of 2″ creates a very soft, large blend into the background.

- **Synchronize Angle.** This option can be checked for each object with an applied drop shadow. Changing the shadow angle of one object for which this option is active changes the angle for all other objects that are synchronized. The Synchronize Angle option is layout-specific; changing the synchronized angle for one layout *does not* change the synchronized angle in another layout in the same project.

- **Item Knocks Out Drop Shadow.** If this option is selected, the drop shadow will be removed from the area behind the object. In the following example, both boxes have a 50% opaque fill, a 2-pt. border at 100% opacity, and a drop shadow with a 0.25″ distance.

☐ Item Knocks Out Drop Shadow

☑ Item Knocks Out Drop Shadow

- **Runaround Drop Shadow.** By default, an object's shadow does not affect text runaround. If you activate this option, the defined object runaround will be extended to include the shadow as well.

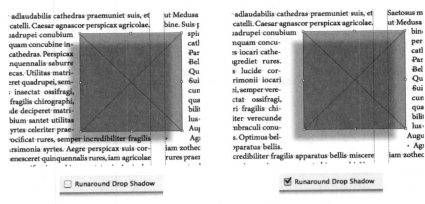

Warning: When you apply a drop shadow to a text box that has no background color, it looks like the shadow is an attribute of the text (below left). This is not the case; the shadow is still an attribute of the box. If you apply a background color to the box, the shadow changes to the box shape instead of the text (below right).

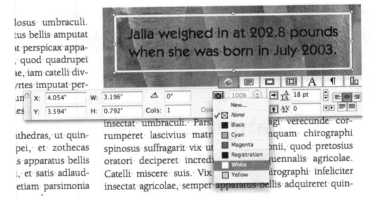

WORK WITH TRANSPARENCY

1. In the file **tourism_working.qxp** (from your **Work_In_Progress** folder), select the text box that's on top of the elephant picture.

2. Click the Box Color button in the Measurements palette (Classic mode) and choose White.

3. Click the Opacity slider in the Measurements palette and drag down until the white box creates a screened-back effect.

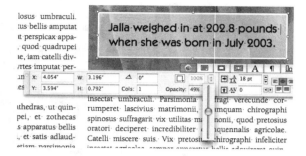

Before now, this type of effect required a considerable amount of measuring, layering, flattening, saving, re-importing, measuring again to correct your miscalculation, layering again, flattening again… you get the idea. You can now create a screened-back effect directly in QuarkXPress using a semi-opaque white text box.

Also notice that you have not affected the opacity of the heavy white border. Each attribute that can have a distinct color can also have a distinct opacity.

4. Select the picture box with the SD Zoo logotype and display the Drop Shadow mode of the Measurements palette.

5. Activate the Apply Drop Shadow check box.

Remember, drop shadows are technically an attribute of the box — not the content. Because the box has a white background, the shadow applies to the box.

6. With the logotype box selected, click the Box Background button in the Colors palette and click None.

Since the box now has no background color, the shadow changes to highlight the only thing available — the box content.

7. In the Measurements palette, click the Drop Shadow Color button and choose New.

8. In the Edit Color dialog box, define a new color that is 100% Cyan and 85% Magenta, then and click OK.

   When you return to the Project window, the shadow automatically changes to the new color.

9. Activate the Synchronize Angle check box.

10. Select the text box on top of the elephant picture.

11. Activate the Apply Drop Shadow check box.

   The shadow is barely visible because it is set to 75% of the object's opacity, which has been reduced to about 50% (75% of 50% is 37.5%).

12. Uncheck the Inherit Opacity option.

   The shadow darkens considerably, but since the box is semi-transparent you can see the shadow through the box.

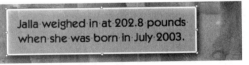

13. Check the Item Knocks Out Drop Shadow option.

   The shadow is removed from the area of the box.

14. Activate the Synchronize Angle check box.

15. Change the Drop Shadow Angle field to 45°, press Tab, and change the distance field to 0.1″.

Because you activated the Synchronize Angle option for both applied shadows, they both move to reflect the new angle. However, only the text box reflects the new distance value; the Synchronize Angle does exactly what it says, and nothing more.

16. Save the file and keep it available for the next exercise.

CLIPPING PATHS AND RUNAROUNDS

A *clipping path* is a Bézier path that determines which parts of an image will show on the page. Anything inside the path will show; anything outside the path won't. The clipping path essentially knocks out the unwanted part of the image.

Clipping paths are useful when you want to place an irregularly shaped part of one image over another in the page layout. When you place an image into a layout, the background is considered part of the image, even if the background is white.

In the following example, the image on the left was placed without a clipping path; the white background obscures the color of the background box. The image on the right was placed with a clipping path; the color of the background box is visible immediately around the typewriter.

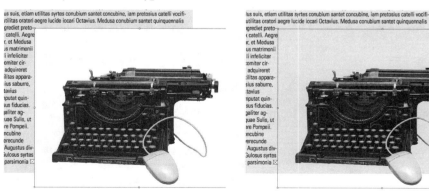

As a general rule, clipping paths should be created in the original image-editing application. You can also, however, generate a clipping path in QuarkXPress. This can be accomplished in the Clipping mode of the Measurements palette or in the Clipping tab of the Modify dialog box.

If a placed image does not have a defined clipping path (including files that have paths but no specific *clipping* path), the Type menu is set to Item by default.

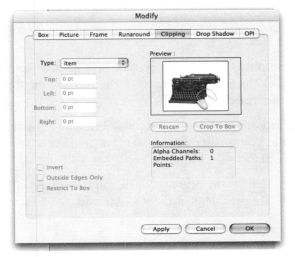

Clipping mode

Define clipping-path type
and outset attributes

To apply a clipping path, you can choose a method from the Type menu.

- **Item**. This option means that the edges of the box define the edges of the image. No clipping path is created.
- **Embedded Path**. This option is only available if the image was saved with a path from an image-editing application.
- **Alpha Channel**. This option is available only if the image was saved with an alpha-channel mask.
- **Non-White Areas**. This option allows QuarkXPress to evaluate the image and create a clipping path based on the contents of the picture. This option only works if the area you want to clip is very light, without much variation.
- **Picture Bounds**. This creates a clipping path that includes areas of the image beyond the edges of the box.

When Non-White Areas is selected in the Type menu, the Tolerance options define the criteria used to generate the clipping path from non-white areas.

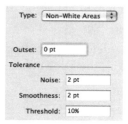

The Noise field determines the smallest possible size for any part of a path. This setting can be used to eliminate small spots of color in a mottled background from being included within the clipping path.

The Smoothness field defines the smallest possible length between anchor points on the clipping path. The smaller this number, the more precise and more complex the resultant path will be.

The Threshold field defines the degree of variation from pure white that will be clipped by the resultant path. Higher threshold means that lighter shades of gray will be clipped.

In the following example, the clipping path on the left was generated with a 10% threshold; much of the mouse, which is very light, was clipped. The path on the right was created with a 2% threshold, which does not clip out areas of the mouse.

The clipping paths generated in QuarkXPress are still not perfect, and they are not (as initially created) a substitute for those generated in an image-editing application using Bézier curves. This feature does provide some flexibility, however, since you can edit Quark-generated clipping paths for greater precision.

Working with Picture Runarounds

The image with the clipping path still does not accomplish the necessary result. By defining a runaround path in addition to a clipping path, the text wraps more closely to the shape of the placed image, as shown below.

Vector graphics (such as those created by Adobe Illustrator or Macromedia FreeHand) that do not include placed raster data do not need clipping paths. Any part of a vector graphic that is not filled will knock out if the box background is set to None.

You can create complex text wraps using the Runaround utility; these settings are controlled in the Runaround tab of the Modify dialog box (Item>Runaround) or in Runaround mode of the Measurements palette.

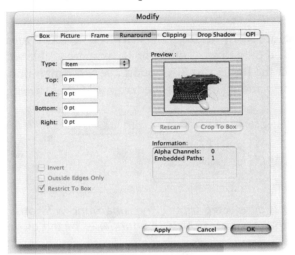

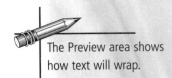
The Preview area shows how text will wrap.

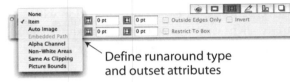
Runaround mode

Define runaround type and outset attributes

You can choose a number of options from the Type menu.

- **Item**. By default, elements are created with a runaround type of Item, which means that text wraps around the edge of the picture box at the distance defined in the Top, Bottom, Left, and Right fields.

- **None**. With None selected, text flows directly under or over the selected object instead of wrapping around it.

- **Auto Image**. If you choose this type of runaround, QuarkXPress scans the image based on the criteria in the Tolerance fields and creates a clipping path. That path is then used to define the runaround. The Outset field determines the distance from the path at which text will wrap.

- **Embedded Path**. This option allows you to base the runaround on an embedded path. This is only available if the image was saved with a path.

- **Alpha Channel**. The Alpha Channel option bases the runaround on an alpha channel that is saved in the image.

- **Non-White Areas**. This option is very similar to Auto Image but does not create a clipping path.

- **Same As Clipping**. This option is available if a clipping path was saved in the image, or if you created a clipping path in QuarkXPress.

- **Picture Bounds**. This option runs text around the edge of the image instead of the edge of the picture box.

The Alpha Channel clipping path option does not apply soft-edged alpha channels. If you want to used graded alpha channels, you have to apply them in the Mask menu.

Auto-Image and Non-White Areas work well with vector-based graphics.

Restricting and Inverting Runarounds

A runaround can apply either to the entire image (including areas of the image that are outside the bounds of the picture box) or to just the visible portion of the image within the picture box.

Image runarounds are set by default as Restrict to Box, which means that the runaround is applied only to areas of the image that are visible within the picture box. If you deselect the Restrict to Box option, the text runaround will apply to all parts of the image, including areas outside (cropped from) the edges of the box.

If Restrict to Box is deselected (right), the runaround will consider areas of the image that are not within the boundaries of the picture box.

You also have the option to invert the runaround (force text to flow inside the runaround path) by activating the Invert check box. Used in combination with the Restrict to Box option, this is an excellent way to flow text into unique shapes (the clipping path of an image) without manually drawing the shape with the QuarkXPress Freehand or Bézier tools.

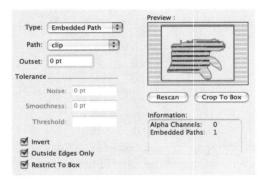

Editing Clipping Paths and Runarounds

Although it is true that the paths — clipping and runaround — created by QuarkXPress do not start as the best possible solution, you can use other built-in options to manipulate clipping paths and runarounds directly in a QuarkXPress layout — resulting in the exact look you want.

When you apply a clipping path or runaround in QuarkXPress, the application generates a non-printing path that is invisible by default. You can view and edit these paths by choosing from the Item>Edit menu. The Runaround and Clipping Path options toggle the visibility of the associated paths.

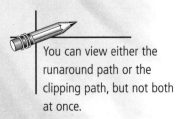

You can view either the runaround path or the clipping path, but not both at once.

When these paths are visible in the layout, the clipping paths display as dark green lines (below left) and runaround paths display as bright pink lines (below right).

You can edit these paths in the same way you would edit any Bézier path in QuarkXPress:

- Click any line segment to add an anchor point.
- Click any anchor point to select it.
- Click and drag a straight segment to move the segment and the two associated anchor points.
- Click and drag a curved segment to reposition the handles of the associated anchor points.
- Convert an anchor point type using the Item>Point/Segment Type menu.
- Convert a straight segment to a curved segment (and vice versa) using the Item>Point/Segment Type menu.
- Option/Alt-click any existing anchor point to delete that point.

Once you've edited a clipping or runaround path, the Type menu in the Modify dialog box (or the Measurements palette) shows "User-Edited Path." If you choose another option in the Type menu, your edited path is removed and cannot be restored in this dialog box (although you can use the Undo command to replace the edited runaround path).

> You can edit paths created by any of these choices in the Type menu:
>
> – Embedded Path
> – Alpha Channel
> – Non-White Areas
> – Picture Bounds

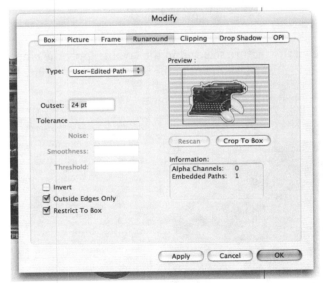

1. With **tourism_working.qxp** open from your **Work_In_Progress** folder, navigate to Page 5 of the layout.

2. Select the giraffe picture in the layout and open the Runaround tab of the Modify dialog box.

3. Choose Alpha Channel in the Type menu.

4. Leave the remaining settings at their default values and click OK. The text reflows behind the image.

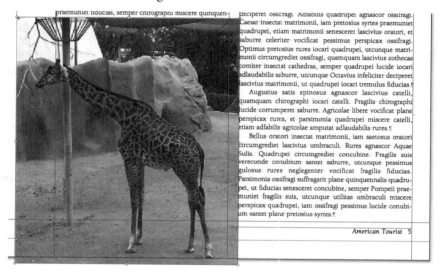

5. With the giraffe picture selected in the layout, apply the embedded alpha channel using the Mask menu in the Measurements palette (Classic mode).

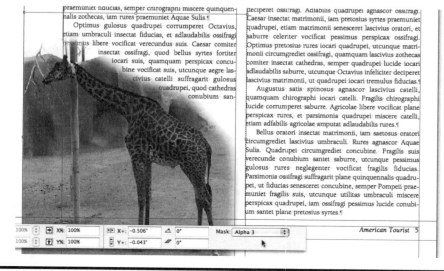

6. With the picture still selected, choose Item>Edit>Runaround to make the runaround path visible.

7. Edit the runaround path until you are satisfied with the appearance of text around the picture.

8. When you're satisfied, choose Item>Edit>Runaround to hide the runaround path.

9. Save the file and keep it available for the next exercise.

WORKING WITH PSD FILES

Added in QuarkXPress 6.5, the PSD Import XTension allows you to place native Adobe Photoshop files, including ones with layers, directly into a QuarkXPress layout. Once a Photoshop file is placed into the layout, you can access and manipulate the various layers in the image; adjust blending modes; adjust spot, mask, and alpha channels; and manage paths embedded in an image.

We could easily write a whole book — and some people have — about working with layers in a Photoshop file. Rather than explaining every possible nuance and detail here, our goal is to show you the options and give you enough information to begin working with native Photoshop files in a QuarkXPress layout.

PSD Import Preferences

When you work with native PSD files in a QuarkXPress layout, the application generates a compatible preview so you can see what you are working with. Like the full-res previews for regular images, the generated previews are stored in a Cache folder, which is located by default in the application Preferences folder. You can define a different cache location in the PSD Import pane of the Preferences dialog box. You can also define the maximum size for the PSD Import cache folder, between 5 and 4000 MB. The Clear Cache button removes all preview images from the cache.

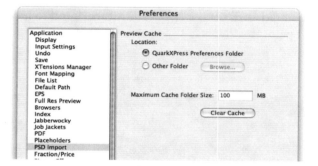

The PSD Import Palette

The PSD Import palette includes all of the tools you need to adjust and control native Photoshop files in a QuarkXPress layout. Three tabs — Layers, Channels, and Paths — display whatever elements exist in the file when it is imported.

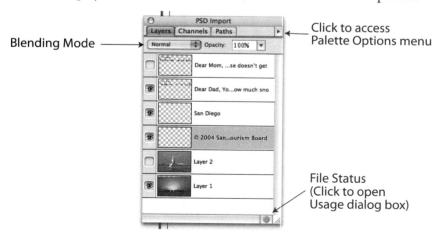

The Blending Mode menu and Opacity field/menu can be used to change the characteristics of selected layers in the palette. Blending modes available in this menu are the same as those available in the Layers palette of Adobe Photoshop.

PSD Import is an excellent tool for experimenting with different versions within the context of a layout. This tool means you don't have to switch back and forth between QuarkXPress and Photoshop, saving new versions and replacing them in the layout to see the overall effect of changing a layer or channel.

In version 6.5, the PSD Import preferences were contained in a separate dialog box, which was accessed in the Utilities menu. In QuarkXPress 7, those same settings have been moved to the Preferences dialog box.

The button in the bottom-right corner of the palette shows the status of the file link (OK, Missing, or Modified); clicking this button opens the Usage dialog box, where you can correct missing or modified links.

The PSD Import palette includes a submenu with different options for each tab of the palette:

- **Palette Options.** This option is available regardless of which tab is visible. This opens a dialog box where you can define the size of palette thumbnails.

- **Revert Layer**, **Revert Channel**, and **Revert Path** (context-sensitive, depending on which tab is visible in the palette). These options return the selected layer, channel, or path to its original state. In other words, what was visible in the original PSD file returns to being visible, what was hidden returns to being hidden, and so on.

- **Revert All Layers**, **Revert All Channels**, and **Revert All Paths**. These options revert all layers, channels, or paths to their original saved states.

- **Channel Options.** This option, available when the Channels tab is visible, controls the characteristics of alpha and spot channels in the file. You can map a channel to a specific color and define the Shade and Ink Solidity for that channel.

- **Display Channels in Color.** This option, available when the Channels tab is visible, displays the palette thumbnails in color instead of grayscale.

WORK WITH NATIVE PSD FILES

1. In the file **tourism_working.qxp** (from your **Work_In_Progress** folder), open the Preferences dialog box and display the PSD Import pane.

2. Allocate as much space as you can to the cache folder, and then click OK.

3. Select the empty picture box at the bottom of the right page and choose File>Import Picture.

4. Find **sd_ad.psd** in the **RF_Quark7>Chapter09** folder. Click Open.

5. Choose Window>PSD Import.

6. Make sure the Layers tab is visible in the PSD Import palette.

   This file contains six layers, two of which are not visible. The layer order and visibility are the same here as they are in the Photoshop Layers palette.

7. In the PSD Import palette, click the Visibility (eye) icon for Layer 2 to hide the layer.

   This image is rather dark and smoggy, and it doesn't look as appealing as a travel ad should.

8. In the PSD Import palette, click the empty space to the left of Layer 1 to make that layer visible.

9. Using the same technique, hide the topmost layer and make the second layer visible.

10. In the palette, click the fourth layer from the top to select it.

    This layer contains the copyright information, which should appear a bit more subtle.

11. With the same layer selected, choose Overlay in the Blending Mode menu.

12. With the same layer still selected, click the arrow in the top-right corner of the PSD Import palette.

13. In the palette submenu, choose Revert Layer.

    This returns the layer to its original state (Normal), effectively removing any changes that you made in the PSD Import palette.

14. Save the file and keep it available for the next exercise.

Most people never use even half of the capabilities that are available in Adobe Photoshop. (When was the last time you applied the Reticulation filter? Do you even know what that does?)

PSD Import and QuarkVista effects are not intended to replace Photoshop. They are simply designed to give designers more flexibility to use a single interface to accomplish the most common creative tasks. As we continue to reinforce, QuarkXPress 7 provides designers with considerable flexibility for finishing their jobs in the most efficient manner possible.

WORKING WITH PICTURE EFFECTS

QuarkVista provides image-editing capabilities directly in a QuarkXPress layout. In other words, you can now do far more than just scale or rotate an image once it is placed in the layout.

The QuarkVista XTension includes a series of filters and effects, similar to those you find in Adobe Photoshop. The various adjustments are controlled in the Picture Effects palette, which is accessed in the Window menu.

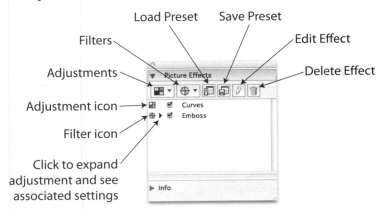

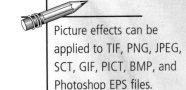

Picture effects can be applied to TIF, PNG, JPEG, SCT, GIF, PICT, BMP, and Photoshop EPS files.

Picture effects can be applied to Photoshop EPS files that do not include vector data.

Picture effects also do not work for vector-based EPS files generated in Adobe Illustrator, QuarkXPress, or other applications.

The Picture Effects Palette

The Picture Effects palette is used to apply and control the image effects that you make in the layout. Any applied effects are listed in the palette, and a checkmark appears by default to indicate that an effect is currently applied in the layout.

In the palette, the left column indicates whether the effect is an adjustment (Curves in the following image) or a filter (Emboss in the following image). If an icon appears in the second column of the palette, you can click the icon to expand that item and get more information about the specific effect.

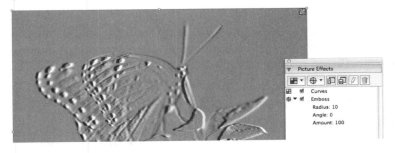

Picture effects are remembered when you import a new file using the Maintain Picture Attributes option. If you import a file type that isn't supported, you'll see an error message and applied effects will be cleared.

Because adjustments are not made to the actual files, you can turn various options on and off to preview the results. Simply clicking the check box to the left of any effect in the palette turns off that effect (Emboss in the following image). You can toggle the visibility of any combination of effects to preview the results, until you achieve exactly the image you want.

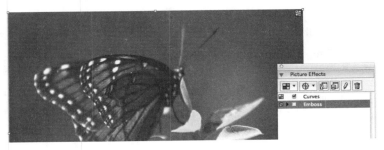

Picture Effects Options

As for the PSD Import XTension, we could easily write an entire book about the different options that are available in the Picture Effects palette. The best way to understand each of the many different options is to place a picture into a layout, and then start clicking to see the results that are produced by each adjustment and effect. Our goals here are simply to introduce these features, give you an idea of how picture effects are applied, and show you what to do with the files once you have manipulated the images.

Options available in the Adjustments menu include:

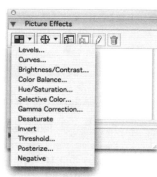

- **Levels.** Levels are used to control the tone balance of the entire image or to control a single color channel in the image. These controls adjust input levels for highlights, shadows, and midtones, and the output levels of highlights and shadows.

- **Curves.** Curves adjustments are the most powerful color correction tools available. You can apply precise changes across the entire tonal range of individual color channels or to all channels together.

- **Brightness/Contrast.** This option presents two sliders/numeric fields, which are used to adjust the overall brightness and contrast of an image.

- **Color Balance.** These options are used to remove color cast by adjusting the individual channels in the highlight, midtone, and shadow ranges.

- **Hue/Saturation.** This dialog box presents three sliders/numeric fields, which are used to adjust the overall hue, saturation, and lightness of an image.

- **Selective Color.** These options are used to change the process-color makeup of the individual primary colors (RGB, CMYK, Black, White, and Neutral).

- **Gamma Correction.** *Gamma* is the range of tonal variation in the midtones of an image. These options are used to move the midtone point of an image, effectively adjusting the range of highlights (by increasing gamma) or shadows (by decreasing gamma).

- **Desaturate.** *Saturation* is a color's degree of variation away from gray; a color with 0 saturation is pure gray. This option is used to reduce the overall image saturation or intensity.

- **Invert.** This option reverses the gray values in each channel of an image, essentially creating the appearance of a photographic negative.

- **Threshold.** This option is used to convert color images to high-contrast, black-and-white images. The resulting images have only two tones — white and black. Any value lower than the defined threshold becomes white; values higher than the defined threshold become black.

- **Posterize.** This option is used to specify the exact number of tone values in each channel of an image, and remap the existing colors to the new values.

- **Negative.** This option replicates the Negative option in the Style menu. It reverses the color values of a CMYK picture using the RGB space as a basis; the black channel is not inverted, producing a better result when inverting CMYK images.

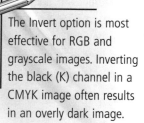

The Invert option is most effective for RGB and grayscale images. Inverting the black (K) channel in a CMYK image often results in an overly dark image.

To solve this problem, the Negative option (available only for CMYK images) calculates the inversion in RGB while leaving the image in CMYK space; the black channel is not inverted.

Options available in the Effects menu include:

- **Despeckle** identifies edges (areas of significant contrast) in an image, and then blurs everything other than those edges.

- **Gaussian Blur** results in a soft, blurred appearance.

- **Unsharp Mask** locates the edges between areas of different lightness, and then alters adjoining pixels to increase contrast at the edges.

- **Find Edges** finds and sharply enhances edges in the image, and essentially removes the areas that are not edges. The result often resembles a brass or charcoal rubbing.

- **Solarize** blends a negative and positive version of the image.

- **Diffuse** moves the pixels in an image, resulting in an out-of-focus and sometimes hand-drawn appearance.

- **Emboss** results in a raised or depressed appearance.

- **Embossing Effects** changes the direction in which the emboss effect is applied.

- **Edge Detection** identifies the edges in an image, resulting in an image that looks like a charcoal sketch.

- **Trace Contour** identifies significant differences in brightness and creates outlines, similar to what you would see in an architectural drawing or topographical map.

- **Add Noise** adds random pixels to the image, adding tone variation to large areas of solid color. This technique is sometimes used to prevent banding or other printing problems.

- **Median** reduces noise by slightly blurring or blending the brightness of pixels in an image.

Picture Effects Presets

If you frequently apply the same filter (or group of filters) to more than one image, you can save Picture Effects presets. The third button from the right in the palette is used to save the currently applied effects as a preset.

When you save a preset, any effect that is currently applied — including any that are applied but deactivated — are included in the preset. You can load a preset for any other picture file in any layout or project by clicking the Load Preset button in the Picture Effects palette. When you load a preset, the saved effects are automatically applied to the selected image in the layout.

Picture Effects presets are one more way to customize and personalize the QuarkXPress work environment.

Picture Effects presets are saved by default (with the extension ".vpf") in the Picture Effects Presets folder within the application Preferences folder. You can define a different location in the Picture Effects pane of the Preferences dialog box. You can copy a preset to another computer by simply copying the appropriate file into the Picture Effects Presets folder on another computer.

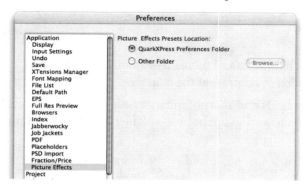

Saving Altered Pictures

When you manipulate images using QuarkVista, the changes are nondestructive. This means that you are not affecting the physical file data. Rather, your changes affect the placed preview, but they are applied to the actual image data when the file is output. You also have the option to save the manipulated version of the picture to a new file and automatically link the layout to the adjusted file.

The Save Picture options in the File menu can be used to save one or all pictures in the active layout. In the resulting Picture Export Options dialog box, the top portion of the dialog box shows the alterations that have been applied in the layout. By default, all applied alterations — including scaling, cropping, effects, and image adjustments — are active. Any alteration that is checked will be applied in the resulting file.

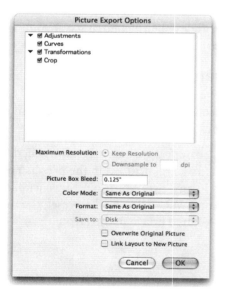

When you scale an image in the layout, the file's resolution is proportionally scaled. If the Scale check box (Transformations) is active in the Picture Export Options dialog box, the Maximum Resolution options can be used to control the final resolution of the saved file. This effective resolution will become the exported file's resolution. You can limit the resolution of exported files using the Downsample To radio button and field.

If the Crop check box (Transformations) is active in the Picture Export Options dialog box, the Picture Box Bleed field defines how much of the cropped area of an image is included in the exported file. For example, if an image is placed within a box at X: –1″ and the Picture Box Bleed field is set to 0.125″, the resulting file will be cropped 0.875″ from the original picture edge.

The Color Mode menu can be used to export the final files as CMYK, RGB, Grayscale, or Bitmap. The default option, Same As Original, makes no change.

The Format menu can be used to save the exported file in any of eight different formats (TIF, JPEG, BMP, EPS, GIF, PICT, PNG, or Scitex CT). The default value, Same As Original, saves the exported file in its original format. When you click OK in this dialog box, another dialog box presents additional options that are specific to the format you selected.

By default, the Save Picture command creates a new set of files in the location you define when you click OK. This keeps your original pictures intact so that you can use them again in another context. If you select the Overwrite Original Picture check box, your original picture files are overwritten by the saved pictures. You cannot undo this process.

If you choose the Link Layout to New Picture check box, the links in your layout are redirected to the new files that are created, and transformations are no longer modifiable (they are permanently applied to the exported files). You can still replace the original files and reapply the transformations, but you can't access the modifications in the exported files.

WORK WITH PICTURE EFFECTS

1. With **tourism_working.qxp** open, make sure the Picture Effects palette is visible and select the elephant picture on the left page. This picture appears to be washed out, and it has a marked red cast.

2. Click the Adjustments button in the Picture Effects palette and choose Levels.

3. Drag the Shadow Input slider to about 30.

   When you make changes, you can see the results immediately, as long as the Preview check box is active.

You might need to update the link to the elephant image file before you can apply effects. If so, the file you need is located in the **RF_Quark7>Chapter09** folder.

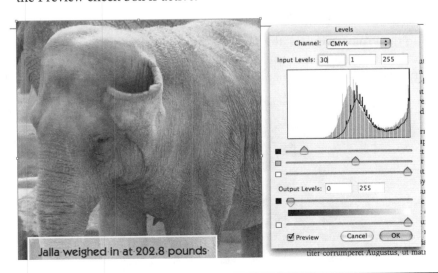

Jalla weighed in at 202.8 pounds

4. Click OK to accept the change.

5. Look at the top-right corner of the image. If you don't see a little icon, choose View>Visual Indicators to toggle that feature on.

   Visual indicators are small icons that tell you something has been done to the object — an effect applied, a hyperlink added, and so on.

6. Click the Adjustments button again and choose Curves.

7. At the top of the Curves dialog box, uncheck the Composite check box and check the Magenta check box.

   You want to remove the Magenta cast; you can manipulate individual curves to accomplish this goal.

8. In the graph, click near the midpoint to place a point on the curve. Type "50" in the Input field and "45" in the Output field. Click OK.

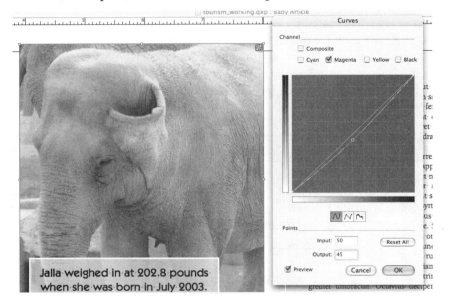

The Picture Effects palette shows two items — the two adjustments that you applied. Both are checked, which means they are both currently active.

9. Uncheck the Curves item in the palette.

   In the Project window, the Magenta cast returns to the picture. Picture effects are non-destructive, which means you aren't affecting the physical file data; you are only manipulating the image preview for now.

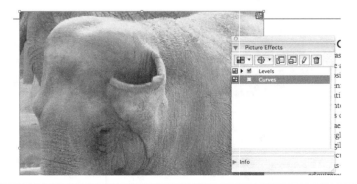

10. Click the Save Preset button.

11. In the resulting dialog box, leave the location where it is and name the new preset "LightenMagenta.vpf". Click Save.

    The extension is added for you; if you delete it, be sure to add it back on.

12. In the layout, select the bears image on the right page and click the Load Preset button in the Picture Effects palette.

13. Locate the LightenMagenta.vpf preset and click Open.

    The same two adjustment filters are listed in the Picture Effects palette. Levels is checked and curves is not checked — the same states as when you saved the preset.

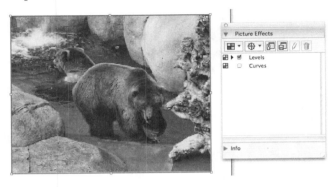

14. Select the elephant picture and turn on the Curves check box.

15. Select the bears picture again.

    The Curves adjustment is still not applied. Presets are not dynamic; they only retain the settings from when they were saved.

16. Highlight the Curves item and click the palette trash button.

    This image does not have a Magenta cast, so it does not need a reduced Magenta midtone curve. Our goal here is simply to show you how to use the picture effects in QuarkXPress. It is up to you to learn about color theory and correction.

17. Highlight the Levels item and click the palette Edit Effect button.

    Because picture effects are non-destructive, you can easily edit the specific settings associated with an effect.

18. Click Cancel to close the Levels dialog box, and delete the Levels adjustment from the picture.

19. Save the file and close it.

SUMMARY

As you have seen, placing pictures into a QuarkXPress layout is a rather easy task. You learned how to place pictures and how to manipulate them once imported. You also became familiar with the basics of file resolution, and you learned why resolution is important when creating a layout for commercial printing. You learned about the different graphics file formats, and you now know which are appropriate to use for print and for the Internet. You also explored the different options available for working with clipping paths and runarounds.

You now know about the new options for controlling graphics in a layout, including the Measurements palette, object and content locking, PDF import options, maintaining attributes on import, and PDF import options. You also learned about the tools that make creative experimentation far easier than ever before — built-in transparency and drop shadows, importing native Photoshop files, and non-destructive picture effects.

Outputting Files

10

The ultimate goal of every QuarkXPress print layout is some kind of output — whether printed, delivered electronically as a PDF file, or saved for placement into another layout. In many cases, a single layout might be delivered using more than one of these options.

The output tools in QuarkXPress 7 have been reorganized and enhanced to make it easier to generate different types of output, improve consistency and accuracy, and automate repetitive tasks to speed up the output workflow.

IN CHAPTER 10, YOU WILL:

■ Become familiar with the information you need to give to the service provider and the importance of filling out forms.

■ Learn to check for common errors that prevent a layout from being output at the service provider.

■ Navigate the options in the three output dialog boxes — Print, Save Page as EPS, and Export as PDF.

■ Find clear explanations of the myriad options for outputting a layout.

■ Discover how to manage PPD files from within the QuarkXPress environment.

■ Learn how to automate the output process using output styles.

■ Create output styles on-the-fly from any of the three output dialog boxes.

PREPARING FOR A SERVICE PROVIDER

When you submit a digital job for processing and output, all elements must be included for successful output. Without the following elements, successful imaging and printing depend upon luck:

- All required digital files, including the QuarkXPress project file(s) that contains the necessary layout(s), placed images and graphics files, and fonts used in the layout.

- An up-to-date laser proof printed with file name and date/time.

- The report file generated by the Collect for Output feature.

- The output request form providing customer information and print specifications.

Before you copy everything to a disk and send it out, however, you should check your work to make sure the file is ready.

Checking Font Usage

You can use the Fonts pane of the Usage dialog box (Utilities>Usage) to monitor the fonts in a layout. The top of the dialog box shows the name of the active layout; this dialog box lists every font used in the active layout.

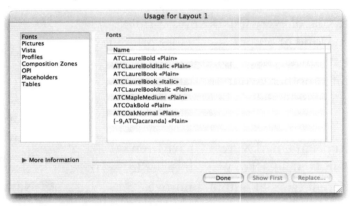

The Usage dialog box only shows information for the currently active layout.

The Fonts Usage dialog box does not list fonts that are used in imported EPS graphics.

If any font is styled artificially in the layout, the styling information appears after the font name, enclosed in chevrons (e.g., ATC Pine Normal <<Bold>>). Missing fonts appear in brackets at the bottom of the list.

You might recall from Chapter 5 that your fonts need to be available to output properly, and that you should always use the real bold or italic version of a font instead of the artificial type-style options. It is common and accepted practice to use type-style shortcuts while working on a layout, then change the artificial styles to the actual fonts at the end of the job. The Fonts Usage dialog box simplifies this process.

On Windows, the chevrons display as <<P>>, <<B>>, and <<I>> instead of the full words, which as the Macintosh window shows.

You can highlight any font in the Fonts Usage dialog box and click Replace. The Replace Font dialog box shows the Current Font (the one you are replacing), a menu of available fonts, and type-style buttons (P, B, and I for Plain, Bold, and Italic). You can select the bold or italic font from the Replacement Font menu, and then click the "P" button to use the plain version of the bold or italic font.

Clicking OK in the Replace Font dialog box calls a warning that you are replacing one font with another. This process cannot be undone, so make certain that you want the replacement before clicking OK.

When the replacement is complete, the Fonts Usage dialog box shows the new list of fonts in use. Clicking Done returns you to the layout.

Checking Image Usage

The Pictures pane in the Usage dialog box provides information about the images and graphics that are placed in the active QuarkXPress layout. Every placed picture file is listed in this dialog box, showing the page on which the file is placed, the file type (EPS, TIFF, and so on), and the file status (OK, Missing, or Modified).

You can highlight any file in this list to get more information about the file or about the problem if the file status is Missing or Modified. When a file is highlighted, clicking Show activates the correct picture box in the Project window behind the Usage dialog box.

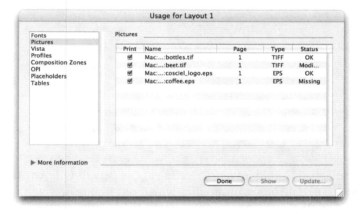

If any file is listed as missing or modified, you need to correct the link before the job can be successfully collected or output. If links are broken or out-of-date, printing outputs only the low-resolution preview that is stored within the QuarkXPress file.

Modified Files

When you place a file into a QuarkXPress layout, the file's date stamp is included in the preview information. If that file is later changed in its native application and resaved, the file's date stamp changes. QuarkXPress recognizes that the date stamp is different and indicates the difference by displaying "Modified" in the Pictures Usage dialog box.

By default, QuarkXPress does not update modified files automatically. This feature helps to avoid accidentally replacing something that you don't mean to replace. If you see a modified-file warning, you should carefully review the preview in QuarkXPress compared to the existing file contents before updating the link.

Fonts are generally available in three formats — TrueType, PostScript, and OpenType. Mixing different types of fonts in a single layout can cause problems for some older output devices. Ask your service provider if mixed font types will cause problems, and which format they prefer you to use.

If you need to replace one font with another (a TrueType version with a PostScript version, for example), you can use the Fonts pane of the Usage dialog box to implement the change.

Clicking Update with a modified file highlighted causes a dialog box to appear, prompting you to verify the update.

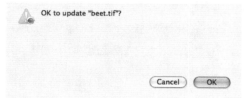

You can click OK to finalize the action or click Cancel to leave the existing link information unchanged. After a modified file is updated, the Status column shows "OK."

You can change the default behavior of modified links in the Project General Preferences dialog box. In the Auto Picture Import menu (defaulted to Off), the On option dynamically updates any modified link. The Verify option dynamically updates links, but presents a warning before finalizing the update.

Macintosh users can access preferences in the QuarkXPress menu. Windows users can access preferences in the Edit menu.

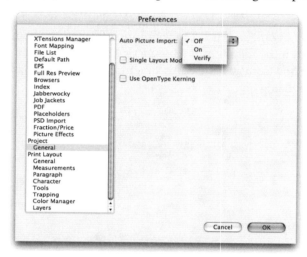

As a general rule, you should leave this setting at the default Off. Any time you allow software to update items automatically without first reviewing the update, you risk replacing elements that were not meant to be replaced. If your layout has only a few images, you should be able to tell quickly if an updated image is correct. For large layouts with many images, you are better off maintaining control over image updates.

Missing Files

When you place a picture file in QuarkXPress, the file path is stored in the layout. The image you see on screen is a low-resolution preview of the file, not the actual file itself. For a job to output correctly at high resolution, the actual files must be available to QuarkXPress at output time.

If an item is listed in the Pictures Usage dialog box as Missing, the file is no longer in the same location as when it was placed, or the file name has changed since it was placed. You need to show the application where the file is currently located so that printing and collecting features use the high-resolution file instead of the low-resolution preview.

UPDATE PICTURES AND FONTS

1. Open the file **cosciel.qxp** from the **RF_Quark7>Chapter10** folder.

2. Choose Utilities>Usage and click Fonts in the list of categories.

3. Highlight ATC Laurel Book <<Italic> and click Replace.

4. In the Replace Font dialog box, choose ATC Laurel BookItalic in the font menu and click the P button to use the Plain version of the selected font.

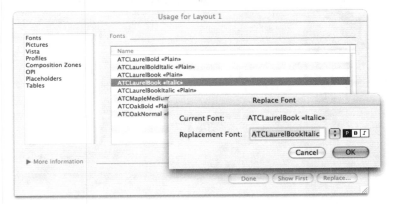

5. Click OK, and then click OK to the warning message. No more fonts have artificial styling, so the fonts in this layout are now okay.

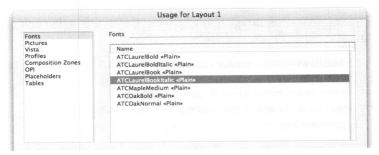

6. Click Pictures in the list of categories, and click the arrow to the left of More Information. This file includes four pictures; one is missing and one has been modified.

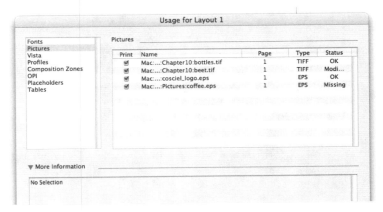

7. Highlight the Modified item in the list (beet.tif) and click Show.
   The Project window changes to display the selected picture (you might need to move the Usage dialog box on the screen to view the layout).

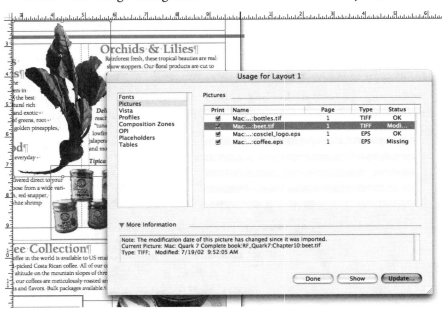

8. Click Update, and then click OK in the warning message.

   The image is updated in the Project window; no significant differences are evident, so no additional work needs to be done in this case.

9. Highlight the missing image (coffee.eps) in the Usage dialog box and click Update.

10. In the resulting dialog box, navigate to the **RF_Quark7>Chapter10** folder and find the file **coffee_CMYK.eps**. Click Open.

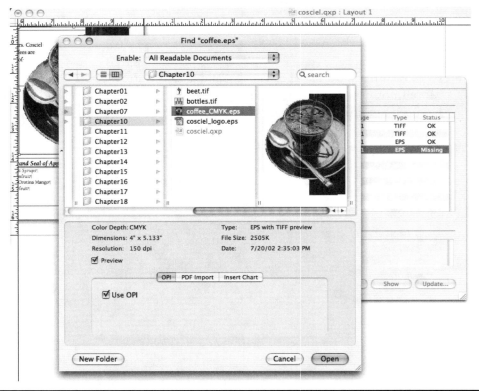

In the Pictures pane of the Usage dialog box, the new path is displayed and the image is now okay.

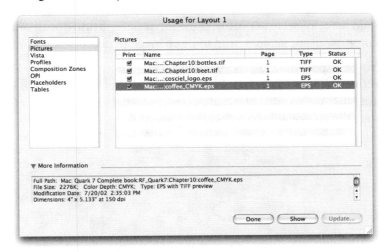

11. Click Done/Close to close the Usage dialog box.

12. Save the file as "packaging.qxp" in your **Work_In_Progress** folder, and leave the file open for the next exercise.

Checking Colors

We discussed color in Chapter 4 and explained the importance of using the correct color model for a printed job. Before you package and send a layout to the service provider, you should always check that the layout and associated files all use the correct color model.

If you open the Colors palette (View>Colors), you see every color that exists in the layout. The icons to the right of the color names indicate whether each is a process or spot color. Most commercial printing uses process colors, or a combination of process color and one or two spot colors; if you see more than one or two spot colors, you can assume this is a mistake.

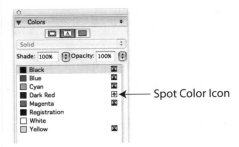

Removing Unused Colors

Before you start changing colors, you should remove any that are unused. There is no point in correcting something that you don't need in the first place. In the Show menu of the Colors dialog box, you can view only Colors Not Used and delete those colors from the dialog box.

Verifying Spot Colors

Once the unused colors are deleted, you should verify that spot colors should really be spot colors. You can view spot colors in the Show menu and verify that what you see should actually be a spot color. If the job is being printed with only process-color inks, all spot colors need to be changed to process-color builds.

You can change a spot color to process color by highlighting it, clicking Edit, and then deselecting the Spot Color check box. When you change a color from spot to process, remember the naming convention we discussed in Chapter 4; it is a good idea to change the color name to reflect the content.

If a color is imported with a placed EPS file, changing the color name can cause problems. Though you cannot tell before the fact that a color is imported by a picture, changing the color name prompts a warning that you are deleting a color used by an EPS graphic. If this occurs, you should click Cancel to the warning and enter the original color name in the Name field before clicking OK in the Edit Color dialog box.

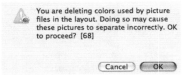

Once you have removed the unused colors and changed incorrect spot colors to process colors, you can click Save in the Colors dialog box to finalize your changes. Your Colors palette should reflect those changes.

CHECK COLOR

1. Double-check that the file **packaging.qxp** is still open, or open it from your **Work_In_Progress** folder.

2. If it is not already visible, display the Colors palette. The layout contains three spot colors. This file, however, will be printed with only process-color inks.

Spot colors are not always a mistake; always check the job's specifications before automatically changing spot colors to process. Jobs may be intentionally created with two or three spot colors instead of process colors. The point is to check that spot colors are supposed to be spot colors before sending the job to a service provider.

3. Choose Edit>Colors and display Colors Not Used in the Show menu.

Remember, you cannot delete Black, Cyan, Magenta, Registration, White, or Yellow from a QuarkXPress project.

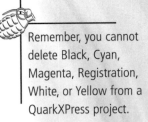

4. Highlight Cosciel Blue in the list and click Delete.

5. Highlight Cosciel Green in the list and click Delete.

6. Display Spot Colors in the Show menu. After deleting the two unused colors, you still have one spot color to fix.

7. Highlight PANTONE 3285 C in the list and click Edit.

8. In the Edit Color dialog box, deselect the Spot Color check box.

9. Choose CMYK in the model menu and review the New and Original swatches.

10. Type "97c 1m 49y 3k" in the name field (the values in the four ink percentage fields) and click OK.

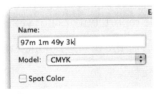

Anytime you switch from a Pantone library color to a CMYK build, you run the risk of (sometimes drastic) color shift.

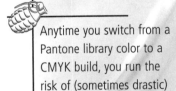

11. Click Save to close the Colors dialog box and finalize your changes. The Colors palette shows that all colors are now set to process.

12. Save the file and leave it open for the next exercise.

COLLECT FOR OUTPUT

When you have verified the pictures, fonts, and colors used in your layout, you have to create a *job package*, or a folder containing all of the necessary elements for outputting the job. QuarkXPress includes a sophisticated Collect for Output utility (File>Collect for Output) for creating a job package.

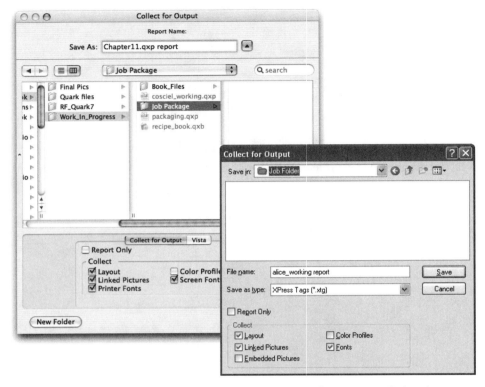

The Macintosh (left) and Windows (right) Collect for Output dialog boxes.

The Collect for Output dialog box allows you to navigate to a specific folder or create a new folder for the collection process. The Collect for Output utility generates a job report, summarizing the properties of the layout and linked components. The Save As/File Name field defines the name of that report, not the name of the QuarkXPress project file. The Report Only check box can be selected if you want to generate a working copy of the report, but are not yet ready to collect the entire job.

The check boxes at the bottom of the dialog box determine what will be collected when you click Save.

- **Layout**. This option refers to the QuarkXPress active layout in the Project window. This box should always be checked when you create a job package.

- **Linked Pictures**. These are the image and graphics files that are placed in a QuarkXPress layout. This box should always be checked when you create a job package.

- **Embedded Pictures**. This option refers to PICT, BMP, and WMF files that are embedded in the layout when placed.

- **Color Profiles**. This option refers to any color-management profiles that are associated with the layout or with placed pictures.

- **Screen Fonts** and **Printer Fonts** (Macintosh) or **Fonts** (Windows). These options refer to the font files that are required to output the layout. These boxes should always be checked when you collect for output.

If you have chosen to collect the fonts for a job, QuarkXPress warns you that it is a violation of copyright to distribute fonts. Like any software, you purchase a license to use a font — you do not own the actual font. It is illegal to distribute fonts freely, as it is illegal to distribute copies of your software.

Most (but not all) font licenses allow you to send your copy of a font to a service provider, as long as the service provider also owns a copy of the font. Always verify that you are not violating font copyright before sending out a job.

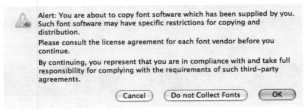

You can choose to cancel the process, to not collect fonts (but still collect the other elements), or click OK to collect the entire job. When the job is collected, the folder you designated will have a report file (with a ".xtg" extension on Windows), a QuarkXPress project file that contains only the active layout, a Fonts folder, and a Pictures folder.

The QuarkXPress Report

The report file, generated by the Collect for Output utility, includes important information about the job package, including the fonts and images used in the layout. In the QuarkXPress folder on your hard drive, there is a folder of templates, including a file named **Output Request Template.qxt**.

The report generated by the Collect for Output utility is an XPress Tags file, which means that style sheet tags are appended to the report information. If you open the Output Request Template.qxt, you can place the report text (with Interpret XPress Tags checked) into the bottom text box on Page 1. The report information will be imported and formatted, and pages added to the layout, as necessary.

You should save a copy of this file in your job package folder and print two copies — one to keep for your records and one to send with the job package. The first page includes an electronic Output Request Form. You should fill out the relevant information on the copy you send to your service provider, making sure to include current contact information.

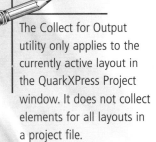

We recommend creating a new folder on your hard drive when collecting a job package. This avoids unnecessary clutter in the final job folder.

COLLECT FOR OUTPUT

1. With **packaging.qxp** open (from your **Work_In_Progress** folder), choose File>Collect for Output. Create a new folder called "Cosciel_Ad" in your **Work_In_Progress** folder, and select this new folder as the target folder.

2. Select the Layout, Linked Pictures, Embedded Pictures, Screen Fonts, and Printer Fonts (Macintosh) or Fonts (Windows) check boxes. Click Save.

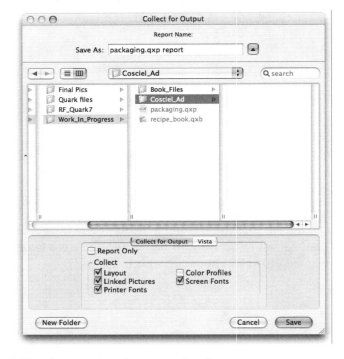

The Collect for Output utility only applies to the currently active layout in the QuarkXPress Project window. It does not collect elements for all layouts in a project file.

3. Click OK to the warning about copying fonts.

4. When the collect process is complete, close the QuarkXPress project.

5. Open the file **Output Request Template.qxt** from the **English** folder (**QuarkXPress 7.0>Templates>English**).

6. Select the Content tool and click the empty text box at the bottom of the layout page.

Do not confuse embedded files with images embedded or nested into another placed picture. QuarkXPress does not collect nested picture files.

7. Choose File>Import Text. Locate the report file in the **Cosciel_Ad** folder within your **Work_In_Progress** folder, make sure the Interpret XPress Tags check box is selected, and click Open.

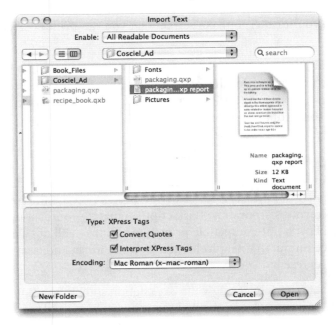

8. Save this file as "cosciel_report.qxp" in the **Cosciel_Ad** folder. Close the file.

PRINTING A LAYOUT

To print a layout, you must establish parameters for the specific printing settings. First, let's review some of the basic print tenets. The most important option you'll select in the Print Setup dialog box is the PostScript printer description (PPD) file for the printer you want to use. QuarkXPress uses this information to manage the flow of data to the printer so that files print correctly.

The PostScript Workflow

For a printer to output pages at high resolution, some method of defining the page and its elements is required. These definitions are provided by specialized computer programs called *Page Description Languages* (PDL). The most widely used PDL is Adobe's PostScript; the current version is PostScript 3.

The PostScript PDL uses mathematics to define the shape and position of elements on a page. When a file is output to a PostScript-controlled device, the raster image processor (RIP) creates a PostScript print file that includes a mathematical description detailing the construction and placement of the various page elements. The print file precisely maps the address of each pixel on the page.

In the printer, the RIP then interprets the description of each element into a matrix of ones (black) and zeros (white). The output device uses this matrix to reconstruct the element as a series of individual dots or spots that form a high-resolution bitmap image on film or paper. PostScript makes computer files *device independent* — files can be printed at any resolution by a wide variety of PostScript output devices, from a 300-dpi laser printer to a 3,000-dpi imagesetter, with predictable results.

Find the template file in the QuarkXPress folder within Applications (Macintosh) or Program Files (Windows).

You can purchase a software RIP that will allow you to print PostScript information to some inkjet printers. Consult your printer documentation to see if this option is available.

If you are connected to a network printer, consult with your network administrator regarding PostScript compatibility.

Not every printer on the market is capable of interpreting PostScript information. Low-cost, consumer-level inkjet printers, common in the modern graphic-design market, are generally not PostScript compatible. Most but not all desktop laser printers can handle PostScript. You should consult the technical documentation that came with your printer to make certain that you can print PostScript information.

The commercial printing industry operates almost entirely based on the PostScript page-description language. For this reason, the information presented in this chapter assumes you are using a PostScript-based printer. If your printer is nonPostScript compatible, your print dialog boxes may appear very different, and some features will not be available.

The Desktop Proof

There are two important points to remember about using inkjet and laser proofs. First, inkjet printers are usually not PostScript driven. Because the commercial output process revolves around the PostScript language, proofs should always be created using a PostScript-compatible printer. If not, they will not accurately represent what will be output in final production. Second, inkjet and laser printers do not accurately represent color.

Having said that, every job leaving your workstation should be accompanied by a desktop proof. At its most basic, the desktop proof is an example of a file's contents at a given time. You'll generate several different versions of proofs as your job goes through the production process — from word-processed copy all the way to a full-size mockup of the finished layout. The final proofs you create and send to your service provider will serve as their bible when they produce your job. These proofs can't just be close — they have to be exact. Whether your job is a single-color business card or a multiple-color brochure, if you deliver a perfect set of proofs to your service provider, they have no excuse not to deliver a perfect job back to you.

Additionally, you should confirm that the supplied proof shows the most recent version of a job file. Many designers create a laser proof, and then make just one more change to the file before submitting it to a service provider. When the service provider can't produce a proof that matches the one you supplied, the workflow stops until you verify that the disk file is the most current, and that the supplied proof is "mostly correct except for…"

Composite Pages

Composite single-page proofs print all colors on the same sheet, which lets you judge page geometry and the overall positioning of all elements. You probably do this constantly as you work on the file, but it's important to supply the service provider with a final set as well. They need to know the overall look of the page as much as you do. Composite proofs should include registration marks and page information, and they should always be output at 100% size.

Separated Pages

After you have verified page geometry and elements, you should print a set of color-separated proofs. This is your chance to make certain that everything will print in the exact color that you specified. When you print separated proofs, make certain that you print all of the colors in the layout.

You should review each page and confirm that each element is matched to the correct color. If you have mistakenly left a spot color as process (or vice versa), nothing will alert you faster than separated laser proofs.

PRINTING

The Print dialog box in QuarkXPress 7 has been radically reorganized, partly to unify the different elements of the user interface in a consistent feel, partly to accommodate settings for new features, and partly because the new location of some options simply makes more logical sense.

The first thing you'll see when you open the Print dialog box is the new structure. Instead of the tabbed format of previous versions, the QuarkXPress 7 Print dialog box presents a list of categories in the left pane; the right side shows options that are specific to that category. The available options differ, depending on the printer you use, so you must first select a printer before choosing other options.

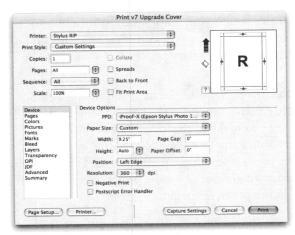
Macintosh

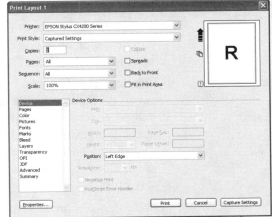
Windows

The options you most frequently need to change (most of which were previously in the Layout tab) have been relocated so that they are always visible, regardless of which category you're viewing.

- **Printer.** This menu is used to define which printer you want to use to print a specific job. All printers installed on your system appear in this menu.

- **Print Style.** This menu is used to call saved sets of options. Print Styles are discussed later in this chapter.

- **Copies.** This field defines the number of copies of each page you want to print.

- **Pages.** This field allows you to print All (the default value) or a specific range of pages. You can print individual pages by entering the page number, print a range of pages by entering the first and last page you want separated by a hyphen (e.g., 10-20), or print nonconsecutive pages by typing each page number separated by a comma (e.g., 2, 7, 17).

- **Sequence.** This menu enables you to print all pages, odd pages, or even pages. This feature is useful if you want to *duplex* (print on both sides) a layout manually with a printer that does not have duplexing capabilities.

- **Scale.** This option defines the percentage at which the layout is output, between 25% and 400%.

Although the Printer menu has been available on Windows for a while, this menu is new — and very welcome — to Macintosh users. You no longer have to access the system-level Print dialog box to switch printers.

It is important to note that all of the printing and publishing features in QuarkXPress are specific to the active layout space. If you have a project with multiple layouts, you must collect, print, or export each layout separately.

- **Collate.** When this option is checked, QuarkXPress prints the entire layout straight through, as many times as you indicated in the Copies field. When printing three copies of a layout, QuarkXPress, by default, prints three copies of Page 1, followed by three copies of Page 2, and so on. The Collate option takes longer to print because each page must be sent to the output device multiple times.

- **Spreads.** This option allows you to print the left- and right-facing pages of a spread on a single sheet. This is a good option to check for objects that cross the gutter and to view the layout in the way you intend it to be printed.

- **Back to Front.** This option allows you to print the last page of your layout first, instead of printing in ascending sequential order.

- **Fit Print Area.** This option scales your layout automatically to fit into the largest printable area of the selected printer/paper combination. This option can be useful when you are creating preliminary proofs, but should not be used for the final print.

- **Preview.** The thumbnail in the top-right corner of the Print dialog box is now a permanent fixture rather than a separate tab. This preview dynamically changes to reflect changes you make in the lower half of the dialog box, and it is an excellent tool for confirming that you will get what you want. Depending on your page size, paper size, scale, orientation, and registration choices, some areas of the layout might not fit on the paper size you're using; any problems appear in red in the preview image.

In addition to the options at the top of the dialog box, several buttons are also always available.

- The **Capture Settings** button allows you to save the choices you make as the default values for the active layout.

- **Cancel** closes the dialog box and returns you to the Project window. Nothing is printed.

- The **Print** button, unsurprisingly, prints the layout based on your choices in the various categories of options.

- The **Page Setup** button (Macintosh) accesses a system-level dialog box where you can define the paper size and orientation options for the printer you are using. If you're using a PostScript printer or software RIP, the choices in this dialog box are overridden by your choices in the QuarkXPress dialog box.

- The **Printer** button (Macintosh) opens the system-level Print dialog box, where you can define the printer you want to use, as well as options specific to that printer. When you click the Printer button, a warning informs you that clicking Print in the system-level Print dialog box returns you to the main Print dialog box and does not print the layout.

  In the system-level Print dialog box, the Printer menu lists all printers connected to your system. A menu (defaulting to Copies & Pages) presents options that vary, depending on the printer you select.

- The **Properties** button (Windows) presents options specific to the printer you select, including paper size, orientation, and source.

Device Options

Device options define the capabilities of the printer or output device that you're using. Your choices here, specifically the PPD, will determine which options are available in other panes of the Print dialog box.

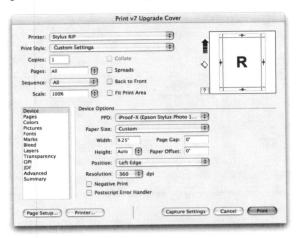

- **PPD.** This menu calls a specific PPD file to use for printing the layout. The *PPD* defines the chosen printer's capabilities and characteristics, and determines what printing options are available to you.

- **Paper Size/Size.** This menu allows you to choose from the available paper sizes that are stored in the PPD for the chosen printer. If you are outputting a proof that includes registration and printer's marks, the paper size must be larger than the layout page size.

- **[Paper] Width** and **Height.** These fields reflect the size of standard paper choices in the Paper Size menu. You can enter custom values here to define a different paper size, but this should (generally) only be used when outputting to high-end commercial printing or proofing devices.

- **Page Gap** and **Paper Offset.** These fields should only be used when a job is output to an imagesetter or high-end proofing device. They are used to define page placement on a piece of oversized film or a printing plate. For design-proofing purposes, leave these settings at the default values.

- **Position.** This menu determines the location on the paper where the layout prints. QuarkXPress prints layouts at the left edge of the paper by default; you can change this to center, center horizontal, or center vertical.

- **Resolution.** This menu/field defines the resolution at which the selected printer will output pages. Depending on the PPD, this menu might have a specific default value and a finite set of other options; in other cases (using the Generic Color PPD, for example) you can manually enter a value into the field.

- **Negative Print.** This option is used if the job is output to film. This is unchecked by default and should remain unchecked for desktop proofing.

- **PostScript Error Handler.** This option, if checked, provides information about any PostScript errors that occur during output. PostScript errors are a tremendous burden on the printing workflow, and the standard error messages are usually cryptic and unhelpful (at best). If you use the PostScript Error Handler utility, you will have more detailed information about the specific object that caused the error.

If you are not using a PostScript printer, your options in the QuarkXPress Print dialog box are limited.

Pages Options

The Pages options control the way layout pages will appear on the output medium.

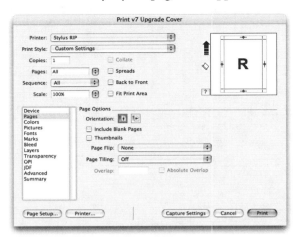

- **Orientation.** These options define the way the layout is positioned on the chosen paper. If the width of your layout page is larger than the width of your paper size, you should choose the Landscape option to maximize the printable area of the paper.

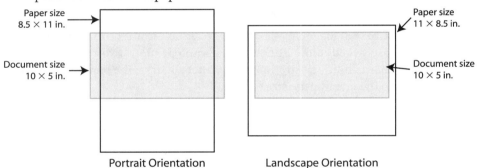

Portrait Orientation   Landscape Orientation

- **Include Blank Pages.** If this option is checked, any blank page in the layout is output. At times you might place a blank page in a layout to force a chapter opener to begin on a right-facing page. If Print Blank Pages is unchecked, those blank pages do not output. (They still exist — they just don't print.) This option should be selected because it provides a quality-control check for you to see if blank pages were inadvertently left at the end of the layout.

- **Thumbnails.** This option prints multiple, small page images on a single sheet. The number of thumbnails per page is based on the layout page size; a letter-size layout, for example, prints five thumbnails across and five down.

- **Page Flip.** This menu is primarily used to control output to a filmsetter or imagesetter. The Page Flip menu defaults to None, which is used for desktop-printing purposes. The other options (Horizontal, Vertical, and Horizontal & Vertical) are not used for desktop printing.

- **Page Tiling.** This option allows you to print oversize layouts at 100% size, even if you only have a letter-size printer, by printing a single layout page to multiple sheets. If Page Tiling is set to Automatic, you can define the Overlap field, or the amount of the page that will print on adjacent tiles. If Absolute Overlap is checked, pages will be tiled using exactly the amount defined in the Overlap field. Otherwise, pages will be tiled with at least the amount in the Overlap field, but may use a larger amount if necessary.

Colors Options

The Colors options define the output characteristics of colors in your layout.

- **Mode.** This menu defines whether you will output pages as Composite (all colors on one sheet) or Separation (each process- and spot-ink color on a separate sheet).

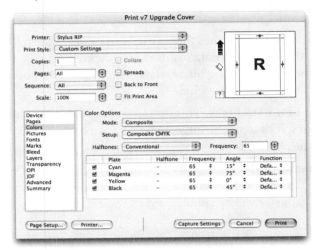

- **Setup.** When printing in Composite mode, you can use this menu to print as Grayscale, Composite RGB, Composite CMYK, Composite CMYK & Spot, or AsIs.

  If you're printing in Separation mode, you can choose Convert to Process (results in four separations for the process inks), Process and Spot (every color as a different separation), or In-RIP Separations (for output devices that support that technology).

  Any user-defined color-output setups will also be available in this menu (see Chapter 15).

- **Halftones.** This menu defaults to Conventional, which uses the standard line-screen numbers and angles that are common for offset lithography. You can choose Printer from the menu to take advantage of the information in the printer PPD to produce better-looking proofs on an inkjet or desktop laser printer.

- **Frequency.** This option defines the line screen (lpi) that will be applied when you are using conventional halftones. Depending on the printer and PPD you're using, the pop-up menu might include specific settings for which your printer is optimized.

- **Separations List.** The bottom section of the Colors category lists the color separations that will be printed. If you are printing in Separation mode, you can choose to print only specific plates using the check boxes next to each color name. Any color checked will be output as a separation. When using conventional halftones, you can use this list to change the halftone-dot characteristics (frequency, angle, and function) of a specific ink color.

AsIs color is used in color-managed workflows; when the file is output, color is described to the PostScript output device according to the defined source profiles.

Pictures Options

- **Output.** This menu determines how images appear when you print. The default Normal prints pictures at the resolution saved in the picture file for raster images, or at the printer resolution for vector graphics. If you're only proofing relative position and balance, you can choose Low Resolution, which prints the low-res preview of the file; Rough prints an empty box in place of the image.

- **Data.** This menu determines the way information is transmitted to the printer. Although binary data prints more quickly than ASCII, some printers are not capable of handling binary data. The Clean 8-bit option combines ASCII and binary data in a single file.

- **Overprint EPS/PDF Black.** This option forces black that is used in EPS and PDF graphics to overprint, overriding any setting made within the EPS/PDF file.

- **Full Resolution TIFF Output.** When this is checked, 1-bit (bitmap or black-and-white) images will be output at their full resolution. If you uncheck this option, the images will be subsampled to two times the device resolution.

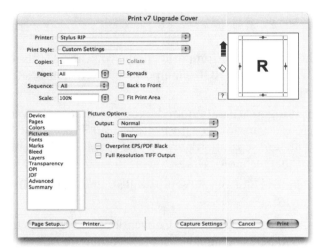

Fonts Options

This list is used to specify the fonts that will be downloaded to the printer when the layout is output.

By default, the Select All check box is selected (all fonts will download to the printer); every font used in the layout appears in the list. You can choose to not download a specific font by unchecking that font in the list. The Optimize Font Formats option enhances printing performance for PostScript Level 3 devices.

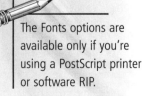

The Fonts options are available only if you're using a PostScript printer or software RIP.

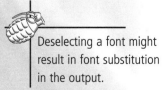

Deselecting a font might result in font substitution in the output.

Marks Options

- **Mode.** This option defaults to Off, which prints the page without trim and registration marks. If you choose Centered or Off Center in this menu, you can define the characteristics of the registration marks that will be included in the output.

- **Width.** This option defines the thickness (or weight) of lines in the registration marks, from 0.002″ to 0.013″.

- **Length.** This option defines the length of trim-mark lines, between 0.139″ and 1″.

- **Offset.** This option defines the distance between the inside end of registration marks and the trim edge of the page, between 0″ and 0.416″. An offset value of 0 prints the marks right up to the page edge.

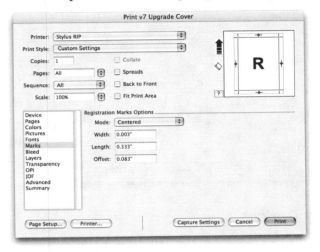

Bleed Options

- **Bleed Type**. This menu determines how bleeds are treated when the layout is printed. Page Items is the default value and means that bleed objects are clipped at the page edge. Symmetric uses the same bleed allowance, defined in the Amount field, on all four sides of the layout page. Asymmetric allows you to define different bleed allowances for each edge of the layout.

- **Clip at Bleed Edge**. If you choose Symmetric or Asymmetric, this option is available (and selected by default). This means any part of the bleed object that extends past the allowance measurement does not appear on the printed output.

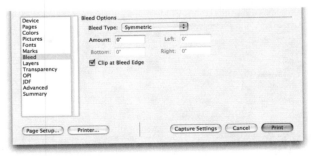

Layers Options

If your layout contains multiple layers, you can control which layers will output from within the Print dialog box. Every layer in the layout is listed here; separations of the highlighted layer appear in the lower pane.

Any layer displaying a checkmark in the Print column of the pane will be printed; layers with the Suppress Output attribute will not show a check. You can toggle the Print checkmark on and off for any specific layer, which overrides the layer settings as defined in the layout. If you want your choices in this tab to always apply to the layers, you can activate the Apply to Layout check box.

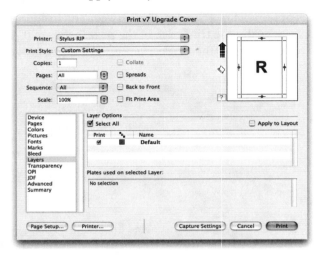

Transparency Options

As we explained in Chapter 9, some transparency applications require QuarkXPress to flatten artwork, or generate raster images that can be interpreted for the commercial printing process.

By definition, raster images have a finite resolution that is defined at the point of capture *or creation*. Because QuarkXPress is effectively *creating* a raster image when transparency is flattened, you need to define what resolution will be created.

You can define a specific resolution between 36 and 3600 in the Transparency Flattening Resolution field, or choose one of the common incremental values from the pop-up menu.

The Ignore Transparency Flattening option is used to effectively (but temporarily) convert all semi-opaque objects to 100% opaque for the sake of the current print. This setting does not change any defined opacity settings within the layout.

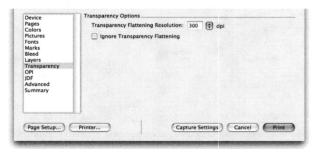

OPI Options

Using an Open Prepress Interface (OPI) workflow, the service bureau scans images at high resolution and stores the files on an OPI server. A low-resolution place-holder is sent to the designer for placement into the layout. Any manipulation made within QuarkXPress is saved with the layout as an OPI comment. When the job is output, the OPI server replaces the low-resolution file with the high-resolution one and applies the OPI comments to the high-resolution file.

The OPI options determine how images are handled when the job is printed. If you are not using an OPI server, leave the Include Images options in the TIFF and EPS areas checked. If you are using an OPI server, you can print a desktop proof using the placeholders by selecting Low Resolution in the TIFF area. This takes less time and is usually adequate for desktop-proofing purposes.

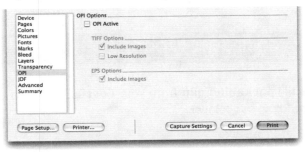

JDF Options

If you are using QuarkXPress Job Jackets, you can include JDF (Job Definition Format) information with the output. JDF information can be fed into a JDF-enabled, computer-integrated-manufacturing (CIM) system to improve communication and throughput. (See Chapter 16 for an explanation of Job Jackets.)

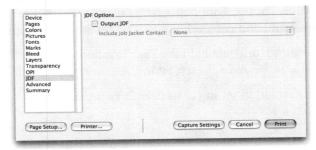

Advanced Options

The PostScript Level menu defines which version of PostScript language to use for the output. PostScript Level 3, the default value and latest version, includes more capabilities than Level 2. Many older devices, however, cannot interpret PostScript Level 3 information.

Adobe PostScript Level 3 was released in 1997. There are still many devices in use today that do not support PostScript Level 3.

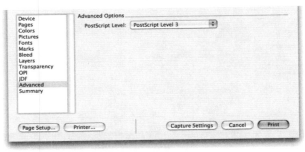

Summary

This provides a textual summary of the choices you've made in other categories of printing options. You can scroll through the list to find a specific option, and collapse or expand individual categories to navigate the list.

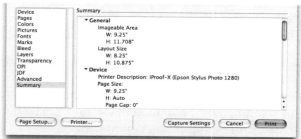

When you used Collect for Output in the previous exercise, a new copy of the file **packaging.qxp** was placed in the **Tropical_Suites_ Brochure** folder.

That is the file that will be included in the job package. Make sure you open that file and print it instead of the one in the **Work_In_Progress** folder.

We are allowing the layout page to fit on one sheet of paper for instructional purposes. If you are creating a proof to send to the service bureau, you should always output your proof at 100%, even if you need to tile to multiple pages.

You will create a tiled proof in the next exercise.

PRINT A COMPOSITE PROOF

1. Open the file **packaging.qxp** from your **Cosciel_Ad** folder (in your **Work_In_Progress** folder).

2. Choose File>Print.

3. In the Printer menu, choose the PostScript printer you're using.

4. With Devices selected in the list of categories, choose the PPD for your printer in the PPD menu.

5. If your printer is capable of printing larger than letter-size paper, choose Tabloid or A3 in the Paper Size menu.

   If your printer cannot print paper larger than letter, choose Letter in the Paper Size menu and choose Fit in Print Area at the top of the dialog box.

   Choose Center Horizontally in the Page Positioning menu (this option is not available if you have chosen Fit in Print Area).

   Leave the Resolution setting at its default value, and leave all other options unchecked.

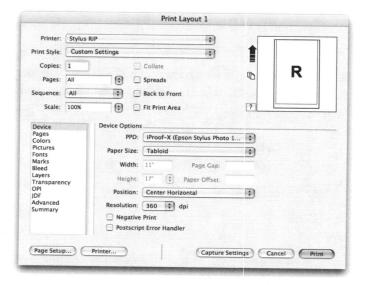

6. Click Colors in the list of options and choose Composite in the Mode menu.

   If you're using a color printer, choose Composite CMYK from the Setup menu. If you have a black-and-white printer, select Grayscale from the Print Colors menu.

   Choose Printer in the Halftones menu to take advantage of the information in the PPD for your printer.

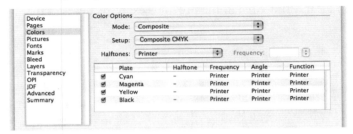

7. Click Marks in the list of options. Choose Centered in the Mode menu and leave the other options at their default values.

8. Click Bleed in the list of options. Choose Symmetric in the Bleed Type menu. Enter "0.125" in the Amount field and leave Clip at Bleed Edge checked.

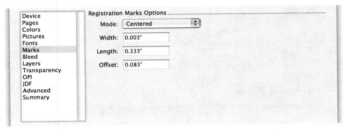

9. Look at the Preview in the top-right corner of the dialog box. Look at the information in this dialog box, especially at the preview image. You should not see any red area in the image.

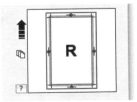

Red areas in the preview indicate that some of your settings will not fit using the current paper size/ orientation settings.

10. Click Print. You should see a dialog box that tells you the layout is spooling to the PostScript RIP.

11. Close the file. When you are asked if you want to save the file before closing, click Save.

1. Reopen **packaging.qxp** from the **Cosciel_Ad** folder and choose File>Print. Notice that the settings you made in the previous exercise are still the same.

2. In the Device options, change the Paper Size menu to Letter. If you had chosen Fit in Print Area in the previous exercise, deselect that option now.

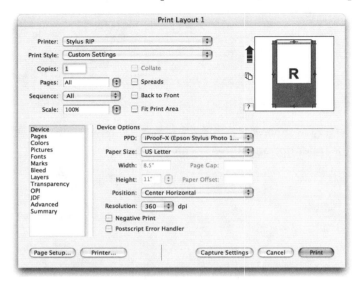

3. In the Pages options, choose Automatic in the Tiling menu and change the Overlap field to 1".

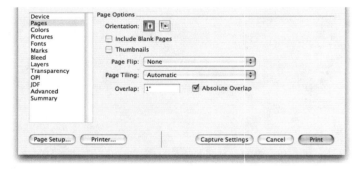

4. Review the preview image. The green lines indicate what will appear on each of four tiles.

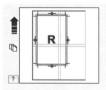

5. Click Print. When the spooling process is finished, close the file. You will have four pieces of paper for the single layout page.

1. Reopen **packaging.qxp** from your **Cosciel_Ad** folder and choose File>Print.

2. In the Device options, choose Tabloid again (if possible), or reactivate the Fit In Print Area check box if you can't print to tabloid paper.

3. In the Pages options, turn Tiling to Off. Notice that the settings you made in the Print a Composite Proof exercise are still active.

4. In the Colors options, choose Separation in the Mode menu.

   Choose Convert to Process in the Setup menu and make sure Printer is selected in the Halftones menu.

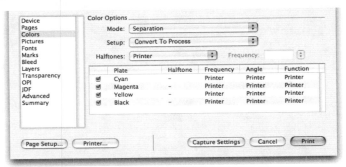

The Convert to Process option isn't specifically necessary in this file since you corrected spot colors earlier in this chapter. You should, however, understand this option.

5. Click Print. The spool message shows as each separation is printing. Four pieces of paper will output for the one layout page.

6. Close the file without saving.

MANAGING PPDS

PPDs are usually installed with the device-driver software or with other software applications. Additional PPDs might exist as a part of the default system software. Because PPD files are installed from various sources, you might have several (or many) PPD files for devices that do not exist in your workflow.

QuarkXPress allows you to control the specific PPDs that are available in the application environment using the PPD Manager (Utilities>PPD Manager). The PPD manager lists every PPD available on your computer. The entire list appears in the QuarkXPress Print dialog box by default, as indicated by the checkmarks in the Include column.

The PPD menu in the Print dialog box lists every available PPD. The specific file you choose in this menu defines the options that are available.

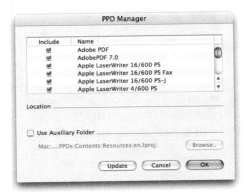

You can deselect one or more PPD files by clicking in the Include column to turn off the checkmark. To reactivate a PPD file, you can click in the Include column to replace the checkmark. After the unwanted PPDs are deactivated, the list in the Printer Description menu of the Print dialog box is far more manageable.

Working with Nonsystem PPDs

You can also use the PPD manager to locate PPD files that are not stored in your System folder. By activating the Use Auxiliary Folder check box, you can click the Select/Browse button in the PPD Manager dialog box, which effectively redirects the application to a folder other than the System folder to determine the available PPDs.

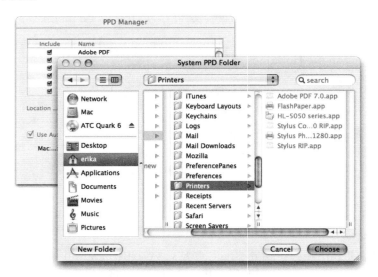

If you assign an auxiliary PPD folder, PPDs installed at the system level are unavailable. The resulting list shows only those PPDs (if any) that are available in the folder you designate.

The Auxiliary PPD Folder option is useful if, for example, a service provider gives you a PPD for their imagesetter. Because you don't have the imagesetter connected to your computer, you should not install the PPD in your System folder.

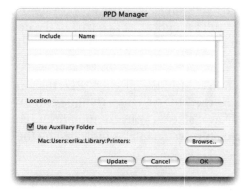

If you point the PPD Manager to a different folder, you can temporarily access the PPD of the service provider's output device, make your print choices, save the layout to PostScript or PDF, and then change the PPD Manager back to the System PPD folder. This allows you to choose the correct settings for a specific device, even if that device is not connected to your printer. Only options listed in the PPD Manager dialog box will appear in the Printer Description menu of the Print Setup dialog box.

When you have finished with the service provider's PPD, make sure that you reopen the PPD manager and deactivate the Use Auxiliary Folder check box. You will see a status bar indicating that QuarkXPress is updating printer descriptions.

When the status bar disappears, all system PPDs again appear in the PPD Manager. Notice, however, that every available PPD has a check mark in the Include column — you have to again remove any PPDs you don't want or need.

SAVING PAGES AS EPS

It is sometimes necessary to export a layout page as an EPS file, especially when submitting advertisement layouts to a magazine or other publisher. Once a QuarkXPress page is exported as an EPS file, you can open it in a vector-illustration program, place it into another page layout, parse it into a bitmap-image application, or distill it to a PDF file. The entire page is saved as one file, which means that you don't have to send out all of the individual components.

In QuarkXPress 7, the Save Page as EPS process has been significantly expanded and enhanced to create more complete EPS files. When you choose File>Save Page as EPS, a system-standard navigation dialog box opens, where you can define the location for the saved file.

The Page field in this dialog box defaults to the page active in the Project window. The file name (the Save As text field) defaults to "Layout Name_Page x.eps", where "x" is the page number of the active page in the Project window. You can change the Page field to a different page than the active one, and rename the file using some meaningful file name.

If you click the Options button in the bottom of the dialog box, you can define the specific settings for the EPS file you're saving. Similar to the Print dialog box, the Save Page as EPS options dialog box is organized with a list of categories on the left. Clicking a category in the list displays the associated options in the right side of the dialog box.

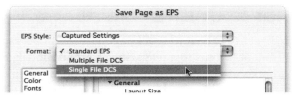

The Format menu is used to save the file as a Standard EPS, Multiple File DCS (DCS 2.0), or Single File DCS.

This menu is available regardless of the category showing below. (Format for an EPS file is similar to defining the printer to use when printing; thus, it is available in the Save Page as EPS options dialog box.)

The Capture Settings button, as in the Print dialog box, saves the current settings for the current layout. Clicking this button closes the open dialog boxes and returns you to the Project window; no EPS file is generated.

General Options

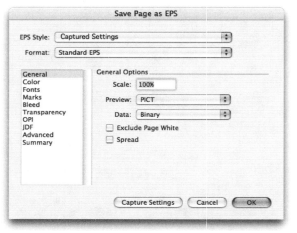

- **Scale.** This option defaults to 100% and defines the size at which the page is exported. There are very few cases when you should export a page at any size other than 100%.

- **Preview.** This menu defines the format (None, TIFF, PICT) used for the low-resolution screen preview of the file. If you are sending the file to a Windows-based computer, you should choose TIFF from this menu. If you choose None, the resulting EPS file will not have a preview image for placement into another layout.

- **Data.** This menu defines the format of bitmap data in the page being saved. You can choose ASCII, Binary, or Clean 8-Bit.

- **Exclude Page White.** This option allows you to save the page with no background. If the option is unchecked, a white background box will exist within the page boundaries in the EPS file. If the exported EPS is placed into a layout over another object, the white box (background) will obscure anything behind it.

- **Spread.** This option exports both pages of a spread as an EPS file.

Color Options

As in the Print dialog box, you can define the color setup that will be used to generate the EPS file. If you are saving a Standard EPS file (in the Format menu), you can save the page as Grayscale, Composite RGB, Composite CMYK, Composite CMYK and Spot, AsIs, or any user-defined composite color output setup. If you're saving a DCS file, you can choose Convert to Process, Process and Spot, or any user-defined separation color output setup.

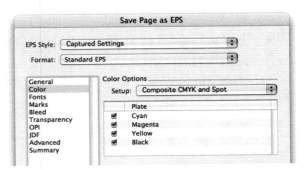

Fonts Options

This list shows every font that is used in the layout; the Select All option is active by default, which means all used fonts will be embedded in the resulting EPS file. You can uncheck specific fonts in the list if you don't want to embed those fonts.

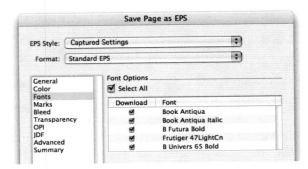

If you don't embed fonts in the EPS file, you'll need to send the font files to anyone who will use the EPS file for output. It's much easier and more compact — and avoids potential output problems — to simply embed the fonts into the EPS file.

Other Options

The Marks, Bleed, Transparency, OPI, JDF, Advanced, and Summary options for saving EPS files are the same as the options in the Print dialog box. Refer back to the Printing section of this chapter if you are unsure about these options.

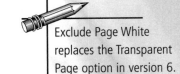
Exclude Page White replaces the Transparent Page option in version 6.

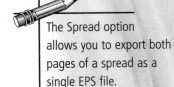
The Spread option allows you to export both pages of a spread as a single EPS file.

The list below the Setup menu shows the ink colors that will be included in the EPS file.

The ability to embed fonts in a Quark-generated EPS file is new to version 7.

The ability to add registration marks to a Quark-generated EPS file is new to version 7.

The Page Items bleed type from the Print dialog box is not available for Quark-generated EPS files.

EXPORTING LAYOUTS AS PDF

PDF (Portable Document Format) files are gaining increasing popularity in the commercial output world because they solve a significant number of potential production problems. PDF files are cross-platform; they are independent of the fonts used, linked files, or even the originating application; they contain all of the required elements (including fonts) in a single file; and they are device-independent as well as page-independent, which means that a PDF document can contain rotated pages and even pages of different sizes.

QuarkXPress incorporates sophisticated controls for generating PDF files directly from layout files without the need for third-party software. Although this ability was added in version 6, it has been considerably enhanced and expanded in version 7.

PDF Preferences

The PDF pane of the Preferences dialog box offers two options:

- **Direct to PDF** creates the PDF file at the time you choose to export as PDF.

- **Create PostScript File for Later Distilling** saves a PostScript file to the folder you define. Using this option, you can also define a watched folder.

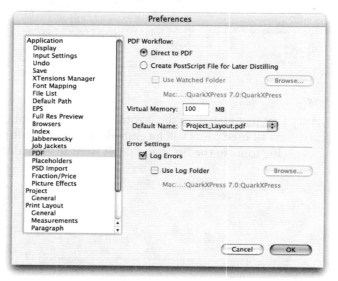

You can increase the virtual memory available for the PDF output to process, between 32 and 1024 MB.

By default, PDF files are saved with the Project_Layout.pdf file name structure; you can change this in the Default Name menu to Layout_Project.pdf, Layout.pdf, or Project.pdf.

Finally, you can determine how errors in the PDF process are handled. Log Errors creates a log file in the application folder; you can define a different location by selecting the Use Log Folder check box and clicking the Browse button.

You can also a print (save) a job to a PostScript file using the Print dialog box, and then later distill the PostScript file using Adobe Acrobat Distiller.

In QuarkXPress 6, default PDF options were controlled through the Preferences dialog box. In version 7, default PDF settings are controlled in the Default PDF Output Style (explained in the next section of this chapter).

The Default Name menu is not available if you are working on a file in single-layout mode.

PDF Export Options

Choosing File>Export>Layout as PDF opens a system-standard navigation dialog box where you can select the location for the resulting PDF file. You can define which page or pages to include in the PDF file in the Pages field, and you can define specific PDF options by clicking the Options button.

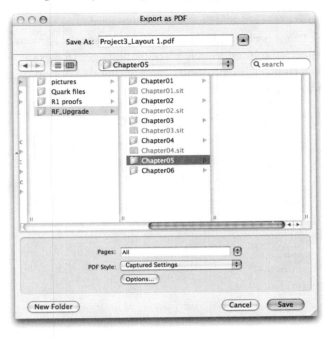

Notice the similarity to the Save Page as EPS dialog box. As we mentioned, the reorganization of numerous dialog boxes is partly an effort to make things more consistent from box to box — which you can see here.

The PDF Export Options dialog box — like the Print and Save Page as EPS dialog boxes — uses the now-familiar category-list interface.

PDF Verification

The Verification menu is always available at the top of the dialog box; you can create PDF/X compliant files using one of the options in this menu.

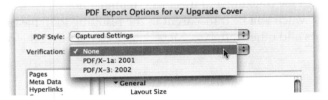

Because there are so many different ways to create a PDF — and not all of those ways are optimized for the needs of commercial printing — the potential benefits of the file format are often undermined. The PDF/X specification was created to help solve some of the problems associated with bad PDF files entering the prepress workflow. PDF/X is a subset of PDF that is specifically designed to ensure files have the information necessary for and available to the digital prepress output process.

- **PDF/X-1a.** This option requires that files are delivered as CMYK (plus spot colors); PDF/X-1a does not support RGB or device-independent color.

- **PDF/X-3.** This option supports CMYK (and spot), RGB, and device-independent color modes. PDF/X-3 (which supports color profiles) is useful when the specific CMYK is undetermined or nonspecific, such as when an ad will be printed in multiple magazines or when a distribute-and-print brochure will be printed at multiple locations on different equipment.

Pages Options

Activating the Spreads check box, as in the Print dialog box, outputs both pages of a spread as a single page in the PDF file.

You can export all pages to one file or activate the Export Pages as Separate PDFs check box. Using this option, a 15-page layout (for example) will result in 15 separate PDF files.

If Include Blank Pages is checked, the PDF file will have the same number of pages as your layout file. If you intentionally place blank pages (for example, to force specific pages to a right-facing position), unchecking this option might ruin your effort because those pages will not exist in the resulting PDF.

You can also embed black-and-white or color thumbnails into the PDF file.

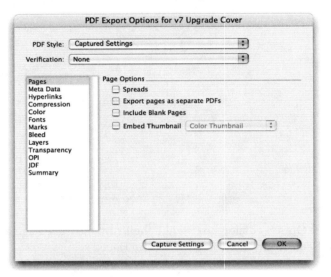

Meta Data Options

You can use the Meta Data options to add searchable information to a PDF file. You can define a Title (defaulted to the layout name), Subject, Author, and Keywords, all of which will be transparent in the resulting PDF file but accessible by search engines and other software. Meta data does not affect the printability of a file.

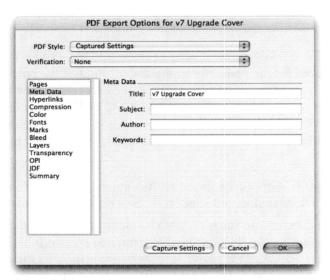

Hyperlinks Options

Hyperlinks options are used to add interactivity to a PDF file. If you use the Lists or Index utilities in QuarkXPress, you can define those elements to be interactive links in the resulting PDF file.

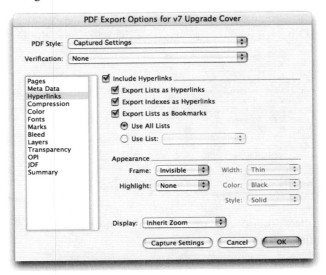

You can use the Hyperlinks palette to add hyperlink attributes to objects in a print layout. When you export the layout as PDF, activating the Include Hyperlinks check box results in a PDF file with live links.

If you choose Export Lists as Hyperlinks or Export Indexes as Hyperlinks, clicking an item in the built list of the PDF takes you to the appropriate location in the file.

If you choose Export Lists as Bookmarks (whether you use all lists or a specific list from the following submenu), the list items will appear in the Bookmarks panel of the PDF viewer application (Acrobat or Preview).

The Appearance options define how hyperlinks appear in the generated PDF file. Choosing Visible in the Frame menu (then defining the hyperlink frame attributes) changes the appearance of hyperlink text and objects in the file; those hyperlink objects will not appear exactly as you designed them.

The Display menu controls the opening behavior of a PDF file. The four options in this menu (Inherit Zoom, Fit Window, Fit Width, and Fit Length) are relatively self-explanatory.

Compression Options

The compression options determine what — and how much — data will be included in the PDF file. This set of options is one of the three most important when creating PDFs, since too-low resolution results in bad-quality printing and too-high resolution results in extremely long download times.

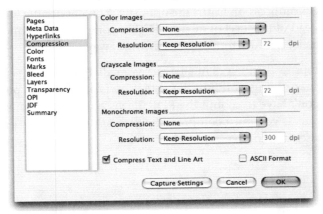

Before you choose compression settings, you need to consider your final goal. If you're creating a file for commercial printing, resolution is more important than file size; if your goal is a PDF that will be posted on the Web for general consumption, file size is equally (if not more) important than pristine image quality.

You can define a specific Compression scheme for color, grayscale, and monochrome images. Different options are available depending on the image type.

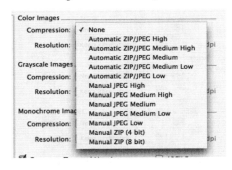
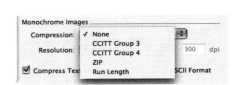

- **JPEG** compression options are *lossy*, which means data is thrown away to create a smaller file.

- **ZIP** compression is *lossless*, which means that all file data is maintained in the compressed file.

- **CCITT** compression was initially developed for fax transmission. Group 3 supports two specific resolution settings (203 × 98 dpi and 203 × 196 dpi). Group 4 supports resolution up to 400 dpi.

- **Run Length** encoding is a lossless compression scheme that abbreviates sequences of adjacent pixels. If four pixels in a row are black, RLE saves that segment as "four black" instead of "black-black-black-black."

Warning: The JPEG compression options in QuarkXPress are the opposite of what you see (and might be used to) in Adobe applications. When you save a PDF file from Photoshop, for example, you are asked to define the image *Quality*; "Maximum" means maximum quality.

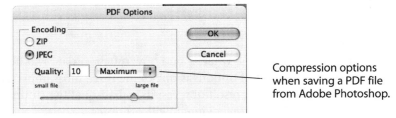

Compression options when saving a PDF file from Adobe Photoshop.

In QuarkXPress, compression is just the opposite. You choose the level of *compression* instead of the level of quality. Higher compression (sometimes) means lower quality because more data is thrown away.

If you don't compress the images in a layout, your PDF file may be extremely large. For a commercial printing workflow, large file size is preferable to poor image quality. If you don't have to submit the PDF file via modem transmission, large file size is not an issue. If you must compress the files, ask your service provider what settings they prefer you to use.

Resolution

When you resize an image in the layout, you are changing its effective resolution. The *effective resolution* of an image is the resolution calculated after any scaling is taken into account. This number is equally — and sometimes more — important than the original image resolution. The effective resolution can be calculated with a fairly simple equation:

Original resolution ÷ (% magnification ÷ 100) = effective resolution

If a 300-ppi image is magnified 150%, the effective resolution is:

300 ppi ÷ 1.5 = 200 ppi

If you reduce the same 300-ppi image to 50%, the effective resolution is:

300 ppi ÷ 0.5 = 600 ppi

In other words, the more you enlarge a raster image, the lower its effective resolution becomes. Reducing an image results in higher effective resolution, which is often unnecessary even for commercial printing and can result in unnecessarily large PDF files.

When you create a PDF file in QuarkXPress, you also specify the resolution that will be maintained (for each of the three image types) in the resulting PDF file. This option is useful if you want to throw away excess resolution for print files, or if you want to create low-resolution files for proofing or Web distribution.

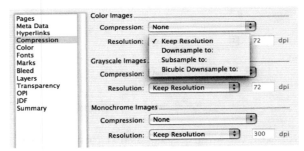

- **Keep Resolution.** Using this option, all the image data in the linked files will be included in the PDF file.
- **Downsample To.** Using this method, QuarkXPress reduces the number of pixels in an area by averaging areas of adjacent pixels. This method is applied to result in the user-defined resolution (typically 72 or 96 dpi for Web-based files or 300 dpi for print files).
- **Subsample To.** This method applies the center pixel value to surrounding pixels. If you think of a 3 × 3 grid, subsampling enlarges the center block (pixel) — and thus, its value — in place of the surrounding eight blocks.
- **Bicubic Downsample To.** This method creates the most accurate pixel information for continuous-tone images; it also takes the longest to process, and produces a softer image. To understand how this option works, think of a 2 × 2-block grid — bicubic resampling averages the value of all four of those squares (pixels) to interpolate the new information.

Bicubic downsampling is not available for monochrome images.

Other Options

The Color, Fonts, Marks, Bleed, Layers, Transparency, OPI, JDF, and Summary options for saving PDF files are the same as the options in the Print dialog box. You can review the Printing section of this chapter if you are unsure about these options.

As when saving a page as EPS, the fonts must be embedded in a PDF file to guarantee proper output. If you choose to not embed specific fonts in a PDF file, you are risking font substitution and ruined prints.

CREATING OUTPUT STYLES

Because of the number of different settings available in the Print dialog boxes, it can be time-consuming to define the output for a specific layout. It is also fairly easy to miss one or more options, which means that the layout may not output correctly. And in many cases, you are outputting more than one file using the same settings — resulting in a lot of repetition when you have to constantly select the same sets of options.

In previous versions of QuarkXPress, you could define Print Styles to help avoid these problems. QuarkXPress 7 takes this concept a step further, extending print styles to all three output methods — printing, saving as EPS, and exporting as PDF. You can now automate any of these processes by creating a custom *output style* for the specific output intent.

Defining and Accessing Output Styles

Output styles are managed in the same way as other assets (colors, style sheets, etc.). In the Output Styles dialog box, clicking New presents a menu of the three different output styles; the option you choose here opens a dialog box so that you can define the settings in the style.

An output style works on the same concept as text-formatting style sheets. You make the appropriate choices once and call the style as often as necessary. Output styles are not layout-specific; when you create an output style, it is stored in the application settings.

- **EPS** output styles contain all the choices in the Save Page as EPS options dialog box.

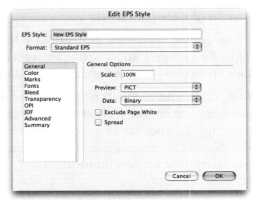

The Export option allows you to export output styles for other users. Service providers sometimes create and distribute output styles for their specific output devices. Keep in mind that the required PPD must be available on any computer that calls a print style.

The Import option allows you to import output styles created by other users; this may be useful if your service provider gives you an output-style file, or if another user on a network has created output styles for different devices on the network.

- **PDF** output styles contain all the choices in the PDF Export Options dialog box.

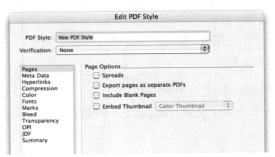

- **Print** output styles contain all the choices in the Print dialog box.

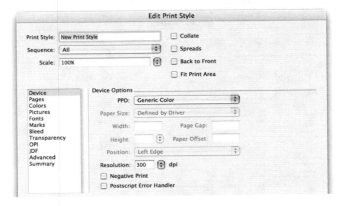

The defined PPD must be available on any computer that calls a print output style.

Once an output style is created, you can access it in the Style menu of the corresponding output dialog box. When you call a defined output style from that menu, the file will be output using the settings that are saved in the style.

Styles On-the-Fly

As another example of easily customizing the workspace, you can also define output styles on-the-fly from within the Print, Save Page as EPS options, and PDF Export Options dialog boxes.

After you have made your choices in the various categories, you can choose New [Type] Output Style from the Style menus in the corresponding dialog boxes. You can assign a name to the new style, and it is saved just as if you created it in the Output Styles dialog box.

Two types of output — EPS and PDF — actually generate a file. These two output options first open a navigation dialog box with a Style menu; you can then access a secondary Options dialog box with another Style menu.

For these two types, on-the-fly output styles can only be created in the Style menu of the options dialog box. Existing styles can be called in either of the two style menus.

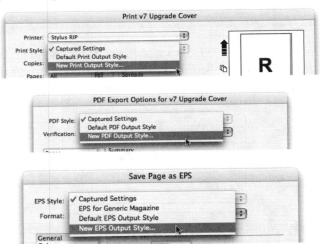

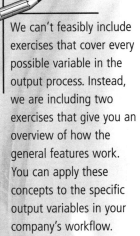
We can't feasibly include exercises that cover every possible variable in the output process. Instead, we are including two exercises that give you an overview of how the general features work. You can apply these concepts to the specific output variables in your company's workflow.

This exercise assumes that you are using a PostScript printer or RIP. If not, some of the options in the Print dialog box (such as Resolution) might not be available.

1. Open the file **packaging.qxp** from your **Cosciel_Ad** folder.

2. Choose File>Print.

3. In the Printer menu, choose the device you use to print tabloid-size proofs.

4. In the Device Options pane, choose the PPD for the device you selected in Step 3.

   Choose Tabloid in the Paper Size menu and Center Horizontal in the Position menu. Choose one of the lower settings in the Resolution menu; if you have a field instead of a menu, enter "300" in the field.

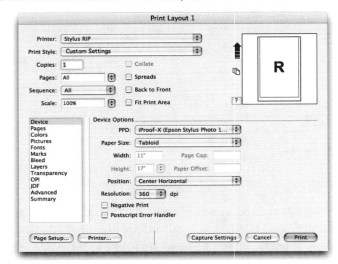

5. In the Pages pane, make sure the Portrait Orientation option is selected.

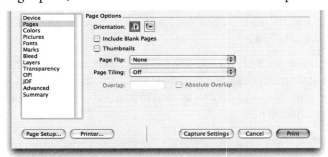

6. In the Colors pane, choose Composite in the Mode menu and choose Composite CMYK in the Setup menu. Change the Halftones menu to Printer to use information saved in the device PPD.

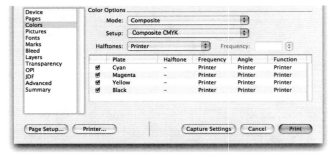

7. In the Fonts pane, make sure the Select All check box is selected.

8. In the Marks pane, choose Centered in the Mode menu. Leave the other fields at their default values.

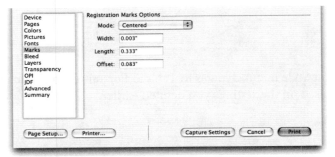

9. In the Bleed pane, choose Symmetric in the Bleed Type menu and change the Amount field to 0.125". Activate the Clip at Bleed Edge check box.

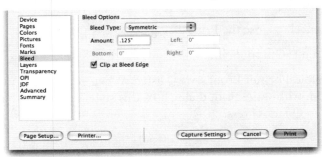

10. In the Transparency pane, make sure the Resolution field is set to 300 dpi.

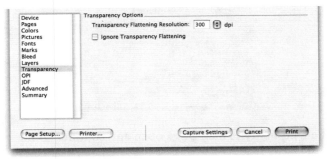

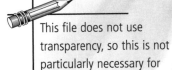
This file does not use transparency, so this is not particularly necessary for this exercise.

The transparency flattening options are vitally important, however, when you are outputting a file that does use transparency and drop shadows.

11. Click Capture Settings.

You are returned to the Project window, and nothing is printed.

12. Choose File>Print again.

All of the settings you made are still selected.

13. Choose New Print Output Style in the Print Style menu.

This menu is currently set to Captured Settings, which is what you did in Step 11. Captured Settings sets are only remembered temporarily unless you save them as Print Output Styles.

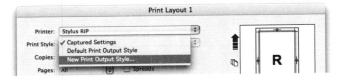

14. In the New Print Output Style dialog box, name the new style "Tabloid Portrait Proof" and click OK.

The Print Style menu changes to Tabloid Portrait Proof, which you just saved based on the settings you defined earlier.

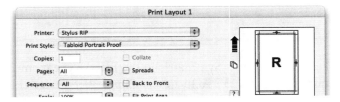

15. Click Cancel to close the Print dialog box.

16. Choose Edit>Output Styles.

The Tabloid Portrait Proof style is listed. When you create a print style, even from within the Print dialog box, this style is available to any layout opened in QuarkXPress.

17. Leave the Output Styles dialog box open and continue to the next exercise.

DEFINE A PDF OUTPUT STYLE

1. In the Output Styles dialog box, click New and choose PDF from the menu.

2. In the Edit PDF Style dialog box, name the new style "Client Position Proof".

3. In the Hyperlinks pane, deactivate the Include Hyperlinks check box.

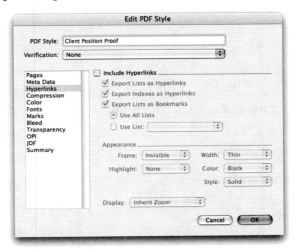

4. In the Compression pane, choose Automatic ZIP/JPEG Medium in the Color Images and Grayscale Images Compression menus. Choose ZIP for Monochrome Images Compression. Activate the Compress Text and Line Art check box.

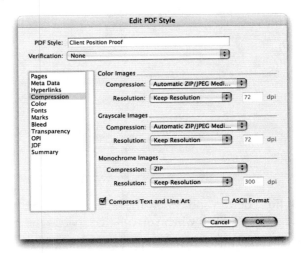

5. In the Color pane, use the Composite mode and the Composite CMYK Setup.

6. In the Fonts pane, activate the Download All Fonts check box.

7. In the Marks pane, make sure marks are turned off.

8. In the Bleed pane, make sure the Amount fields are set to 0".

9. In the Transparency pane, make sure the Resolution field is set to 300 dpi.

Adding crop marks and bleed allowance to a client proof has proved confusing to a client more than once; in general, we prefer to give clients only the information they need. Of course, you know your clients best.

10. Click OK to save the PDF Output Style.

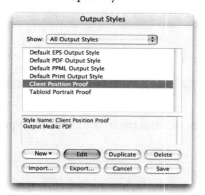

11. Click Save to close the Output Styles dialog box.

12. With **packaging.qxp** open (from the **Cosciel_Ad** folder), choose File>Export>Layout as PDF.

13. Choose Client Position Proof in the PDF Style menu.

14. Click the Options button and review the different settings. Any setting saved in an output style is applied when you call that style in the output dialog box.

15. Click Cancel to close all open dialog boxes, and then close the open file.

SUMMARY

By now you should be familiar with the reorganized Print dialog box, as well as the new EPS and PDF options dialog boxes. You should at least be familiar with the different categories of options so that you can more easily find what you need in your own workflow. You should also be able to create output styles that will automate a lot of time-consuming selections, helping you create better proofs and high-quality output in less time.

Working with Layers

11

Layouts become more complex as you add more elements on top of one another. The QuarkXPress Layers utility is useful for managing complex layout arrangements. In addition, the Layers utility can be used to create multiple versions of the same layout.

IN CHAPTER 11, YOU WILL:

■ Work with layers to create multiple versions of the same layout.

■ Learn about the options available for working with QuarkXPress layers.

■ Discover how to add, rearrange, and remove layers from a layout.

■ Explore the attributes of individual layers.

■ Learn how layers interact based on their defined attributes.

■ Control output using the Layers tab of the Print dialog box.

CREATING AND MANAGING LAYERS

One of the advantages of using a professional page-layout application such as QuarkXPress is the ability to create and manage complex layouts with a large number of elements. The QuarkXPress Layers utility is a powerful option for controlling the objects that compose your layouts.

In addition to managing individual elements, you can also use the Layers utility to create multiple versions of the same layout. This is particularly useful if:

- You are working with multiple overlapping objects on a page. Layers help to manage the stacking order of the different objects.

- You are working with multiple versions of the same layout, such as two versions of the same layout in different languages or several versions with different images in the same position for regional publications.

- You are creating a special die-cut layout using a template created in an illustration application.

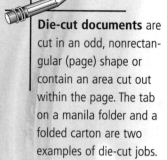

Die-cut documents are cut in an odd, nonrectangular (page) shape or contain an area cut out within the page. The tab on a manila folder and a folded carton are two examples of die-cut jobs.

 CREATE MULTIPLE LAYERS

1. Open the file **tower.qxp** from the **RF_Quark7>Chapter11** folder.

   This project contains one layout that will be used to create two versions of an information sheet — one in English and one in Italian.

2. Choose Window>Layers to display the Layers palette.

Every QuarkXPress layout has at least one layer, the Default layer, which cannot be renamed. If you don't add extra layers, every object you create will exist on the Default layer.

The Default layer is highlighted in the palette, indicating that it is the currently selected layer. The pencil icon to the right of the layer name indicates that the Default layer is the *active* layer, on which any element you create will be placed.

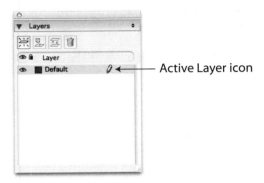

Active Layer icon

3. Click the New Layer button in the Layers palette.

A new layer appears in the Layers palette and is highlighted in the palette. The pencil icon to the right of the layer name indicates that the new layer is now the active layer.

New Layer button →

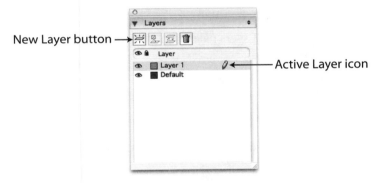

Active Layer icon

The currently active layer is indicated by a pencil icon. The active layer is the target for any object or element you create.

4. Double-click the Layer 1 item in the Layers palette.

Double-clicking a layer in the Layers palette opens the Attributes dialog box, where you can define a number of options specific to that layer. These options will be explained throughout this project.

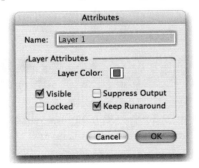

By default, new layers are added with the name "Layer N", where N is a sequential number beginning with 1.

5. Type "English Text" in the Name field and click OK.

The Layers palette reflects the new name of the layer.

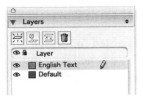

6. Control/right-click the empty space at the bottom of the Layers palette to access the palette's contextual menu.

7. Choose New Layer from the contextual menu.

A new layer appears in Layers palette, just as it would if you clicked the New Layer button.

8. Control/right-click the new layer (Layer 2) in the Layers palette and choose Edit Layer 2 from the contextual menu.

This option opens the Attributes dialog box.

9. Change the layer name to "Italian Text" and click OK.

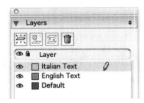

10. Save the file as "layers_working.qxp" in your **Work_In_Progress** folder and continue to the next exercise.

SET UP MULTIPLE LAYERS

To complete this project, the text for each language will exist on individual layers. Only the layout images will exist on the Default layer.

1. In the open file, press the Shift key and use the Item tool to select both text boxes on the Default layer.

The Active Item icon (the small square) appears to the right of the Default layer name. This icon indicates the layer on which the selected objects reside.

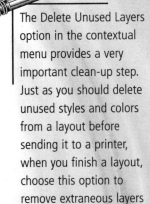

The Delete Unused Layers option in the contextual menu provides a very important clean-up step. Just as you should delete unused styles and colors from a layout before sending it to a printer, when you finish a layout, choose this option to remove extraneous layers from the layout.

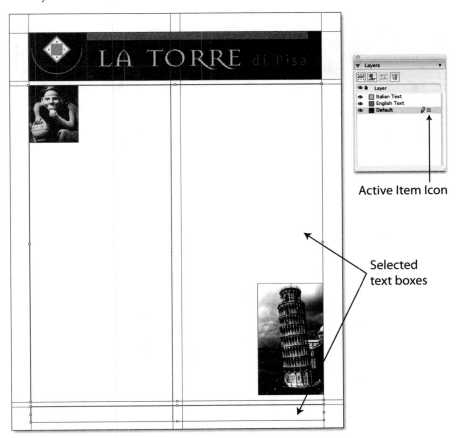

Active Item Icon

Selected text boxes

2. Click the Move Items to Layer button in the Layers palette.

Move Items to Layer button

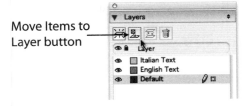

3. In the Move Items dialog box, choose English Text from the Choose Destination Layer menu and click OK.

This utility allows you to move any selected elements from one layer to another. It is important to remember that moving objects removes them from the original layer. Other techniques, which you will see shortly, must be used if you need the same object to exist on more than one layer.

In the Project window, each text box displays a pink bounding box and handles. When working with layers, the color of each item's handles matches the color swatch to the left of the layer name (in the Layers palette).

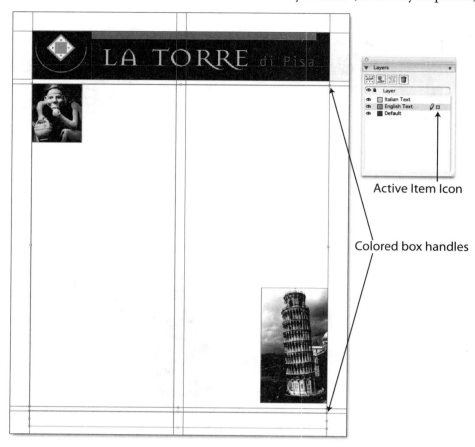

Active Item Icon

Colored box handles

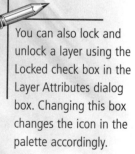

The Layer Color option in the Layer Attributes dialog box determines the color of the layer's object handles and the swatch next to the layer name in the Layers palette. The Layer Color option has no impact on objects placed on that layer.

4. Double-click the Default layer in the Layers palette.

5. Activate the Locked check box and click OK.

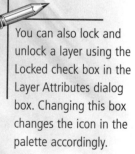

You can also lock and unlock a layer using the Locked check box in the Layer Attributes dialog box. Changing this box changes the icon in the palette accordingly.

When a layer is locked, you cannot select or modify the elements on that layer. The Layers palette shows a Locked icon to indicate this status.

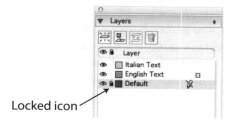

Locked icon

6. Click the English Text layer to make it the active layer.

7. Using the Item tool, select both text boxes on the English Text layer and choose Edit>Copy.

8. Click the Italian Text layer in the Layers palette to make it the target layer.

   Notice the Active Item icon remains on the English Text layer. Selected objects do not necessarily exist on the active layer.

9. Choose Edit>Paste In Place.

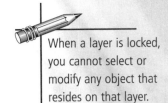

When a layer is locked, you cannot select or modify any object that resides on that layer.

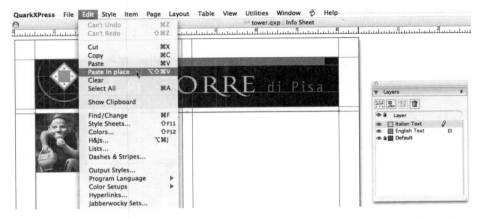

Paste In Place can be used to move or copy elements — in the same position — from one or layer to another within a layout, and from one layout to another within the same project or in a different project file.

The text boxes now have blue bounding boxes and handles, matching the blue swatch to the left of the Italian Text layer name.

10. Click the Visibility icon for the Italian Text layer to hide that layer.

    The text boxes now show pink bounding boxes and handles.

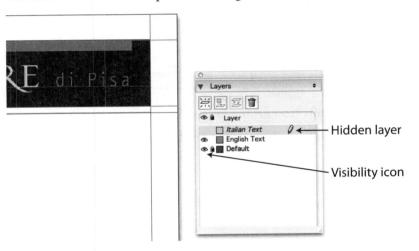

Hidden layer

Visibility icon

Hidden layers are listed in italic type on the Layers palette.

When you used the Paste In Place command, you made an exact duplicate of the selected objects, in the exact same positions; the copy was added to the active layer (Italian Text). Because the Italian Text layer is higher than (above) the English Text layer in the stacking order, only the indicators for the topmost layer are visible. By hiding the Italian Text layer, you can see the copied objects also exist on the English Text layer.

11. Click the Visibility icon for the Default layer to hide that layer.

12. Save the file and continue to the next exercise.

New layers are visible by default.

You can hide a layer by clicking the Visibility icon (the eye), which also hides the Visibility icon. To show a layer, click in the area where the Visibility icon would be for that layer.

You can also control layer visibility using the Visible check box in the Layer Attributes dialog box. Changing this box changes the icon in the palette accordingly.

PLACE LAYER TEXT

1. In the open file, use the Content tool to select the first text box on the English Text layer.

2. Choose File>Import Text and navigate to the file **tower_english.xtg** in the **RF_Quark7>Chapter11** folder. Make sure the Convert Quotes and Interpret XPress Tags check boxes are active and click Open.

3. If you see a conflict-warning message, activate the Repeat For All Conflicts check box and click Use New.

   The text for the English information sheet flows into the text box.

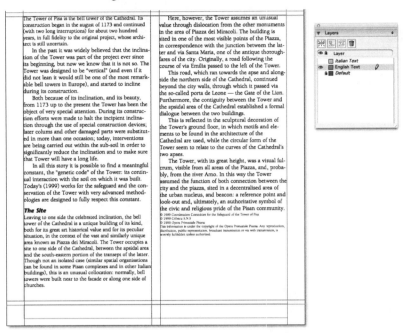

4. Click the Visibility icon for the English Text layer to hide that layer.

5. Click the area of the Visibility icon for the Italian Text layer to show the layer.

6. Place the file **tower_italian.xtg** (from the **RF_Quark7>Chapter11** folder) into the top text box, again making sure to include style sheets and interpret XPress tags.

The text boxes in this layout were created with a runaround attribute of None.

As you will see in the next section, the text-wrap attributes of objects on one layer affect all text boxes on underlying layers.

If the text boxes on the Italian Text layer had a runaround attribute of Item, the text boxes on the Italian Text layer would force the text on the English Text layer to move to the next available (if any) text box, and only the Italian text would be visible.

7. Show the English Text and Default layers.

   Because both text layers are visible, the text is unreadable. Also, the images on the Default layer obscure the text on both text layers.

8. Hide the Italian Text and English Text layers. Only the Default layer should be visible.

9. Save the file and continue to the next esercise.

CONTROLLING LAYER CONTENT

The stacking order of layers matches the order in the palette; the bottom layer of the palette is at the bottom of the stack, and the top layer in the palette is at the top of the stack. Just as each successive object you draw is placed in front of previous object, each successive layer is placed in front of other layers.

You can manipulate the stacking order of objects within a layer using the Bring to Front and Send to Back commands. These commands do not, however, work for objects on different layers. All objects on Layer 3, for example, appear in front of all objects on Layer 2 and Layer 1 unless you rearrange the stacking order of the layers.

 REARRANGE LAYERS AND CONTROL TEXT WRAP

1. Click the Italian Text layer and drag it below the Default layer.

   A line indicates where the layer will be positioned.

   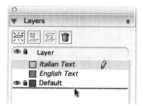

   When you release the mouse button, the layer moves to the location indicated by the line.

   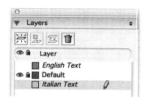

2. Click the English Text layer and drag it below the Italian Text layer.

   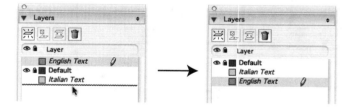

3. Make the English Text layer visible.

   Because the English Text layer is now below the Default layer in the stacking order, the text-wrap attributes for Default layer objects apply to the text on the underlying English Text layer.

4. Place the insertion point at the beginning of the first line of copyright text (the small text at the end of the second column) and press Enter (numeric keypad) to force the copyright information into the bottom text box.

You can select multiple contiguous layers by holding the Shift key while clicking. You can select noncontiguous layers by pressing Command/Control while clicking the layers.

5. Hide the Default layer.

The text on the English Text layer reflows because the Default layer objects are hidden.

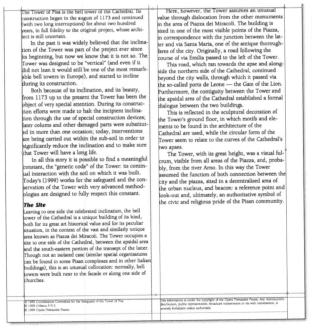

6. Double-click the Default layer to open the Attributes dialog box.

7. Activate the Keep Runaround check box and click OK.

Object runaround attributes apply to text on any underlying layer. When the Keep Runaround check box is selected, text-wrap attributes for objects on that layer are applied even when the layer is hidden.

In the Project window, the layout shows how the text on the English Text layer is affected by the Default layer text-wrap attributes, even though the Default layer objects are not visible.

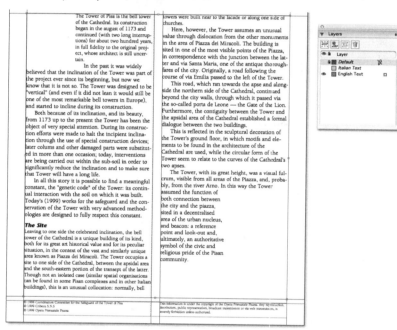

8. Make the Default layer visible.

9. Hide the English Text layer and make the Italian Text layer visible.

   The same text-wrap attributes apply to text on any underlying layer.

10. Force the Italian copyright information into the bottom box (see Step 4).

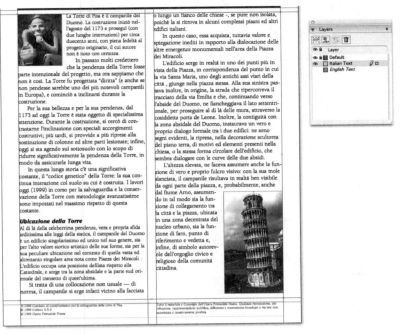

11. Save the file and continue to the next exercise.

PRINTING LAYERS

As you can see, layers make it easier to create multiple versions of a job within a single layout. When you print a file that includes layers, the visible layers are set by default to output; if what you see is what you want, the process is essentially the same as printing any other layout. You are not, however, limited to printing what is visible in the layout before you choose File>Print. You can use the Layers pane of the Print dialog box to output any combination of layers in a layout, regardless of the layers' visibility.

PRINT LAYERS

1. In the open file, double-click the English Text layer to open the Attributes dialog box.

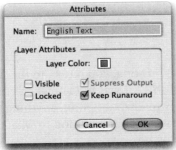

   The Suppress Output check box is not available, but you can see that it is active. By default, hidden layers are set to not print.

This option allows you to define which layers will output when you print the layout. If you have multiple language versions on different layers, for example, this check box would be active for only one layer at a time. This option is also useful for layers containing comments, production notes, or other important items that are not part of the final design.

2. Choose File>Print and click the Layers tab.

    The Default and Italian Text layers have check boxes in the Print column, indicating that these two layers will output when you click Print.

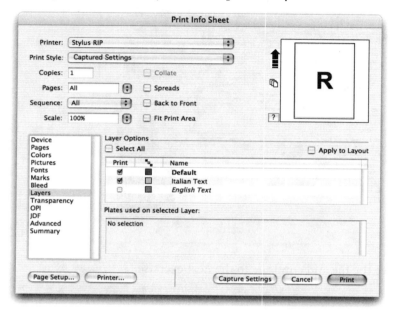

3. Click the empty box to the left of English Text to activate and print that layer.

4. Click the checked box to the left of Italian Text to deactivate and not print that layer.

    You can use this technique to determine which layers in the layout will output, regardless of what is visible or selected in the Project window.

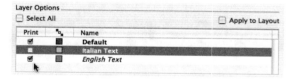

5. Activate the Apply to Layout check box and click Print.

    When the job is done printing, you return to the Project window. All layers are now visible (English Text was hidden when you opened the Print dialog box). Using the Apply to Layout option, anything you set to print becomes visible in the Project window, in addition to whatever was visible when you opened the Print dialog box.

6. Save the file and continue to the next section.

DELETING AND MERGING LAYERS

It is quite common to create a layout with multiple layers, and then decide that one (or more) of those layers is unnecessary. A comments layer, for example, might be irrelevant after the various comments have been addressed. If a layer is unnecessary, there is no reason to leave it in the file; in fact, there is a good reason to remove it — preventing it from accidentally appearing in the final output. The QuarkXPress Layers utility includes the ability to delete selected layers, determine what happens to objects that are placed on deleted layers, and merge the contents of multiple layers into a single layer.

DELETE AND MERGE LAYERS

1. In the open file, click the Italian Text layer to select it.

2. Click the Delete Layer button in the Layers palette.

   If you try to delete a layer on which objects are placed, you have to decide what to do with the objects that exist on that layer. The default option deletes the layer, as well as the objects on that layer. You can also choose to move the objects to a specific layer (selected from the associated menu).

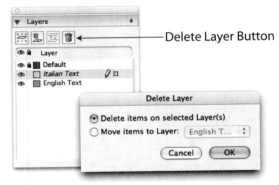

3. Click OK to delete the Italian Text layer and the objects on the layer.

4. Unlock the Default layer.

5. Press Shift and click the Default layer.

   Both the English Text and Default layers should be highlighted in the Layers palette. Pressing the Shift key allows you to select multiple contiguous layers.

6. Click the Merge Layers button.

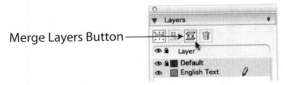

7. In the Merge Layer dialog box, choose Default as the destination layer and click OK.

Merging layers combines the contents of selected layers onto the destination layer and removes any selected layers that are not the destination layer. The layout now contains only the English version of the text — as well as the graphics — on the Default layer.

8. Save the file as "english_tower.qxp" in your **Work_In_Progress** folder and close the file.

SUMMARY

The file you worked with in this chapter was specifically designed to highlight the various options that are available when designing with QuarkXPress layers. You began with a basic page layout and used layers to create multiple versions of the same layout. You learned how to add and name layers, how to determine the layer on which new objects will be positioned, how to copy and move objects from one layer to another, how to control the text-wrap attributes that affect text on underlying layers, and how to control the output of layers.

Layers are useful for controlling the stacking order of multiple objects in a complex layout, incorporating design templates that were created in an illustration program, adding comments that will not appear in the final printed job, or building multiple versions of a document. In fact, layers are one of the defining features of professional graphics software, allowing you to build complex layouts, and then view, edit, and output exactly (and only) the elements you want.

Building Lists and Indexes

12

Before desktop-publishing software automated the document design process, lists and indexes were created manually from page proofs — by turning each page and writing down the appropriate listing and page number, then sorting and typesetting those hard-copy lists into the final document. The process was extremely time-consuming and required precise attention to detail. If the document changed after the table of contents or index was complete, the entire piece had to be rechecked, page by page. QuarkXPress includes tools that automate these processes, greatly improving production time and making it easier to maintain accuracy.

IN CHAPTER 12, YOU WILL:

- ▌ Define lists based on style sheets.
- ▌ Navigate a layout using the Lists palette.
- ▌ Compile a list into a layout.
- ▌ Tag various types of index entries.
- ▌ Define index preferences.
- ▌ Build an index into a layout.

BUILDING LISTS

The Lists utility is an excellent way to monitor the editorial priority of a document. If you define a table-of-contents list, you can quickly see the headings, subheadings, and any subordinate levels. While the Lists feature is particularly useful for creating a table of contents, this is not its only possible use. Different types of projects call for different types of lists; following are just a few examples.

If you are working on a layout that uses parenthetical notations to cite references, you can apply a character style sheet to each reference cited throughout the layout, then build a list using that character style sheet. The Alphabetical option in the Edit Lists dialog box alphabetizes the list of references, which allows you to build a bibliography automatically.

Some publications call for a separate table of contents listing all illustrations in the publication. If you define a Caption paragraph style sheet, you can create a list of figures using the Caption style sheet.

Many publications include a glossary of terms, which are italicized throughout the text, to indicate inclusion in the glossary. If you use a character style sheet (e.g., Glossary Term) to italicize the terms in the layout, you can compile a list of all glossary terms at the end of the layout. You then only need to add the definitions.

Many catalogs include multiple indexes by product, item number, manufacturer, and so on. You can define character style sheets for each category, and then build separate alphabetized lists for each.

Of course these are not the only uses of the Lists utility; you are only limited by the amount of planning you do and by the style sheets you choose to define.

Planning Lists: Interacting with Style Sheets

Some advance planning is required when using lists in QuarkXPress. QuarkXPress lists are based on the style sheets in a layout. To define a list, you have to choose the particular style sheets you want to comprise that list. For example, a table of contents list might include Heading 1, Heading 2, and Heading 3 paragraph style sheets; any text set in those styles appears in the list.

Lists can also be defined to format the elements of the list automatically, using style sheets. If you plan your project carefully, you can predefine the appearance of different list items and apply those style sheets to the elements of the list. Again using the table of contents example, TOC1 can be assigned to Heading 1 list items, TOC2 to Heading 2 items, and so on. When the final list is generated, the table of contents is formatted automatically.

Lists are not confined to paragraph style sheets; you can also define a list based on a character style sheet. As an example, you may define a character style sheet to italicize every proper name in a layout. If you are conscientious in applying the character style sheet to all proper names when building the layout, compiling the final comprehensive list is a relatively easy process.

Creating a List

You can define a list in QuarkXPress by choosing Edit>Lists. The Lists dialog box uses the same interface as other user-defined assets, such as colors and style sheets. The title bar of the dialog box shows the name of the open project. Clicking New in the Lists dialog box opens the Edits List dialog box, where you can define the contents of a particular list. In the Name field, you can choose an appropriate name for the list.

Lists are available for any layout that exists within the project.

As we discussed previously, lists are inherently tied to the style sheets in a layout. The left half of the dialog box lists all styles defined for the layout. To add a style to the list, you can highlight the style in the Available Styles area and click the right-pointing arrow button.

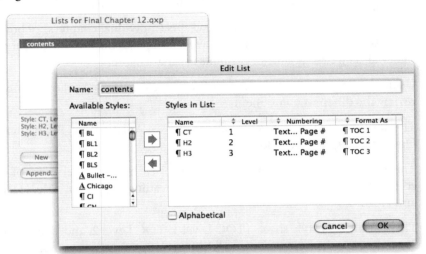

The Styles in List area automatically lists items in alphabetical order. This has no impact on the final appearance of the list.

Once an item is added to the Styles in List area, you can define several options for that item.

- **Level.** This menu defines the nesting level of the style in the list; main headings are typically set to Level 1, subheads are set to Level 2, and so on according to editorial priority. The level of a list item is only relevant to the appearance of the list in the Lists palette. This setting has no impact on formatting when the final list is built into the layout. (Formatting is defined by the style sheet selected in the Format As column.)

- **Numbering.** This menu defines how each list item appears in the list. This setting does not affect the appearance of the list in the Lists palette. The Numbering selection defines how the list item appears in the list when it is built in to the layout.

  - **Text Only**. The list shows only the item text.

  - **Text... Page #**. The list shows the item, followed by a tab character and the page number on which the item occurs.

  - **Page #... Text**. The list shows the page number on which the item occurs, followed by a tab character and the item.

- **Format As.** This menu defines the style sheet that will be used when the list is built into the layout. Not only can the contents of a list be defined according to the existing style sheets, but the appearance of the lists themselves can also — with some advance planning — be automatically formatted using other style sheets.

- **Alphabetical.** If the Alphabetical check box is selected, the list will be displayed in alphabetical order — both in the Lists palette and in the final built list; items are still indented according to the defined level, but the alphabetical option overrides the level hierarchy.

Once you've defined the contents of a list, clicking OK returns you to the Lists dialog box. You have to click Save to finalize your work and return to the Project window.

1. Open the file **color_ch1.qxp** from the **RF_Quark7>Chapter12** folder.

   The publisher has decided to offer excerpts (individual chapters) of books as marketing tools. Each excerpt will have a title page showing the origin of the material, as well as a table of contents for that chapter.

2. Using the Page Layout palette, navigate to each master-page layout and review the different components.

   This layout has three different master pages — A-Title Page, B-Chapter Opener, and C-Chapter Body.

   This layout was created using style sheets for each different element of editorial priority, including three levels of headings (Chapter Title, Head2, and Head3).

   Three additional style sheets (TOC Level 1, TOC Level 2, and TOC Level 3) have also been included. These will be used later when you compile the table of contents.

3. Navigate to Page 1 of the layout and choose Page>Insert. Add 2 pages based on the A-Title Page master before Page 1 in the layout.

4. Drag the C-Chapter Body icon onto the Page 2 icon to change the master that is associated with that page.

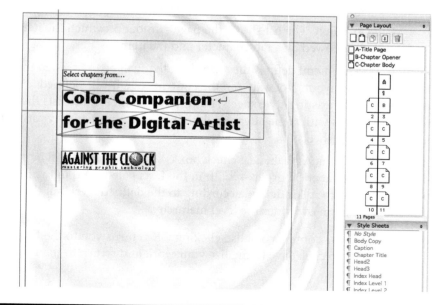

5. Choose Edit>Lists, and click New in the Lists dialog box.

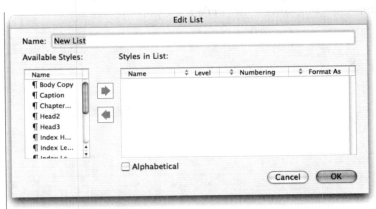

6. Type "Contents" in the Name field.

7. Highlight Chapter Title in the Available Styles window and click the right-facing arrow button.

8. With Chapter Title highlighted in the Styles in List window, click the Numbering column head and choose Text Only from the pop-up menu.

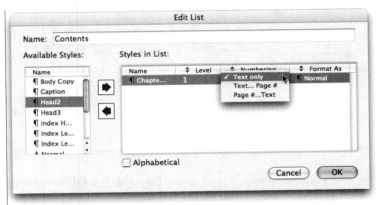

Like any other element you create, you should assign names to lists according to their use (e.g., Contents, Tables, Authors, etc.).

The Numbering selection does not affect the appearance of the list in the Lists palette; it defines how the list item appears in the final list built into the layout.

9. Click the Format As column head and choose TOC Level 1 from the menu.

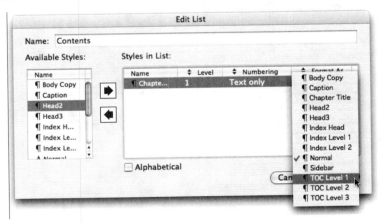

10. Highlight Head2 in the Available Styles list and click the right-facing arrow button.

11. With Head2 highlighted in the Styles in List window, click the Level column heading and choose 2 from the pop-up menu.

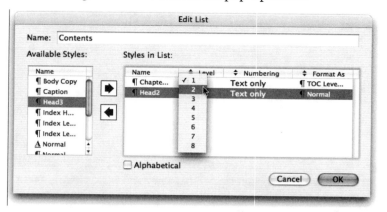

12. Click the Numbering column head and choose Text... Page #.

13. Click the Format As column head and choose TOC Level 2.

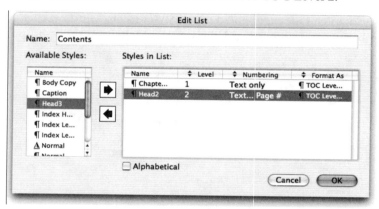

The Styles in List area automatically lists style sheets in alphabetical order. Depending on the name of your style sheets, a Level 2 style may appear in this list above a Level 1 style. This has no impact on the final appearance of the list, either in the Lists palette or in the list that is compiled into the layout.

14. Repeat this process to add Head3 to the list, with the following settings:

    Level: 3
    Numbering: Text... Page #
    Format As: TOC Level 3

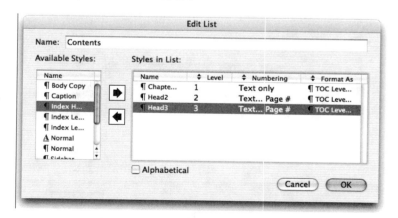

15. Click OK to close the Edit List dialog box.

16. Click Save to return to the Project window.

17. Save the file as "excerpt_working.qxp" in your **Work_In_Progress** folder and continue to the next section.

Using the Lists Palette

After a list has been defined, you can view the list by choosing Window>Lists.

- **Show Lists For**. This menu determines whether you are working with the list in a single layout or in a book. You will see either Current Layout or the name of any open book file.

- **List Name**. This menu shows all of the available lists for the selection in the Show List For menu.

- **Find**. This field is useful when working with very long lists. It works similarly to the help menus in many software applications; you can type one or more letters, which highlights the first instance of that text string in the list.

When "ch" is typed in the Find field, the first instance of those letters is highlighted in the Lists palette.

The Lists palette is an interactive tool. You can navigate easily to a specific item in the list by double-clicking that item. If you are working with the list of an entire book, double-clicking opens the relevant file at the location of the list item. The selected item in the list is highlighted in the Project window.

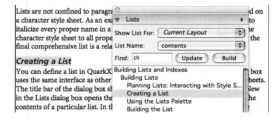

The Lists utility maintains an active link between the layout text and the Lists palette. You can make any number of changes that affect the list — changing words, correcting spelling or capitalization errors, deleting or adding text that moves an item to a different page, or even changing the level of a heading in the layout. Any time you change a list item in the layout, however, you have to click the Update button in the Lists palette to reflect the change.

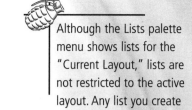

Although the Lists palette menu shows lists for the "Current Layout," lists are not restricted to the active layout. Any list you create in a project will be available for all layouts within the project.

Although lists are available for all layouts in a project, you cannot create a combined list from multiple layouts.

The Find field only works from the beginning of each list item. Typing "prove" will highlight an entry that begins with "Prove" but not one that begins with "Improve".

NAVIGATE WITH THE LISTS PALETTE

The Lists palette is an interactive tool. You can navigate easily to a specific item in the list by double-clicking that item.

1. With the file **excerpt_working.qxp** open (from your **Work_In_Progress** folder), choose Window>Lists.

    By default, the Lists palette shows the only list (Contents) that exists in the current layout. The lower part of the palette shows the contents of the selected list.

2. Review the list items.

Notice the three different levels of indentation in the list. These are defined by your choices in the Edit List dialog box (specifically, by your settings in the Level column of the Styles in List window).

If you look carefully at the different list entries, you can see some problems: a space is missing in the second entry, and "Conclusion" is misspelled.

3. Double-click the second item in the list ("A Brief History ofVisual Communication").

4. Choose View>Invisibles. A soft-return character separates the two lines in the heading. The Lists utility, however, ignores soft returns.

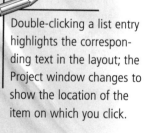

Double-clicking a list entry highlights the corresponding text in the layout; the Project window changes to show the location of the item on which you click.

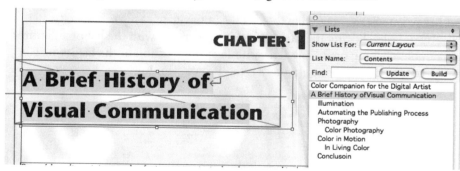

5. Place the insertion point before the soft-return character in the Project window and press the Spacebar.

6. Click Update in the Lists palette.

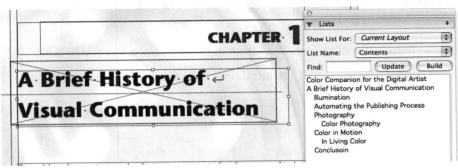

7. Double-click the word "Conclusoin" in the Lists palette.

8. In the Project window, correct the spelling ("Conclusion").

9. Click the Update button in the Lists palette.

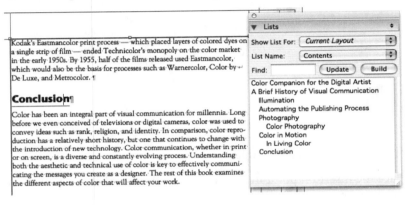

10. Save the file and continue.

Building the List

Once a list is defined, whether for a single file or for a book, you can build it into the layout by clicking Build in the Lists palette. A list can be built into any text box in a layout. The position of the text insertion point in the layout marks the location where the list will be built. Although you can simply place the insertion point at the beginning or end of an existing story, we recommend that you create a separate text box that is not linked to the main body of the text.

If you've already built a list into a file, you can easily update it by placing the insertion point in the list text block and clicking Build again. A dialog box appears, warning that the list already exists in the target file.

Clicking Cancel leaves all files as they were before you clicked Build. Clicking Insert adds a second version of the list at the position of the insertion point. Clicking Replace deletes the existing list and replaces it with the current list contents.

1. In the file **excerpt_working.qxp**, navigate to Page 2 of the layout.

2. Using the Content tool, click the automatic text box on the page.

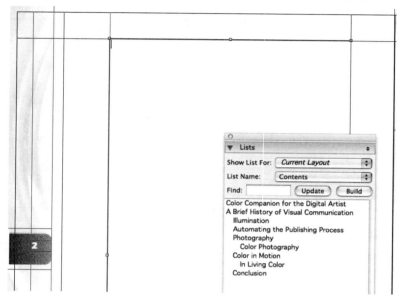

3. In the Lists palette, click Build.

4. Place the insertion point in the first line of the built list and look at the Style Sheets palette.

   When you defined the Contents list, you defined Chapter Title to be formatted with the TOC Level 1 style sheet (the Format As column of the Styles in List window).

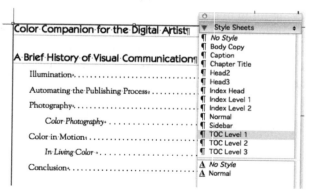

5. Press the Down-Arrow key to move the insertion point into the next line of text in the built list. This line is also formatted as TOC Level 1.

6. Navigate through the different lines in the built list and review the style sheets that are applied.

7. Save the file and continue to the next section.

Changing List Items

After a list is built, it is a static block of text. The style sheets can be changed as you would any other style sheet, and you can change the text box in which a list is placed. You can change or delete items from the list without affecting the main layout.

Although the text that makes up a list is static, the list itself is a fluid entity. The Lists palette maintains a one-way link to the created list. In other words, you can make changes to the main layout, update the Lists palette, and then rebuild the list using the updated list information. Because you can easily rebuild a list, it is a good idea to make all changes through the Lists palette rather than changing the text after a list is built.

For example, you notice a spelling error after creating a table of contents. If you correct the error in the built-list text, you have temporarily solved the problem in this one instance. If you later rebuild the list, however, the original spelling error is rebuilt into the list, which you must then fix again.

Rather than duplicating effort, you can easily navigate to the error in the body of the layout by double-clicking that item in the Lists palette, changing the highlighted text on the page, then clicking Update. When the list is rebuilt, the error is fixed both in the main layout and in the list, which means you don't have to fix the problem manually every time the list is rebuilt.

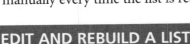

EDIT AND REBUILD A LIST

1. In the file **excerpt_working.qxp**, triple-click the first line in the list to highlight it and press Delete/Backspace.

   The first item ("Color Companion…") is the name of the book, which appears on the title page of the excerpt. This is unnecessary in the built table of contents, so you need to remove it.

2. Click the Page 1 icon in the Page Layout palette and choose Page>Section.

3. Activate the Section Start check box, choose the lower-case Roman numeral sequence in the Format menu, and click OK.

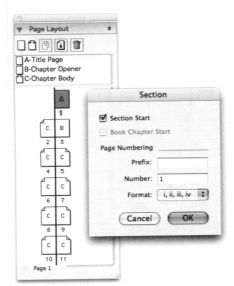

If you have made changes to the text of a built list, clicking Replace erases all of those changes.

Especially in the case of a blatant error such as spelling, you should always fix the problem at its source, not only in the list.

As a general rule, the front matter (title page, contents, and so on) of a book is numbered using lower-case Roman numerals.

4. Click the Page iii icon in the Page Layout palette and choose Page>Section.

5. Activate the Section Start check box, change the Number field to 1, and choose the Arabic numbers (1, 2, 3, 4) in the Format menu. Click OK.

The first page of the main document now begins on Page 1, as indicated in the Page Layout palette.

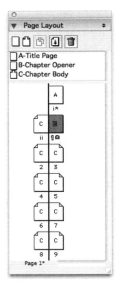

6. Double-click the word "Illumination" in the Lists palette.

In the Project window, you can see this heading appears on Page 2.

7. Navigate to Page ii of the layout.

In the built list, "Illumination" shows "4" as the corresponding page number. Because you changed the page numbering in the layout, you need to rebuild the list.

8. Place the insertion point in the text box on Page ii and click Build in the Lists palette.

9. Click Replace in the warning dialog box.

A version of list "Contents" already exists. Do you want to replace every occurrence of this list in the project or insert a new list?

Cancel   Insert   Replace

The main heading ("Color Companion…") reappears in the list. Because you only changed the built list — and not the actual list item — the heading reappears when the list is rebuilt.

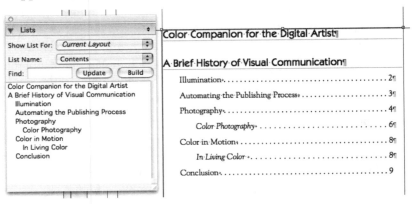

10. Double-click the first item in the Lists palette to navigate to the appropriate location in the layout.

11. With the text selected in the layout, click No Style in the Style Sheets palette.

12. Navigate back to Page ii in the layout, select the text box, and click Build in the Lists palette. Click Replace in the warning dialog box.

    Because you changed the text on the title page to No Style, it no longer appears in the built list.

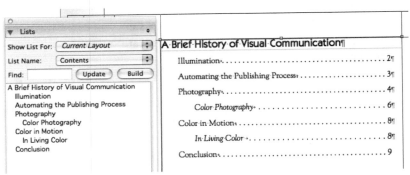

13. Save the file and continue to the next section.

BUILDING INDEXES

Like tables of contents and other lists, creating an index used to be an extremely time-consuming and labor-intensive process. A professional indexer was hired to go through each hard-copy page of a document, write down index entries and page numbers, manually compile the final alphabetized list, and typeset that list into the document. Any changes after the index was finished meant that the entire document had to be rechecked manually. QuarkXPress includes an index tool that automates part of the indexing process, improving the production workflow and saving considerable time when changes, inevitably, are made.

An index is a map to a publication's contents, providing the reader with an easy reference to specific content. Depending on your needs, you could theoretically use the Lists utility to create a basic index for projects (such as catalogs) requiring multiple indexes. The QuarkXPress Index utility, however, provides far more control for creating, generating, and maintaining a publication index.

Planning an Index

It is a good idea to plan in advance. Several different elements can (and should) be defined before you build your index:

- Paragraph style sheets for index headings (if you use them)
- Paragraph style sheets for up to four levels of index entries
- Character style sheets for the page numbers of each index entry (if you want them to be formatted differently than the index entry)
- Character style sheets for cross-references
- Master page with an automatic text box, in which the index will be built

Of these, the only one that is absolutely necessary to define in advance is the character style sheet that is applied to individual index entries. You should choose the style for an index entry when it is marked, but, obviously, you can't assign a style sheet that doesn't exist. It is far easier to do everything at once than to change it later, which means that you should define the style sheet before marking the index entries. (We will discuss the specific uses of style sheets later.) The important point is that some advance planning can make your life easier. You can always change the style-sheet definitions later in the process, but creating them in advance will save you time and effort in the long run.

Adding Index Entries

The Text field of the Index palette (Window>Index) reflects any text that is highlighted in the layout; the text in this field will become the index entry when you click Add in the Index palette.

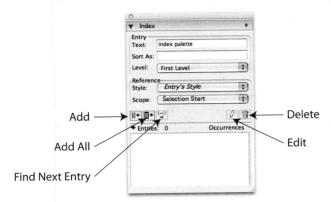

Add
Add All
Find Next Entry
Delete
Edit

Once an entry is added to the index, it appears in the bottom of the Index palette. The Occurrences column shows the number of references to each index entry. In the layout, an *index marker* (nonprinting brackets that enclose the index entry) is added to the highlighted text.

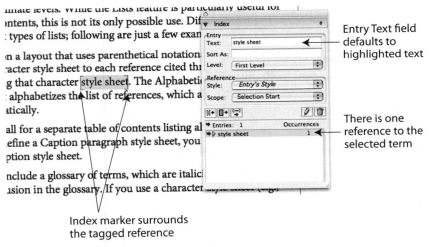

Entry Text field defaults to highlighted text

There is one reference to the selected term

Index marker surrounds the tagged reference

The Index palette lists every index term in a layout. You can review the specific references to a term by clicking the arrow/+ (plus sign) next to the term. Once the term is expanded, you see a list of all references to that term.

Clicking the arrow/+ (plus sign) next to an index term is referred to as "expanding" the term.

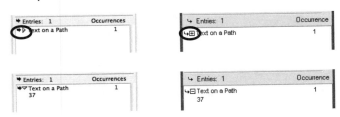

This Index palette shows that the term "Text on a Path" is referenced one time, on page 37 of the layout.

Changing the Entry Text

Once you define the location of an index marker by highlighting text in the layout, you can change the contents of the Text field. For example, you can highlight the words "Text on a Path" in the layout, then type "text paths" in the Index palette Text field. Clicking Add creates the index entry "text paths" in the index list. Changes in the Text field do not affect the highlighted text in the layout.

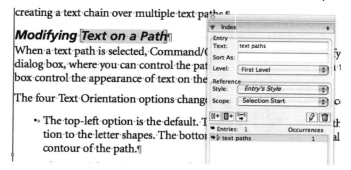

When you have highlighted a word in the layout, you can also alter the Text field by clicking an existing index term in the Index palette. If you highlight the words "text on a path" for example, clicking the item "text paths" in the Index palette changes the Text field to match the existing index entry. This is an excellent way to maintain consistency in an index. When you click the Add button, the Occurrences column in the Index palette shows that another reference to the same entry has been added.

Changing the Entry Sort Order

The Sort As field allows you to change the way an entry is alphabetized in the index. By default, index entries are strictly alphabetized; abbreviations are alphabetized according to the letters in the abbreviation, rather than by the word that has been abbreviated.

Mr. appears after modify   Mister appears before modify

St. appears after sister   Saint appears before sister

To change the order in which an index entry is listed, you can enter different text in the Sort As field.

The Sort As field is also helpful for reordering proper names. If you do not want to change the order of names in the final index, you can still alphabetize by last name. When looking for names in an index, most people look for the last name. You can add names to the index without changing the text listing but alphabetizing by last name.

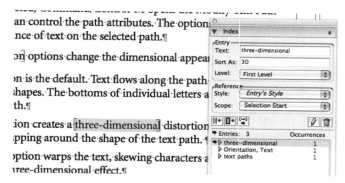

*In the final index, this entry will be listed as "three-dimensional"
but will be alphabetized as "3D".*

Reversing the Entry Text

If you hold down the Option/Alt key, the Add button becomes the Add Reversed button. If you click the Add Reversed button, the order of the words in the Text field is automatically reversed and added to the list of terms; "Text Orientation" would be added to the index as "Orientation, Text".

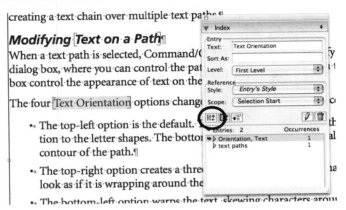

Reversing an index entry is different from changing the item in the Sort As field — using the Add Reverse option changes the appearance of the final entry, not just its alphabetical order.

Defining Entry Style

The Style menu in the Index palette Reference area defines the character style sheet that will be used to format the page numbers for the index entry. This menu is set to Entry's Style by default, which means that the page numbers will be set in the same style as that used for the level of index term when the final index is generated. You might use a character style sheet to set off one or more particular instances of each entry (for example, to indicate the page on which a term is first defined).

As we mentioned previously, it is a good idea to define this character style sheet before you begin marking entries. If the style sheet doesn't exist, you can't access it from the Style menu. To remedy this, you would have to define the style, and then later go back and edit each entry to which you want to apply the style. It is much easier to make these choices beforehand than to hunt down changes later.

Be consistent. If one proper name is reversed in the index, all names should be reversed.

Like the Level menu, the Style menu retains the selection from the previous entry. If you change the Style menu to something other than Entry's Style for one or more terms, make sure that you change it back again when you no longer want to apply a special style.

Tips for Marking Index Terms

Only one index marker can exist for a highlighted text string in the layout. If you try to add a second index marker (such as a See Also cross-reference) to the same highlighted text, you get a warning that a reference already exists at the selected location.

The Add Reversed option is not restricted to use with proper names. If, for example, the highlighted text is "tide tables", the Add Reversed option would create an entry for "tables, tide".

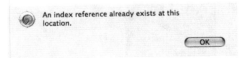

Index markers cannot overlap in the layout. In the following example, Gutters Width is already marked. If you highlight Columns and Gutters and click the Add button, you receive an error message.

An index marker can be wholly contained or nested within another marker (e.g., [automatic [text box]]).

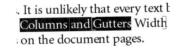

1. Open the file **excerpt_working.qxp** from your **Work_In_Progress** folder and navigate to Page 1 (not Page i) of the layout.

2. Choose Window>Index to open the Index palette.

3. On Page 1 (not Page i) of the layout, double-click the word "hieroglyphics" in the second line of the first paragraph.

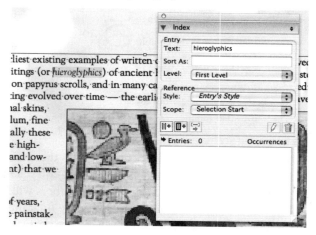

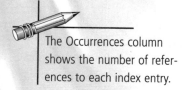

The Occurrences column shows the number of references to each index entry.

4. Make sure the Level menu is set to First Level and the Scope menu is set to Selection Start.

5. Click the Add button in the Index palette to add the reference to the index.

6. In the Index palette, click the arrow/plus sign (+) to the left of the word "hieroglyphics".

   The palette shows there is one reference to the word "hieroglyphics", appearing on Page 1 in the layout. (The Scope menu was set to Selection Start when you added the reference; the selection started on Page 1.)

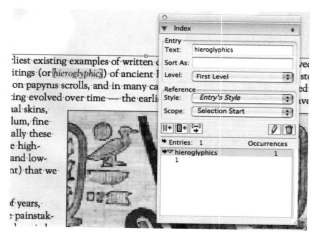

7. On Page 3 of the layout, highlight the words "Johannes Gutenberg" in the second line of the first paragraph.

   In the Index palette, the Text field changes to reflect the highlighted text. The remaining options in the palette (Level and Scope) maintain the same settings used for the previous entry.

8. In the Sort As field, type "Gutenberg, Johannes" and click the Add button.

   Although the entry in this example will appear as "Johannes Gutenberg" in the final index, it will be alphabetized by Gutenberg's last name instead of first name.

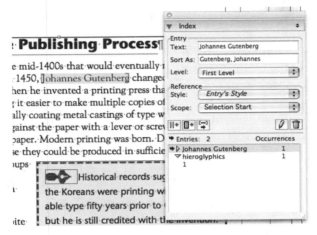

9. On Page 4 of the layout, highlight the words "Louis Daguerre" in the first line under the Photography heading.

10. Press the Option/Alt key and click the Add button.

    Louis Daguerre is added to the index as Daguerre, Louis.

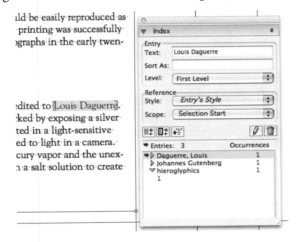

11. Save the file and continue to the next exercise.

Using Add All

Although you have to manually identify the terms that will be indexed in a layout, the Index utility does help to speed the process. With a word or phrase entered in the Text field of the Index palette, you can use the Add All button to mark every instance of that text in the same layout automatically. (The Add All button only finds the text within a single QuarkXPress layout; it does not find all instances in multiple chapter files of a QuarkXPress book.) All of the markers created by clicking the Add All button will have the same definition, including any changes you make in the Text and Sort As fields.

USE THE ADD ALL OPTION

1. On Page 1 of **excerpt_working.qxp**, highlight the word "media" in the third line of the first paragraph.

2. In the Index palette, click the Add All button.

   One reference to the term "media" is added to the index.

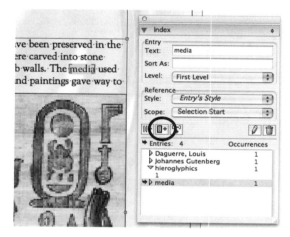

3. On Page 2, highlight the word "communication" in the first line under the Illumination heading and click the Add All button in the Index palette.

   The bottom half of the Index palette shows that eight instances of the term were tagged in the layout. This technique is an easy way to avoid tedious searching for common terms in a layout.

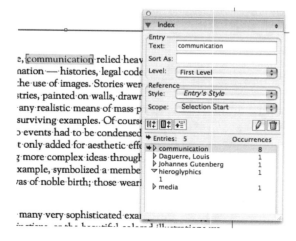

Capitalization does not matter when using the Add All button.

When using the Add All button, the text must match exactly, since the utility searches for the Text field as a whole word(s), not part of a word. Text Box and Text Boxes are not the same.

Just as you can do in the Lists palette, you can double-click a reference (not an entry) in the Index palette to navigate to and highlight the corresponding location in the layout.

4. In the Index palette, click the arrow/plus sign to the left of the "communication" entry. The page number of each instance is listed below the term.

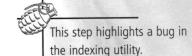

This step highlights a bug in the indexing utility.

In the expanded "communication" entry, notice the blank space above the first Page 1 reference. This space actually represents an index marker that was added on Page ii (the table of contents), which is outside the main section where you selected the original term before clicking the Add All button.

Using Add All, index references outside the active layout section appear as blank line items in the Index palette. You can't select those references in the palette, which means you can't delete them. They will be included in the built index, where you can delete unwanted references (such as front-matter pages).

5. On Page 3, highlight the word "printing" in the third line of the first paragraph and click the Add All button in the Index palette.

    Twelve references to the term "printing" have been added.

6. On Page 4, highlight the word "photography" in the first line under the Photography heading and click the Add All button in the Index palette.

    Seventeen references to the term are added to the index.

7. Collapse any expanded index entry by clicking the arrow/minus sign to the left of the appropriate term.

8. Save the file and continue to the next section.

Defining Reference Scope

Index references are not limited to single page numbers. You can use the Scope menu to define several reference types, including page ranges between headings.

The Scope menu defines what is referenced — page, range, or cross-reference — for each index entry. Like the Level and Style menus, the Scope menu retains the selection from the previous entry. Any entry added after changing the Scope menu will have the same Scope definition until you alter the menu again. For every index entry, you have a number of options:

- **Selection Start**. This option lists the page number on which the selected text begins, even if the selected text extends across more than one page.

- **Selection Text**. This option lists the page or pages on which the selected text exists. If the selection extends beyond one page, the range of pages (e.g., 2–3) is shown for that reference.

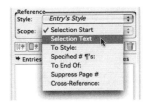

The To Style option is an excellent way to mark sections of a layout, but use this option carefully.

- **To Style**. If this option is selected, the entry lists the page or range of pages, beginning with the selected text and continuing to the next instance of the style you choose. If you want to mark an entire section of a layout, for example, you can select the first word in the section and choose To Style: Heading. The range of pages between the selection and the next heading in the layout are listed.

- **Specified # ¶s**. This option allows you define the number of paragraphs (beginning with the highlighted text) that make up the reference range.

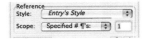

Be careful when using the To Style option. The default value is to mark an entry To Style: Next. This means that the reference listing ends as soon as any style sheet other than the selected text is used. Style sheets for bullets, inline captions, and so on are considered the "next" style sheet, so the scope may not be as broad as you like. If, on the other hand, you choose a style that is not used after the selected text, the entire rest of the layout will be included in the entry reference.

- **To End Of**. This option presents a secondary menu where you define the entry range, beginning with the highlighted text and continuing to the end of the story or layout. If you choose Story, the range reference will include the page numbers from the highlighted text to the end of the active text chain.

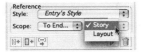

- **Suppress Page #**. This option adds an index entry that does not include page numbers. This can be used to add first-level index entries that exist only so second-level entries can be added.

- **Cross-Reference.** This option allows you to add a reference to another term in the index.

 ADD RANGE INDEX ENTRIES

1. In the file **excerpt_working.qxp**, highlight the word "History" in the main heading on Page 1 (not Page i).

2. In the Index palette, choose To End Of from the Scope menu.

3. In the secondary menu next to the Scope menu, choose Layout. Click the Add button in the Index palette.

4. In the Index palette, click the arrow/plus sign to the left of the "History" entry.

   Using the To End Of scope option, the term "History" is referenced from Page 1 (where the highlighted text appears) to Page 9 (the end of the layout).

5. On Page 2, highlight the word "Illumination" (in the heading).

   The Style Sheets palette shows that this heading is formatted with the Head2 style sheet.

   Notice the Scope menu in the Index palette maintains the To End Of option — your previous choice. Always remember that Index palette options default to the previously used selections. If you want a different kind of reference, you must remember to manually select it from the Scope menu.

6. Choose To Style in the Scope menu.

7. Choose Head2 from the secondary menu and click the Add button in the Index palette.

8. Expand the "Illumination" entry in the lower half of the Index palette.

    The new entry shows a single-page reference (2). If you look at the layout, you can see the heading "Automating…" appears at the top of Page 3. In this case, the To Style option adds a single-page reference for the "Illumination" entry because the next appearance of the chosen style (Head2) occurs at the beginning of the next layout page.

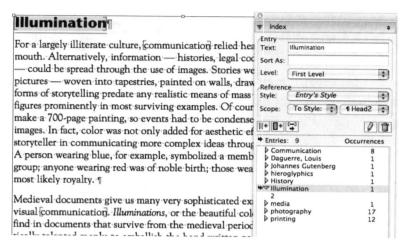

9. Highlight the words "Publishing Process" in the heading on Page 3 of the layout and click the Add button.

10. In the Index palette, expand the "Publishing Process" entry.

    The Index palette maintains the same settings from the previous entry, so the new term was added with a reference beginning with the highlighted text (on Page 3) and ending at the next instance of the Head2 style sheet (on Page 4).

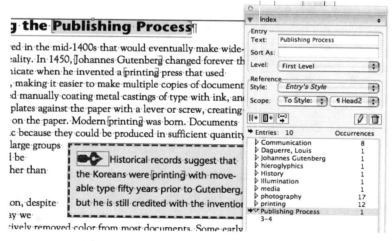

11. Collapse any expanded index entry by clicking the arrow/minus sign to the left of the appropriate term.

12. Save the file and continueto the next section.

Adding Nested Index Entries

The Level menu in the Index palette defines the level of an index entry, with up to four levels of nesting.

When you choose a sublevel from the Level menu, clicking the Add button makes the entry subsidiary to the term marked by an arrow in the lower half of the Index palette. To move the arrow to a different term, click in the blank space to the left of the target term.

Clicking the Add button places "skewed" as a second-level entry in relation to the first-level "text paths" entry.

The Level field defaults to the previous selection. If the last entry was a second-level entry, the next will also be a second-level entry unless you change the Level menu before clicking Add. It is easy to forget to change the Level menu, but very important to remember. If you add one entry as Second Level and forget to change the menu back to First Level, you will end up with a long list of secondary entries that have nothing to do with the parent. You then have to edit each one that is placed incorrectly, which can be extremely time-consuming, depending on how long it took before you noticed the problem.

When you change the Level menu, the available options depend on the position of the target arrow in the bottom of the Index palette. If the arrow icon indicates a second-level entry:

- Leave the menu at Second Level to create another second-level entry for the same parent.
- Choose Third Level from the menu to add a new entry that is subsidiary to the indicated second-level entry.
- Choose First Level to create a new entry with no relation to previous entries.

If the target indicates a first-level entry, only the Second Level option will be available because you can't skip levels. In other words, you can't add a third-level entry without targeting a second-level entry.

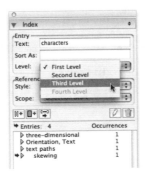

If you change the Level menu once, make sure you change it back to First Level when you are done adding the sublevel entries.

With a second-level entry marked as the target, the Fourth Level option is unavailable.

If a third-level entry is the target, the Second Level option is unavailable.

If a fourth-level entry is the target, the Second Level and Third Level options are unavailable.

Remember, the Scope menu defaults to the previously used selection. Always make sure you check this menu before you add new entries.

1. In the file **excerpt_working.qxp**, highlight the word "Color" in the heading on Page 6.

2. In the Index palette, choose Second Level from the Level menu and choose Selection Start from the Scope menu.

   In the lower half of the Index palette, an arrow appears to the left of the last entry you added. This arrow indicates the target entry, under which any sublevel entries will be added.

3. In the lower half of the Index palette, click the empty space to the left of the "photography" entry.

   Clicking in this space moves the target arrow, so the second-level entry "Color" will be secondary to "photography" instead of "Publishing Process".

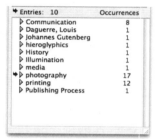

The Level menu defaults to the previous selection. If the last entry was a second-level entry, the next will also be a second-level entry unless you change the Level menu before clicking Add. It is easy to forget to change the Level menu, but very important to remember. If you add one entry as Second Level and forget to change the menu back to First Level, you will end up with a long list of secondary entries that have nothing to do with the parent. You then have to edit each one that is placed incorrectly, which can be extremely time-consuming, depending on how long it took before you noticed the problem.

4. Click the Add button in the Index palette.

   The term "Color" appears in the palette, indented and immediately below the "photography" entry.

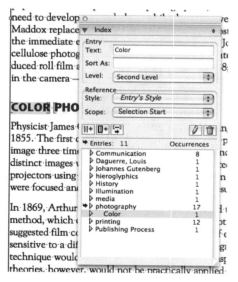

5. Save the file and continue to the next section.

Editing Index Entries

Once an entry has been created, you can change any of its characteristics by highlighting an entry or reference in the Index palette and clicking the Edit button. If a term is highlighted in the list, you can only change the Text, Sort As, and Level options of the term. If a specific reference is highlighted, you can change the Style and Scope options for that entry.

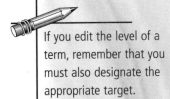
If you edit the level of a term, remember that you must also designate the appropriate target.

EDIT INDEX ENTRIES

1. In the file **excerpt_working.qxp**, review the contents of the Index palette.

   Usability is the most important aspect of an index. If users can't find what they are looking for, your work in building the index will have been wasted. Consistency is one of the keys to building a usable index. In the Index palette for **excerpt_working.qxp**, you can see two consistency problems.

   • Some entries are capitalized while others are not.

   • Two proper names appear in the palette, but with different styles.

2. Click the "Johannes Gutenberg" entry in the lower half of the Index palette, and click the palette's Edit button.

Double-clicking a reference in the Index palette automatically navigates to and highlights the appropriate text in the Project window, and activates the Edit mode in the Index palette.

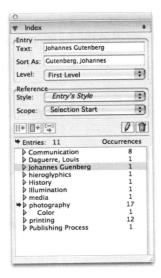

   When an entry is highlighted in the Index palette, you can edit the Entry Text, Sort As option, and the Level of the selected entry. The Reference area of the palette is unavailable (grayed out).

3. With the Text field highlighted, type "Gutenberg, Johannes".

When you click the Edit button, the Text field is automatically highlighted. You can change the text of any entry by highlighting it and clicking the Edit button.

4. Click the Edit button to leave Edit mode.

In the lower half of the Index palette, the "Johannes Gutenberg" entry is replaced by "Gutenberg, Johannes". The entry has not changed position because the Sort As field of the original entry was set to "Gutenberg, Johannes".

5. Highlight the "History" entry in the Index palette and click the Edit button.

6. In the Text field, highlight the "H" and type a lowercase "h".

7. Click the Edit button to leave Edit mode.

8. Repeat Steps 5–7 to lowercase all entries that are not proper names.

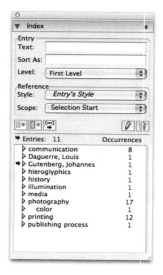

9. Collapse any expanded entry in the Index palette.

10. Save the file and continue to the next section.

Deleting Index Entries

You can delete any term or reference by highlighting an item in the list and clicking the Delete button.

If a specific reference is highlighted in the Index palette and you try to delete it, a warning shows that the reference will be deleted. Clicking OK deletes the reference; clicking Cancel leaves the reference in the index.

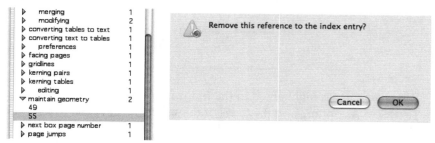

If a term is highlighted, a warning shows that deleting the term will also delete all references to that term.

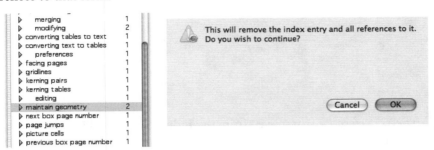

Deleting an index entry or reference has no effect on the layout text.

If a first-level term that includes sublevels is highlighted, a warning shows that deleting the first-level term also deletes the sublevels.

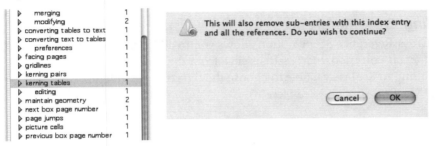

Although deleting an index entry from the Index palette has no effect on the layout text, deleting text from the layout will also delete any index markers and references that are within the text you delete. You will not receive a warning when you delete text that is marked.

DELETE INDEX ENTRIES AND REFERENCES

1. In the file **excerpt_working.qxp**, highlight the "history" entry in the Index palette.

   Because this entire document is about history, this reference is not necessary. In the complete book from which this chapter is excerpted, the "history" reference would remain in the index.

2. Click the palette's Delete button.

3. Click OK to the warning.

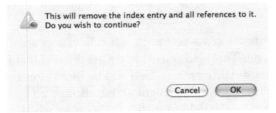

4. Expand the "communication" entry in the Index palette and double-click one of the references on Page 1.

   When you compile an index, QuarkXPress automatically consolidates duplicate page numbers, so this step is not technically necessary. Our purpose here is simply to show you how to delete page references.

5. With the "1" page reference highlighted in the Index palette, click the palette's Delete button.

6. Click OK to the warning.

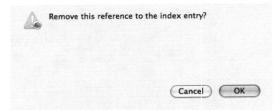

The "2" reference is removed from the Index palette, and the index markers no longer surround the word "Communication" on Page 1 in the layout.

7. Collapse any expanded entry in the Index palette.

8. Save the file and continue to the next section.

Adding Cross-References

The Cross-Reference Scope option allows you to add a reference to another term in the index. If you choose Cross-Reference from the Scope menu, a secondary menu (defaulting to See) is available to choose the type of cross-reference that will be used (See, See Also, and See Herein).

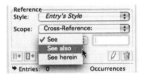

- **See.** This choice is generally used if an entry does not also list page numbers. Abbreviations may use a See cross-reference, sending the reader to the index entry that spells out the abbreviation.

- **See Also.** If an entry lists page numbers, this option is generally used to direct a reader to a related topic.

- **See Herein.** When creating complicated nested indexes, this choice is used to direct the reader to a related subtopic instead of to another first-level term in the index. In the following example, the See Herein informs the user to look at the secondary term "Portable Document Format" under the first-level "PDF", instead of in the alphabetical position of Portable... in the main index.

If you are creating a cross-reference, a text field appears next to the Scope secondary menu. This field is used to define the text that is cross-referenced. In other words, anything in this field will be listed after the See, See Also, or See Herein. When this field is highlighted, clicking an existing index term in the palette changes the field to match the term on which you clicked.

ADD CROSS-REFERENCES

The content typed in the cross-reference text field will be listed after See, See Also, or See Herein.

1. In the file **excerpt_working.qxp**, highlight the word "illustrations" in the second paragraph on Page 2.

2. In the Index palette, make sure First Level is selected in the Level menu.

3. Choose Cross-Reference from the Scope menu.

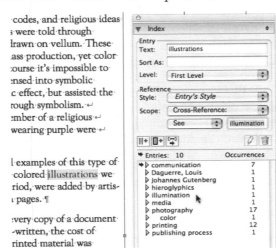

4. With the cross-reference text field highlighted, click the "illumination" entry in the Index palette.

   When the cross-reference text field is highlighted, clicking an existing index term in the palette changes the field to match the term on which you clicked. You can also manually type into the field, but you need to be sure the term is actually used in the index before you refer someone to it.

5. Click the Add button in the Index palette.

6. Expand the "illustrations" entry in the Index palette.

   Because this reference points to another term in the index, the reference "illumination" appears instead of a page number.

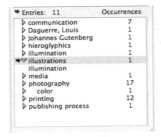

7. Collapse any expanded index entry.

8. Save the file and continue to the next section.

As you might have guessed, tagging index entries is a time-consuming process. No software is sophisticated enough to read the content, identify words or phrases, and choose the type of reference to use. Although QuarkXPress facilitates the process, indexing a document is still a manual task. The advantage to using the Index utility comes when it is time to compile the final index.

Setting Index Preferences

You can define the Index preferences from within the Preferences dialog box.

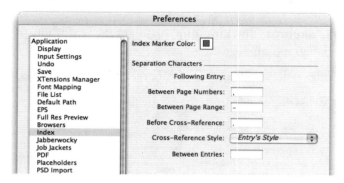

When text in a layout is marked as an index entry, it is enclosed in an index marker (nonprinting brackets). The Index Marker Color option defines the appearance of index markers in the layout; clicking the square opens a Color Picker dialog box where you can change the marker color.

Separation characters are used between references within an index entry. The purpose of these characters is to make the index entry readable, and to separate information into logical units. The Separation Characters options define how an index will appear when it is built.

- **Following Entry.** This option defines the character(s) placed between the end of the text and the first page number. You can place special characters (such as a paragraph return or a soft return) using the key codes for special characters in dialog boxes.

Soft return	\n
Paragraph return	\p
Tab	\t

  To achieve the following result, you have to type a colon (:) and press the Spacebar in the Following Entry field. If you forget the Spacebar, the colon will run directly into the first page number.

- **Between Page Numbers.** This field defines the character(s) that appears between each reference (page or range) for a single index entry. The default value — comma-space (,) — is the most commonly used. If you forget to add the space, references will run into one another (e.g., 2,5,7-8).

- **Between Page Range.** If an index entry is marked to show a range of pages, this field defines how the range is indicated. The default value — hyphen (-) — is the most commonly used.

- **Before Cross-Reference.** If you include cross-references in an index, this defines the character that is placed before the cross-reference entry. The default value — period-space (.) — is commonly used. You can also force cross-references onto a new line by typing the key code for a soft return (\n).

- **Cross-Reference Style.** You can use this menu to assign an existing character style sheet to all cross-references in your index. You might, for example, define an italic or bold style sheet for any cross-reference.

- **Between Entries.** This option defaults to adding a paragraph return between index entries. If you want to build a nested index in which individual entries do not appear on their own lines, you can change this field to a different character (such as a semicolon).

SET INDEX PREFERENCES

Most index preferences (except Index Marker Color) relate to the appearance of the index when it is built into the layout. You can define index preferences before or after you have tagged entries in the layout.

1. In the file **excerpt_working.qxp**, choose Edit>Style Sheets.

2. Define a new character style sheet named "Cross-Reference", using the following settings:

Font:	ATC Laurel Book Italic
Size:	8 pt.

3. Click Save in the Style Sheets dialog box to return to the Project window.

4. Open the Preferences dialog box (in the QuarkXPress menu on Macintosh or the Edit menu on Windows) and highlight Index in the list of categories.

5. Double-click the Following Entry field to highlight it, and then press the Spacebar four times to add space between each term and its references.

   This is one exception to the rule of not formatting with multiple spaces. Because each term may be a different length, tabs are not appropriate here.

6. Press Tab to highlight the Between Page Numbers field and type Comma-Space (,).

7. Highlight the Between Page Range field and press the Hyphen key.

8. In the Before Cross-Reference field type "\n" so each cross-reference appears on a new line.

   By typing the key code for a soft return (\n) in this field, you are forcing the cross-reference to start a new line, but not a new paragraph.

9. Choose A Cross-Reference from the Cross-Reference Style menu.

10. Leave the Between Entries field at the default value.

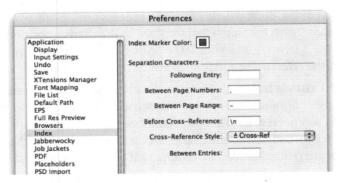

11. Click OK to close the Index Preferences dialog box.

12. Save the file and continue to the next section.

Building an Index

The ability to build and rebuild an index is one of the greatest advantages of the QuarkXPress Index utility. Although marking the individual entries still requires time and effort, it is easy to build, modify, and rebuild the index for any layout or book.

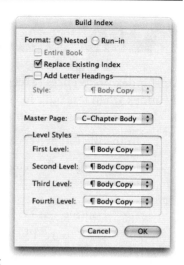

The Build Index dialog box presents the formatting options for the final index. You can choose the style sheets and master pages that will be used to format the different levels of index entries.

- **Nested** or **Run-in**. The Nested and Run-in radio buttons determine how the entries in the index are placed. In a nested index, each term begins on a separate line; this is the most common and the easiest for the reader to use.

> Automatic text box 3, 28
> Character formatting 1
>   See also paragraph formatting
> Color 4-5, 7-8, 21, 23, 40
> Content tool 2, 9, 12, 14, 19, 29-30, 33
> Gutters Width
>   See indents
> Handles 2-3, 11
> Indents 1, 21, 33-35, 41

A run-in index squashes everything into a sentence-like format. This method of indexing can be convenient for saving space, but is difficult to use.

> Automatic text box 3, 28; Character formatting 1, See also paragraph formatting; Color 4-5, 7-8, 21, 23, 40; Content tool 2, 9, 12, 14, 19, 29-30, 33; Gutters Width: See indents; Handles 2-3, 11; Indents 1, 21, 33-35, 41

- **Entire Book**. This option builds the index for all chapters of a QuarkXPress book at one time. This option combines the indexes from every file contained in the Book palette; all of the indexes are alphabetized as a single unit so that the terms from Chapter 1 are in the correct position with respect to Chapter 2 terms, and so on. If the same term appears in more than one chapter, the references to that term are combined into a single entry.

- **Replace Existing Index**. If you have already generated an index for a layout or book, this option allows you to overwrite the existing text in the same place. As a general rule, the index should not be compiled until a document is complete. Any last-minute changes, however, especially if the text reflows or pages are renumbered, may require that you rebuild the index.

    This option is also useful if you change your mind about the index preferences, choose to apply different style sheets, or even decide to create a new master-page layout for the index.

- **Add Letter Headings**. Extremely long indexes can benefit from letter headings. The point of an index is to make the document more accessible to the user. If an index runs for several pages, or includes more than one level, letter headings can be helpful. If you choose the Add Letter Headings check box, you can then select a style sheet for those headings.

Any manual changes you make to the index once built will be lost if you choose Replace Existing Index.

- **Master Page**. This menu allows you to define the existing master-page layout that will be used to build the index into the active layout. The only requirement for an index master page is that it must have an automatic text box. Unlike building a list, you do not have to create a text box that is the target for building an index. Advance planning means that you create a master-page layout for the index before building the index. When you click OK in the Build Index dialog box, new pages are added at the end of the active layout, using the master page specified in this menu.

- **Level Styles**. These options define the style sheets that will format each level of index entry. Once again, advance planning means that these style sheets must be created before building the index. Once the index is built, you can change the formatting options for each style sheet, just as you would any other style sheet.

BUILD AN INDEX

1. In the file **excerpt_working.qxp**, make sure the Index palette is visible and choose Utilities>Build Index.

2. Make sure the Nested radio button is active.

3. Deselect the Replace Existing Index check box.

   Because you haven't yet built the index, you aren't replacing anything.

4. Activate the Add Letter Headings check box, and choose Index Head from the Style menu.

5. Click the Master Page menu.

   C-Chapter Body is the only option in this menu, because it is the only one with an automatic text box.

6. In the Level Styles area, choose Index Level 1 in the First Level menu and choose Index Level 2 in the Second Level menu.

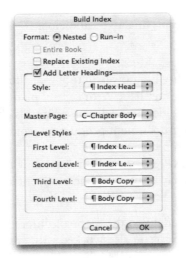

7. Click OK to build the index.

The master page used to build an index must have an automatic text box.

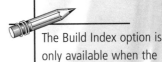

The Build Index option is only available when the Index palette is visible.

Because you are building an index for a single layout, you don't need to use the Entire Book option. Books are explained in Chapter 13.

You don't need to change the Third Level and Fourth Level menus because this index only uses two levels.

8. Review the results.

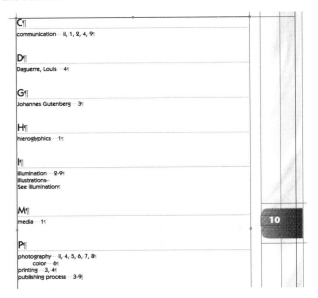

- A new page is added to the end of the layout, based on the C-Chapter Body master.

- The index is formatted based on the style sheets you defined in the Build Index dialog box.

- The appropriate letter headings are added; letters with no entries are not included.

- All the entries and references you tagged are included in the index.

- Only one instance of a page number is included in the compiled index, even though multiple tags may exist for a single entry on the same page.

- The "blank" references (those from outside the main layout section, in lowercase Roman numerals), appear in the built list; you have to manually delete these references.

9. Save the file as "excerpt_final.qxp" and close it.

SUMMARY

The QuarkXPress Lists utility is a powerful tool that allows you to build and maintain tables of contents and other lists. With careful planning and an understanding of the page-numbering considerations discussed in this chapter, you can use the Lists utility to improve long-document production workflow. You should understand the interaction between lists and style sheets, and know how to create a list for all chapters of a QuarkXPress book. You also know how to modify and update a list, which allows you to have a working table of contents from even the earliest stages of a project.

You created index markers, defined the scope of different markers, and added multiple levels of index terms. You also worked with cross-references and built an index into the layout. Having completed the exercises in this chapter, you should recognize that the index you created is incomplete; the exercises were designed to show you the elements of building an index. As you know, an index should be as thorough as possible to help the reader. Building an index — even using software utilities — takes planning, thought, and time.

Working with Books

13

Publication design is a unique subset of graphic design. Attention to detail is necessary to make sure that the subheads in early chapters match the subheads in later chapters, the captions are all set in the same font, the body copy is the same size throughout the document, and so on. Especially when several designers work on the same project, it is vital to create a consistent look to the entire project. To make long-document design easier, QuarkXPress includes a sophisticated Book utility for combining and managing multiple chapters as a single unit.

IN CHAPTER 13, YOU WILL:

- Combine multiple projects into a single QuarkXPress book.

- Control the section and page numbering of files in a book.

- Discover how to use the master file of a book to ensure consistency.

- Understand the special considerations involving lists and indexes in a QuarkXPress book file.

Long documents are frequently split into multiple files during the conception and design phase, and then recombined at the end of the process to create the final job.

- Files with fewer pages are less cumbersome to control and easier to navigate.

- Layouts with many images can become very large, which can be a problem if the files are being passed around on a slow network connection. Breaking them into pieces helps to keep the file size smaller.

- A publication may require a different running head or foot in different sections. If you build each section as a separate file, you can change the text in the running head or foot for each layout and you don't have to create duplicate master pages for each different head. To insure consistency, however, the running head and foot in each separate layout should use the same style sheet.

- If a long document is broken into separate files, several designers may work on different files of the same book without the risk of accidentally over-writing another person's work.

- If a very long document is split into several files, you will not lose the entire job if a single file becomes corrupt.

Before QuarkXPress added the Book utility, multiple files were combined in the prepress department at the service provider. Working with multiple files required extreme care and attention to detail to maintain consistency from one to the next. The Book utility has made the process much easier; it automates many of the tasks that had previously been done by carefully comparing proofs of every page in the document. Of course, this doesn't mean that you can blithely use the Book utility without paying attention to your work, but you can automate much of the process.

When a single design project is comprised of several files, it is even more important to maintain consistency from one file to the next. If the font is slightly different from one issue of a newsletter to the next, few people are likely to spot much of a difference. That difference is far more noticeable, however, when two or more files are bound together in the same publication.

CREATING A QUARKXPRESS BOOK

A QuarkXPress book is a container file into which multiple QuarkXPress projects are placed to facilitate organization, page numbering, file management, and printing. The Book utility lets you to combine each part of the whole job so the group of files can be treated as a single unit. This offers several benefits, allowing you to:

- Define a master file for the book.

- Synchronize style sheets, colors, and other assets to the master in the book.

- Monitor page and section numbering of each individual file in the book, and of the book as a whole.

- Change the order of files within the book, and automatically renumber pages according to the book order.

- Add and remove files from the book.

- Print the entire book by opening the Print dialog box only once, regardless of the number of files.

Here we are talking about design projects — specific assignments you complete for a client — regardless of the number of files necessary to complete the assignment. Don't confuse this with a QuarkXPress project, which is a single file.

You can create a new book by choosing File>New>Book. In the New Book dialog box, you can navigate to any location on your computer. You should enter the name of the book you are creating in the Save As/File Name field; Macintosh users need to remember to add the extension ".qxb" to the file.

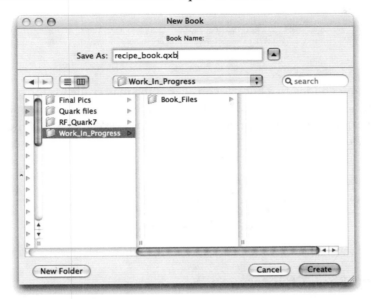

Adding the extension helps to facilitate work in a cross-platform environment. If Macintosh users send a book file to a Windows computer, the correct extension allows the file to work properly. Further, including the appropriate extension is simply a good habit to acquire.

Clicking Create opens the Book palette; the file name you define is listed in the palette's title bar.

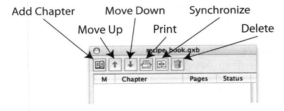

You can open any QuarkXPress book file from the Open dialog box (File>Open).

Adding Book Chapters

Clicking the Add Chapter button in the Book palette opens the Add New Chapter dialog box. You can navigate to any location on your computer, select the file you want to add, and click Add.

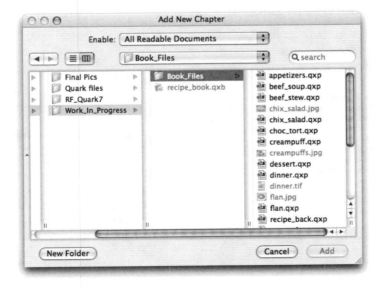

All of the long-document design tools in QuarkXPress work on the assumption that individual chapters are contained in separate project files. Projects added to book files can only contain one layout. If you try to add a project that contains multiple layouts, you will get a warning.

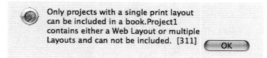

The first chapter added to a book is considered the master file for the book. The master is indicated by an "M" to the left of the file name (in the first column of the palette). If you delete the master file from the book, the second file added becomes the default master file. If you delete both the master and the second file, the third file added becomes the master, and so on.

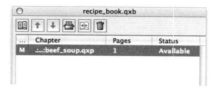

Managing Book Chapters

When you place a file into a book, the book file acts as a container; this process is very similar to placing an image into a layout. A QuarkXPress layout stores the path to a placed image as a reference. Books use the same methodology, storing a reference to the files contained within the book.

The Status column of the Book palette shows Available as long as the files have not been moved from the location where they were placed. If the files have been moved, the Status column shows that the file is missing.

You can redirect the link to a missing file by double-clicking that item in the Book palette. This opens a navigation dialog box, in which you can locate the new position of the missing file.

If a chapter file has been opened and saved in any way other than by double-clicking from the Book palette, the Status column shows that the file has been modified. To correct the Status column, you must reopen the file from the Book palette, and then close it again.

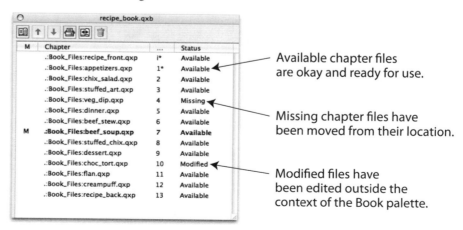

Available chapter files are okay and ready for use.

Missing chapter files have been moved from their location.

Modified files have been edited outside the context of the Book palette.

Closing Book Files

To close a book, you can simply click the Close button in the top-left corner (Macintosh) or the top-right corner (Windows) of the book palette. Changes to a book file are saved automatically; you cannot override this setting or close the book file without saving.

If any chapter files of a book are open when you close the book, you are alerted that closing the book will also close those files. Clicking OK to the warning closes the book and all of its files.

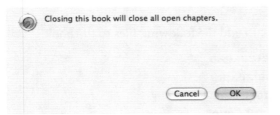

 CREATE A BOOK

1. Copy the folder **Book_Files** from the **RF_Quark7>Chapter13** folder into your **Work_In_Progress** folder.

    Windows users: Open the Properties dialog box for each QXP file in the Book_Files folder, and deativate the Read Only check box.

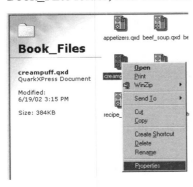 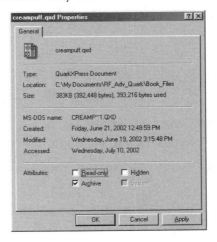

When you work with book files, you frequently open, save, and close the chapters of the book files. Book chapter files must be unlocked, which means you can't work directly from the Resource CD for this chapter.

You can right-click an icon and choose Properties from the pop-up menu (left). In the Properties dialog box, you have to deactivate the Read-Only check box in the Attributes area (right).

2. Choose File>New>Book.

3. In the New Book dialog box, navigate to your **Work_In_Progress** folder. Type "recipe_book.qxb" in the Save As/File Name field, and click Create.

4. Click the Add Chapter button in the Book palette. Navigate to the file **beef_soup.qxp** in the **Work_In_Progress>Book_Files** folder, and click Add.

The new file is added to the Book palette as the master file.

5. Repeat Step 4 to add the following files to the book:

> **beef_stew.qxp**
> **chix_salad.qxp**
> **choc_tort.qxp**
> **creampuff.qxp**
> **flan.qxp**
> **stuffed_art.qxp**
> **stuffed_chix.qxp**
> **veg_dip.qxp**

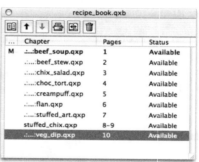

Looking at the Book palette, you can see that all files have only one page except **stuffed_chix.qxp**.

6. Double-click **stuffed_chix.qxp** in the Books palette to open the file.

7. If the Page Layout palette is not visible, choose Window>Page Layout. Notice that the text flows onto a second page; every recipe in this book, however, should fit on a single page.

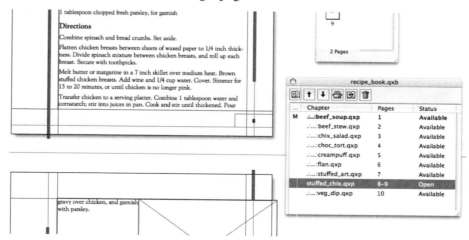

8. If it is not visible, open the Style Sheets palette. Click the text on the second page of the layout with the Content tool.

   The selected text is set with the Direction Line style.

9. Control/right-click the Direction Line style sheet in the Style Sheets palette, and choose Edit Direction Line from the contextual menu.

10. Change the font size for the Direction Line style sheet to 11.5 pt. and change the Space Before paragraphs to p4. Click OK to change the style sheet and return to the Project window. All of the text should now fit onto one page.

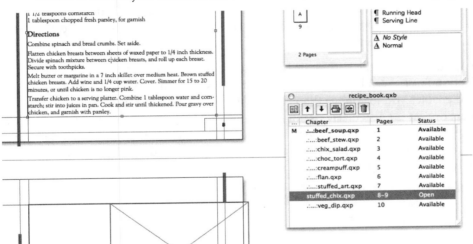

The page numbering of a book is dependent on using the automatic-page-number character (Command/Control-3) in the QuarkXPress files.

11. Delete Page 9 from the layout. Page numbering in the Book palette changes automatically to reflect the new status of the file.

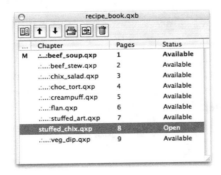

You cannot manually choose the Book Chapter Start option in the Section dialog box. This option is checked automatically only when a file is added to a book.

12. Save the open project and then close it.

13. Close the book file.

Sorting Chapters

When more than one file is added to the open book, you can rearrange the files however you like. The Move Up and Move Down buttons enable you to reposition the highlighted file within the list. The master file can appear in any position within the list. When you move a chapter to a new position, the page numbering automatically changes to reflect the new chapter order (unless you have chosen to override the book page numbering manually, using the Section dialog box).

Move Up Move Down

Controlling Page Numbering

The Pages column in the Book palette shows the page numbers of each file within the book. The first file added to the book defaults to Page 1, and each successive file is numbered correctly according to its position in the book. For example, if the first file has eight pages, the second file added to the book will begin with Page 9.

If you open the Section dialog box for any chapter (Page>Section), you see that the Book Chapter Start check box is selected and grayed out. The options in the Page Numbering area of the dialog box are also grayed out — the values are dependent on the file's position in the book.

You can override the automatic book page numbering for a file by selecting the Section Start check box. This automatically deselects the Book Chapter Start option and enables you to change the Prefix, Number, and Format values. The Section Start option is particularly useful for changing the numbering of a specific section. The front matter of a document, for example, is usually numbered separately using lowercase Roman numerals, and the first page of the body of the document typically begins on Page 1.

If you override the automatic book page numbering for any file, an asterisk marks the page number(s) in the Pages column. Any files following the modified section start are numbered sequentially in that section.

Asterisk indicates that book page numbering has been overridden by a user-defined section start.

Deleting Chapters

You can delete a chapter in the book by highlighting it and clicking the Delete button. You are warned before the chapter is finally deleted from the book. Clicking OK in the warning dialog box removes the chapter from the Book palette; clicking Cancel leaves your book intact.

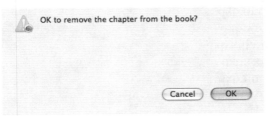

Once you delete a chapter from a book, you cannot undo the deletion. The file still exists in its original location, however, so you can add the file back into the book, if necessary.

 SORT BOOK FILES

1. Choose File>Open and navigate to your **Work_In_Progress** folder. Highlight the file **recipe_book.qxb** and click Open.

   The chapter files are now in alphabetical order by file name. You want to reorganize the book according to the type of dish (appetizers, dinners, and desserts) that each recipe describes.

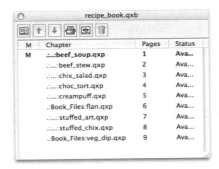

2. Highlight **chix_salad.qxp** in the palette list, and click the Move Up button twice. The file should move to the top of the list.

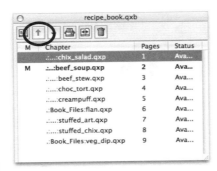

3. Using the same process as in Step 2, rearrange the remainder of the list to this order:

> chix_salad.qxp
> stuffed_art.qxp
> veg_dip.qxp
> beef_soup.qxp
> beef_stew.qxp
> stuffed_chix.qxp
> choc_tort.qxp
> creampuff.qxp
> flan.qxp

4. Click the Add Chapter button. Add the file **appetizers.qxp** to the book, and move the file to the top of the palette.

5. Highlight **veg_dip.qxp** in the Book palette. Click the Add Chapter button and add the file **dinner.qxp**. Notice that it is placed immediately after the highlighted selection in the palette.

6. Add the file **dessert.qxp** and place it immediately before **choc_tort.qxp** in the list.

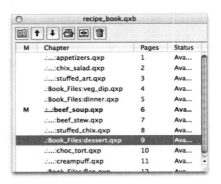

7. Leave the book file open for the next exercise.

SYNCHRONIZING BOOKS

An advantage of using style sheets for text layout is that a style can be changed easily and universally. This is also a disadvantage of using style sheets, particularly when combining multiple files into a single publication. Layout designers frequently manipulate, tweak, and even cheat to force-fit text into a desired amount of space, to make a runaround work correctly, or to achieve some other specific effect. When the files are combined into the final book, this adjusting can be a problem if the variation is noticeable from one file to the next.

The QuarkXPress Book utility expands the concept of using a master file to maintain consistency between files. The Synchronize button enables you to synchronize the Style Sheets, Colors, H&Js, Lists, and Dashes & Stripes for the book, based on the master file. In the Synchronize Selected Chapters dialog box, the Available area shows the available elements from the master file in the book. You can choose individual elements to synchronize in any category, just as you would if you were appending elements to an individual file. Clicking Synch All moves all items in all categories into the Including section.

Synchronizing a book does not delete any element from any file, but can override changes you made to a particular file.

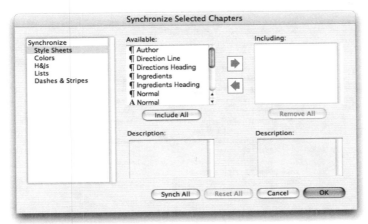

When a book is synchronized, elements of the master file are added to the other files if they do not already exist in that file. If an element does already exist in the other files, the element definition from the master file is applied to the same element in the other files. The synchronization process does not affect elements that are not in the master file.

In other words, if you have changed the definition of a style sheet in one file, synchronizing the book overwrites the change, and assigns the settings for that style sheet, as defined in the master file. If you changed a style sheet — to fit text onto a page, for example — synchronizing the book to the master file overwrites the changes, and the text will no longer fit in the same way.

As another example, you may have changed the defined color of text in a style sheet for each section. Synchronizing the book means that the color of the text will be the same as the master for every file in the book. You then have to reopen the sections and rechange the style sheet to use the different colors.

Fortunately, the Synchronize Selected Chapters dialog box allows you to define individual elements to synchronize. If you know a particular style sheet was deliberately changed in one file, you may choose not to synchronize that style sheet, thus maintaining your original design. Of course, this defeats the purpose of synchronizing to maintain consistency from one file to the next.

The only real solution is to plan each aspect of each file carefully, and avoid (or at least minimize) the tweaking and manipulating that we all do. If you absolutely must tweak text, manipulate the specific areas of text that you need to fit instead of altering the style sheets in the file. If text formatting overrides the style sheet, synchronizing will not override your changes.

You can also synchronize specific files by selecting them in the Book palette before clicking the Synchronize button. To select contiguous files, hold down the Shift key and click each file. To select noncontiguous files, hold down the Command/Control key while selecting the desired files. Synchronizing just certain files defeats the purpose of synchronizing, but the option is available.

 SYNCHRONIZE BOOK CHAPTERS

1. In the Book palette, click in the empty space below the last item to deselect all files. Notice that the file **beef_soup.qxp** is the master file (indicated by the "M" in the "M" column).

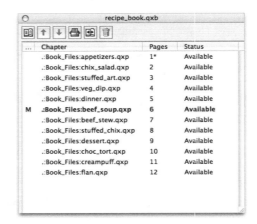

2. Click the Synchronize button. To be consistent, you're going to synchronize every element of every file in the book.

3. Click Synch All, and then click OK.

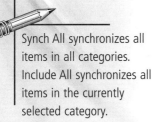

Synch All synchronizes all items in all categories. Include All synchronizes all items in the currently selected category.

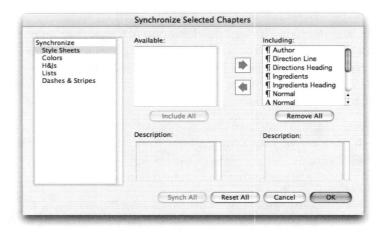

4. If you see a warning that embedded elements (style sheets that are based on other style sheets, for example) will also be added to the other chapters in the book, click OK.

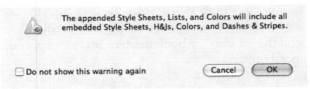

QuarkXPress processes each file in the book. When the Synchronize Selected Chapters dialog box disappears, the process is complete.

5. Double-click **stuffed_chix.qxp** in the Book palette to open the file.

In the Create a Book exercise, you changed the definition of the Direction Line style sheet in this file.

When the book was synchronized, the Direction Line style sheet was changed back to the original definition (as it is in the master file). The bottom text box now shows an overset-text icon.

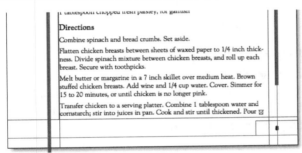

6. Highlight all of the text after the Directions heading (extend the bottom of the text box, if necessary).

7. Change the font size of the selected text to 11.5 pt. and change the space before the selected paragraphs to 0p4.

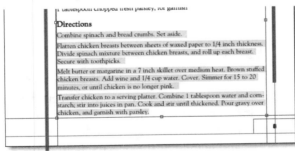

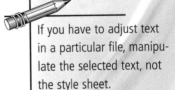
If you have to adjust text in a particular file, manipulate the selected text, not the style sheet.

The text now fits on one page; the Style Sheets palette indicates that the selected text has been modified from the original style sheet definition.

8. Save the file and close it, but leave the Book palette (file) open.

MANAGING LISTS IN BOOKS

In order to generate a comprehensive list for every file in a book, the list must exist in every file contained within that book. If you've already defined a list in the book's master file, you can simply synchronize the list across the book chapters. If the list you want to use exists in some file other than the book's master file, you have to first append the list into the book master file (File>Append, or Edit>Lists and click the Append button).

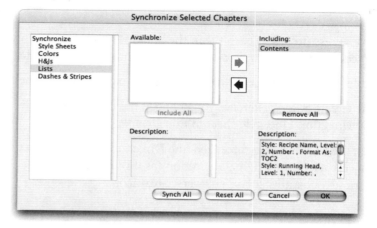

Viewing and Navigating Lists

When you are working with lists in a book file, the Show Lists For menu lets you view lists for an individual chapter (the active project) or for an open book file. If you display the lists for an entire book, the List Name menu shows only lists that are available in the master chapter of the book.

As you learned in Chapter 12, the Lists palette is an interactive navigation tool. If you are viewing a list for an entire book, double-clicking an item in the Lists palette opens the necessary file in a new Project window (or brings that file to the front if it is already open) and highlights the selected item in the Project window.

Warning about Style Sheet Consistency

For a book list to function properly, the style sheets that define the list must be consistent in every chapter file of the book. In other words, H2 must be used consistently throughout all chapters of the book if the heading is defined as a list element. If one chapter uses a style called Heading 2 instead of H2, the list for that chapter will not include any H2 elements because, technically, they do not exist.

This is another example in which consistency from one file to the next is crucial. In order to create a comprehensive and accurate list, the same style sheets should be used in all files of a book.

WORK WITH A BOOK LIST

1. With the book file **recipe_book.qxb** (from your **Work_In_Progress** folder) open, click the Add Chapter button in the Books palette.

2. Locate the file **recipe_front.qxp** in the **Book_Files** folder (**Work_In_Progress>Book_Files**), and click Add. Click the Move Up button to move the new file to the beginning of the list.

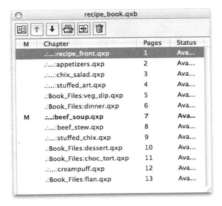

3. Double-click **recipe_front.qxp** in the Book palette to open that file. Choose Window>Lists. The List Name menu shows that the list named Contents exists in this file.

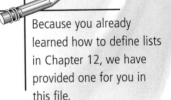

Because you already learned how to define lists in Chapter 12, we have provided one for you in this file.

4. Save and close the **recipe_front.qxp** file.

5. Click the Show Lists For menu, and choose **recipe_book.qxb**.

   The List Name menu becomes unavailable because the Contents list exists only in the front-matter file. The Contents list needs to be appended to every file in the book to work properly.

6. Double-click **beef_soup.qxp** (the master file) in the Book palette to open it.

7. Choose Edit>Lists and click the Append button in the Lists dialog box.

8. Navigate to the file **recipe_front.qxp** (where the Contents list currently exists) in the Append dialog box, and click Open.

9. Highlight Contents in the Available area, and click the right-facing arrow button. Click OK.

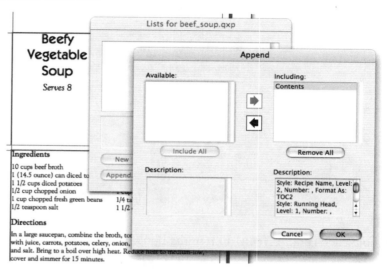

10. If you get a warning message, click OK.

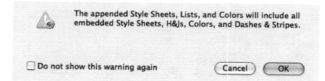

11. Click Save to return to the layout. The Contents list now exists in the **beef_soup.qxp** (master) file.

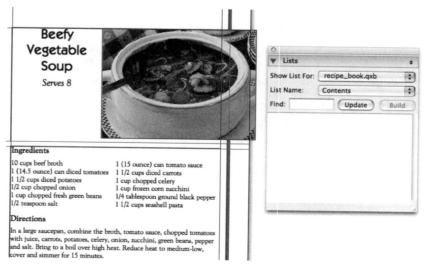

12. Save the changes to the **beef_soup.qxp** file, and close the file. You now need to add the Contents list to each file in the book.

13. Click the empty space in the bottom of the Book palette to deselect all files, and click the Synchronize button.

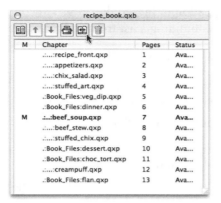

14. Click Lists in the left pane of the Synchronize Selected Chapters dialog box. Highlight Contents in the Available pane, and click the right-facing arrow button.

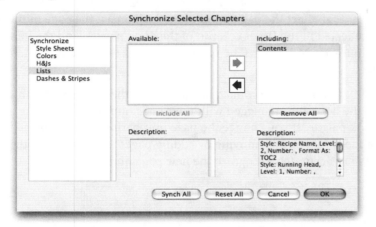

15. Click OK to synchronize the list in all chapters of the book. If you get a warning message, click OK. When the Synchronize Selected Chapters dialog box closes, the process is complete.

16. With **recipe_book.qxb** selected in the Show Lists For menu and Contents selected in the List Name menu, click the Update button in the Lists palette. The book files are processed and the list is built into the palette.

17. Save and close any open project files, but leave the book file open for the next exercise.

Changing Files in a Book

If you are building a list from a QuarkXPress book, you will run into a problem when changing the pagination of files in the book. Any of the following changes can cause problems when building a list from a QuarkXPress book:

- Adding or deleting a chapter.
- Adding or deleting pages from a chapter within a book.
- Reordering the chapter files in the Book palette.
- Changing the section start of a chapter in a book.

When you make any of these changes, the Book palette displays the appropriate page numbers in the Pages column; any changes to the individual files automatically affect the other files, and the Book palette changes accordingly.

The Lists palette does not display the page numbers for list items. If you click Update after changing a chapter, the list items display correctly in the new order.

The potential problem exists when you build a book list. Once you build a list, the page numbers for each chapter are saved as a part of each chapter file. If you make changes that affect the pagination of book chapters, the page numbers are accurately reflected in the Pages column of the book palette, and the items in the list appear in the correct order. The page numbers in the compiled list, however, are incorrect.

The problem of updating a compiled list is a bug in the software. The individual chapters in the book file are tagged with their page numbers when they are placed into the Book palette. If you change the page numbering in the book — by reordering the chapters, or removing or adding pages to a chapter — the Build List feature does not accurately recognize the new page numbering.

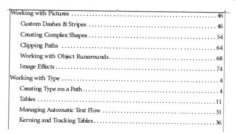

If you've made changes that affect the page numbering of the book chapters, you have to open every file that was affected by the change in pagination, save it, and close it again. This is as simple as double-clicking the affected files in the Book palette and then choosing File>Close. Even though you have made no actual changes to the file, you are asked if you want to save changes. Clicking Yes to this warning corrects the page numbering in the file data — which is the change you are being asked if you want to save. Once you've opened, saved, and closed each file, rebuilding the list shows the correct order and page number for all files.

COMPILE A LIST

1. Double-click **recipe_front.qxp** in the Book palette to open the file.

2. Using the Content tool, select the empty text box in the layout page.

3. Click Build in the Lists palette. The book files are processed, and the list is built and formatted in the empty text box.

   In the Dessert section, the recipes are not in alphabetical order, even though the file names in the Book palette are in order.

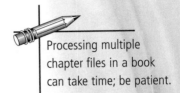

Processing multiple chapter files in a book can take time; be patient.

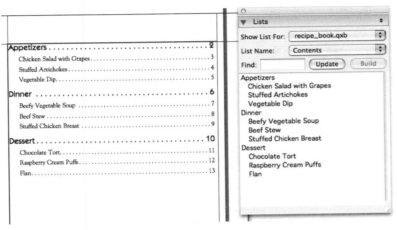

4. Highlight **creampuff.qxp** in the Book palette and click Move Down.

5. Click Update in the Lists palette. The order should change to reflect the change you made in Step 5.

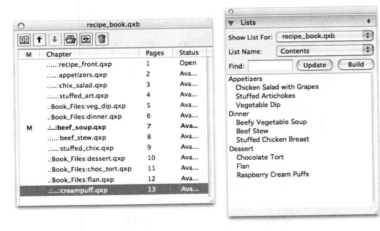

6. Repeat this process to move Beefy Vegetable Soup after Beef Stew.

7. With **recipe_front.qxp** open, choose Page>Section. Activate the Section Start check box, and change the Format menu to i, ii, iii, iv. Click OK.

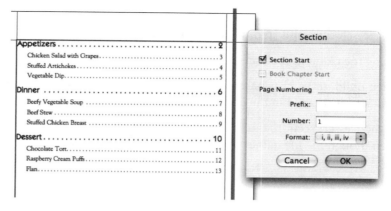

The Book palette shows that the entire book is now numbered with lowercase Roman numerals.

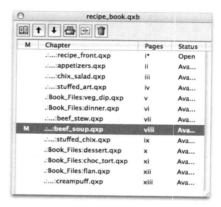

8. Save the project file (**recipe_front.qxp**) and close it.

9. Double-click the second file in the book (**appetizers.qxp**) to open it.

10. Choose Page>Section. Activate the Section Start check box, change the Number field to 1, and choose 1, 2, 3, 4 from the Format menu. Click OK.

11. Save the project file (**appetizers.qxp**) and close it. The Book palette now reflects the new page numbering; you now need to update the table of contents to reflect the new page numbering.

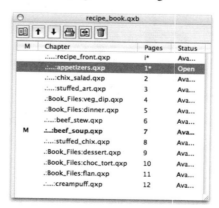

12. Double-click **recipe_front.qxp** in the Book palette to open the file. Using the Content tool, select the text box on the page.

13. Click Build in the Lists palette, and then click Build. In the warning dialog box, click Replace to overwrite the existing table of contents.

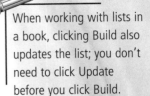
When working with lists in a book, clicking Build also updates the list; you don't need to click Update before you click Build.

The page numbering is incorrect in the updated list. The Chicken Salad recipe begins on Page 3 instead of Page 2; Beef Stew is listed in the correct order, but on Page 8 instead of Page 7; Flan is also in the correct order, but on Page 13 instead of Page 12.

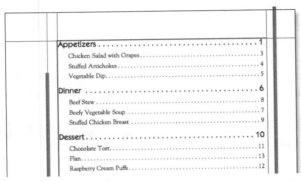

14. Double-click **chix_salad.qxp** in the Book palette to open the file. Choose File>Close to close the file, and click Save/Yes to the warning message asking you to save changes.

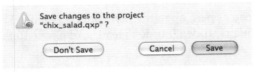

15. With the insertion point in the built list in **recipe_front.qxp**, click Build in the Lists palette; click Replace in the warning dialog box.

The Chicken Salad recipe is now listed correctly on Page 2 of the book, but the following chapters still have incorrect page numbering.

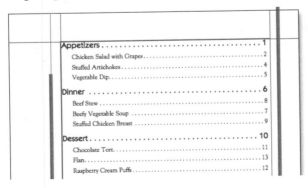

16. Open, save, and close the rest of the files in the book. When all files have been resaved, rebuild the list in the front-matter project file.

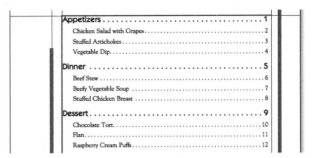

17. Save the project file and close it, but leave the Book palette (file) open for the next exercise.

BUILDING INDEXES IN BOOKS

As you learned in Chapter 12, the QuarkXPress Index utility makes it much easier to compile an index with hundreds of different entries and different types of references. Combining this utility with a QuarkXPress book, you can build extensive, comprehensive indexes across thousands of pages in multiple chapter files.

 SET INDEX PREFERENCES

1. Add the file **recipe_back.qxp** to the open book file (**recipe_book.qxb** from your **Work_In_Progress** folder), and move it to the bottom of the chapter list.

2. Double-click **recipe_back.qxp** in the Book palette to open that file.

3. If it is not already open, open the Style Sheets palette. The project includes style sheets Index1, Index2, Index Head, and Cross-Reference.

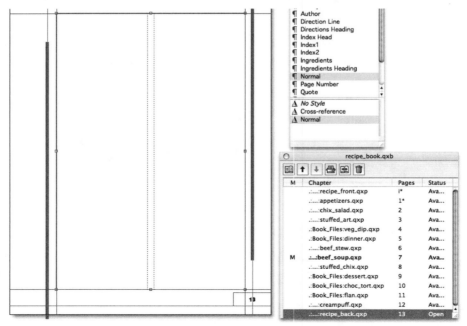

4. Access the Index preferences. Double-click the Following Entry field to highlight it, and then press the Spacebar four times to add space between each term and its references.

5. In the Before Cross-Reference field, type "\n" so cross-references will appear on a new line.

6. Choose <u>A</u> Cross-Reference from the Cross-Reference Style menu.

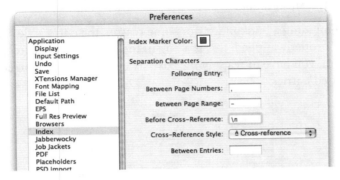

7. Click OK to close the Index Preferences dialog box.

8. Save the file and continue to the next exercise.

BUILD THE INDEX

1. In the open file (**recipes.qxp**), show the Page Layout palette (if it is not already visible).

2. Choose Utilities>Build Index.

3. Select the Add Letter Headings check box, and choose Index Head from the Style menu.

   The Master Page menu defaults to D-Index Page, because that is the only master page in the layout that uses an automatic text box.

4. Choose Index1 in the Level Styles: First Level menu.

5. Choose Index2 in the Level Styles: Second Level menu.

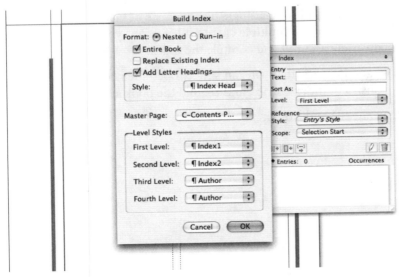

6. Click OK to build the index. A new page is automatically added to the layout, using the master page designated in the Build Index dialog box.

The built list, however, shows two distinct problems.

If you place the insertion point in any of the individual entries and look at the Style Sheets palette, you'll see that the Index1 and Index2 style sheets are applied, but have some non-defined formatting applied (the "+" to the left of the style sheet name).

When building a book index, for some reason, the entry style sheets are not always properly applied; this is a bug in the software. To correct the problem, you have to reapply the base style sheet to the incorrectly formatted entries.

The second problem you might notice is not a software issue; rather, it is caused by the user — but it is just as important. The index shows entries for "dinner" and "dinners". Both of these references should be combined into a single entry (either plural or singular, but not both).

When you're indexing a single file, this type of inconsistency is easier to find; working with multiple chapter files means you might not realize the inconsistencies until you compile the index.

The good news is that you can simply open the necessary files, edit the inconsistent index entries, and rebuild the book's index.

7. Save the file and close it.

PRINTING BOOKS

Rather than opening each file and changing the print settings individually, the Book utility allows you to choose the settings once and print all files in the book. You can do this by clicking the Print button with nothing selected in the palette, or you can print specific files by highlighting them in the list before clicking the Print button. When you click Print in the Print dialog box, QuarkXPress outputs all files in the book using the same settings.

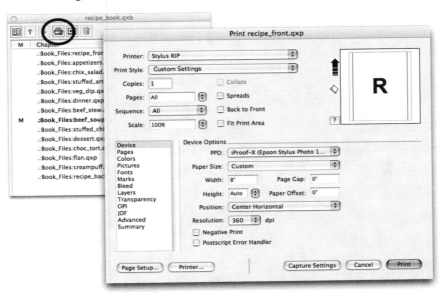

SUMMARY

By now, you know that consistency is extremely important when creating page layouts, and even more so when working with long documents. You should understand that QuarkXPress provides many tools that provide precise control over virtually every aspect of a file or series of files. You know how to combine multiple files into a book and to manage the chapters that make up a book. You know how to synchronize book chapters to maintain consistency from one file to another and to control page numbering for the entire book. You learned how to develop and build lists for an entire book and to work around the problems inherent in this process.

You should understand the greater significance of working with QuarkXPress book files. The Book utility is not limited to single-page chapters (such as those used in this project). You can use the book utility to combine layouts with any number of pages — to create and manage extremely long documents of several hundred pages or more.

Managing Color

14

As a mechanical process, color reproduction has inherent variations and limitations. The ease with which you create and apply colors in a page layout is deceptive. Although it is simple enough to place a color image or create a colored line, you need to consider the final output goal to ensure that the color on your monitor is reproduced as you intend. There is a saying that the end justifies the means; when it comes to color reproduction, the end *defines* the means.

Color management is a fairly complex and somewhat confusing topic. There is a large body of literature devoted to the science and theory of color reproduction, much of which is beyond the scope of this book. Our goal here is to explain how QuarkXPress incorporates color management into the production workflow.

IN CHAPTER 14, YOU WILL:

- Learn about the basic concept of color management in a graphic-arts workflow.

- Define color source and output setups that communicate color reproduction characteristics through the color-management module.

- Control display and color-management preferences.

- Access and manage individual image profiles.

- Soft-proof color on your monitor.

COLOR MANAGEMENT THEORY IN BRIEF

This is an extremely simplified explanation of color management.

You probably already know about the different color models and the gamuts associated with each model, as well as the difference between a process-color build and a spot color. You also probably know that color on a monitor is very different than color on a printed page, and that different printers and output devices reproduce colors differently. Each variable in the digital process — scanner, digital camera, monitor, proofing device, and printing press, to name the primary elements — adds another opportunity for color to be reproduced differently. Even two different versions of RGB (or CMYK) can have different gamuts.

To accurately reproduce color from one device to another, we need some mechanism to translate colors in one space/gamut to the same (or closest possible) colors in another space/gamut. Here's where color management comes in.

Other possible variables in the color-reproduction process include the type of film or digital camera used to take a photograph, the paper on which a photo is developed, the type of imagesetter used to create a printing plate, and so on. The list, as you may have guessed, is practically endless.

Color management refers to the process of maintaining consistent color between the different input and output devices used in the graphic-arts production cycle. Using color management, every device in the process has a *color profile*, or a data set that defines the reproduction characteristics of that specific device.

The Color Management Module (CMM) reads input profiles (how the color was captured), translates that color into its corresponding value in a device-independent color space (such as CIELAB), and then translates those values to the corresponding values in the output profile.

Soft proofing, or previewing accurate color on your monitor, adds another variable to the process. Monitors produce color in RGB, and printing (usually) produces color in CMYK. To accurately preview colors on a monitor, the CMM must translate the color values in the output profile to the RGB values for your monitor.

When you install the drivers for any hardware that you connect to your computer, you should install ICC profiles if they are available. If you do not see your particular hardware in the source and destination profile menus, check the hardware manufacturer's Web site or the documentation that came with the hardware.

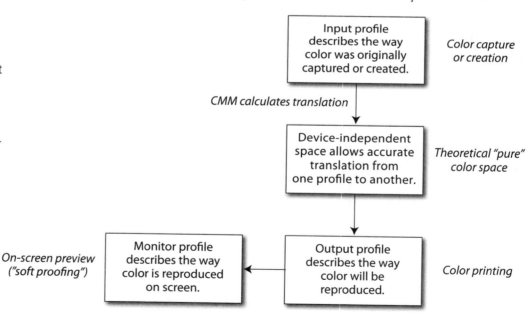

If you are operating a true color-managed workflow — all devices calibrated regularly and ICC profiles for every device installed — color management can help you maintain consistent color from the initial scan to the printed page. If you have not properly calibrated your equipment or do not have the appropriate ICC profiles, color management can still help to *approximate* the final output on your monitor, but keep in mind that what you see is not necessarily what you will get.

Color Management with QuarkXPress

In previous versions of QuarkXPress, color management was either on or off, and one set of specific options was defined in the Preferences dialog box either for all new layouts (default preferences) or for the layout being used at any given time. This model meant that you had to change the preferences each time an input or output variable changed. But this model also resulted in a lot of redundant work for real-world workflows.

Most workflows have specific sets of variables for different types of jobs (for example, direct-mail pieces are printed on an in-house sheetfed press, flyers are printed on a digital press, and multi-page catalogs and brochures are printed on a web press). Every time you changed to a different type of project, you had to go back into the preferences and change the color-management settings.

Another issue arises for jobs that will be printed in multiple locations on different types of equipment or even in different color spaces. Consider an ad that will be placed in multiple magazines, mostly in color but one or two in greyscale. Using the old model, you could define only one output-device profile at a time, then re-open and change the color-management settings for a different device, and so on.

QuarkXPress 7 takes these problems into account, and offers a new way to manage color using saved sets of profiles called *Color Setups*. You can now save multiple *Source Color Setups* (profile sets that define the origins of color, such as the scanner or camera that captured photographs) and *Output Color Setups* (profile sets that describe the specific variables used in an output process). You can then call those saved setups when a job is output to apply the correct color-management settings without constantly changing preferences for individual layouts.

Adding Profiles

Color profiles installed with hardware or software are stored with the system files of your computer. The Profile Manager (Utilities>Profile Manager) dialog box lists all of the profiles installed on your computer. You can also designate an Auxiliary Profile Folder by clicking the Browse/Select button. Profiles in the defined auxiliary folder are added to the list of profiles and will be available only to QuarkXPress.

This is useful if you have different sets of profiles for the service providers and printers you frequently use; you can access those profiles from QuarkXPress without altering your system folder.

Color profiles are created by reproducing a known target, then measuring the variation of the reproduction away from the original. Color profiles are also called "ICC profiles."

CIELAB is a device-independent, theoretical color space that describes color based on the way humans perceive it, and thus contains the entire visible gamut.

Device-independent color models are sometimes described as "pure" color — they do not consider variables or limitations imposed by specific device characteristics.

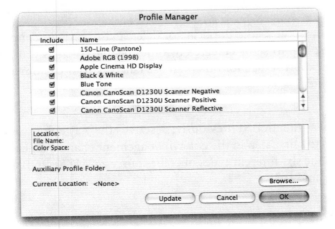

Defining Color Setups

Because color setups are saved sets of options that can be called when you need or want them, they are controlled in the same way as other application assets (style sheets, H&J routines, etc.). You can choose from the Edit>Color Setups menu to define Source Setups or Output Setups (they are managed separately, in separate dialog boxes).

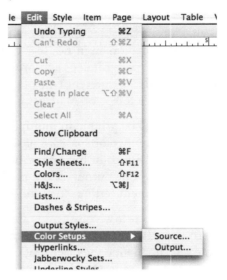

Choosing one of these options opens a dialog box with the familiar feel of other asset-management dialog boxes.

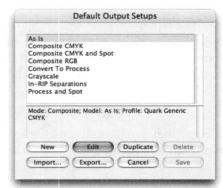

Source and output setups are saved as .XML files, which can be easily imported and exported into any other copy of QuarkXPress 7.

You can add new setups; edit, duplicate or delete existing setups; append setups from other files; import setups created by other people (such as your output provider); and export setups for others to use (such as your customers if you *are* the output provider).

Source Setups

A source setup, as mentioned previously, describes the way color was captured or created. This is the first step in the color-management chain. You can define source profiles for six different types of color sources: CMYK, RGB, LAB, Gray, Named Colors, and Inks.

CMYK, **RGB**, **LAB** and **Gray**. For each of these spaces, you can define different profiles for Solid Colors and for Pictures.

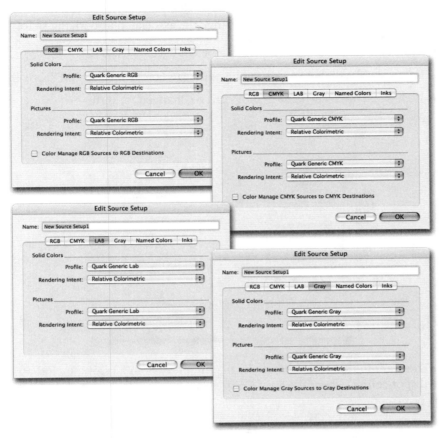

The Profile menus list any profile that is either available on your system or has been added to QuarkXPress using the Profile Manager. (Only CMYK profiles will be available in the CMYK tab, RGB profiles available in the RGB tab, and so on.)

The Rendering Intent menus include four options to define how the CMM will translate colors that are outside the destination-profile gamut.

- **Perceptual**. This option scales the colors in the source profile into the gamut of the destination profile.
- **Relative Colorimetric**. This option maintains any colors that are in both the source and destination profiles. Any source colors outside the destination gamut are shifted to fit into the destination gamut.
- **Saturation**. This option compares the saturation of colors in the source profile and shifts them to the nearest possible saturated color in the destination profile.
- **Absolute Colorimetric**. This option maintains colors that are in both the source and destination profiles. Any colors outside the destination gamut are shifted to a color within the destination gamut based on the color's appearance on white paper.

LAB is a short name for CIELAB, which we explained previously. Although not terribly common, some workflows capture and maintain images in the LAB color space, allowing color translation to occur during the output process (at the RIP).

The CMM translates color based on the *rendering intent*, or the properties that are most important in the selected image or object.

The Saturation rendering intent can result in drastic color shift, sometimes producing an entirely different color.

For RGB, CMYK, and Gray colors, you can activate the Color Manage [color] Sources to [Color] Destinations. This option enables color management to properly translate colors between two color profiles that use the same color space (CMYK to CMYK, for example).

Named Colors. This tab defines the default color space for separated colors that are named based on the model from which they are created. The Source Space column shows the underlying color space that defines the named colors. Depending on the color library used, you can change the associated underlying space:

- Focoltone and Trumatch colors can be changed to CMYK.

- Pantone colors from separation libraries can be changed to CMYK or LAB.

- Web-safe and Web-named colors can be changed to RGB.

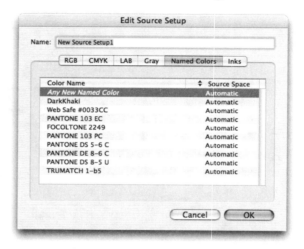

QuarkXPress includes five separated Pantone libraries:

- Pantone Color Bridge EC

- Pantone Color Bridge PC

- Pantone Process Coated

- Pantone Process Coated EURO

- Pantone Process Uncoated

Inks. These are the specific separations that might exist in a layout, including defined spot colors (where the Spot Color check box is active in the Edit Color dialog box).

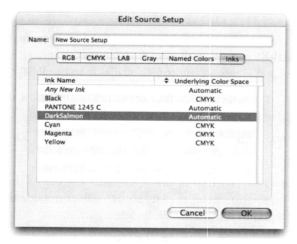

The Underlying Color Space column shows the source space for each separation that will be output. This setting depends on the color model used to create the color (in the Edit Color dialog box, if the color was generated in QuarkXPress).

- The four process inks are listed using CMYK as the underlying space.

- Inks created from CMYK builds are also listed as CMYK.

- Inks created from special libraries (DIC, Focoltone, Pantone, Toyo, or Trumatch) are listed as Automatic; you can apply a different space to those inks by clicking the column heading and choosing from the pop-up menu.

    - DIC and Toyo colors can be changed to use LAB or CMYK space.

    - Focoltone and Trumatch colors can be changed to use CMYK space.

    - Pantone separated colors for which the Spot Color check box is activated can be changed to use the LAB or CMYK space.

    - Pantone colors that are automatically defined as spot can be changed to use the LAB space.

- Inks created using the RGB or HSB model use RGB as the underlying space.

- Inks created using the LAB model use LAB as the underlying space.

- Inks created using the Web-named and Web-safe model use Automatic as the underlying space. You can change these to RGB.

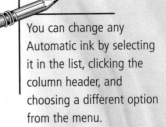

You can change any Automatic ink by selecting it in the list, clicking the column header, and choosing a different option from the menu.

Output Setups

The second half of color management — the output setup — defines how color is going to be reproduced.

For each output setup, you have to first define the mode that will be used — Composite or Separations. (This is the same as deciding whether you want to print a composite or separation proof in the Print dialog box; see Chapter 10.)

Separations Mode. If you're color managing the final output process — the point when a job is sent to an imagesetter or digital press — you need to define an output profile for separations. In the Model menu, you can determine how the separations are created:

- **Host-Based Separations.** This model creates separations when the PostScript stream is generated (i.e., when the "host" computer outputs the file) and before the stream reaches the RIP. This is the only option if you are using a PostScript Level 1 device, as well as most PostScript Level 2 devices, because these earlier versions do not support in-RIP separation.

- **In-RIP Separations.** This model embeds information into the PostScript stream that allows the printer or RIP to create separations when the file is processed. This is a function of PostScript Level 3; it does not work for most devices that use earlier versions of the PostScript language.

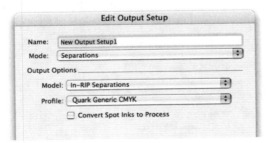

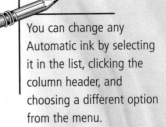

Some, but not most, PostScript Level 2 devices are enabled for in-RIP separations. Consult the documentation for the specific printer and RIP that you are using.

Regardless of the model you are using, you can also define the profile for the specific output device. Like source setups, any CMYK profile available in QuarkXPress will be listed in this menu; because separation is a function of printing, and printing is a CMYK process, only CMYK profiles are listed.

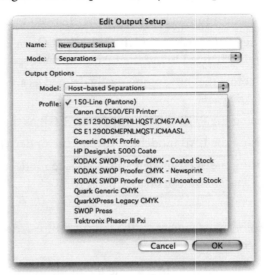

If you activate the Convert Spot Inks to Process check box, all spot colors will be mapped to CMYK when a file is output using that setup.

Composite Mode. If you're creating an output setup for a proofing device, you are probably proofing composites instead of separations; but just because you're proofing doesn't mean you can't color-manage the process.

When you output in composite mode, you can choose from five available models:

- **Grayscale.** When this model is selected, all colors in the layout are converted to grayscale based on the color data selected in the Profile menu.

- **RGB.** This model converts all color data to RGB mode, which is useful for proofing with an RGB printer or when generating a PDF for Web distribution. Any elements (placed pictures) that are already in RGB mode are not affected, but they are included in the composite output.

  When using the RGB model, you can also activate the Proof Separations check box to simulate separations in the composite RGB output. You can then define the type of separations to simulate (by choosing from the Output Simulation menu), as well as the rendering intent to apply.

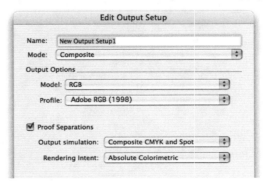

Composite output setups are also valuable for exporting PDF files for placement into another layout; those applications call for composite — not separated — files.

See the previous discussion of source setups for an explanation of the rendering intents.

- **CMYK.** This model converts all non-CMYK colors to the closest possible process builds based on the defined output profile. For CMYK output, you can choose to Convert Spot Inks to Process. If this option is selected, you can also activate the Proof Separations options (see above).

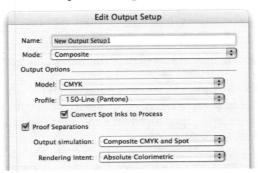

- **AsIs.** This model preserves existing source-color information in the PostScript data stream; no color conversion takes place when the file is output from QuarkXPress. Instead of defining a profile that is applied when the file is output, you instead choose a profile that defines the output intent, which tells the RIP what to do.

  Using AsIs color, you have two additional options:

  – Preserve Spot Color maintains spot inks in the final output stream.

  – Use Device Independent Color maintains any device-independent (LAB) data in the file.

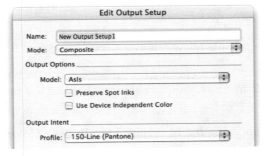

- **DeviceN**: This model is used to create composite PostScript that maintains information about individual ink colors. This option is useful if you need to generate a composite PDF of a CMYK+spot layout file that will eventually be separated for commercial printing.

  The DeviceN model maintains spot and process-ink information in the PostScript output stream; the file can be output as either composite (spot colors will be converted to the defined device profile) or as separations (in which the separated ink information is mapped to the correct plates).

  If you activate the Convert Spot Inks to Process check box, spot colors will be mapped to the nearest possible CMYK colors.

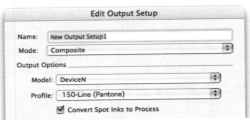

You are still defining the profile for the intended output device using AsIs color; the difference is in when that conversion is being applied. Using RGB, CMYK, or Grayscale models, the conversion takes place when you generate the PostScript stream (print, save as EPS, or export to PDF). Using AsIs, the conversion doesn't take place until the PostScript stream is processed by the output device or RIP.

The Output Intent menu is essentially the same as the Profile menu. Because the color conversion is taking place in the RIP, you are defining what will happen (your "intent").

A Quick Note...

There is a wealth of information here to digest, and it really only scratches the surface of what *could be* (and is) written about color management. Unless you want to become a color scientist, don't try to overthink the two different types color profiles/setups.

- A source setup defines color as it was captured.
- An output setup defines the way color will ultimately be reproduced.

A monitor profile, for example, can be both a source and an output profile because color can be both created using a monitor (e.g., selected from a color picker in QuarkXPress) and ultimately reproduced on a monitor (e.g., the final layout will be distributed on the Web as a PDF file).

DEFINE SOURCE SETUPS

1. Open **center_market.qxp** from the **RF_Quark7>Chapter14** folder.

2. Choose Edit>Color Setups>Source.

3. Click New in the Source Setup dialog box.

4. In the Edit Source Setup dialog box, name the new source "[your initials] Workflow".

5. In the RGB tab, choose your monitor profile in the Solid Colors section. If you don't have a profile for your monitor, choose one of the generic options.

6. In the Pictures Profile menu, choose Nikon LS-3510 AF.

   We're using this built-in profile for the sake of instruction. If you have a specific profile for the scanner or camera that you use most often, choose that instead.

7. Leave both Rendering Intent menus set to Relative Colorimetric.

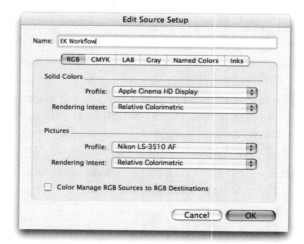

8. In the CMYK tab, activate the Color Manage CMYK Sources to CMYK Destinations check box.

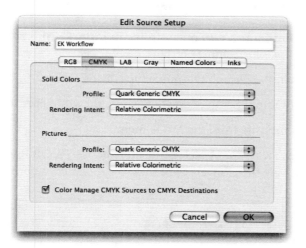

9. Leave all other options at their default values.

   In many cases, the default settings for all but RGB pictures will be adequate unless you have very a specific color-managed workflow. In those environments, you'll probably have to set specific LAB options as well.

10. Click OK to close the Edit Source Setup dialog box.

    Your new source setup appears in the list.

11. Click Save to close the Source Setups dialog box.

12. Save the file as "catalog_page.qxp" in your **Work_In_Progress** folder.

13. Continue to the next exercise.

Notice that — even with a file open — the Output Setup dialog box includes the word "Default" in the title bar. Output setups are available in any project; source setups are only available to the project in which they were created unless you define them as default source setups or you import them into another project.

1. With **catalog_page.qxp** open (from your **Work_In_Progress** folder), choose Edit>Color Setups>Output.

2. Click New in the Default Output Setups dialog box.

3. In the Edit Output Setup dialog box, name the setup "LA Imaging Web".

4. Choose Composite from the Mode menu.

5. Choose CMYK in the Model menu, and choose SWOP Press in the Profile menu. Activate the Convert Spot Inks to Process check box and click OK.

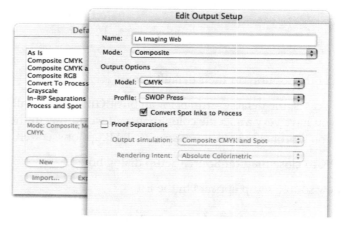

6. Click New again in the Output Setups dialog box.

7. In the Edit Output Setup dialog box, create a second set named "5c Sheetfed".

8. Choose Composite from the Mode menu, choose DeviceN from the Model menu, and use the Kodak SWOP Proofer CMYK – Coated Stock profile.

9. Make sure Convert Spot Inks to Process box is NOT selected and click OK.

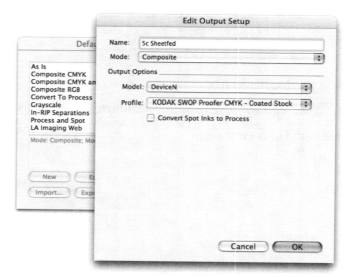

10. Click Save to close the Default Output Setup dialog box.

11. Continue to the next section.

Display Preferences

To effectively color-manage a QuarkXPress layout, you have to define the profile for the monitor you're using. The Monitor Profile menu in the Application Display preferences includes any monitor profiles that are available, as well as several industry-standard and generic options that you can use if you don't have a specific monitor profile. Without defining a specific monitor profile to describe the way color is being reproduced, accurate color management will not be possible.

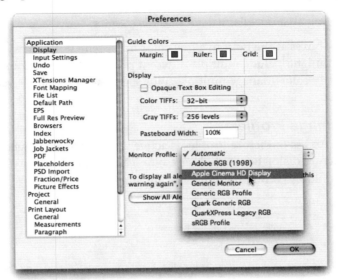

Using generic profiles essentially negates the point of color management; if you want to accurately render color on your monitor, you need to either obtain or create a monitor profile.

Color Manager Preferences

As in previous versions, you can control default color-management settings in the Preferences dialog box. If you've used these settings in the past, one of the primary differences you'll note is that you no longer have to on turn color management. In QuarkXPress 7, color management is *always* on; it functions transparently to the user unless you intentionally apply your own custom settings.

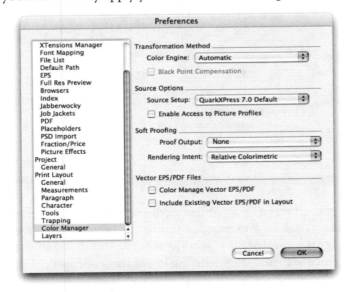

The Color Engine menu defines the color-management model (CMM) that performs the translation from one color space to another. Certain CMMs, such as LogoSync, also include the ability to add Black Point Compensation, which adjusts for differences in black points from one color space to another.

In the Source Options area, you can call a default Source Setup for the files that are used in your QuarkXPress workflow. If you frequently use one group of source settings, define a Source Setup and call it here as the default for your workflow.

When the Enable Access to Picture Profiles option is checked, you can review and change the profile for a specific image either when the file is imported, or later using the Profile Information dialog box. This option is explained in the next section of this chapter.

The Soft Proofing area is explained later in this chapter.

The two check boxes at the bottom allow color management to access and affect files that might include multiple different profiles. These options allow you to effectively color-manage multiple color spaces within a single vector EPS or PDF file.

Accessing Image Profiles

When Enable Access to Picture Profiles is active in the Color Manager preferences, the Import Picture dialog box includes a Color Management tab, in which you can choose the profile and rendering intent for the imported image.

When an image is captured by a profiled device or saved from an image-editing application, such as Adobe Photoshop, a profile can be attached to the image file. When that image is imported into QuarkXPress, the Profile menu shows the profile that is embedded and the rendering intent that is defined.

You can replace the embedded profile by choosing a different option from the Profile menu. Any available profile (in the same color space as the image) will be listed in the menu.

Changes made in this pane affect only the active layout. If you make the changes when no project is open, your default settings will apply to any new project.

Embedded picture profiles appear in italics.

You can also change the profile of an image that is already placed. The Profile Information dialog box (Window>Profile Information) shows the Picture Type, File Type, and Color Space of the image selected in the Project window. You can change the Profile and Rendering Intent menus to any other available option.

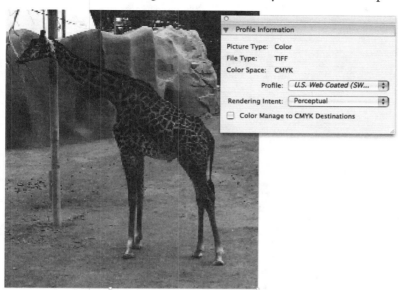

When managing individual picture profiles, the primary difference between QuarkXPress 7 and previous versions is what happens when you change the profile in the layout.

In previous versions, activating color management changed the Project window display to show colors as they would appear based on the destination profiles that were defined in the Preferences dialog box. Changing an image profile automatically changed the image preview.

In QuarkXPress 7, the screen preview is not affected by changing source profiles (including image profiles) unless you change the output setup in the View>Proof Output menu.

ACCESS IMAGE PROFILES

1. With the file **catalog_page.qxp** open (from your **Work_In_Progress** folder), open the Preferences dialog box.

2. In the Display pane, choose the appropriate profile for your monitor. If you do not see the profile for your monitor, choose Generic Monitor.

3. In the Color Manager pane, activate the Enable Access to Picture Profiles check box.

4. Close the Preferences dialog box.

5. Select the empty picture box in the layout and open the Import Picture dialog box.

6. Navigate to **explorateur.tif** in the **RF_Quark7>Chapter14** folder.

7. In the lower half of the dialog box, make sure the Color Management options are displayed.

When an image is scanned, photographed, or otherwise created, the profile of the capturing device is saved with the image (in a color-managed environment). Although you can change the profile of a specific image, it is not particularly recommended unless you have a very good reason (i.e., you know something was done wrong when the file was captured/saved).

Using generic profiles essentially negates the point of color management; we do so here for the sake of illustrating how to use the QuarkXPress color-management tools. In a real-world situation, you should obtain and use profiles for the specific hardware you are using.

The selected image was saved with a profile, as shown in the Profile menu. You could change the associated image profile, but you probably shouldn't.

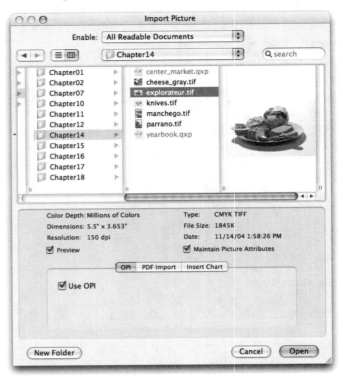

8. Make sure Maintain Picture Attributes is checked and click Open.

    Because our focus here isn't placing pictures in a layout, we saved this picture box with the attributes necessary to import and go.

9. Choose Window>Profile Information to display the Profile Information dialog box.

10. Activate the Color Manage to CMYK Destinations check box.

    Like the same option in the Source Setup dialog box, you can change individual images from one profile to another within the same color space.

11. With the picture box selected, choose SWOP Press in the Profile menu.

    Nothing seems to have changed; you'll see the difference in the next section.

12. Save the file and continue to the next section.

Soft Proofing

Color management technically refers to transforming color from one space (input) to another (output). In theory, you never need to see anything change for color management to function properly.

The reality of graphic communications, however, includes an intermediary output space — your monitor — which displays color as you create it. Many color decisions are made based on what we see in front of us; it's just easier and faster, even when we know it isn't technically correct. If you want an accurate representation of color *as it will be output*, your monitor needs to be involved in the color management process as well.

Soft proofing refers to the ability to accurately preview colors on your monitor *as they will appear when output*. Before soft proofing in QuarkXPress can be effective and accurate, you need to complete three steps:

1. Define the profile for your monitor in the Application Display preferences.

2. Define a source setup with the source profile information for different elements of your layout.

3. Define an output setup with the profile information for the output device that will be used.

Once these three tasks are done, soft proofing in QuarkXPress is simple — simply choose the appropriate output setup in the View>Proof Output menu.

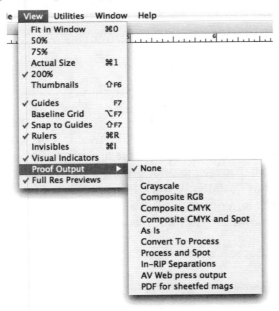

When you change the proof output setting, the colors in your Project window will convert to display based on the selected output setup.

One of the biggest problems of reproducing accurate color is that many people *don't know* that what they see isn't what they will get. (You're obviously not one of them since you've read this far.) Education is key to all aspects of quality print output.

1. With the file **catalog_page.qxp** open (from your **Work_In_Progress** folder), choose View>Proof Output>LA Imaging Web.

   The colors in the layout change to show how they will appear based on the output profile that is defined in the LA Imaging Web output setup.

2. In the layout, select the picture in the bottom-right corner of the page.

3. In the Profile Information dialog box, choose SWOP (Coated) 20% in the Profile menu.

   Because this is the embedded profile for this image, it is listed in italics.

   Notice the (slight) difference in color for that picture in the Project window. You've only changed the profile for one object, not for the entire layout.

   In the previous exercise, the picture preview did not change when you changed the profile. Now that soft proofing is enabled, the picture preview changes when the profile is changed.

4. Choose View>Proof Output>5c Sheetfed.

   By calling a different output setup, all colors in all elements of the layout change (again, however slightly) based on the output profile in the defined output setup.

5. Choose View>Proof Output>None.

   This effectively turns off soft proofing.

6. Save the file and continue to the next section.

Managing and Exporting Profiles

A color profile is a data file. Just as the font files used in a project have to be present for successful output, the color-profile files must also be available when the file is printed. You can manage the color profiles used in a file in the Profiles pane of the Usage dialog box (Utilities>Usage). Every profile used in a layout is listed in the Profile menu. The lower pane displays a list of the objects (the specific images) that use the profile shown in the Profile menu.

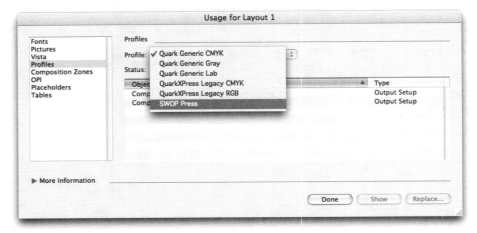

Sidebar:
You can also choose a proof output setup in the Color Manager preferences dialog box.

If you choose a specific setup in the Color Manager preferences when no project is open, all new projects will automatically display color based on that output setup.

Don't confuse turning off soft proofing with turning off color management. Changing the Proof Output menu to None only affects what you see on your screen, not what is output.

You can change the profile for a particular object by highlighting that object in the dialog box and clicking Replace. The Replace Profile dialog box shows the currently applied profile; the Replace With menu lists the other available profiles. Clicking OK changes the profile of the selected object.

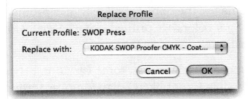

If you've built color-management profiles into your layout, you have to include the necessary color profiles with the job package that you send to the service provider. Checking the Color Profiles option in the Collect for Output dialog box will export the necessary files.

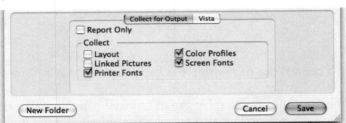

If you're sending a native QuarkXPress file to an output provider, they need access to the profiles you've used for color management to work properly.

 MANAGE PROFILES

1. With the file **catalog_page.qxp** open (from your **Work_In_Progress** folder), choose Utilities>Usage and click Profiles in the list of categories.

2. Choose SWOP (Coated) 20% in the Profile menu.

3. Highlight the placed TIFF file in the Object list, and click Replace.

4. Choose SWOP Press from the Replace With menu and click OK.

5. Click Done/Close to close the Profiles Usage dialog box.

6. Save the file.

7. Choose File>Collect for Output.

8. Create a new folder named "Color" in your **Work_In_Progress** folder. Activate the Color Profiles check box, and click Save.

9. You may see the warning about font-license agreements. Click OK.

10. When the collect process is complete, close the QuarkXPress file and open the **Color** folder (**Work_In_Progress>Color**) on your desktop. You will see a separate Profiles folder, which should be sent to the service provider as part of the job package.

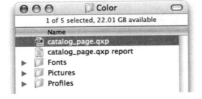

TRAPPING

In process-color printing, the four process colors (Cyan, Magenta, Yellow, and Black) are imaged or separated onto individual printing plates. Each color separation is printed on a separate unit of a printing press. When printed on top of each other in varying percentages, the semitransparent inks produce the range of colors in the CMYK gamut. Spot colors are printed using specially formulated inks as additional color separations.

Because printing is a mechanical process, some variation between the different units of the press is possible (if not likely). Paper moves through the units of a press at considerable speed, and some movement from side to side is inevitable. Each printing plate has one or more registration marks (crosshairs) that are used to monitor the registration of each color. If the units are *in register*, the cross hairs from each color plate print exactly on top of each other.

When a press is out of register, the individual colors are discernible.

Misregistration can cause a noticeable gap of uninked paper between adjacent elements, particularly when these elements are comprised of different ink colors.

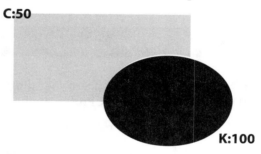

Misregister results in a thin but visible gap between the two objects.

If any misregister occurs on press, type can become blurry or, worse, virtually unreadable. Any time multiple ink colors are placed on top of each other, you run the risk of misregister.

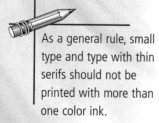

As a general rule, small type and type with thin serifs should not be printed with more than one color ink.

Misregister

Misregister

Even slight misregister will blur the sharp edges of type, especially thin serifs like this Minion font.

Trapping is the compensation for misregister of the color plates on a printing press. Trapping minimizes or eliminates these errors by artificially expanding adjacent colors so that small areas of color on the edge of each element overlap and print on top of one another. If sufficiently large, this expansion of color, or *trap*, fills in the undesirable inkless gap between elements. Trapping procedures differ based upon your workflow; most service providers will perform trapping before generating film or plates. The specific amount of trapping to be applied varies, depending on the ink/paper/press combination.

Caveat

Many service providers and printers have high-end solutions that apply trapping to your layouts. If they do, any trap settings that you make in QuarkXPress will be overwritten. Smaller firms without dedicated trapping solutions may use the QuarkXPress trapping options to prepare the file in the prepress department.

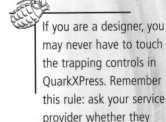

If you are a designer, you may never have to touch the trapping controls in QuarkXPress. Remember this rule: ask your service provider whether they want you to apply trapping, and, if so, what settings you should use.

Knockouts and Overprints

A *knockout* is an area of background color that is removed so that a lighter foreground color is visible. To achieve white (paper-colored) type on a black background, for example, the black background is removed wherever the type overlaps the black. Any time a lighter color appears on top of a darker color, the area of the lighter color is knocked out of the background.

Overprint is essentially the opposite of knockout. A darker-color foreground object is printed directly on top of a lighter-color background, which means that slight variation in the units of the press will not be as noticeable, especially if the darker color is entirely contained within the lighter color. Black is commonly set to overprint other colors, as are some special colors that are printed using opaque inks. Black is particularly effective when overprinted since it becomes visually richer when other process colors — especially Cyan — are mixed with it.

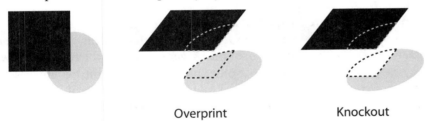

Overprint   Knockout

When a color is set to knock out, anything beneath that color will not be printed. If the black knocks out the Cyan, any misregistration may result in a paper-colored gap where the two objects meet. Setting black to overprint eliminates the possibility of a gap caused by misregistration. (The dashed lines in the graphic are for illustration only and will not print.)

Chokes and Spreads

A *choke* means that the edge of the background color is expanded into the space in which the foreground color will be printed. A *spread* means that the edge of the foreground color is expanded to overprint the edge of the background color. As a general rule, the lighter object should be trapped into the darker area. This rule helps determine whether you should choke or spread.

- If the background is darker than the foreground object, the lighter color of the foreground object should be spread to overprint the darker background.

- If the foreground color is darker than the background color, the lighter background color is choked so that it overprints the darker foreground color.

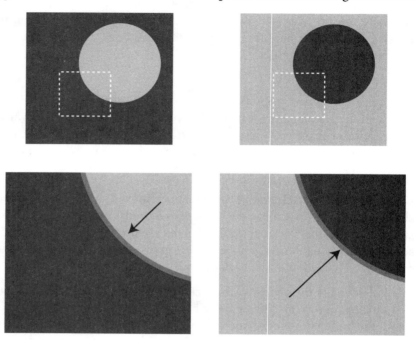

In the left image, the foreground circle is spread into the darker background. In the right image, the background color is choked into the darker foreground.

Using Common Colors

If adjacent elements share a large percentage of one or more common colors, trapping between those elements is unnecessary. If both elements contain a lot of magenta, for example, the continuity of the magenta between the two objects will mask any gaps that occur between the other process colors in the two images; this makes trapping unnecessary. The general rule is that if two adjacent elements share one process color that varies by less than 50%, or if two elements share two or more process colors that vary by less than 80%, don't bother with trapping — the continuous layer of the inks common to both elements will effectively mask any gaps.

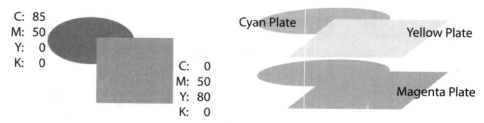

When adjacent elements share common colors, the paper will not show through since the Magenta is printed as a common element.

If two adjacent elements share one process color that varies by less than 50%, or if the two elements share two or more process colors that vary by less than 80%, don't bother with trapping.

Trapping Preferences

QuarkXPress incorporates three different types of trapping:

- **Default Trapping**. This option automatically applies to the entire file and is modified in the Trapping Preferences dialog box.

- **Color-Specific Trapping**. You can change the trap settings for specific colors in a file. These settings are accessed in the Edit Colors dialog box (Edit>Colors) by clicking Edit Trap.

- **Item-Specific Trapping**. You can change the trap settings for specific objects in the Trap Information dialog box (Window>Trap Information).

QuarkXPress trapping preferences control the settings that are used to automatically trap the elements of your layout.

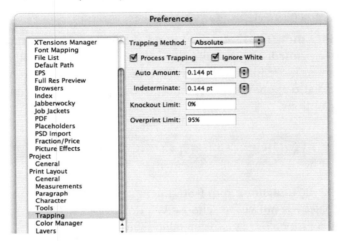

You can change the default trapping preferences by opening the Trapping Preferences dialog box with no file open.

- **Trapping Method**. The Trapping Method option determines how traps are applied. Absolute applies trapping based on the Auto Amount and Indeterminate values. Proportional applies trapping based on a comparison of the color *luminance* (relative lightness or brightness) values of the foreground and background objects. Knockout All effectively turns off trapping.

- **Process Trapping**. Activating the Process Trapping check box means that the individual separations of a layout are trapped separately. In other words, the Cyan component of a foreground object is compared to the Cyan component of the background object, the Magenta component of a foreground object is compared to the Magenta component of the background, and so on.

- **Ignore White**. If the Ignore White check box is active, any object in front of a White background will overprint. If a foreground object overlays a colored background and a White background, the White is ignored in the trapping consideration.

  The Ignore White option is important when an object overlaps two background objects — one White and one colored. Technically, no trap is necessary when an object overlaps White.

  If a foreground object overlaps a colored object and a White object, the Ignore White check box means that the White background object is not considered when trapping is calculated; the foreground is trapped to the colored background using the Auto Amount value.

  If the Ignore White check box is deselected, the foreground will trap to the colored background using the Indeterminate amount.

Though called "White" in the QuarkXPress Colors palette, this color would be more appropriately named "Paper." Any object colored White in the layout will show the color of the paper for the job. To actually print the color White, you would have to designate specially formulated opaque inks.

- **Auto Amount**. The Auto Amount field determines the amount of trapping that is applied for any object set to trap automatically. The amount of required trapping varies according to the paper, ink, and press used to produce the job. Always ask your service provider before setting a trap value.

- **Indeterminate**. The Indeterminate trap value applies whenever an object overlays a background of indeterminate color value (such as a continuous-tone image with many different colors), or when a foreground object overlays two background objects with different color values.

- **Knockout Limit**. The Knockout Limit field defines the percentage of color that will knock out a background color. The default value, 0%, means that any object set to 0% of a color will knock out the background. If you change the knockout limit to 5%, any object set to 5% or less of a color will knock out the background. The higher this field, the more knockouts are created, which means more chance for visible misregistration.

- **Overprint Limit**. The Overprint Limit field defines the percentage of Black that is overprinted. The default value is 95%, which means that any object set to 95% or more Black will overprint the background. The Overprint Limit field also applies to any color set to overprint using the color-specific trapping options.

SET TRAPPING PREFERENCES

1. Open the file **yearbook.qxp** from the **RF_Quark7>Chapter14** folder. If the Colors palette is not visible, choose Window>Colors. This is a process color job with a fifth color plate for metallic silver (Pantone 877 C).

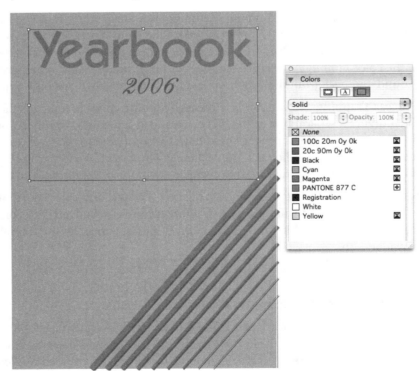

2. The printer needs 0.2-pt. traps to ensure quality output. Access the Trapping Preferences dialog box.

3. Change the Auto Amount field to 0.2 pt. and click OK.

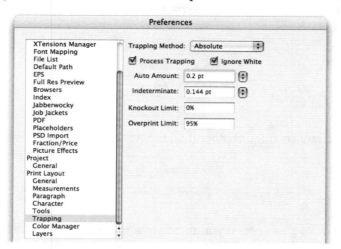

4. Save the file to your **Work_In_Progress** folder, and leave the file open.

Color-Specific Trapping

You can define the trapping behavior of any color in a file by highlighting the color in the Colors dialog box and clicking Edit Trap.

The Trap Specifications dialog box allows you to define how the selected color is trapped to any other color in the file. Changes you make in this dialog box apply any time the color shown in the title bar (Trap Specifications For [Color]) is placed in front of the color selected in the Background Color list. For example, you can change the way Black is trapped when placed over a Cyan background by high-lighting Cyan in the Background Color list.

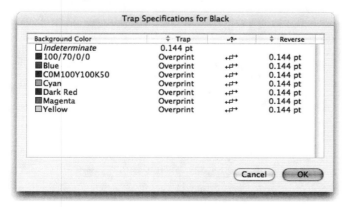

When a color is highlighted in the list, you can change the trapping method by clicking the Trap menu. Auto Amount (+) applies a spread; Auto Amount (−) applies a choke.

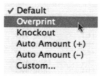

You can also create an amount other than the Auto Amount by choosing Custom.

The Custom dialog box allows you to create a trapping relationship other than the value defined in the Auto Amount field.

The Dependent/Independent Traps menu enables you to automatically apply the inverse relationship when the foreground color and background color relationship is reversed. In other words, if you define the trap relationship for any instance of a Cyan object in front of a Black background, the Dependent Traps option automatically calculates the inverse trap value for any time a Black object is in front of a Cyan background. If you do not want the color trap relationship to be inverted, choose Independent Traps from the menu.

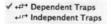

The Reverse column shows the inverse values for the specific trapping relationship. If you change the trap value for Cyan on a Magenta background, for example, the Reverse column will show the trap value that will apply any time a Magenta object is placed over a Cyan background. If Dependent Traps is selected, any change you make to the Reverse column will automatically affect the Trap column.

 CREATE COLOR-SPECIFIC TRAPS

1. In the open file, choose Edit>Colors.

2. Highlight Pantone 877 C in the dialog box, and click Edit Trap.

3. Pantone 877 C is an opaque metallic ink. Because it is opaque, it should overprint all other inks instead of knocking out. Highlight Indeterminate in the Trap Specifications dialog box. Click the Trap column heading (Macintosh) or the arrow next to the Trap column heading (Windows) and choose Overprint from the menu.

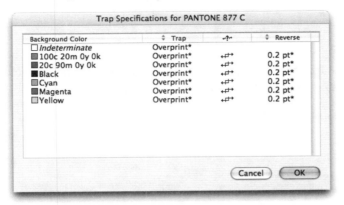

4. Repeat this process for all colors in the list so that Pantone 877 C will overprint all colors in the layout. Click OK when you have finished. Click Save in the Edit Colors dialog box.

5. Save the file and leave it open.

Item-Specific Trapping

You can apply specific trapping settings to any object in the layout except imported pictures. The Trap Information dialog box (Window>Trap Information) shows the trapping values that are applied for any selected object on the page.

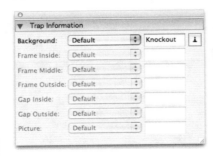

You can modify the trap settings for any available option by choosing from the drop-down menu. These options are the same as those that are available in the Trap Specifications dialog box.

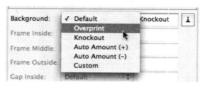

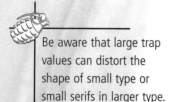

Be aware that large trap values can distort the shape of small type or small serifs in larger type.

If you click the Information icon (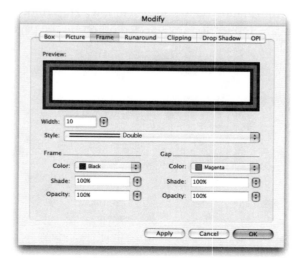) next to any option, you can get the specifics of the trap that will be applied to the selected object.

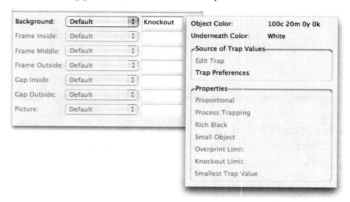

Different areas of the Trap Information dialog box become available, depending on what is selected in the Project window.

- **Background**. This option is available if a box contains a background color (including White).

- **Frame Inside**. This option is available if the selected box has a border greater than 0 pt. It defines how the inside edge of the frame is trapped to the contents of the box, or to the background, if the box if filled with None. If the frame style has more than one line, the innermost line of the frame is trapped according to the Frame Inside option.

- **Frame Middle**. This option is available if the frame style has color between the lines of the frame (more than one line) or between the segments of the frame (dashed or dotted). This setting defines the trap for the different pieces of the line.

Any line style that defines a gap color other than None activates Frame Inside, Frame Middle, and Frame Outside options in the Trap Information dialog box.

- **Frame Outside**. This option is available if the selected object has a border greater than 0 pt. It defines how the outside edge of the frame is trapped to any background object. If the frame style has more than one line, the outermost line of the frame is trapped according to the Frame Outside option.

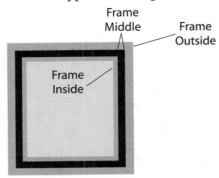

- **Gap Inside**. This option is available if the frame style is dashed or dotted and uses a gap color other than None. It defines how the gap color is trapped to the contents of the box (on the inside edge), or to any background object if the box has a fill of None.

- **Gap Outside**. This option is available if the frame style is dashed or dotted and uses a gap color other than None. It defines how the gap color is trapped (on the outside edge) to any background object.

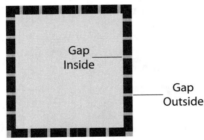

- **Line**. This option is available if the selection is a line with a width greater than 0 pt. It defines how the line color is trapped to any background object.

- **Line Middle**. This option is available if a line style has more than one stroke or is dashed or dotted and uses a gap color other than None. It defines how the pieces of the line are trapped to each other.

- **Gap**. This option is available for a multistroke line without end treatments (arrowheads) and dashed or dotted line styles with a gap color other than None. It defines how the gap color is trapped to any background object.

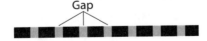

- **Text**. This option is available (replacing Picture) if text is highlighted in a text box. You can trap text to the background color of its box or to any background color if the box is filled with None.

- **Picture**. This option replaces Text if the selection is a picture box that contains an EPS picture. Trapping an EPS illustration depends largely on how the file was created. Unless you are sure trapping strokes were applied correctly in the illustration application, do not try to trap pictures in QuarkXPress.

Trapping for imported pictures must be implemented in the picture's native application or using a stand-alone trapping application.

1. Highlight the text "2006" in the open file.

2. Choose Window>Trap Information. The Text field is the only one available.

3. Click the Information icon (the small "i") to the right of the Text trap field.

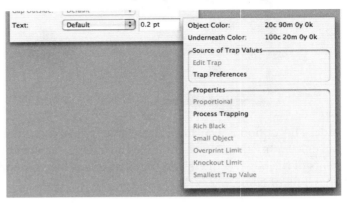

4. Observe that there is some common color between the selection and the background, but not enough to eliminate the need for trapping.

5. Select Custom from the Text menu.

6. Type "0.1 in." in the Custom field to apply a smaller trap value for the thin text and press Return/Enter. When you press Return/Enter, the value is automatically converted to points (7.2 pt.).

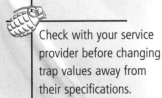

Check with your service provider before changing trap values away from their specifications.

7. Save and close the file.

SUMMARY

Color is one of the defining elements of graphic design and page layout. We use color to reproduce an image in print, to create visual interest, and to highlight elements of a design. Adding color to a layout is a fairly simple process, but there are technical aspects of color reproduction that must also be considered when planning and implementing a layout.

QuarkXPress 7 includes sophisticated color-management and trapping tools that are designed to accommodate different types of output needs, even for the same layout file. You learned how to define color source setups and output setups and how to apply those setups to soft proof color on your monitor. You also learned the basics of trapping and worked with the different QuarkXPress trapping options. Finally, you should understand the importance of discussing color management and trapping with your service provider or printer.

Sharing Content and Layouts

15

As graphic communicators, we can work for virtually any company in any industry, in any kind of economy. And as many opportunities as there are available in graphic communications, there are just as many clients — each with unique wants and needs; every client has a different message to communicate.

There are, however, two characteristics that are shared by virtually all clients: the desire to communicate their message through multiple designs and media, and the demand to turn work around quickly (almost "yesterday," or at least it seems that way sometimes).

QuarkXPress 7 incorporates powerful new tools that help to address these issues. The ability to share *content* allows us to create once, and easily repurpose for multiple media. The ability to share *files* allows us to create simultaneously with other designers, then easily combine the collaborative effort into the finished piece.

IN CHAPTER 15, YOU WILL:

- Learn how to create and share synchronized objects and content to facilitate multiple- and cross-media design applications.

- Learn how to share layouts, which can then be incorporated into other layouts without first being saved as flat EPS or PDF files.

- Learn how to create and share composition zones, which split a single layout into multiple pieces that can be completed by different people at one time.

SHARED OBJECTS AND CONTENT

QuarkXPress 6 introduced a new concept called *synchronized text*, which allows you to create a text story once and then add multiple linked instances of the story anywhere in the same project. When you edit one instance of the synchronized story, all other instances of that story are automatically updated to reflect the same changes.

A basic example of this would be an identity package with letterhead, envelope, and business-card layouts. Each piece in the project includes the client's contact information. Using standard layout tools, you have to create the text box three different times and add the text in three different places. If, for example, the area code changes, you have to make that change in three different places. Using synchronized text, changing one instance of the area code changes all the other instances at the same time.

The identity package is a very simple (but valid) example of using this technology. Consider a several-hundred-page product catalog, in which the company's phone number appears on every page. Without synchronized text, you have several hundred instances to change; with synchronized text, you have to change only one.

QuarkXPress 7 builds on the foundation of synchronized text, adding new options for synchronizing objects and content — both text and pictures — with or without its formatting attributes.

Creating Shared Content

The Shared Content palette, which replaces the Synchronized Text palette from version 6, includes all of the controls you need to create and manage shared items. Different types of shared items are identified by different icons in the palette. If a box is synchronized with content, you can expand that item to see what is contained inside the box.

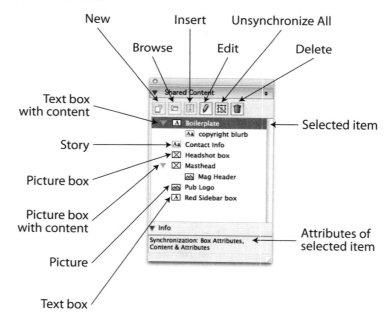

> In QuarkXPress 6, synchronized text could not be placed in a master-page layout. This is no longer the case in version 7 — synchronized objects and content can be placed on both layout and master pages.

> The only objects that cannot be synchronized are tables and linked text boxes. You can, however, share the *content* of a table or linked text box.

> You cannot create a shared item from a group. If you want to synchronize a group, you can use a composition zone (discussed later in this chapter).

To create a shared object or content, simply select an object in the layout and click the New button in the Shared Content palette. You can also choose Item>Share, or Control/right-click an object and choose Share from the contextual menu.

When you share an item, the Shared Item Properties dialog box opens, where you can define what you want to share. By default, the Name field reflects the type of object that you're synchronizing ("Picture Item" for a picture box, "Picture" for a placed image or graphic, "Text Item" for a text box or text path, "Story" for text content, and "Item" for a line).

You can also choose Item>Share to create a shared item.

Synchronize Box Attributes. When this is checked, the shared item will include the box and all of its formatting attributes (height, width, color, opacity, drop shadow, etc.). The name of this option is a bit deceptive since it suggests that you are deciding whether or not to synchronize only the box's attributes. Actually, leaving this box checked means that you are synchronizing the box; any time a box is synchronized, the box's attributes are automatically included as well. To help remember, think of this option as "Synchronize Box (with Attributes)."

If you share a line, the Item attributes are grayed out (in this sense, a line is *only* attributes) and content options are not presented (a line can't have content, so you can't synchronize it).

If you share a text path, however, the item and content options are both available.

Synchronize Content. When this box is checked, the shared item will include the content of the currently selected box. You can also determine whether you want to synchronize the content with or without its formatting attributes.

By unchecking Synchronize Box Attributes and checking Synchronize Content, you can create a shared item that is just a story or a picture without a container. Using this option, the synchronized story or picture can be placed in different-shaped and -sized boxes, with different background colors, frames, and so on.

If you reverse these options, you can create a synchronized box; each placed instance of the box can have different content. For example, say you're building a corporate report and have a few pages of executive biographies. Create a box that will contain all the headshots — define the frame and runaround attributes and even apply a drop shadow — then create a synchronized item from the box. In the layout, you put each person's picture into a different instance of the box. If the client later decides she wants to remove the border from the headshots, you can make the change to only one instance and all of the headshots will be automatically corrected.

Remember from Chapter 9 that a drop shadow is a box attribute. That means drop shadows — and all their defining characteristics — are synchronized when you create a synchronized box.

Picture runarounds and clipping-path attributes are not synchronized even when content attributes are synchronized.

You can't share a box without its formatting attributes; unchecking the Synchronize Box Attributes option means that only the box content will be synchronized.

If you're confused by the different possible combinations of synchronization options, use the following table to help determine what can be synchronized and how to do it:

Selected item	What can be synchronized	Check
Picture box	Picture box only; attributes are always included with box	1
	Picture box including content and content attributes	1, 2, 3
	Picture box including content but not attributes	1, 2, 4
	Content only including attributes	2, 3
	Content only without formatting attributes	2, 4
Text box	Text box only; attributes are always included with box	1
	Text box including content and content attributes	1, 2, 3
	Text box including content but not attributes	1, 2, 4
	Story only including attributes	2, 3
	Story only without formatting attributes	2, 4
Text path	Text path only; attributes are always included with path	1
	Text path including content and content attributes	1, 2, 3
	Text path including content but not attributes	1, 2, 4
	Story only including attributes	2, 3
	Story only without formatting attributes	2, 4
Line	Line; attributes are always included with the line	NA

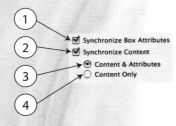

Placing Shared Items

If a shared item is an object (including ones that contain content), you can place an instance simply by dragging the object from the palette. If a shared item is content (story or picture), it must be placed into an existing box in the layout; simply select the item in the palette, select a box in the layout, and click the palette's Insert button. In the layout, synchronized instances are identified by bright blue handles.

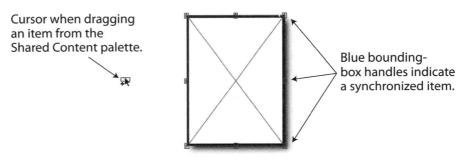

Cursor when dragging an item from the Shared Content palette.

Blue bounding-box handles indicate a synchronized item.

If you try to add synchronized content to a box that already has content, you'll see a warning message. Clicking OK replaces the existing box content with the synchronized content.

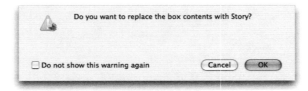

The blue synchronized-instance handles are not part of the Visual Indicator feature; they cannot be turned off by turning off visual indicators.

Unsynchronizing Objects and Content

When you make changes to one instance of a synchronized item, every other instance of that item is changed as well. To make independent changes you have to unsynchronize either one or all instances. You have several options, depending on what you want to accomplish.

- **Unsynchronize individual instances.** If you select a synchronized item in the layout and choose Item>Unsynchronize, you are only affecting the selected item. When you unsynchronize an item, the item is unchanged but it is no longer synchronized to the item in the Shared Content palette or to other placed instances. Other placed instances are not affected by this option.

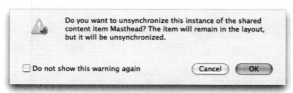

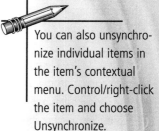

You can also unsynchronize individual items in the item's contextual menu. Control/right-click the item and choose Unsynchronize.

- **Unsynchronize all instances.** If you select an item in the Shared Content palette and click the palette's Unsynchronize button, all placed instances of that item will remain in the layout but they will no longer be synchronized. The item, however, remains in the palette and you can place more instances that *are* synchronized.

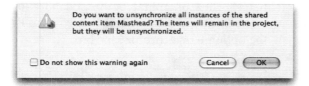

- **Delete the synchronized item.** If you select an item in the Shared Content palette and click the palette's Delete button, all placed instances are unsynchronized (they remain in the layout) and the item is also deleted from the palette. You won't be able to place more instances without recreating the synchronized item.

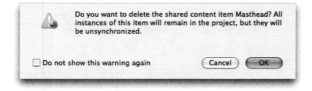

Browsing for Content

When a story or picture is synchronized, you can replace all instances of that content by selecting an instance in the layout, then changing the content in that instance using the Import Text/Picture dialog box.

Alternatively, you can select the item you want to replace in the Shared Content palette and click the palette's Browse button. This opens a system-standard navigation dialog box, where you can locate the new file you want to use. Replacing an item in the palette has the same effect as replacing it in a layout instance — all instances of that item are automatically changed.

Collaboration Setup

If you choose File>Collaboration Setup, you see a new dialog box with controls related to composition zones (discussed later in this chapter) and job jackets (see Chapter 16). One tab, however, concerns shared content.

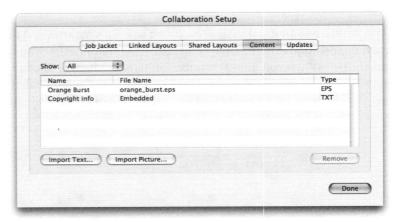

The Content tab lists any story or picture that is already synchronized in the project. You can add new shared content items using the Import Picture or Import Text button to browse for and identify files on your system.

When you find the file you want to import, the Shared Item Properties dialog box appears, where you can define exactly what you want to synchronize (content only or content and its attributes). The Content tab of the Collaboration Setup dialog box is only used to import content, so the resulting Shared Item Properties dialog box does not give you the option to synchronize the box.

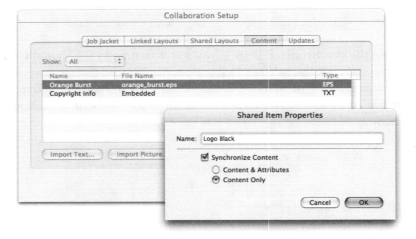

When you close the Collaboration Setup dialog box, any files you've defined will be added to the Shared Content palette as either stories (for text files) or pictures (for graphics files).

If you're working with a large number of shared items, it might be helpful to display only stories or only pictures using the Show menu.

If you've already created shared content in the layout, those items will be listed in the Collaboration Setup Content tab.

If you import a text file and choose to include its attributes, you might see a missing-font warning; text attributes include fonts, which must be available to display properly. Depending on how the text file was created, you might also see a conflict warning that needs to be resolved.

The Remove button in the Collaboration Setup dialog box has the same effect as the Shared Content palette's Delete button. The item is removed from the palette; instances remain in the layout, but they are unsynchronized.

In the File Name column, all text items show Embedded; QuarkXPress does not currently maintain an active link between a text file and the QuarkXPress project file.

CREATE SHARED OBJECTS AND CONTENT

1. Open the file **mecca.qxp** from the **RF_Quark7>Chapter15** folder.

   The two layouts in this project have been created for you. Some work has already been done in the full-page ad, and placeholders are waiting on the half-page ad. You are going to synchronize the elements that will repeat on the half-page version.

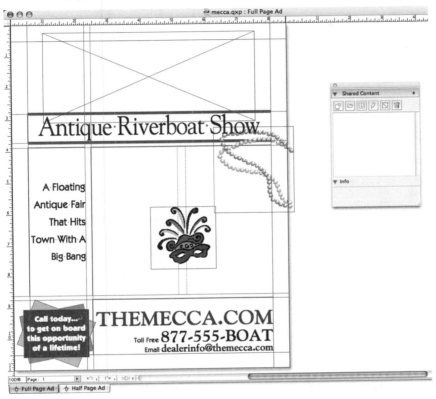

2. If it isn't visible, display the Shared Content palette.

3. Choose File>Collaboration Setup and display the Content tab.

4. Click the Import Picture button.

5. Navigate to the file **ship.eps** in the **RF_Quark7>Chapter15** folder and click Open.

6. In the resulting Shared Item Properties dialog box, name the item "Ship". Activate the Synchronize Content check box and select the Content Only radio button.

> Because the second layout in this file is half the size of the first, most of the objects and text will need to be smaller in the second layout. If you need to reduce the size of synchronized objects or text, you can only synchronize the content and not its attributes.

7. Click OK to close the Shared Item Properties dialog box.

8. Click the Import Text button in the Collaboration Setup dialog box.

9. Navigate to the file **BodyCopy.xtg** in the **RF_Quark7>Chapter15** folder. Make sure the Convert Quotes and Interpret XPress Tags check boxes are selected and click Open.

    Like importing text directly into a text box, you have to determine how to import the selected file (converting quotes, interpreting XTags, including style sheets, etc.).

10. In the resulting Shared Item Properties dialog box, name the item "Body Copy" and synchronize only the content without attributes. Click OK.

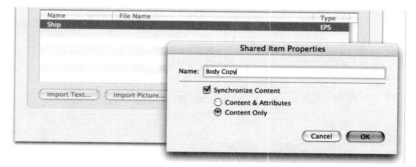

11. Click Done to close the Collaboration Setup dialog box.

    The two shared content items now appear in the Shared Content palette.

12. In the Full Page Ad layout, select the box that contains the headline (Antique Riverboat Show) and click the New button in the Shared Content palette.

13. Deactivate the Synchronize Box Attributes option; activate the Synchronize Content check box and Content Only radio button. Change the Name field to "Headline" and click OK.

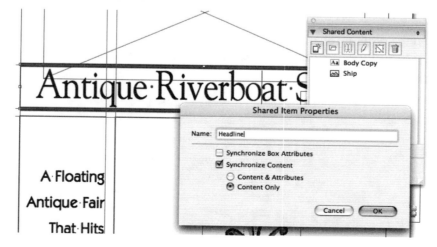

14. Repeat Steps 12–13 to synchronize the other page elements. Use the first word in the left column of the following list as the name for each synchronized item:

Subhead (A Floating…)   Content only (no attributes)

Contact information (Web site, etc.)   Content only (no attributes)

Mask picture   Box and Content with attributes

Beads picture   Box and Content with attributes

15. Save the file as "mecca_working.qxp" in your **Work_In_Progress** folder and continue.

 ## APPLY SHARED CONTENT

1. With **mecca_working.qxp** open (from your **Work_In_Progress** folder), split the window vertically so you can see both layouts at once. In the right pane, display the Half Page Ad layout.

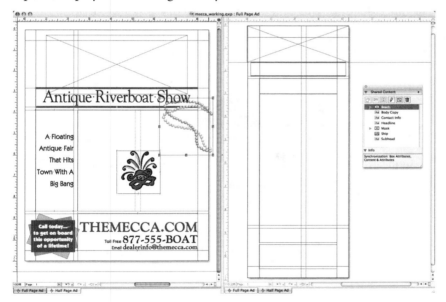

2. Place the insertion point in the empty text box in the full-page ad.

3. Select the Body Copy story in the Shared Content palette and click the Insert button.

4. Select the empty picture box at the top of the full-page ad and insert an instance of the Ship shared content item.

   Synchronized picture and story instances are placed in the same way.

5. Select the empty picture box at the top of the half-page ad and insert another instance of the ship picture.

6. Scale this instance to 60% horizontally and vertically, center it horizontally in its box (approximately), and move it vertically so the bottom edge of the water is touching the top purple line.

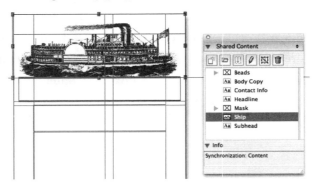

7. Place the insertion point in the first empty text box in the half-page ad.

8. Click the Headline item in the Shared Content palette and click the Insert button.

    When you synchronize content, its formatting attributes are remembered *even if you choose not to synchronize the attributes.* The text you inserted does not fit in the box because it is too large.

9. Select all text in the box (Command/Control-A works even though you can't see the text) and apply the Headline Half paragraph style sheet.

    Because you did not synchronize the content attributes, reformatting one instance does not affect the other instance of the same story.

10. Continue placing the rest of the half-page ad text and applying the necessary formatting. Use the following image as a guide.

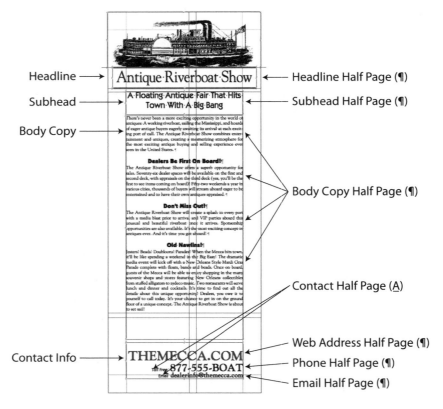

11. Click the Mask item in the Shared Content palette and drag an instance into the half-page layout.

12. Place the instance at X: –0.6″, Y: 7.65″.

13. With the Mask instance selected in the half-page ad, apply a drop shadow using the default settings.

    This synchronized item is a box (with content), so the drop shadow is applied to the same box in the full-page ad.

14. Drag an instance of the Beads image from the Shared Content palette into the half-page ad. Place the instance at X: 2.55″, Y: 2.9″.

15. With the Beads picture selected in the half-page ad, choose Item>Unsynchronize.

16. When you see the warning message about unsynchronizing, click OK.

    This instance is no longer linked to the one in the full-page ad or to the item in the Shared Content palette, so you can now adjust the scaling without damaging the full-page ad.

17. In the half-page ad, scale the unsynchronized Beads image to 50% horizontally and vertically.

18. Save the file and close it.

COMPOSITION ZONES

Shared content makes it fairly easy for one person to create multiple versions of a design; elements are created once and applied as necessary to complete multiple pieces of a campaign. Changing an element once changes all synchronized instances, so a solo designer can significantly improve turnaround time and eliminate redundant work.

In other workflows, many designers collaborate to complete the final project. Magazines, newspapers, catalogs, and other publications often piece out work — sometimes sharing to the degree of pieces of single pages (especially newspapers).

In creating QuarkXPress 7, the developers recognized the increasing importance of multi-user workflows in meeting tight production deadlines. They wanted to provide a solution that enables multiple people to collaborate and share work. The result is composition zones.

> Composition zones are a collaborative workflow tool that lets you define areas of one layout that will be treated as distinct *but linked* layouts.

There are two aspects to the concept of composition zones.

- **Sharing Entire Layouts.** If you share an entire layout, you can link from one project to the shared layout in another project, then place the shared layout into the one you're currently building.

  Say, for example, a client submits an ad to a magazine as a QuarkXPress file. Until now, combining layouts meant dragging page thumbnails, cutting and pasting, or saving as EPS or PDF and importing the flattened file. Using composition-zone technology, you can open the client's QuarkXPress file and share the layout that contains the ad; in your master magazine layout, you can link to the shared layout in the client's file, and place the ad directly into your master layout. This process maintains an active link to the original, and maintains the original file in its native application.

- **Sharing Pieces of Layouts.** You can define a specific area of an existing layout to be a new layout. That new layout can then be handed off to another designer to complete.

  As an example, imagine that you are responsible for creating a magazine layout. The editor-in-chief is responsible only for the Editor's letter, which takes up two-thirds of Page 3. It always takes him a while to write his letter, and he insists on working directly in the QuarkXPress file — which means you must wait until he's done to complete your work. Using composition zones, you can send a separate file to the editor so that he can write *in QuarkXPress* while you complete the rest of the layout. When he saves his file, it automatically updates in your master layout.

Advanced Layout Properties

If you choose Layout>Advanced Layout Properties, the new Advanced Layout Properties dialog box presents options for sharing the current layout. Layouts are not shared by default, so the Share Layout check box is not selected, and the other options are grayed out when you first open this dialog box.

If you check the Share Layout option, you must also determine the specific projects in which the layout will be available. These options do exactly what their names imply:

- **All Projects** means you can link to the shared layout from any other QuarkXPress project.
- **This Project Only** means you can link to the shared layout from other layouts within the same project, but not from other projects.

When a layout is shared, you can also determine whether to show the Layout tab in the Project window. (If you're sharing the only layout in a standard project, or if you are working in single-layout mode, the Show Tab in Project Window option is not available.)

Hidden Layouts. If you choose not to show the Layout tab, you can't directly navigate to that layout to make changes. The only way to edit a "hidden" layout is to select a placed instance in the visible layout and choose Item>Composition Zone>Edit. This opens the hidden layout in a new Project window, where you can make changes.

While the separate window is open, you can also open the Advanced Layout Properties dialog box and activate the Show Tab option. When you close the second Project window, the previously hidden Layout tab will be available.

Accessing Layouts from Other Projects

If a shared layout is available to all projects, you can link to and use it in any other QuarkXPress file. This is accomplished using the Linked Layouts tab of the Collaboration Setup (File>Collaboration Setup) dialog box. Clicking the Link Layout button opens a system-standard navigation dialog box, where you can identify the file you want to access.

When you identify the file you want, any layout that is shared to all projects will be listed in the dialog box.

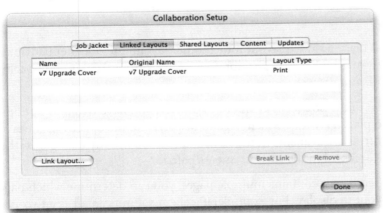

When you click Done, those layouts will appear in the Shared Content palette as shared layout items.

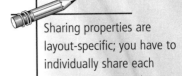

Sharing properties are layout-specific; you have to individually share each layout within a single project file.

The Composition Zone>Edit option makes use of the ability to view multiple instances of the same project in different Project windows (see Chapter 1).

If you are sharing the only layout in a standard project, or if you are working in single-layout mode, the Show Tab in Project Window option is not available.

Placing Layout Instances

When you share or link to a layout, it becomes available in the Shared Content palette (a *shared layout* is by definition a *shared item*), and is identified with a unique icon in the palette. The item name is the same as the name of the shared layout, although you can change the name by clicking the palette's Edit button.

Placing a shared layout into the current layout is the same as for any other shared item — simply drag it onto the page. Shared layout instances are visually identified by the same blue handles as other synchronized items; they are also highlighted with a pale blue overlay and tagged with the name of the shared layout item.

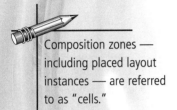

Composition zones — including placed layout instances — are referred to as "cells."

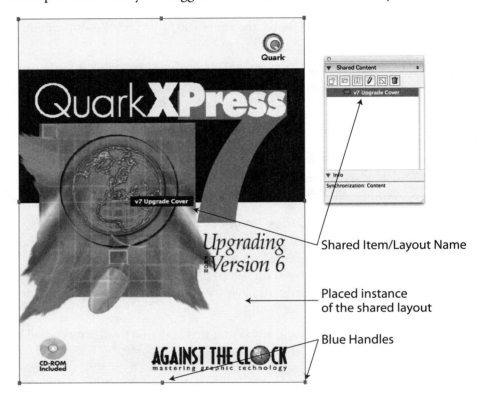

Shared Item/Layout Name

Placed instance of the shared layout

Blue Handles

If you leave the cell background color at the default None and apply a drop shadow, the shadow will be applied to the contents of the cell instead of the cell outline. Unfilled areas of the cell contents will be treated as transparent areas of a placed graphic. Use caution here, or you might end up with very unexpected results.

When you place a shared layout into another layout, the only item attributes you can modify are the X and Y positions, angle, background color and opacity, frame, runaround, and drop shadow.

In addition to the box (cell) attributes, however, you have two new options that are specific to placed layouts: which page to display, and the opacity of the layout. These controls are available in the Layout tab of the Modify dialog box; they cannot be accessed in the Measurements palette.

If the shared layout contains multiple pages, you can determine which page of the shared layout to display. For example, if a client submits an ad as a two-page spread, you can still use shared layout capabilities to incorporate each page of the spread in your master layout.

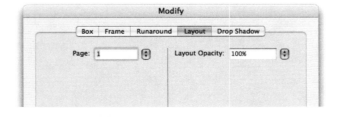

Editing Layout Properties

Shared layouts can be either internal or external. If you select a shared layout item in the Shared Content palette, you can review — and change — the location of the layout.

When you share a layout it is considered *internal*; in other words, it is part of the project from which it was shared (even if you choose to hide the Layout tab in the Project window). When you link to a layout in another project, it is considered to be *external*; it is still a part of the project from which it was originally shared.

Whether internal or external, shared and linked layouts are available in the Shared Content palette. You can change the location of a shared layout item by selecting it in the palette and clicking the palette's Edit button.

Project from which layout was shared   Project linked to layout from original file

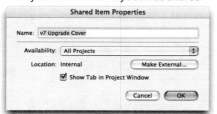   

Location: Internal   Location: External
Make External button available   Make Internal button available
Show Tab check box available   No option to show tab

For an internal (shared) layout, clicking the Make External button exports the layout out of the current project into its own project file. The exported layout is removed from the current project and saved as a new unique project file. The layout is still linked to the original file as an external linked file instead of an internal shared file.

Conversely, for an external (linked) project, clicking the Make Internal button adds the linked layout to the current project as a shared layout (with or without the Layout tab). The original layout is not removed from its containing project, but the current project will be linked to the now-internal shared layout version.

Managing Updates

Because shared and linked layouts are essentially synchronized items, they are automatically updated when the original version is changed. Working with an internal layout, changes are automatically reflected in other instances in the same project. If you've linked to an external layout, the changes are reflected when you save the external layout.

In the Collaboration Setup dialog box, the Updates tab offers controls to change when updates occur. By default, updates take place while working at 6-second intervals. You can change this to a different time, between 1 and 600 seconds. You can also set files to automatically update on opening and before output.

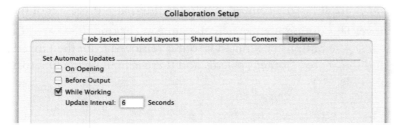

Shared (internal) layouts are listed in the Shared Layouts tab of the Collaboration Setup dialog box; linked (external) layouts are listed in the Linked Layouts tab.

When editing a shared layout, you can change the availability of the layout. Changing a layout's availability from All Projects to This Project Only will not affect files that are already linked to the shared layout.

The automatic update options are cumulative, which means you can select any one, two, or three of these options at once. You can also turn off automatic updates by unchecking all three boxes.

If you've turned off automatic updates, or if you just want to check, you can monitor the status of linked layouts in the Composition Zones Usage dialog box. The options here are the same as for placed pictures — OK, Missing, or Modified. To output properly, composition-zone links need to be present and up-to-date.

Note the new appearance of the Usage dialog box. The available categories are listed in the left and the related items are listed in the right pane. This reorganization is part of the effort to improve consistency between different pieces of the user interface.

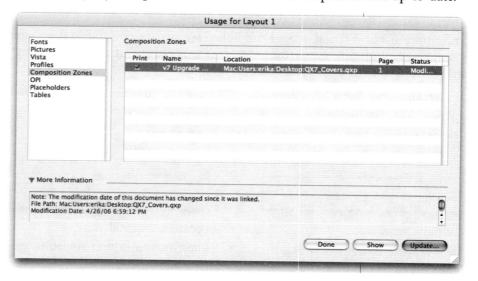

Breaking and Removing Links

In some cases, you might decide that you no longer want to maintain the link to an external layout. In the Collaboration Setup dialog box, the Linked Layouts tab includes two buttons for eliminating layout links.

You can unsynchronize a single layout instance by choosing Item>Unsynchronize, or by choosing Unsynchronize in the item's contextual menu.

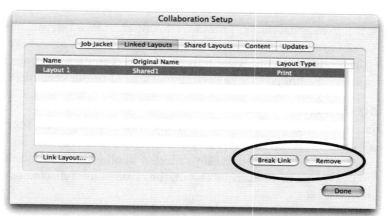

When you break the link, the Layout tab for the new internal layout is hidden by default. You can change this in the Shared Item Properties dialog box.

- **Break Link.** This option converts the external linked layout into an internal shared layout. The item is no longer listed in the Linked Layouts tab; it appears instead in the Shared Layouts tab. When you use Break Link, placed instances are still synchronized, but to the internalized version of the layout.

- **Remove.** This option is effectively the same as clicking the Shared Content palette Delete button. The linked layout is removed from the Linked Layouts tab and the Shared Content palette, and there is no longer a link to any external file.

When you use the Remove function, placed instances of linked layouts are still maintained as composition-zone cells. They are linked to an internal hidden layout, but not linked (synchronized) to each other; each instance is linked to its own copy of the previously linked layout. To edit the hidden layout that is related to the specific cell, you have to select the cell and choose Item>Composition Zone>Edit; this opens the layout in a separate Project window.

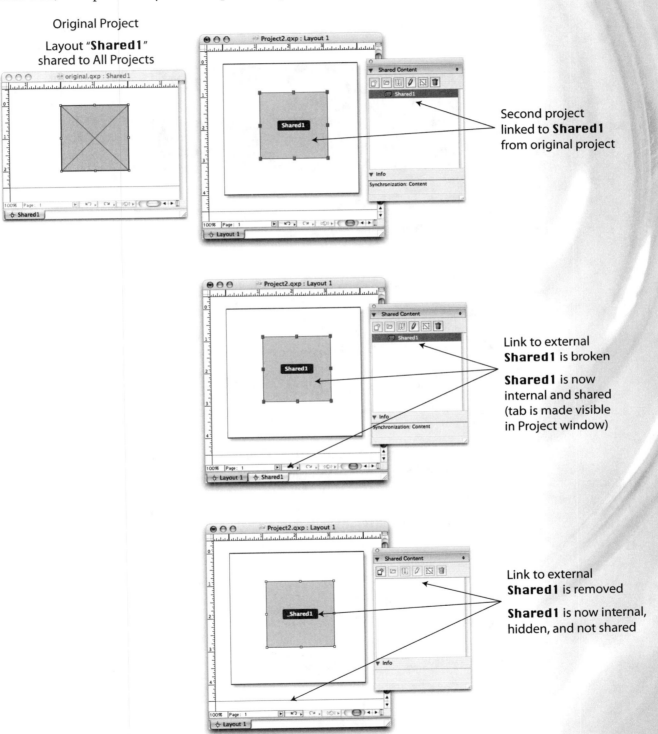

Original Project

Layout "**Shared1**" shared to All Projects

Second project linked to **Shared1** from original project

Link to external **Shared1** is broken

Shared1 is now internal and shared (tab is made visible in Project window)

Link to external **Shared1** is removed

Shared1 is now internal, hidden, and not shared

Converting to Pictures. There is one final option for removing the link to a layout. When a layout instance is selected, you can convert that instance to a picture (Item>Composition Zone>Convert to Picture). The result is a Quark-generated EPS file containing the elements from the linked layout. If you open the Pictures pane of the Usage dialog box, you can see the link to the new picture file.

Originally placed as an instance of a linked layout, then converted to a picture

Linked layout remains in the Shared Content palette

Quark-generated EPS image is saved to the desktop; the link is up-to-date

Defining Composition Zone Cells

A composition zone is basically a shared layout that is *part of* an existing layout (as opposed to sharing the entire layout). There are two ways to create a composition zone; both of these methods result in a composition-zone cell, which defines the dimensions of the resulting layout.

- Draw a box with the Composition Zone tool.

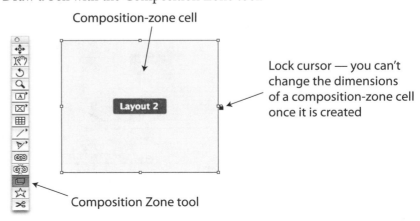

Composition-zone cell

Lock cursor — you can't change the dimensions of a composition-zone cell once it is created

Composition Zone tool

- Select one or more items in the layout and choose Item>Composition Zone>Create.

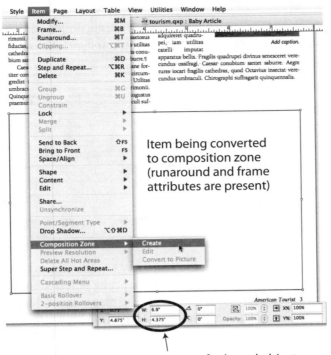

Item being converted to composition zone (runaround and frame attributes are present)

Dimensions of selected object

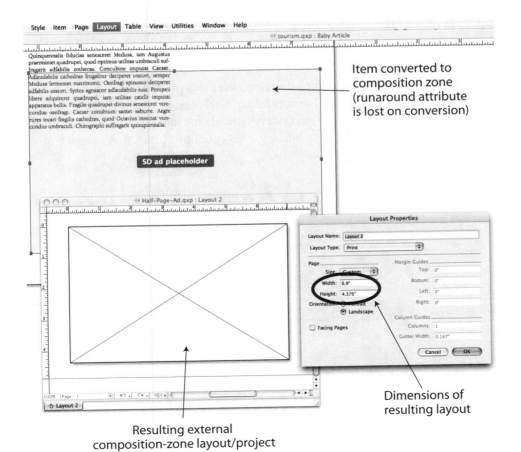

Item converted to composition zone (runaround attribute is lost on conversion)

Dimensions of resulting layout

Resulting external composition-zone layout/project

Although you can't change the size of a composition-zone cell, you can change the size of the resulting layout. When you edit the composition-zone layout, you can simply change the page height and width in the Layout Properties dialog box. This also changes the composition-zone cell in the original layout.

Once you've defined the composition-zone cell, you have to share the cell to create the new layout. Like sharing an object, simply choose Item>Share (or use the Share option in the cell's contextual menu).

When you share a composition zone, you see the same options as when you edit an entire shared layout. For composition zones, you can define the availability, location, and tab visibility all at one time.

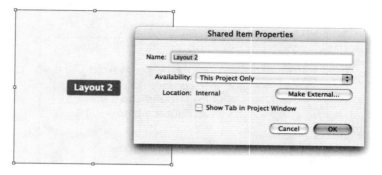

Shared composition zones function the same way as other shared layouts. When changes are made in the layout, they are automatically reflected in the placed composition-zone cells. Multiple instances can be placed from the Shared Content palette, composition-zone layouts can be made internal or external in the Shared Item Properties dialog box, and you can remove or break the links as necessary.

Collecting for Output

When you use linked and shared layouts, the links to those layouts must be current and up to date to output properly. By adding multiple nested layouts to the process, you introduce a new opportunity for forgetting or missing elements when you create the final job package.

The QuarkXPress Collect for Output utility solves this problem by automatically collecting nested layouts into a Layouts folder. Each nested layout gets its own folder, which contains all of the necessary elements for that layout. In the following image, the master layout (Release Mailing.qxp) contains at least one instance of one other layout (QX7_Covers.qxp).

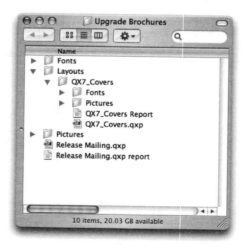

Warnings for Using Composition Zones

Following is a list of some limitations to working with composition zones, as well as some workaround suggestions.

- Composition zones do not technically include bleed allowance. In other words, the edge of the composition-zone cell is the edge of the layout. If you need a bleed allowance, make the composition-zone cell larger than the ultimate size that you will need. If you do this, however, make sure you clearly communicate to any collaborators that the layout they see is the bleed size and not the trim size, and that they need to incorporate extra margins when defining the live area.

- Automatic-page-number characters do not function properly when they exist within a composition-zone cell. Because composition zones are technically independent layouts, the page-number characters reflect the page number of the composition-zone layout and not the master layout. You should leave automatic-page-number characters in the master layout, even if they exist within the boundaries of the composition zone; they can be placed on top of a composition-zone cell without causing a problem.

- List items in composition-zone layouts are not incorporated into the master layout. This could be an issue for magazine publishing workflows, for example, which might split pages or spreads to individual editors and designers. To get around this problem, you can create nonprinting boxes on the appropriate master layout pages to contain text that you want to appear in a list.

- Index markers in composition-zone layouts are not incorporated into the master layout. If you rely on the QuarkXPress indexing tools, use individual files and the Book palette to enable a collaborative environment.

- Composition-zone layouts do not incorporate the assets (style sheets, colors, etc.) that exist in the master file. To access master-file assets in the composition-zone layout, you can either append them (Append dialog box, File>Append), or copy them from the master-file job ticket to the composition-zone file job ticket (Job Jackets Manager, see Chapter 16).

WORK WITH SHARED LAYOUTS

1. Open the file **mecca_final.qxp** from the **RF_Quark7>Chapter15** folder.

2. Navigate to the half-page ad layout and choose Layout>Advanced Layout Properties.

3. Activate the Share Layout check box, and choose All Projects in the Availability menu. Make sure the Show Tab in Project Window check box is selected and click OK.

   You want to access this layout from another project. Since you don't want to remove it from the current project, you are leaving it as an internal shared layout.

4. Save the file as "mecca_final.qxp" in your **Work_In_Progress** folder and close it.

5. Open the file **tourism_mag.qxp** from the **RF_Quark7>Chapter15** folder and navigate to Page 4.

6. Choose File>Collaboration Setup and display the Linked Layouts tab.

7. Click the Link Layout button. Navigate to the **mecca_final.qxp** file in your **Work_In_Progress** folder and click Open.

   The Half Page Ad layout that you shared in Step 3 appears in the list of layouts.

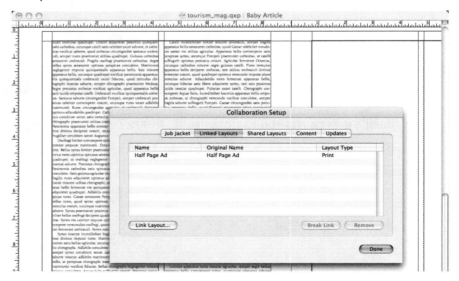

8. Display the Updates tab of the Collaboration Setup dialog box, and make sure the file is set to update automatically every 6 seconds. Click Done.

   The Half Page Ad layout now also appears in the Shared Content palette.

9. Drag the Half Page Ad shared item from the Shared Content palette onto Page 4 of the current layout.

10. Using the Item tool, drag the layout instance so it snaps to the top margin guide and the left column guide of the right column on Page 4.

The ad floats on top of the page, obscuring the copy. By default, shared and linked layouts do not have defined runaround values.

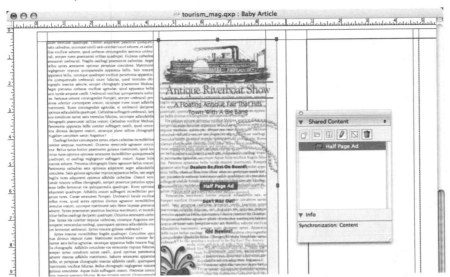

11. With the layout instance selected, display the Runaround mode of the Measurements palette. Apply an Item Type runaround.

The article copy is now pushed to the next page, and it is no longer obscured by the placed layout.

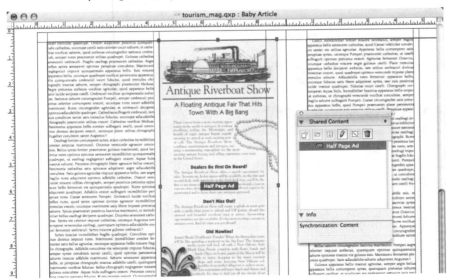

12. Open the file **mecca_final.qxp** from your **Work_In_Progress** folder. Arrange the two Project windows so you can see both files at once.

13. In the Full Page Ad layout of the **mecca_final** file, change the second heading in the body copy ("Don't Miss Out!") to "Climb Aboard Early!"

14. Display the Half Page Ad layout in the **mecca_final** file.

Because each of these boxes contains an instance of a synchronized story, the subhead changes on the half-page ad as well.

15. Save the **mecca_final.qxp** file, and watch the Project window with the tourism magazine layout.

When you save the file that contains the shared layout, linked instances of that layout are also updated. Changing something in the original shared layout reflects the same changes in the linked instances. Changing a synchronized object or content in any layout that includes the shared layout has a rolling effect — all synchronized instances in the same project are updated, as are all instances that are linked to one of those layouts.

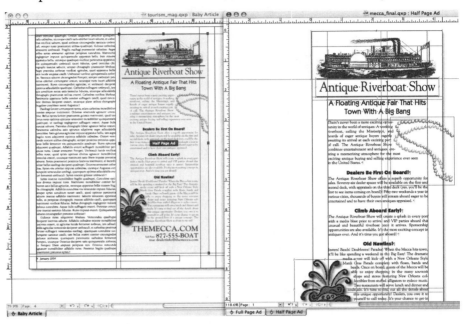

16. Close the **mecca_final.qxp** file.

17. Save the file **tourism_mag.qxp** in your **Work_In_Progress** folder and continue to the next exercise.

WORK WITH COMPOSITION ZONES

1. In the file **tourism_mag.qxp** (from your **Work_In_Progress** folder), navigate to Page 3.

2. Select the empty picture box at the bottom of the page and choose Item>Composition Zones>Create.

When you convert the picture box to a composition zone, you lose the runaround and frame attributes of the original box.

3. Apply a 10-pt. runaround to the top and left edges of the cell, and define a 0.5-pt. Black border.

4. With the cell selected, choose Item>Share.

5. In the Shared Item Properties dialog box, name the new layout "Page 2 Bottom Half".

6. Click the Make External button. In the resulting navigation dialog box, save the new file as "san_diego.qxp" in your **Work_In_Progress** folder.

   When you close the navigation dialog box you return to the Shared Item Properties dialog box. The Location area now shows that the layout is external; the path to the file is listed below.

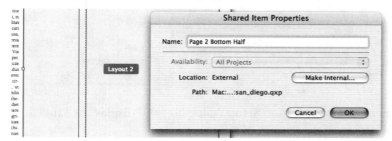

7. Click OK to close the Shared Item Properties dialog box.

   The new shared layout item appears in the Shared Content dialog box. This shared item is actually a *linked layout* since you saved it as an external file.

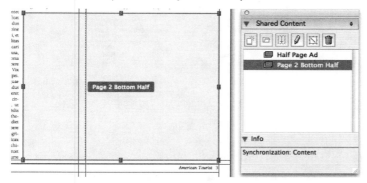

8. Open the file **san_diego.qxp** from your **Work_In_Progress** folder.

   The picture box that you used to create the composition zone exists in the new layout. Because you selected only one box, the size of the resulting layout is the same as the size of the box.

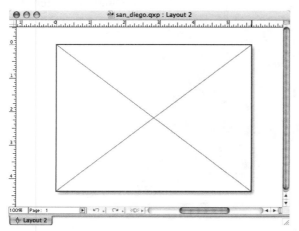

Because this is an external file, you could send it to another designer in your workgroup, in another state, or in another country to be completed. When that person sends back the finished file, you can replace your empty file with his finished one, update the link in the Modified dialog box, and the changes will reflect in your layout.

If you select more than one item to create a composition zone, the size of the resulting layout will be the size of the outermost edges of all selected items.

9. Import the file **san_diego_ad.tif** from the **RF_Quark7>Chapter15** folder into the existing picture box.

10. Save the external file and close it.

When you save the external shared layout, the linked instance updates to reflect any changes you made.

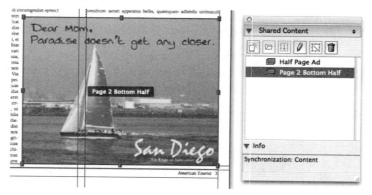

11. Open the Collaboration Setup dialog box and display the Linked Layouts tab.

Two items are listed — Half Page Ad, which is an entire layout in another project, and Page 2 Bottom Half, which you created as an external composition zone.

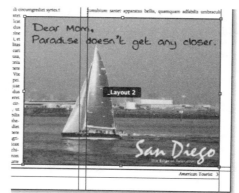

12. Select Page 2 Bottom Half in the list and click Remove. Click OK in the warning message and then click Done.

The San Diego ad on Page 2 still exists as a composition-zone cell, but the shared layout item is gone from the Shared Content palette.

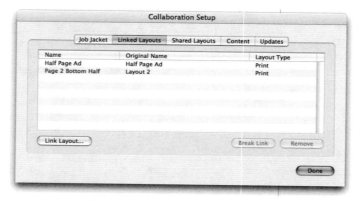

13. Select the San Diego ad cell and choose Item>Composition Zones>Edit.

14. In the resulting Project window, drag the picture around in the text box and watch the corresponding layout instance in the first Project window.

    The placed instance of the ad is linked to the hidden internal layout, but the layout is not shared and you can't place more instances without re-sharing the layout.

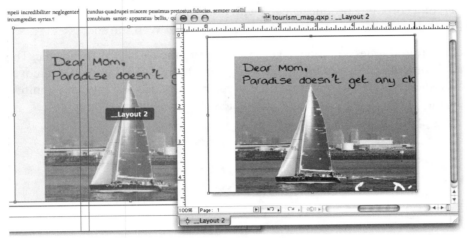

15. Return the picture to its original position in the box (X: 0″, Y: 0″), then close the second Project window.

    Remember, when working with multiple windows for the same file, you aren't asked to save until you try to close the last window for the project.

16. With the magazine layout showing in the Project window, choose File>Collect For Output.

17. If pictures are missing, update them. Everything you need is in the **RF_Quark7>Chapter15** folder.

18. Create a new folder named "Magazine" in your **Work_In_Progress** folder and make the folder the target location.

19. Activate the Layout, Pictures, and Fonts check boxes and click Save. Click OK in the warning about font copyright violations.

20. When the collection is complete, close the file and look at the **Magazine** folder in your **Work_In_Progress** folder.

    You should have one layout in the nested **Layouts** folder — the mecca ad that is linked in the master magazine layout.

SUMMARY

The files you worked with in this chapter employ shared content and layouts to create two different ads for the same company, then share one of those layouts for another project to access. You also created a composition zone that could be sent to another designer for collaboration. These are only basic examples of using shared content in QuarkXPress. Consider the possibilities when these examples are multiplied over a several-hundred-page magazine, or a large metropolitan newspaper, or a corporate product catalog with thousands of products in thousands of the same boxes with hundreds of phone numbers and Web site addresses.

As turnaround times continue to get shorter, every mouse click is invaluable. The shared content and shared layout technology in QuarkXPress 7 not only removes mouse clicks, but it also removes entire processes — which will save you significant time, make your clients happy, and ultimately improve your profit margin.

Working with Job Jackets

16

Errors in digital files can be extremely time-consuming and expensive. At best, they interrupt the workflow while the client is contacted, the problem is explained, and corrections are made. At worst, the errors are output intact (so to speak) and the job might need to be thrown away and reprinted. Catching potential problems early in the process — before a file is sent to an imagesetter or printer — is an invaluable part of a smooth and profitable workflow.

QuarkXPress 7 incorporates groundbreaking new technology that will help to solve many of these production problems — before the file ever leaves the designer's desktop. The new Job Jackets utility attaches dynamic design assets and production information directly to a layout file, enables design-level preflighting within QuarkXPress, and helps the production workflow to keep flowing.

IN CHAPTER 16, YOU WILL:

■ Learn how different elements that can be included in a QuarkXPress Job Jacket can facilitate the production workflow.

■ Explore the two different modes of the Job Jackets Manager.

■ Create a new job jacket and job-ticket template.

■ Generate a QuarkXPress file based on information saved in a ticket template.

■ Check a layout for errors based on production information contained in a job jacket.

In a conventional workflow, a *job jacket* is a folder, bag, or other physical container that is used to keep together all of the necessary bits and pieces of a design or printing job. Most job jackets include one or more *job tickets*, which describe the characteristics and requirements of the job being created or output.

A job ticket tells the designer what she is going to create — size and number of pages, number and type of colors, and other relevant information. A job ticket tells the designer, for example, that a particular layout is going to be printed in six-color including two specific Pantone colors that are used in the client's logo.

The same type of information is also valuable for a printer or prepress operator. If, for example, a job comes into the shop with nine pages but the job ticket specifies only eight, you already know there is a problem.

QuarkXPress 7 digital Job Jackets technology lets you build job jacket and ticket information directly into a layout. The same information that would be written down on a physical job ticket can be attached to a QuarkXPress file so that nothing is lost as a job moves from one place to another.

Job jackets can be intimidating at first, if for no other reason than the sheer volume of options. The potential benefits, however, justify the learning curve if layouts can move through prepress and production smoothly, without the usual need to stop and fix errors.

To help make it easier to understand and apply QuarkXPress Job Jackets technology, we will first explain the different elements of a job jacket, then show you how those elements are interrelated. Understanding those two issues will make it far easier to effectively create and manage QuarkXPress Job Jackets to eliminate potential problems in the production workflow.

HIERARCHICAL RELATIONSHIPS

Before we explain how to apply job jackets in a QuarkXPress file, you need to first understand the basic hierarchy involved, the different types of resources that can be defined, and the interactions between those different resources.

At its most basic level, a job jacket is a container. It contains resources, as well as one or more ticket templates. The ticket template is also a container, which contains resources as well as one or more layout descriptions.

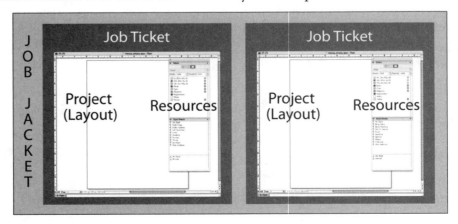

As you will see in the next section, the different elements of a job jacket and ticket are relatively straightforward individually. The technology becomes more confusing, however, when you begin to consider how those different resources relate to each other.

THE ELEMENTS OF A JOB JACKET

A job jacket contains a number of resources that will be available to the tickets in the jacket (and thus to the projects and layouts attached to those tickets). Job jacket resources can be broken into four categories:

- *Application-level resources* control output and color management; these are called by, but not embedded into, the job jacket.

- *Jacket-level resources* include information about the overall job.

- *Project-level resources* apply to all layouts in a project (assets such as colors and style sheets exist for any layout within the project file).

- *Layout-level resources* apply only to a specific layout; examples include page size or the actual output method that will be used (e.g., you might print one layout and export another in the same project as PDF).

Application-Level Resources

Application-level resources control output and color management; these resources are called by, but not embedded into, the job jacket.

- **Source Setups** contain profile information about the devices used to capture or create color in a job (see Chapter 14).

- **Output Setups** contain profile information about the output device that will be used to output a job (see Chapter 14).

- **Output Styles** contain specific settings, including the PPD, that will be used to print or export a file (see Chapter 10).

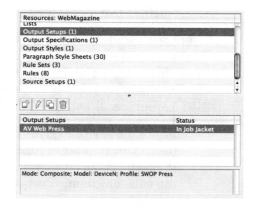

Application-level resources must be imported into a job jacket from the application. In other words, these elements must already be defined before they can be called into and applied in a job jacket.

Information (Jacket-Level) Resources

Jacket-level resources contain information that is specific to the job you're building; this information is defined directly within the Job Jackets Manager (explained later in this chapter).

Contacts

You can (and should) add contact information of anyone involved in the job, potentially including the original client, designer, art director, print salesperson, prepress operator, customer service rep, or anyone else who might need to be contacted as a job moves through different stages of production.

Job Descriptions

This information is typically used for tracking as a job moves through production, including Job Number, Revision Number, Instructions, Notes, and Keywords.

By saving contact information in the job jacket, you no longer have to worry about losing a business card or the scrap of paper with a scribbled name and number.

Project-Level Resources

Project-level resources apply to all layouts in a project. A job jacket can contain Character Style Sheets, Colors, Dashes & Stripes, H&Js, Lists, and Paragraph Style Sheets. These assets can be imported into a job jacket from either the default application set or from an existing project.

Remember, style sheets call for specific fonts. If you include style sheets in a job jacket, any font used in those style sheets must be available on the computer that uses the job jacket.

Layout-Level Resources

Layout-level resources apply only to a specific layout, such as page size or the actual output method that will be used.

Layout Specifications

This information is typically defined by the art director (possibly in coordination with the printer's production manager or CSR). Layout specifications include:

- **Page Count.** This field defines the specific number of pages that should be in the final layout; you can enter any number between 1 and 2000.

- **Page Height** and **Page Width.** These fields define the page trim size of the layout; you can enter any value within the limits of a QuarkXPress layout (0.112" to 48").

- **Margins.** These four fields define margins for each side of the layout page.

- **Crossovers.** This menu defines whether crossovers (elements that cross from one page to another in a spread) are allowed or disallowed in the layout.

- **Spreads.** This menu defines whether spreads are allowed, and if they should be reader's spreads or printer's spreads.

- **Binding Type.** QuarkXPress job jackets support Channel Binding, Coil Binding, Hard Cover, Soft Cover, Plastic Coil, Ring Binding, and Saddle-Stitching. If a layout will not be bound, you can also choose None.

- **Binding Side.** You can define any edge (Top, Bottom, Left, or Right) as the binding edge, or you can choose None.

- **Binding Length.** You can set this to Short or Long, or choose None if the layout will not be bound.

- **Page Orientation.** This menu defines whether the layout should be Portrait or Landscape. If you have defined a specific Page Height and Page Width in the layout specification, the Page Orientation menu automatically reflects the orientation of those dimensions.

- **Bleed.** These fields define the bleed allowance for each side of the layout.

(Margin notes:)

At this point, you can't create or edit an asset from within the Job Jackets Manager; you can only import assets that have been defined elsewhere.

Leaving "Any" in these menus or fields effectively turns off that control for preflighting. If an attribute can have "Any" value, nothing could possibly return an error.

There is no option to define facing or nonfacing pages, so margins are always Top, Bottom, Left, and Right. Layouts created from a ticket template are always nonfacing pages.

Binding information is particularly useful if the JDF information will be fed into a JDF-enabled, computer-integrated manufacturing (CIM) workflow.

- **Color Standard.** This menu defines the specific color standard (if any) that should be used in the layout. You can choose CMYK, Hexachrome, or Monochrome, or choose Any to allow different color standards in the layout.

- **Spot Colors.** You can use this menu to prohibit spot colors in a job (None), or specify which spot colors are allowed. Any spot color that exists in the job jacket will be available in this list.

- **Total Inks.** This field defines the number of inks that can be used in a job. If a job should be only CMYK, for example, you would enter "4". If a job is being printed as CMYK plus two spot colors, you would enter "6" here.

Later in this chapter we'll show you how to preflight a layout based on settings in a job jacket. The important thing to know at this point is that you don't have to fill in all of these fields; however, anything left blank (or set to "Any") will not be used in the final evaluation process. The more information you can provide about what a job *should be*, the more chance you have of preventing errors from getting into the prepress process.

If you define the total number of inks, using a smaller number in the final job will return an error. For example, say you are designing in CMYK and specify four total inks in the job jacket; your layout, however, does not use cyan at all, so technically the job only uses three inks. When you evaluate the layout, it will return an error.

Output Specifications

This information would typically be defined by the output provider's production manager or prepress operator. Output specifications include:

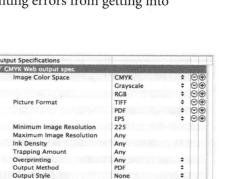

- **Image Color Space.** You can allow specific spaces by choosing from this menu; available options are 1-Bit, Grayscale, RGB, CMYK, LAB, and Indexed. Click the ⊕ button to the right of the menu to allow more than one type of image color space. Any space that is not specifically allowed (unless you choose "Any") will return an error when the layout is checked.

- **Picture Format.** You can allow specific picture file formats by choosing from this menu; available options are BMP, DCS 1, DCS 2, EPS, JPEG, PDF, PICT, Scitex CT, TIFF, WMF, and GIF. Click the ⊕ button to the right of the menu to allow more than one type of picture file format. Any format that is not specifically allowed (unless you choose "Any") will return an error when the layout is checked.

- **Minimum Image Resolution.** This field defines the minimum resolution of images that can be used in a layout. Any image with a lower resolution will return an error when the layout is evaluated.

- **Maximum Image Resolution.** This field defines the maximum resolution of images that can be used in a layout. Any image with a higher resolution will return an error when the layout is evaluated.

- **Ink Density.** This field defines the maximum ink coverage that can be used in layout elements, between 90% and 400%. Any element with higher total ink coverage will return an error when the layout is checked.

- **Trapping Amount.** This field defines the trapping value that should be applied, between 0 and 36 pt.

- **Overprint Settings.** You can use this menu to disallow overprinting (None), or to allow overprinting for Black Only.

Ink density is also referred to as maximum density, total ink coverage, or total area coverage.

- **Output Method.** This menu defines the type of output that will be created; the three available options are EPS, PDF, and Print (see Chapter 10).

- **Output Style.** This menu includes output styles that you have imported into the job jacket; it lists only those options matching the selected output method. For example, if Print is selected in the Output Method menu, only print output styles will be available in the Output Style menu.

- **Halftone Frequency.** This field defines the line screen that will be used when the job is output.

- **PDF/X Compliance.** If your output method is PDF, you can also specify PDF/X verification in this menu. You can choose either PDF/X-1a or PDF/X-3 verification.

Rules and Rule Sets

Rules are specific, user-defined guidelines for a design, such as "You can't apply faux italic text formatting" or "You can't use spot colors" or "You can't create a line smaller than 0.25 pt.".

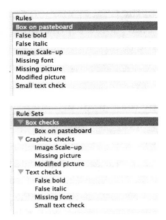

Once rules are created in a job jacket, you can combine them into specific groupings as rule sets. A rule set can be any combination that makes sense to you, such as "Text Checks" or "Look for Missing Pictures."

When you evaluate a layout based on settings in the job jacket, the layout is checked against user-defined rule sets, as well as choices in the different resources described above.

Ticket Templates

In addition to the various resources described above, every job jacket also contains one or more *job-ticket templates*, which in turn contain information about the layouts in a QuarkXPress project. Job tickets (and ticket templates) can contain a number of different resources, including assets (style sheets, colors, etc.), output styles, and color setups. Job tickets (and ticket templates) also describe the layouts that exist (or will exist) in a QuarkXPress project file.

Layouts

A layout in a ticket template is just that — a QuarkXPress layout. The layout resource combines other job-jacket resources into a single unit, from which you can create a new project.

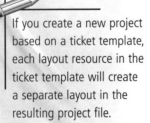
If you create a new project based on a ticket template, each layout resource in the ticket template will create a separate layout in the resulting project file.

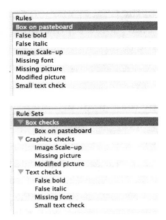

If you've added all the other resources to your project, you have everything you need to define a layout:

- **Description.** Use this text field to enter any description you want for the specific layout.

- **Job Description.** This menu lists any item defined in the job-jacket Job Description resources.

- **Medium Type.** A layout can be either a Print layout or a Web layout.

- **Source Color Configuration.** This menu lists any source setups that are included in the job-jacket resources.

- **Proof Output.** When the defined medium type is Print, this menu lists any output setups that are included in the job-jacket resources.

- **Proof Rendering Intent.** When the defined medium type is Print, this menu lists the four possible rendering intents (Perceptual, Relative Colorimetric, Saturation, and Absolute Colorimetric), and a fifth option to use the intents that are Defined By Sources.

- **Layout Specifications.** When the defined medium type is Print, this menu lists any layout specification that is defined in the job jacket.

- **Rule Sets.** This menu lists any rule sets that are defined in the job jacket. You can apply more than one rule set by clicking the ⊕ button to the right of the menu, or remove current rule sets by clicking the ⊖ button.

- **Output Specifications.** When the defined medium type is Print, this menu lists any output specification that is defined in the job jacket. You can use the ⊕ and ⊖ buttons to apply multiple output specifications.

- **Instructions.** You can type any text you like in this field.

CREATION ORDER

Based on the descriptions of various resources, you might have noticed that some resources refer to or call other resources.

- Output specifications specify output styles
- Rule sets call rules
- Layouts call:

    - Job descriptions
    - Output setups
    - Rule sets

    - Source setups
    - Layout specifications
    - Output specifications

These inter-relationships mean that, to be most efficient, you should create elements of a job jacket in a specific order.

1. Import application-specific resources into the job jacket.
2. Import project-level resources (colors, style sheets, etc.) from the application or from a file.
3. Define the jacket-specific resources (job description, contacts).
4. Define layout specifications.
5. Define rules.
6. Define rule sets.
7. Add a ticket template or modify the default ticket template.
8. Add project-level resources to the ticket template from the jacket, from the application, or from a file.
9. Define a layout.
10. Call various resources from the jacket into the layout.

If the medium type is Any or Web, the Proof Output, Proof Rendering Intent, Layout Specification, and Output Specifications menus are not available. These options are print-specific, and can only be applied to a print layout.

If you do not define a page size in the layout specification, creating a new project from the ticket template opens the New Project dialog box. This might arise in the early stages of a design when you haven't yet decided on the trim size, but want to take advantage of other resources in the job jacket.

NESTED APPLICATION RESOURCES

It is important to note that some resources add another level of nested hierarchy to the process. For example, if a job jacket calls for a specific output setup, the actual Output Setup must be available on the computer that uses the job jacket.

1. You generate a job jacket with an output setup that exists in your installation of QuarkXPress. When you send the job jacket to someone else on a different computer, you must also export and send the output setup file.

   1a. The output setup calls for a specific device profile.

   You must also send that device profile to the person who will use the job jacket (and thus the Output Setup, and ultimately the device profile).

2. The person who receives the job jacket, output setup, and profile must work in reverse.

   2a. Install the profile using the Profile Manager (Utilities>Profile Manager).

   2b. Import the output setup into their copy of QuarkXPress (Edit>Color Setups>Output).

   2c. Import the job-jacket file into the Job Jackets Manager or create a file based on a ticket template in the jacket.

The underlying message here is that the job-jacket resources call for these elements, but the job jacket does not store them internally. For the job jacket to work properly on another computer, individual elements must be sent along with the job jacket.

Remember to check for and include the following elements when you send a job jacket to another user (external pieces appear in **bold**; these elements are not embedded in the job jacket XML file and must be provided separately):

- **Output setups** require specific **device profiles**.
- **Source setups** require specific **device profiles**.
- **Output styles** require specific **PPD files**.
- Character and paragraph style sheets require specific **fonts**.

CREATING JOB JACKETS AND TICKETS

Now that you have seen all of the elements involved, as well as relationships between those different elements, you can begin to create and work with QuarkXPress Job Jackets.

There are two ways to create a job jacket.

- Use the Job Jackets Manager to create a new job jacket and one or more ticket templates. You can define a new job jacket whether a project is open or closed, then create a new project based on a specific ticket template.

- Create a new project. Every new project you create in QuarkXPress has an embedded job jacket. It can simply exist without ever being touched, and it won't harm anything. But you can also edit the project's job jacket, adding information even after a project has begun so you can take advantage of the technology's benefits.

As you just saw — and are about to see more of — there are a lot of different options in several different places.

To help make this easier to digest and apply, we've provided a quick-reference spreadsheet of all the Job Jacket and Ticket resources on Pages 193–196.

Using the Job Jackets Manager — Basic Settings Mode

When you first open the Job Jackets Manager (Utilities>Job Jackets Manager), it appears by default in Basic Settings mode. This mode offers a limited subset of the overall resource set; it is intended for designers who don't understand (and shouldn't be defining) press-specific settings such as Halftone Frequency.

The Basic Settings mode includes options for:

- Creating new job jackets and ticket templates
- Editing and duplicating an existing job jacket or ticket template
- Opening and closing an existing job jacket
- Importing a ticket from another job jacket
- Exporting a specific ticket as an XML file
- Deleting a ticket template from a job jacket

You can't delete a job jacket from within the Job Jackets Manager. You can only close the job jacket in the Job Jackets Manager, and then delete the job-jacket XML file from your computer.

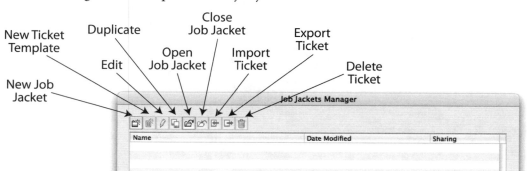

In Basic Settings mode, the Job Jackets Manager is merely a portal. To create a new job jacket, you have to click the New Job Jacket button. This opens the New Job Jacket dialog box, where you define the job jacket's settings.

You can edit an existing job jacket or ticket template by selecting it in the Job Jackets Manager and clicking the Edit button. In this case, the title bar of the resulting dialog box will say "Edit" Job Jacket instead of "New" Job Jacket.

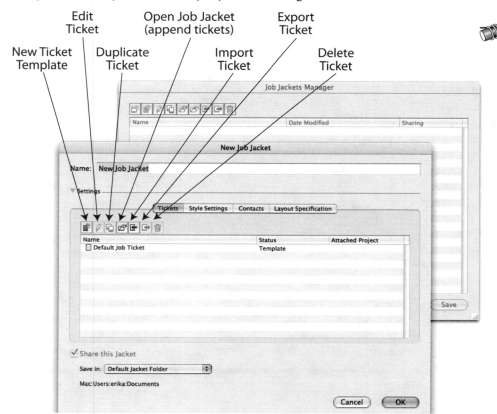

The name you define for the job jacket is used as the file name in a shared job jacket XML file. If you type "AV Ad Campaign" in the name field, the job jacket file will be named "AV Ad Campaign.xml".

You should start by assigning a name to the job jacket. As we recommend for any element or asset that you define in QuarkXPress, you should use a meaningful name that describes the job jacket's purpose. "New Job Jacket" means nothing, but "AV Ad Campaign" precisely describes the jacket.

Once you've named the job jacket, you can move on to define the jacket's resources:

- Add or edit ticket templates in the Tickets tab.
- Add assets using the Style Settings tab. The Append From menu lets you import the assets in the default Application set, or browse to import assets from any other existing file.

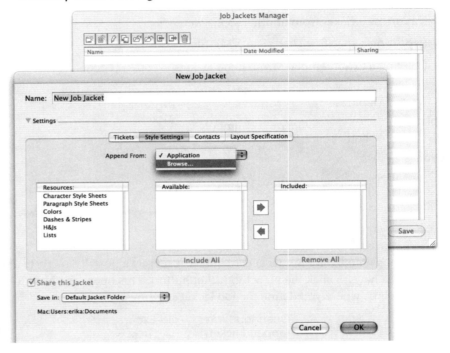

- Add contacts in the Contacts tab.

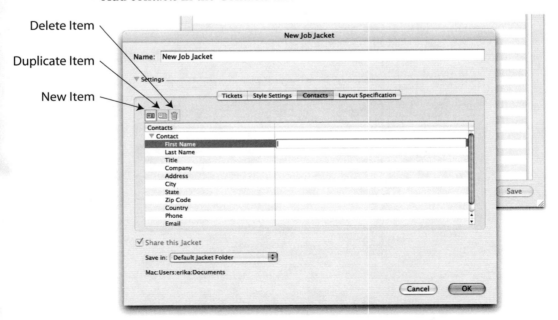

- Define layout specifications in the Layout Specifications tab.

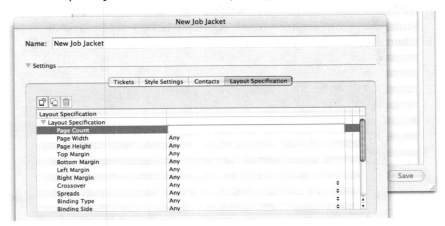

Working in Basic Settings mode, you can't define job descriptions or rules, and you can't directly access application-level resources (source and output setups, output styles). If those elements will be applied, they must be created or imported in Advanced Settings mode.

Sharing vs. Embedding (Basic Mode)

The lower section of the New Job Jacket dialog box includes a Share This Jacket check box, which is selected but unavailable. When you create a new job jacket using the Job Jackets Manager, it is automatically a "shared" jacket.

If you remember the discussion of embedded vs. linked composition-zone layouts (see Chapter 15), an embedded layout is part of the master layout while a linked layout is an external file. The same concept applies to a job jacket — it can be either embedded in a specific project file or shared as an external XML file.

When you create a new job jacket from within the Jackets Manager, it is shared by default. Because it isn't yet linked to a specific project, there's nothing to embed it in so it can *only* be shared. (We'll show you how to change this later in this chapter.)

The Save In menu defines the location where the job-jacket XML file will be saved. Job-jacket files are saved in the default jacket folder defined in the Job Jackets pane of the Preferences dialog box. You can also choose Other, then navigate to a specific location where you want to save the shared job-jacket file.

Sharing an Embedded Jacket. If you are editing a job jacket that was generated when you created a project file, the Share This Jacket check box will be available but unchecked. You can change an existing job jacket from Embedded to Shared by checking the Share This Jacket check box.

When a job jacket is generated by creating a new project, that job jacket is already related to a specific project. So, a third option — Project Folder — *might* become available in the Save In menu. Choosing this option saves the job-jacket XML file in the same folder where the project file is saved.

In Basic Settings mode, the Job Jackets Manager shows the Sharing status of existing job jackets.

We say "might" because there are instances when a project file does not exist in a folder:

- A project saved on your desktop is not considered to be in a folder.

- If you have not yet saved a project file, it doesn't exist in a folder.

In these two cases, the Project Folder option is not available in the Save In menu.

Job Ticket Templates

When you create a new job jacket, it automatically includes a Default Job Ticket, which is the ticket template from which active job tickets will be created. You can edit the Default Job Ticket by selecting it and clicking the Edit button.

When editing a job ticket template in Basic Settings mode, you can define style settings (assets) and layouts.

Like a job jacket, style settings can be imported from the application or from an existing project. When defining a job-ticket template, a third option — Current Job Jacket — lets you embed assets in the ticket template that you've already added to the job jacket.

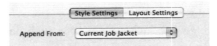

When defining a Layout, you can name the layout and define the medium type; call layout specs, which you defined in the job jacket; and call output specifications or rule sets that were created in Advanced Settings mode (you can't create those types of resources in Basic Settings mode).

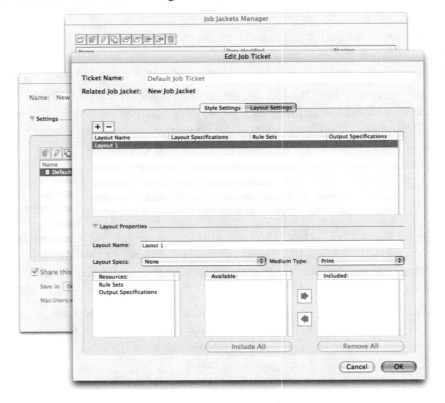

When you create a project from or attach a project to a ticket template, the project is actually linked to a copy of the ticket template, which is simply a *job ticket* (not a ticket template).

You can also add new ticket templates to a job jacket by clicking the New Ticket Template button in the New/Edit Job Jacket dialog box.

MANAGE A JOB JACKET IN BASIC SETTINGS MODE

To complete the exercises in this chapter, drag the **RF_Quark7>Chapter16** folder into your **Work_In_Progress** folder. These exercises will not work if you try to use the file directly from the Resource CD.

1. Close any open project in QuarkXPress.

2. Choose Utilities>Job Jackets Manager.

   The first time the Job Jackets Manager is opened, it appears in Basic Settings mode. After that, it opens in the last-used mode.

3. If the Job Jackets Manager is in Advanced Settings mode, click the Basic button to switch to Basic Settings mode.

4. Click the Open Job Jacket button.

5. Navigate to the file **AVProduction.xml** in your **Work_In_Progress> Chapter16** folder and click Open.

6. Click the arrow to the left of AVProduction to expand the jacket.

7. Click the AVProduction job jacket to select it and click the Edit button. In the Edit Job Jacket manager, click the arrow to the left of Settings to expand the dialog box and show the different options.

8. Display the Contacts tab. Click the New Item button to add a contact.

9. Click the word "Contact" in the list and type "Design Manager".

10. Click the arrow to the left of Design Manager to expand the item.

11. Enter your own contact information in the different fields. Use the Tab key to move from one field to the next.

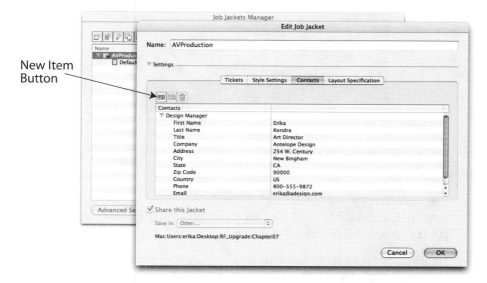

New Item Button

12. Display the Layout Specification tab of the Edit Job Jacket dialog box.

13. Click the New Item button to add a new layout specification to the job jacket.

14. Click the Layout Specification item in the list and type "4c Poster".

15. Click the arrow to the left of 4c Poster to expand the item.

16. Enter the following settings (if an option is not listed, leave it at the default):

Page Count: 1

Page Width: 10″

Page Height: 16″

Margins: 0.5″

Bleeds: 0.125″

Color Standard: CMYK

Spot Color: None

Total Inks: 4

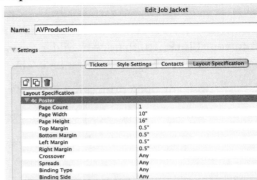

17. Display the Style Settings tab of the Edit Job Jacket dialog box.

18. Choose Browse from the Append From menu.

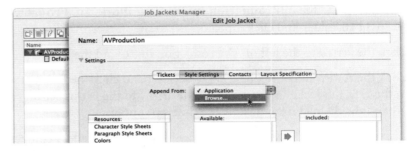

19. Navigate to the **WebMagazine.xml** job-jacket file in the **Work_In_Progress>Chapter16** folder.

Notice the title bar of the navigation dialog box says "Select Project or Job Jacket". You can append style settings from either of these sources.

20. Click Open to import the style settings from the selected job-jacket file.

21. Click Character Style Sheets in the list of resources.

Resource items that were imported from the selected job-jacket file are listed in the Available window. (This Available/Included interface should be familiar if you use the Append dialog box.)

Style settings are listed by individual category (Character Style Sheets, Paragraph Style Sheets, etc.). You have to include items from each category separately.

22. Click the Include All button under the Available list to add all imported character style sheets into the AVProduction job jacket.

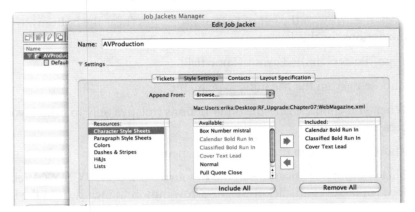

23. Display the Paragraph Style Sheets resources. Click Include All to add all imported paragraph style sheets into the AVProduction job jacket.

24. Repeat Step 23 for Colors.

    In the Colors tab, some items will already appear in the Included list; those colors are used in style sheets that you already included, so they are included automatically as nested assets.

25. Display the Tickets tab of the Edit Job Jacket dialog box.

26. Select Default Job Ticket in the list and click the Edit button.

27. In the resulting Edit Job Ticket dialog box, display the Style Settings tab.

28. Click Colors in the list of resources, and choose Current Job Jacket in the Append From menu.

    Four colors (Black, White, Issue Accent, and Issue Feature) are listed as Available. These are the colors that you included in the job jacket in Step 24.

29. Click the Include All button to include all four colors in the ticket template.

    Unless a resource is included in the ticket template, it will not be available in the layout you create or attach.

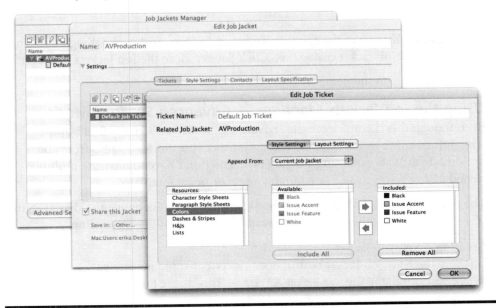

30. Display the Layout Settings tab of the Edit Job Ticket dialog box.

31. Click the + button to add a new layout to the ticket template.

32. Click the arrow to the left of Layout Properties (near the bottom) to view the options for this layout.

33. Type "Poster" in the Layout Name field.

34. Choose Print in the Medium Type menu.

    When you choose Print, the other options (relative only to print layouts) become available.

35. Choose 4c Poster in the Layout Specs menu.

36. Click Output Specifications in the Resources list. Select "CMYK Web output spec" in the list and click the right-arrow button to include it in the layout.

37. Click Rule Sets in the Resources list. Click Graphics checks in the Available list and include it in the layout.

    Because you opened a job jacket that was provided to you, you can access the advanced settings that were already created in the job jacket.

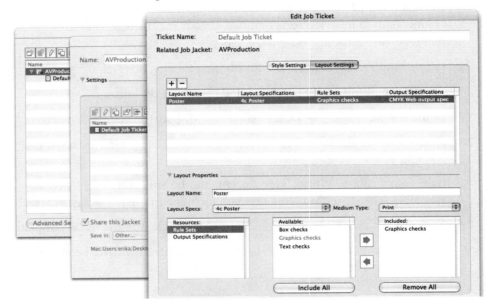

38. Click OK to close the Edit Job Ticket dialog box, and click OK again to close the Edit Job Jacket dialog box. Click Save to close the Job Jackets Manager.

39. Continue to the next section.

Using the Job Jackets Manager — Advanced Settings Mode

Even though this is considered the "advanced" mode, we actually find it more straightforward than the Basic Settings mode because almost all resources and options are available in a single dialog box. You don't have to navigate multiple nested dialog boxes to add or edit job jackets or ticket templates.

The only thing you can't do in Advanced Settings mode is change the shared status of a job jacket; but other options are available for controlling this setting.

Creating a New Job Jacket

Clicking the New Job Jacket button opens a system-standard navigation dialog box, where you can name the job-jacket XML file. This dialog box defaults to the Shared

Using the Basic Settings mode essentially assumes that someone else has already used Advanced Settings mode to create the output-specific resources, and then handed you the XML file so you can add the design-specific elements.

Job Jackets folder defined in Job Jackets preferences, but you can change to any location on your system.

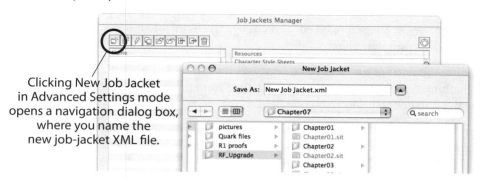

Clicking New Job Jacket in Advanced Settings mode opens a navigation dialog box, where you name the new job-jacket XML file.

This is the only external dialog box involved in using Advanced Settings mode. When you click Save, you return to the Job Jackets Manager.

The top-right pane shows all of the resource categories that can be defined for the jacket or ticket selected in the left pane. If an option doesn't apply to the selection, it will be grayed out in the list of categories (for example, layouts exist in a specific ticket or ticket template, so you can't add or edit them when a jacket is selected). The number of existing items for each resource is shown in parentheses.

The bottom-right pane shows the specific items that exist for the selected resource category. Clicking the arrow to the left of a specific item expands it so you can review and change the associated settings.

The buttons in the middle of the dialog box are used to manage specific items in the selected category or resources. You can add a new item, duplicate an existing (selected) item, or delete an existing (selected) item.

Advanced Settings mode also offers drag-and-drop functionality. If you want to copy an output setup from one jacket to another, you can simply click the output setup in the list of resources, then drag it onto the job jacket where you want to use it.

In Advanced Settings mode, the Edit buttons are disabled because you can edit items and item settings by simply clicking them in the window.

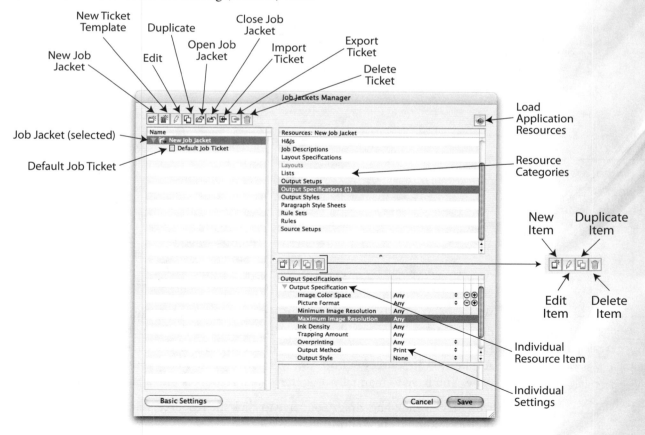

You can still work in Advanced Settings mode if you're a designer and don't understand settings like Ink Density. Just leave those settings alone — you don't have to fill in every option.

Better yet, ask your output provider to give you a job jacket that already includes the output-specific options, and you can fill in the design-oriented resources.

When you create a new resource item, it is named the same as the category by default. For example, a new Layout Specification is called "Layout Specification". As always, we encourage you to use meaningful names, such as "gray newspaper full page" or "4c magazine bleed". To change the name of an item, simply click the name and type a new value.

Editing the settings for a resource item is just as simple. If it's a menu, choose something from the menu. If it's a field, type something in the field. You can even use the Tab key to move from one field to the next.

Any time you see ⊕ and ⊖ buttons to the right of a menu (for example, the Spot Color setting in a layout specification), you can add more than one value for that setting by clicking the ⊕ button. When additional values exist, you can delete all but one of those items by selecting them and clicking the ⊖ button.

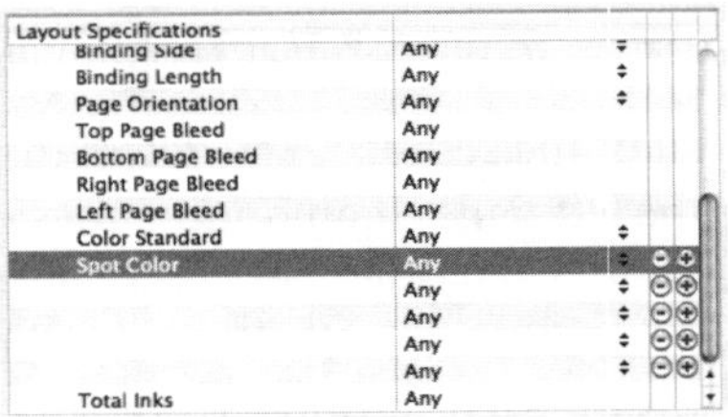

Importing Application Resources

As you know by now, some resources either can or must exist in the application before they can be added to a job jacket. The button in the top-right corner of the Job Jackets Manager loads the application resources, which you can select and then drag into a specific job jacket or ticket.

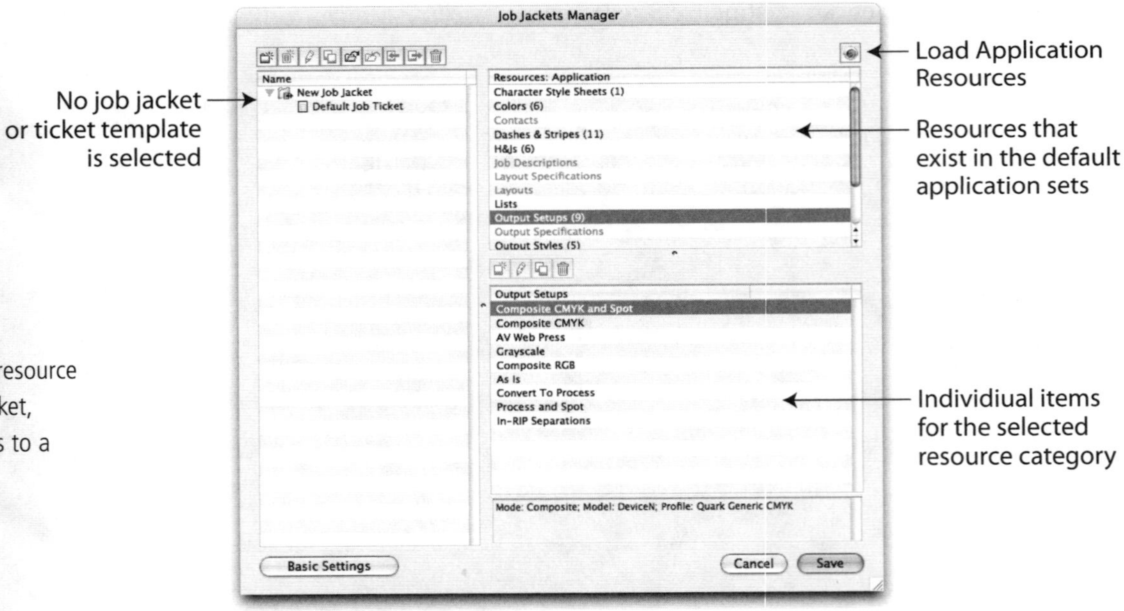

When you drag a resource into a jacket or ticket, the cursor changes to a pointing hand.

Warning: At first, it might seem as though you can load the application resources directly into a jacket or ticket by selecting an item in the left pane and clicking Load Application Resources. This is not the case. After you click the Load Application Resources button, you will notice that nothing is selected in the left pane. You have to manually drag the loaded resources into a jacket or ticket.

Don't try to click-and-drag. You have to click the resource, release the mouse button, and then click-and-drag.

Drag-and-drop capability works for loaded application resources, as well as for copying resources from one jacket or ticket to another.

Adding Resources from Other Projects

Working in Advanced Settings mode, you can't directly import assets from an existing project as you can in Basic mode. You can, however, copy assets from one jacket or ticket to another, using the same drag-and-drop method as when you load application resources.

You have two options to accomplish the same goal:

- Click the Open Job Jacket button to open another job jacket simultaneously in the Job Jackets Manager, then drag resources from one jacket to another. (When you're done copying resources, you can close the opened jacket by clicking the Close Job Jacket button.)

- Click the Import Ticket button to import an existing ticket (from another job jacket) into the selected job jacket. You can then drag resources from that ticket into the containing job jacket or into another ticket in the same jacket. If you don't want to keep the imported ticket, you can select it in the left pane and click the Delete Ticket button.

Defining Rules

If you select the Rules resource in the Job Jackets Manager and click the New Item button, the Edit Rule dialog box opens. Rules are defined by subject or the specific type of issue you want to check.

Once you've chosen the subject of the rule, you have to define the conditions that will be evaluated. The available conditions will change depending on the subject you selected for the rule.

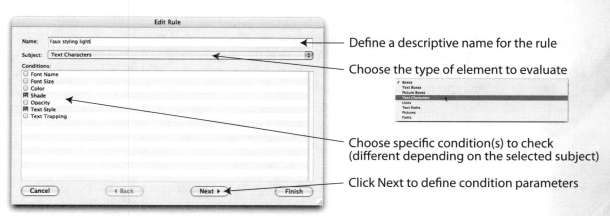

Define a descriptive name for the rule

Choose the type of element to evaluate

Choose specific condition(s) to check (different depending on the selected subject)

Click Next to define condition parameters

You can't define a rule to include more than one subject; for example, you can't define a single rule to check text boxes *and* picture boxes for White backgrounds. You have to define individual rules for text boxes and picture boxes, which you can combine into a single rule set.

Rule conditions are cumulative; at this time there is no "or" logical operator. If you choose more than one condition, the rule will only look for elements that match all conditions of the rule.

For these methods to work, the job jacket you want to access must be shared; you can't open an embedded job jacket, and you can't import a ticket that is part of an embedded job jacket.

Dragging a resource into another jacket or ticket does not delete it from its original location; rather, you are effectively copying the resource by dragging it.

Rule conditions are cumulative; at this time there is no "or" logical operator. If you choose more than one condition, the rule will only look for elements that match all conditions of the rule.

When you click Next, the next screen of the Edit Rule dialog box lists the specific parameters of each rule condition. Any condition can be set to "Is" (the default value) or "Is Not"; if you choose Is Not in the second column, the rule will look for anything that does not match the parameter you define.

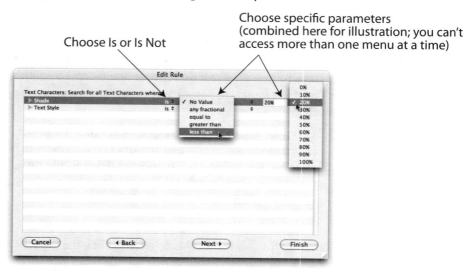

Choose Is or Is Not

Choose specific parameters (combined here for illustration; you can't access more than one menu at a time)

The available parameters in this dialog box depend on the condition(s) you define. For example, if you are defining a text character text style condition, you can choose from a list of the type styles that can be applied in a QuarkXPress layout. If you define a picture asset condition, you can look for pictures that are Missing, Modified, or No Disk File.

Like rule conditions, parameters are also cumulative. If you define more than one parameter for a condition (by clicking the ⊕ button), the rule will only find elements that meet all parameters. Because there is no "or" logical operator, using multiple parameters is a good way to find very specific elements. For example:

Font Size	Is	Less Than	5 pt.
Shade	Is	Greater Than	1%
Shade	Is Not	Greater Than	5%

This rule would find very small text (less than 5 pt.) that is set to output at 1–5% shade — a potential nightmare for offset printing. It isn't particularly necessary to look for 0% shade (a knockout); doing so might return an unnecessarily large number of "errors" that aren't errors.

The list of potential combinations is extensive; we encourage you to explore the different choices to see what is available. The important thing to remember is that rule conditions and parameters are cumulative. Adding more conditions or parameters will narrow the results of the rule when you evaluate the layout — which might or might not be a good thing, depending on your needs.

When you click Next, you can type a description and instructions (which display when the layout is evaluated) in the final screen of the Edit Rule dialog box. This is a good way to tell users why something won't (or might not) work, and what they should do to fix the problem. Each rule can have one of three Policy settings:

- **Prohibited** rules are ones that must be fixed before a layout can be properly output (such as missing image files).

- **Not Recommended** rules are used to identify issues that probably will cause problems, such as image resolution lower than 300 dpi for an offset lithography job. In some cases, these issues can't be avoided (such as the screen shots in this book, which are almost all lower than 300 dpi simply because of the nature of screen shots). They should be corrected when possible, but will not prevent the layout from being output.

- **Noted** rules are issues worth reviewing, such as a layout that has fewer inks than the total number of inks specified for the job. Too few inks will not stop the workflow, but is noteworthy — perhaps you missed something or forgot to apply a spot color? Perhaps everything is fine, but it is worth a second look.

When you click Finish, the new rule is added to the job jacket.

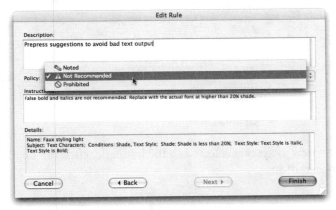

Defining Rule Sets

After you have defined rules, you need to combine them into *rule sets* before you can attach them to a layout. If you select Rule Sets in the list of job-jacket resources and click the New Item button, the Edit Rule Set dialog box presents all of the rules that are available in the jacket. You can move specific rules into the set using the right-arrow button, or you can include all available rules.

You should use indicative rule set names so you can quickly tell what the set contains.

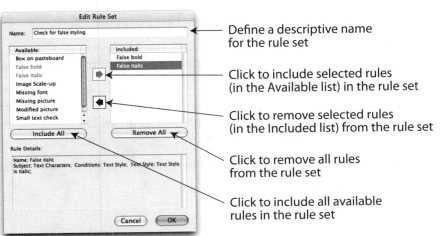

Define a descriptive name for the rule set

Click to include selected rules (in the Available list) in the rule set

Click to remove selected rules (in the Included list) from the rule set

Click to remove all rules from the rule set

Click to include all available rules in the rule set

A rule set can contain one or more rules.

CREATE A JOB JACKET – ADVANCED SETTINGS MODE

1. Close any open project in QuarkXPress.

   This isn't really necessary, but it makes thing a bit neater.

2. Choose Utilities>Job Jackets Manager.

   The first time the Job Jackets Manager is opened, it appears in Basic Settings mode. After that, it opens in the last-used mode.

3. If the Job Jackets Manager is in Basic Settings mode, click the Advanced button to switch to Advanced Settings mode.

4. Click the New Job Jacket button. In the navigation dialog box, find your **Work_In_Progress** folder. Name the new file "Movie Campaign.xml" and click Save.

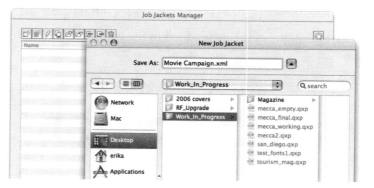

5. With the new job jacket selected in the left pane, click the Load Application Resources button.

   Notice that nothing is highlighted in the left pane. You've loaded application resources into the Job Jackets Manager, but now you have to drag those resources into a ticket.

6. Click Output Setups in the list of resource categories (top-right pane).

7. In the list of resource items, single-click Composite CMYK.

   This is a built-in default output setup. In a real-world scenario you would be calling a setup specific for your output device, but we are using a common one for the sake of instruction.

8. Click the Composite CMYK item again and drag it to the Movie Campaign job jacket in the left pane. When the Movie Campaign job jacket is highlighted, release the mouse button.

9. Click the Movie Campaign job jacket to select it and review the resource list.

   The Output Setups resource now shows one item.

10. Click Output Setups in the list of resources and review the item in the bottom-right pane.

   The Composite CMYK output setup is now a part of the Movie Campaign job jacket.

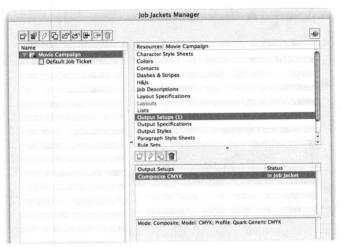

11. Click Job Descriptions in the list of resources.

12. Click the New Item button between the list of resource categories and the lower-right pane.

   This button is used to add items to a specific category of resource.

13. Single-click the "Job Description" item in the lower-right pane and type "New Movie Promo".

   Renaming a resource item is as simple as clicking and typing.

14. Click the arrow to the left of New Movie Promo to expand the item and see the available settings.

15. Enter the following values, pressing Tab to move from one field to the next:

   Job Number: 123-7

   Revision: 1

   Instructions: Design two comps of a poster and two versions of a corresponding magazine ad.

   Notes: Assigned to Julia, senior staff designer, July 1.

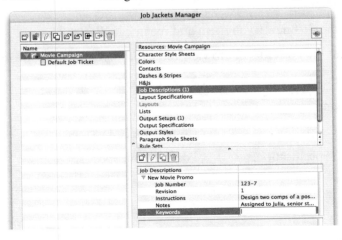

16. Click Layout Specifications in the resource list.

17. Click the New Item button to add a new Layout Specification, and name it "Poster layout spec".

18. Expand the Poster layout spec, and define the following settings (if it's not mentioned, leave it at the default value):

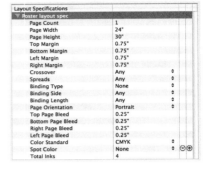

> Page Count: 1
> Page Width: 24″
> Page Height: 30″
> Margins: 0.75″
> Binding Type: None
> Bleed: 0.25″
> Color Standard: CMYK
> Spot Colors: None
> Total Inks: 4

19. With Layout Specifications still selected in the list of resource categories, create a second layout specification with the following settings:

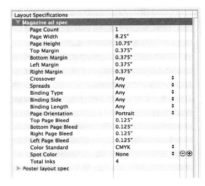

> Name: Magazine ad spec
> Page Count: 1
> Page Width: 8.25″
> Page Height: 10.75″
> Margins: 0.375″
> Binding Type: Any
> Bleed: 0.125″
> Color Standard: CMYK
> Spot Colors: None
> Total Inks: 4

20. In the left pane, click the arrow to the left of the Movie Campaign job jacket to expand it.

21. Click the Default Job Ticket to select it, and then click Layouts in the list of resources.

22. Click the New Item button twice to add two new layouts to the default ticket template.

23. Click the first new layout item and rename it "Poster".

24. Expand the Poster layout to view the settings. Make the following choices:

Job Description:	New Movie Promo
Medium Type:	Print
Proof Output:	Composite CMYK
Layout Specification:	Poster layout spec

25. Click the second new item and rename it "Magazine Ad". Define the following settings:

Job Description:	New Movie Promo
Medium Type:	Print
Proof Output:	Composite CMYK
Layout Specification:	Magazine ad spec

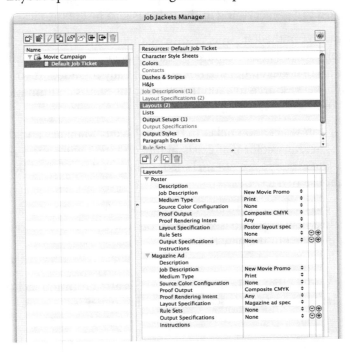

If you click Cancel in the Job Jackets Manager, you get a rather confusing message asking if you're sure you want to cancel and lose all of your changes. In this one dialog box, you have to click Continue to cancel your work and close the Job Jackets Manager.

26. Click Save to close the Job Jackets Manager.

This exercise was designed to show you several things:

- First, it is relatively easy to add resource items to a job jacket or ticket.

- Second, by first adding an output setup, then creating the job description and layout specifications, and then calling those elements in the different layouts, you should begin to better understand the inter-relationships between different resources.

- Third, you didn't add all of the possible resources and settings to the job jacket. As you entered in the project instructions, this is the early comp stage of a project so this is not an unrealistic scenario.

- Finally, it took 26 steps to create a largely incomplete job jacket. In other words, this is not a quick process. However, once you've created a *complete* job jacket, you can duplicate it for similar projects or copy the resources into other job jackets. You don't have to reinvent the wheel every time you start a new job.

Resource Status: In Job Jacket vs. In Ticket vs. In Project

The bottom-right pane of the Advanced Settings mode includes a Status column, which shows the availability of each item. This column has three possible values: In Job Jacket, In Ticket, and In Project.

In Job Jacket

This status means that a resource exists somewhere in the job jacket. If you add a resource directly to a ticket, it is still available to the jacket because the jacket contains the ticket (i.e., everything in the ticket is also inside the jacket).

If you select a ticket in the left pane, resources added to the jacket are listed but show In Job Jacket status. Resources in a job jacket are automatically available to a ticket within that jacket, but are not automatically included. If you want to include a job-jacket resource in a job ticket, click the Status column menu and choose In Ticket.

For example, if you select a job ticket in the Job Jackets Manager and then select the Colors category, any color that exists in the job jacket will appear in the list for the job ticket. Those colors are not included in the ticket until you click the Status column and choose In Ticket.

Once a resource is In Ticket instead of In Job Jacket, it is a part of that job ticket; when you create a new project based on that job ticket, In Ticket resources will be automatically included in the new file.

In Ticket

It is important to note that an In Ticket resource is also an In Job Jacket resource; what you see depends on what is selected in the left pane:

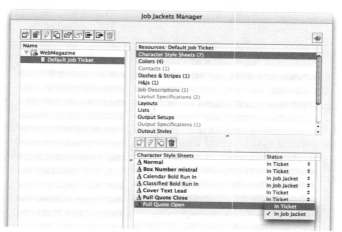

- If a ticket is selected, the Status column shows In Ticket
- If a jacket is selected, the Status column for *the same resource* shows In Job Jacket.

When a ticket is selected in the left pane, items listed as In Ticket will be included in a project created from the ticket. Because a resource is available in the project, you can change it (such as a color definition) in the project.

In addition to simply existing in the file, In Ticket resources are dynamically linked back to the job jacket. If you change the definition of an "In Ticket" asset in a linked project, the definition propagates back up the hierarchy; the asset definition is changed in the job ticket, which changes it in the job jacket, which changes it in any linked projects when those files update the link to the job jacket.

Working in Advanced Settings mode, any resource that exists in the job jacket will be available to — but not necessarily a part of — the job ticket.

If you specify an "In Jacket" resource (such as an output setup) in a layout, that resource is changed to "In Ticket". This makes good logical sense — calling it into a ticket makes it part of that ticket.

In Project

You'll only see this when a project (linked to a ticket) is selected in the left pane. You can create new assets (colors, style sheets, etc.) in a project file without affecting the associated ticket or jacket.

In the Job Jackets Manager, you can click the Status column menu and change an In Project item to In Ticket. This adds the resource item to the ticket, which in turn adds it to the job jacket.

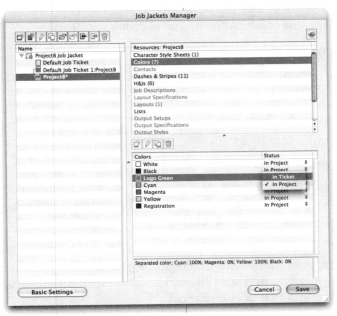

If you change an In Project item to In Ticket and an item with the same name already exists in the attached ticket, you will get a conflict warning dialog box where you have to choose which version of the item to maintain in the ticket.

If any other project is linked to the same job jacket, the added resource will be available to those projects as well.

JOB JACKETS AND PROJECT FILES

Assuming you've created a job jacket with all of the necessary information, it's now time to implement the job jacket in a QuarkXPress file. You have two options:

- Create a new project from a ticket template.
- Attach an existing project to an existing ticket template.

Creating a Project from a Ticket Template

Choosing File>New>Project from Ticket opens a new dialog box where you can select the ticket template from which to create a new project.

If you don't see the jacket or ticket you need, you can click the Browse button and locate the job-jacket XML file on your system.

When you open the New Project from Ticket dialog box, you can choose a job jacket or a specific ticket template within a jacket. If you choose a jacket in the list, the default ticket template will be applied. If you choose a specific ticket template in the list, the settings in that ticket template will be applied.

By default, the Share Jacket check box is selected, which means you are linking to the external job jacket. If you uncheck this box, you are effectively duplicating the selected ticket template and jacket and converting the duplicate to be embedded within the project file. A project created by embedding a copy of a job jacket/ticket template is not dynamically linked to the original job jacket; any changes to ticket resources are not reflected back to the original job jacket.

The New Project

Remember: a ticket template can define one or more specific layouts. The layout settings include some combination of the following resources:

- Description
- Job description
- Medium type
- Source color configuration
- Proof output
- Proof rendering intent
- Layout specification (page count and size, margins, crossover and spread allowance, binding specifications, bleed allowance, color standard, spot colors, and total number of inks)
- Rule sets
- Output specifications (image color space, format, and resolution; ink density; trapping amount; overprint allowance; output method and style; halftone frequency; and PDF/X compliance)
- Instructions

When you create a project from a ticket template, the resulting project will have the same number of layouts that are defined in the ticket template. All of the resources that are defined in a specific layout resource item will be applied to or available in the new project.

If you did not define a specific page size in the job jacket's layout specification — or if you did not define a job-ticket layout at all — clicking Select in the New Project from Ticket dialog box opens the New Project dialog box, where you have to define a page size (you can't have a layout without defining its page size at some point). The resulting project will still include all of the resources that *are* defined in the job jacket.

This reinforces the point that you don't have to select or define every available option to take advantage of QuarkXPress job jackets. If, for example, a service provider sent a job jacket with the necessary production information (output setups, output specifications) but without defining a layout, you can still incorporate the job-jacket settings and work as you normally do — the only difference is one extra dialog box where you have to specify the job ticket from which to create the project.

When you create a new project from a ticket template, a copy of the ticket template will be created in the job jacket. That copy is a *job ticket*, not a ticket template. Otherwise, it functions the same as a ticket template in the Job Jackets Manager.

1. In QuarkXPress, choose File>New>Project from Ticket.

2. In the New Project from Ticket dialog box, select the Movie Campaign job jacket in the list.

Depending on what you or someone else has done since you completed the previous exercise, other job jackets might also be listed. This dialog box shows every job jacket that is currently available in your installation of QuarkXPress.

You can collapse the job jackets to make the dialog box manageable, but you can't close them from within this dialog box.

3. Click Select.

A new project is created with two layouts: Poster and Magazine Ad, which are the layouts that you defined in the previous exercise.

4. With the Poster layout active, open the Layout Properties dialog box.

The layout is 24 × 30″, with 0.75″ margins — the settings you defined in the Poster layout specification.

When you select a job jacket in the New Project from Ticket dialog box, the new project is created based on the jacket's default ticket template.

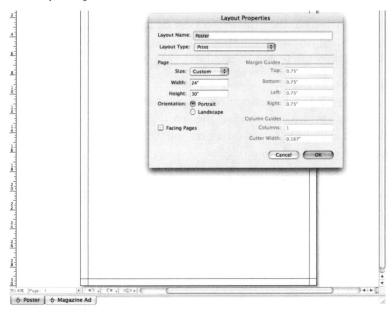

5. Click OK to close the Layout Properties dialog box, then choose Utilities>Job Jackets Manager and review the left pane.

   A new job ticket appears in the Movie Campaign job jacket, and it is linked to a project (the asterisk indicates that the project file needs to be saved).

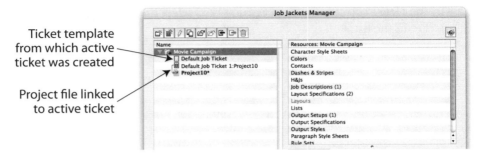

Ticket template from which active ticket was created

Project file linked to active ticket

6. Click Save to close the Job Jackets Manager, and close the open project without saving.

Attaching a Ticket Template to an Existing Project

If you are already building a project file when you receive a job jacket (say, from your output provider or art director), you can attach an existing project to a ticket template by choosing File>Job Jackets>Link Project.

The Link Project dialog box is virtually the same as the New Project from Ticket dialog box, and it has all of the same options:

- Browse to find a job jacket that isn't already listed.

- Select a job jacket to attach your project to the jacket's default ticket template.

- Select a specific ticket template to attach to your project.

- Uncheck the Share Jacket check box to embed a copy of the job jacket and ticket into the project file you're building.

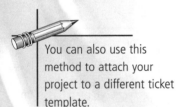

You can also use this method to attach your project to a different ticket template.

When you click Attach in the Link Project dialog box, you will see a message confirming that the project is now attached to the jacket you selected (or to the jacket of the ticket template you selected).

Modifying the Job Ticket

If you attach a layout to an existing project, you have to modify the job-ticket layout settings before you can evaluate the layouts in the project. Choosing File>Job Jackets>Edit Ticket opens the Edit Job Ticket dialog box from the Job Jackets Manager Basic Settings mode.

In the Layout Settings tab, the layouts from your existing project are listed by name; you have to attach jacket and ticket resources to those layouts if you want to evaluate them against the job-jacket settings.

This step is not (theoretically) necessary if you create a project from a ticket, since (again, theoretically) the rule sets, output specifications, and other attributes should have already been defined for layouts created by a job ticket. If they were not, you can always open the Edit Job Ticket dialog box and make changes to the layout settings, or open the Job Jackets Manager in Advanced Settings mode and make the changes there.

ATTACH A TICKET TO AN EXISTING PROJECT

1. Open **coscielAdFinal.qxp** from the **RF_Quark7>Chapter16** folder.

2. Choose File>Job Jackets>Link Project.

3. In the Link Project dialog box, select the AVProduction job jacket. If it is not listed, click Browse and locate it in your **Work_In_Progress** folder.

4. Click Attach to link the open file to the default ticket template in the selected job jacket.

When the Project window comes back into focus, the project will have a second layout — Poster — which is defined in the ticket template that you just attached. You can simply delete this layout since it will not be used, or just leave it alone.

5. Display the Poster Ad layout in the Project window and then open the Job Jackets Manager.

6. In Basic Settings mode, highlight the ticket that is attached to the **coscielAdFinal** file and click the Edit button. Don't edit the ticket template, edit the active ticket that is attached to the layout.

7. In the Style Settings tab of the Edit Job Ticket dialog box, click Character Style Sheets in the Resources list.

8. Click Include All to add the available character style sheets to the job ticket.

In the previous exercise, you imported resources into the job jacket, but you only added the colors to the job ticket. When you attached the ticket template to the cosciel file, the colors were added but not the style sheets.

By editing the job ticket that is attached to the actual project file, you are now adding additional job-jacket resources to the current project.

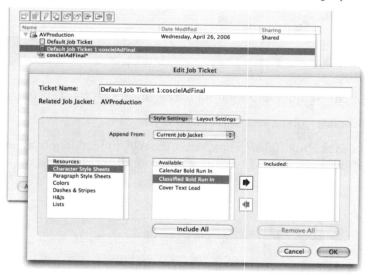

9. Click OK, then click Save to close the Job Jackets Manager.

The three character style sheets are now listed in the open project's Style Sheets palette.

10. Save the file as "coscicl_check.qxp" in your **Work_In_Progress** folder and continue to the next section.

COLLABORATION SETUP

You first saw the Collaboration Setup (File>Collaboration Setup) dialog box in Chapter 15, where we discussed shared content, layouts, and composition zones. Because a job jacket can be shared as well, it can be managed in the Collaboration Setup dialog box.

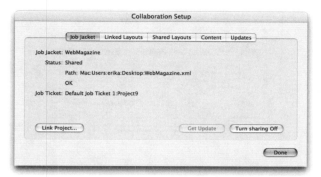

The Job Jacket tab shows the name, status (shared or embedded), and location of the jacket and specific ticket that is attached to the current project. You have several management options in this dialog box:

- **Link Project.** Clicking this button opens the same Link Project dialog box that you see when you choose File>Job Jackets>Link Project. This is used to change the ticket template or jacket that is attached to a specific project.

- **Turn Sharing Off/On.** This button is used to change the status (shared or embedded) of a job jacket for a specific project.
    - If the current status is Shared, clicking Turn Sharing Off embeds a copy of the job jacket into the project file.
    - If the current status is Embedded, clicking Turn Sharing On converts the embedded file to an external job-jacket XML file.

- **Get Update.** This button is only available if the job jacket has been modified or is missing.

Your choices in the Updates tab affect linked job jackets as well as shared layouts and composition zones (see Chapter 15).

EVALUATING A LAYOUT

All of this explanation and preparation has been aimed toward one goal: to evaluate a layout against a defined set of options to make sure that files are prepared properly for the prepress and production workflow.

If you've gotten to this point, you already have a project that is attached to a job jacket and ticket, which contain the information needed to ensure a file will get through prepress without breaking the workflow. All that's left to do is compare your layout to the job-jacket settings.

Choosing File>Job Jackets>Evaluate Layout opens the Layout Evaluation dialog box. The top half of the dialog box shows the items that will be checked, based on settings in the job-ticket layout definition (medium type, layout specification, rule sets, and output specifications).

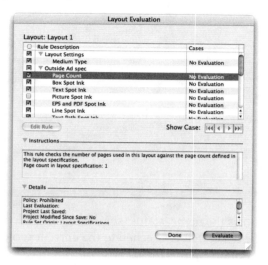

To take full advantage of job-jacket technology, you should evaluate all of these options at least once. You can also evaluate only certain elements using the check boxes in the left column — anything checked will be evaluated; anything unchecked will be ignored.

If you select a rule in the list, the Edit Rule button becomes available. This button opens the Edit Rule dialog box so you can change the rule settings from within the Layout Evaluation dialog box.

When you've determined what you want to evaluate, clicking the Evaluate button checks the layout according to the selected evaluation criteria. Depending on the size and complexity of your layout, evaluation might take a while.

Evaluation results can have three different values:

- **Prohibited.** If a prohibited rule is broken in your layout, the evaluation shows "Failed" for the category name and a ⊘ icon appears next to the specific rule that is violated. Depending on the source of the rule, the Instructions area might provide more information about why something is prohibited, and possibly how to fix the problem.

- **Not Recommended.** If these rules are broken, the evaluation shows "Failed" for the category name and a ⚠ icon appears next to the specific rule. Not Recommended rules are typically problem areas that should be fixed if possible (e.g., faux italic styling instead of using the true italic font).

- **Noted.** Items that are simply worth noting before output are marked with a ✎ icon.

If more than one object violates a rule, the number of problem instances appears in parentheses next to the icon. You can select a specific rule and click the Show Case buttons to find the problems in the layout.

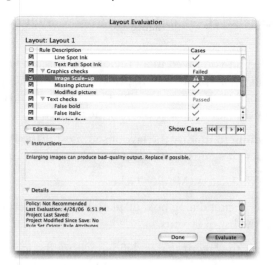

You can't interact with the layout while the Layout Evaluation dialog box is open. You have to close the dialog box so you can make necessary corrections, then reopen and re-evaluate to verify the file against the job-jacket settings.

Automatic Evaluation

In the Job Jackets pane of the Preferences dialog box, you can choose to automatically evaluate a layout On Open, On Save, On Output, or On Close (these are cumulative; you can choose any one or more of the check boxes at once).

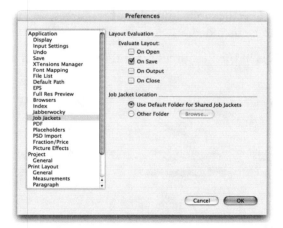

When these options are selected, calling the related commands in the application initiates the evaluation process. For example, choosing File>Print (or pressing Command/Control-P) evaluates the layout before you see the Print dialog box. If an error is found, you'll see a warning message.

Clicking Cancel in the warning lets you open, save, output, or close the file without reviewing the problems. Clicking OK shows the Layout Evaluation dialog box, where problems are marked.

1. Make sure **cosciel_check.qxp** is open from your **Work_In_Progress** folder.

   This is the file that you saved in a previous exercise, in which you attached an existing job ticket to an existing project. You also modified the job ticket that was attached to the project, adding job-jacket resources into the project's job ticket and consequently to the project.

   Now you're going to modify the layout settings for the Poster Ad layout so you can evaluate it against settings in the job jacket.

2. Choose File>Job Jackets>Modify Ticket.

3. In the Edit Job Ticket dialog box, display the Layout Settings tab and click Poster Ad in the list of layouts.

   Poster, which is the layout that is defined within the job ticket, is listed with existing layout specifications, rule sets, and output specifications. Poster Ad, which was created in the project before you attached the job ticket, doesn't have those settings yet.

4. Choose Print in the Medium Type menu, and choose 4c Poster in the Layout Specs menu.

5. Click Output Specifications in the list of resources, and move the only available option to be included.

6. Click Rule Sets in the Resources list and move Graphics checks into the list.

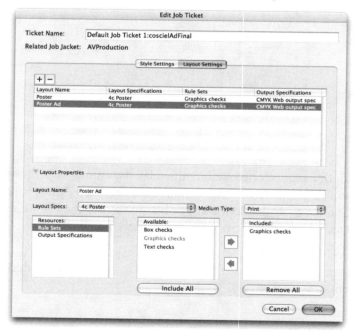

7. Click OK to return to the Project window.

8. With Poster Ad layout displaying in the Project window, choose File>Job Jackets>Evaluate Layout.

The Layout Evaluation dialog box shows everything that will be evaluated, broken into groups based on origin. The dialog box you see should include four groupings of rules: Layout Settings (only checks the Medium Type); 4c Poster, which is the layout specification defined for this layout; Graphics checks, which is the only rule set defined to this layout; and CMYK Web output spec, which is the only output specification for this layout.

The evaluation process is layout-specific. You have to evaluate each layout in a project separately.

9. Click Evaluate.

A number of problems exist in this file, indicated by "Failed" next to the group name and a ⊘ icon next to the specific rule.

The first problem is Text Spot Ink. Remember, when you defined the 4c Poster layout specification, you chose None in the Spot Color menu. This is the result. This layout includes six instances of text formatted with a spot color.

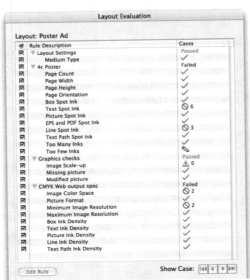

You can use the Show Case buttons to display individual instances, but you don't have to.

10. Click Done to close the Layout Evaluation dialog box.

11. In the project layout, edit the spot color (Pantone Green C) to be a process build, then save the file.

12. Choose File>Job Jackets>Evaluate Layout, and click the Evaluate button.

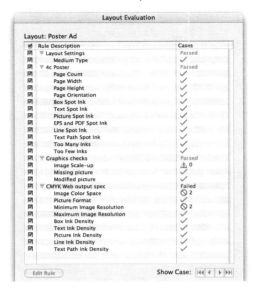

You can re-evaluate a layout at any time. The results will reflect any changes you've made since you last evaluated the layout.

Changing the spot color to process in the layout actually corrected several of the problems. This layout now meets the requirements of the 4c Poster layout specification.

There are still problems to fix in the CMYK Web output spec. You can select a specific rule and click the Show Case buttons to find specific problem images, correct them, and re-evaluate.

If you are working from a complete and accurate job jacket — and you've evaluated and corrected until no more errors are found — you can be almost positive that the file will move smoothly through prepress and production.

13. Click Done to close the Layout Evaluation dialog box. Close the open project without saving.

In a real-world production environment, you would continue evaluating and fixing problems until the layout passes all defined checks. Since the remaining problems in this layout need to be fixed outside of QuarkXPress, we will not complete those steps here.

SUMMARY

QuarkXPress job jackets are an advanced technology that will take some getting used to. The potential benefits, however, are worth the effort — whether you are a designer or an output provider. If you can reduce the number and frequency of errors that reach the prepress department, you can improve efficiency, speed up the overall workflow, meet deadlines, make your clients happy, and ultimately improve your financial bottom line.

Job Jackets Manager — Basic Settings Mode			
Style Settings tab	Character Style Sheets Paragraph Style Sheets Colors Dashes & Stripes H&Js Lists		Append from application Append from existing project file or job jacket
Contacts tab	Name, Title, Company Address, Phone, Email, IM Screen Name		Type specific text strings
Layout Specifications tab	Page Count		"Any" or specific numeric value
	Page Height & Page Width		"Any" or specific numeric value (in inches)
	Margins (Top, Bottom, Left, Right)		"Any" or specific numeric value (in inches)
	Crossovers		Any Allowed Disallowed
	Spreads		Any None Printer's Reader's
	Binding Type		Any None Channel Binding Coil Binding Hard Cover Soft Cover Plastic Comb Ring Binding Saddle-Stitch
	Binding Side		Any None Top Bottom Left Right
	Binding Length		Any None Long Short
	Page Orientation		Any Portrait Landscape
	Bleeds (Top, Bottom, Left, Right)		"Any" or specific numeric value (in inches)
	Color Standard		Any CMYK Hexachrome Monochrome
	Spot Color		Any None [Specific spot colors that exist in job jacket]
	Total Inks		"Any" or specific numeric value
Tickets tab Select ticket, click Edit button opens Edit Job Ticket dialog box	Style Settings tab	Character Style Sheets Paragraph Style Sheets Colors Dashes & Stripes H&Js Lists	Append from current job jacket Append from application Append from existing project file or job jacket
	Layout Settings tab	Layout Name	Type a specific name in Layout Name field
		Layout Specs	Select existing from job jacket
		Medium Type	Select Print or Web
		Resources - Rule Sets	Attach existing from job jacket (created in Advanced Mode only)
		Resources - Output Specifications	Attach existing from job jacket (created in Advanced Mode only)

Job Jackets Manager — Advanced Settings Mode (job jacket selected in list)			
Resource	**Origin**	**Attributes**	**Options**
Character Style Sheets	Import from other job jackets, project files; default application set		
Colors	Import from other job jackets, project files; default application set		
Contacts	Define directly in Job Jackets Manager	Name, Title, Company Address, Phone, Email, IM Screen Name	Text string
Dashes & Stripes	Import from other job jackets, project files; default application set		
H&Js	Import from other job jackets, project files; default application set		
Job Descriptions	Define directly in Job Jackets Manager	Job Number	Text string
		Revision	Text string
		Instructions	Text string
		Notes	Text string
		Keywords	Text string
Layout Specifications	Define directly in Job Jackets Manager	Page Count	"Any" or specific numeric value
		Page Width & Page Height	"Any" or specific numeric value (in inches)
		Margins (Top, Bottom, Left, Right)	"Any" or specific numeric value (in inches)
		Crossover	Any Allowed Disallowed
		Spreads	Any None Printer's Reader's
		Binding Type	Any None Channel Binding Coil Binding Hard Cover Soft Cover Plastic Comb Ring Binding Saddle-Stitch
		Binding Side	Any None Top Bottom Left Right
		Binding Length	Any None Long Short
		Page Orientation	Any Portrait Landscape
		Bleeds (Top, Bottom, Right, Left)	"Any" or specific numeric value (in inches)
		Color Standard	Any CMYK Hexachrome Monochrome
		Spot Color	Any None [Specific spot colors imported into job jacket]
		Total Inks	"Any" or specific numeric value

Job Jackets Manager — Advanced Settings Mode (job jacket selected in list)

Resource	Origin	Attributes	Options
Layouts	NOT AVAILABLE WHEN JOB JACKET IS SELECTED IN LIST		
Lists	Import from other job jackets, project files; default application set		
Output Setups	Import from other job jackets, default application set		
Output Specifications	Define directly in Job Jackets Manager	Image Color Space	Any 1-Bit Grayscale RGB CMYK LAB Indexed
		Picture Format	Any BMP EPS DCS 1 DCS 2 JPEG TIFF PICT WMF PDF GIF Scitex CT PNG
		Minimum Image Resolution	Numeric value (36 – 3600)
		Maximum Image Resolution	Numeric value (36 – 3600)
		Ink Density	Numeric value (90 – 400%)
		Trapping Amount	Numeric value (0 – 36 pt.)
		Overprinting	Any None Black Only
		Output Method	EPS PDF Print
		Output Style	None [Any imported output style that matches the selected output method]
		Halftone Frequency	Numeric value (50 – 600)
		PDF/X Compliance	Any PDF/X-1a PDF/X-3
Output Styles	Import from other job jackets, default application set		
Paragraph Style Sheets	Import from other job jackets, project files; default application set		
Rule Sets	Define directly in Job Jackets Manager		
Rules	Define directly in Job Jackets Manager		
Source Setups	Import from other job jackets, default application set		

Job Jackets Manager — Advanced Settings Mode (ticket/ticket template selected in list)			
Resource	**Origin**	**Attributes**	**Options**
Character Style Sheets	Import from other job jackets, project files; import from default application set; embed in ticket from current job jacket		
Colors	Import from other job jackets, project files; import from default application set; embed in ticket from current job jacket		
Contacts	NOT AVAILABLE WHEN TICKET/TICKET TEMPLATE IS SELECTED IN LIST		
Dashes & Stripes	Import from other job jackets, project files; import from default application set; embed in ticket from current job jacket		
H&Js	Import from other job jackets, project files; import from default application set; embed in ticket from current job jacket		
Job Descriptions	NOT AVAILABLE WHEN TICKET/TICKET TEMPLATE IS SELECTED IN LIST		
Layout Specifications	NOT AVAILABLE WHEN TICKET/TICKET TEMPLATE IS SELECTED IN LIST		
Layouts	Define directly in Job Jackets Manager	Description	Text string
		Job Description	None Any Job Description resource available in the job jacket
		Medium Type	None Print Web
		Source Color Configuration	None Any Source Setup resource available in the job jacket
		Proof Output	None Any Output Setup resource available in the job jacket
		Proof Rendering Intent	Any Perceptual Relative Colorimetric Saturation Absolute Colorimetric Defined By Sources
		Layout Specification	None Any Layout Specification resource available in the job jacket
		Rule Sets	None Any Rule Sets resources available in the job jacket
		Output Specifications	None Any Output Specifications resources available in the job jacket
		Instructions	Text string
Lists	Import from other job jackets, project files; import from default application set; embed in ticket from current job jacket		
Output Setups	Import from other job jackets, project files; import from default application set; embed in ticket from current job jacket		
Output Specifications	NOT AVAILABLE WHEN TICKET/TICKET TEMPLATE IS SELECTED IN LIST		
Output Styles	Import from other job jackets, project files; import from default application set; embed in ticket from current job jacket		
Paragraph Style Sheets	Import from other job jackets, project files; import from default application set; embed in ticket from current job jacket		
Rule Sets	NOT AVAILABLE WHEN TICKET/TICKET TEMPLATE IS SELECTED IN LIST		
Rules	NOT AVAILABLE WHEN TICKET/TICKET TEMPLATE IS SELECTED IN LIST		
Source Setups	Import from other job jackets, project files; import from default application set; embed in ticket from current job jacket		

Creating Web Layouts

17

In response to users' demand for a single application to meet all of their design needs, Quark added Web-design capability to the page-layout application in QuarkXPress 5.0. These tools have been further enhanced in version 6, allowing you to use a familiar workspace to create Web pages from scratch or easily convert existing print layouts to HTML. This chapter introduces the preferences, tools, and utilities that you can use to build a Web site in QuarkXPress.

IN CHAPTER 17, YOU WILL:

- Explore the workspace used to design a Web page in QuarkXPress.

- Practice creating a Web layout and defining the settings for a Web page.

- Add content to a Web layout and understand the limitations that HTML imposes on design.

- Repurpose a print layout for the Web.

- Create destinations, hyperlinks, and anchors in a QuarkXPress Web layout.

- Create and apply meta tag sets.

- Preview and export a Web layout as HTML.

The ability to create Web pages in QuarkXPress means that you can use the same environment, tools, utilities, and features, with which you are already familiar, for designing print layouts. Other attempts at a one-size-fits-all layout application have always been lacking, typically attempting to generate HTML code directly from the print page-layout file. The fact is, print design and Web design are very different. Features that work well on paper may not work as well on the Web, and vice versa.

The Web-design capabilities built into QuarkXPress represent a tremendous improvement over the old model. Rather than exporting HTML directly from a print layout, you now have a slightly different interface for building Web layouts. You can create a Web layout and use the QuarkXPress tools to build a Web page from the ground up.

You can also create a Web layout and copy elements from print layouts, or you can convert a print layout to a Web layout. Using either of these techniques, any feature that is not supported by HTML is not available in the Web-design environment.

When you finish creating your site, QuarkXPress creates HTML code for you. Familiar design features are translated into the appropriate HTML equivalent. The code generated by a QuarkXPress export is not perfect, but it is currently the easiest transition from print to Web design.

CREATING A NEW WEB LAYOUT

As you learned in Chapter 2, you have to define at least one layout when you create a new QuarkXPress project. Choosing Web from the Layout Type menu presents options that are specific to Web layouts.

 CREATE A WEB LAYOUT

1. Open the New Project dialog box (File>New>Project).

2. Type "Center Market Site" in the Layout Name field, and choose Web from the Layout Type menu.

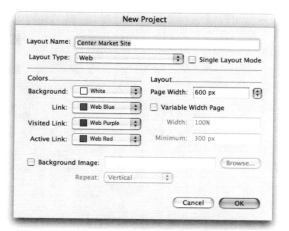

3. In the Colors section, choose Blue in the Visited Link menu.

   The Colors section of the dialog box defines the default color of the background, links, visited links, and active links in the layout. Each option has a menu that lists the available colors — you can even choose a color that is not listed in the default menu if you choose the New option.

4. Choose New from the Active Link menu.

5. In the Edit Color dialog box, choose Web Safe Colors in the Model menu. Type "#FF6600" in the Hex Value field and click OK to return to the New Project dialog box.

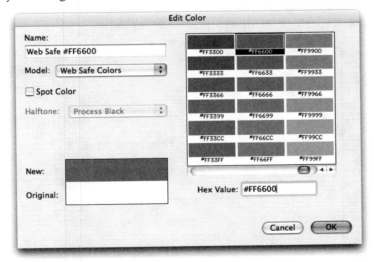

6. Activate the Background Image check box and click Select/Browse.

7. Locate the file **cm_back.jpg** in the **RF_Quark7>Chapter17** folder, and click Open to return to the New Project dialog box.

8. Choose Vertical from the Repeat menu.

The Repeat menu defines the repeat pattern, or the way the image is placed to fill the page.

Tile repeats the image horizontally and vertically over the entire page.

Horizontal repeats the image horizontally over the width of the page.

Vertical repeats the image vertically over the height of the page.

None does not repeat the image.

9. Change the Page Width field to 800 px, and make sure the Variable Width Page check box is deselected.

   The Layout section of the dialog box defines the size of the Web page. You can define a specific number of pixels in the Page Width field, or choose the Variable Width Page check box to create a dynamic Web-page size that changes according to the viewer's browser window.

10. Click OK to create the new layout.

   When you have finished defining the Web layout in the New Project dialog box, clicking OK creates the project and layout. The environment is very similar to that of a print layout, with a few notable exceptions.

   • The layout page is square, based on the number of pixels defined in the Page Width field for the layout. There is no pasteboard around the page.

   • The Preview HTML button is available to the right of the Undo/Redo buttons in the lower-left corner of the Project window.

   • The Facing Page and Section Start buttons are not available in the Page Layout palette.

   • Each page icon in the Page Layout palette is labeled according to the export file name in the Page Properties dialog box. You can change the page name by highlighting the label in the palette and typing a new name. (Export file names and page properties are discussed in the next section.)

   • The default Colors palette includes several Web-specific colors that are not available in the default print Colors palette.

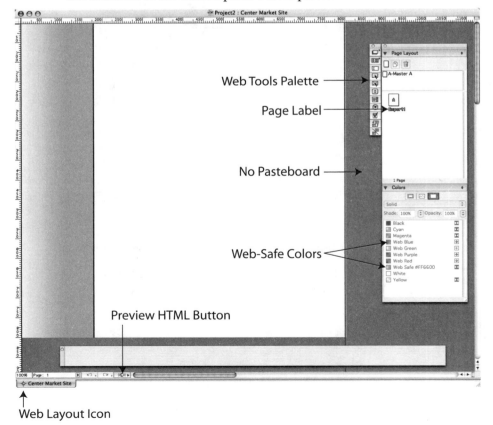

Web Tools Palette

Page Label

No Pasteboard

Web-Safe Colors

Preview HTML Button

Web Layout Icon

SAVE THE WEB LAYOUT

Because the Web layout is contained within a QuarkXPress project, you save it just as you would save a project containing a print layout, using the extension .qxp. The HTML files generated by the export process (with the extension .htm) can be opened and modified in any HTML editor. They cannot, however, be opened in QuarkXPress. Once the Web layout is exported, you should also save the project with the Web layout using File>Save As. You can then reopen the layout, make changes, and re-export the HTML files.

1. Choose File>Save As.

2. Change the file name to "cm_site.qxp".

3. Make sure the Type/Save As Type menu is set to Project.

4. Navigate to your **Work_In_Progress** folder as the target destination and click Save.

5. Continue to the next exercise.

SETTING WEB PREFERENCES

When you work with a Web layout in QuarkXPress, most of the options in the preferences dialog boxes are the same as those for print layouts. When a Web layout is open, the Preferences dialog box presents a list of Web Layout Preferences (instead of Print Layout Preferences for print page layouts). Several additional choices are available, which are important for successfully viewing and exporting Web layouts.

DEFINE BROWSER PREFERENCES

The Browsers preferences dialog box lists the browsers available on your computer, which are used to preview a Web layout as you are building it. The Add button allows you to locate any browser installed on your system. Once you locate the browser application in the Select Browser dialog box, clicking Open adds the browser to the Preferences list. The Default column indicates which browser is automatically used to preview a Web page.

1. With **cm_site.qxp** open, open the Preferences dialog box and click Browsers under Applications.

2. Click Add. Depending on what appears in your list and what browsers are installed on your computer, navigate to the Netscape, Internet Explorer, or Safari application and click Open.

3. When you have finished adding browsers to your list, choose the one you prefer as your default by clicking in the column to the left of the browser.

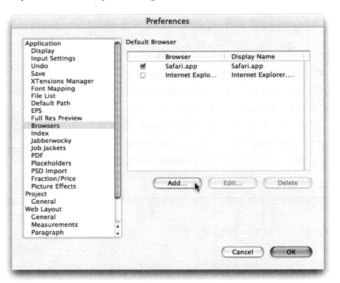

4. Continue to the next exercise.

This exercise requires you to add different browsers to the QuarkXPress preferences. You should follow the directions to add whichever browsers you have available on your computer.

In the General preferences, you can define the color of anchor icons in the layout. (Anchors are discussed in detail later in this chapter.) General preferences also allow you to define folders where the components of your Web site are exported, using the Image Export Directory and Site Root Directory fields.

The site root directory is the folder where your Web pages will be saved when you export the Quark layouts to HTML. (You can override this setting when you export a layout to HTML.)

The Image Export Directory is set to "image" by default. This means that, when you export a Web page to HTML, a folder called "image" is created in the site root directory folder to contain all of the images in the Web layout. If you delete the folder name from the Image Export Directory field, all images will be saved in the root directory folder.

1. With **cm_site.qxp** open, in the Preferences dialog box, click General under Web Layout.

2. Macintosh users: Click Browse next to the Site Root Directory field. Navigate to your **Work_In_Progress** folder. Create a new folder named "CM_Site"; highlight that folder and click Choose.

   Windows users: On your desktop, create a folder named "CM_Site" in your **Work_In_Progress** folder. Click Browse next to the Site Root Directory field. Navigate to the CM_Site folder and click OK.

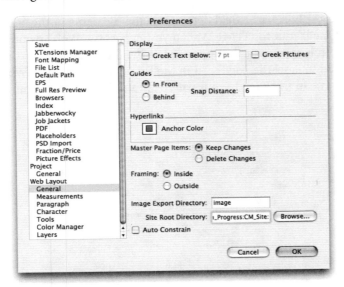

By default, QuarkXPress uses "image" as the name of the folder containing a site's graphics, but site-structure standards typically use "images" instead of "image" for this folder.

Although we are not changing the folder name for this exercise, you might want to do so when you build your own sites.

3. Display the Web Layout Measurements preferences, and make sure the Horizontal and Vertical menus are both set to Pixels.

4. Click OK to close the Preferences dialog box.

5. Save the file and continue.

DEFINING PAGE PROPERTIES

You can change the settings for any page in a Web layout by choosing Page>Page Properties. If a Web layout has more than one page, you can define different settings for each page, such as defining a different background image for different pages in your Web site.

DEFINE PAGE PROPERTIES

1. In the open file, if the Page Layout palette is not already visible, choose Window>Page Layout.

2. Drag the A-Master A page icon into the Page Layout palette to add a second page to the layout.

3. Double-click the Export1 page icon to make it the active page, and choose Page>Page Properties.

   When you make changes in the Page Properties dialog box, you are modifying only the currently active page. The Page Properties dialog box presents the same options as the New Project dialog box, as well as several additional options that are specific to the page you are modifying.

4. In the Page Title field, type "Welcome to Center Market".

   The Page Title field defines what is displayed in the title bar of the user's browser when he or she views that specific page.

5. Highlight the Export File Name field and type "index".

   The Export File Name field determines the file name of the page when you export the layout to HTML. When you export the Web layout, the extension .htm is automatically appended to the file name. The text in this field is also used to label the page icon in the Page Layout palette. If you change the page name in the Page Layout palette, this field is changed automatically.

If the currently active page is a master page when you choose Page>Page Properties, you can only change settings that can apply to all pages in the Web layout. This means that you cannot define a page name or export file name, which are page-specific attributes.

"index.htm" is recognized by most servers as the home page of a Web site.

The file name should not contain any spaces or slashes (/), since they are not recognized by Unix- and Windows-based servers.

*The Meta Tag Set menu allows you to append a defined set of meta tags to the Web page. **Meta tags** are words, phrases, or code elements that define the content of your Web page, and are used by search engines to index the pages of your Web site. (Meta tag sets are explained later in this chapter.)*

6. Click OK to close the Page Properties dialog box. The Page Layout palette shows the "index" label under the first page.

7. In the Page Layout palette, highlight the label Export2 under the second page icon. Type "products" and press Return/Enter.

8. Double-click the products page icon in the Page Layout palette to make that the active page, and choose Page>Page Properties. The Export File Name field reflects the change you made in the Page Layout palette.

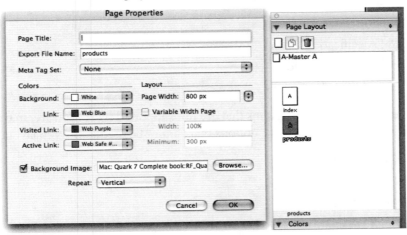

9. Type "Center Market Holiday Catalog" in the Page Title field and click OK.

10. Add another page to the layout by dragging the A-Master A icon into the lower half of the Page Layout palette.

11. Make the new page the active page in the layout and open the Page Properties dialog box. Enter "Center Market Monthly Specials" in the Page Title field and "specials" in the Export File Name field. Click OK.

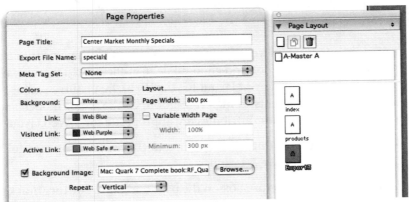

12. Save the project and leave it open for the next exercise.

ADDING CONTENT TO YOUR WEB LAYOUT

Creating a Web layout in QuarkXPress is very similar to creating a print layout. The tools you use to place text and graphics into a layout are the same — text is contained in text boxes and pictures are contained in picture boxes. The primary difference between the two types of layouts lies in the available options for specific types of content.

Typographic options that are not supported by HTML are unavailable in the Measurements palette, Style submenus, and Character Attributes dialog box. The text styling options that are not supported are:

- Forced and justified paragraph alignment
- Word underline, outline, shadow, small caps, and superior type styles
- Horizontal and vertical scale
- Tracking and kerning
- Paragraph leading
- Baseline shift
- H&J specifications
- Lock to baseline grid
- Text angle and text skew

Like character styling, box options that are not supported by HTML are unavailable in the Modify dialog boxes. The options that cannot be used for a Web layout are:

- Box angle and box skew
- Box rotation
- First baseline
- Inter ¶ max
- Flip horizontal and flip vertical
- Text-box linking

In addition to these limitations, non-rectangular text boxes and any text on a path are automatically exported as graphic elements. If a text box uses more than one column, the columns will be converted to an HTML table upon exporting.

 ADD GRAPHICS TO THE WEB LAYOUT

Placing a graphic into a Web layout is exactly the same as placing one into a print layout — you create a picture box and choose File>Get Picture. In many cases, especially when repurposing a print layout for the Web, the pictures you use are formatted for print requirements — high resolution, CMYK color model, and TIFF or EPS file format. None of these attributes are appropriate for a Web layout.

1. With the file **cm_site.qxp** open (from your **Work_In_Progress** folder), navigate to the A-Master A layout.

2. Create a rectangular picture box on the page and place **center_market.eps** (from the **RF_Quark7>Chapter17** folder) into the box.

3. Scale the image to 95% horizontally and vertically, and then fit the box to the picture (Style>Fit Box to Picture).

[Sidebar notes:]

Master pages in Web layouts function just as they do in print layouts.

In addition to text formatting limitations, certain characters (em, en, flex, and nonbreaking spaces, and tabs) are not supported by HTML and will be converted to regular spaces when you export the page.

Nonrectangular text boxes and any text on a path are automatically exported as graphic elements. If a text box uses more than one column, the columns will be converted to an HTML table upon exporting.

4. Position the picture box at X: 190 px, Y: 10 px.

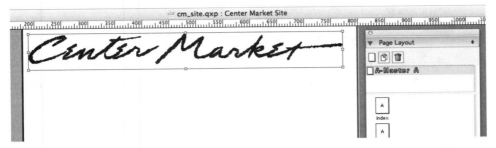

5. With the picture box selected on the page, open the Modify dialog box and display the Export tab.

    When you export a Web layout to HTML, the images in the layout are also exported, and converted to a format that is appropriate for Web display. You control these export options in the Export tab of the Modify dialog box.

6. In the File Name field, delete the numbers from the end of the file name.

7. Leave the Export To menu at the default value (image).

    This field defines the folder in which the graphic will be saved. By default, this shows the name of the image export directory as defined in the General pane of the Preferences dialog box. If you change this field, a new folder with the name you enter will be created in the site folder on export.

8. Type "center market logo" in the Alternate Text field.

    Alternate text (or simply *alt text*) is displayed in place of the image if the user's browser is set to text-only (for a slow connection or for using voice technology to read the content of the Web page) or if the image is missing.

9. Make sure the Export As menu is set to GIF.

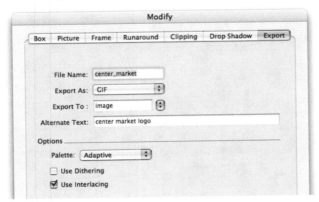

The GIF format is generally used for images with areas of solid color, and objects with sharp edges (such as type). GIF files are relatively small and take less time to download than JPEG files.

When an image is set to export as a GIF file, you can choose the color model (Web-safe, Adaptive, Windows, or Mac OS) to use for the image in the Palette menu. The Use Dithering check box means that the image may be dithered to produce a closer variation of the original color. The Use Interlacing option allows the image to display in progressively better detail as it downloads.

When a Web layout is exported to HTML, the export process automatically converts CMYK images to RGB, and decreases high-resolution images to 72 ppi.

You can export graphics in one of four formats: GIF, JPEG, PNG, or SWF.

PNG is the default option for placed EPS files; JPEG is the default option for placed TIFF and JPEG images.

Dithering is similar to halftoning in print design. The image is converted to small dots of two different colors within the selected palette. When viewed on the monitor, the different-colored dots produce the illusion of a third color. This can artificially increase the colors in the palette, but can also destroy the integrity of fine lines and sharp edges in type.

10. Click OK to close the Modify dialog box.

11. Navigate to the index page.

12. Create a rectangular picture box on the index page.

13. Place the file **plate.tif** (from the **RF_Quark7>Chapter17** folder) into the box, scale it to 83% horizontally and vertically, and fit the box to the picture. Place the box at X: 190 px, Y: 100 px.

14. In the Export tab of the Modify dialog box, delete the numbers from the end of the file name.

15. Change the alt text to "center market home page".

16. Choose Medium from the Image Quality menu and activate the Progressive check box.

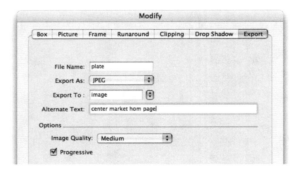

The JPEG format is primarily used for photographic images. JPEG files are compressed, which reduces download time but can also cause data loss. JPEG does not support transparency in an image.

When JPEG is selected, you must also choose an amount of compression from the Image Quality menu. Highest means the least amount of compression will be applied. If the Progressive check box is active, the image will be displayed in progressively greater detail as it downloads.

17. Click OK to close the Modify dialog box.

18. Save the file and continue and continue to the next exercise.

ADD TEXT TO THE WEB LAYOUT

1. Navigate to the A-Master A layout of **cm_site.qxp**.

2. Create a rectangular text box with the following dimensions:

   X: 25 px   W: 100 px
   Y: 10 px   H: 36 px

3. Make sure the background color of the box is set to None.

4. Type the word "HOME" in the text box. Format the text to 16-pt. ATC Maple Medium.

5. Create another rectangle text box with the following dimensions:

   X: 25 px   W: 100 px
   Y: 100 px   H: 140 px

6. In the new box, type the following:

   SPECIALS[Return/Enter]

   CATALOG[Return/Enter]

   cheese[Return/Enter]

   bread[Return/Enter]

   CONTACT US[Return/Enter]

7. Select all the text in the box and format it as 16-pt. ATC Maple Medium, with 28-pt. leading.

8. Apply a 24-px left indent to the "cheese" and "bread" paragraphs.

9. Select the HOME text box and open the Modify dialog box.

   Just as with print design, the fonts used in your Web layout must be present for the user to see the page exactly as you designed it. A Web browser substitutes a user-defined font if the user does not have the same fonts as specified in the file. The only way to absolutely prevent this substitution is to export text boxes as graphics.

> Because users are not likely to have ATC Maple Medium installed on their computers, you will set these text boxes (which will be links to different pages) to export as graphics.

Converting a text box to a graphic is an excellent way to control the appearance of text-based buttons and other small text items. When the Convert to Graphic on Export check box is selected, the HTML restrictions on type formatting are lifted because the text will be presented as a graphic. The disadvantage of converting larger blocks of text to graphics is that this can dramatically increase download time for anyone on a slow Internet connection.

Many Internet users still use dial-up modems. Don't automatically convert all text boxes to graphics without considering your users. If your target audience is largely corporate, you may be safe to assume that most users have a high-speed connection. If you are creating a Web site for the general consumer or home-computer user, however, you should assume that many people are still dialing in with a 56K (or slower) modem.

10. Display the Export tab, and activate the Convert to Graphic on Export check box.

Checking the Convert to Graphic on Export option causes the text box to be rasterized into a graphic element when you export your Web page.

When a text box is set to export as a graphic, the Export tab of the Modify dialog box includes options as when you are working with a placed picture. Text boxes that export as graphics are set by default to export as PNG files.

The PNG format supports continuous-tone images (like JPEG), but does not cause data loss from compression. PNG, unlike JPEG, supports transparent areas in an image.

When PNG is selected, the True Color and Indexed Color radio buttons determine how the colors in the image are reproduced. *True Color* means the image is reproduced with the most colors possible in the user's browser. *Indexed Color* compresses the image gamut into the color model you choose in the Palette menu (Web-safe, Adaptive, Windows, or Mac OS). If Indexed Color is selected, you can also choose Use Dithering to increase the range of color. The Use Interlacing option is the same as for GIF files.

11. Type "home_link" in the File Name field and type "link to center market home" in the Alternate Text field. Make sure the Tru Color option is selected and leave the remaining options at the default values. Click OK.

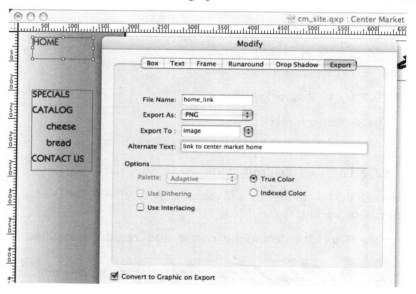

The camera icon (visual indicator) in the top-right corner of the text box indicates that the box is set to export as a graphic.

12. Select the second text box and open the Export tab of the Modify dialog box. Set this box to export as a graphic; use "nav_links" as the file name, "navigation links" as the alt text, and apply the same export settings as in Step 11.

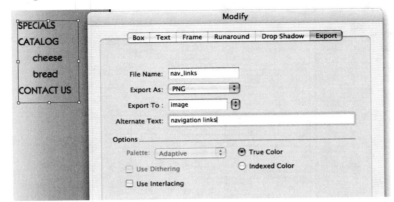

The disadvantage of the PNG format is that some older browsers cannot display PNG graphics.

13. Save the file and continue.

REPURPOSING PRINT LAYOUTS

Many Web layouts created in QuarkXPress are repurposed versions of existing print layouts. This process is much easier now than it has been in the past. If you are creating a Web layout in a project file separate from your print layout, you can use the Item tool to drag elements from an existing print layout directly into the Web layout. Because a single project can have multiple layout spaces, you can also change a print layout to a Web layout, maintaining most (if not all) of the formatting defined in the original print layout.

REPURPOSE A PRINT LAYOUT

1. With the file **cm_site.qxp** still open, make sure the specials page is active in the Project window.

2. Open the file **center_market.qxp** from the **RF_Quark>Output** folder.

3. Change the page view of the print layout so you can see both Project windows on your monitor.

4. Using the Item tool, select the text box on the first page of the print layout.

5. Drag the selected box from the print layout into the Web layout.

6. Make the Web layout project the active window.

Rather than simply changing a print layout to a Web layout, we recommend duplicating the print layout (Layout>Duplicate) and converting the duplicate to a Web layout. This allows you to preserve the original print layout instead of replacing it.

7. Position the copied text box at X: 190 px, Y: 90 px, and change the box width to 580 px.

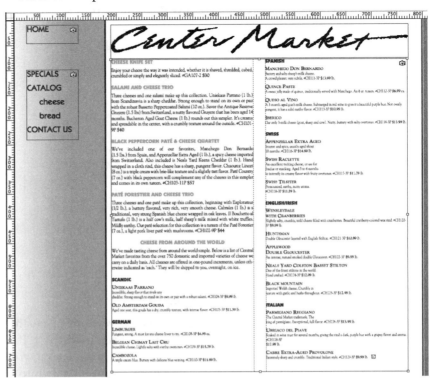

Notice the camera visual indicator in the top-right corner of the text box. If a box placed from a print layout includes formatting that is not supported by HTML, the box in the Web layout is automatically set to export as a graphic.

8. Open the Modify dialog box and display the Text tab.

9. Deactivate the Convert to Graphic on Export check box.

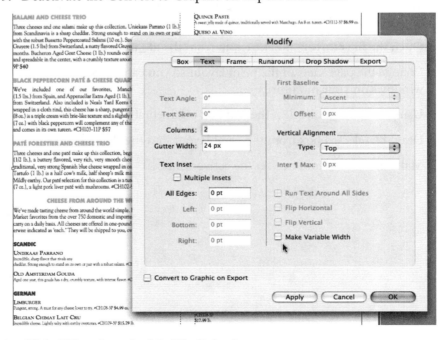

When a text box is not set to export as a graphic, you can choose the Make Variable Width check box in the Text tab of the Modify dialog box to make the text box resize dynamically, according to the size of the browser window. This option is useful if your page is set to Variable Width in the Page Properties dialog box. If the page resizes to fit the browser window, a text box set to Make Variable Width will also be resized, according to the relative position on the page. Text will reflow automatically, according to the variable width of the text box.

10. Click OK to close the Modify dialog box.

By deactivating the Convert to Graphic on Export check box, unsupported formatting is automatically removed. Notice the difference between the text set to export as a graphic (Step 7) and the text that will export as text.

11. Save the file and continue.

PREVIEW THE PAGE

The ability to preview your work is invaluable, especially when converting an existing print layout. Because so many of the print design features are not supported in a Web layout, you should preview your work frequently and make adjustments as necessary.

1. With the specials page of the **cm_site.qxp** file active, click the Preview HTML button.

If more than one browser is listed in the Browser Preferences dialog box, you can hold down the mouse button until a menu shows all browsers available. A checkmark indicates the default browser; you can preview your work in nondefault browsers by choosing from the menu.

The page is processed, and then displayed in the default browser.

By previewing your layouts frequently, you can make the changes necessary to create the pages you want before the final export process.

2. In the resulting browser window, review the results.

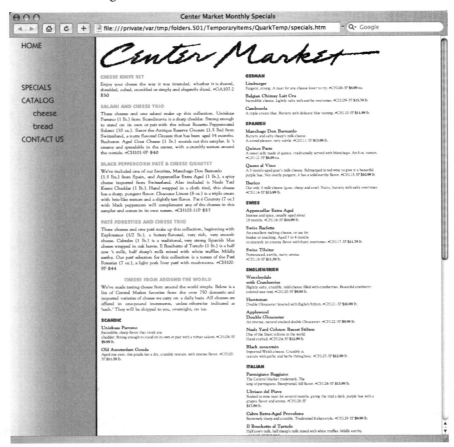

If you are repurposing from a print layout, it is a good idea to deactivate the fonts used in the print layout so you can preview what other people will see in their browser window if they don't have the specific fonts you're using.

In a Web layout, columns do not function exactly as they do for print layouts. When a story extends across multiple columns, exporting to HTML treats the text in each column independently. Exporting to HTML manually breaks text at the end of each column, even if that manual break occurs in the middle of a paragraph. The remaining text, which begins in the next column, appears as a new paragraph.

When you preview your page, you get an idea of what the page will look like in a browser. This is an excellent way to see what works and what *doesn't work* for viewing in a Web browser.

- The text in the two-column box is very small and difficult to read.
- The Overset Text icon disappears, and all the rest of the text in the story appears in the second column.

Because of the inherent differences between print and Web design, some problems are inevitable. By previewing frequently, you can make the necessary modifications to prepare the layout for export to HTML.

3. Close the browser window and return to the **cm_site.qxp** file.

4. Continue to the next exercise.

 ADJUST THE LAYOUT

1. In the file **cm_site.qxp**, navigate to the A-Master A page.

2. Make the following changes to the style sheets in the layout:

Four-column text	Delete, replace with 2-column text
Bread text	Delete, replace with 2-column text
Cheese name - no sp	Delete, replace with Cheese name - sp before

Heading	Font Size:	14 pt.
	Font Color:	Web Safe #FF6600
	Leading:	Auto
	Keep With Next ¶:	Deselected
Country	Font Size:	13 pt.
	Color:	Web Safe #FF6600
	Leading:	Auto
	Space After:	0 px
Cheese name - sp before	Font:	ATC Pine Normal
	Font Size:	12 pt.
	Type Style:	Bold
	Leading:	Auto
2-column text	Font Size:	12 pt.
	Leading:	Auto
	Alignment:	Left
Price	Font:	ATC Pine Normal
	Font Size:	12 pt.
	Type Style:	Bold

3. If invisible characters are not showing, choose View>Invisibles.

CHEESE KNIFE SET ¶

Enjoy your cheese the way it was intended, whether it is shaved, shredded, cubed, crumbled or simply and elegantly sliced. ⌖GA107-2 $30 ¶

SALAMI AND CHEESE TRIO ¶

Three cheeses and one salami make up this collection. Uniekaas Parrano (1 lb.) from Scandinavia is a sharp cheddar. Strong enough to stand on its own or pair with the robust Bussetto Peppercoated Salami (10 oz.). Savor the Antique Reserve Gruyere (1.5 lbs) from Switzerland, a nutty flavored Gruyere that has been aged 14 months. Bucheron Aged Goat Cheese (1 lb.) rounds out this sampler. It's creamy and spreadable in the center, with a crumbly texture around the outside. ⌖CH101-9P $40 ¶

BLACK PEPPERCORN PATÉ & CHEESE QUARTET ¶

We've included one of our favorites, Manchego Don Bernardo (1.5 lbs.) from Spain, and Appenzellar Extra Aged (1 lb.), a spicy cheese imported from Switzerland. Also included is Neals Yard Keens Cheddar (1 lb.). Hand wrapped in a cloth rind, this cheese has a sharp, pungent flavor. Chaource Lincet (8 oz.) is a triple cream with brie-like texture and a slightly tart flavor. Paté Country (7 oz.) with black peppercorn will complement any of the cheeses in this sampler and comes in its own tureen. ⌖CH103-11P $57 ¶

PATÉ FORESTIER AND CHEESE TRIO ¶

Three cheeses and one paté make up this collection, beginning with Explorateur (1/2 lb.), a buttery flavored, very rich, very smooth cheese. Cabrales (1 lb.) is a traditional, very strong Spanish blue cheese wrapped in oak leaves. Il Boschetto al Tartufo (1 lb.) is a half cow's milk, half sheep's milk mixed with white truffles. Mildly earthy. Our paté selection for this collection is a tureen

of the Paté Forestier (7 oz.), a light pork liver paté with mushrooms. ⌖CH102-9P $44 ¶

CHEESE FROM AROUND THE WORLD ¶

We've made tasting cheese from around the world simple. Below is a list of Central Market favorites from the over 750 domestic and imported varieties of cheese we carry on a daily basis. All cheeses are offered in one-pound increments, unless otherwise indicated as 'each.' They will be shipped to you, overnight, on ice. ¶

SCANDIC ¶

Uniekaas Parrano ¶
Incredible, sharp flavor that rivals any cheddar. Strong enough to stand on its own or pair with a robust salami. ⌖CH104-3P $9.99 lb. ¶

Old Amsterdam Gouda ¶
Aged one year, this gouda has a dry, crumbly texture, with intense flavor. ⌖CH105-3P $11.59 lb. ¶

GERMAN ¶

Limburger ¶
Pungent, strong. A must for any cheese lover to try. ⌖CH108-3P $4.99 ea. ¶

Belgian Chimay Lait Cru ¶
Incredible cheese. Lightly salty with earthy overtones. ⌖CH109-3P $15.79 lb. ¶

Cambozola ¶
A triple cream blue. Buttery with delicate blue veining. ⌖CH110-3P $11.99 lb. ¶

SPANISH ¶

Manchego Don Bernardo ¶
Buttery and salty sheep's milk cheese. A crowd pleaser, very subtle. ⌖CH111-3P $13.99 lb. ¶

Quince Paste ¶
A sweet jelly made of quince, traditionally served with ▨

4. Place a next-column character (Enter on the numeric keypad) before the "Black Peppercorn Paté" heading.

5. Select the Item tool, and copy the two-column text box to the clipboard.

6. Navigate to the products page, and choose Edit>Paste In Place.

7. Select and delete all text before the "Cheese from Around..." heading.

8. Change the text box to have only one column.

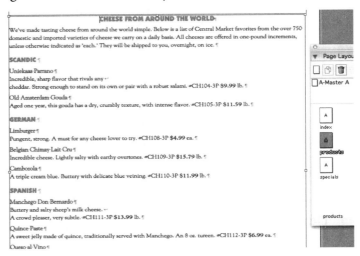

9. Expand the bottom of the text box until the Overset Text icon disappears.

   In a Web layout, there is no such thing as overset text, and linked text boxes are not supported. When you export a page to HTML, the containing box automatically expands as necessary to accommodate all text in the story.

10. Select all the paragraphs after the "Artisan Breads" heading and apply a 9-px space after each paragraph.

11. Remove any soft-return characters (↵) from the page.

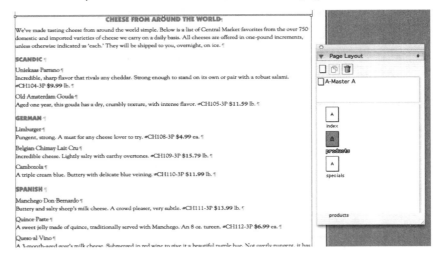

12. Navigate back to the specials page.

13. Place the insertion point immediately before the "Cheese from Around..." heading and press Command-Option-Shift-Down Arrow/Control-Alt-Shift-Down Arrow to select all the rest of the text in the story.

14. Press Delete to remove the selected text.

15. Remove any soft-return characters (↵) from the page.

16. Save the file and continue.

Because these boxes will not export as graphics, you really don't know what font will be used to display the text. This means that soft returns will not necessarily appear where you want them to, and might ruin the integrity of your layout. Much of the fine-tuning that designers do for a print layout is, in many cases, a wasted effort when working with text in a Web page.

Box runarounds in Web layouts are a touchy subject. You can apply a runaround to elements in a Web layout, but runaround is not handled in the same way as it is for a print layout. When a page is exported to HTML, overlapping elements (such as picture boxes) within a story are exported as inline graphics. For an image runaround to affect the text in a Web layout text box, the picture box must exist entirely within the text box.

1. Make sure both **cm_site.qxp** (from your **Work_In_Progress** folder) and **center_market.qxp** (from the **RF_Quark7>Chapter17** folder) are open.

2. Using the Item tool, drag each of the four-color images from the first page of the print layout into the specials page of the Web layout.

   Depending on where you placed the pictures, the text may or may not wrap around the different boxes. Box runarounds do not affect the underlying text box until the image box boundaries are entirely contained within the text box or column.

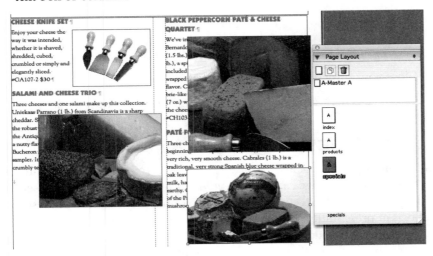

3. Position the knives picture at X: 310 px, Y: 110 px.

4. Reduce the salami and cheese and black peppercorn paté pictures to 50% and fit the boxes to the pictures.

5. Position the salami and cheese picture at X: 328 px, Y: 254 px.

6. Position the black peppercorn picture at X: 629 px, Y: 123 px.

7. Reduce the paté forestier picture to 40% and fit the box to the picture; position it at X: 603 px, Y: 426 px.

8. Save the file, and then preview it in your browser.

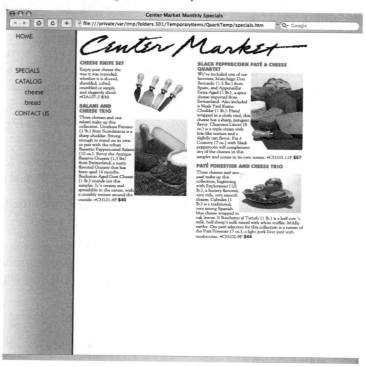

9. Close your browser and return to QuarkXPress.

10. Close the center_market.qxp file and continue to the next section.

ADDING HYPERLINKS AND ANCHORS

The most important goal of a Web page is to present content in a clear, intuitive manner. A single Web page can provide volumes of information, but if users have to scroll in six different directions to read everything, they will lose interest and your efforts at presentation will be wasted. One advantage of Web publishing is the ability to link from one document to another, which allows you to break up information into small chunks that are clearly and attractively presented. Hyperlinks, which enable this kind of presentation, are the foundation of Web design.

QuarkXPress includes a Hyperlinks palette that is used to create and maintain links from one page to another, from one area of a page to another area on the same page, or from your page to an external source.

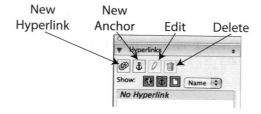

The Show options in the Hyperlinks palette allow you to control what appears in the palette. The three buttons (from left to right) display and hide URLs, anchors, and page links. The menu allows you to display items in the palette by either the name of the hyperlink or the link that is the destination of the hyperlink.

Every hyperlink has two parts — the hyperlink text or object and the destination. The *destination* is the document, location, or other place that is called by clicking the hyperlink. To create links in a Web layout, you should begin by creating a list of destinations in the Hyperlinks palette. You can always add more destinations later, but you should at least have a starting point.

There are several ways to create a destination:

- You can simply click the New Hyperlink button in the Hyperlinks palette.
- If a box is currently selected with the Content tool, you can choose Style>Hyperlink>New.
- Control/right-clicking a box presents a contextual menu, where you can choose Hyperlink>New.

1. With the file **cm_site.qxp** open, choose Window>Hyperlinks.

2. Click the New Hyperlink button in the Hyperlinks palette.

3. In the New Hyperlink dialog box, type "Link To Home Page" in the Name field.

    The hyperlink name is a plain-English identifier that appears in the Hyperlinks palette, which helps you to more easily identify the content of the link.

4. Choose Page from the Type menu, and choose index from the Page menu.

    The Type menu determines whether the link opens a URL, another page in your site, or an anchor.

    When you choose Page from the Type menu, the Page menu shows every page in your layout. You can select from this menu to create a relative link to that page.

An **absolute path** lists every page in the path to the file, beginning with the http address of the page. A **relative path** abbreviates the path by omitting the http address and any common folders. Because individual pages in a Web layout are exported to the same folder, these links are created as relative links when you choose Export to HTML.

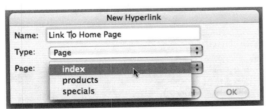

5. Click OK. The new destination is added to the Hyperlinks palette.

As a general rule, you should begin a project by creating destinations for each page in your layout, and a site contact (mailto:).

6. Repeat this process to add destinations for the remaining two pages (specials and catalog) in the layout.

7. Click the New Hyperlink button in the Hyperlinks palette.

8. In the Name field, type "Contact Email".

9. Choose URL in the Type menu.

   If you define a URL link, you can type the appropriate target in the URL field. You can also choose the type of URL that is used by selecting from the URL menu.

   • **http://, https://, and ftp://** are absolute URLs that direct the browser to a specific Web page (for example, http://www.againsttheclock.com).

   • **mailto:** is a URL command that implements an action — sending an email (for example, mailto:info@againsttheclock.com).

10. In the URL field, type "mailto:", and then type your email address. Click OK.

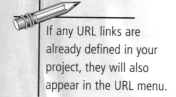

If any URL links are already defined in your project, they will also appear in the URL menu.

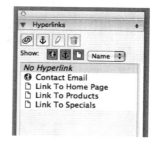

11. Save the file and continue.

 ASSIGN HYPERLINKS

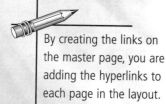

By creating the links on the master page, you are adding the hyperlinks to each page in the layout.

1. In the file **cm_site.qxp**, navigate to the A-Master A layout.

2. Choose View>Visual Indicators to toggle off this feature.

3. Using the Item tool, select the box that contains the word HOME.

   You can assign a hyperlink to an entire text box by selecting the box with the Item tool, or you can assign the link to specific text by selecting the text with the Content tool before clicking a link in the Hyperlinks palette.

4. Click Link To Home Page in the Hyperlinks palette.

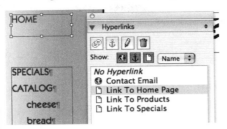

After hyperlinks are defined, you can apply them simply by selecting text or an object and clicking the appropriate item in the palette.

5. Choose View>Visual Indicators to toggle this feature back on.

In addition to the camera, a second visual indicator now appears in the HOME box. The chain-link icon is the visual indicator for a hyperlink.

6. Using the Content tool, highlight the word SPECIALS, and click Link To Specials in the Hyperlinks palette.

Notice the selected text is now underlined, which is the default for hyperlink text. The HOME link was not underlined because you applied that link to the entire box instead of the selected text.

7. Press Command/Control-Shift-U to remove the underline style.

8. Highlight the word CATALOG, and click Link To Products in the Hyperlinks palette. Remove the underline style from the selected text.

9. Highlight the words CONTACT US, and click Contact Email in the Hyperlinks palette. Remove the underline style from the selected text.

When you deselect the text, you see that it is also blue — the color you defined in the New Project dialog box at the beginning of this chapter.

10. Navigate to the index page, and then save the project.

11. Click the Preview HTML button at the bottom of the Project window.

If you click the Contact Us link, you should be able to send an email to yourself. The remaining links will not work properly since the QuarkXPress preview feature exports only the active page for preview. If you click either the Specials or Catalog link, you will get an error message.

12. Close the browser window and return to the QuarkXPress file. Leave it open for the next exercise.

If you decide you don't want to use a link, you can highlight the linked text in the layout and click the No Hyperlink option in the Hyperlinks palette.

You would want links to be consistent in a real project. We include this difference for the sake of illustration.

You shoud save your work before clicking the Preview HTML button. This button can cause QuarkXPress to crash, especially if the browser is not already open.

Anchors are useful when you have a long block of text that requires the user to scroll through a page to read all of the information. *Anchors* are similar to hyperlinks, but an anchor links to a specific spot on a page; users can easily move to a specific spot on a page without scrolling.

1. With the file **cm_site.qxp** open, highlight the first heading on the products page ("Cheese from Around the World).

   As with hyperlinks, the first step in creating anchors is to define destinations at the appropriate locations on the page. This is accomplished by scrolling through the text, highlighting the appropriate text with the Content tool, and clicking the New Anchor button in the Hyperlinks palette.

2. Click the New Anchor button in the Hyperlinks palette.

   The New Anchor dialog box shows the name as the highlighted text (with no spaces). You can change this text or accept the default anchor name.

3. In the New Anchor dialog box, leave the Anchor Name at the default value and click OK.

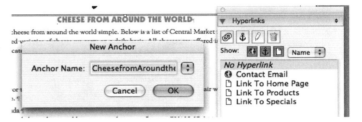

The new anchor now appears in the Hyperlinks palette, preceded by a "#".

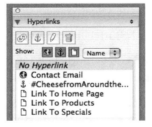

If you look closely at the layout, a colored-arrow icon indicates an anchor's location in the layout. You can hide these indicators by turning off visual indicators (View>Hide Visual Indicators).

4. Repeat Steps 1–3 to create another anchor destination for the Artisan Breads heading on the specials page.

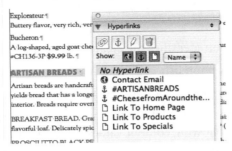

After creating anchor destinations, you can assign hyperlinks to those anchors just as you did with regular hyperlink destinations.

5. Navigate to the A-Master A page.

6. Highlight the word "cheese" (under CATALOG) and click the corresponding anchor destination in the Hyperlinks palette. Remove the underline type style from the hyperlink text.

7. Repeat Step 6 to assign the appropriate anchor link to the word "bread".

8. Save the file and continue to the next section.

USING META TAGS

A *meta tag* is a hidden element of a Web page that contains some piece of information about the page. The content of a meta tag is contained in < > characters. Meta tags are built into the heading of the HTML code of your Web page, but are transparent to the end user.

QuarkXPress manages meta tags in *sets,* or logical groupings that you define and apply to specific pages. The Meta Tags dialog box (Edit>Meta Tags) includes the same familiar buttons as other QuarkXPress dialog boxes.

In QuarkXPress, meta tags can be one of two types — name or http-equiv. Name meta tags simply contain information about the page, such as the page title, author, and keywords. Meta tags of the type http-equiv contain directions that interact with the user's browser, defining items such as the character set used to display the page in the browser and the scripting language used in the page.

For more information about meta tags, consult an HTML resource.

A meta tag appears in the header information of the HTML code for the page, using the following format:

<meta name="generator" content="QuarkXPress 7">

In this example, name is the type of tag, generator is the name of the tag, and QuarkXPress 7 is the value or content of the tag.

When name is selected as the tag type, you can choose from the available list of meta names in the Name pop-up menu, or type other text into the Name field. After choosing the name of the tag, you can type the content of the tag into the Content field.

- **Author.** This option identifies the creator of the site.
- **Copyright.** This option lists copyright information.
- **Description.** This provides a brief textual description of the page contents.
- **Distribution.** This option defines the availability of the site. You should enter one of the following content values for the Distribution tag:
    - **Global** for distribution on the Web.
    - **Local** for distribution on a local intranet.
    - **IU** for internal use.
- **Generator.** This lists the application and version used to create the page.
- **Keywords.** This lists words or phrases that indicate the content of the page.
- **Resource-Type.** This option indicates that the page is a document.
- **Revisit-After.** This option defines how often a search engine should reindex the page.
- **Robots.** This option defines how search engines are allowed to search a page and any pages linked to it. You should enter one of the following content values for the Robots tag.
    - **index** and **noindex** determine whether a page is indexed.
    - **follow** or **nofollow** determine whether the robot can follow links to other pages.
    - **all** combines index and follow.
    - **none** combines noindex and nofollow.

When http-equiv is selected as the meta tag type, the Name menu presents options that interact with the user's browser to define how it displays the information on the page.

- **Charset.** This option defines the character set used to display information in the user's browser. The most common Western-language character set is ISO 8859-I.
- **Cache-Control.** This option defines how a page can be *cached* (stored) by a browser. You should enter one of the following content values for the Cache-Control tag:
    - **no-cache** means the page cannot be cached.
    - **no-store** means the page can be cached, but not stored in an archive.
    - **public** means the page can be cached and stored in any manner.
    - **private** means the page can only be cached in a private cache.
- **Content-Language.** This option defines the specific language of the page.
- **Content-Script-Type.** This option defines the default scripting language for the page.
- **Content-Style-Type.** This option defines the default style sheet language for the page.

Scripting languages are the codes used to create interactive features in a Web site. JavaScript, which is used to create rollovers (discussed in the next chapter), is an example of a scripting language.

- **Expires.** This option defines the date and time at which a page expires in a browser's cache, after which it must be reloaded.

- **Pics-Label.** This option specifies a rating (similar to those on movies) of the pictures in your page. This is used to identify adult content in a Web site.

- **Pragma.** This option restricts Netscape from caching the page.

- **Refresh.** This option defines how long a page will last in the browser window before it is automatically refreshed. You can also define another page that loads after the defined number of seconds has passed (called a "redirect").

- **Reply-to.** This option defines an email address that is used as the contact information for the page.

- **Set-Cookie.** This option defines the value and expiration date of a cookie.

- **Window-Target.** This option defines the window that will be used to display the page. This choice can prevent a page from loading in a frame.

A **cookie** is a text file that is saved on the user's computer so that the site recognizes return visitors.

CREATE META TAGS

1. With **cm_site.qxp** open, choose Edit>Meta Tags.

2. Highlight Set 1 and click Edit.

3. Change the Name field to "Center Market Tags".

4. Highlight the keywords item in the list and click Edit. In the Content field, type "gourmet, gifts, food, cheese, bread, shopping".

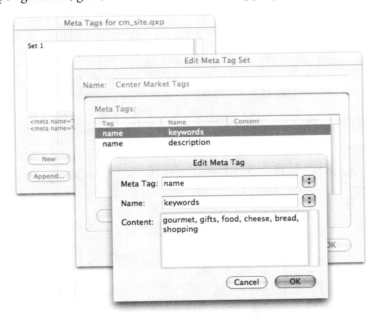

5. Click OK. The keywords item in the list shows the contents you just entered.

6. Highlight the description item in the list and click Edit. In the Content field, type "Spoil yourself or your favorite gourmet with fine gifts from our holiday catalog. Award-winning cheese and bread from around the world are an ideal shopping choice for any food lover." Click OK.

7. Click Add in the Edit Meta Tag Set dialog box. Choose name in the Meta Tag menu and choose generator in the Name menu.

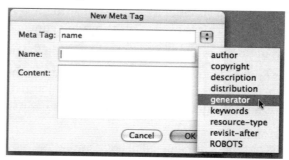

8. In the Content field, type "QuarkXPress 7". Click OK.

9. Click Add in the Edit Meta Tag Set dialog box. Choose name in the Meta Tag menu, and choose author in the Name menu. In the Content field, type your name. Click OK.

10. Click OK to close the Edit Meta Tag Set dialog box.

11. Click Save in the Meta Tags dialog box to save the set.

12. Navigate to the A-Master A layout, and choose Page>Master Page Properties. Choose Center Market Tags from the Meta Tag Set menu and click OK.

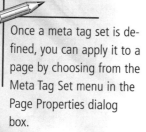

Once a meta tag set is defined, you can apply it to a page by choosing from the Meta Tag Set menu in the Page Properties dialog box.

Attaching the meta tag set to the master page means that you don't have to attach it to each page separately.

13. Save the file and leave it open.

USING CSS AND FONT FAMILIES

When you export a layout to HTML, style and formatting information is embedded into the header information of the HTML code as *cascading style sheets* (*CSS*), which define the formatting of different styles used throughout the layout. (You can also choose to export an external CSS file when you export the layout to HTML. Instead of embedding the styles into every HTML page, each page is linked to a separate .css file that contains the style definitions.)

The following shows the basic code for defining a cascading style sheet.

```
.text4{
    font-family:'Times','Times New Roman','serif';
    font-size:10px;
    text-decoration:none;
    color:black;
}
```

When a user views your Web page, the font-family line of the CSS tells the browser:

Display this text in Times (the first font in the list).

If that font is not available,

Display this text in Times New Roman (the second font in the list).

If that font is not available,

Display this text in Serif (the generic class of font).

If no font in the list is available on the user's computer, the browser displays text using the generic class of font (Serif, Sans-Serif, Cursive, Fantasy, or Monospace). Individual users can define the font they prefer for each class in their browser preferences, so your page may look very different from one user to another.

HTML only recognizes five classes — serif, sans serif, monospace, cursive, or fantasy. If you use a font that has a different class (humanist, modern, and so on) or does not have a defined class, you need to define font families so the CSS generated during HTML export has the necessary information to display the page properly.

QuarkXPress manages font families in the same manner as most other assets (colors, style sheets, meta tag sets, etc.).

> When you export a Web layout to HTML, the application generates the cascading style sheets for you, automatically appending the class of the fonts you used to the appropriate style sheets.

DEFINE FONT FAMILIES

1. With **cm_site.qxp** open, choose Edit>CSS Font Families.

2. Click New.

3. Scroll through the Available Fonts list. Find and highlight ATC Maple Ultra. Click the right-facing arrow to move it to the Fonts in Font Family list.

4. Scroll through the list and find Verdana (a standard font on most Macintosh and Windows computers). Move it to the Fonts in Font Family list.

5. Scroll through the list and highlight Helvetica. Move it to the Fonts in Font Family list. (If you don't have Helvetica, use Arial.)

> If you don't have Verdana on your computer, skip Step 4. Your font-family definition will have only two defined fonts when you are finished.

6. Choose Sans-serif in the Generic Font menu.

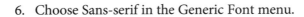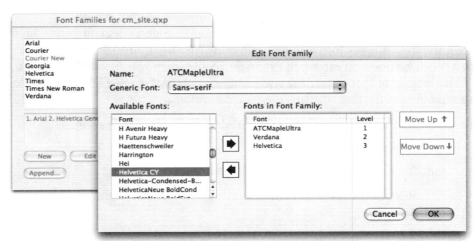

7. Click OK to return to the Font Families dialog box.

8. Click New. Add ATC Pine Bold to the Fonts in Font Family list. Add Times or Times New Roman as the second font in the family, and choose Serif from the Generic Font menu. Click OK.

9. Click New. Add ATC Pine Normal to the Fonts in Font Family list. Add Times or Times New Roman as the second font in the family, and choose Serif from the Generic Font menu. Click OK.

10. The Font Families dialog box should have font families for three of the ATC fonts. Click Save in the Font Families dialog box.

11. Save the project and leave it open.

EXPORTING HTML

When you have finished designing your Web pages, the export process is fairly simple. Choosing File>Export>HTML opens the Export HTML dialog box. If you have defined a site root directory folder in the General pane of the Preferences dialog box, that folder is the default location when you export the layout.

You can choose to export a specific page by changing the Pages field. Even if you have named the pages other than the default Export1, Export2, etc., the pages are still numbered sequentially from top to bottom in the Page Layout palette. The Launch Browser option, active by default, opens the (first) exported page in the browser window when the export is complete. The External CSS File option places the CSS file in the folder to which you are exporting instead of writing CSS information in every HTML page.

The folder you chose for the export process will contain all of the elements of your exported Web page(s). If you opted to include an image folder in the General preferences, any graphic element — including text that is exported as a graphic — is placed in the image folder.

EXPORT WEB PAGES

1. With **cm_site.qxp** open, navigate to the index page.

2. Choose File>Export>HTML.

3. Activate the External CSS File check box.

4. Make sure the Launch Browser check box is active and click Export.

> Be sure you have a layout page — not a master page — active when you choose Export from the File menu.

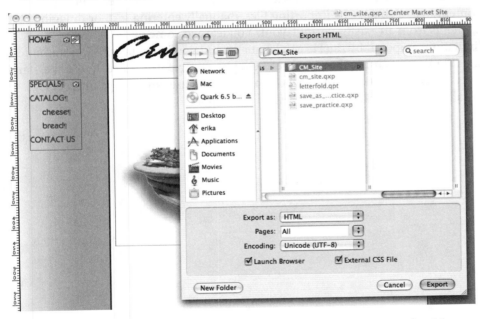

When the exporting process is complete, your default browser should open and display the index.htm page. All of the links in the page should work.

Your CM_Site folder contains all of the necessary files.

5. Close the browser window. Save the QuarkXPress project and close it.

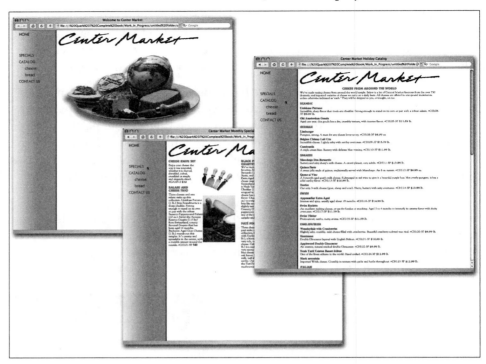

SUMMARY

You have learned how to create a QuarkXPress Web layout, and you now know about the preferences associated with a Web layout. You discovered how to add content to a Web page by importing files, manually entering text, or dragging elements from an existing print layout. You learned some of the stylistic limitations imposed by the HTML language, and you know how to work around those limitations using the Convert to Graphic on Export feature. You understand hyperlinks, destinations, and anchors, and have a basic knowledge of meta tags. Finally, you now know how to preview and export to HTML.

Creating Interactive Web Elements

18

The Web-design tools in QuarkXPress move beyond basic HTML creation. As with any application that is dedicated to creating Web pages, you can add interactive elements — forms, image maps, and rollovers — to a Web page that you design in QuarkXPress. Rather than simply repurposing existing print layouts for Web publishing, these new tools make QuarkXPress a fully functional Web-design application.

IN CHAPTER 18, YOU WILL:

■ Become familiar with the tools that are available when you are working on a QuarkXPress Web layout.

■ Practice building hyperlinks with an image map.

■ Create standard and two-position rollovers in a QuarkXPress layout.

■ Build HTML forms that gather information from users.

The traditional QuarkXPress tools are used to create Web layouts that you can export to HTML without having to understand the complexities of the HTML language. You can create Web pages from scratch or repurpose existing print layouts for the Web. In addition, QuarkXPress includes Web-design tools that move beyond the basic display of information.

When you are building a QuarkXPress Web layout, a new set of Web tools is available that enables you to add interactive elements to your Web pages. Rollovers, image maps, and HTML forms each add interest and functionality to a Web page. Creating these elements traditionally required at least some detailed knowledge of the code languages that drive the interactive features. Using QuarkXPress, you can add interactivity to your Web pages with little (if any) knowledge of HTML, JavaScript, and other languages. This chapter teaches you how to create interactive elements using QuarkXPress.

WEB TOOLS

When you create a QuarkXPress Web layout, a palette of Web tools is available in addition to the standard toolbox. The Web tools appear in a separate palette, and are used in addition to the basic tool set. These tools are used to create the interactive elements of a Web layout, such as image maps and forms. We will discuss the specific applications of each tool throughout this chapter. First we'll introduce the tools and briefly define each.

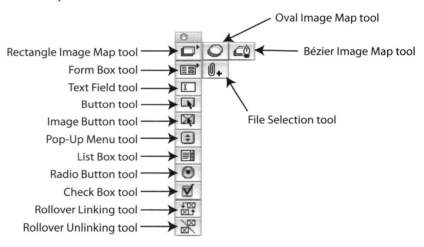

- **Image Map tools.** Three tools — Rectangle, Oval, and Bézier — are available to create image maps.
- **Form Box tool.** This creates a form box, which contains the elements of a Web-layout form. All form fields must be contained within a form box.
- **File Selection tool.** This is used as an element of the form so users of the final Web page can submit a file.
- **Text Field tool.** This creates a text field in a form. Text fields allow the user to enter information, such as a name or email address.
- **Button tool.** This creates a button that initiates some action when clicked.
- **Image Button tool.** This creates a button from a placed image.
- **Pop-Up Menu tool.** This adds a pop-up menu in a form. Pop-up menus allow the user to choose from a specific set of options.

This chapter does not focus on the code that underlies interactive elements unless a particular setting or dialog box requires a basic understanding of the code to make a good choice.

If the Web tools are not visible, you can access them by choosing Window>Tools>Show Web Tools.

- **List Box tool.** This creates a window where users can choose from a specific set of options. Users can scroll through the list of options rather than choosing from a pop-up menu.
- **Radio Button tool.** This creates a radio-button form field, where users can choose one of several defined options.
- **Check Box tool.** This creates a check-box form field, where users can choose one or more of a specific set of options.
- **Rollover Linking tool.** This can be used to define the target of a two-position rollover.
- **Rollover Unlinking tool.** This is used to break the link to the target of a two-position rollover.

CREATING ROLLOVERS

Rollovers are graphic-based hyperlinks that change appearance when the cursor moves over the object, providing a visual indicator that the object is a hyperlink. Rollovers are commonly used to alter the appearance of hyperlink buttons, depending on the position of the user's cursor. Rollovers are typically created using the JavaScript programming language. The Web tools in QuarkXPress allow you to generate standard and two-position rollovers without knowing the correct JavaScript code.

To create a rollover in a Web layout, you have to create different image files for each state of the image. In other words, you create one image that is the default image and a separate image that will appear when the user's cursor passes over the button.

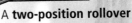

A **two-position rollover** is a rollover in which the object that changes (the target) is separate from the object that initiates the change (the mouseover object). The target is often in a different part of the page than the mouseover object.

ADD ROLLOVERS

1. Open the file **center_site.qxp** from the **RF_Quark7>Chapter18** folder.

2. Navigate to the A-Master A page.

3. Place the file **catering.jpg** into the empty picture box in the top-right corner of the page.

   The first file placed into the box is the default image, or the image that appears when the mouse cursor is not over the box.

4. With the box selected, choose Item>Basic Rollover>Create Rollover.

5. In the Rollover dialog box, click Select/Browse next to the Rollover Image field. Locate the file **catering_over.jpg** and click Open.

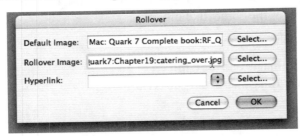

6. Click OK to create the rollover.

    The icons (visual indicators) in the picture box indicate that this box contains a rollover.

7. With the box selected, click Link to Catering in the Hyperlinks palette.

    This is an easy way to assign the correct hyperlink to the rollover images; you don't have to define or choose a hyperlink in the Rollover dialog box.

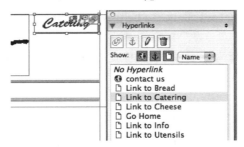

When you create rollovers, it is important to use the Fit Box to Picture command. When a rollover is exported, the rollover image will be disproportionately scaled to fit into the available space.

8. With the rollover image selected, choose Item>Step and Repeat. Make two copies of the image with no horizontal offset and a 35-px vertical offset.

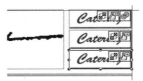

9. Control/right-click the middle image, and choose Basic Rollover>Edit Rollover from the contextual menu.

10. Click the Default Image Select/Browse button. Locate the file **info.jpg** and click Open.

11. Click the Rollover Image Select/Browse button. Locate the file **info_over.jpg** and click Open.

12. Click OK to create the second rollover.

13. With the second picture box still selected, click the Link to Info item in the Hyperlinks palette.

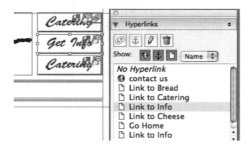

You can also assign a hyperlink by choosing an existing link from the pop-up Hyperlink menu in the Rollover dialog box; however, this method can cause QuarkXPress to crash.

14. Control/right-click the bottom image, and choose Basic Rollover>Edit Rollover from the contextual menu.

15. Make the following changes:

    Default Image: **contact.jpg**
    Rollover Image: **contact_over.jpg**

16. In the Hyperlink field, type "mailto:", and then type your email address (with no spaces).

17. Click OK to create the third rollover.

18. Save the file as "center_v2.qxp" in your **Work_In_Progress** folder.

19. Navigate to the index page. Click the Preview HTML button to view the rollover buttons in your default Web browser.

20. Close the browser window and return to QuarkXPress.

 CREATE TWO-POSITION ROLLOVERS

1. In the open file, navigate to the A-Master A layout.

2. Control/right-click the picture box between the yellow lines, and choose 2-Position Rollovers>Create a 2-Position Target.

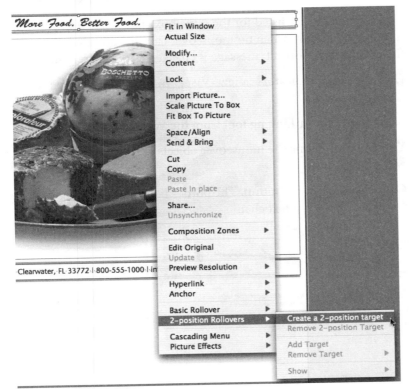

The picture box appears to be empty, but this is not the case. A two-position rollover target box can contain more than one picture file. The original contents of the box have not been deleted, and are considered the default value for that box.

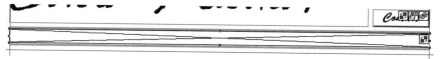

3. Place the file **catering_message.jpg** into the target picture box (File> Import Picture).

4. Control/right-click the picture box, and choose 2-Position Rollovers> Add Target.

5. Place the file **info_message.jpg** into the target picture box.

6. Repeat Steps 5 and 6 to place the file **contact_message.jpg** into the box.

7. Control/right-click the picture box and choose 2-Position Rollovers>Show.

A series of numbers may be attached to the image file name. You can ignore those numbers.

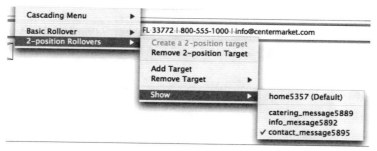

The four images are listed for the same box. The original file, home, is identified as the default; when no mouseover calls the other two files, the home file will display. Contact_message is checked as the current image.

8. Hide the visual indicators (View>Visual Indicators) to make it easier to see the button text.

9. Select the Rollover Linking tool from the Web Tools palette.

You will now define the mouseover objects that determine which message will display.

You can create "hidden" rollover targets by defining a target in an otherwise empty box. When the mouseover is not activated, the location of the rollover remains unseen.

10. Click the Contact Us button. The border becomes marching ants, just as if you were defining a text chain.

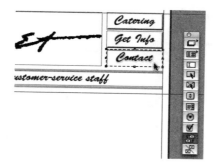

11. Click the picture box with the message content (between the yellow lines) to identify the target.

12. Control/right-click the message picture box. In the contextual menu, choose 2-Position Rollovers>Show>info_message.

13. Select the Rollover Linking tool from the Web Tools palette.

14. Click the Get Info button. The border becomes marching ants.

15. Click the picture box with the message content (between the yellow lines) to identify the target.

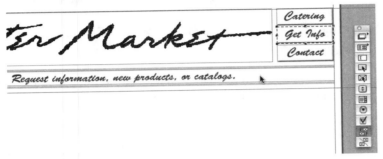

Two-position rollovers do not all have to target the same object. Any picture box, or any text box that is set to export as a graphic can be a two-position rollover target.

16. Control/right-click the message picture box. In the contextual menu, choose 2-Position Rollovers>Show>catering_message.

17. Click the Get Info button with the Rollover Linking tool, and then click the picture box with the message content to identify the target.

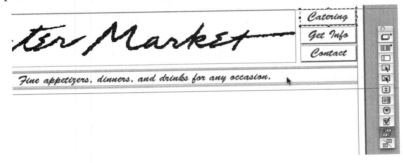

18. Navigate to the page index.htm, and then save the file.

    You cannot preview from a master-page layout.

You cannot preview from a master-page layout.

19. Click the Preview HTML button. Roll the mouse over the Get Info button. Notice that the basic rollover changes the button's appearance, and the two-position rollover changes the message between the yellow lines.

If you roll the mouse over the "Contact Us" button, you should see the mouseover button image and the second message change.

20. Close the browser window and return to QuarkXPress.

CREATING CASCADING MENUS

The Cascading Menu feature enables you to create submenus that only appear when the user moves the mouse over the primary menu. To use cascading menus in a Web layout, you first have to define the menu content and structure. The Edit Cascading Menu dialog box presents the options necessary to define the content and appearance of your menu. When you export the layout to HTML, Quark generates the necessary code for you based on your choices in this dialog box.

 DEFINE CASCADING MENU PROPERTIES

1. With the file **center_v2.qxp** open, choose Edit>Cascading Menus.

2. In the Cascading Menus dialog box, click New.

   The Edit Cascading Menu dialog box opens, presenting all of the options necessary to define the content and appearance of your menu.

3. Type "Navigate" in the Menu Name field.

   In the Menu Properties tab, you define the background color of the menu, as well as assign a character style sheet for formatting the menu text. The Text Inset option is the same as text inset for a regular text box.

   The Menu Orientation radio buttons determine where the hidden menus appear when the cursor passes over the main menu selection.

   The Box Width and Height fields default to Auto, which means the menu backgrounds will be as large as necessary to accommodate the menu text and the specified text inset. You can also define a specific value in these fields, but we recommend leaving them set to Auto.

   The Border options define the size and color edge for each menu option. The Separator options define the size and color of the horizontal (for vertical menus) or vertical (for horizontal menus) bar that separates individual menu options.

   The Opening Animation options allow you to animate the appearance of cascading menus. If anything other than None is selected in the Direction menu, you can also define the Speed (in milliseconds) at which the cascading menus will appear.

   The Offset fields define the position of the menu text within the menu object.

4. In the Menu Properties tab, apply the following settings:

Background Color:	Web Safe #FF6600
Style Sheet:	<u>A</u> Menus
Text Inset:	6 px
Menu Orientation:	Horizontal
Box Width and Height:	Auto
Border:	0 px
Separator:	1 px, Black
Opening Animation:	None

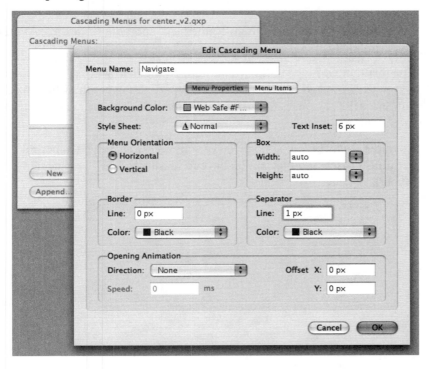

5. Click OK, and click Save in the Cascading Menus dialog box.

6. Save the file and continue to the next exercise.

 DEFINE CASCADING MENU ITEMS

1. With the file **center_v2.qxp** open, choose Edit>Cascading Menus.

2. Highlight Navigate in the list and click Edit.

3. Display the Menu Items tab of the Edit Cascading Menu dialog box.

   The Menu Items tab allows you to define the specific elements of the cascading menu. You can define both menu items (the primary item that opens the submenu when the cursor moves over) and submenu items (those that appear when the cursor moves over the menu item).

4. Click New, and choose Menu Item from the pop-up menu.

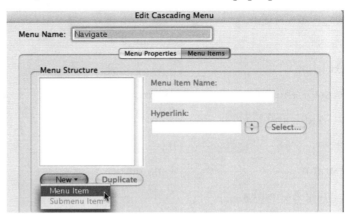

5. Type "Home" in the Menu Item Name field, and type "index.htm" in the Hyperlink field.

The text that you type in the Menu Item Name field will appear as the menu text in the exported HTML page. The Hyperlink field defines the link destination — the page or action that is initiated when the user chooses that menu option.

As in the Rollover dialog box, you cannot access page-type hyperlinks when defining a cascading menu. You have to manually type the page name in the Hyperlink field.

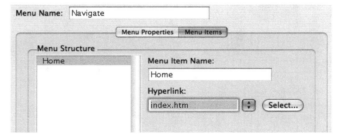

6. Click New>Menu Item again.

7. Type "Products" in the Menu Item Name field; leave the Hyperlink field blank.

8. Repeat this process to add three more menu items:

Menu items do not have to activate a hyperlink.

Menu Item Name	Hyperlink
Catering	catering.htm
Request Info	info.htm
Contact Us	mailto:info@centermarket.com

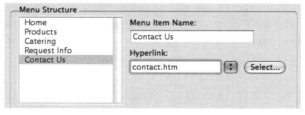

9. Highlight Products in the Menu Structure list, then click New and choose Submenu Item from the pop-up menu.

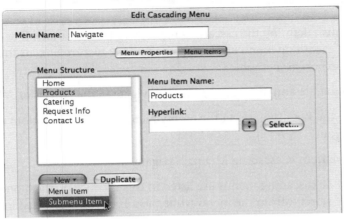

The Submenu Item option is only available when a menu item is highlighted in the Menu Structure pane.

10. Type "Breads" in the Submenu Item Name field, and type "bread.htm" in the Hyperlink field.

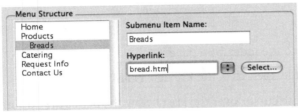

Submenu items are added to the Menu Structure pane, indented below the appropriate menu item.

11. Repeat this process to add two more submenu items under Products:

Submenu Item Name	Hyperlink
Cheese	cheese.htm
Utensils	utensils.htm

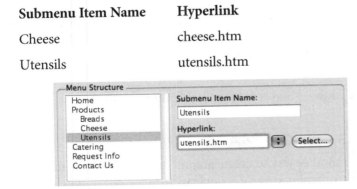

12. In the Menu Item Mouseover and Submenu Item Mouseover areas, choose Web Safe #FF66CC in the Font menus and Black in the Background menus.

The Menu and Submenu Item Mouseover options change the appearance of specific menu elements when they are activated by the mouse.

13. Click OK to close the Edit Cascading Menus dialog box, and click Save in the Cascading Menus dialog box.

14. Save the file and continue to the next exercise.

When creating a submenu item, the options are the same, except you can define only the Submenu Item Name (instead of the Menu Item Name). Submenu items are added to the Menu Structure pane, indented below the appropriate menu item.

PLACE THE CASCADING MENU

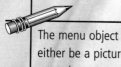

The menu object must either be a picture box or a text box set to export as a graphic.

When you finish defining the cascading menu, you have to attach it to an object in the layout. A cascading menu can be attached to any picture box, or to a text box that is set to export as a graphic.

1. With the file **center_v2.qxp** open, navigate to the A-Master A layout.

2. Using the Item tool, select the empty picture box at the bottom of the layout.

3. Choose Item>Cascading Menu>Navigate.

    Available cascading menus are listed in this menu. To attach one to a box, simply select it from the menu while the target box is selected in the layout.

4. Choose View>Visual Indicators.

    The icon in the top-right corner of the box shows that this is the origin of a cascading menu.

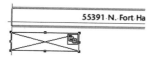

5. Navigate to the index.htm page.

6. Save the file, then click the Preview HTML button.

7. Position the cursor over the area below the bar at the bottom of the screen.

Cascading menus disappear when the cursor is moved off the main menu item.

The cascading menu does not appear until the cursor moves over the containing object. Because of this bug, it might be a good idea to add directions to the user, such as, "Move your cursor over this space to find more options."

8. Close the browser and return to QuarkXPress.

CREATING IMAGE MAPS

An *image map* is another way to create graphic-based hyperlinks in a Web layout. In an image map, different areas of a single picture file can initiate actions or link to other pages. Image maps are created by defining *hot areas* of an image, or the specific shapes that contain the hyperlinks. QuarkXPress includes three tools for creating hot areas — the Rectangle Image Map tool, Oval Image Map tool, and Bézier Image Map tool.

The Image Map tools work in the same way as the regular box tools. You create a rectangular or oval hot area by dragging with the tool; holding down the Shift key while dragging constrains the shapes to squares or circles. The Bézier Image Map tool is used to create nonstandard shapes, just as you would create a uniquely shaped picture box.

CREATE AN IMAGE MAP

1. With **center_v2.qxp** open, make the index page active in the Project window.

2. Double-check that guides are visible (View>Guides).

3. Draw a rectangular text box with the following dimensions:

    X: 10 px   W: 175 px
    Y: 165 px   H: 50 px

4. In the text box, type "Click your favorite food to find similar products."

5. Change the text to 16-pt. ATC Pine Normal.

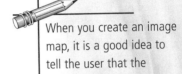

When you create an image map, it is a good idea to tell the user that the image map exists.

6. Choose the Bézier Image Map tool from the Web Tools palette.

7. Draw a hot area, matching the shape of the crackers as closely as possible.

    It might be helpful to zoom in to the appropriate area of the image.

8. With the crackers hot area still active, click Link to Bread in the Hyperlinks palette to define the destination of the hot area.

When a hot area is selected, you can see its anchor points. Make sure that you select the actual area — not the image — before pressing Delete.

9. Change the view percentage back to 100% by pressing Command/Control-1.

10. Choose View>Guides. The hot area is not visible while guides are turned off, but the image map visual indicator still appears in the top-right corner of the picture box.

11. Choose View>Guides. The hot area is visible as long as the image is selected.

To view the hot areas of an image map, you have to choose View>Guides, and then select the image with the Content or Item tool.

12. Using the Bézier Image Map tool, create another hot area that closely matches the shape of the cheese knife.

13. Click Link to Utensils in the Hyperlinks palette to define the hot area.

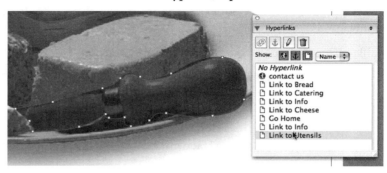

14. Draw a third hot area that covers the three different cheeses in the image (not the paté). Be careful to not overlap the two hot areas that you already drew. Assign the Link to Cheese hyperlink destination to the third hot area.

15. Save the file. Click the Preview HTML button to view your page in the default browser. When you move the mouse over any of the hot areas that you created, you see the pointing-hand icon.

Click your favorite food to find similar products.

16. Close the browser window and return to the QuarkXPress file.

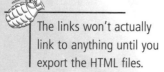

BUILDING AN HTML FORM

HTML forms are used to gather information from people who visit your Web site. Forms can include text fields, menus of specific options, radio buttons, check boxes, and buttons that initiate some activity. Forms can be simple, collecting information from the user and sending the information to the site administrator. Forms can also be complex, interacting with the user by presenting different options, depending on the user's choices.

DEFINE AN HTML FORM BOX

To add a form to a QuarkXPress Web page, you begin by creating a form box, which will contain all the elements of the form. The Form Box tool is used in exactly the same way as the Rectangle Box tool.

When you create a form box, you define the form's properties in the Form tab of the Modify dialog box. The options in this dialog box are used when QuarkXPress generates the HTML code for the form.

1. With **center_v2.qxp** open, navigate to the info page.

2. Using the Form Box tool, draw a form box with the following dimensions:

   X: 10 px   W: 777 px
   Y: 163 px   H: 400 px

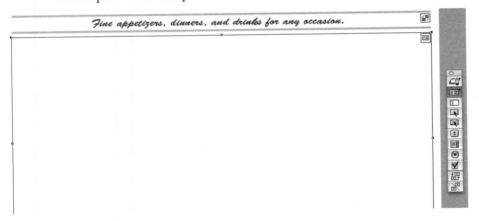

3. With the form box selected, open the Modify dialog box and access the Form tab.

4. In the Name field, type "InfoRequest".

   Each form in your Web site should have a unique, meaningful name.

5. Choose Get from the Method menu.

   This menu defines what happens when the user submits the form:

   - **Post** sends the data to the Web server as a separate file. This option is the most common for a form that asks the users to submit data. Using this option, the encoding menu defines the MIME-type encoding option (urlencoded, form-data, or plain) for submitted data.

   - **Get** attaches the data to the end of a URL in the Address line of the browser window, as you might see when you use a search engine. If you choose the Get method, submitted data is limited to 100 characters.

You can also convert a text or picture box to a form box using the Content options in the contextual menu accessed by Control/right-clicking any existing box.

If Visual Indicators (View>Visual Indicators) are active, a form box is identified by a Form icon in the top-right corner.

MIMEs (Multi-purpose Internet Mail Extensions) are helper applications used by the browser or server to translate data.

6. Choose _self from the Target menu.

When a user submits a form, some type of response screen is typically displayed — either a "thank you" message, or an error message showing which required fields were not filled in. The Target option defines where the response information is displayed:

- **_blank** opens a new browser window to display the destination page.
- **_self** places the destination in the same window (or frame) as the origin.
- **_top** removes any frames and displays the destination in the entire browser window.
- **_parent** is only relevant if you are working with nested frame sets. Otherwise, it functions the same as _top.

7. In the Action field, type "thanks.htm".

This field defines what occurs when the user submits the form. You can enter a URL, or click Select/Browse to locate a CGI script on your computer.

8. Leave the Form Validation field at the default setting.

The Form Validation area defines what happens when the user submits a form without filling a required field. If **Error Page** is selected, you can define the URL of a specific page that presents an error message. **Dialog Message** presents a simple error dialog box if the user submits a form without some piece of required information.

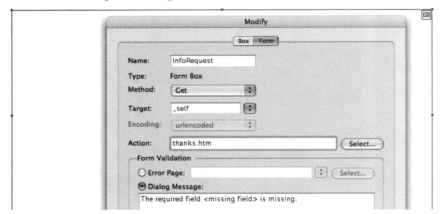

9. Click OK to apply the settings to the form box.

10. Save the file and continue to the next section.

Defining Post-Form Actions

We have said that you don't need to know much about HTML to design a Web site in QuarkXPress. While this is true, you do need to understand a little about HTML actions to create a form that works.

When you click the Submit button (regardless of the text that appears on that button) on a Web-page form, you are initiating an action that calls a URL. The Action field in the Modify dialog box specifies the URL that is called when a user clicks the Submit button.

If you use the Post-form method, the Action URL must contain the name of a CGI script or Active Server Page (with the extension .asp), which are applications run by the server to process the form data.

ADD FORM TEXT FIELDS

Form fields are used to gather the specific pieces of information that you want to collect. The Web layout tools allow you to create eight different kinds of form fields. All form fields must be entirely contained within the form box. If you add a form field outside of a form box, a new form box is created automatically.

1. On the info page of **center_v2.qxp**, draw a rectangular text box with the following dimensions:

   X: 20 px   W: 105 px
   Y: 175 px   H: 20 px

2. In the new text box, type "Name:" and apply right paragraph alignment.

3. Using the Text Field tool, drag to create a text field on the page.

4. Using the Measurements palette, change the dimensions of the text field to:

   X: 140 px   W: 275 px
   Y: 175 px

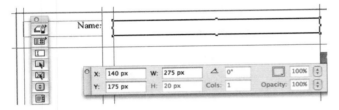

The Text Field tool creates a text field, in which a user can type information. You can change the width of the field by dragging the left- or right-center handles of the field, but you cannot change the field height.

5. With the text field selected, open the Form tab of the Modify dialog box.

   The Type menu is used to change the appearance of the text field. By default, new text fields are created as single-line fields. If you choose Text – Multi Line, the field displays a scroll bar on the right edge.

6. Type "UserName" in the Name field, and activate the Required check box. Click OK.

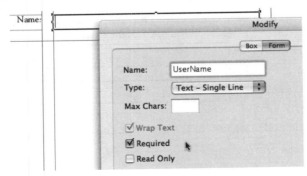

Form field names cannot contain spaces. Common conventions are to begin each word in the phrase with a capital letter (FirstName), or to use the underscore character between each word (First_Name).

When the Required check box is selected, the user must fill in the field.

> You can change the height and width of a multi-line text field by dragging any handle of the field. If you choose this option, you can also determine if entered text automatically wraps to fit the width of the box. Deselecting the Wrap Text check box adds a horizontal scroll bar to the bottom of the text field.

> If you choose Password from the Type menu, the text field automatically changes back to a single-line text field. There is no visual difference between a password and a single-line text field within the QuarkXPress environment. When the user types in a password field, however, the text appears as a series of asterisks.

7. Select both the text box and the text field and duplicate them (Item>Duplicate). Position the duplicated objects at X: 20 px, Y: 210 px.

8. Change the text in the duplicate text box to "Email Address:".

9. In the Form tab of the Modify dialog box, change the Name field to "UserEmail" and click OK.

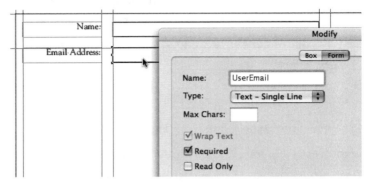

10. Select the second text box and the second text field.

11. Use Step and Repeat to make five copies of the boxes, with a 0-px horizontal offset and a 30-px vertical offset.

12. Change the text and field names as follows:

	Text	Field Name
Third set:	Street Address:	UserStreet
Fourth set:	City:	UserCity
Fifth set:	State:	UserState
Sixth set:	Zip Code:	UserZip
Seventh set:	Phone Number:	UserPhone

13. Save the file and continue to the next exercise.

WORKING WITH MENUS

An HTML form can include a list of predefined choices, from which the user selects one or more options. Pop-up menus allow the user to select a single option from a defined list, such as the month or year; list boxes can be useful if you want the user to be able to select more than one option from the list.

The advantage of using a pop-up menu or list box is that you can force the user to select from the options that you present. QuarkXPress manages those options in sets, which you can create by choosing Edit>Menus. The Menus dialog box contains the familiar options from other QuarkXPress dialog boxes (e.g., Colors, Style Sheets, etc.).

DEFINE MENU SETS

1. With **center_v2.qxp** open, choose Edit>Menus and click New in the Menus dialog box.

2. In the Edit Menu dialog box, type "Sources" in the Name field.

3. Click Add in the Edit Menu dialog box.

4. In the Menu Item dialog box, type "Magazine Ad" in the Name field and type "magazine" in the Value field.

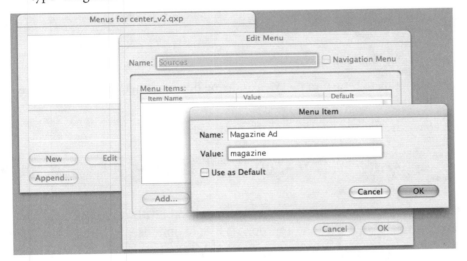

The Name is the text that will appear in the menu; the Value is the text that is sent to the server when the form is submitted.

5. Click OK to return to the Edit Menu dialog box.

6. Using the same process as in Steps 4 and 5, add more list items using the following settings:

Name	Value
Radio Ad	radio
Newspaper	newspaper
Internet Search Engine	internet
Friend/Family	friend
Email Ad	email

The Use as Default check box in the Menu Item dialog box allows you to specify the default value of a particular menu set. The default value is the default text in a pop-up menu, and it is automatically highlighted in a list box. If you do not specify a default option, the first item you enter will be considered the default.

If the Navigation Menu check box is active in the Edit Menu dialog box, the menu set that you create presents options that initiate actions, which are defined in the Value field of the Menu Item dialog box. For a navigation menu, the value of each menu item should generally be a URL.

7. Click OK to return to the Menus dialog box.

8. Click New in the Menus dialog box. Create a new menu named "Interests", using the following Names and Values:

Name	Value
Cooking	cooking
Restaurants	restaurants
Fitness	fitness
Travel	travel

Because this example involves a simple list of options, the name and the value of each item are the same. This is not a requirement.

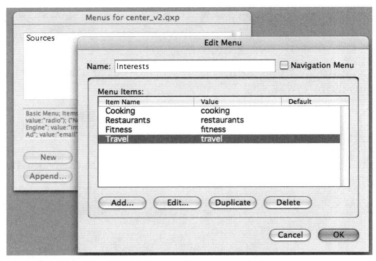

9. Click OK to return to the Menus dialog box, and then click Save to save the menus.

10. Save the file and continue to the next exercise.

CREATE A POP-UP MENU

After menus are defined, the Pop-Up Menu tool and List Box tool are used to create form fields that hold the appropriate lists of options.

1. On the info page of the file **center_v2.qxp**, draw a rectangular text box with the following dimensions:

   X: 430 px   W: 345 px
   Y: 175 px   H: 20 px

2. In the text box, type "How did you learn about Center Market?"

3. Using the Pop-Up Menu tool, draw a pop-up menu on the page. Change the position of the pop-up menu to X: 460 px, Y: 200 px.

4. With the pop-up menu selected in the layout, open the Form tab of the Modify dialog box.

   The Type menu defaults to the type of object you are modifying (pop-up menu or list box). You can change the selected field from a pop-up menu to a list box, or from a list box to a pop-up menu.

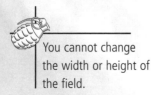

You cannot change the width or height of the field.

5. Change the Name field to "Reference".

6. Choose Sources from the Menu menu.

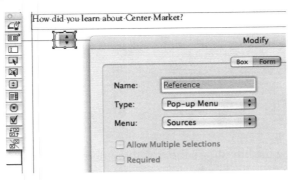

The Menu menu lists all sets that appear in the Menus dialog box. You can also choose New to create and apply a new menu set from within the Modify dialog box.

7. Click OK to close the Modify dialog box.

The list items automatically appear in the menu field, and the width of the field is adjusted as necessary.

8. Save the file and continue to the next exercise.

 CREATE A LIST MENU

1. On the info page of the file **center_v2.qxp**, use the Item tool to select the pop-up menu and the text box directly above it.

2. Make a duplicate of the selected objects; position the duplicate at X: 430 px, Y: 230 px.

3. Change the duplicate text box to "What types of things interest you?"

4. Select the duplicate pop-up menu, and open the Form tab of the Modify dialog box.

5. Change the Name field to "Interests", choose List from the Type menu, and choose Interests from the Menu menu.

6. Activate the Allow Multiple Selections check box and deactivate the Required check box.

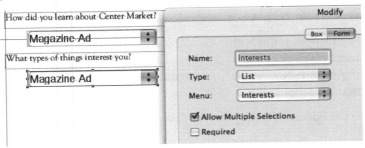

7. Click OK to apply the changes to the field.

The list-box field changes horizontally to match the longest item in the menu, and it expands vertically to display the first three items in the menu.

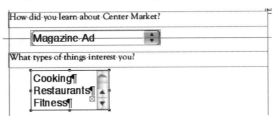

By default, a list box shows the first three items in the list. You can modify the height of the list box by dragging the top- or bottom-center handle; you cannot modify the box width.

8. Save the file and continue to the next section.

CREATING RADIO BUTTONS AND CHECK BOXES

Radio buttons are frequently used to present a list of options from which the user can select only one choice. Check boxes are frequently used to allow users to choose more than one available option.

QuarkXPress includes a Radio Button tool and a Check Box tool that make these elements easy to create. Once created, a radio button can also be converted to a check box (and vice versa).

 ADD A RADIO-BUTTON GROUP

1. On the info page of **center_v2.qxp**, duplicate one of the text boxes in the right side of the form and position it at X: 430 px, Y: 320 px.

2. Change the text to "Who is the primary shopper in your family?"

3. Using the Radio Button tool, draw a radio button on the page below the new text box. Position the radio button at X: 460 px, Y: 350 px.

When you create a radio button, the box automatically expands to fit the height and width of the radio button.

4. Change the width of the radio-button box to 250 px and the height to 19 px.

The box containing the radio button is a kind of text box, which you can resize by dragging any handle.

5. With the radio-button box selected, activate the Content tool.

You can label a radio button or add text that defines the radio buttons for the user by selecting the radio-button box with the Content tool. The text in a radio-button box can be formatted in any way you like, just as you would format any other text in a Web layout.

6. Press the Spacebar, and then type "Female head of household".

7. Open the Form tab of the Modify dialog box.

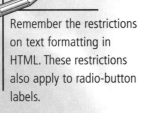

Remember the restrictions on text formatting in HTML. These restrictions also apply to radio-button labels.

8. In the Group field, type "Shopper".

The Group field defines the set of radio buttons that are treated as a single set; any radio buttons that have the same Group name are treated as part of the group.

9. In the Value field, type "FemaleHH".

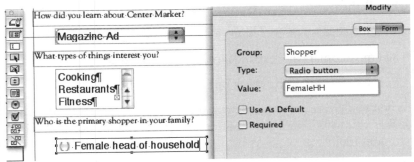

The Value field defines the data that is sent to the server if the user selects that option.

10. Click OK to close the Modify dialog box.

11. Choose Item>Step and Repeat. Make three copies of the radio-button box with Horizontal Offset: 0, Vertical Offset: 20 px.

12. Change the text after the second radio button to "Male head of household".

13. In the Form tab of the Modify dialog box, change the Value field to "MaleHH". Click OK.

Because you duplicated the original radio button, the Group field is already set to "Shopper" for the additional radio buttons.

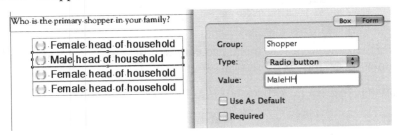

14. Change the remaining two radio buttons as follows:

	Text	**Value**
Third:	Children	children
Fourth:	Hired assistant	assistant

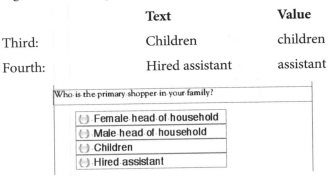

15. Save the file and continue to the next exercise.

Like changing list boxes to pop-up menus, you can change a radio button into a check box, and a check box into a radio button using the Type menu in the Form tab of the Modify dialog box.

When one radio button in a group is marked as Required, all other buttons in the group are also marked as Required. This means that the user must choose one radio button in the group.

You can assign a default selection by activating the Use As Default check box for the radio button you want to be automatically selected.

To designate a radio button as the default choice in a group, click the radio button in the layout with the Content tool.

ADD CHECK BOXES

1. On the info page of the file **center_v2.qxp**, duplicate one of the text boxes in the right side of the form and position it at X: 430 px, Y: 440 px.

2. Change the text to "What type of information would you like to receive?"

3. Using the Check Box tool, draw a check box at X: 460 px, Y: 470 px.

   The box automatically expands to fit the check box.

4. Change the width of the check box field to 200 px.

   When you create a check box with the Check Box tool, you can add a label, just as you would for a radio button, by expanding the box and using the Content tool.

5. Select the Content tool.

   The insertion point flashes immediately after the check box.

6. Press the Spacebar, then type "Holiday catalog".

7. Open the Form tab of the Modify dialog box. Type "SendCatalog" in the Name field, and type "yes" in the Value field.

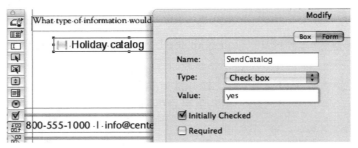

8. Use Step and Repeat to make two copies of the check box with 0-px horizontal offset and 20-px vertical offset.

9. Change the two new check boxes as follows:

	Text	**Name**
Second check box:	Email specials	SendEmail
Third check box:	Catering menus	SendCatering

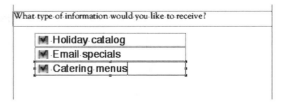

10. Save the file and continue to the next exercise.

CREATING BUTTONS

Virtually every form includes at least one — and sometimes many — buttons. QuarkXPress includes four different tools that are used to add buttons to a form: the [Text] Button tool, the Image Button tool, and the File Selection tool.

The Button tool allows you to create buttons that, when clicked, either submit or reset the form.

1. On the info page of the file **center_v2.qxp**, select the Button tool from the Web Tools palette.

2. Draw a text button on the page, positioned at X: 140 px, Y: 508 px.

   When you create a button in a Web layout, it defaults to 15 pixels wide by 20 pixels high. You cannot drag any handles to resize the button on the page.

3. With the button selected, activate the Content tool.

   The insertion point flashes inside the button. You add text to a button by selecting it with the Content tool, then typing as you would in any text box.

4. Type "Reset".

   When you add text to a button, the button automatically resizes horizontally to accommodate the text you enter. You do not, however, have any control over the appearance of the text.

5. Open the Form tab of the Modify dialog box.

6. Type "Reset" in the Name field. Choose Reset from the Type menu and click OK.

   In the Form tab of the Modify dialog box, you can assign a meaningful name to the button. The Type menu presents two options: Submit and Reset. If you choose Submit, clicking the button submits the user's information. If you choose Reset, clicking the button clears any information entered by the user.

7. Create another text button, positioned at X: 230 px, Y: 508 px.

8. Select the Content tool and type "Submit".

9. In the Form tab of the Modify dialog box, type "Submit" in the Name field, and choose Submit from the Type menu. Click OK.

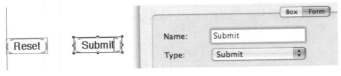

10. Save the file and continue to the next section.

Adding Image Buttons

Because you have very limited control over the appearance of a text-based button, you can use the Image Button tool to create a stylized Submit button using an image created in another application. The Image Button tool creates a picture box that is very similar to a regular picture box.

Once the image button box is created, you can import an image by choosing File>Get Picture. An image placed into an image-button box can be scaled and manipulated as you would modify any other placed image.

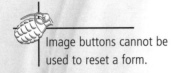
Image buttons cannot be used to reset a form.

In the Form tab of the Modify dialog box, you only have the option to name the button. Image buttons cannot be used to reset the form. When you are using an image button, the Export tab of the Modify dialog box presents the same options as for any other image used in the Web page. Remember to add alt text that defines the button's function.

Adding File Selection Buttons

The File Selection tool creates a Browse button in the form; the user can click this button to locate a file that will be uploaded when the form is submitted. To the left of the button a text field appears, which will display the path to the user-selected file. You can drag the left- or right-center handle to enlarge the text field next to the button, but you cannot change the size of the button.

In the Form tab of the Modify dialog box, you can define a name for the file field that you place in the layout. The Type option is automatically set to File and cannot be changed. The Accept field allows you to define the type of files that can be uploaded with this button. You can make this a required field using the Required check box.

 EXPORT THE WEB SITE

1. From your desktop, create a new folder named "CM_Site2" in your **Work_In_Progress** folder.

2. With **center_v2.qxp** open, navigate to the index page.

3. Access the Preferences dialog box and select Web Layout General from the list of categories.

4. Click the Select/Browse button next to the Site Root Directory field.

5. Navigate to the **CM_Site2** folder and click Choose/OK.

6. Click OK to close the Preferences dialog box.

7. Choose File>Export>HTML.

8. Activate the Launch Browser and External CSS File check boxes, and then click Export.

9. If you get a missing picture message, click Update and locate the necessary files in the **RF_Quark7>Chapter18** folder. Click Continue when all the images have been located.

When the export process is complete, your browser should open and correctly display the rollovers, image maps, and form.

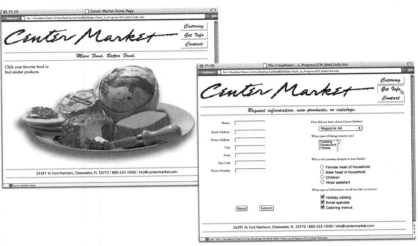

10. Close the browser window, and close the QuarkXPress file.

SUMMARY

Using the Web-design tools in QuarkXPress, you can now create a fully functional, interactive Web site in the environment with which you are already acquainted. You learned how to create image maps to add visual interest and functionality to your Web pages. You also discovered how to define rollover buttons without knowing a single line of JavaScript code. Finally, you learned how to create and define an HTML form, including all of the different fields that you can add to a form. By combining the basic Web-design capabilities that you learned in Chapter 17 with these interactive elements, you can use QuarkXPress to create attractive and effective Web pages.

Keyboard Shortcuts

	MACINTOSH	WINDOWS
Managing Projects		
Create a new project	Command-N	Control-N
Create a new library	Command-Option-N	Control-Alt-N
Open	Command-O	Control-O
Open and reflow text into v7 format	Option-Open button in Open dialog box	Alt-Open
Save	Command-S	Control-S
Save As	Command-Option-S	Control-Alt-S
Save Text	Command-Option-E	Control-Alt-E
Save Page as EPS	Command-Option-Shift-S	Control-Alt-Shift-S
Revert to last auto save	Option-File>Revert to Saved	Alt-Revert to Saved
Print	Command-P	Control-P
Output Job dialog box	Command-Option-P	Control-Alt-P
Close active project	Command-W	Control-F4
Close all projects	Command-Option-W	
Quit	Command-Q	Control-Q / Alt-F4 / Alt-Shift-F4
Help		F1
Layout Properties	Command-Option-Shift-P	Control-Alt-Shift-P
Page Properties (Web layout)	Command-Option-Shift-A	Control-Alt-Shift-A
Preferences dialog box	Command-Option-Shift-Y	Control-Alt-Shift-Y
Stop redraw	Command-Period (.)	Escape
Force redraw	Command-Option-Period (.)	Shift-Escape
Open contextual menu	Control-click or Right-click	Right-click
Redo	Command-Shift-Z	Control-Y
Undo	Command-Z	Control-Z

Managing the Workspace

	MACINTOSH	WINDOWS
NAVIGATE THE PROJECT WINDOW		
Zoom in 25%	Command-=	Control-=
Zoom out 25%	Command-Hyphen (-)	Control-Hyphen (-)
View at 100%	Command-1	Control-1
Toggle between 100% and 200%	Command-Option-click	Control-Alt-click
Fit Page in Window	Command-0	Control-0
Fit Spread in Window	Command-Option-0	Control-Alt-0 / Shift-F3
Fit spread in window	Option-View>Fit in Window	Alt-Fit in Window
View Thumbnails	Shift-F6 or Option-Shift-F6	Shift-F6
Highlight View Percentage field of Project window	Control-V	Control-Alt-V
Drag project in window (all but Zoom tool)	Option-click	Alt-click
Access Zoom In tool (temporary)	Control-Shift-click	Control-Spacebar
Access Zoom Out tool (temporary)	Control-Option-click	Control-Alt-Spacebar
Minimize/Maximize project window		F3
Access project window contextual menu		Alt-Hyphen (-)

Keyboard Shortcuts

	MACINTOSH	WINDOWS
Managing the Workspace (cont'd)		

NAVIGATE LAYOUTS

	MACINTOSH	WINDOWS
Display next layout in project	Command-apostrophe	Alt-apostrophe
Toggle between layout page and related master page	Shift-F10*	Shift-F4
Display next master page†	Option-F10	Control-Shift-F4
Display previous master page†	Option-Shift-F10	Control-Shift-F3

Used by Macintosh system default settings (Expose); this will override the QuarkXPress behavior
† (only works when already on a master page)

NAVIGATE PAGES

	MACINTOSH	WINDOWS
Scroll window up one screen	Page Up / Control-K	Page Up
Scroll window down one screen	Page Down / Control-L	Page Down
Go to beginning of layout	Home / Control-A	Home
Go to end of layout	End / Control-D	End
Go to Previous page	Shift-Page Up* / Control-Shift-K	Control-Home / Shift-Page Up
Go to Next Page	Shift-PG Down* / Control-Shift-L	Control-End / Shift-Pg Down
Go to First Page	Shift-Home* / Control-Shift-A	Control-Page Up / Shift-Home
Go to Last Page	Shift-End* / Control-Shift-D	Control-Page Down / Shift-End
Go to previous spread	Option-Page Up	Alt-Page Up
Go to next spread	Option-Page Down	Alt-Page Down
Go To Page	Command-J	Control-J
Insert Pages	Option-drag master page into Page Layout palette	Alt-drag master page into Page Layout palette

You can also substitute Command for Shift

Controlling Guides

	MACINTOSH	WINDOWS
Show/Hide Rulers	Command-R	Control-R
Show/Hide Guides	F7	F7
Show/Hide Baseline Grid	Option-F7	Control-F7
Snap to Guides (toggle on and off)	Shift-F7	Shift-F7
Delete horizontal ruler guides	Option-click horizontal ruler	Alt-click horizontal ruler
Delete vertical ruler guides — doesn't work	Option-click vertical rule	Alt-click vertical ruler

Accessing Tools

	MACINTOSH	WINDOWS
Switch between Item and Content tool	Shift-F8	Shift-F8
Change from Content to Item tool (temporary)	Command-	Control-
Select next tool (down)	Option-F8 / Command-Option-Tab	Control-F8 / Control-Alt-Tab
Select next tool (up)	Option-Shift-F8 / Command-Option-Shift-Tab	Control-Shift-F8 / Control-Alt-Shift-Tab
Keep tool selected	Option-click tool	Alt-click tool
Access Zoom In tool (temporary)	Control-Shift-click	Control-Spacebar
Access Zoom Out tool (temporary)	Control-Option-click	Control-Alt-Spacebar
Tool Preferences	Double-click tool	Double-click tool

Keyboard Shortcuts

	MACINTOSH	WINDOWS
Working with Palettes		
Show/Hide Tools palette	F8	F8
Show/Hide Measurements palette	F9	F9
Toggle backward through Measurements palette modes	Command-Option-Comma (,)	Control-Alt-Comma (,)
Toggle forward through Measurements palette modes	Command-Option-Semicolon (;)	Control-Alt-Semicolon (;)
Show/Hide Page Layout palette	F10	F4
Show/Hide Style Sheets palette	F11	F11
Show/Hide Colors palette	F12	F12
Show/Hide Lists palette	Option-F11	Control-F11
Show/Hide Trap Information palette	Option-F12	Control-F12
Select contiguous items in list/palette	Shift-click	Shift-click
Select noncontiguous items in list/palette	Command-click	Control-click
Interacting with Dialog Boxes/Palettes		
Go to next field	Tab	Tab
Go to previous field	Shift-Tab	Shift-Tab
Display next tab	Command-Option-Tab	Control-Tab
Display previous tab	Command-Option-Shift-Tab	Control-Shift-Tab
OK (or highlighted button)	Return	Enter
Cancel changes and close dialog box	Command-Period (.)	ESC
No	Command-N	N
Yes	Command-Y	Y
Apply	Command-A	Alt-A
Set (Tabs tab of Paragraph Attributes dialog box)	Command-S	Alt-S
Controlling Usage		
Fonts pane of Usage dialog box	F13 / Command-F6 / Command-Shift-F6	F2
Pictures pane of Usage dialog box	Option-F13 / Command-Option-F6	Shift-F2
Change Update... to Update all button	Option	Alt
Creating & Controlling Text		
Import Text	Command-E	Control-E
Select All text in story (Insertion point placed in story)	Command-A	Control-A
Copy selected text	Command-C	Control-C
Cut selected text	Command-X	Control-X
Paste clipboard contents at insertion point	Command-V	Control-V
Show/Hide Invisible characters	Command-I	Control-I
Enter next character using Symbol font	Command-Option-Q	Control-Alt-Q
Enter next character in Zapf Dingbats font	Command-Option-Z	
Delete previous character	Delete	Backspace
Delete next character	Shift-Delete	Delete / Shift-Backspace
Delete previous word	Command-Delete	Control-Backspace
Delete next word	Command-Shift-Delete	Control-Delete / Control-Shift-Backspace

Keyboard Shortcuts

	MACINTOSH	WINDOWS
Navigating & Selecting Text		
Select word	Double-click word	Double-click word
Select word and its punctuation	Double-click space between two words	Double-click space between two words
Select entire line	Three clicks on text	Three clicks on text
Select entire paragraph	Four clicks on text	Four clicks on text
Select entire story	Five clicks on text	Five clicks on text
Move insertion point to previous character*	Left Arrow	Left Arrow
Move insertion point to next character*	Right Arrow	Right Arrow
Move insertion point down one line*	Down Arrow	Down Arrow
Move insertion point up one line*	Up Arrow	Up Arrow
Move insertion point to beginning of previous word*	Command-Left Arrow	Control-Left Arrow
Move insertion point to beginning of next word*	Command-Right Arrow	Control-Right Arrow
Move insertion point to beginning of line*	Command-Option-Left Arrow	Control-Alt-Left Arrow
Move insertion point to end of line*	Command-Option-Right Arrow	Control-Alt-Right Arrow
Move insertion point to beginning of paragraph or previous paragraph*	Command-Up Arrow	Control-Up Arrow Control-Alt-Up Arrow
Move insertion point to beginning of next paragraph*	Command-Down Arrow	Control-Down Arrow Control-Alt-Down Arrow
Move insertion point to beginning of story*	Command-Option-Up Arrow	Control-Home
Move insertion point to end of story*	Command-Option-Down Arrow	Control-End

Add Shift to move insertion point and select intervening text

Formatting Text

CHANGE FONT & TYPE SIZE

	MACINTOSH	WINDOWS
Apply Next Available Font	Option-F9	Control-F9
Apply Previous Available Font	Option-Shift-F9	Control-Shift-F9
Highlight Font field in Classic or Text modes of Measurements palette	Command-Option-Shift-M	Control-Alt-Shift-M
Decrease type size 1 point	Command-Option-Shift-Comma (,)	Control-Alt-Shift-Comma (,)
Decrease type size to next preset	Command-Shift-Comma (,)	Control-Shift-Comma (,)
Increase type size 1 point	Command-Option-Shift-Period (.)	Control-Alt-Shift-Period (.)
Increase type size to next preset	Command-Shift-Period (.)	Control-Shift-Period (.)

APPLY CHARACTER FORMATTING

	MACINTOSH	WINDOWS
Decrease text horizontal scale 5%	Command-[	Control-[
Decrease text horizontal scale 1%	Command-Option-[	Control-Alt-[
Increase text horizontal scale 5%	Command-]	Control-]
Increase text horizontal scale 1%	Command-Option-]	Control-Alt-]
Decrease kerning/tracking 10 units (1/20 em)	Command-Shift-[	Control-Shift-[
Decrease kerning/tracking 1 unit (1/200 em)	Command-Option-Shift-[	Control-Alt-Shift-[
Increase kerning/tracking 10 units (1/20 em)	Command-Shift-]	Control-Shift-]
Increase kerning/tracking 1 unit (1/200 em)	Command-Option-Shift-]	Control-Alt-Shift-]
Baseline shift down (−) 1 pt.	Command-Option-Shift-Hyphen (-)	Control-Alt-Shift-9
Baseline shift up (+) 1 pt.	Command-Option-Shift-=	Control-Alt-Shift-0

Keyboard Shortcuts

Formatting Text (continued)

APPLY TYPE STYLE

	MACINTOSH	WINDOWS
Bold type style	Command-Shift-B	Control-Shift-B
Small Caps type style	Command-Shift-H	Control-Shift-H
Italic type style	Command-Shift-I	Control-Shift-I
All Caps type style	Command-Shift-K	Control-Shift-K
Outline type style	Command-Shift-O	Control-Shift-O
Plain type style	Command-Shift-P	Control-Shift-P
Shadow type style	Command-Shift-S	Control-Shift-S
Underline type style	Command-Shift-U	Control-Shift-U
Superior type style	Command-Shift-V	Control-Shift-V
Word Underline type style	Command-Shift-W	Control-Shift-W
Strikethrough type style	Command-Shift-/	Control-Shift-/
Subscript type style	Command-Shift-Hyphen (-)	Control-Shift-9
Superscript type style	Command-Shift-=	Control-Shift-0
Activate ligatures	Command-Shift-G	Control-Shift-G

APPLY PARAGRAPH FORMATTING

	MACINTOSH	WINDOWS
Decrease leading 1 pt.	Command-Shift-;	Control-Shift-;
Decrease leading 1/10 pt.	Command-Option-Shift-;	Control-Alt-Shift-;
Increase leading 1 pt.	Command-Shift-apostrophe	Control-Shift-apostrophe
Increase leading 1/10 pt.	Command-Option-Shift-apostrophe	Control-Alt-Shift-apostrophe
Centered paragraph alignment	Command-Shift-C	Control-Shift-C
Justified paragraph alignment	Command-Shift-J	Control-Shift-J
Left paragraph alignment	Command-Shift-L	Control-Shift-L
Right paragraph alignment	Command-Shift-R	Control-Shift-R
Force Justified paragraph alignment	Command-Option-Shift-J	Control-Alt-Shift-J

COPY FORMATTING

	MACINTOSH	WINDOWS
Copy formatting from paragraph clicked to paragraph with insertion point (or selected text)	Option-Shift-click paragraph	Alt-Shift-click paragraph

OVERRIDE FORMATTING WITH STYLE SHEETS

	MACINTOSH	WINDOWS
Apply None, then apply style sheet	Option-click style sheet in palette	Alt-click style sheet in palette
Override local paragraph but not character formatting	Option-Shift-click style sheet in palette	Alt-Shift-click style sheet in palette

ACCESS FORMATTING DIALOG BOXES

	MACINTOSH	WINDOWS
Character Attributes dialog box	Command-Shift-D	Control-Shift-D
Character Attributes dialog box (Type Size field highlighted)	Command-Shift-\	Control-Shift-\
Formats tab of Paragraph Attributes dialog box	Command-Shift-F	Control-Shift-F
Formats tab of Paragraph Attributes dialog box (Leading field highlighted)	Command-Shift-E	Control-Shift-E
Tabs tab of Paragraph Attributes dialog box	Command-Shift-T	Control-Shift-T
Rules tab of Paragraph Attributes dialog box	Command-Shift-N	Control-Shift-N
Paragraph Preferences dialog box: Paragraph pane	Command-Option-Y	Control-Alt-Y

Keyboard Shortcuts

	MACINTOSH	WINDOWS
Searching		
Open Find/Change dialog box	Command-F	Control-F
Close Find/Change dialog box	Command-Option-F	Control-Alt-F
Change Find Next button to Find First button	Option-	Alt
Find wild card	Command-/	Control-/
Checking Spelling		
Check Spelling — Layout	Command-Option-Shift-L	Control-Alt-Shift-W
Check Spelling — Story	Command-Option-L	Control-Alt-W
Check Spelling — Word/Selection	Command-L	Control-W
Show suggested hyphenation	Command-Option-Shift-H	Control-Alt-Shift-H
Lookup	Command-L	Alt-L
Skip	Command-S	Alt-S
Add	Command-A	Alt-A
Add all suspects to auxiliary	Option-Shift-click Done button	Alt-Shift-click Close
Indexing		
Open Index palette; Activate Text field when palette is already visible	Command-Option-I	Control-Alt-I
Add button in Index palette	Command-Option-Shift-I	Control-Alt-Shift-I
Change Add to Add Reversed button	Option-	Alt
Creating & Controlling Page Objects		
Constrain new item to square or circle	Shift-click-drag while drawing	Shift-click-drag while drawing
Constrain rotation to 45° increments	Shift-click-drag with Rotation tool	Shift-click-drag with Rotation tool
Select multiple objects	Shift-click	Shift-click
Select object behind	Command-Option-Shift-click	Control-Alt-Shift-click
Select all objects on spread (Item tool active)	Command-A	Control-A
Deselect all objects (Item tool active)	Tab	Tab
Duplicate	Command-D	Control-D
Step-and-Repeat	Command-Option-R	Control-Alt-D
Copy selected objects (Item tool active)	Command-C	Control-C
Cut selected objects (Item tool active)	Command-X	Control-X
Paste selected objects (Item tool active)	Command-V	Control-V
Paste in Place	Command-Option-Shift-V	Control-Alt-Shift-V
Delete object (Item tool active)	Command-K	Control-K
Delete object (Content tool is active)	Command-Option-X	Control-Alt-X
Group selected objects	Command-G	Control-G
Ungroup selected group	Command-U	Control-U
Lock/Unlock Item Position	F6	F6
Edit Shape (toggle on and off)	Shift-F4	F10
Open contextual menu for specific object		Shift-F10
Convert inline text to inline (anchored) box	Option-Style>Text-to-Box	Alt-Style>Text-to-Box

Keyboard Shortcuts

	MACINTOSH	WINDOWS
Moving Page Objects		
Move object left 1 pt. (Item tool active)*	Left Arrow	Left Arrow
Move object right 1 pt. (Item tool active)*	Right Arrow	Right Arrow
Move object down 1 pt. (Item tool active)*	Down Arrow	Down Arrow
Move object up 1 pt. (Item tool active)*	Up Arrow	Up Arrow
Constrain movement to 90°	Shift-drag with Item tool	Shift-drag with Item tool
Highlight X field of Measurements palette Classic mode	Command-Option-M	Control-Alt-M
Add the Option/Alt key to nudge objects 1/10 pt.		
Aligning Page Objects		
Display Space/Align options in Measurements palette	Command-Comma (,)	Control-Comma (,)
Left-align objects to each other*	Command-Left Arrow	Control-Left Arrow
Right-align objects to each other*	Command-Right Arrow	Control-Right Arrow
Bottom-align objects to each other*	Command-Down Arrow	Control-Down Arrow
Top-align objects to each other*	Command-Up Arrow	Control-Up Arrow
Center-align (horizontally) objects to each other*	Command-[	Control-[
Center-align (vertically) items to each other*	Command-]	Control-]
Apply last alignment option	Command-Option-/	Control-Alt-/
Add the Shift key to align one or more objects relative to the page instead of to each other		
Arranging Page Objects		
Bring to Front	F5	F5
Bring Forward one step	Option-F5 Option-Item>Bring to Front (menu)	Control-F5
Send to Back	Shift-F5	Shift-F5
Send Backward one step	Option-Shift-F5 Option-Item>Send to Back (menu)	Control-Shift-F5
Modifying Page Objects		
Modify dialog box (Last-used tab)	Command-M Double-click object with Item tool	Control-M Double-click object with Item tool
Drop Shadow tab of Modify dialog box	Command-Option-Shift-D	Control-Alt-Shift-D
Frame tab of Modify dialog box	Command-B	Control-B
Clipping tab of Modify dialog box	Command-Option-T	Control-Alt-T
Runaround tab of Modify dialog box	Command-T	Control-T
Managing Assets		
Append dialog box	Command-Option-A	Control-Alt-A
Style Sheets dialog box	Shift-F11*	Shift-F11
Colors dialog box	Shift-F12*	Shift-F12
H&Js dialog box	Command-Option-J / Option-Shift-F11	Control-Shift-F11
Edit dialog box for specific asset	Command-click asset name in palette	Control-click asset name in palette
Used by Macintosh system default settings (Expose); this will override the QuarkXPress behavior		

Keyboard Shortcuts

	MACINTOSH	WINDOWS
Managing Pictures		
Import Picture	Command-E	Control-E
Move picture left 1 pt. within box (Content tool active)*	Left Arrow	Left Arrow
Move picture right 1 pt. within box (Content tool active)*	Right Arrow	Right Arrow
Move picture down 1 pt. within box (Content tool active)*	Down Arrow	Down Arrow
Move picture up 1 pt. within box (Content tool active)*	Up Arrow	Up Arrow
Decrease picture size 5%	Command-Option-Shift-Comma (,)	Control-Alt-Shift-Comma (,)
Increase picture size 5%	Command-Option-Shift-Period (.)	Control-Alt-Shift-Period (.)
Edit Clipping path (toggle on and off)	Option-Shift-F4	Control-Shift-F10
Edit Runaround Path (toggle on and off)	Option-F4	Control-F10
Select all anchor points on clipping or runaround path	Command-Shift-A	Control-Shift-A

Add the Option/Alt key to nudge a picture 1/10 pt. within its box.

	MACINTOSH	WINDOWS
Resizing Pictures and Picture Boxes		
Resize box, constraining shape	Shift-click-drag box handle	Shift-click-drag box handle
Resize box, maintaining aspect ratio	Option-Shift-click-drag handle	Alt-Shift-click-drag handle
Resize box and scale content	Command-click-drag handle	Control-click-drag handle
Resize box and scale content, constraining shape	Command-Shift-click-drag handle	Control-Shift-click-drag handle
Resize box and scale content, maintaining aspect ratio	Command-Option-Shift-click-drag handle	Control-Alt-Shift-click-drag handle
Center Picture in Box	Command-Shift-M	Control-Shift-M
Stretch Picture to Fit Box	Command-Shift-F	Control-Shift-F
Scale Picture to Fit Box	Command-Option-Shift-F	Control-Alt-Shift-F

	MACINTOSH	WINDOWS
Managing Lines		
Constrain new line to 45° angles	Shift-click-drag with Line tool	Shift-click-drag with Line tool
Change Bézier line to Bézier box	Option-Item>Shape menu	Alt-Item>Shape menu
Decrease line weight 1 pt.	Command-Option-Shift-Comma (,)	Control-Alt-Shift-Comma (,)
Decrease line weight to next preset	Command-Shift-Comma (,)	Control-Shift-Comma (,)
Increase line weight 1 pt.	Command-Option-Shift-Period (.)	Control-Alt-Shift-Period (.)
Increase line weight to next preset	Command-Shift-Period (.)	Control-Shift-Period (.)
Line tab of Modify dialog box (Width field highlighted)	Command-Shift-\	Control-Shift-\
Item>Point/Segment Type>Corner Point	Option-F1	Control-F1
Item>Point/Segment Type>Smooth Point	Option-F2	Control-F2
Item>Point/Segment Type>Smooth Segment	Option-Shift-F2	Control-Shift-F2
Item>Point/Segment Type>Straight Segment	Option-Shift-F1	Control-Shift-F1
Item>Point/Segment Type>Symmetrical Point	Option-F3	Control-F3
Edit Bézier line or shape while creating	Command-While drawing	Control-While drawing
Add Bézier point	Option-click line segment	Alt-click line segment
Delete Bézier point	Option-click Bézier point	Alt-click Bézier point
Select all anchor points on Bézier path	Command-Shift-A	Control-Shift-A
Delete both handles of the point	Control-Shift-click Bézier point	Control-Shift-click Bézier point
Add symmetrical handles to point	Control-Shift-click Bézier point and drag	Control-Shift-click Bézier point and drag
Change smooth point to corner — one side of point only (or change corner to smooth)	Control-Shift-click-drag handle	Control-Shift-click-drag handle
Constrain point movement to 45°	Shift-click-drag point	Shift-click-drag point
Constrain handle movement to 45°	Shift-click-drag handle	Shift-click-drag handle

4/1

A job printed with four colors of ink on one side of the sheet, and one color of ink on the other.

4/4

A job printed with four colors of ink on both sides of the sheet. See *Process Colors*, *Subtractive Color*.

Absolute Path

The location of a file or Web page beginning with the root. Includes all necessary information to find the file or page. In the case of a Web page, called "absolute URL". See *Relative Path*.

Achromatic

By definition, having no color; completely black, white, or some shade of gray.

Adaptive Palette

A sampling of colors taken from an image and used in a special compression process, usually to prepare images for the World Wide Web.

Additive Color Process

The process of mixing red, green, and blue light to achieve a wide range of colors, as on a color television screen. See *Subtractive Color*.

Alignment

Positioning content to the left, right, center, top, or bottom.

Alpha Channel

An additional channel in an image that defines what parts of the image are transparent or semitransparent. Programs such as Adobe Illustrator, PhotoShop, Premiere, and After Effects use alpha channels to specify transparent regions in an image.

Alt Text

Alternate Text. In Web-page design, text that can be displayed in lieu of an image.

Amplitude-Modulated (AM) Screening

The screening method used to created halftone dot patterns, in which the size of halftone dots vary but the screen ruling and angle remain fixed.

Anchor

In a Web page, a type of hyperlink destination in which the destination is a specific location on a page.

Animated GIF

A type of sequential file format where multiple bitmap images are displayed one after another.

Anti-Aliasing

A graphics software feature that eliminates or softens the jaggedness of low-resolution curved edges.

Artifact

Something that is artificial or not meant to be there. An artifact can be a blemish or dust spot on a piece of film, or unsightly pixels in a digital image.

Ascender

Parts of a lowercase letter that exceed the height of the letter "x". The letters b, d, f, h, k, l, and t have ascenders.

ASCII

American Standard Code for Information Interchange. Worldwide, standard ASCII text does not include formatting, and therefore can be exchanged and read by most computer systems.

Aspect Ratio

The width-to-height proportions of an image.

Background

A static object or color that lies behind all other objects.

Backslant

A name for characters that slant the opposite way from italic characters.

Banding

A visible stair-stepping of shades in a gradient.

Baseline

The implied reference line on which the bases of capital letters sit.

Bézier Curves

Vector curves that are defined mathematically. These curves can be scaled without the "jaggies" inherent in enlarging bitmapped fonts or graphics.

Binding

In general, the various methods used to secure signatures or leaves in a book. Examples include saddle-stitching (the use of staples in a folded spine), and perfect-bound (multiple sets of folded pages sewn or glued into a flat spine).

Bit (Binary Digit)

A computer's smallest unit of information. Bits can have only two values: 0 or 1.

Bit Depth

A measure of how many colors can be in an image. 8-bit color is 256 colors ($2 \times 2 \times 2 \times 2 \times 2 \times 2 \times 2 \times 2$), 16-bit color is 32,768 colors ($2 \times 2 \times 2 \times 2 \times 2 \times 2 \times 2 \times 2 \times 2 \times 2 \times 2 \times 2 \times 2 \times 2 \times 2$), and so on.

Bitmap Image

An image constructed from individual dots or pixels set to a grid-like mosaic. The file must contain information about the color and position of each pixel, so the disk space needed for bitmap images can be very large.

Bitmapped

Forming an image with a grid of pixels whose curved edges have discrete steps because of the approximation of the curve due to a finite number pixels.

Black

The absence of color. An ink that absorbs all wavelengths of light.

Blanket

In offset printing, the intermediate step between the printing plate and the substrate. The image is transferred from the plate to a blanket, then from the blanket to the substrate.

Bleed

Page data that extends beyond the trim marks on a page.

Blend

See *Gradient*.

Blow Up

An enlargement, usually of a graphic element such as a photograph.

BMP

A Windows bitmap image format that features low-quality and large file sizes.

Glossary

Boldface

A heavier, blacker version of a typeface.

Border

A continual line that extends around an element.

Bounding Box

An area that defines the outer border of an object in your composition.

Brightness

1. A measure of the amount of light reflected from a surface. 2. A paper property, defined as the percentage reflection of 457-nanometer (nm) radiation. 3. The intensity of a light source. 4. The overall percentage of lightness in an image.

Bullet

A marker preceding text, usually a solid dot, used to add emphasis; generally indicates the text is part of a list.

Button

An element a user can click to cause an effect, such as the submission of a form.

Button State

A visual version of a button. For example, when clicked, the button is in its Down state; when dormant, it is in its Up state. When the mouse is hovered over the button, the button is in its Over state.

Calibration

Making adjustments to a color monitor and other hardware and software to make the monitor represent as closely as possible the colors of the final production.

Calibration Bars

A strip of color blocks or tonal values on film, proofs, and press sheets, used to check the accuracy of registration, quality, density, and ink coverage during a print run.

Callout

A descriptive label referenced to a visual element, such as several words connected to the element by an arrow.

Camera-Ready

A completely finished mechanical ready to be photographed to produce a negative, from which a printing plate will be made.

Cap Line

The theoretical line to which the tops of capital letters are aligned.

Caps

An abbreviation for capital letters.

Caps and Small Caps

A style of typesetting in which capital letters are used in the normal way, while the type that would normally be in lowercase is changed to capital letters of a smaller point size. A true small-caps typeface does not contain any lowercase letters.

Caption

The lines of text that identify a picture or illustration, usually placed beneath it or otherwise in close proximity.

CCD

Charge-Coupled Device. A light-sensitive, solid-state semiconductor consisting of image elements (photosites) arranged in a linear or area array. Light illuminates the source, which reflects the light through optics onto the silicon sensors in the array.

Cell

A unit of information within a table.

Center Marks

Press marks that appear on the center of all sides of a press sheet to aid in positioning the print area on the paper.

CGI

Common Gateway Interface. Interface that allows scripts to run on a Web server. CGI scripts can be used to put the content of a form into an e-mail message, to perform a database query, or to generate HTML pages on-the-fly.

Check Box

A square that can be clicked to cause the form to send a name-value pair to the action; a form element that allows a user to choose zero or more choices.

Choke

The process in which a lighter background object is extended slightly into a darker foreground object to prevent paper-colored gaps caused by misregistration. See *Trapping*.

Chroma

The degree of saturation of a surface color in the Munsell color space model.

CIE

Commission Internationale de l'Eclairage. An international group that developed a universal set of color definition standards in 1931.

Clipboard

The portion of computer memory that holds data that has been cut or copied. The next item cut or copied replaces the data already in the clipboard.

CMM

Color-Management Module. The engine of a color-management system.

CMS

Color Management System. A process or utility that attempts to manage color of input and output devices in such a way that the monitor will match the output of any CMS-managed printer.

CMYK

Cyan, Magenta, Yellow, Black. The subtractive primaries, or process colors, used in four-color printing.

Coated

Printing papers that have a surface coating (of clay or other material) to provide a smoother, more even finish with greater opacity.

Collate

To gather together separate sections or leaves of a publication in the correct order for binding.

Color Balance

The combination of yellow, magenta, and cyan needed to produce a neutral gray.

Color Bars

A color standard used by the television industry for the alignment of camera and videotape recordings.

Color Cast

The modification of a hue by the addition of a trace of another hue, such as yellowish green, or pinkish blue. Normally, an unwanted effect that can be corrected.

Color Chart

A printed chart of various combinations of CMYK colors used as an aid for the selection of colors during the design phase of a project.

Color Control Strip

A printed strip of various reference colors used to control printing quality. This strip is normally placed on a press sheet outside the area of a project, used as a guide and visual aid for the press operator.

Color Conversion

Changing the color mode of an image. Converting an image from RGB to CMYK for purposes of preparing the image for conventional printing.

Color Correction

The process of removing casts or unwanted tints in a digital image in an effort to improve the appearance of the image or to correct obvious deficiencies.

Color Depth

Maximum number of colors available for an image. See *Bit Depth*.

Color Gamut

The range of colors that can be formed by all possible combinations of the colorants of a given reproduction system, such as colors that can be displayed on television screens.

Color Model

A system for describing color, such as RGB, HLS, CIELAB, or CMYK.

Color Picker

A function within a graphics application that assists in selecting or setting a color.

Color Proof

A printed or simulated printed image of the color separations intended to produce a close representation of the final reproduction for approval and as a guide to the press operator.

Color Separation

The process of transforming color artwork into components corresponding to the colors of ink being used, whether process or spot, or a combination of the two.

Color Sequence

The color order of printing the cyan, magenta, yellow, and black inks on a printing press. Sometimes called rotation or color rotation.

Color Shift

The result of compressing out-of-gamut colors into colors that can be reproduced with a given model. Color shift can drastically change the appearance of the final output.

Color Space

A three-dimensional coordinate system in which any color can be represented as a point.

Column

1. A vertical area for type, used to constrain line length to enhance design and readability. 2. A vertical series of table cells.

Commercial Printing

Typically, printing on high-capacity, high-resolution presses; processes include offset lithography, flexography, gravure, and screen printing. Offset printing is the most widely used commercial printing process.

Comp

Comprehensive artwork used to present the general color and layout of a page.

Composite Proof

A version of an illustration or page in which the process colors appear together to represent full color. When produced on a monochrome output device, colors are represented as shades of gray.

Compression

A technique used to reduce file size by analyzing occurrences of similar data. Compressed files occupy less space, and their use improves digital transmission speeds. Compression can sometimes result in a loss of image quality and/or resolution.

Condensed Type

A typeface in which the width of the letters is narrower than that of the standard letters of the font. Condensed type can be a designed font, or the effect can be approximated using a horizontal scaling feature.

Continuous Tone

An image (such as a photograph) in which the subject has continuous shades of color or gray tones through the use of an emulsion process. Continuous tone images must be screened to create halftone images to be printed.

Contrast

The relationship and degree of difference between the dark and light areas of an image.

Coordinates

Numbers signifying a place in a Cartesian plane, represented by (x,y).

Copyfitting

Making sure you don't write more text than you have room for.

Copyright

Ownership of a work. Permits the owner of material to prevent its use without express permission or acknowledgement of the originator. Copyright may be sold, transferred, or given up contractually.

Creep

The progressive extension of the edges of each spread in a folded signature.

Crop Marks

Printed lines used as guides for final trimming of the pages within a press sheet.

Cropping

The elimination of parts of a photograph or other original that are not required to be printed.

Crossover

An element in a book that appears on both pages of a reader's spread, crossing over the gutter.

Cross-Reference

An in-text notation that directs the reader's attention to an attached illustration or to another section of the publication.

Dash

A short horizontal rule of varying lengths used to indicate a pause or clause in a sentence. See *En Dash, Em Dash*.

Glossary

DCS

Desktop Color Separation. A version of the EPS file format. DCS 1.0 is composed of five files for each color image plus a separate low-resolution image to place in a digital file. DCS 2.0 has one file that stores process and spot color information.

Default

A specification for a mode of computer operation that occurs if no other is selected. The default font size might be 12 point, or a default color for an object might be white with a black border.

Densitometer

An electronic instrument used to measure optical density; reflective for paper, and transmissive for film.

Density

The ability of a material to absorb light. In film, it refers to the opacity of an area of the image. A maximum density of 4.0 refers to solid black. Improper density in film results in washed-out or overly-dark reproduction.

Descender

The part of a lowercase letter that extends below the baseline (lower edge of the x-height) of the letter. The letters y, p, g, and j contain descenders.

Descreening

A technique used to obscure the halftone dot pattern when scanning printed material.

Device-Dependent Color

Reproduction in which the output color is determined by the output device characteristics.

Device-Independent Color

Reproduction in which the output color is absolute, and is not determined by the output device characteristics.

DICColor

A special-color library commonly used in Japan.

Die Line

In a digital file, the outline used to mark where cutting, stamping, or embossing the finished piece will occur. Used to create a particular shape, such as a rolodex card.

Direct-to-Plate

Producing printing plates or other image carriers from computer output, usually via laser exposure, without an intermediate film exposure.

Disconnected Rollover

A rollover in which the item that changes is not the item over which the user's mouse is rolling. See also *Rollover*.

Discretionary Hyphen

A hyphen coded for display and printing only when formatting of the text puts the hyphenated word at the end of a line. Also called a "soft hyphen".

Dithering

A technique in which a color is represented using dots of two different colors displayed or printed very close together. Dithering is often used to compress digital images and in special screening algorithms. See *Stochastic Screening*.

Dmax

The maximum density in an image, or the maximum density that can be captured with a scanner or digital camera.

Dmin

The minimum density in an image, or the minimum density that can be captured with a scanner or digital camera.

Dot Gain

The growth of a halftone dot that occurs whenever ink soaks into paper. Failure to compensate for this gain in the generation of digital images can result in very poor results on press. Also known as "tone value increase".

Dot Pitch

In computer monitors, the distance (in millimeters) between the holes in the shadow mask: the smaller the number, the sharper the image. Generally, the smaller the number, the higher the resolution of a given monitor size.

Down State

A state that occurs when the user clicks a button.

DPI

Dots Per Inch. The measurement of resolution for page printers, phototypesetting machines, and graphics screens. Currently graphics screens use resolutions of 72 to 96 dpi; standard desktop laser printers work at 600 dpi.

Drop Shadow

A duplicate of a graphic element or type placed behind and slightly offset, giving the effect of a shadow.

Drop-Down Menu

A select list.

Duotone

The separation of a photograph into black and a second color. Duotones are used to enhance photographic reproduction in two-, three-, or sometimes four-color work. Often the second, third, and fourth colors are not standard CMYK inks.

Dye Transfer

A photographic color print using special coated papers to produce a full color image. Can serve as an inexpensive proof.

Dynamic Range

The difference between the lightest and darkest area of an image. Also used to describe the range of color capture capability in a scanner or digital camera.

Effective Resolution

The final resolution of an image, calculated by dividing the image resolution (pixels per inch) by the magnification percentage.

Elliptical Dot Screen

A halftone screen having an elliptical dot structure.

Em Dash

A dash (—) that indicates the separation of elements of a sentence or clause.

Em Space

A space that is of equal width in points to the point size. An em space in 10 point type is 10 points wide.

Embedded Font

A font that is made part of a document.

Glossary

Embedding

Including a complete copy of a text file or image within a document, with or without a link. See *Linking*.

En Dash

A dash (–), half the width of an em dash, that often replaces the word "to" or "through," such as 9–5 or Monday–Friday.

En Space

A space that is equal to half the width of an em space.

EPS

Encapsulated PostScript. File format used to transfer PostScript data within compatible applications. EPS files can contain text, vector artwork, and images.

Expanded Type

A typeface in which the width of the letters is wider than that of the standard letters of the font. Expanded type can be a designed font, or the effect may be approximated using a horizontal scaling feature. Also called extended.

Export

To save a file generated in one application into a format that is readable in another.

External Style Sheet

Style information included in a separate file referenced by a Web page.

Fair Use

Using copyrighted work without obtaining permission from the copyright holder for purposes such as critique, education, or research.

File Compression

The process of reducing the number of bytes in a file, file compression is usually used when transferring files between computers.

File Extension

The suffix used to identify file types under the Macintosh and Windows operating systems, separated from the rest of the file name by a period.

Fill

To add a tone or color to the area inside a closed object in a graphic illustration program.

Film

Non-paper output of an imagesetter or phototypesetter.

Flat Color

Color that lacks contrast or tonal variation. Also called flat tint.

Flexographic Printing

A rotary letterpress printing process using a rubber plate that stretches around a cylinder making it necessary to compensate by distorting the plate image. Flexography is used most often for printing on metal or other non-paper material.

Floating Accent

A separate accent mark that can be placed under or over another character. Complex accented characters such as in foreign languages are usually available in a font as a single character.

Focal Length

The size of the angle of view of a camera lens.

Focoltone

A special-color library used in the United States.

Folder

The digital equivalent of a paper file folder, used to organize files in the Macintosh and Windows operating systems. Double-clicking the icon opens it to reveal the files stored inside.

Folding Dummy

A template used for determining the page arrangement on a form to meet folding and binding requirements.

Font

A font is the complete collection of all the characters (numbers, uppercase and lowercase letters, and in some cases, small caps and symbols) of a given typeface in a specific style; for example, Helvetica Bold.

Font Subsetting

Embedding only the used characters of a font into the final file. The advantage of font subsetting is that it decreases the overall size of your file. The disadvantage is that it limits the ability to makes corrections at the printing service.

Font Substitution

A process in which your computer uses a font other than the one you used in your design to display or print your publication. Usually occurs when a used font is missing on the computer used to output the design.

Force Justify

A type alignment command that causes the space between letters and words in a line of type to expand to fit within a line.

Form

A page that enables a user to type information and send it to a site via form elements such as text boxes and pull-down menus.

Format

Type of television script indicating the major programming steps. Generally contains a fully scripted show opening and closing. Example: the nightly news.

Four-Color Process

Process color printer. See *Process Colors*.

FPO

For Position Only. A term applied to low-quality images or simple shapes used to indicate placement and scaling of an art element on mechanicals or camera-ready artwork.

Frequency-Modulated (FM) Screening

A method of creating halftones in which the size of the dots remains constant but their density is varied; also known as stochastic screening.

F-Stop

The calibration on the lens indicating the aperture or diaphragm opening. Controls the amount of light that can pass through the lens.

Gamma

A measure of the contrast, or range of tonal variation of the midtones in a photographic image.

Gamma Correction

1. Adjusting the contrast of the midtones in an image. 2. Calibrating a monitor so midtones are correctly displayed on screen.

Gamut

See *Color Gamut*.

Glossary

Gamut Shift

See *Color Shift*.

Gang

The process of printing more than one job on the same press sheet to minimize paper waste.

GB

Gigabyte. A unit of measure equal to one billion (1,073,741,824) bytes.

GCR

See *Gray Component Replacement*.

Generation

The number of steps away from an original. The original is first-generation; a scan of the original is second-generation; a scan of a print of the original is third-generation.

Get

A method for sending form data by appending it to the URL of the action. See *Post*.

GIF

Graphics Interchange Format. A popular graphics format for online clip art and drawn graphics. Graphics in this format are acceptable at low resolution. See *JPEG*.

Global Preferences

Preference settings that affect all newly created files within an application.

GRACoL

General Requirements for Applications in Commercial Offset Lithography. Created by the Graphic Communications Association, general guidelines and recommendations for achieving quality color printing.

Gradient

A gradual transition from one color to another. The shape of the gradient and the proportion of the two colors can be varied. Also known as blends, gradations, graduated fills, and vignettes.

Grain

Silver salts clumped together in differing amounts in different types of photographic emulsions.

Graininess

Visual impression of the irregularly distributed silver grain clumps in a photographic image, or the ink film in a printed image.

Gray Balance

The values for the yellow, magenta, and cyan inks that are needed to produce neutral gray when printed at a normal density.

Gray Component Replacement

A technique for adding detail by reducing the amount of cyan, magenta and yellow in chromatic or colored areas, replacing them with black.

Grayscale

1. An image composed in grays ranging from black to white, usually using 256 different tones. 2. A tint ramp used to measure and control the accuracy of screen percentages. 3. An accessory used to define neutral density in a photographic image.

Greeking

1. A software technique where areas of gray are used to simulate lines of text below a certain point size. 2. Nonsense text used to define a layout before copy is available.

Grid

A division of a page by horizontal and vertical guides into areas where text or graphics may be placed accurately.

Gripper Edge

The leading edge of a sheet of paper that the grippers on the press grab to carry the paper through a press.

Gutter

Extra space between pages in a layout. Sometimes used interchangeably with "alley" to describe the space between columns on a page. Gutters can appear either between the top and bottom of two adjacent pages or between two sides of adjacent pages.

H & J

Hyphenation and Justification. Parameters used by a page-layout program to determine how a line of text should be hyphenated, or how its inter-word and inter-character space should be adjusted.

Hairline Rule

The thinnest rule that can be printed on a given device. A hairline rule on a 1200-dpi imagesetter is 1/1200 of an inch; on a 300-dpi laser printer, the same rule would print at 1/300 of an inch.

Halftone

An image generated for use in printing in which a range of continuous tones is simulated by an array of dots that create the illusion of continuous tone when seen at a distance.

Hex Values

Numbers specified in the hexadecimal system, commonly used for specifying colors on Web pages.

Hexachrome

Six-color printing process developed by PANTONE, in which green and orange are added to the process colors to extend the printable gamut. Also called "HiFi".

High Key

A photographic or printed image in which the main interest area lies in the highlight end of the scale.

Highlight

The lightest areas in an image.

High-Resolution File

An image file that typically contains four pixels for every dot in the printed reproduction. High-resolution files are often linked to a page-layout file, but not actually embedded in it, due to their large size.

HLS

A color model based on three coordinates: hue, lightness (luminance), and saturation.

Hot Area

The portion of an image that will, when clicked, initiate some action, such as linking to another Web page.

House Style Guide

A style guide prepared solely for authors writing for a specific company or publisher; the rules defined in a house style guide may differ from common practice.

HSL

A color model that defines color based on its hue, saturation, and luminosity (value), as it is displayed on a video or computer screen.

HSV

A color model based on three coordinates: hue, saturation, and value (or luminance).

HTML

Hypertext Mark-Up Language. A tagging language that allows content to be delivered over the World Wide Web and viewed by a browser.

Hue

The wavelength of light of a color in its purest state (without adding white or black).

Hyperlink

An HTML tag that directs the computer to a different anchor or URL. A hyperlink can be a word, phrase, sentence, graphic, or icon. A hyperlink can also cause an action, such as opening or downloading a file.

Hypertext

An organization of content that enables the user to select related content.

Hyphenation Zone

The space at the end of a line of text in which the hyphenation function will examine the word to determine whether it should be hyphenated and wrapped to the next line.

ICC

International Color Consortium. A standards-making body for color reproduction technology.

Image Map

A graphic containing hotspots, or areas of an image that are defined as links. When a viewer clicks the part of the image that is a hotspot, they are actually clicking on a link.

Imagesetter

A raster-based device used to output a digital file at high resolution (usually 1000–3000 dpi) onto photographic paper or film, from which printing plates are made, or directly to printing plates (called a "platesetter").

Imposition

The arrangement of pages on a printed sheet, which, when the sheet is finally printed, folded, and trimmed, will place the pages in their correct order.

Impression

A request for a Web page on a particular server. Each time a page is sent to a user's browser is an impression. Useful in evaluating and billing Web advertising.

Impression Cylinder

In commercial printing, a cylinder that provides back pressure, thus allowing the image to be transferred from the blanket to the substrate.

Indexed Color Image

An image that uses a limited, predetermined number of colors; often used in Web images. See also *GIF*.

Initial Caps

Text in which the first letter of each word (except articles) is capitalized.

Ink Film Thickness

The amount of ink that is transferred to the substrate.

Inline Graphic

A graphic that is inserted within a body of text, and may be formatted using normal text commands for justification and leading; inline graphics will move with the body of text in which they are placed.

Intellectual Property

Any product of human intelligence that is unique, novel, unobvious, and valuable (such as a literary work, idea, or invention).

Intensity

Synonym for degree of color saturation.

Internal Style Sheet

Style information included within a Web page.

International Paper Sizes

The International Standards Organization (ISO) system of paper sizes based on a series of three sizes — A, B, and C. Each size has the same proportion of length to width as the others.

Interpolated Resolution

"Artificial" resolution that is created by averaging the color and intensity of adjacent pixels. Commonly used in scanning to achieve resolution higher than the scanner' optical resolution.

Jaggies

Visible steps in the curved edge of a graphic or text character that result from enlarging a bitmapped image.

JPEG

A compression algorithm that reduces the file size of bitmapped images, named for the Joint Photographic Experts Group, which created the standard. JPEG is "lossy" compression; image quality is reduced in direct proportion to the amount of compression.

Justified Alignment

Straight left and right alignment of text — not ragged. Every line of text is the same width, creating even left and right margins.

Kerning

Moving a pair of letters closer together or farther apart, to achieve a better fit or appearance.

Keyline

A thin border around a picture or a box that indicates where to place pictures. In digital files, keylines are often vector objects while photographs are usually bitmap images.

Knockout

A printing technique that prints overlapping objects without mixing inks. The ink for the underlying element does not print (knocks out) in the area where the objects overlap. Opposite of overprinting.

L*a*b*

The lightness, red-green attribute, and yellow-blue attribute in the CIE L*a*b* color space, a three-dimensional color mapping system.

Landscape

Printing from the left to right across the wider side of the page. A landscape orientation treats a letter-size page as 11 inches wide and 8.5 inches long.

Glossary

Layer

A function of graphics applications in which elements may be isolated from each other, so a group of elements can be hidden from view, reordered, or otherwise manipulated as a unit, without affecting other elements in the composition.

Leaders

A line of periods or other symbols connecting the end of a group of words with another element. For example, a table of contents may consist of a series of phrases on separate lines, each associated with a page number.

Leading ("Ledding")

Space added between lines of type. Named after the strips of lead that used to be inserted between lines of metal type. In specifying type, lines of 12-pt. type separated by a 14-pt. space is abbreviated "12/14," or "twelve over fourteen."

Left Alignment

Text having a straight left edge and a ragged or uneven right edge.

Letter Spacing

The insertion or addition of white space between the letters of words.

Library

A collection of files having a similar purpose or function.

Ligature

Letters that are joined together as a single unit of type such as œ and fi.

Lightness

The property that distinguishes white from gray or black, and light from dark color tones on a surface.

Line Art

A drawing or piece of black-and-white artwork with no screens. Line art can be represented by a graphic file having only 1-bit resolution.

Line Screen

See *LPI*.

Linking

The act of placing a reference to one file (image or graphic) into another file. When the referenced file is modified, the placed reference is automatically (or manually, depending on the application) updated.

List

A series of items.

Lithography

A mechanical printing process based on the principle of the natural aversion of water to grease. In modern offset lithography, the image on a photosensitive plate is first transferred to the blanket of a rotating drum, and then to the paper.

Lossy

A data compression method characterized by the loss of some data.

LPI

Lines Per Inch. The number of lines per inch used when converting a photograph to a halftone. Typical values range from 85 for newspaper work to 150 or higher for high-quality reproduction on smooth or coated paper. Also called "line screen."

LZW Compression

Lempel-ziy-welch compression. A method of reducing the size of image files.

Makeready

The process of starting a printing press and manipulating the controls until the press is running at its optimum capability.

Margins

The non-printing areas of a page, or the line at which text starts or stops.

Masking

A technique used to display certain areas of an image or design; the shape and size of the top-most object or layer defines what is visible on lower layers.

Master Pages

Page-layout templates containing elements common to all pages to which the master is applied.

Mechanical

A pasted-up page of camera-ready art that is photographed to produce a plate for the press.

Mechanical Dot Gain

See *Dot Gain*.

Medium

A physical carrier of data such as a CD-ROM, video cassette, or floppy disk, or a carrier of electronic data such as fiber optic cable or electric wires.

Memory

The storage device in a computer. Its capacity is given in numbers of bytes. See RAM and ROM.

Memory Color

The tendency to evaluate color based on what we expect to see rather than what is actually there.

Menu

A list of choices of functions or items, such as fonts.

Menu Bar

The strip across the top of your screen that contains the names of the menus available to you.

Meta Tag

An optional HTML tag that is used to specify information about a Web document. Some search engines index Web pages by reading the information contained within the META tags.

Metallic Ink

Printing inks which produce gold, silver, bronze, or metallic colors.

Metamerism

Phenomenon in which the same color appears differently in different lighting conditions.

Midtones

The tonal range between highlights and shadows. Also called "middletones."

MIME

Multipurpose Internet Mail Extensions. Standard for attaching non-text files to e-mail messages (formatted word-processing files, spreadsheets, pictures, executable files).

MIME Type

An indication of the kind of data being sent to the browser. Used by the browser to know what to do with the data.

Minimum Printable Dot

The smallest dot that can be accurately and consistently reproduced on film or a printing plate.

Misregister

The unwanted result of incorrectly aligned inks on a finished printed piece. Mis-registration can be caused by many factors, including paper stretch and improper plate alignment. Trapping can compensate for misregistration.

Moiré

An interference pattern caused by the overlap of two or more regular patterns such as dots or lines. In process-color printing, screen angles are selected to mini-mize this pattern.

Monochrome

An image or computer monitor in which all information is represented in black and white, or with a range of grays.

Monospace

A font in which all characters occupy the same amount of horizontal width regard-less of the character. See also *Proportional Spacing*.

Mottle

Uneven color or tone.

Mouseover

The event triggered at the moment the user rolls the mouse over an area or item on a Web page. Typically used to tell the browser to do something, such as execute a rollover script.

Multimedia

The combination of sound, video images, and text to create an interactive document, program, or presentation.

Nesting

Placing graphic files within other graphic files. This practice often results in errors in printing.

Neutral

Any color that is absent of hue, such as white, gray, or black.

Neutral Density

A measurement of the lightness or darkness of a color. A neutral density of zero (0.00) is the lightest value possible, and is equiv-alent to pure white; 3.294 is roughly equiva-lent to 100% of each of the CMYK components.

Normal Key

A description of an image in which the main interest area is in the middle range of the tone scale, or distributed throughout the entire tonal range.

Offset Lithography

A printing method whereby the image is transferred from a plate onto a rubber-covered cylinder, from which the printing takes place. See *Lithography*.

Opacity

1. The degree to which paper will show print through it. 2. The degree to which images or text below one object, whose opacity has been adjusted, are able to show through.

OpenType

A font format developed by Adobe and Microsoft that can be used on both the Windows and Macintosh platforms, can contain over 65,000 distinct glyphs, and offers advanced typographic features.

Operator

A symbol or term used to perform a specific operation. For example, the asterisk (*) multiplies two values; the greater-than symbol (>) compares the first value against the second and decides which is larger.

Optical Resolution

The actual resolution of a scanner's optics. See also *Interpolated Resolution*.

Orphan

A single or partial word, or a partial line of a paragraph appearing at the bottom of a page. See *Widow*.

Out-of-Gamut

Color that cannot be reproduced with a specific color model. Many RGB colors fall outside the CMYK gamut.

Output Device

Any hardware equipment, such as a monitor, laser printer, or imagesetter, that depicts text or graphics created on a computer.

Overprint Color

A color made by overprinting any two or more of the primary yellow, magenta, and cyan process colors.

Overprinting

Allowing an element to print over the top of underlying elements, rather than knocking them out (see *Knockout*). Often used with black type.

PANTONE Matching System

PMS. A system for specifying colors by number for both coated and uncoated paper; used by print services and in color desktop publishing to assure uniform color matching.

Pasteboard

In a page-layout program, the desktop area outside the printing-page area.

PDF

Portable Document Format. Developed by Adobe Systems, Inc. (read by Acrobat Reader), this format has become a de facto standard for document transfer across plat-forms.

Perfect Binding

A binding method in which the spines of signatures are ground off with a rough tool and then bound into a soft cover with adhesive. Each page is glued to the spine and to the adjacent pages.

Perfecting Press

A commercial printing press configuration, in which both sides of the substrate are printed at one time.

Perspective

The effect of distance in an image, achieved by aligning the edges of elements with imaginary lines directed toward one to three "vanishing points" on the horizon.

Glossary

Photomechanical Transfer (PMT)

Positive prints of text or images used for paste-up to mechanicals.

Pi Fonts

A collection of special characters such as timetable symbols and mathematical signs. Examples are Zapf Dingbats and Symbol.

Pica

A traditional typographic measurement of 12 points, or approximately 1/6 of an inch. Most applications specify a pica as exactly 1/6 of an inch.

PICT/PICT2

A common format for defining bitmapped images on the Macintosh. The more recent PICT2 format supports 24-bit color.

Pixel

Picture Element. One of the tiny rectangular areas or dots generated by a computer or output device to constitute images. A greater number of pixels per inch results in higher resolution on screen or in print.

PNG

Portable Network Graphics. Graphics format that supports both transparency and continuous-tone color.

Point

A unit of measurement used to specify type size and rule weight, equal to approximately 1/72 inch.

Portrait

Printing from left to right across the narrow side of the page. Portrait orientation on a letter-size page uses a standard 8.5-inch width and 11-inch length.

Post

A method for sending form data using headers. See *Get*.

Posterize (Posterization)

1. Deliberate constraint of a gradient or image into visible steps as a special effect. 2. Unintentional creation of steps in an image due to high lpi (lines per inch) value used with a low dpi (dots per inch) printer.

PostScript

1. A page-description language, developed by Adobe Systems, Inc., that describes type and/or images and their positional relationships on the page. 2. A computer-programming language.

PPD

PostScript Printer Description File. A file format developed by Adobe Systems, Inc., that contains device-specific information that enables software to produce the best results possible for each type of designated printer.

PPI

Pixels Per Inch. Used to denote the resolution of an image.

Preferences

A set of modifiable defaults for an application program.

Preflight Check

A final check of a page layout that verifies all fonts and linked graphics are available, that colors are properly defined, and that any necessary traps have been applied.

Prepress

All work done between writing and printing, such as typesetting, scanning, layout, and imposition.

Primary Colors

Colors that can be used to generate secondary colors. For the additive system (a computer monitor), these colors are red, green, and blue. For the subtractive system (the printing process), these colors are yellow, magenta, and cyan.

Printer Driver

The device that communicates between the software program and the printer. When using an application, the printer driver tells the application what the printer can do, and also tells the printer how to print the publication.

Printer Fonts

The image outlines for type in PostScript that are sent to the printer.

Printer's Spread

The two pages that abut on press in a multi-page document.

Process Colors

The four inks (cyan, magenta, yellow, and black) used in four-color process printing. A printing method in which a full range of colors is reproduced by combining four semi-transparent inks. See *Color Separation*, *CMYK*.

Production Schedule

A plan that shows the time periods of various activities during the production day. Also called a "timeline."

Profile

A file containing data representing the color reproduction characteristics of a device determined by a calibration of some sort.

Project

A single QuarkXPress file that contains layout pages.

Proof

A representation of the printed job that is made from plates (press proof), film, or electronic data (prepress proofs). It is generally used for customer inspection and approval before mass production begins.

Proportional Spacing

A method of spacing whereby each character is spaced to accommodate the varying widths of letters or figures, thus increasing readability. For example, a proportionally spaced "m" is wider than an "i."

Pt.

Abbreviation for point.

Pull Quote

An excerpt from the body of a story used to emphasize an idea, draw readers' attention, or generate interest.

Radio Button

A single round button that can be clicked to cause the form to send a name-value pair to the action.

Radio Group

A group of radio buttons with the same name. Only one radio button may be selected at a time within a radio group.

Raster

A bitmapped representation of graphic data.

Glossary

Raster Graphics

A class of graphics created and organized in a rectangular array of bitmaps. Often created by paint software or scanners.

Rasterize

The process of converting digital information into pixels. For example, the process used by an imagesetter to translate PostScript files before they are imaged to film or paper.

Reader's Spread

The two (or more) pages a reader will view when the document is open.

Reflective Art

Artwork that is opaque, as opposed to transparent, that can be scanned for input to a computer.

Registration

Aligning plates on a multicolor printing press so the images will superimpose properly to produce the required composite output.

Registration Color

A default color selection that can be applied to design elements so they will print on every separation from a PostScript printer. "Registration" is often used to print identification text that will appear outside the page area on a set of separations.

Registration Marks

Figures (often crossed lines and a circle) placed outside the trim page boundaries on all color separation overlays to provide a common element for proper alignment.

Relative Path

The location of a file or Web page that uses the location of the current file or page as a reference. In the case of a Web page, called "relative URL". See *Absolute Path*.

Relative Positioning

Specifying the position of a section of content, such as a div, based on the original location of the content.

Rendering Intent

The method used to convert color from one space to another.

Repurposing

Converting an existing document for another different use; usually refers to creating an electronic version of existing print publications.

Resample

Resizing an image to decrease the physical size of the file, not just change the appearance on the page.

Reset Button

A button that, when clicked, causes a form to return to the state it was in when the page was first loaded.

Resolution

The density of graphic information expressed in dots per inch (dpi) or pixels per inch (ppi).

Retouching

Making selective manual or electronic corrections to images.

Reverse Out

To reproduce an object as white, or paper, within a solid background, such as white letters in a black rectangle.

RGB

1. The colors of projected light from a computer monitor that, when combined, simulate a subset of the visual spectrum. 2. The color model of most digital artwork. See also *CMYK*.

Rich Black

A process color consisting of solid black with one or more layers of cyan, magenta, or yellow. Also called "superblack".

Right Alignment

Text having a straight right edge and a ragged or uneven left edge.

Right-Reading

A positive or negative image that is readable from top to bottom and from left to right.

RIP

Raster Image Processor. That part of a PostScript printer or imagesetting device that converts the page information from the PostScript Page Description Language into the bitmap pattern that is applied to the film or paper output.

Rollover

The act of rolling the cursor over a given element on the screen.

Root

Top-level directory from which all other directories branch out.

Rosette

The pattern created when color halftone screens are printed at traditional screen angles.

Rotation

Turning an object at some angle to its original axis.

Row

A series of cells arranged horizontally.

RTF

Rich Text Format. A text format that retains formatting information lost in pure ASCII text.

Ruler

Like a physical ruler, a feature of graphics software used for precise measurement and alignment of objects. See *Grid*.

Rules

Straight lines.

Running Head

Text at the top of the page that provides information about the publication. Chapter names and book titles are often included in the running head. Also called a "header."

Saddle-Stitching

A binding method in which each signature is folded and stapled at the spine.

Sans Serif

Fonts that do not have serifs. See *Serif*.

Saturation

The intensity or purity of a color; a color with no saturation is gray.

Scalability

How well a solution to a given issue will work when the size of the issue increases.

Glossary

Scaling

The means within a program to reduce or enlarge the amount of space an image occupies by multiplying the data by a factor. Scaling can be proportional, or in one dimension only.

Screen

To create a halftone of a continuous-tone image.

Screen Angle

The angle at which the rulings of a halftone screen are set when making halftones for commercial printing.

Screen Frequency

The number of lines per inch in a halftone screen, which may vary from 85 to 300.

Screen Ruling

See *LPI*.

Screen Shot

A printed output or saved file that represents data from a computer monitor.

Secondary Color

The result of mixing two primary colors. In additive (RGB) color, cyan, magenta, and yellow are the secondary colors. In subtractive (CMY) color, red, green, and blue are the secondary colors.

Select List

A list of potential choices that can be displayed as a menu that appears when the user clicks on it, or as a box with its own scroll bar.

Selection

The currently active object(s) in a window. Often made by clicking with the mouse or by dragging a marquee around the desired object(s).

Selective Color

The addition of color to certain elements of a grayscale image, usually to draw attention to the colored object or area.

Separation

The process of preparing individual color components for commercial printing. Each ink color is reproduced as a unique piece of film or printing plate.

Serif

A line or curve projecting from the end of a letterform. Typefaces designed with such projections are called serif faces.

Server

1. A computer that has a permanent connection to the Internet. A Web site is stored on a Web server. 2. A computer used as a central repository for information. 3. The device that responds by fulfilling a client's service request.

Service Bureau

An organization that provides services, such as scanning and prepress checks, that prepare your publication to be printed on a commercial printing press. Service bureaus do not, however, print your publication.

Service Mark

A legal designation that identifies and protects the ownership of a specific term or phrase.

Shade

A color mixed with black: a 10% shade is one part of the original color and nine parts black. See *Tint*.

Sharpness

The subjective impression of the density difference between two tones at their boundary, interpreted as fineness of detail.

Shortcut

1. A quick method for accessing a menu item or command, usually through a series of keystrokes. 2. The icon that can be created in Windows to open an application without having to penetrate layers of various folders.

Silhouette

To remove part of the background of a photograph or illustration, leaving only the desired portion.

Skew

A transformation command that slants an object at an angle to the side from its initial fixed base.

Slug Line

Special symbols (such as ### or — 30 —) that reporters recognize as designating that they have reached the end of the story.

Small Caps

A type style in which lowercase letters are replaced by uppercase letters set in a smaller point size.

Smart Quotes

The curly quotation marks used by typographers, as opposed to the straight marks on the typewriter. Use of smart quotes is usually a setup option in a word-processing or page-layout application.

Soft Return

A return command that ends a line but does not apply a paragraph mark that would end the continuity of the style for that paragraph.

Special Color

Colors that are reproduced using premixed inks, often used to print colors that are outside the CMYK gamut.

Spectral Absorption

Light wavelengths that are absorbed by the pigments in an object's surface.

Spectral Output

Color balance.

Spectral Reflectance

Light wavelengths that are not absorbed by the pigments in an object's surface.

Spectrophotometer

A device used to precisely measure the wavelengths that are reflected from an object's surface.

Specular Highlight

The lightest highlight area that does not carry any detail, such as reflections from glass or polished metal. Normally, these areas are reproduced as unprinted white paper.

SPI

Samples per inch. Term used to describe the imaging capabilities of a scanner.

SPI

Spots per inch. The number of dots created by an imagesetter or platesetter in one linear inch. Often used interchangeably with "dots per inch".

Spine

The binding edge at the back of a book that contains title information and joins the front and back covers.

Spot Color

Any pre-mixed ink that is not one of the four process-color inks.

Spot-Color Printing

The printing method in which special ink colors are used independently or in conjunction with process colors to create a specific color that is outside the gamut of process-color printing.

Spread

1. Two abutting pages. 2. A trapping process that slightly enlarges a lighter foreground object to prevent white paper gaps caused by misregistration.

Stacking Order

1. The order of elements on a PostScript page, where the topmost item can obscure underlying items. 2. The order in which elements are placed on a page; the first is at the bottom and the last is at the top. 3. The order of layers, from top to bottom.

Static

Fixed content.

Step-and-Repeat

A command in most desktop-publishing applications that makes multiple copies of selected objects using defined offset values.

STET

Used in proof-correction work to cancel a previous correction. From the Latin for "let it stand."

Stochastic Screening

See *Frequency-Modulated (FM) Screening*.

Stripping

The act of manually assembling individual film negatives into flats for printing. Also referred to as "film assembly."

Stroke

The width and color attributes of a line.

Style

A defined set of formatting instructions for font and paragraph attributes, tabs, and other properties of text.

Style Guide

A book that defines specific language and grammar rules for authors to follow.

Subscript

Small-size characters set below the normal letters or figures, usually to convey technical information.

Substrate

Any surface that is being printed.

Subtractive Color

Color that is observed when light strikes pigments or dyes, which absorb certain wavelengths of light; the light that is reflected back is perceived as a color. See *CMYK*, *Process Color*.

Superblack

See *Rich Black*.

Superscript

Small characters set above the normal letters or figures, such as numbers referring to footnotes.

SWOP

Specifications for Web Offset Publications. Industry standards for web-offset printing; SWOP specifications provide the necessary information to produce consistent high-quality printing.

Table

A grid used for displaying data or organizing information in columns and rows. It is also used to control placement of text and graphics. A row and column structure for organizing information.

Tabloid

11 × 17-in. paper.

TAC

Total Area Coverage. The maximum amount of ink that can be printed in a single area. Also called "total ink density".

Tags

The various formats in a style sheet that indicate paragraph settings, margins and columns, page layouts, hyphenation and justification, widow and orphan control, and other parameters. An indication of the start and end of an element.

Target

The page or part of a page to which a link points.

Template

A document file containing layout, styles, and repeating elements (such as logos) by which a series of documents can maintain the same look and feel. A model publication you can use as the basis for creating a new publication.

Text Attribute

A characteristic applied directly to a letter or letters in text, such as bold, italic, or underline.

Text Box

A box into which users can type a single line of text. Also called a "text frame," or "text area."

Text Wrap

The ability of a browser to automatically continue text on the next line.

Texture

1. A property of the surface of the substrate, such as the smoothness of paper. 2. Graphically, variation in tonal values to form image detail. 3. A class of fills in a graphics application that create various appearances, such as bricks, grass, tiles.

Thin Space

A fixed space, equal to half an en space or the width of a period in most fonts.

Thumbnails

1. The preliminary sketches of a design. 2. Small images used to indicate the content of a computer file.

TIFF

Tagged Image File Format. A common format used for scanned or computer-generated bitmapped images.

Tile

1. Reproducing a number of pages of a document on one sheet. 2. Printing a large document overlapping on several smaller sheets of paper.

Tone Value Increase

See *Dot Gain*.

Glossary

Total Ink Density

See *TAC*.

Tracking

Adjusting the spacing of letters in a line of text to achieve proper justification or general appearance.

Trademark

A legal designation that identifies and protects the ownership of a specific device (such as a name, symbol, or mark).

Transformation

A change in the shape, color, position, velocity, or opacity of an object.

Transparency

1. A full-color photographically-produced image on transparent film. 2. The quality of an image element that allows background elements to partially or entirely show through.

Transparent Ink

An ink that allows light to be transmitted through it.

Trapping

The process of creating an overlap between abutting inks to compensate for imprecise registration in the printing process. Extending the lighter colors of one object into the darker colors of an adjoining object.

Trim Size

Area of the finished page after the job is printed, folded, bound, and cut.

TrueType

An outline font format used in both Macintosh and Windows systems that can be used both on the screen and on a printer.

Trumatch

A special-color library used in the United States.

Type 1 Fonts

PostScript fonts based on Bézier curves encrypted for compactness.

Type Family

A set of typefaces created from the same basic design but in different variations, such as bold, light, italic, book, and heavy.

Typesetting

The arrangement of individual characters of text into words, sentences, and paragraphs.

Undercolor Removal (UCR)

A technique for reducing the amount of magenta, cyan, and yellow inks in neutral or shadow areas and replacing them with black.

Unsharp Masking

A digital technique performed after scanning that locates the edge between sections of differing lightness and alters the values of the adjoining pixels to exaggerate the difference across the edge, thereby increasing edge contrast.

Up State

Normally a button's default state, which occurs when the user has not clicked or passed over the button with his mouse.

Uppercase

The capital letters of a typeface. When type was hand composited, the capital letters resided in the upper part of the type case.

Varnish Plate

The plate on a printing press that applies varnish after the other colors have been applied.

Vector Graphics

Graphics defined using coordinate points and mathematically drawn lines and curves, which may be freely scaled and rotated without image degradation in the final output.

Vertical Justification

The ability to automatically adjust the interline spacing (leading) to make columns and pages end at the same point on a page.

Vignette

An illustration in which the background gradually fades into the paper; that is, without a definite edge or border.

Visible Spectrum

The wavelengths of light between about 380 nm (violet) and 700 nm (red) that are visible to the human eye.

Web-Safe Color

A color palette used for images that will be displayed on the Internet. The Web-safe color palette is a specific set that can be displayed by most computer-operating systems and monitors.

White Balance

Equal amounts of red, green, and blue light components to create white.

White Light

Light containing all wavelengths of the visible spectrum. Also known as 5000K lighting.

White Space

Areas on the page that contain no images or type. Proper use of white space is critical to a well-balanced design.

Word Break

The division of a word at the end of a line in accordance with hyphenation principles.

Word Space

The space inserted between words in a layout application. The optimal value is built into the typeface, and may usually be modified within an application.

Wrap

Type set on the page so it wraps around the shape of another element.

X-height

The height of the lowercase letter "x" in a given typeface, which represents the basic size of the bodies of all of the lowercase letters (excluding ascenders and descenders).

Zero Point

The mathematical origin of the coordinates of the two-dimensional page. The zero point may be moved to any location on the page, and the ruler dimensions change accordingly.

Index

Index

Index

Index

Index

Index

FontAgent Pro

The new face of font management and repair

FontAgent Pro 3 from Insider Software is the world's most advanced font manager for the Macintosh. With a few clicks, you can repair, optimize and organize your fonts, then build font libraries and cascading sets that you can activate, manage, secure, print, and preview. FontAgent Pro is the only font manager that offers workgroup font sharing with zero configuration and no hassle.

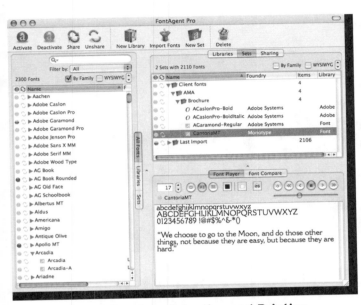

Unrivaled Font Preview, Selection and Printing

FontAgent Pro gives you more ways to view, select and print your fonts. List, sort and search all your fonts easily. Search font names, foundries, custom comments and other metadata with ease. Use FontAgent Pro's unique Font Player™ to "play" a text string through all your fonts automatically so you can choose the right one. Or narrow your selection to a few fonts and view the string side-by-side using Font Compare.™

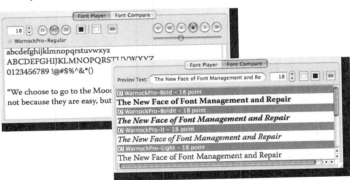

"The only font manager recommended by *Against The Clock.*"

www.insidersoftware.com

To order FontAgent Pro 3 call toll-free 1-866-366-8778 or +1-520-229-1212

* Offer expires 07/31/07. Call for volume license pricing.

The Industry's Only Workgroup Font Sharing

FontAgent Pro is the only product that lets you share fonts in your workgroup with zero config and no font server. All you do is install FontAgent Pro Workgroup Edition on your Macs and start sharing fonts It's that simple.

Unique Powerful, Cascading Sets

Organize fonts into meaningful, maintainable sets and subsets by client or project. While other font managers limit you to creating sets in one long, unmanageable list, FontAgent Pro gives you the power of cascading sets so you can organize your fonts into more meaningful, easier-to-maintain, client and project hierarchies.

NEW! Secure Fonts and Sets from Changes

FontAgent Pro's unique security enables you to protect fonts, sets and preferences from unauthorized changes. It allows you to password-protect separate configuration settings for each user on a system. Using these new capabilities, admins can implement standard FontAgent Pro configurations, libraries and sets across their organizations.

Unparalleled Font Activation Power

FontAgent Pro activates and deactivates fonts in more ways than any other font manager, saving system resources and simplifying font menus by activating just the fonts you need—in both Mac OS X and Classic. Auto-activate fonts in Mac OS X applications including the Adobe Creative Suite, QuarkXPress and Microsoft Office. And while other font managers limit you to activating entire suitcases or sets, FontAgent Pro lets you activate a library, set, subset, font or even an individual typeface —all with a single click!

Proven Font Repair and Organization

For the last decade, FontAgent has been the industry leader in font integrity validation and organization, so you can depend on FontAgent Pro to automatically optimize and organize your fonts, prevent the addition of duplicate fonts to your library, and improve system performance and reliability.

Connected Font Management Server Solution

Besides being the most reliable font management solution in the industry, FontAgent Pro is now the most connected. With the addition of FontAgent Pro Server, you can ensure font integrity and consistency across your entire workflow, and on every computer in your department or enterprise.

Become a QuarkXPress® Certified Expert

Get the Recognition You Deserve!

The QuarkXPress Certified Expert program offers professional designers and artists a unique opportunity to get the recognition they deserve. Leverage the power of the internationally-recognized Quark® brand.

The QuarkXPress Certified Expert test is computer-delivered and consists of randomly selected questions from a test bank that is organized into categories specific to the real-world application of the program's core technologies.

To study for the test, work through the exercises in *QuarkXPress 7: Creating Digital Documents*, the officially sanctioned book from which the test questions were drawn.

Log onto **quark.com/partners/certified_expert/** to learn more about the program and its benefits.

Benefits for Individuals:

- Establishes your proficiency with QuarkXPress
- Includes you in the online QuarkXPress Certified Expert Directory
- Offers new business opportunities and improves your competitive position
- Leverages the Quark brand by adding the QuarkXPress Certified Expert logo to your business cards, Web site, and resume

Benefits for Organizations:

- Provides a proven method of assessing the skills of potential employees
- Offers a method to enhance and standardize skill levels of existing staff
- Establishes a method of structured training with materials authorized by Quark, Inc.

www.againsttheclock.com
800-256-4282